Location and Change

Location and Change

Perspectives on Economic Geography

Michael J. Healey and Brian W. Ilbery

OXFORD UNIVERSITY PRESS · 1990

Oxford University Press, Walton Street, Oxford OX2 6DP

Oxford New York Toronto
Delhi Bombay Calcutta Madras Karachi
Petaling Jaya Singapore Hong Kong Tokyo
Nairobi Dar es Salaam Cape Town
Melbourne Auckland
and associated companies in
Berlin Ibadan

Oxford is a trade mark of Oxford University Press

Published in the United States
by Oxford University Press, New York

British Library Cataloguing in Publication Data
Healey, Michael, 1949–
Location and change : perspectives on economic geography.
1. Economic conditions. Geographical aspects
I. Title II. Ilbery, Brian W.
330.9
ISBN 0–19–874154–5
ISBN 0–10–874155–3 pbk

Library of Congress Cataloging in Publication Data
Healey, Michael.
Location and change : perspectives on economic geography /
Michael J. Healey and Brian W. Ilbery.
1. Geography, Economic. I. Ilbery, Brian W. II. Title.
HF1025.H4 1990   330.9–dc20   90–7202
ISBN 0–19–874154–5
ISBN 0–19–874155–3 (pbk.)

Typeset by Latimer Trend & Company Ltd, Estover, Plymouth
Printed in Great Britain by Wm Clowes Ltd, Beccles, Suffolk

To our parents; and
Chris, Lauren, and Ruth;
Lynne, Gareth, and James

Preface

The late 1980s is an exciting time to be writing a textbook concerned with the location and spatial evolution of economic activity. During the last twenty-five years the world economy has experienced both a major recession and a partial recovery. Over the same period, major changes have occurred in the relative importance of different economic sectors, with most developed market economies experiencing a loss of employment in their primary and manufacturing industries, and a growth of employment in their service industries. A fundamental feature of economic changes such as these is that they vary markedly in their nature and extent between and within countries, giving rise to shifting patterns of growth and decline, disadvantage and opportunity at a variety of spatial scales. Documentation and analysis of the causes, characteristics, and consequences of these changes have emerged as a central research focus in the social sciences. The resulting literature is rich in detail but deficient in the broad overviews and insights which are essential to foster a general understanding of the geography of economic activity.

The idea for this book developed from a new course in economic geography which we began teaching in October 1986. Unfortunately there was no suitable textbook available then, or now, which covered the topics we felt to be important or adopted the kind of integrated approach which we wished to use. The framework for the book was developed during the first year of teaching the course and we spent the following two years researching, writing, and revising the chapters. The book integrates the treatment of different economic sectors by adopting a structure which aims to provide a broad understanding of the evolution of the economic landscape. Recent trends and theoretical developments in the subject are emphasized and most of the chapters use a range of examples from different economic sectors.

A key argument, which runs throughout the book, is that processes of economic change and spatial patterns of economic activity are interrelated and interdependent and an understanding of either requires an appreciation of the role of the other. As a consequence of emphasizing the close links between the way an economy is organized and its geography, the book brings together a wide range of work by geographers, economists, planners, regional scientists, and others. This means that, although the book developed out of an undergraduate course in economic geography, much of the material covered is also relevant to courses at a variety of levels in economic development, business studies, and planning. No previous knowledge of geography or economics is assumed.

The emphasis of the book is on understanding the processes which lead to contrasts and changes in spatial patterns of economic activity in developed market economies, particularly North America and Britain and, to a lesser extent, Australia and mainland Europe. However, the need to view change in a global context means that some examples are also taken from developing market economies and planned economies. The book is divided into four parts. The first is concerned with concepts and methodology. After outlining some of the main features of recent economic changes and their spatial impacts, different theoretical perspectives on economic location and change are assessed. Part II, the longest in the book, discusses the context of change and systematically examines the factors influencing the evolution of the economic landscape. Part III is concerned with applying the theoretical perspectives and factors discussed in Parts 1 and II to case studies of recent changes in the spatial pattern of economic activity drawn from different economic sectors. The final part examines the geography of economic change at a variety of spatial scales, from the international to the local, and assesses the environmental impacts of economic change.

The individual chapters follow in a logical order, but readers should find little difficulty in selecting those sections and chapters which are most relevant to the level and type of course that they are following. Cross-referencing between chapters is used to enable other places in the text where related material or ideas are discussed to be found. The index enables the identification of the various places where the key concepts and terms used in the book are mentioned. Each chapter ends with a summary of the main points covered. An important feature of the book is the extensive bibliography of approximately 900 items which should help those wishing to investigate the subjects discussed in more detail.

The length of the bibliography indicates our debt to numerous other research workers whose ideas and analyses we have drawn on freely. A book of this nature could not have been written without the assistance of many others. First our thanks must go to our students who over the last few years have helped us, often without realizing it, to clarify our thinking about much of the material we have included. If the book helps future generations of students to appreciate the importance of the geography of economic activity and to understand more readily how the economic landscape evolves, our labours will have been worth while. The granting to each of us of a term of partial study leave greatly aided us in the writing of this book. Consequently we are especially grateful to David Smith and colleagues in the Department of Geography, Coventry Polytechnic, for facilitating and covering for our absence.

We are much indebted to Doug Watts and David Clark, who made numerous helpful comments on various drafts of the book. Thanks are also due to Andy Pratt and other colleagues for their suggestions on various sections. Their comments challenged us to rethink and clarify many of our ideas. At the end, of course, we alone are responsible for any errors and inadequacies which may remain. A particular tribute is due to Shirley Addleton who expertly and skilfully drew the figures. We typed the manuscript ourselves, as befits the age of word processors, although Joy Summers and Joan James gamely took on the onerous task of typing the bibliography. Thanks are also due to Andrew Schuller of Oxford University Press for his encouragement and patience. Last, but not least, our greatest debt is owed to our respective families. Our parents, wives, and children have inspired and guided us in their different ways throughout our endeavours and it is to them that we dedicate this book.

Michael J. Healey
Brian W. Ilbery

Coventry
September 1989

Acknowledgements

The authors and publishers wish to thank the following who have kindly given permission for the use of copyright material.

FIG. 2.3: from R. Knowles and J. Wareing, *Economic and Social Geography*, Heinemann (1986). By permission of Heinemann Publishers (Oxford) Limited.

FIG. 3.1: from D. B. Grigg, *An Introduction to Agricultural Geography*, Hutchinson (1982). By permission of Unwin Hyman Limited.

FIG. 3.3: from M. L. Parry, in *Transactions of the Institute of British Geographers* (1975). By permission of The Institute of British Geographers.

FIGS. 3.6 and 3.7: from M. G. A. Wilson, in the *Annals of the Association of American Geographers*, 58 (1968). By permission of the Association of American Geographers.

FIG. 4.1a: from R. J. C. Munton, in *Tijdschrift voor Economische en Sociale Geografie*, 67 (1976). By permission of The Royal Dutch Geographical Society, KNAG.

FIG. 4.2: from R. J. C. Munton, in *Area*, 9 (1977). By permission of The Institute of British Geographers.

FIGS. 4.3 and 4.4: from D. W. Owen *et al.*, in *Regional Studies*, 18, Cambridge University Press (1984). Reproduced by permission of David Owen.

FIG. 4.6: from H. D. Watts, *Industrial Geography*, Longman (1987). By permission of Longman Group Limited.

FIG. 4.7: from M. F. Dunford and D. C. Perrons, *The Arena of Capital*, Macmillan (1983). By permission of Macmillan (London and Basingstoke).

FIG. 4.8: from A. R. Townsend, in *Regional Studies*, 20, Cambridge University Press (1986). Reproduced by permission of the author.

FIG. 4.9: from C. M. Mason, in *Quarterly Review* (May 1987). By permission of National Westminster Bank PLC.

FIG. 5.1: from R. T. Dalton, in *East Midland Geographer*, 5 (1971). By permission of *East Midland Geographer*.

FIG. 5.2: from H. D. Watts, in *Regional Studies*, 12, Cambridge University Press (1978). Reproduced by permission of the author.

FIG. 5.7: from P. Tyler and M. Kitson, in *Urban Studies*, 24 (1987). By permission of *Urban Studies*.

FIG. 5.9: from David Keeble *et al.*, in *Regional Studies*, 16, Cambridge University Press (1982). By permission of David Keeble.

FIG. 6.2: from P. Hall *et al.*, *Western Sunrise: The Genesis and Growth of Britain's Major High Tech Corridor*, Allen & Unwin (1987). By permission of Unwin Hyman Limited.

FIG. 6.3: from A. Markusen *et al.*, *High Tech America*, Allen & Unwin (1986). By permission of Unwin Hyman Limited.

FIG. 6.5: from D. Rowe, in UK Science Park Association, *Science Parks as an Opportunity for Property and Venture Capital Investment* (1988). By permission of UK Science Park Association.

FIG. 6.6: from Louis T. Wells, Jr. (ed.), *The Product Life Cycle and International Trade*, Harvard Business School Press (1972). By permission of Harvard Business School Press.

FIG. 6.7: from Ronald F. Abler, John Adams, and Peter R. Gould, *Spatial Organization: The Geographer's View of the World*, Prentice-Hall (1971). By permission of Ronald F. Abler.

FIG. 7.2: from D. E. Keeble, in W. F. Lever (ed.), *Industrial Change in the United Kingdom*, Longman (1987). By permission of Longman Group Limited.

FIG. 7.3: from H. D. Watts, *The Large Industrial Enterprise: Some Spatial Perspectives*, Croom Helm (1980). By permission of Croom Helm Limited.

FIG. 7.4: from M. J. Healey and H. D. Watts, in W. F. Lever (ed.), *Industrial Change in the United Kingdom*, Longman (1987). By permission of Longman Group Limited.

FIG. 8.2: from I. R. Bowler, *Geography*, 71 (1986). By permission of The Geographical Association.

FIG. 8.3: from I. R. Bowler, 'Recent Developments in the Agricultural Policy of the EEC', *Geography*, 61 (1976). By permission of The Geographical Association.

FIG. 8.5: from E. J. Malecki, in *Environment and Planning C*, 2 (1984). By permission of Pion Ltd.

FIG. 8.6: from P. W. Daniels, *Service Industries Growth and Location*, Cambridge University Press (1982). By permission of Cambridge University Press.

FIG. 8.7: from Peter Hall, *Urban and Regional Planning*, Allen and Unwin (1985). By permission of Unwin Hyman Limited.

FIG. 9.1: from K. B. Raitz and C. Mather, in the *Annals of the Association of American Geographers*, 61

(1971). By permission of the Association of American Geographers.

FIG. 9.2: from M. E. Buchanan, in *Australian Geographical Studies*, 13 (1975). By permission of *Australian Geographical Studies*.

FIG. 10.3: from L. E. Edwards, in *Environment and Planning A*, 15 (1983). By permission of Pion Ltd.

FIG. 10.4: from A. S. Mather, *Land Use*, Longman (1986). By permission of Longman Group Limited.

FIGS. 11.1, 11.2, and 11.3: from various issues of *FAO Production Yearbook*, Food and Agriculture Organization of UN. By permission of Food and Agriculture Organization.

FIG. 12.2a: from D. Keeble, *Industrial Location and Planning*. Methuen (1976).

FIG. 12.2b, c, d: from HMSO, Department of Employment statistics. By permission of The Controller of Her Majesty's Stationery Office.

FIG. 12.6: from J. Holmes's data, in K. Chapman and G. Humphreys, *Technical Change and Industrial Policy*, Basil Blackwell (1987). By permission of Basil Blackwell Limited.

FIG. 13.1: from D. B. Johnson, in *International Journal of Retailing* (1987). By permission of MCB University Press.

FIG. 13.2: from the *Register of Managed Shopping Schemes* (1987). By permission of The Data Consultancy (URPI Group Ltd.).

FIG. 13.3: from A. Kellerman, in *Geoforum*, 16 (1985). Reproduced by permission of Pergamon Press PLC.

FIG. 13.5: from P. W. Daniels, *Service Industries: A Geographical Appraisal*, Methuen (1985). By permission of Methuen & Co.

FIG. 13.6: from J. D. Lord and C. D. Lynds, in *GeoJournal*, 9 (1984). Reproduced by permission of Kluwer Academic Publishers.

FIG. 14.2: from D. E. Keeble, in R. Chorley and P. Haggett, *Models in Geography*, Methuen (1967). By permission of Methuen and Co.

FIG. 15.1: from P. Haggett, *Geography: A Modern Synthesis*, Harper and Row (1983).

FIG. 16.2: from HMSO, Department of Employment statistics. By permission of The Controller of Her Majesty's Stationery Office.

FIG. 16.3: data from the *Employment Gazette*, April 1985 and November 1988. By permission of The Controller of Her Majesty's Stationery Office.

FIG. 17.1a: data from D. M. Smith, *Human Geography: A Welfare Approach*, Edward Arnold (1977). By permission of Edward Arnold (Publishers) Ltd., (Division of Hodder & Stoughton).

FIG. 17.1b: data from J. Bale, in *Area*, 10 (1978). By permission of The Institute of British Geographers.

FIG. 17.2a: from C. Rose, in *New Scientist*, 14 Nov. 1985. FIG. 17.2b, d: F. Pearce, in *New Scientist*, 4 Dec. 1985.

FIG. 17.3: from C. M. Wood *et al.*, *The Geography of Pollution: A Study of Greater Manchester*, Manchester University Press (1974). By permission of Manchester University Press.

Although every effort has been made to trace and contact copyright holders, this has not always been possible. We apologize for any apparent negligence.

Contents

xii   Contents

IV. The Geography of Economic Change

List of Figures

List of Tables

I Concepts and Methodology

1

Economic Change and Location

1.1 A framework for analysis

Change is a characteristic feature of the modern world. Some economic changes are sudden and traumatic, for example the quadrupling of oil prices in 1973/4 by members of OPEC (Organization of Petroleum Exporting Countries); some are long term and progressive, such as the increase in the level of economic development in the countries of Western Europe over the last 150 years; while others fluctuate, such as the level of unemployment. The superimposition of these different types of economic change with different frequencies and severities at different locations means that the way national and local economies evolve varies over time and from place to place.

Economic changes then are the norm and stability is the exception. Of critical importance for the subject of this book is that the impact of these economic changes is felt unevenly between places. Thus, for example, indigenous supplies of oil in North America enabled the rise in price in the United States to be less than in European countries, which for the most part lacked these resources. Similarly the increase over the last century and a half in the level of economic development in Western Europe generally benefited the core areas more than the peripheral areas. The contrasts between places, to which such economic changes have contributed, have in turn had an impact on the nature of the processes of change themselves. Thus the oil price rise in Europe, one of the major markets for oil, made it more economic to exploit previously marginal oil resources, such as those under the North Sea. Similarly the existence of spatial contrasts in the levels of economic development within Europe have been used by multinational firms in their attempts to maintain and increase their profitability. For example, in recent years they have been attracted to locate some of their assembly operations in the peripheral areas by the fall in transport costs and the reduction in the level of skill required for many operations

Spatial contrasts are not, therefore, simply a response to economic changes (Massey, 1984a). There is a two-way relationship between economic change and location. Spatial contrasts in turn influence the functioning of economies (Fig. 1.1). Economic processes do not operate on the point of a needle, they function in a spatial environment in which distance, movement, and the differences between places all have an effect. The costs of overcoming distance affect the profitability of businesses; while differences in the costs of labour from one place to another can influence how production is organized, with labour-intensive technologies being used in low labour-cost areas, such as South and South-East Asia, and capital-intensive technologies being used to produce identical products in the relatively high labour-cost areas of the developed

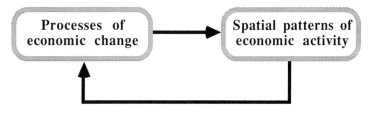

FIG 1.1 The relationship between processes of economic change and spatial patterns of economic activity

market economies. So to understand spatial patterns of economic activity it is necessary to understand how economic processes (and indeed social and political processes as well) operate, but equally, in order to understand how economies operate an appreciation of the effects of space is required.

The need to clarify the processes influencing the changing location of economic activity is becoming more important as there are indications that the general rate of change is speeding up. This is most clearly seen with the rates of technological change. The rapid developments in micro-electronics and biotechnology that are occurring currently are reducing the 'life-cycle' of many products as the period between innovation and obsolescence falls. Change in economic activity as a whole is also often described in terms of cycles. Booms and recessions occur every few years, while some research workers have identified longer cycles associated with technological revolutions, which are of the order of fifty years or so. These changes can result in major shifts in the structure of economies. For example, at the end of the nineteenth century there was a shift from an era based on steam power, railways, and steel to one increasingly dominated by electric power, chemicals, and the motor industry.

Some areas gain from economic change while others lose. This spatial unevenness is felt at all geographical scales. Thus the shift in industrial structure beginning at the end of the nineteenth century, which witnessed the growth of the motor industry among others, benefited particular nations such as the United States. It also affected regions within countries, such as the Mid-West in the United States and the West Midlands in Britain, and individual communities, such as Detroit and Coventry. Intriguingly, these same places suffered some of the most rapid rates of industrial decline in the 1970s and early 1980s as their economies went into recession and the post-1945 shift of economic growth consolidated in countries such as Japan and West Germany, regions such as the 'Sunbelt' of the United States and the 'South' of Britain, and communities such as Silicon Valley (south of San Francisco) and Cambridge, England.

The main aim of this book is to provide a broad understanding of the processes which lead to contrasts and changes in spatial patterns of economic activity. There are two main kinds of

spatial pattern of economic activity. One is concerned with the *location* of various establishments including factories, warehouses, offices, and shops; while the other is concerned with *land uses* such as agriculture and forestry. Although there are overlaps between these two categories and it is possible to discuss the location of farms and forest sites and land uses such as industrial estates and office parks, the distinction is useful because it emphasizes two different analytical approaches. In the first case the economic activity is taken as given and the analysis is concerned with how its location pattern has evolved; in the second case the location is taken as fixed and the analysis concerns the changing land uses and activities which occupy that location.

The analysis of economic location and land use can occur at a variety of spatial scales from the international through the regional down to that of the local economy. These different geographical scales are interrelated, they are 'nested' one within another. Thus changes at one spatial scale are affected by changes at other scales. Hence to understand spatial contrasts in economic activity in, say, Britain, it is necessary to consider not only factors internal to the country but also processes operating externally, such as the relationship with the European Community and the changing role of Britain in the world economy. This issue of interdependence between spatial scales is one which reoccurs at several points in subsequent chapters.

It is important to understand why extraction, production, and services occur in certain places and the way the patterns develop over time because they affect the incomes and social well-being of people living in different areas. The way the economic landscape evolves also raises significant implications for policy and the environment. What, for example, can local and central governments do to alleviate the effects of economic decline on particular areas? Should they attempt to divert growth industries to declining areas or will this impair the efficiency of the firms? What effect does the increasing use of fertilizers and factory farming methods in developed market economies have on the environment?

Book structure

In seeking to make clear the processes which lead

to contrasts and changes in spatial patterns of economic activity, this book is divided into four parts. Part I is concerned mainly with *concepts and methodology*. It seeks to introduce some of the main features of recent economic changes and their spatial impacts (Chapter 1) and to evaluate the main theoretical perspectives on both economic change and the location of economic activity and its evolution (Chapter 2). Part II, the longest in the book, is entitled *the context of change*. It is concerned with answering three main questions:

1. What are the characteristics of the factors which influence where economic activities are located and the uses to which land is put?
2. How have these characteristics changed over time, and how do they vary over space?
3. What effects do the temporal and spatial variations in the factors have on the geography of economic activity?

The material is presented in seven main chapters concerned with the physical context (Chapter 3), factors of production (Chapter 4), demand, transport, and linkages (Chapter 5), the technological context (Chapter 6), the organizational context (Chapter 7), the political context (Chapter 8), and the social and cultural context (Chapter 9). The emphasis varies between the chapters according to the nature of the factor being discussed. For example, the physical context chapter stresses the effect of spatial variations in the physical environment on the geography of economic activity rather than temporal variations, because many aspects of the physical environment are slow to change. The last chapter in this part of the book (Chapter 10) deals with the way in which these various factors influence decisions about the use of land and the location of economic activity.

Part III examines *applications*. Its concern is to apply the theoretical perspectives and factors discussed in Parts I and II to case studies of recent changes in the spatial pattern of economic activity drawn from the primary (Chapter 11), manufacturing (Chapter 12), and service (Chapter 13) sectors. The final section of the book, Part IV, is entitled *the geography of economic change*. Following a chapter on international economic change (Chapter 14), two chapters are concerned with regional economic change; the first considers the nature of regional economic change and

assesses a variety of theories (Chapter 15), while the other examines three case studies at different spatial scales and discusses the nature of regional economic policies and their strengths and weaknesses (Chapter 16). The final chapter of the book examines the environmental impacts of economic change and how these vary from place to place (Chapter 17).

The interrelationships between the different chapters are summarized in Figure 1.2. The diagram emphasizes that:

1. the space economy is affected by macroeconomic changes, modified by various contextual factors;
2. the processes of change may be interpreted using a variety of theoretical perspectives on location and economic change; and
3. the international, regional, and local responses to economic change in turn influence the nature and operation of the processes of change.

In the remainder of this introductory chapter some of the chief features of recent economic changes and their spatial manifestations are briefly outlined. To start with a few comments are made on the development of the world economy since 1970 and then attention concentrates on recent changes in developed market economies, the main focus of this text. Further details of most of these economic and spatial changes, along with additional examples, are contained in the main body of the text.

1.2 The changing world economy

Perhaps the most significant economic change following the Second World War, and especially after the late 1960s, has been the development of *the world economy*. One of the main features of this global economy is the increasing interdependence between places. Thus what is happening in the economies of Britain, Belgium, Brazil, or Bulgaria or the cities of Seattle, Seoul, Southampton, or Sydney is 'determined increasingly by their role in systems of production, trade and consumption which have become global in scope and complex in structure' (Knox and Agnew, 1989 p. 3). As Johnston (1984 p. 446) notes: 'there

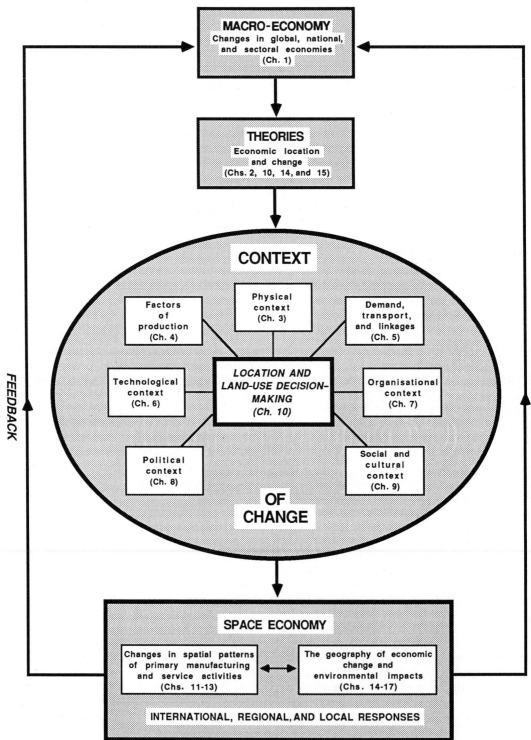

FIG 1.2 The changing macro- and space-economies: a framework for analysis

is but one world economy, to which all places are linked, to a greater or lesser degree'. A striking illustration of the interdependence of different parts of the world economy is the emergence of the debt crisis in many Third World countries. One of the major contributants to this was an indirect result of the dramatic rise in oil prices during the 1970s. Much of the sudden increase in wealth of the members of OPEC flowed into the international banking system, which found willing borrowers in the developing countries who were desperate for capital to invest in new technology and infrastructure. The scale of borrowing undertaken, together with the subsequent increase in interest rates, led to a crisis in some countries who are unable to meet the costs of servicing their long-term debts (i.e. meeting the costs of both interest charges and repayments) (Knox and Agnew, 1989).

This example helps show that the processes of economic change have decisively shifted in the last few decades from national economies to the world economy. It is perhaps no accident that some of the major success stories in economic development terms over the last twenty years—Japan, West Germany, and South Korea—have based their national policies on the world economic system. The account which follows of recent changes in the world economy draws heavily on the work of Drucker (1986) and Thrift (1986).

Over the last two decades the global economy has experienced three major changes. First, the production of raw materials, both agricultural and mineral, has come to play a much smaller role in the world system. Few major countries, with the exceptions of Japan and the Soviet Union, rely on food imports. Furthermore, considerable reductions have been made in the demand for minerals, metals, and forest products, as less are required for a given level of output in older products, and the new high-technology (microchip) industries make use of few raw materials. These changes have contributed to a fall in the prices of raw materials, which by 1986 had reached their lowest level in recorded history, in relation to prices for manufactured goods and services.

The second major change in the world economy is that trends in manufacturing employment are becoming increasingly unrelated to trends in manufacturing production. Manufac-

turing employment in developed market economies, particularly blue-collar jobs, is declining, while output is increasing. Thus it is not the developed market economies which are becoming *deindustrialized*; it is their labour forces. The agricultural sectors of developed market economies have experienced a similar trend of 'jobless growth' (Morgan and Sayer, 1983a p. 22), although for a longer period, with production continuing to rise while employment levels have declined. An important implication of jobless growth in manufacturing industries is that differences between places in their cost of labour is becoming of decreasing importance as a factor influencing trends in industrial location.

The third change in the world economy is that flows of capital, rather than trade in goods and services, have become the driving force of the world economy. The 'real' economy has been swamped by what Drucker calls a 'symbol' economy, dominated by capital movements, exchange rates, and credit flows. These two economies are operating increasingly independently. Exchange rates can determine differences in labour costs between countries, and domestic currencies have become subordinate to such pseudo-currencies as the Eurodollar (i.e. US dollars held outside the United States). Capital has, therefore, become more footloose and internationalized. Multinational corporations and banks have become truly global, spreading world-wide and penetrating such newly industrializing countries (NICs) as Mexico, South Korea, and Brazil. Such foreign direct investment takes three main forms:

1. The obtaining of raw materials, as with bauxite for aluminium.
2. The penetration of the markets of countries that cannot be penetrated by exports (e.g. because of tariff barriers).
3. The use of cheap labour to produce goods for re-export to the home market or third markets.

The world economy has, therefore, been restructured since the early 1970s and this has affected the geography of employment opportunities. In particular, the international distribution of economic activities has changed. In other words a *new international division of labour* has emerged. As production processes have become more standardized, enabling them, after a short period of training, to be carried out by unskilled workers, multinationals have increasingly located the different stages of production in different places. The tendency has been to maintain head office and research and development (R. & D.) functions in the core areas of developed economies, while relocating lower-level assembly functions so as to benefit particularly from the cheap but disciplined labour within developing countries. Thus there has been a relative shift in manufacturing employment in favour of the developing countries. However, the decline in the relative significance of labour costs suggests that this new international division of labour may be a temporary phenomenon, more characteristic of the 1970s and 1980s than the 1990s and the early twenty-first century.

Changes in the geography of production have been matched by the growth in the international service economy, particularly finance, marketing, and business services of all kinds. One major result of the world-wide growth of these corporate functions has been the formation of *world cities*. Such cities can be identified at three hierarchic levels:

1. *True international centres*, such as London, New York, and Tokyo, which contain the headquarters and branch offices of major, global companies and banks.

2. *Zonal centres*, which have important financial links with particular zones of the world, for example, Los Angeles and Singapore.

3. *Regional centres*, which specialize in providing space for the regional headquarters of corporations serving particular regions, such as Miami, acting as a node for US multinationals in Latin America, and Honolulu, for US multinationals in Asia.

The world is 'shrinking' as the time taken for travel and communications has reduced and this has encouraged the world economy to become more integrated than ever before and for the links between multinationals, banks, and countries to strengthen. This new economic order has important implications for the developed market economies.

1.3 Changes in developed market economies

With the emergence of the new world economy the mature industrial countries are playing a different role than previously. Whereas under the old international division of labour they were virtually the only source of manufacturing exports, under the new international division of labour the emergence of the newly industrializing countries has meant that many of the staple industries of the developed market economies have come in for severe competition. Partly as a consequence of their changing role many developed countries underwent a period of deindustrialization and high unemployment in the early 1980s which was made more severe by the general weakness of the world economy at that time. Faced with these problems they have had to undertake a series of major adjustments: including the promotion of small firms; the development of new technologies; the attraction of foreign investment; and the protection of certain industries against imports (Dicken, 1986). Adjustments such as these, which are discussed in detail later in the book, are relatively recent. Over a longer period of time the distribution of employment in the different economic sectors changes as the economy of a country develops.

An economy is usually divided into three economic sectors, or types of economic activity:

1. *The primary sector*, which is engaged in the exploitation of the earth's resources and includes agriculture, forestry, fishing, mining, and quarrying. The output from this sector, in the form of commodities and raw materials, often becomes the input for the next sector.

2. *The secondary sector*, which includes manufacturing, construction, and utilities (e.g. gas and water) and involves transforming the primary products into usable goods. Value is added in each successive process.

3. *The tertiary sector*, which provides services, often intangible in form, to other producers (producer services) and the general public (consumer services). This sector involves a wide range of functions, from wholesaling and retailing to the provision of business, personal, and entertainment services.

The distinction between these sectors is not, however, always clear-cut. This is because most statistics which are compiled using this schema consign industries to sectors on the basis of the *main activity of the establishment*. The problem is that many establishments are involved in activities from more than one sector. For example, many large establishments in the primary and manufacturing sectors also have tertiary activities, such as accountancy, marketing, and warehousing functions on site. If the employer decides either to move one of these functions to a different location, such as a detached head office, or to subcontract the function to a specialist employer in the tertiary sector, then the statistics will appear to show a loss of employment and output from the primary or secondary sector and an increase in the tertiary sector, whereas all that has really happened is an organizational change (Healey, 1983; 1991).

The employment structure in the different sectors of developed economies can usually be distinguished from the developing economies of the Third World. In particular, developed economies employ lower numbers in the primary sector and higher numbers in the secondary and tertiary sectors. However, this has not always been the case and in the early stages of the evolution of developed market economies the primary sector was the major employer. This demonstrates the dynamic nature of employment structure, with a general tendency for employment in the primary sector to decline over time.

These different *stages of economic development* are conceptualized in the Fisher–Clark model (Fisher, 1935; Clark, 1940). This is essentially a three-sector stages model, based on advanced industrial countries, which depicts a sequential shift in employment structure, from agriculture (primary sector) into manufacturing (secondary sector) and then into services (tertiary sector) (Fig. 1.3). The model is descriptive rather than explanatory and does not identify the processes bringing about structural shifts. It suggests that the pattern of change is broadly consistent for all industrial societies. The ideas of Fisher and Clark gained support and further development when Bell (1974) suggested a *post-industrial society* was emerging, in which the tertiary sector was becoming the main locus of economic growth. This new dynamism is particularly associated with the utilization of knowledge and information, suggesting that a fourth sector—an *information* sector, including services such as finance, insurance,

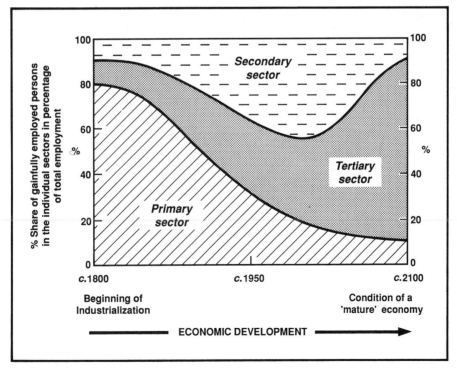

FIG 1.3 Employment structure and economic development in developed market economies (*source*: based on Hurst, 1974 p. 17)

real estate, business services and community, social and personal services—may need to be added to the standard three-sector model.

Six main reasons may be suggested for the growth of employment in the service sector in mature industrial economies (Gershuny and Miles, 1983; Howells and Green, 1986).

1. An increase in demand for services from final consumers as societies become richer.
2. An increase in demand for 'intermediate' or 'producer' services, such as finance, market research, and advertising.
3. A slower rate of increase of labour productivity in the service sector relative to manufacturing.
4. The subcontracting or 'externalization' of services, such as accountancy, by some manufacturing companies. These services would previously have been classified as manufacturing activities.
5. An increase in the internationalization of services, ranging from banking to fast-food, and public relations to car-hire.
6. The emergence of new service activities, such as computer programming and video shops.

There is also an important spatial dimension to the relationship between economic development and the economic sectors, because areas vary in their economic structure and the way their economies evolve. This idea may be illustrated by examining examples of changes in the structure of employment at two different spatial scales—the international and the regional. Singelmann (1978), for example, identifies three types of industrial transformation that have been experienced by different groups of countries:

1. *Western Europe* (United Kingdom, France, West Germany, and Italy), where the decline in the primary sector was replaced by employment in the secondary sector between 1900 and 1930. This was an intermediate step before the transfer of employment to services in the tertiary sector.
2. *United States and Canada*, where employment in the secondary and tertiary sectors initially grew in parallel, before the subsequent relative decline in manufacturing saw the gap in employment between the secondary and tertiary sectors widen.
3. *Japan*, where the proportion employed in services has been consistently higher than in the secondary sector. Singelmann explains this in terms of the country's ability to replace labour with technology and thus miss the dependence on manufacturing employment normally associated with economic development.

Singelmann's ideas suggest, therefore, that the Fisher-Clark thesis may only be applicable in a European context.

Nevertheless, many developed market economies (not just European) have experienced a clear shift from manufacturing to service employment. This process of *tertiarization* has been most marked in the United States, where seven out of ten Americans produced services rather than goods in 1983, but it is also important in such

TABLE 1.1 Employment changes in advanced industrial countries, 1973–1983

	USA		UK		West Germany		Japan	
	000s	%	000s	%	000s	%	000s	%
Agriculture etc	−31	−0.1	−96	−1.4	−553	−3.3	−1 740	−2.8
Industry	+28	+0.0	−2 600	−1.8	−2 202	−1.9	+360	+0.2
Services	+15 772	+2.6	+1 475	+1.0	+993	+0.8	+6 080	+2.1
goods	+4 884	+1.8	+118	+0.2	−284	−0.5	+2 410	+1.5
information	+10 888	+3.3	+1 357	+1.7	+1 277	+1.8	+3 670	+2.9
TOTAL	+15 770	+1.7	−1 224	−0.5	−1 762	−0.7	+4 740	+0.9
Replacement ratios								
Services/manufacturing		14.23		0.67		0.59		16.43
Information/goods		—		0.52		0.58		—

Source: Hall (1987a p. 98).

economies as West Germany, the United Kingdom, and Japan (Hall, 1987*a*). However, sharp differences also exist in the degree to which these four countries have compensated for manufacturing job losses (i.e. *deindustrialization*) by gains in service employment (Table 1.1). The virtual stagnation in manufacturing employment in the USA between 1973 and 1983 was more than compensated by a massive gain (15 million) in service employment, especially in information-handling services (finance, insurance, real estate, business services, and community, social, and personal services). In contrast, the United Kingdom lost over 2.5 million jobs in manufacturing (a classic example of deindustrialization); which were not made up by the modest growth in service jobs (1.5 million), again mostly in information services. The large discrepancy between the USA and the United Kingdom is depicted in Table 1.1 by *replacement ratios*, which show that 14.23 service jobs were gained for every manufacturing job lost in the United States, compared to a ratio of just 0.67 for the United Kingdom. A similar magnitude of difference occurred between Japan and West Germany, leading Hall (1987*a*) to conclude that in successful economies, such as the United States and Japan, employment gains in both goods-handling and information-handling services compensate for relatively modest manufacturing losses.

International differences in employment trends hide notable regional contrasts. In the United Kingdom, for example, three groups of regions can be identified on the basis of employment changes between 1971 and 1981 (Hall, 1987*a*):

1. Greater London, West Midlands, North-West, and Northern regions, where manufacturing decline was severe and the growth in the service sector (especially information handling) was lower than the national average.
2. Yorkshire and Humberside, Wales and Scotland, where manufacturing decline was greater than the national average but performance in the goods-handling sectors and information services was better.
3. The rest of the South-East, the South-West, East Anglia, and the East Midlands, which experienced an absolute gain in overall employment and where the less than average decline in manufacturing was more than compensated by a strong performance in goods-handling and information services.

Regions, of course, also hide important internal differences between, for example, inner cities, suburbs, and rural areas. This kind of *scale problem* is fundamental to studies of economic change and location.

The focus of this section, so far, on changes in employment structure may give the impression that the primary and secondary sectors of developed market economies are declining. Indeed the term *post*-industrial, used to describe the growth of the service sector and the development of the information economy, suggests that primary and manufacturing industries are no longer important. This is misleading for two reasons. First, it ignores variations occurring within sectors. For instance, within manufacturing many developed market economies are experiencing *reindustrialization*, in the sense of various processes of new investment and growth. Keeble (1989*a*) argues that in the European Community these include a resurgence of new and small firms; a rapid growth of 'high-technology' industry; widespread adoption of new computer-based technologies by existing industries; and a surge of new, inward multinational investment, particularly from Japan and America.

The second reason why it is misleading to think of the primary and secondary sectors as declining is that it is important to distinguish between the contribution of the different sectors to providing jobs, and their contribution to the economy and to land use. Although employment in services in developed market economies has been growing rapidly in recent decades, there has been little shift from goods to services in terms of output, which illustrates the weakening of the relationship between manufacturing employment and output discussed in the last section. For example, in the United States, when output is measured in constant dollars, there has been very little change in the share contributed by services since 1961 (Table 1.2). Certainly, in terms of wealth production and level of overseas earnings many primary and secondary industries are not only very significant but are also expanding. Indeed, many researchers (e.g. Fothergill and Gudgin, 1982) consider these sectors to be comprised largely of *basic* or exporting activities, while most of the service sector is *non-basic*, as its output is mainly for internal consumption. This argument can be taken too far and it can be shown that many services are productive, can stimulate economic growth in other sectors, and are increasingly

TABLE 1.2 Shares of employment and gross national product in the United States by sector, selected years, 1948–1976

	1948	1961	1976
EMPLOYMENT[a]			
Agriculture	10.8	6.9	4.2
Industry[b]	43.2	38.6	35.1
Services	46.0	54.5	60.7
GNP (1972 dollar)			
Agriculture	5.8	4.3	2.9
Industry[b]	43.0	40.7	40.7
Services	51.3	55.0	56.3

[a]Full-time equivalent persons engaged.
[b]Industry includes mining, construction, manufacturing, transportation, communications, and public utilities.

Source: Stanback (1979 p. 3).

being traded internationally (e.g. Daniels, 1983; Marshall *et al.*, 1988). It remains true, however, that a great deal of employment in services, as much as one half in one estimate (Cohen and Zysman, 1987), is more or less dependent directly on demand from the manufacturing sector. This raises again the issue of the blurring of the boundaries between sectors. For example, Hall (1988, p. 158) suggests that:

in a realistic accounting framework, much of the apparent growth of service jobs should really be reclassified to manufacturing; the fact that manufacturing employment declines, while informational jobs increase, arises from restructuring of the manufacturing sector, whereby productivity gains are obtained on the shop floor while ancillary service jobs are contracted out to specialized operations like accountancy, advertising, and legal services.

In the special case of the primary sector, there is a further reason for the continued interest of geographers in that much of the sector, principally agriculture and forestry, is an extensive user of land. Changes affecting these industries thus have an important impact on the evolution of the rural landscape.

Two of the key processes which contribute to changes in output and employment structure are technological and organizational changes, both of which have significant impacts on the spatial pattern of economic activity. For example, the reduction in the friction of distance, brought about by improvements in transport, has encour-

aged the intensification and specialization of agriculture. The greater freedom in choice of location has allowed particular agricultural activities to concentrate to a greater extent in those areas which are most suited for their production, because they provide, for instance, a better physical, economic, or political environment.

In manufacturing, technological innovations such as computer-assisted design and computer-based inventory and production control have encouraged a shift away from assembly-line systems of production to small-batch production and new job flexibility. This emerging kind of organization of production is called *flexible specialization*. This new flexibility has been aided and quickened by changes in consumer tastes, away from the items of standard mass production and towards differentiation and individual specialization. The increasing demand for a flexible workforce is encouraging economic growth away from older industrial areas dominated by assembly-line techniques and their associated trade union structures to 'new industrial spaces' (Scott, 1988), such as the craft industrial agglomerations around Emilia Romagna in Italy and the high-technology complexes of Orange County and Silicon Valley in California and Sophia Antinopolis in France. In Britain, Martin (1988*a*) suggests that the transition to flexible specialization has been associated with a divergence in economic fortunes at both regional and local levels, though there is a danger of assuming such organizational changes have a specific geographical outcome.

Flexible specialization, with its dependence on information technology, has furthermore led to an increased demand for producer services and helped to blur the distinctions traditionally drawn between the three economic sectors. These distinctions have been further complicated by the growth in importance of the *informal economy*, especially in the construction and service industries. The informal economy comprises the small but increasing part of the economy that goes unreported. It consists of an *underground economy* and a *self-service economy*. The former includes undeclared employment, self-employment, and multiple job-holding and has increased significantly since the economic crisis of the mid-1970s. It has been estimated that up to 10 per cent of all service activities in the United Kingdom will have gone unrecorded by 1990 (Lambooy and Renooy, 1985, cited by Howells and Green,

1986). The latter has witnessed a displacement to some extent of consumer services by manufactured goods operated by the consumers themselves (hence self-service); this includes a growth in DIY, automatic dishwashers and washing-machines, and the production of home-grown vegetables and fruit (Gershuny, 1978).

1.4 Summary

- This book is concerned with understanding the processes which lead to contrasts and changes in spatial patterns of economic activity (i.e. both the location of economic activities and the uses of land).
- It is important to understand the evolution of the economic landscape because it affects the social and economic well-being and opportunities of people living in different areas. It also influences the distribution of environmental impacts. Both these raise significant issues for the development of policies.
- There is a circular relationship between the processes of economic change and the location of economic activity. The impact of economic changes is felt unevenly between places. These spatial contrasts in turn provide opportunities and constraints which affect the operation of the processes of economic change.
- The different spatial scales are interrelated. To explain economic change in a particular area it is necessary to examine factors both internal and external to that area. Increasingly these external processes are operating on a global scale as the links between multinational enterprises, financial institutions, and countries strengthen.
- Among the important recent changes in the global economy are the decline in the production of raw materials, the weakening of the relationship between trends in manufacturing employment and production, and the increas-

ing significance of capital flows as a force driving the world economy.
- Both manufacturing and service activities are becoming more international, leading to a new international division of labour and the development of a hierarchy of world cities. The shift of manufacturing to low labour cost countries may, however, not be a long-term phenomenon.
- Developed market economies are also evolving as they adjust to the changing world economy. Most have entered a post-industrial phase characterized by an information society. Their primary and manufacturing sectors, however, remain important in terms of output, wealth generation, and land use. Although the number of jobs provided directly by the primary and secondary sectors is falling, much employment in services is more or less dependent on demand from these other sectors.
- Among the recent processes of change operating in developed market economies are tertiarization, deindustrialization, and reindustrialization. It has further been suggested that a system of flexible specialization is emerging based on a combination of technological and organizational changes. There has also been a recent growth in the informal economy.
- The geographical ramifications of these processes have yet to be fully revealed, although clearly economic changes result in considerable international and regional differences. Indeed, as is shown later in the book, some trends may result in both a concentration and dispersal of economic activities and these spatial responses may change over time.

This variability in the spatial outcomes of economic change presents geographers with an exciting challenge in the search for explanations. A number of theoretical perspectives which geographers use to help them understand economic change and location are reviewed in the next chapter.

2

Changing Theoretical Perspectives

Chapter 1 outlined the major economic and spatial changes occurring in the world economy and developed market economies. This chapter is concerned with the different theoretical approaches that have been developed to explain both economic change and the location of economic activity. The two are interrelated because theories of economic change have a spatial interpretation; indeed, it is increasingly being argued that, in the development of location theories, locational change needs to be assessed in the context of changes occurring in the national and world economy. Theories of economic change and location permeate the whole book and so it is important to grasp their main characteristics at this early stage. Further aspects of these (and other) theories are developed at various points throughout the text, particularly in the context of location and land-use decision-making (Chapter 10.1) and international and regional economic change (Chapters 14.2, 14.3, and 15.2).

Theoretical approaches to economic location and change have themselves changed over time. For example, the first major theory of economic change considered here—long wave theory—was proposed and further developed in the 1920s and 1930s, before being revived with the onset of world economic recession in the late 1970s. This period of considerable economic change (Chapter 1) witnessed the development of two further theoretical perspectives on economic change—world system theories and regulationist theories (see Section 2.1). A similar process of evolution, with three major theoretical perspectives, has characterized geographers' concern with economic location since the 1950s. The 1960s were dominated by neoclassical approaches to economic location, whereas the 1970s and 1980s favoured behaviouralism and structuralism respectively (see Section 2.2). Although the relative importance of these theoretical approaches has

changed over time, it needs to be stressed that one approach has not completely replaced another; proponents of each perspective are still active, ensuring a healthy theoretical debate. Indeed, the 1980s have been characterized by greater integration between the two sets of theories. Geographers are paying more attention to processes of economic change in their location theories and economists/social scientists are increasingly recognizing the importance of spatial differences in economic change.

This chapter is, therefore, divided into two main parts. In the first, the main characteristics of the three theories of economic change are outlined, with the different emphases they place on national and international structures being stressed. In the second, theories of the location and locational change of economic activity are reviewed and their main limitations listed.

2.1 Theories of economic change

Different theoretical frameworks have been developed to explain the nature of economic change in both the world and developed market economies. A major feature of the theories is the varying degree of emphasis placed upon the importance of history, the internal structure of an economy, and international relations (Harris, 1988). Three groups of theories are considered here: first, *long wave theories*, which suggest that economic change occurs in cycles and is associated with major shifts taking place over fifty years or so in the prevailing technologies; secondly, *world system theories*, which treat the world system as the fundamental unit of analysis and argue that economic change in any country can be understood only be examining the international economy as a whole; and thirdly, *regulationist theories*, which take the national economy as the frame of reference and explain economic change in terms of distinct historical phases, each characterized by a particular type of production system.

Long wave theories

The world recession of the late 1970s and early 1980s revived a long-running debate about the occurrence, in capitalist economies, of cycles which have gone from boom to bust and back to boom again. These 'long waves' have occurred approximately every half a century from the Industrial Revolution onwards and coincided with major changes in technology. Whereas most authorities now accept the existence of these long waves of economic activity, or *Kondratieff cycles* as they are usually called, the extent to which technological change is a cause or an effect of them is more contentious (Hall, 1985; M. Marshall, 1987; Preston, 1987). It is clear though that each Kondratieff cycle is associated with the application of a set of significant technological innovations. These *technological revolutions* (Schumpeter, 1939), *technological paradigms* (Dosi, 1983), or *new technological systems* (Freeman *et al.*, 1982) concern not only new products, but also new processes, new forms of transport

and communications and, some suggest, innovations in the organizational, managerial, and institutional environment as well. Significantly, different countries and different regions have been associated with the development of each technological revolution (see Chapter 15.2).

Kondratieff (1935), a Russian economist writing in the 1920s, identified three waves of economic expansion and contraction based on the movement of commodity prices since the late eighteenth century. The first of these waves coincided with the Industrial Revolution in Britain in the first half of the nineteenth century; the second saw industrial expansion in Europe and the Victorian depression of the 1880s; while the third coincided with the imperialist expansion of Britain, Germany, and the United States, reaching its climax in 1914. Had Kondratieff lived, he might have correctly forecast the economic depression of the 1930s, and a fourth cycle which began with the long post-war boom and was followed by descent into international recession in the late 1970s and 1980s. Extrapolating forward, a fifth cycle may be expected, beginning in the mid-1990s (Fig. 2.1).

Although Kondratieff's work was highly descriptive, he did suggest that the triggering mechanism for these cycles of economic activity is

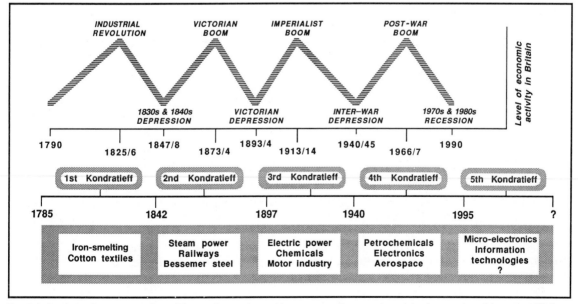

FIG 2.1 A schematic representation of innovation cycles and long waves of economic activity (*source*: based in part on Hall, 1981*a*, p. 535 and M. Marshall, 1987 p. 99)

technological development, which creates new economic opportunities and thus generates economic expansion. It was another fourteen years before this explanation was developed by Schumpeter (1939). He argued that at certain points in history a bunching of innovations occurs which together produce a rapid economic expansion. Schumpeter related the first Kondratieff cycle to developments in iron-smelting and cotton-spinning and weaving; the second to steam power, the railways, and Bessemer steel; and the third to electric power, chemicals, and the beginnings of the motor industry. Followers of Schumpeter have subsequently related the fourth Kondratieff cycle to developments in petrochemicals, electronics, and aerospace industries. Not surprisingly, there has been much speculation about which technologies may herald the start of a fifth Kondratieff cycle (e.g. Hall, 1985 and 1987b; Harris and McArthur, 1985). It is clear from examining earlier cycles that many of the key innovations leading to economic expansion reach the stage of commercial applicability in the recession phase of the previous cycle. On this basis, Freeman (1986) suggests that micro-electronics and the associated information technologies will be the key innovations of the next technological paradigm rather than biotechnologies, which are too new, and still less nuclear technology, which is currently too costly and limited in its operation.

Supporting evidence for Schumpeter's thesis of the bunching of innovations comes from a detailed analysis of hundreds of technical innovations by Mensch (1979). He identifies 1764, 1825, 1886, and 1935 as the peak years in which the clustering of innovations occurred. The regularity of the cycle led him to predict that 1989 would be the next 'radical year of history'. This innovation cycle, he argues, corresponds almost exactly to the long waves of the Kondratieff cycle (Fig. 2.1).

According to Schumpeter and Mensch, bunching of innovations is the key to understanding long waves of economic activity. They argue that there is a kind of *internal* automatic, regulating system within capitalist economies; the fall in profits which accompanies the onset of a recession stimulates a search for investment in new profitable opportunities, supplies the incentive to find commercial opportunities, and provides the demand to find commercial applications for earlier inventions (hence the bunching of innovations). Such a bunching, therefore, can be explained in terms of low profits and the adventurous entrepreneurship of industrial leaders. As each innovation works its way through, the market for a particular range of goods becomes saturated, profits fall and the cycle starts over again.

Others dispute this explanation. For example, members of the Science Policy Research Unit at Sussex University argue that the important phenomenon is not a statistically observable bunching of innovations, but rather the speed of the diffusion bandwagon *after* the basic innovations (Freeman et al., 1982). Freeman and his co-workers have presented evidence which suggests that rapid diffusion of new technologies is characteristic of economic upswings rather than depressions. Significantly, they and others (e.g. Mandel, 1980; Perez, 1983; M. Marshall, 1987) emphasize that long waves of economic activity are more a function of the social, economic, and political relationships in which particular forms of technology are developed and diffused, rather than anything inherent in the new technologies themselves. In other words, they see the waves as triggered by *exogenous* forces. For example, both the Sussex team and Mandel believe that the long wave starting around the time of the Second World War was partly triggered by the rearmament boom of the 1930s, by the war itself, and by the subsequent Cold War (Hall, 1985; Preston, 1987).

Long wave theories are, therefore, essentially historical and have considerable support in the academic literature. However, the theories do not attempt to understand spatial relationships and fail 'to explain how long waves are generated at the international level or the mechanisms by which national economies' cyclical movements are linked' (Harris, 1988 p. 29).

World system theories

The second group of theories explaining economic change, world system theories, are not concerned with cycles of change within national economies. Instead, they explain the evolution of a world economy in terms of the international character of the capitalist system; the internal structure of each nation's economy is of little significance (Amin, 1976). Wallerstein (1974), the main proponent of world system theories, envisages an evolving capitalist market system in which individual countries are subordinate to a structured world system. The world system is the unit of analysis (Harris, 1988), which can be used to understand economic change within both developed market economies generally and regions and localities of specific countries.

A major element of world system theories concerns the emergence of a new international division of labour in the 1970s (Chapters 1.2 and 14.3), where 'commodity production is being increasingly subdivided into fragments which can be assigned to whichever part of the world can provide the most profitable combination of capital and labour' (Frobel *et al.*, 1980 p. 14). As a consequence, it is argued that trade takes place in a world market, where commodities or semi-finished parts are either exported/imported or transferred from one country, or branch of a multinational company, to another. Supporters of world system theories suggest that this new international division of labour was generated by three forces, which 'came together' in the 1970s (Frobel *et al.*, 1980; Thrift, 1986; Harris, 1988):

1. The availability of large reserves of cheap labour in the Third World and newly industrializing countries for employment in industrial processes.
2. The development of new methods of transport and communication.
3. The subdivision of manufacturing processes so that each operation can be performed with minimal skills.

Multinational companies, the main beneficiaries of these forces, have subdivided their stages of production on a spatial basis and transferred much of the more labour-intensive work to Third World countries. This has led to mass redundancies, high unemployment, and deindustrialization in many developed economies, notably those heavily dependent on multinational companies (e.g. the United Kingdom). According to world system theories, therefore, in order to understand economic change at regional and local levels, the operation of the international economy has to be examined.

It is on this last point that world system theories have received most criticism. As Knox and Agnew (1989 p. 97) contend, 'it is clearly not the case . . . that the world economy now runs rampant over national economies without check or restraint in either underdeveloped or developed countries.' By relegating the internal structure of national economies to a position of insignificance, world system theories suggest that the main trends outlined in Chapter 1.3—tertiarization, deindustrialization, reindustrialization, flexible specialization, and the emergence of information and informal economies—have nothing to do with the internal policies of different governments, local labour markets, trade-unionism, and the decisions of individual entrepreneurs. Harris (1988) points to two further fundamental objections. First, world system theories are over-dependent on one type of economic activity—large-scale multinationals—whereas most studies of national economies are paying increasing attention to small and medium-sized manufacturing concerns as well and the ways in which such firms are interacting with financial institutions and the expanding tertiary sector. Secondly, they do not explain why the three forces mentioned (reserves of cheap labour, subdivision of manufacturing processes, and new methods of transport and communication) culminated in the 1970s; their history is ignored, as are other forces creating change in economic activity.

Regulationist theories

In contrast to world system theories, which see the main mechanisms of change occurring at the global scale, the third group of theories concerned with economic change—the regulationist theories—believe that the main forces for change occur within national economies. Aglietta (1979; 1982) and Lipietz (1984; 1986), the main authors to outline a detailed theoretical framework of regulation, view the world economy as consisting of relations between national economies and being shaped by them rather than by a world system.

The term 'regulationist' derives from the central concern of these theories to examine how production and growth (accumulation) in advanced capitalist economies are regulated and why one regime of accumulation is replaced by another. Each regime of accumulation is dominated by a particular mode of production (the way in which human societies organize their productive activities) and brought to an end by *internal* changes in the economic system. Capitalist economies have, therefore, according to regulationist theories been characterized by a succession of accumulation regimes, although these have not occurred in the regular/cyclical sequence suggested by long wave theories.

Regulatory mechanisms can be analysed at two levels (Harris, 1988): first, within a country; and secondly, between countries. The former include mechanisms that attempt to overcome recurring disequilibria and achieve some sort of balance in the economy. This could be done through regulating the relations between capital and labour for example, involving such mechanisms as the role of market forces in determining prices and wages, the system of management and wage payments, the policies of the state towards income control and welfare provision, and the banking system. The main mechanism regulating the economic relations between nations is the international finance system (Chapter 1.2). Of particular concern here is the way in which the dominance of nations has changed over time; dominance is usually based on finance and the financial centre of the world economy changed from London to New York, which in turn is now being challenged by Japan and Europe.

Regulationists argue, therefore, that structural changes within a nation's economy can be explained by a breakdown in one mode of production and a shift towards a new one. In the 1970s and 1980s, a major shift occurred in methods of production and the labour process (the way in which labour is organized); this led to a decisive move from Fordism to neo-Fordism (see Chapters 4.2, 6.1, 7.1, 7.2, and 15.2 for more details of changes in the labour process). Fordism, characterized by mass production and consumption, assembly-line techniques (with large-scale investment in inflexible fixed plant), state intervention in the management of the economy, and collective bargaining, was regulated by the continuous growth of purchasing power which, in turn, was encouraged by escalating wages, strong unions, state monetary and fiscal policies (with full employment), and a supportive welfare system. According to the regulationist school, economic growth encouraged the search for market opportunities on a world scale, helping to foster global trade links.

However, problems with Fordism began to appear, notably the rigidity of mass production, increasing costs of production, labour militancy, and worker morale. Economic growth started to falter and many developed market economies experienced deindustrialization and rationaliza-

tion, just as multinationals 'switched' parts of their production to Third World countries in an attempt to maintain Fordist processes. Government policies attempted to revitalize economic growth, through such measures as wage controls, but Aglietta (1979) argues that the developments which brought Fordism to an end were beyond the control of any individual nation and were the result of competition between nations. In particular, he points to the development of new forms of international money (e.g. the Eurodollar) and technological convergence in productivity levels, which reduced the superiority of US industry and raised that of European and Japanese industry.

These developments in turn led to a more flexible regime of accumulation known as neo-Fordism (Blackburn et al., 1985). Regulationists interpret neo-Fordism as being characterized by increased flexibility in production technologies, labour processes and markets, and patterns of consumption. Aided by technological developments in computer-assisted design and computerized production control, small-batch processing has become economical. This has permitted geographical decentralization, as parts can be produced in many different locations and ordered for assembly in batches. With the breakdown of large factories and rigid work hours, labour has also been geographically decentralized, large-scale unionism has declined, and the state has abandoned its commitment to full employment and corporate arrangements with management and the unions.

Regulationist theories, therefore, have a number of positive attributes. First, they have a strong historical dimension. Secondly, they have an important international dimension, which is created and conditioned by rivalry and interactions between national states rather than by a world system. Thirdly, they allow an examination of the internal structure of a country, where for example the initiatives of local governments to attract industry to their areas can be researched. As Knox and Agnew (1989 p. 97) remark, 'the crux of the present situation is the coexistence of the national and global structures within the world economy.' However, regulationist theories have not escaped criticism. Massey (1988a) suggests that they do not show how important Fordism was or how its dominance was established. Similarly, there is some discussion as to whether a new phase of accumulation (neo-

Fordism) has actually begun or whether recent economic restructuring represents an attempt to extend the life of Fordism (Hudson, 1988; Chapter 15.2).

Geographers have begun to incorporate spatial elements into these theories of economic change, especially those concerned with long waves and regulation. World system theories have also been applied by geographers, but at this scale of analysis much depends on macro-economic policies of individual countries (Chapter 14.3), in which geographers have little expertise. Moreover, world system theories pay little attention to the internal structure of national economies and thus cannot explain intranational variations in economic location and change.

The interest in long wave and regulationist theories shown by geographers can be related to their desire to understand how capitalist economies develop unevenly over space. For example, within the Regulationist school Fordism was associated with mass production and consumer goods industries. Spatially, this led in Britain to a concentration of economic activity near the two major conurbations: London in the South-East and Birmingham in the West Midlands (Chapter 15.2). Northern regions, by contrast, continued to be dominated by older (heavy) industries. The pattern of uneven development at that time was, therefore, between expansion in the South-East and West Midlands and decline elsewhere. With the breakdown of Fordism, production became more geographically decentralized, mainly in search of cheap labour. This involved a movement of industry to the Third World and to the peripheral areas in the United Kingdom for example. In turn, the move to neo-Fordism, with its more flexible production systems, is leading to a further redistribution of industry into new areas of high technology like the M4 Corridor and the Cambridge district (Chapter 6.2). The overall result of different regimes of accumulation is an increasingly unequal national geography (Martin, 1988a).

Long wave theories can similarly be linked to the changing nature of uneven spatial development. For example, Hall (1985) suggests that each Kondratieff cycle was important in different parts of the United Kingdom (see Chapters 6.2 and 15.2). He believes that the fifth cycle is likely to occur in areas associated with neo-Fordism because of the presence of scientific research and high-technology industries. Others (e.g. Freeman, 1986) agree with the location of the fifth Kondratieff cycle but disagree that it will be caused by technology within the area. Instead, they relate the location of high-tech industries in the Cambridge and M4 areas to the regional bias of R. & D. expenditure towards the South-East (Chapter 8.3), the traditional industrial structure of northern regions, the unequal availability of venture capital (Chapter 4.3), and the local-planning environment for small firms. M. Marshall (1987) further developed the link between long wave and regulationist theories and argued that the two theories could be combined to help explain the complex phenomenon of uneven geographical development. Most of these ideas have emerged from within the structuralist approach to economic location, which is one of three major approaches developed to explain the changing distribution of economic activity; these form the focus of attention in the next section.

2.2 Theories of economic location and locational change

This section examines three main theoretical approaches to economic location and demonstrates how their relative importance has changed over time. It deals with the philosophy surrounding the changing approaches to explanation rather than the applied nature of decision-making, which is covered in Chapter 10. As attention is concentrated mainly on theoretical developments since the 1950s, a few statements concerning earlier approaches to explaining economic location seem appropriate.

Traditional studies in economic geography were of an *idiographic* nature (stressing the unique) and involved collecting digests of factual information about economic production and trade within and between different parts of the world. Emphasis was placed upon generating large statistical gazetteers on the import and export patterns of particular commodities (e.g. cotton, tea, silk) and on individual regions ('capes' and 'bays' geography—Johnston, 1987). Regional differences, or areal differentiation, were highlighted (Hartshorne, 1939). For example, O. E. Baker described the uniqueness of different agricultural regions of the world in a series of

papers in *Economic Geography* during the 1920s
and 1930s. The similarities between places were
ignored. Explanations of these patterns of economic activity were usually expressed in terms of
the physical environment (Wooldridge and East,
1958). For example, it was assumed that physical
factors such as soils and climate 'determined' the
distribution of agricultural regions (determinism).

Idiographic studies and determinism became
the subject of increasing criticism during the
1950s. Three criticisms in particular can be highlighted here:

1. They encouraged the increasing fragmentation of economic geography, as researchers
   became specialists in particular regions and/
   or products.
2. They usually concentrated on *how* economic
   phenomena were located and not on *why*
   they were so spatially arranged.
3. They failed to aid the development of generalization and thus theory.

The last criticism may appear rather harsh, as it
has recently been questioned whether such generalizations can be derived (see later discussion of
structuralist approaches).

In response to these criticisms, economic geography experienced a change in direction. This
involved a shift from idiographic to *nomothetic*
studies (stressing the general) and a movement
away from simple description of location patterns
and towards the identification of processes creating such patterns. Three major theoretical perspectives have dominated studies of economic
location since the 1950s—neoclassical (in the
1960s), behaviouralism (in the 1970s), and structuralism (in the 1980s)—and these form the focus
of attention in the rest of this chapter.

Neoclassical approaches

A *positivist* science seeks to establish generalizations and theories and following Schaefer's (1953)
famous paper on the formulation of laws in
geography, economists and geographers became
interested in the science of spatial relations. Attempts were made to develop generalizations and
principles in economic geography and the search
for regularities in patterns of economic activity
emerged as a main focus of interest. It was
assumed that:

1. there is an identifiable order to the material
   world,
2. people are rational decision-makers, reacting in the same way to given stimuli,
3. people have complete knowledge and seek
   to maximize profits,
4. economic activity takes place within a freely
   competitive manner and on a uniform land
   surface (although this was often only the
   starting-point of more complex models).

Emphasis was placed on the development of
models and theories of economic activity, within a
spatial context. Traditional economic theory
(*neoclassical*) was used by both geographers and
economists to model patterns of land use (see
Isard, 1956; 1960; Bunge, 1966; Harvey, 1969*a*).
The derived patterns were the result of *deductive*
reasoning (reasoning from general principles) and
not observation; for this reason, most models
developed in economic geography at the time
were *normative*. They simply stipulated patterns
of agriculture, industry, and services that should
occur, given a number of assumptions about the
processes at work. Most of these processes were
held 'constant' and the models concentrated upon
the interrelationships between just a few factors
and their spatial consequences. Often using
statistical/mathematical procedures, these *partial
equilibrium models* produced an 'optimal' location
and/or land-use pattern, where profits were maximized and/or costs were minimized. Distance
was assumed to be a predominant influence on
human behaviour and spatial patterns could be
accounted for by examining the relationship
between distance and transport costs. Other factors discussed in the 'context of change' section of
this book were either ignored or assumed not to
have sufficient locational significance to be
incorporated into the models (Chorley and Haggett, 1967). A more *inductive* approach to model-
building was often added at a later stage, where
the distorting effect of local factors on the 'ideal'
pattern was examined (Abler, Adams, and Gould,
1971).

Such an approach to economic geography suggested that the explanation of spatial patterns
could be found from within the patterns themselves. This represented a major advance on idiographic studies and was quickly adopted during
the 1960s; the approach was admirably synthes-
ized in Harvey's (1969*a*) classic work on *Explana-*

tion in Geography. Examples of neoclassical approaches to location theory can be described for each of the three main economic sectors. Although proposed well before the 1960s, the significance of such approaches was not appreciated until that decade. In agriculture, von Thünen's model of land use (1826) provides the classic example (Hall, 1966; Morgan and Munton, 1971), whereas in industry Weber's model (developed in 1909) is the one most commonly discussed (Weber, 1929; Hurst, 1974; Smith, 1981). Similarly, Christaller's central place theory, proposed in 1933, typifies normative approaches to modelling the distribution of settlements and services (Christaller, 1966; Daniels, 1985a). These particular models and their numerous modifications and extensions have been examined in detail in standard geography texts (e.g. Abler, Adams, and Gould, 1971; Hurst, 1974; Lloyd and Dicken, 1977; Boyce and Williams, 1979). Such detail is not repeated here but certain features of the models of von Thünen, Weber, and Christaller need to be outlined.

All three are based on rather unrealistic assumptions, including perfect knowledge and rational economic behaviour, maximization of profits, and (in the cases of von Thünen and Christaller) a linear relationship between distance and transport costs (e.g. transport costs are directly proportional to distance) and a homogeneous physical environment, often referred to as an isotropic surface. In each model, the key variable is distance. For example, von Thünen's theory of agricultural land use, written in 1826 (Hall, 1966), is based on the concept of *economic rent*, which simply defined is the difference between income and costs. Economic rent is, in turn, controlled by distance and the cost of transporting the farmer's output to the market (Fig. 2.2a). Consequently, the theory predicts that bulky and perishable products will be produced close to the market.

Within this general theory, von Thünen developed two models: first, a crop model, where there would be a zonal organization of crops around a market; and secondly, an intensity model, where land-use intensity would decline with distance from the market (Fig. 2.2a). The concentric circle pattern was later modified by the inclusion into the models of a navigable river and a minor market centre. Von Thünen's ideas provided a useful framework for examining patterns

of agriculture and his theory has been both modified (Peet, 1969; Kellerman, 1977) and applied at numerous geographical scales (Horvath, 1969; Griffin, 1973; Ewald, 1976; Chisholm, 1979) in different parts of the world.

Weber's (1929) theory of industrial location follows a similar format to von Thünen's. In the first instance, Weber assumed that industry would locate where the costs of production and distribution would be minimized. According to his theory, the most important of these costs was transport and Weber demonstrated their effect with the use of locational triangles (Fig. 2.2b). The point of least transport costs (P) depends on whether the industry is weight-gaining or weight-losing. For example, in weight-gaining industries such as bottling, baking, and car-assembly a market-oriented location is attractive; conversely, such weight-losing industries as iron-smelting and pulp and paper industries prefer, according to the theory, to locate near to the sources of raw materials.

Modifications were then made to this basic framework by examining the distorting effects of labour costs and agglomeration. Weber realized that an industry could be attracted to a point of least labour costs, if the savings in labour costs offset extra transport costs. To accommodate this, Weber derived lines of equal total (assembly and distribution) transport costs (*isodapanes*) for helping to determine the least cost site. In Fig. 2.2b, cheap labour is found at points L_i and L_{ii} and would reduce costs by 40p per unit of production. Thus, any location within the 40p isodapane (e.g. L_i) would be more profitable than point P; an industry would not locate at L_{ii} because this would increase costs. Finally, Weber noted the tendency for industry to agglomerate. He demonstrated how firms may be prepared to incur increased transport and labour costs if production rises sufficiently to lead to an overall reduction in the unit costs of production. In the model, this is the point where the critical isodapanes intersect (Fig. 2.2b). Weber's ideas were applied with some success to the Swedish paper industry (Lindberg, 1953) and the Mexican steel industry (Kennelly, 1954–5); they have been summarized in the work of Lloyd and Dicken (1977) and Smith (1981).

Central place theory is similarly based on certain assumed laws of human behaviour, from which was developed a model of the size, spacing,

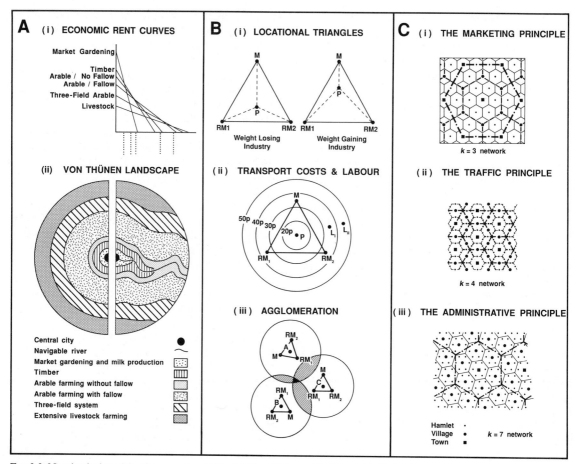

FIG 2.2 Neoclassical models of economic activity: (*a*) Von Thünen; (*b*) Weber; (*c*) Christaller

and function of settlements. Christaller (1966) excluded manufacturing towns and developed an idealized system of hexagonal market areas based on two basic concepts: *threshold* and *range*. The former is the minimum level of demand needed to maintain a service and the latter is the maximum distance a consumer is willing to travel to purchase that service. From these concepts, a hierarchy of service centres was envisaged, with a large number of small (low-order) centres providing basic services and increasingly smaller numbers of high-order centres providing more specialized goods in addition to the basic services. Three types of settlement pattern were modelled (Fig. 2.2*c*). First, a system known as *k* = 3 hierarchy (*marketing principle*), where second-order centres for example were envisaged to serve three times the area and three times the population of first-order centres. Similarly third-order centres

would serve hinterlands that are three times the size of second-order centres. In such a hierarchy, the number of settlements at progressively less specialized levels follows the geometric progression 1, 3, 9, 27 . . . (Knowles and Wareing, 1976). Secondly, a *k* = 4 hierarchy (*transport principle*), where the progression would be 1, 4, 16, 64 . . . , could develop in regions where transport costs are particularly important. The *k* = 4 solution maximizes the number of central places on straight-line routes. Finally, a *k* = 7 hierarchy (*administrative principle*) would develop when, for administrative reasons, it is necessary to group centres even more strongly. A greater concentration on high-order centres thus occurs, in the sequence 7, 49, 343 . . . , so that districts of practically equal area and population are created, in the centre of which lies an administrative capital.

Christaller (1966) emphasized that any of these

principles could influence the distribution of central places and, not surprisingly, empirical evidence of such hierarchies were soon being reported in different parts of the world, from China and Sri Lanka to the USA (see Johnston, 1964; Berry, 1967; Everson and Fitzgerald, 1969). Most studies were concerned with the distribution of consumer services and there was little or no reference to the information-dependent producer services (Daniels, 1985a).

There can be no doubting the value of such neoclassical models for providing a framework for empirical studies or their marked impact on studies of economic location. Indeed, Berry (1967 p. 12) observed that 'a theory or model, when tested and validated, provides a miniature of reality and therefore a key to many descriptions.' However, it was this emphasis on description rather than explanation that provided the main criticism of neoclassical approaches to economic location. A detailed critique of such 'spatial science' is not possible here (see Johnston, 1986 and 1987), but some of the main limitations can be listed:

1. The neoclassical assumptions of *economic man*, the maximization of profits, complete knowledge, and the perfect ability to use knowledge are untenable. Non-economic motives are also relevant to an understanding of economic behaviour.

2. Most models of this type are devoid of empirical content and thus are unrealistic.

3. It is not possible to derive explanations from just within the descriptions themselves as the processes creating spatial variations in the distribution of economic activity are often external to the actual patterns. Consequently, in seeking explanations at the level of the individual 'firm' the models lack real explanatory power.

4. Most models are static in nature and the social and economic changes which have occurred since their development are far from those predicted by classical theory. For example, the growth of large farm businesses and multinational enterprises (see Chapter 7.1) defies the notion of perfect competition (where knowledge of all data are available to all competitors and where all resources are perfectly divisible and mobile).

5. Neoclassical models ignore both the importance of history and the position of the firm within the total economic system. Location behaviour should not be isolated from its historical context.

6. The social system within which economic activity is modelled is taken for granted and so the models are independent of cultural and behavioural reality. As Massey (1984a) demonstrates, there are no such things as spatial processes but rather there are social processes and relationships which have a spatial form (see Chapter 9). As the models were developed within a particular social context, they must refer to particular situations only. It follows, therefore, that they have no universal application.

In summary, neoclassical approaches to economic geography can be criticized for seeking explanation at the level of the individual firm, farm, or office, for building abstract models in which real world decisions are treated as additional factors, and for ignoring the historical conditions in which firms are operating.

Behavioural approaches

Disillusionment with the type of deductive model-building exercises which dominated the spatial science 'era', together with changes in the real world (e.g. growth of large organizations/firms) which made such assumptions about perfect competition even less tenable, led, in the 1970s, to the adoption of behavioural approaches to the study of economic location and locational change. Models were proving to be rather poor descriptions of reality and attention began to be directed more towards *inductive* reasoning (from the parts to the whole) and the micro-scale. Behaviouralists considered the individual to be the main motive force in economic affairs and behaviour was inductively investigated, in an attempt to discover generalizations. Much of behaviouralism, like neoclassical approaches, was seeking generalizations; however, the former was based on what actually occurs (at the individual level) rather than on an idealized (group) view of behaviour. Emphasis became centred on a wider range of 'variables' that help shape patterns of economic activity, including motives, values, preferences, perceptions, and opinions. Large data sets were compiled and analysed using statistical techniques. Consequently, the earliest behavioural studies in economic geography were merely an appendage to the spatial science paradigm (pattern of thought). However, whilst neoclassical theories helped to strengthen links between economic geographers and economists, behaviouralism developed the relationship between geographers and sociologists and psychologists.

Behaviouralism stresses the non-optimal behaviour of entrepreneurs and attempts to produce alternative theories to those based on 'economic man'. Attention is focused more on the processes creating spatial variations in economic activity than on the actual patterns. The decision-making process is a major area of concern and many decision-making models relating to agriculture, manufacturing, and services have been formulated (see Chapter 10.1). These models draw attention to two important points concerning the location of economic activity and the distribution of land uses: first, that decision-makers do not have perfect information when making their locational choices, or perfect ability to use it; and secondly, that conscious decisions are often made knowing that they are not optimal and that profits will not be maximized. The second point emphasizes the complexity of locational choice and land-use decision-making, where many other factors beside profit may be involved (e.g. of a social and environmental nature). Indeed, the behavioural approach argues that businesses may attempt to satisfy multiple goals which, as well as profit, could include security, growth, risk minimization, self-preservation, and satisfaction.

One attempt to conceptualize the relationship between the amount of information available to decision-makers and their ability to use it was Pred's (1967; 1969) behavioural matrix. The matrix represented an attempt to provide an understanding of decision-making at the margin of transference (point of change from one land use to another). The two axes of the matrix are the amount of information available (vertical) and the ability to use that information (horizontal) (Fig. 2.3); economic man is located in the bottom right-hand corner. A farmer or entrepreneur's position on the horizontal axis will be influenced by such factors as size of business, age, level of education, and aspiration levels, whereas on the vertical axis his or her place will, in part, be influenced by location, reflecting the nature and importance of information flows (possibly in a distance decay fashion from urban areas).

Pred replaced the idea of profit maximization with Simon's (1957) notion of *satisficing behaviour* (see below) and recognized that, whilst

entrepreneurs in different positions in the matrix will vary in their decisions, it is possible for two businesses at the same position in the matrix to react to given stimuli in contrasting ways and thus make different locational decisions. In relation to agriculture, for example, land-use patterns are likely to overlap in a disorderly way, distorting the distinct concentric pattern as envisaged by von Thünen (Fig. 2.3).

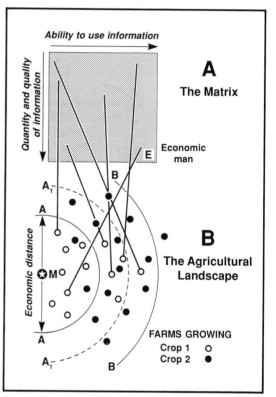

FIG 2.3 The behavioural matrix and agricultural location (*source*: Ilbery, 1985a p. 36)

An element of chance and uncertainty is involved in nearly all forms of decision-making and Pred attempted to show how some entrepreneurs will become more informed over time and thus 'shift' through the matrix towards economic man; similarly, the less informed are likely to be eliminated. However, this takes little account of one of the main foci of this book—changes in the external environment. With major changes occurring in regional policy for example (see Chapter 8.3), entrepreneurs become less informed and may experience what Pred (1969) terms a *parametric shock*, forcing them to move back through the matrix towards the top left-hand corner. By the time industrialists become well informed of these policy changes, new measures may be introduced. This is one reason why optimal patterns of economic activity are unlikely, except by chance.

Although useful conceptually, the behavioural matrix was intended only as a hypothetical device. It has received little empirical testing (see Chapter 10.1), mainly because of the difficulty of accurately locating the cell in the matrix to which an entrepreneur belongs. Harvey (1969*b*) criticizes it as being an over-simplification of the complex nature of behaviour.

Risk and uncertainty are important concepts in behavioural geography. They help to emphasize that entrepreneurs are unlikely to be optimizers and are more likely to be *satisficers*. First advanced by Simon (1957) and applied in a study of Swedish farming by Wolpert (1964), the satisficer concept suggests that entrepreneurs will do the best they can on the basis of the information they acquire. The tendency to adopt the first 'satisfactory' decision from a range of possible alternatives was shown to be a dominant characteristic among farmers in Sweden. In comparing actual labour productivity in farming with a normative model of potential labour productivity, Wolpert (1964) attributed the large discrepancies to the farmers' desire for a satisfactory solution and the degree of aversion to risk and uncertainty. However, 'satisficing' is an ambiguous concept (Harvey, 1969*a*) because it uses personal considerations and chooses the best (most reasonable) of a limited number of choices. It is not clear whether a deliberate sub-optimal decision has been made or whether an attempt to make the best decision has, because of uncertainty, resulted in a sub-optimal decision.

Game theory represents a further attempt to provide a solution to decision-making, taking into account an entrepreneur's incomplete knowledge. The theory introduces probabilistic formulations into decision-making, associated with conditions of uncertainty, and is concerned with the rational choice of strategies (e.g. land uses, locations) in face of competition from an opponent, usually the environment. The basic principles are outlined elsewhere (Found, 1971; Ilbery, 1985*a*) and have been applied mainly in agricultural situations (Gould, 1963; Agrawal and Heady, 1968; Cromley, 1982). However, game-theoretic

models have been the subject of numerous criticisms, ranging from a failure to incorporate the whole set of factors affecting decision-making behaviour to an inability to explain the patterns they simulate (see Ilbery, 1985*a*).

Behavioural studies of economic location have been concerned mainly with long-term decision-making, as this has a major impact on the economic landscape (e.g. choice of crops, location of factories, choice of shopping centres). Most work has been of an empirical nature, seeking to 'measure' perceptions, attitudes, and behaviour, and to derive generalizations from case studies (Walmsley and Lewis, 1984). Examples can be drawn from all economic sectors and include surveys of farmers' decision-making behaviour (Ilbery, 1978, 1983*c* and *d*, 1985*a* and *b*; see Chapter 11.3); decision-making within individual firms and locational change in industry (Hamilton, 1974; Townroe, 1975; Healey, 1981*a*; Krumme, 1981; Carr, 1983; Hayter and Watts, 1983; see Chapter 10.2); and studies of office location and shopping choice and consumer behaviour (Potter, 1977; 1979; Timmermans, 1979 and 1981; Edwards, 1983). Most of these studies have collected information on the attributes of farms, firms, and other businesses and attempted to relate these to the behaviour of individuals, thereby inferring an explanation. Factors affecting locational and land-use decisions have also been elicited.

Other behavioural studies of economic activity have divorced themselves from positivist methodologies and adopted a more *humanistic* approach (see Walmsley and Lewis, 1984; Johnston, 1986). These have relied heavily on description and the literal reconstruction of the world as seen through the eyes of the individual whose behaviour is to be understood. *Humanism* denies the existence of the 'objective' world studied by positivists and concentrates upon the perceived worlds of decision-makers. Humanistic approaches study unique events and attempt to 'break away from the preoccupation with scientific method and quantification and to study instead distinctly human traits such as meaning, feeling and emotion' (Walmsley and Lewis, 1984 p. 162). However, a concentration on the feelings and perceptions of just a few decision-makers renders the derivation of generalizations impossible and humanistic approaches have, like earlier behavioural studies in a positivist mould, been criticized for failing to develop theory (Olsson, 1978; Ley, 1981).

Behaviouralism has highlighted the need to incorporate the motives of entrepreneurs into explanations of the changing patterns of economic activity. However, it has been the subject of mounting criticism (Massey, 1979a; Bunting and Guelke, 1979) and some of the more important points can be listed here:

1. It has failed to solve the problems associated with earlier neoclassical approaches, especially in terms of poor explanation. Massey (1979a) described the behavioural approach as pure description and merely a variant of neoclassical approaches, and Walmsley and Lewis (1984) warned that it runs the risk of substituting description for explanation. In modelling economic behaviour, geographers have simply highlighted the existence of variations in behaviour and not explained them; emphasis has been placed on *how* decisions are made, rather than on *why* firms and farmers, for example, choose respectively, a particular location or crop.

2. Too much emphasis has been placed on the attitudes of individual entrepreneurs and too little on behaviour itself. Attitudes and behaviour are often (and wrongly) assumed to be synonymous. It does not follow, for example, that just because an industrialist has a favourable attitude towards a particular area he or she will behave accordingly and move there. There remains comparatively little work on real behaviour.

3. Approaches developed under the behavioural 'umbrella' have varied considerably in content and there is no generally accepted methodology. This has hindered the search for generalizations and the identification of strong empirical regularities in behaviour; indeed, studies have demonstrated the great variety in economic behaviour (e.g. North, 1974). Consequently, the development of theory has been slow and it could be argued that the behavioural approach has made little contribution to the development of theory explaining economic location.

4. Behaviouralism places too much emphasis on choice; it takes much of the material world as given and examines how people operate within it. Yet, it is possible to explain how an individual acts only within the constraints set for him or her. One cannot ignore constraints in the economic system; for example, a proper explanation of consumer behaviour cannot be obtained without analysing why a particular set of alternatives (shopping centres) is there in the first place.

5. In separating the individual business from the broader 'environment', too much autonomy is afforded to factors at the 'firm' level. The wider processes operating in the economic system and society are ignored, and the importance of history and the uniqueness of places are underplayed. As Johnston (1986 p. 128) expounds, 'the study of economic geography cannot be isolated from the more general study of socio-spatial structures.'

Structuralist approaches

According to this theoretical perspective, space is what an economy makes of it and the economic landscape is the product of the overall structure of the economic system in which individual decision-makers operate. Structuralism thus adopts a more holistic approach than behaviouralism and argues that behaviour is constrained by wider social, political, and economic processes. This suggests that parts cannot be considered independently of wholes; for example, class and culture, rather than individual values and ideas, are the main determinants of behaviour.

Consequently, structuralist explanations of location and land-use patterns attempt to relate the changing geography of economic activity to the underlying structure of society and to economic and social relations. For example, whilst neoclassical approaches to economic location may accept that 'low wages encourage employment growth' is an adequate explanation for job creation in an area, structuralism argues that it is necessary to ask why there are low wages in some areas and not others in the first place (Watts, 1987). According to structuralists, the answer to the latter lies in the structure of the capitalist society in which the firm works.

Boddy (1987 p. 36) admirably summarizes the importance of structural approaches to explanation:

They place particular emphasis on the analysis of production itself rather than simply on 'location factors', they see production as an essentially social process structured by capital–labour relations and the wider political and ideological context, they situate empirical analyses in their wider national, international and historical context, and finally, they place emphasis on the role of labour and the nature of the labour process as a key element in the production process.

Structuralists believe that a crucial factor in the development of any spatial structure is the way in which surplus capital is circulated, concentrated, and utilized in space (Johnston, 1987; Chapter 10.1). With the increased mobility of capital (Chapter 4.3), uneven spatial development (see Section 2.1) is a necessary precondition for the process of capital accumulation. Consequently, the restructuring of capital occurs at numerous scales: e.g. world economy, nation state, and the city. This helps to create what Massey (1984b) terms *spatial divisions of labour* (i.e. what types of job people do where) (see Chapters 4.2 and 15.2).

Economic geographers adopting a structuralist perspective are particularly interested in the macro socio-economic processes which underlie spatial patterns of economic activity (hence their interest in long wave and regulationist theories of economic change), although the actual details of the spatial impacts may not always be examined. For example, the reasons for differential rates of economic development between places may be advanced, without examining which places experienced which rates. A dominant feature of structuralism, therefore, is that explanations of economic patterns (or observed phenomena in the *superstructure*) cannot be found from within the patterns themselves. In other words, explanations will not be obtained solely through an empirical study of the economic sectors. Instead, there is a need to examine the general structures or processes which underpin the economic patterns. These processes or mechanisms are 'hidden' in the *infrastructure*, which cannot be observed; it is possible only to theorize about its nature. Consequently, much structuralist work has involved developing theories about the nature of the infrastructural processes and relating these to the patterns in the superstructure (see also Chapter 10.1).

The superstructure is itself founded on the prevailing mode of production (as espoused in regulationist theories), which over time builds up internal contradictions and is replaced by another mode (e.g. shift from tribalism to feudalism to capitalism). A historical sequence is thus developed, where one mode of production is superseded by another; consequently, structuralists argue that locational and land-use decisions are specific to a certain time period. As an economic system does not return to the same point, even within a particular mode of production, the situation facing entrepreneurs is never repeated. Explanations, therefore, should be time (and also place) specific and, for this reason, structuralists reject the use of models which seek to generalize about location and land-use patterns.

An example of the structuralist approach may make the ideas easier to follow. Changes in the location of an industry, for example, are—according to structuralists—a function of two main groups of factors (Massey, 1981) (Fig. 2.4). First, there are *changes in economic conditions* which affect the *requirements of production*. In other words, changes in the national and international economic environment lead to changes in the demands that an industry makes of locations. It is assumed that in developed market economies the main demand made by firms is for profitable locations. However, the requirements for profitable production, in, for instance, the extent of mechanization, vary between firms and between industrial sectors. The second group of factors is the *changing geographical environment*. For instance, the locational opportunities for profitable production may alter in response to changes in say population distribution or transport technology. So, to understand the recent shifts in the

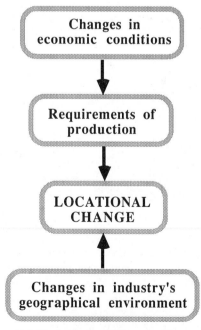

FIG 2.4 A structuralist framework for examining changes in industrial location (*source*: based in part on information in Massey, 1981 p. 307)

location of an industry it is necessary, according to a structuralist approach, to examine recent changes in both the industry's production requirements and its geographical environment (for an application of this framework see Chapter 12.2).

Much structuralist work has been theoretical in content. This is typified by the increasing interest shown by rural and agricultural geographers in the economic, social, and political structures within which agriculture has been restructured and the food chain operates (Wallace, 1985; Marsden *et al.*, 1986*a* and *b*; Marsden, 1988; Le Heron, 1988). In advocating a structuralist approach to the study of capitalist agricultural systems, Marsden *et al.* (1986*b*) outline four main 'areas' for study which would help to redefine agricultural geography:

1. *Uneven development*, whereby capital penetrates different regions at different times.
2. *Conceptualization of the family labour farm*, whereby the different transformations it makes to capitalization need to be explored. Wallace (1985) suggests that an issue of considerable theoretical and political interest is whether the basis of agricultural production remains sufficiently different from other sectors of the economy for small-to-medium-sized family businesses to survive as the 'modal' group of operators and, indeed, to prosper.
3. *Agriculture and state policy*, whereby government policies have supported the family farm but inadvertently encouraged the penetration of agriculture by outside capitals (e.g. from industry).
4. *Geographical and historical specificity*, whereby local studies are required to understand the process of uneven development. Historically, different areas developed different agricultural systems and this initial uniqueness is important in understanding the spatial ramifications of agricultural change.

The 1980s have, however, been characterized by an increase in empirical studies, within the broad field of economic change and restructuring. Most have concentrated upon the geographically unique outcomes of general underlying processes. One of the earliest was Massey and Meegan's (1982) analysis of the processes affecting the geography of job loss (see Chapter 10.2 for details). The three processes identified in that study—

intensification, investment and technical change, and rationalization—have been applied to individual companies such as British Shipbuilders, Plessey, and Metal Box (Peck and Townsend, 1984), and to particular industries like steel (Morgan, 1983), the semiconductor industry (Cooke *et al.*, 1984), and the electronics industry in South Wales and the M4 Corridor (Morgan and Sayer, 1985). The last example is typical of the increased interest in locality-based studies, including work on the Lancaster area (Murgatroyd and Urry, 1983) and the Bristol region (Boddy and Lovering, 1986; Boddy *et al.*, 1986), and culminating in the Economic and Social Research Council's (ESRC) initiative on the 'changing urban and regional system' in Britain (Cooke, 1989).

Some of this work has adopted a *realist* approach, which recognizes that individuals make choices within the constraints set by economic processes (Sayer, 1984). *Realism* aims to explain the causes of events (e.g. what makes things happen) and does not search for regularities or generalizations. The study of causation is not dependent on the number of times an event occurs; it requires *intensive* research programmes (see Chapter 10.1) which examine causal processes in a particular case or cases (Johnston, 1987). This is in contrast to *extensive* research, characteristic of positivist approaches to economic location. Sayer (1982*a*) made the important distinction between 'rational abstraction' and 'chaotic conception'. The former 'isolates a significant element of the world which has some unity and autonomous force' whereas the latter 'combines the unrelated and divides the indivisible' (Sayer, 1982*a* p. 71). Much behavioural work in industrial geography, for example, has been concerned with 'components of change' analyses and examined employment change in terms of openings, closures, movements in or out, and *in situ* change (Keeble, 1976; Watts, 1987). These 'components' are fine as descriptive categories but they represent a classification based on outcomes rather than causes and are an example of a chaotic conception because each 'component' (e.g. *in situ* job loss) may relate to a range of different causes (e.g. intensification, rationalization, partial relocation—non-chaotic conceptions). 'Closure', for example, is not a category with explanatory power; it is an outcome of underlying forces and so does not explain why it occurred.

Earlier approaches to industrial change can be criticized on similar grounds. For example, Fothergill and Gudgin (1982) explain the urban–rural shift in manufacturing employment in Britain mainly in terms of one factor—the lack of space for physical expansion in urban areas (the constrained location hypothesis; see Chapters 4.1 and 16.2). As Boddy (1987 p. 64) complains, this is 'in total disregard for the range of processes underlying the spatial restructuring of employment'. The causal processes at work in this instance may not be spatial in nature; they probably reflect the character of productive capacity itself in the older industrial areas and not a lack of space. It may well make more economic sense to replace old capacity with new investment and this provides the opportunity to relocate in rural areas, where a new spatial division of labour can be exploited. Any attempt to relate spatial patterns to spatial causes is likely to represent a 'chaotic conception'. Realists argue, therefore, that classifications should be based on processes like rationalization and intensification rather than on outcomes like closures and movements.

Although structuralism is comparatively new in human and economic geography, it has not escaped criticism, most notably from Hamnett (1977), Duncan and Ley (1982), and Walmsley and Lewis (1984). The main points of discussion are as follows:

1. In recognizing that economic geography would be incomplete without an examination of wider processes, the macro-economy has been over-emphasized. As a consequence, the world of 'lived experience' is underplayed (Johnston, 1987) and little attention has been devoted to real events in specific places and at specific times (Johnston, 1980). By concentrating on the development of a general theory of political economy, structuralist approaches in economic geography have been guilty of using 'fragments of reality to illustrate the theory rather than using theory to provide insights into the real world' (Walmsley and Lewis, 1984 p. 24).

2. Structuralists are opposed to the idea of sovereign decision-makers, and individuals within a particular social class are assumed to behave in a standardized manner. 'Each class is given a type of consciousness or ideology which individuals appear to internalize *en masse*' (Duncan and Ley, 1982 p. 40). A strong flavour of economic deter-

minism, so characteristic of spatial science, thus prevails in structuralism.

3. In assuming that all individual behaviour is 'determined' by larger structures, the importance of variations in economic behaviour at the level of the individual firm, farm, or office is ignored. However, individuals are not 'passive units in an overall plan' (Walmsley and Lewis, 1984 p. 24) and Hamnett (1977 p. 143) describes this as 'throwing the baby out with the bath water'. Structuralism has been criticized, therefore, for being a one-sided analysis, where attention is focused on constraints and choices are left to look after themselves. Clearly people do make choices, within a set of constraints, and realism has attempted to accommodate this point within its methodology.

4. A question mark hangs over whether structuralist ideas are really geographical if they ignore the details of the superstructure (i.e. actual patterns of economic activity). Theorizing about processes operating in the infrastructure is often aspatial. Realism has allowed some of these fears to be allayed, although it remains largely theoretical and untested and also has a tendency to be deterministic (Chapter 10.1).

2.3 Summary

This chapter has, in the space available, outlined briefly the major characteristics and limitations of the different theoretical approaches to both economic location and change. A basic dichotomy of methodologies exists between the two groups of theories, with one stressing economic change and the other emphasizing location and locational change. However, they are essentially dealing with related topics and thus their interrelationship should be stressed and further developed. This is beginning to happen, especially with structuralists applying ideas from long wave and regulationist theories of economic change in an attempt to explain uneven geographical development.

● Differences in philosophy are also clearly apparent within each group of theories. For example, the major contrasts between theories of economic change can be related to different geographical scales of analysis and to the varying importance attached to history. In theories of economic location, the major difference lies between neoclassical and behavioural approaches to explanation, which search for general principles, and structuralism, which argues that they do not exist.

- While long wave theories relate cycles of economic change to shifts in prevailing technologies, regulationist theories explain economic change in terms of distinct historical phases, each characterized by a particular type of production system. World system theories differ again in arguing that economic change in any particular area can be understood only by examining the international economy as a whole.

- Theories of economic location and locational change have developed and varied in importance over time. Neoclassical theories seek their explanations in terms of an idealized (group) view of economic behaviour, which contrasts with behavioural approaches and their emphasis on what actually occurs at the individual level. Structuralists criticize the behaviouralists' assumption of freedom of choice and argue that behaviour is constrained by wider social, political, and economic processes. A compromise is offered by realists who recognize that choices are made within constraints.

- All of the theoretical frameworks outline in this chapter continue to be employed in studies of economic location and change, suggesting that this subject area has been characterized by a healthy and continuous process of evolution rather than a series of separate 'revolutions'. Elements of all the different theories are used in this book and it is for this reason that this chapter has tended to emphasize the limitations rather than the advantages of each theoretical perspective. It is impossible to cover both aspects fully in a single chapter and it is hoped that readers will, as they make their way through the subsequent chapters, be able to list what they believe to be the relative merits of the different theoretical approaches, as well as better appreciating their weaknesses.

- This book adopts an integrated approach to the study of economic location and change, drawing heavily upon the different theoretical perspectives developed from within studies of economic location in particular (and complemented by theories of economic change where relevant). Such an approach is aptly summarized by Johnston (1980 p. 411): 'a combination of behavioural and positivist approaches, sensibly geared to the problem being studied and set within a structuralist framework, should allow a better explanation of actual patterns.' Despite this, some caution should be exercised in using such a 'mix and match' approach in that different approaches ask different types of questions and are underpinned by different philosophies.

The next part of the text is concerned with an examination of some of the many factors which affect economic location and change (Chapters 3 to 9); these are then combined in a discussion of location and land-use decision-making (Chapter 10).

II   The Context of Change

3

The Physical Context

Economic systems are dynamic and patterns of economic activity change in response to different sets of circumstances. Whilst the physical environment remains fairly static in the short to medium term, the extent to which it acts as a constraint on the location and distribution of economic activities varies over time, according to such considerations as technological developments and changing supply/demand relationships. The physical environment, therefore, sets broad limits within which economic relationships influence specific locations; as these economic relationships change so the location and distribution of economic activity also changes.

Two fundamental points with regard to the effect of physical factors need to be made at the outset: first, the physical environment does not act in a deterministic manner and can be overcome, for example, with positive changes in the price received for minerals and agricultural products; and secondly, the isotropic surface assumed in neoclassical models of economic location is untenable (Chapter 2.2), as macro and micro variations in physical conditions will always exist, providing opportunities for and constraints upon economic development.

It is possible, therefore, to relate patterns of primary, secondary, and tertiary activity to the opportunities and constraints presented by the physical environment. However, it is within the primary sector, and especially in agriculture and the extractive industries, that the constraints of the physical environment in particular are most apparent and discussed. Consequently, this chapter concentrates upon the 'physical context' of agriculture and mining and attempts to demonstrate how the constraints imposed by the physical environment vary in relation to changing economic conditions.

3.1 Natural resources and the physical environment

An important concept concerning land and physical conditions is that of natural resources. These can be of two broad types: renewable and non-renewable. The former are biological and relate to the vegetative or animal components of the environment, and are thus important in agriculture, whilst the latter are inorganic 'stock', as in mineral resources. A further important distinction is between resources and reserves. *Resources* are dynamic, constantly changing as the circumstances of exploitation alter. They can be defined as all deposits of a material (i.e. mineral) for which uses exist, whether or not the deposit can be worked profitably (Bradbeer, 1986). Resources may, therefore, be known, but not economically or technologically recoverable, or they may be inferred to exist but not, as yet, discovered (Spooner, 1981). The part of the resource stock that is capable of profitable working, under existing economic and political conditions and with the available technology, is known as a *reserve*. Reserves are developed from resources, through the application of technology, capital, and expertise, and are defined more by economic than physical criteria.

The concept of a resource is, therefore, both cultural and functional. Indeed, the perception of any resource does not rely on physical properties, but on a range of cultural factors. Spooner (1981 p. 9) summarizes the situation well: 'The term resource does not apply to a material or an object, but to a value placed upon a material, in view of the function it may perform or the operation in which it may take part.' Resources are not, they become (Zimmerman, 1951). They are inseparable from human wants and capabilities and change in response to an increase in knowledge and economic and social development. Location helps to determine whether or not a resource becomes a reserve. For example, small-scale iron-ore deposits were a reserve in eighteenth-century Britain, but are ignored today as higher quality ore from large-scale deposits abroad can be imported more cheaply.

Resources can be classified into four main groups:

1. *Ubiquities*, which occur everywhere, as in oxygen for steel making
2. *Commonalities*, which are widely occuring and often occupy extensive areas, as in agricultural land and forestry, and sands and gravels.
3. *Rarities*, which occur in very few places, as in diamonds (e.g. South Africa) and nickel (e.g. eastern Canada).
4. *Uniquities*, which occur in one place only, as in cryolite (flux for aluminium) in Greenland.

This classification demonstrates that resources have *place utility* (a measure of satisfaction with respect to a given location); indeed, locational differences in the distribution of resources can help to explain the spatially variable nature of economic development. The relationship between resources and economic development is a complex one, but many regions have developed from an important initial resource endowment, such as coal. If aided by multiplier and backwash effects, in the form of employment generation and increased purchasing power, a region can prosper through a process of cumulative causation into 'self-sustaining growth' (see Section 3.3 and Chapter 15.2 for further exemplification of these processes).

3.2 Agriculture and the physical environment

Traditional approaches to agricultural geography were characterized by attempts to identify and delimit agricultural regions on the basis of such physical criteria as climate and soils (Whittlesey, 1936; Symons, 1967). Implicit in this work was the idea that spatial differences in farming practices were a function of differences in the physical environment. Such determinism did not, how-

ever, lead to a satisfactory environmental theory of agricultural location (Grigg, 1982). This failure can be related to the large number of influences that affect the spatial patterning of farm types, of which physical factors represent only one group. It is the constantly changing interaction between physical and human factors that affects patterns of agricultural land use, an interaction made even more complex by two further influences: first, the dynamic nature of agriculture, where changes in economic relationships (e.g. demand changes, changing government policies) lead to an imbalance between physical and economic 'environments'; and secondly, the personal characteristics of farmers and their varying attitudes towards, and perceptions of, risk avoidance and changes in mechanization, methods, and crop and livestock types.

It follows, therefore, that there 'are very few, if any, situations where physical factors are either all-important or of no account in the (changing) distribution of agricultural practices' (Ilbery, 1985a p. 9). This situation relates to two factors in particular—scale and crop type. The importance of physical constraints becomes clearer as the scale of analysis increases and at larger scales it is possible to correlate variations in agriculture with environmental conditions, as has been demonstrated in Europe (Clout, 1971), America (Michaels, 1982), and Britain (Briggs, 1981). At the micro scale, however, differences in farm management practices and farmer characteristics are likely to be more important in explaining variations in agricultural land use. Similarly, the biological and physical requirements of crops differ, with some needing specific conditions and others being suited to a wide range of environments and subjected to such bio-physical constraints as disease (see example of hops in Chapter 11.2). The classic example of the former is maize in the US Mid-West, where the spatial limits of production have been shown to be clearly defined by physical controls (Morgan and Munton, 1971).

Maize is, in fact, often used to demonstrate the importance of two concepts in relation to agriculture and the environment: first, the ecological optimum; and secondly, the margins of cultivation. The former argues that for every crop there are minimum requirements of moisture and temperature without which it will not grow, and also maximum conditions beyond which growth ceases (Grigg, 1982). As conditions vary from crop to crop, different 'margins of cultivation' exist. These ideas are graphically portrayed in Fig. 3.1, where climatic conditions deteriorate regularly in all directions from a central point (the ecological optimum), until the absolute or physical margins of production are approached (where it is either too wet, too dry, too hot, or too cold). Cultivation rarely takes place near the physical margins and instead farmers operate well within the 'economic' margins, where returns from the crop (income) are higher than production costs. Whilst the absolute limits of production are fixed (except for new crop varieties), the economic margins are dynamic and change in response to either an improvement or deterioration in economic conditions. With a fall in prices and/or a rise in production costs (price–cost squeeze), the economic margins may 'move' further away from the physical limits and towards the optimum area. In this situation, farming practices would increasingly seek those areas offering a *comparative advantage* (the greatest ratio of advantage over other areas or the least ratio of disadvantage). This in turn would encourage a changing pattern of regional specialization in agriculture

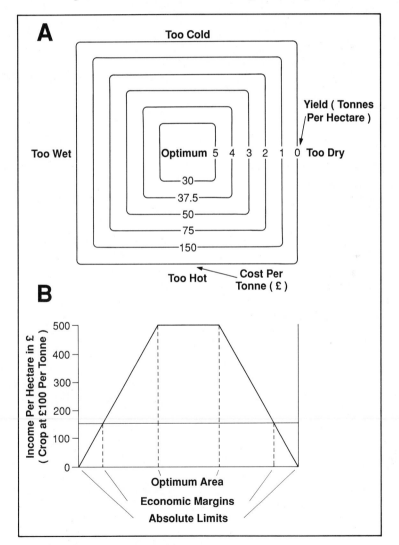

FIG 3.1 The ecological optimum and margins of cultivation.
(*source*: Grigg, 1984 p. 115)

(Winsberg, 1980; Bowler, 1981). A good example of this process is the changing pattern of vegetable specialization in England, away from the Vale of Evesham (poorer quality land) to the Fens (higher quality land) (Ilbery, 1985c). Conversely, favourable economic conditions (as present for so long under the operation of the Common Agricultural Policy of the EC) could shift the economic margins towards the absolute limits. This partly helps to explain the westward shift in cereal farming in England since the mid-1970s.

The relationship between physical and economic margins is, therefore, a complex one and has been examined in case studies in both Finland (Laaksonen, 1979; Varjo, 1979) and Scotland (Parry, 1975; 1976). Finland is a country crossed by the absolute limits, or physical margins, of several crops, and crop failures occur from time to time. Harvest yields are necessarily related to climatic factors and Varjo (1979) envisaged that

the progressive southward movement in the cultivation limits of different cereal crops (Fig. 3.2a) was a response to deteriorating climatic conditions. Indeed, a climatic amelioration in the 1930s and a deterioration in the 1940s caused the physical margins of cultivation to shift first northwards and later southwards. Since the 1950s, however, climatic conditions have remained fairly stable, yet violent southward movements of the margins continued to occur, especially during the 1960s. Varjo explains this apparent anomaly in terms of economic factors and market considerations and declining profitability in particular. Between 1960 and 1974, the output of spring wheat required to cover overall costs rose from 700 kg/ha to 1600; similar increases were recorded for barley and oats, from 800 to 1760 and 860 to 1750 kg/ha respectively. These changes were responsible for the 'retreat' of the economic margins, where cereal yields succeeded in covering

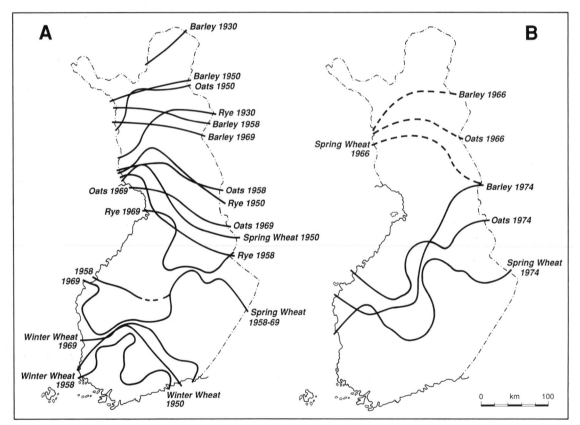

Fig 3.2 Physical and economic margins of agriculture in Finland: (a) changing northern limits of production for cereal crops, 1930–69; (b) changing economic margins for spring wheat, barley, and oats, 1966–74
(source: Varjo, 1979 pp. 227, 231)

input costs (Fig. 3.2*b*). Varjo (1979) suggests that in reality the economic margins were even further south than indicated because farmers' wages had been excluded from the analysis. With falling profit margins, farmers attempted to cut costs by reducing fertilizer applications. This in turn helped to increase the number of crop failures, especially in northern districts.

Similar physical and economic margins are identified by Parry (1975; 1976) in a study of abandoned farmland in the Lammermuir Hills of south-east Scotland. Over 20 per cent of the existing moorland had been used for agricultural practices at some time; 9 per cent (4890 ha) before 1860 and 12 per cent (6500 ha) between 1860 and 1970. Parry thought that climatic deterioration had caused the physical (absolute) margins of cultivation to retreat 'downhill'. This was examined in relation to oats, the only crop with commercial potential on the higher slopes of the Lammermuir Hills. The cultivation of oats was shown to be sensitive to climatic conditions and, using three indicators of climatic change—exposure (average windspeed), summer wetness (potential water surplus), and summer warmth (accumulated temperature)—Parry demonstrated how the absolute limit to production had fallen by 140 metres between 1300 and 1600.

By 1860, the physical margin (upper climatic limit) was established at between 320 and 350 metres above sea-level. However, an economic margin (lower climatic limit) was also identified within the foothills. The location of this lower limit was 'largely the product of the economic and social incentives to cultivation operating at any one time' (Parry, 1975 p. 3). When the upper and lower climatic limits of marginal land were compared with the distribution of abandoned land before 1860 (Fig. 3.3), a strong correlation was obtained, indicative of a causal relationship.

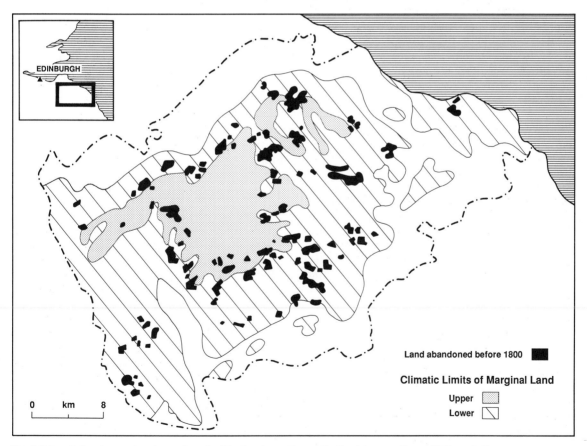

FIG 3.3 Land abandonment and margins of cultivation in south-east Scotland (*source*: Parry, 1975 pp. 4, 6)

Undoubtedly, therefore, the slow deterioration in climate since 1300 had reduced the potential for successful cereal cultivation in the marginal uplands. Yet, Parry (1975 p. 11) stressed that 'climatic deterioration was not, of course, the most important factor behind the abandonment of land', a proper explanation of which could only be obtained by examining such factors as the decay of monastic farming systems, fluctuations in demand, and soil exhaustion. It was, however, because of climatic change that high-altitude farming had become particularly sensitive to socio-economic conditions.

Given both the economic depression of the late 1970s and early 1980s in most developed economies and the *price–cost squeeze* in agriculture (where the costs of inputs increase at a greater rate than the price of outputs), it is not surprising that interest has been shown in the relationship between environmental factors and the yield of particular crops (Gillooly and Dyer, 1979; Briggs, 1981; Michaels, 1982). Farmers have increasingly sought the 'best' physically endowed areas (ecological optimum) for their enterprises, in an attempt to raise profits and gain a comparative advantage over other farmers in either the same area or elsewhere. At regional and national scales, a process of agricultural specialization will occur (Bowler, 1986), whereby areas concentrate upon those crops for which they have a *comparative advantage*; other products can easily be imported as a system of trade develops. The relationship between physical and economic influences on farming is, therefore, a very dynamic one, causing the margins of cultivation to shift over space and time. There will always be physical constraints to agriculture, in terms of climate, soils, and topography. However, it is their interaction with changing economic conditions that helps to determine both changing patterns of agricultural land use and the margins of production.

3.3 Mineral resources: physical constraints and economic opportunities

Most minerals occur in limited locations which, for physical and geological reasons, are often remote and inaccessible, with low population densities. It is not surprising, therefore, that the more accessible resources are exploited early.

Mining usually takes place in regions offering few advantages for other forms of economic activity. In addition, the non-renewable character of minerals means that production has a restricted life span, after which the local economy will decline (unless other activities can be substituted for mining).

The distribution of mining is necessarily related to the fixed location of mineral deposits. However, the geography of mining is far from simple, being influenced by a complexity of location factors, summarized by Warren (1973 p. 6) as 'the response of enterprise to the known geological facts, though conditioned by the availability of capital and labour, by political considerations, planning controls and, very importantly, by the legacy from past patterns'. As with agriculture, therefore, it is the interaction between physical and economic considerations that influences patterns of mining activity. This interaction is aptly demonstrated in the following quotation from Bradbeer (1986 p. 100): 'the prospects for ... (mineral extraction) ... rest not only on the physical endowment, but also on the complex process of resource appraisal. This involves the assessment of geological conditions, technologies of extraction and processing, market forces, demand and price, and the statutory and fiscal framework of mineral industries.' The complexity of locational decision-making in mining is enhanced by the changing relative importance of such influencing factors.

Physical factors and mining

The changing patterns of mining are, therefore, related to two crucial sets of factors—physical and economic—with the latter increasingly overcoming the former. Physical constraints to mining affect costs of production and thus net returns and include the quality and quantity of deposits, geological conditions, and climate. Together, such factors help to determine the margins of production. The quality of a deposit refers to its mineralogical content, which is the amount of mineral/metal per tonne of ore; this ranges from a very low percentage to over 70 per cent and can, therefore, have a significant effect upon working costs. Quality varies spatially, with exploitation again depending on costs and supply/demand patterns. For example, high-quality underground minerals will be ignored if lower-quality but open cast ones are available. Conversely, iron-ore is not mined around the American Great Lakes unless it has a mineral content of over 30 per cent; in the United Kingdom it has consistently been mined at less than 20 per cent, because of a lack of alternative higher-quality sources. Quite often metamorphic rocks contain a range of mineral compounds, which may add to the economic viability of mining (Hay, 1976).

Although high-quality minerals may be found in large deposits, there is often an inverse relationship between quality and quantity (Fig. 3.4). The best-quality deposits are usually concentrated in few places, whereas deposits of lower quality can be widely distributed. All other things being equal (which they seldom are), higher-quality deposits will be exhausted first, increasing the demand and economic viability of lower-grade sources. This has occurred in copper-mining, where known deposits with a mineralogical content of over 50 per cent have been 'worked out'. A shortage of supply has led to the mining of copper with as low a content as 0.8 per cent. Previous waste can, therefore, become commercially viable, causing old metal slag heaps to be reworked. Similarly, if the mineral is located in an inaccessible area that is lacking in basic infrastructure, it is the quantity as well as the quality of the deposit which helps determine whether or not it becomes an economically viable reserve.

A good example of this latter situation involves the thick and plentiful beds of high-quality iron-ore in the harsh physical environment of the Labrador trough in eastern Canada. Although discovered in the 1890s, ore was not shipped until the completion, in 1953, of a 571 km railway from Seven Islands, on the St Lawrence, to Schefferville (Fig. 3.5). The sub-arctic conditions re-stricted mining to the summer months and it was the combination of high quality (> 50 per cent) and quantity (> 400 million tonnes) that made the operation economic. Similar developments occurred further south at Gagnon with the building of a rail link to the expanding town of Port Cartier, which could accommodate 100 000 ton tankers. Whilst the ore deposit was of lower quality (35 per cent), it was upgraded to 65 per cent pellets, which were dry and capable of being transported throughout the winter. Together, these developments enabled Canada to become an important exporter of iron-ore, primarily to the USA and Europe.

Even if quality and quantity are both high, adverse geological conditions can make mining uneconomic. Ore that is either difficult to separate or contained in deep underground beds that are folded and faulted may not become a reserve, whereas lower-grade deposits in favourable geological conditions could be commercially viable.

Economic factors and mining

A range of physical factors, therefore, helps to shape the changing pattern of mining operations. However, as with agriculture, the extent to which they act as a constraint to production depends on such economic factors as production and transfer costs. The former vary spatially, according to the presence or absence of infrastructure, the cost of labour, rates of absenteeism, taxes, and social security payments. The latter are a function of location and are affected by market/distance relationships. Transport costs tend to decline proportionately with increasing distance (tapering effect) (Chapter 5.2) and this can have a greater discriminating effect on mines in close proximity to the market than on those located further away (Hay, 1976).

Minerals have both *unit* and *place value*. The former is the ratio of value to weight (McCarty and Lindberg, 1966) and is related to distance from the market and the possibility of substitution. Deposits of sand and gravel, for example, have low unit value and their price is strongly influenced by transport costs. They have few substitutes as sources of aggregates and their value is highly dependent upon the place in which they are found. There tends to be an inverse relationship between unit and place value,

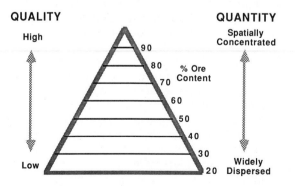

FIG 3.4 The quality/quantity pyramid in mining

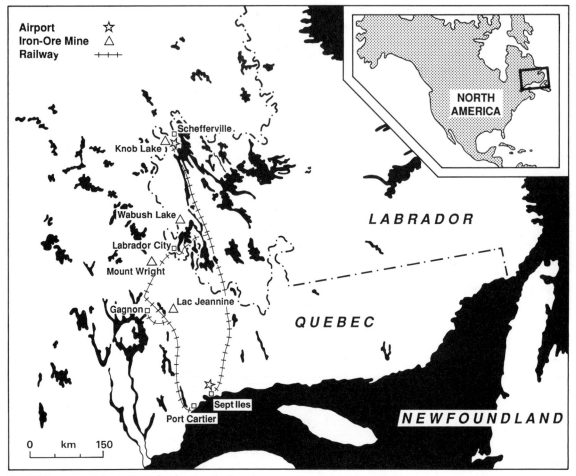

FIG 3.5 Iron-ore mining in the Labrador trough, Canada

although technological developments in transport (e.g. oil and gas pipelines) have permitted exploitation further from the market than unit value would otherwise suggest.

If one assumes favourable geological conditions, least-cost principles suggest that pits near to the market will be exhausted first, with new pits further away becoming more economic over time. Such temporal shifts in patterns of production formed the basis of simple models of mining developed by Wilson (1968) and Hay (1976). The former used least-cost principles to demonstrate how mining on a hypothetical coalfield would develop through time. Assuming one thick, continuous seam dipping gently from the outcrop, one market and shipping point, and one mode of transport, different stages of development were likely to occur (Fig. 3.6):

1. Simple tunnelling into the outcrop. With transport costs increasing with distance from a central shipping point, the first mines 'should locate on those sections of the outcrop closest to or most accessible from this point' (Wilson, 1968 p. 79). As these become exhausted, further pits, at greater distances from the shipping point, will open along the outcrop.

2. Shaft-mining develops as it becomes more economical to mine coal at greater depths, but closer to the shipping facilities. Again, those areas nearest the market or export point would be worked.

3. Further developments in shaft-mining occur in less favourable locations and at even greater depths and distances from the market. The combination of depth and distance that gives the least total cost is the optimum one.

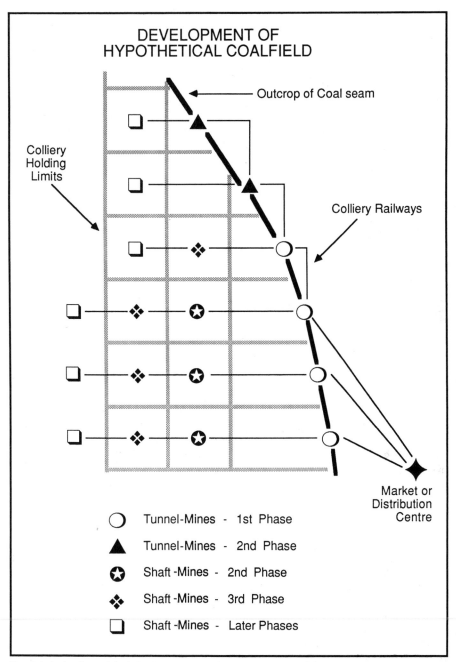

DEVELOPMENT OF
HYPOTHETICAL COALFIELD

Outcrop of Coal seam

Colliery
Holding
Limits

Colliery Railways

Market or
Distribution
Centre

○ Tunnel-Mines - 1st Phase

▲ Tunnel-Mines - 2nd Phase

✪ Shaft -Mines - 2nd Phase

❖ Shaft -Mines - 3rd Phase

▢ Shaft -Mines - Later Phases

FIG 3.6 A simple model of the development of a hypothetical coalfield (*source*: Wilson, 1968 p. 79)

Although aware of the model's many limitations, Wilson applied it with some success to three coalfields in New South Wales, Australia. In particular, the early stages of development in the South Maitland coalfield could be explained by the least-cost hypothesis (Fig. 3.7). Later stages saw similar shifts in location to those suggested in the model, but they could be better explained in terms of the end of the life cycle of the original pits than by least-cost principles. However, the model did not account for the secondary reworking of pits, especially the scavenging on coal tips.

The importance of least-cost principles would seem to have declined over time as other economic factors have influenced more modern mining developments. However, they can still be important, as demonstrated by British Coal's (formerly the National Coal Board) drift mine near Selby in Yorkshire (North and Spooner, 1976). The location of the mine was influenced by both mining and transport costs, avoiding the difficult Bunter Sandstones but taking advantage of nearby existing rail routes. This has not always been the case, as demonstrated by British Coal's proposals for a three-mine complex in the Vale of Belvoir (north-east Leicestershire), which was first rejected and finally reduced to a single construction at Ashfordby on environmental grounds (see below).

Technological change and economies of scale have increasingly reduced the importance of place value and hence market proximity on mining operations. Developments in transportation have allowed the working of lower-grade deposits away from the market, just as new and large extraction and processing technologies have reduced production costs, generated scale economies, and permitted an (increasing) localization of production in certain areas. A trend towards large-scale, low-grade mining, serving larger markets over wider distances can thus be discerned. This has been accompanied by corresponding changes in organizational structure, whereby individual mining entrepreneurs, with

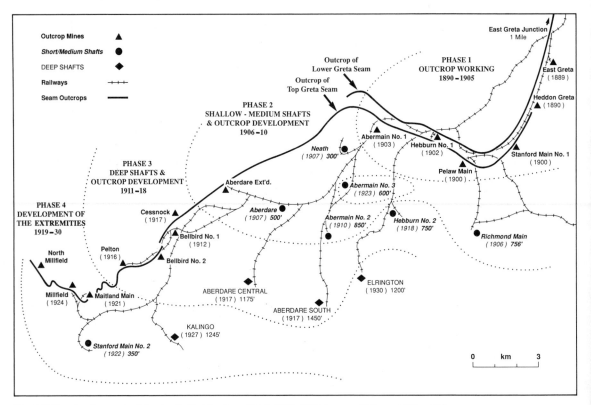

FIG 3.7 The development of the South Maitland coalfield, 1890–1930 (*source*: Wilson, 1968 p. 87)

their seemingly less rational location behaviour, have been progressively replaced by a concentration of ownership in the hands of more rational corporate organizations. As with other industries (Chapters 11, 12, and 13), mining has become more capital-intensive and vertically integrated with mineral-using manufacturers.

Improved processing technology can help to overcome the physical constraint to mineral production. This, together with government aid and political uncertainties abroad, permitted a renewed interest in the Cornish tin industry in the 1960s and 1970s (Goodridge, 1966; Blunden, 1970; Hewison and Whitmarsh, 1981). Three new mines were opened in west Cornwall between 1971 and 1976, at Pendarves, Wheal Jane, and Mount Wellington, and employment in tin-mining rose to 1500 by 1977 (Spooner, 1981). The £5.3 million project at Mount Wellington was aided by a £0.8 million development grant and a £0.8 million government loan. Success was, however, short-lived. Pendarves went bankrupt in 1973 and was taken over by St Piran. The withdrawal of grants in 1977 caused further decline and in 1978 Mount Wellington closed, supposedly because of poor-grade ore and water problems; Wheal Jane soon followed, for the same reasons. A more likely explanation for the closures was, according to Spooner (1981), mismanagement by Consolidated Goldfields, especially as both Mount Wellington and Wheal Jane were taken over and reopened in 1979 by an international mining group including Rio Tinto Zinc, before closing again in the mid-1980s. The revival in the Cornish tin industry was, therefore, related to changing economic circumstances (e.g. the price of tin and the awarding and withdrawing of government grants) and provides a good example of 'politically induced economic development in Britain' (Warren, 1973 p. 240).

Indeed, political factors and planning decisions have played an increasing role in the geography of mining. In Britain, exploitation of state-owned minerals requires planning permission, which is the responsibility of County Planning Authorities. Unfortunately, national policies are very general and there is a lack of a coherent policy framework for minerals (Roberts and Shaw, 1982). This creates conflict when applied to specific proposals, as witnessed at the public inquiry for the coal-mines in the Vale of Belvoir. Most planning inquires are weighed in favour of the developer, on the basis of providing jobs in areas with little alternative employment. Nevertheless, the Vale of Belvoir project was reduced from a three- to one-mine complex on environmental grounds. The growth in conservation/pressure groups has stimulated a greater resistance to new developments, even within traditional mining areas. This has been demonstrated quite clearly in the resistance in the late 1980s to British Coal's proposals to develop a large mine beneath farmland at Hawkhurst Moor on the outskirts of Coventry. Environmental opposition stems from an increase in affluence and leisure time, which conflicts with the growing scale of mining operations in peripheral rural areas. Society is becoming less tolerant of the adverse effects of mining and environmental considerations are now an integral part of planning procedures.

Mining and economic development

It is clear from the above analysis that physical constraints to mining may be overcome with changing economic conditions. It should also be clear that mineral resources can present opportunities and play an important role in regional economic development (see also Chapters 15 and 16). Consequently, it is worth looking briefly at the three-stage model of mining and regional development suggested by Spooner (1981):

1. *Minerals dominant phase*, where the early stages of mining may have a positive influence on development in resource frontier regions. Minerals can encourage linkages with succeeding stages of production and ancillary industries, where infrastructure provision and multiplier effects could lead to cumulative and self-sustaining growth (Perloff and Wingo, 1961). However, this is not automatic, especially with the trend towards larger-scale mines controlled by corporate structures. In such a situation, the benefits of mineral exploitation are unlikely to remain in the region, but instead will 'leak back' (backwash) to the headquarters of the corporate companies (in the core). The mining of fuel minerals today, for example, is less likely to have the same lasting effects on regional development than coal produced in the past. This relates to many factors, including the capital- rather than labour-intensive nature of oil and gas, their relative ease of transport and global politics.

2. *Mining regions as depressed areas*, where the movement to manufacturing and service activities, the increasing range of minerals available, and developing technology enable the market rather than the resource to become the dominant locating factor. As a consequence, the resource region is likely to decline, with an over-reliance on one mineral helping to inhibit growth of new forms of production. The 'regional problem' is thus born, necessitating government-based regional policies (Chapter 15).

3. *Mining revival and return to resource frontier*, where the incentive to mine indigenous minerals is renewed, as in the case of Cornish tin. This can be explained by such factors as rising mineral prices (as the economies of large-scale production become exhausted), balance of payments problems, political uncertainty, and hostility among many of the developing economies supplying minerals, government tax concessions, and incentives, and regional policy grants for mining in 'development' areas. However, an important countervailing force has been the growth in environmental opposition, as society becomes less tolerant of the problems created by mining developments (Chapter 17).

3.4 Summary

Unlike most factors examined in the context of change section of this book, the physical environment is fairly static in the short to medium term. However, it provides both opportunities and constraints for economic change and sets broad limits within which economic relationships affect the changing distribution of economic activity. This chapter has concentrated mainly upon the constraints imposed by the physical environment on economic change within agriculture and mining in particular. Certain pertinent points can be made:

● The constraints imposed by the physical en-

vironment do not remain constant but vary according to changing economic conditions.

● It is important to distinguish between resources and reserves. The latter are developed from the former through the application of technology, capital, and expertise.

● Although physical factors do not determine changing patterns of agricultural land use, they cannot be ignored and increase in importance as the scale of analysis changes from micro to macro.

● The relationship between physical and economic margins is a complex and dynamic one. An improvement or decline in economic conditions will cause the economic margin to expand towards or retreat from the physical margin respectively. A process of regional specialization typifies agriculture during periods of economic recession as crops and livestock become concentrated into areas offering a physical comparative advantage.

● The changing geography of mining is far more complex than the simple distribution of mineral deposits and is affected by the dynamic relationship between physical and economic margins of production.

● The application of neoclassical least-cost principles to mining, where the pits nearest the market are exhausted first, seems less relevant today. Other economic factors (e.g. technological change, economies of scale, labour, and capital) have helped to reduce the significance of physical distance. However, environmental concern (e.g. pressure-group activity) is a factor of increasing importance.

● The physical environment, and resource endowment in particular, can also play a more positive role in the process of regional economic development.

One set of economic relationships which affects economic location and change involves the 'factors of production'. These factors are systematically examined in the next chapter.

4

Factors of Production

Among the many factors affecting land use and the location of economic activity are what economists call 'factors of production'. Academic researchers have traditionally focused attention on three factors of production—land, labour, and capital—although entrepreneurship or management (Chapters 7 and 10) and technology (Chapter 6) are sometimes also included under this heading. Surprisingly, of the three traditional factors of production, only land was considered in the earliest location theories (e.g. von Thünen); labour and capital (especially their cost) were thought to be less significant as location factors. Indeed, geographers were, for a long time, guilty of underestimating the role of factors of production in helping to explain the locational dynamics of economic activity, especially manufacturing and service activities (Lever, 1987a). More recently and with the changing patterns of employment and the restructuring of businesses, the study of factors of production has gained a new impetus (Watts, 1987). To one research team, for example, the 'primacy of labour over all other market factors influencing industrial location' needs to be stressed (Walker and Storper, 1981 p. 497).

Clearly then, factors of production should be considered in any examination of locational change in the distribution of economic activities. Within this broad context, it is necessary to make some basic observations, before providing more detailed insights into the importance of each factor in turn:

1. Factors of production represent inputs into the economic system. They are necessarily interrelated and combine with other inputs to mould the economic landscape.
2. The demand for land, labour, and capital varies over space and time and according to economic sector. For example, variations in the numbers employed in the different economic sectors have already been discussed (Chapter 1.3). Similarly, different products and industries require varying combinations of the factors of production; for example, contrast the labour-intensive clothing industry with the more capital-intensive motor vehicle industry (Chapter 12), both of which also use different amounts of land.
3. The factors of production are themselves very unevenly distributed over space. This is true at most geographical scales of analysis, but is particularly pronounced at the international scale. Countries may have plentiful land resources but little labour and capital to exploit them; others may have plenty of labour but little capital. Rarely do all three coincide spatially.
4. Land, labour, and capital markets become very complex as economies mature over time. All economic systems are dependent on land and labour, but capital is often missing from peasant subsistence economies.
5. The possibility of substituting one factor of production for another increases with time and spatial differences in costs may be offset by varying the proportions in which they are utilized (Estall and Buchanan, 1980). Often capital replaces labour, sometimes in an attempt to overcome a problem of a shortage of land. The balance between capital and labour is central to regulationist theories of economic change, discussed in Chapter 2.1.

The main point to emerge from this preamble is that the relative importance of factors of production varies spatially, temporally, and sectorally. However, it is very difficult either to generalize about the changing locational importance of factors of production or to isolate the specific spatial effects of any one particular factor. In the space available, it is not possible to examine in detail all aspects of each factor of production.

Consequently, discussion focuses attention on the geographical and temporal importance of four main dimensions of each factor of production: type, mobility, availability, and cost.

4.1 Land

With the exception of land reclamation schemes such as the Zuider Zee in the Netherlands and the loss of land due to rising sea-levels, land is effectively fixed in supply and an immobile factor of production. However, the use to which it can be put is flexible and land is a vital consideration for both intensive and extensive users of space. Consequently, the discussion will first concentrate on agriculture before considering the secondary and tertiary sectors. Neoclassical theory suggests that the actual location of land (e.g. in relation to distance from the market), leads to a spatial differentiation of both farming types and the intensity of agricultural land use. With improved technology and a corresponding decline in the importance of transport costs, the importance of location in relation to the market has been reduced. Instead, agricultural land use is more likely to be distributed on the basis of land quality, tenure, and cost.

The physical characteristics of land vary spatially (and temporally in terms of resources—see Chapter 3) and, whilst the chemical and biological properties of land are rarely locational factors in the secondary and tertiary sectors, the morphology of the landscape can act as a constraint on the siting of factories, offices, and hypermarkets. Within the primary sector, however, the production potential of land is influenced by its quality. Reference to land capability and land-use capability maps in the United Kingdom, produced by the Ministry of Agriculture, Fisheries and Food (MAFF, 1968) and the Soil Survey (1977) respectively, indicates that land is far from being a homogeneous factor of production, with marked spatial variations in quality occurring, often within relatively small areas (Ilbery, 1985a). These classifications identify five and seven grades of land quality respectively and it is intimated that farming types will vary accordingly. Such a deterministic approach to the analysis of agricultural land use is not being advocated here, for as Tarrant (1974 p. 119) remarked, 'good and bad quality farming is not

restricted to good and bad quality land.' Other aspects of land, that disrupt such a simple association, thus need to be considered. One of these is land tenure.

Systems of land tenure vary enormously between regions and countries, from communal tenure and *latifundia* (large landed estates) to freehold and tenancy (Hurst, 1974), and have fundamental effects on farm size structures, levels of land fragmentation, and thus land-use patterns. In Western capitalist economies, the main contrast is between tenancy and owner-occupancy. The latter has increased significantly: in the United Kingdom, for example, the amount of agricultural land farmed by owner-occupiers increased from around 11 per cent at the beginning of the twentieth century to over 60 per cent in 1985. Similarly in the USA, nearly 90 per cent of all farms are wholly or partly owner-occupied. Ownership confers greater freedom of choice upon the farmer than tenancy, where agreements may be quite restrictive towards certain types of farming. However, tenancy may carry greater profits, a point that can only reinforce the importance of non-economic motives in land ownership among farmers (Denman, 1965).

Remarkably little is known about land ownership patterns in the United Kingdom; privacy and confidentiality prevail. One thing that is clear is that historical patterns of land ownership have undergone considerable change. Massey and Catalano (1978) identify four changes in particular:

1. A decline in the great private estates of large landowners, especially of the landed aristocracy. Nevertheless, these still account for approximately 20 per cent of the total land area; this form of inherited ownership rather than purely capitalistic land ownership helps to distinguish the United Kingdom from the USA and other European countries.

2. A major change from tenancy to owner-occupancy.

3. The increasing role of state agencies in land ownership. Over 20 per cent of the total land area is now controlled by such bodies as the Forestry Commission (see Chapter 11), nationalized industries, Local Authorities, and conservation organizations.

4. The entry into direct land ownership, especially in the early 1970s, by private property

companies, insurance companies, and pension funds (see below).

Whilst land is a means to an end and a condition of production for the large number of fairly small, owner-occupied farm units, it is a form of investment for the financial sector, where the sole objective is a return on capital. Such diverging attitudes towards land ownership are not uncommon elsewhere and have been clearly portrayed in a study of social relations and conflict in farming in north-east Brazil (Massey and Phillips, 1985). Three types of land ownership are important in the area, each with different methods of establishing ownership and valuing land:

1. *The old fazendas*, where social structures are hierarchical and land ownership is the basis of social power, rather than the use to which the land is put. Indeed, large parts of the fazendas are left uncultivated.

2. *Commercial estates* or modern fazendas, where capitalistic development and profit maximization through agricultural production represent the overriding purpose. Monoculture is often the result and sugar-cane production is currently the most profitable activity.

3. *Peasantry*, where uncultivated land on the old fazendas has been occupied by subsistence farmers (without legal title). A period of continuous cultivation is seen as the basis for a claim to land ownership. The small plots of land are intensively worked for internal consumption. In this case, land is a source of security and survival, not power and/or profit. Land use is usually mixed, comprising different crops and livestock.

With reduced profit margins in farming, resulting from the price-cost squeeze (see Chapters 3.2 and 11.2) and the rise in land prices in the early 1970s, sale and leaseback became an increasingly popular form of tenure. This involved the farmer selling his land, usually to an institutional buyer, with an agreement (lease) to continue farming that land for a specified time. The farmer thus has a new source of capital to invest in the farm (or elsewhere), although he forfeits any subsequent capital gain in the value of his property and has to pay a rent (Munton, 1977). Sale and leaseback would become a very attractive form of tenure if a wealth tax was introduced (Haines, 1982).

Land is, therefore, a saleable commodity and commands a price, which depends upon the vari-ability of demand. The price of land varies spatially, reflecting its availability, quality, and location. Prices are higher for good-quality land (often on larger farms) in 'core' areas than for lower-quality land in 'peripheral' locations. They can be particularly high on the urban fringe, where land-use competition between agriculture, industry, commerce, and housing is intense. In such a situation, agriculture usually 'loses out', although the farmer can use the potential windfall profit (especially if the land has planning permission for development) to invest in less expensive land further away. A gradient of declining land values with distance from urban areas exists, which may affect both the intensity and type of agricultural land use practised. An 'urban' effect can be seen in the pattern of land prices in the United Kingdom and the USA (Fig. 4.1).

In England and Wales, prices rose from an average of £570 per ha in 1969 to just over £2000 in 1973, before 'falling back' with the onset of economic recession caused by rising oil prices and then rising again in the mid-1980s. The sudden rise in prices was due to a significant short-term injection of money into the agricultural land market from two sources (Munton, 1976): first, investment firms began to invest in agricultural land in the belief that land was an under-valued but essential natural resource that would increase in value due to inflationary trends; and secondly, tax concessions to urban fringe landowners selling land for urban development released considerable sums of money for reinvestment in the rural land market. Spatially, the maximum regional price reached in any one six-month period between 1969 and 1971 was highest in the more urbanized southern area and East Anglia and declined quite rapidly with distance towards the South-West, Wales, and northern regions (Fig. 4.1a). Although much lower in the USA, land prices also increased quite spectacularly, from $33 per ha in 1960 to $260 in 1981, and are highest in the more urbanized states, most notably California in the West and Illinois and the contiguous states of Maryland, New Jersey, Connecticut, and Rhode Island in the East (Fig. 4.1b). Such regional variations in land prices are greater than for any other factor of production.

A major factor causing land prices to rise, therefore, was the speculative behaviour of institutional buyers in the land property market. Fuelled by rapid inflation, a heavy inflow of funds

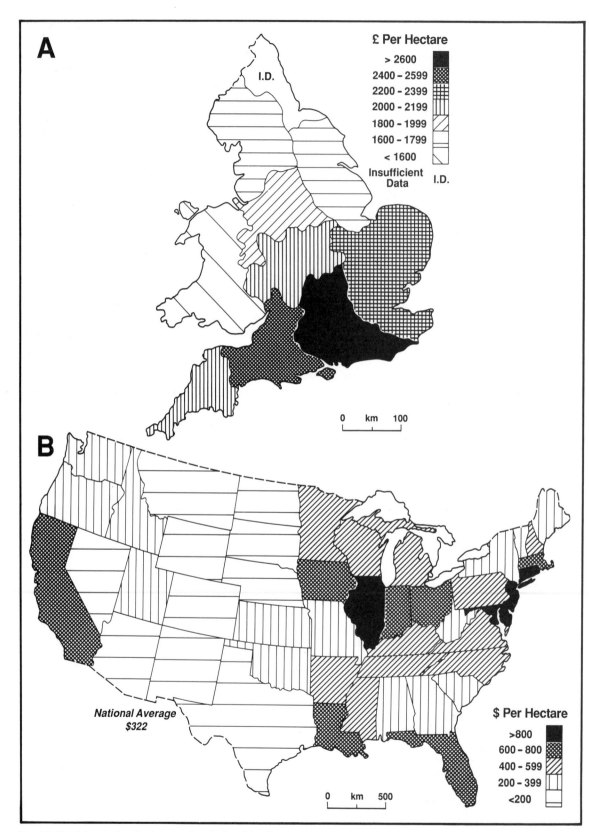

FIG 4.1 Spatial variations in the cost of agricultural land: (*a*) England and Wales, 1969–71; (*b*) United States, 1981 (*source*: (*a*) Munton, 1976 p. 209; (*b*) Ilbery, 1985*a* p.104)

in the early 1970s, and reduced rates of corporation tax on investment income announced in the 1965 Finance Act, insurance companies, pension funds, and unit trusts began to buy agricultural land in the United Kingdom in 1970; in 1973, 28 per cent of agricultural land sold (12 150 ha) was bought by institutions (Country Landowners Association, 1973). In a detailed survey of auctioneers' transactions, Munton (1976) was able to show how the proportion of land acquired by financial institutions increased from 3.6 per cent in 1971 to 22.8 per cent in 1973, before falling back to 9.5 per cent in 1974 (Table 4.1). The table also demonstrates how the institutions were prepared to pay more for their land, although this in part reflected the tendency to 'buy large, economically viable holdings in the agriculturally favoured areas of East Anglia and the mid-south of England' (Munton, 1976 p. 211). Between 1972 and 1974, they spent 83 per cent in just these two regions and when the prices in the South-East rose excessively, attention was directed further north, first into East Anglia and then into Lincolnshire and Humberside. Indeed, when the 112 000 ha of land owned by 14 major institutions were mapped at the county scale (Fig. 4.2), 46 per cent fell within the counties of Norfolk, Lincolnshire, Humberside, and Cambridgeshire (Munton, 1977). Once established, the pattern was reinforced as it became possible to reduce costs by acquiring local or adjacent properties to existing ones.

Economic recession and rising interest rates caused the price of land to fall in real terms from the mid-1970s until the mid-1980s, but it is clear from this discussion that the different 'characteristics' of land vary over both space and time, with concomitant effects on the 'economic' use to which it can be put.

In the secondary and tertiary sectors, such large quantities of land are rarely required and land costs are not as critical in the cost structure of a firm, although they may play an important role at particular points in a plant or office's history (Watts, 1987). Consequently, interregional differences in land costs do not represent an important locational factor, although intra-regional and intra-urban variations can be important. Smith (1981) for example, identifies distinct spatial differences in building costs within the USA and Keeble (1976) notes that cheaper land prices were a contributory factor encouraging the movement of firms from the South-East and West Midlands to Development Areas between 1967 and 1970. Indeed, the decentralization of industry from urban areas has been related to differential land costs, with the urban/rural shift reflecting higher operating costs in urban areas (Lever, 1982). However, there is disagreement over this theory and other researchers have suggested that the availability rather than cost of land is more important (see below).

Land is a necessary input to the production process and a number of financial and institu-

TABLE 4.1 Properties bought by institutions in England and Wales

	Acreage %	Average price paid (£/ha)	Average size of purchase (ha)
1971			
Institutions	3.6	587.1	115.3
Other purchasers	96.3	720.3	52.2
1972			
Institutions	22.4	1 530.4	197.9
Other purchasers	77.6	1 301.9	53.3
1973			
Institutions	22.8	2 164.2	161.9
Other purchasers	77.2	1 946.9	49.1
1974			
Institutions	9.5	1 881.1	145.9
Other purchasers	90.5	1 673.9	43.0

Source: Munton (1976 p. 211).

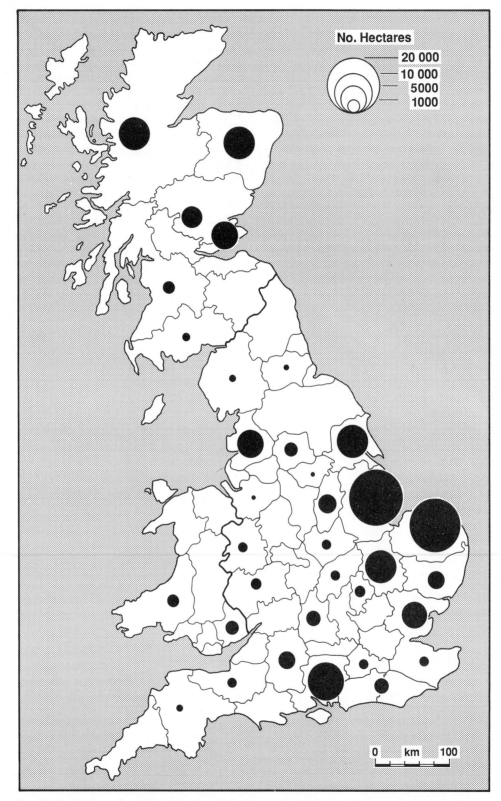

FIG 4.2 Distribution of agricultural land owned by financial institutions, 1975 (*source*: Munton, 1977 p. 33)

tional constraints upon its supply exist. Few industrial and office firms engage in large-scale land ownership for other than their own use and most companies tend to own the land on which they operate. Once located, therefore, the capital invested becomes immobile (see Section 4.3), although a firm could decide to move from a constrained, but valuable, urban site to a modern, purpose-built, rural site in order to generate surplus capital for other needs. In contrast, property developers enter the land market for profit and begin providing standardized single-storey buildings for industry and service activities, usually to rent but also sometimes to buy. These developers may be spatially selective in their purchasing of land, but there has been little research on this (Fothergill et al., 1987). Market demand is a crucial factor in this context, suggesting a concentration of activity in the more urbanized core areas. Indeed the total demand for floorspace has been increasing in the United Kingdom. This partly relates to developers of industrial and office buildings rejecting the reuse of existing sites (usually in urban areas) because of high costs in both site preparation and obtaining large enough parcels of suitable land; instead preference is given to green-field (rural) sites, which are cheaper and more environmentally attractive. Urban areas are thus disadvantaged in terms of the quality, quantity, and cost of land. Initially,

therefore, the decentralization of industry would appear to be a function of land costs.

However, Fothergill and Gudgin (1982) have argued that the availability rather than cost of land has been the critical factor in encouraging the urban/rural shift. Indeed, the supply of land and property for industry varies markedly from place to place and Fothergill et al. (1987) identify a 'mismatch' between manufacturing employment change and industrial floorspace in the regions of the United Kingdom. Between 1967 and 1985, all regions except East Anglia experienced a decline in employment, whereas most regions (except the North-West, South-East, and Yorkshire and Humberside) increased their amount of floorspace. When examined at the urban/rural scale, the mismatch was even greater. The largest change in manufacturing employment (1967–81) occurred in London (−46.9 per cent), followed by the conurbations (−40.3) and the free-standing cities (−29.8); a regular fall with declining size was identified, until the rural areas (+7.6) were included (see also Chapter 16.2). Regarding industrial floorspace, reversals were recorded only for London (−23.2) and the conurbations (−11.9); elsewhere floorspace increased, with the smaller settlements experiencing the greatest growth (i.e. small towns +28.7 and rural areas +52.1). Upon comparing the two sets of statistics, it is immediately clear that the growth in

TABLE 4.2 Changes in industrial floorspace by type of area in England, 1974–1985

	Cities[a]	Towns and rural areas
STOCK IN 1974 (million m^2)	129.2	97.8
	as % of stock	
New units	+ 6.5	+13.6
Extensions	+ 8.1	+15.6
Change of use	+ 5.0	+ 6.4
ALL ADDITIONS	+19.6	+35.6
Complete demolitions	− 6.9	− 4.8
Other	−21.1	−22.3
ALL REDUCTIONS	−28.0	−27.1
NET CHANGE	− 8.4	+ 8.5

[a] London, conurbations, and free-standing cities.

Source: Fothergill et al. (1987 p. 95).

floorspace in rural areas was much larger than their growth in employment. A summary of changes in industrial floorspace between urban and rural areas, for the 1974–85 period, is provided in Table 4.2. The net decline of − 8.4 per cent in London, the conurbations, and free-standing cities was more than balanced by the + 8.5 per cent growth in small towns and rural areas.

These differences led Fothergill and Gudgin (1982) to conclude that the urban/rural shift reflected changes in the stock of floorspace. Nevertheless, this did not explain why new units or extensions were more likely in rural than urban areas. Two contributory factors need to be considered (Watts, 1987): first, new plants can only be established where there is adequate land (for buildings of the right shape, size, and location); and secondly, existing plants can only expand *in situ* if adjacent land/buildings are available. Consequently, the constrained location hypothesis was advocated (Fothergill and Gudgin, 1982; Fothergill *et al.*, 1987), whereby a lack of land next to existing property in urban areas acted as a restraint for access, expansion, and development of new technologies and caused a movement to cheaper, purpose-built sites in either the suburbs or rural areas. A contributory factor in the process was the increasing amount of inner-city land being acquired by local authorities for redevelopment schemes, thus reducing the amount available on the 'open market'. Faced with a shortage of space, firms wishing to expand have two possible options: first, to forgo growth because of the constrained site and attempt to overcome the land problem by displacing labour and increasing capital investment in new equipment (although this in itself often necessitates more space e.g. a single rather than multi-storey building to take the increased 'load'); or secondly, to divert production elsewhere.

A similar set of circumstances can be identified in the tertiary sector, where there has been a major growth in private land ownership by property companies. Changes in office location and employment, for example, are increasingly the result of deliberate investment decisions made by just a few people (Bateman, 1985; Daniels, 1985*a*). Irrespective of the demand for office floorspace, new property development can be related to the purchase of land (or buildings) by financial institutions and property companies, on the basis that land is a secure asset. Once again,

such investments are likely to be spatially selective: at the regional scale, central locations are favoured at the expense of peripheral ones, thus intensifying the core–periphery dichotomy in office development; at the local scale, urban and the more accessible/pleasant suburban sites are preferred to distant rural locations. Most office growth has occurred on inner-city sites (Barras, 1979 and 1981), often moving into premises vacated by decentralizing manufacturing firms.

Property developers, themselves financed by institutions, have taken full advantage of the major post-war development boom and purchased and/or developed land and property in order to collect a rent. Three 'areas' in particular were important in the United Kingdom (Massey and Catalano, 1978): first, city-centre reconstruction, dominated by Ravenseft Properties who, working with local authorities, redeveloped Plymouth, Exeter, Hull, Sheffield, and Coventry; secondly, shopping redevelopments and out-of-town centres; and thirdly, office development, initially in London (where permits were issued for over 30 million square feet of new building between 1954 and 1960), and then in more provincial centres, when office development permits were difficult to obtain in London (see Chapter 8). Over 50 per cent of post-war offices up to 1966 were built by developers and 80 per cent of the new building was in the London region.

Land represents an important input to all economic systems. Variations in the quality, availability, and cost of land encourage locational change in especially the secondary and tertiary sectors. Increasingly, it is the land property market and the actions of financial institutions and property developers in particular that provide the key to understanding the role of land as a factor of production.

4.2 Labour

The importance of labour as a factor of production varies between economic sectors, specific businesses, and different places. Although the locational 'pull' of labour has declined and manufacturing and tertiary 'firms' have become increasingly footloose, it can still exert a considerable influence in terms of the four characteristics discussed in this chapter (type, mobility, availability, and cost). As these characteristics are themselves subject to spatial variations, labour is seen as a critical factor in geographical studies of economic activity (Clark, 1981; Walker and Storper, 1981; Storper and Walker, 1984; Dicken, 1986). For example, Dicken (1986) shows how, at the global scale, labour has become a very important location factor, especially in terms of type (skill) and cost, and Keeble (1976) demonstrates how, at the regional scale, the availability and cost of female, non-unionized, labour influenced the decision of selected clothing firms to move to the peripheral and more rural areas of Great Britain.

A region's labour force, in terms of its mix of skills, sex, and education, is fairly stable in the short term (Watts, 1987), being both occupationally and geographically immobile. 'Labour is far less mobile geographically, particularly over greater distances, than other factors such as capital and technology' (Dicken, 1986 p. 125). Labour is strongly place-bound and ties to an area are not easily severed. Migration of workers tends to be selective towards young males and skilled professional people and the strong periphery to core pattern of labour migration in Western Europe in the early 1970s, for example, was predominantly of unskilled young males (King, 1975). However, this was not of a permanent nature and return migration to the peripheral areas was common (King, 1979).

One of the best example of labour immobility, both occupationally and spatially, comes from the farming industry, especially among the operators of small farms (Gasson, 1969). This reflects the importance of a family tradition, independence, and an outdoor way of life. However, the phenomenon relates more to farm owners and their families than to farm labourers. With the latter, the 'drift from the land' has been considerable, reflecting a range of 'push' and 'pull' factors. In the USA, for example, the agricultural labour force fell from 9.9 million in 1950 to less than 3.5 million in 1985; similarly in England and Wales, the number of workers declined from 800 000 in 1950 to under 270 000 in 1985. Increasing numbers of farm operators are also leaving the industry altogether or becoming part-time; the latter has become particularly important on the urban fringe and in physically marginal areas.

With labour being a fairly immobile factor of production, attention needs to be directed away from mobility and towards the availability or supply of labour. The normal indicator of labour supply is the size of the *labour pool* (the number of people available for work). This can affect the location of secondary and tertiary activities, especially during periods of full employment. In the United Kingdom, the labour supply increased by 3 per cent between 1971 and 1981, although this consisted of a rapid decline in metropolitan areas and a corresponding growth in rural areas (Table 4.3). Two measures of the size of labour pool are usually employed. The first is the *participation* or *activity rate*, defined as the proportion of the total population of a given age-group in work. This is influenced by the demographic (age/sex/marital

TABLE 4.3 Change in the number of economically active residents in the main metropolitan areas, 1971–1981

	Change in economically active population (%)	
	Metropolitan area	Urban core[a]
Greater London	− 32.4	n.a.
West Midlands	− 7.9	− 12.5
Greater Manchester	− 5.8	− 20.9
Merseyside	− 7.1	− 17.0
West Yorkshire	− 2.0	− 4.8
South Yorkshire	− 0.1	− 7.0
Tyne and Wear	− 2.6	− 7.6
GREAT BRITAIN	+ 2.9	+ 2.9

[a] Inner London, Birmingham MB, Manchester MB, Liverpool MB, Leeds, Sheffield, and Newcastle upon Tyne.

Source: Hasluck (1987 p. 65).

status) structure of an area's population, together with its density and distribution. Activity rates are not constant, but vary over time and space in response to patterns of migration, the changing role of women in the labour force and the growth in part-time employment (see below). They tend to be higher for males than females, with the latter (until recently) being particularly low in peripheral areas. Male activity rates are normally over 70 per cent, but these have been declining as more older men are retiring early and more younger people are receiving extended education (Hasluck, 1987). Spatially, male activity rates are below average in metropolitan labour markets and are declining at a greater than average rate. However, female rates have increased significantly, from 55 to 61 per cent between 1971 and 1981 in the United Kingdom (49 to 57 per cent for married women). These also vary spatially, and are higher in the North-West, West Midlands and the South-East than in Wales and the South-West; similarly in the USA, they vary from 47 per cent in Alabama to 62 per cent in Nevada (Watts, 1987). At the urban scale, these increases do not show because of out-migration, which has coincided with a sectoral shift in the pattern of employment in the 1970s towards women and the service sector. Over time, spatial differences in female activity rates have been reduced through a process of convergence and 'areas with the lowest historical levels of female participation have experienced the greatest increase' (Hasluck, 1987, p. 69).

A second measure of the size of labour pool is the *unemployment rate*. Rising unemployment was characteristic of many Western nations between the mid-1970s and the mid-1980s, with rates being subject to extreme areal variations (Townsend and Peck, 1985b). The spatial pattern of unemployment is complicated by varying rates between such divergent groups as ethnic minorities, women, and the young. At an international level, unemployment in the European Community (EC), for example, rose from 2.5 per cent in 1973 to 12.9 per cent in 1987, when over 15 million people were out of work. Figures ranged from a low of 1.9 per cent in Luxembourg to over 18 per cent in Ireland. The regional dimension has been exacerbated, with marked differences between the ten strongest (< 5 per cent) and ten weakest (> 20 per cent) regions in the Community (Ilbery, 1986). However, it is not only the peri-

pheral fringes of the EC that have been experiencing increasing rates of unemployment, as the problem is also acute in the more central and industrial regions with higher production levels. Similar regional contrasts, although with a smaller range, were reported for the USA in the late 1970s, from 12.3 per cent in Michigan to 3.6 per cent in Oklahoma (Watts, 1987).

In the United Kingdom, the number of jobs for males fell by three million between 1966 and 1984, whilst jobs for females increased by 1.28 million (Lever, 1987a). Unemployment rose sharply in the early 1980s, from 1.8 million in 1979 to a peak of 3.3 million in 1985. At the regional scale, rates of unemployment in 1985 ranged from over 20 per cent in Northern Ireland to less than 10 per cent in the South-East, although there was some regional convergence up to 1983, before divergence again returned. At the local scale, unemployment for both males and females has increased in virtually every local labour market area (LLMAs) and a distinct north–south dichotomy is apparent. North of a line drawn from the Severn to the Wash, the increase in unemployment was significant and for males the rise was most acute in the industrial heartland of metropolitan England (Fig. 4.3). South of this line, the increase in unemployment was relatively small, except in the extreme South-West and, for males, in metropolitan London (Owens et al., 1984). At the urban scale, over one million manufacturing jobs were lost in the inner cities between 1951 and 1981, with a further one million in the outer areas of conurbations and the free-standing cities (Hasluck, 1987). Rates of unemployment are related to the size of settlement, with the highest rates and largest increases occurring in the principal cities. However, the greatest rise occurred in the West Midlands conurbation which previously had low unemployment; this suggests some convergence in metropolitan unemployment rates over time. Reasons for major job losses in the inner cities include deindustrialization, a spatial reorganization of production, and changes in the type and conditions of employment (see below). For example, cities tend to contain traditionally skilled, manual, and unionized labour and have low reserves of female labour; characteristics that are associated with high job loss.

By examining differences in the supply of labour and the number of jobs available, imbalances in the labour market can be calculated. This

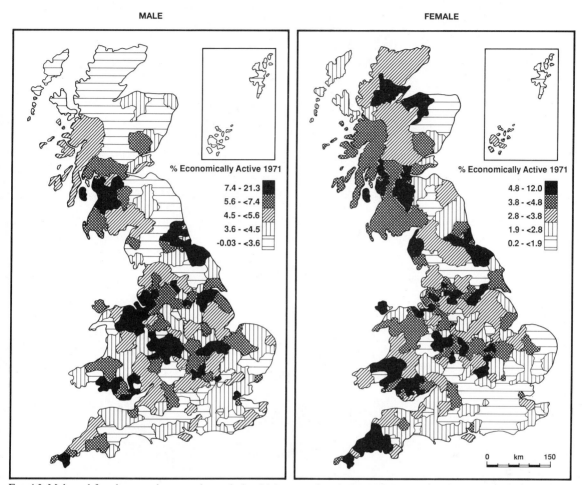

MALE   FEMALE

% Economically Active 1971

7.4 - 21.3
5.6 - <7.4
4.5 - <5.6
3.6 - <4.5
-0.03 - <3.6

% Economically Active 1971

4.8 - 12.0
3.8 - <4.8
2.8 - <3.8
1.9 - <2.8
0.2 - <1.9

0   km   150

FIG 4.3 Male and female unemployment change in local labour markets in Great Britain, 1971–81 (*source*: Owen *et al.*, 1984 p. 477)

was undertaken in an analysis of 'job shortfalls' (or labour demand deficiency) between 1971 and 1981 for the 280 LLMAs in the United Kingdom by Owens *et al.* (1984). A shortfall of jobs is a measure of 'the extent to which employment creation in an area between two dates failed to match the increase in labour supply' (p. 470), and on this basis the 280 LLMAs were classified into seven main types, of which the first three are characterized by surpluses and the last four by shortfalls (Fig. 4.4):

1. *Rapid growth*, comprising areas with high employment growth, job surpluses and in-migration e.g. Peterborough, Milton Keynes, and Telford.

2. *Low supply growth*, where low population and activity rate increases led to a shortage of labour. This group of LLMAs is comprised mainly of coastal resort and retirement areas in England and Wales.

3. *Slow growth*, where low employment growth was offset by even slower labour force growth because of out-migration. The 77 LLMAs are essentially non-metropolitan in nature and include Hertford, Ipswich, and Gloucester.

4. *High supply*, where an increase in labour supply was swamping a remarkably high employment growth and thus leading to increased unemployment e.g. Oxford, Basildon, Aldershot, and Rugby.

5. *Slow decline*, characterized by slow employ-

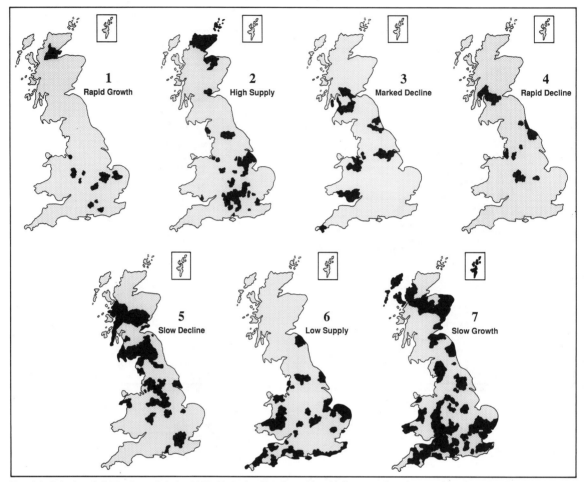

FIG 4.4 'Job shortfalls' in Great Britain, 1971–81: a classification of local labour markets (*source*: based on data in Owen *et al.*, 1984 pp. 486–7)

ment decline and a small increase in labour supply, and where unemployment was offset by reduced activity rates e.g. the traditional industrial areas of Yorkshire, East Midlands, and Lancashire.

6. *Marked decline*, characterized by a large decline in the demand for males and a rapid increase in female supply. High unemployment is the result, as in South Wales and other traditional steel-making areas.

7. *Rapid decline*, where there were very rapid falls in labour demand, intensified by increases in labour supply. The result was massive job shortfalls and out-migration. This was particularly pronounced in such metropolitan labour markets

as Merseyside, Greater Manchester, West Midlands, Clydeside, and Tyne and Wear.

The results suggest distinctive north-south, regional and urban/rural contrasts and in order to examine possible spatial relationships, Owens *et al.* (1984) recast the data in tabular form (Table 4.4). The table suggests some relationship between job shortfalls and urban size, although there is considerable variation between LLMAs of the same size category, as indicated for the 156 towns. Similarly at the regional scale, distinct differences emerge between the 'better off' southern region and the worse affected heartland and peripheral regions. This is confirmed and further

TABLE 4.4 Local labour market experience at different spatial scales in Great Britain

Labour markets in order of increasing job shortfalls	Better than average			Worse than average
	Rapid growth	Low supply and slow growth	High supply and low decline	Marked and rapid decline
(a) BY URBAN SIZE				
London dominant	—	—	1	—
Conurbation domin.	—	—	—	5
Provincial domin.	—	2	3	—
Cities	—	16	26	19
Towns	9	75	44	28
Rural	3	33	13	3
TOTALS	12	126	87	55
(b) BY REGIONAL LOCATION				
London metropolit.	3	15	13	—
Other southern[a]	4	62	14	3
Heartland[b]	4	25	38	19
Peripheral[c]	1	24	22	33
TOTALS	12	126	87	55
(c) BY NORTH/SOUTH DIVIDE				
Southern				
Dominants	—	2	2	—
Subdominants	3	18	13	—
Service towns	—	20	—	—
Other freestanding	2	25	9	1
Rural areas	2	12	3	2
Northern				
Dominants	—	1	5	10
Subdominants	3	11	18	27
Service towns	—	6	5	1
Other freestanding	1	10	22	13
Rural areas	1	21	10	1
TOTALS	12	126	87	55

[a] South of the Severn/Wash line.
[b] Midlands, North-West, and Yorkshire.
[c] Northern, Scotland, and Wales.

Source: Owens *et al.* (1984 pp. 483, 484).

highlighted when a north/south contrast is drawn. As Owens *et al.* (1984 p. 485) commented, 'patterns of change in labour market conditions are seen to reflect not a single spatial process but a range of processes, operating at different spatial scales.' This in turn has important implications for the location of economic activity and the spatial restructuring of the British economy (see below).

A major consequence of increasing unemployment has been the development of *dual labour markets* (Hasluck, 1987; Lever, 1987a; Watts, 1987), where jobs can be divided into *primary* and *secondary* sectors. The former enjoys high wages and good conditions (security, promotion, and specific training) and access is limited by education and skills; external mobility is low. In contrast, the latter is characterized by low wages, poor jobs, and uncertainty of employment and there is little if any career prospects. Consequently, mobility between (unskilled) jobs is high and disadvantaged groups (the young, elderly, females, and ethnic minorities) get trapped in the secondary sector. With unemployment having a distinctly spatial character, the primary and secondary sectors of the dual labour market become spatially separated (between prosperous core areas and poorer peripheral areas), leading to a spatial division of labour (see below). As a further consequence of rising unemployment, labour supply exceeds demand in every skill category and so people 'take on' jobs below their qualifications (deskilling). Such a process makes it even more difficult for those out of work to gain employment (Lever, 1987a).

It would appear, therefore, that with high rates of unemployment labour supply is not a critical locating factor (although skill shortages can still occur); the cost of labour may be more important. Differences in the cost of labour exist at numerous geographical scales, as well as between different industries and occupations. The major contrasts in wage levels occur at the international level (Fig. 4.5), especially between developed and developing countries. This has undoubtedly been a vital factor in influencing the 'global shift' (Dicken, 1986), where some multinationals have relocated their mass-production units to the cheaper labour areas of the Third World (Chapters 7.2 and 14.3). It is more difficult to demonstrate regional differences in labour costs, although they definitely exist in the USA, for example, and, on a smaller scale, in the United Kingdom. In the former, a distinct north/south divide is apparent, with labour costs in the South being 20 per cent below the national average (Watts, 1987). Estall and Buchanan (1980) comment upon the contrasts between the low cost areas of Mississippi and North Carolina and the high cost areas of Michigan and California, as well as upon spatial differences in supplementary payments (holiday pay, sickness benefit pensions, redundancy pay,

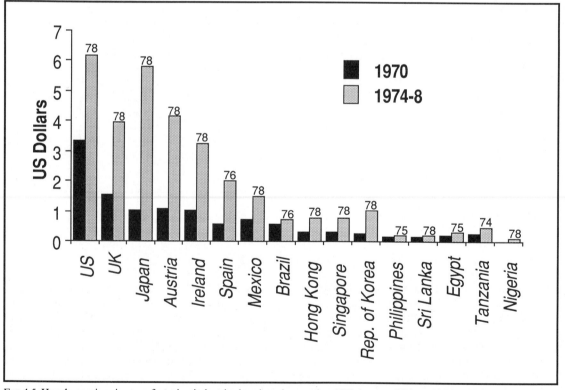

Fig 4.5 Hourly earnings in manufacturing industries in selected countries, 1978 (*source*: Dicken, 1986 p. 125, derived from Peet, 1983 p. 134)

national insurance), where a distinction can be drawn between the less liberal southern states and the more liberal north-eastern states. Such differences are a function of the relative immobility of labour at the interregional scale, as well as between skills and jobs. Selective mobility can also enhance regional differences in labour costs, between poorer 'sending' and more prosperous 'receiving' regions.

Spatial differences in labour costs are not, however, simply a function of wage levels, but are related to productivity, turnover rates, absenteeism, and labour relations, all of which have a spatial expression. These factors are interrelated and low wage areas in either the Third World or peripheral rural areas in Western economies, for example, are not necessarily attractive if they are characterized by low productivity and a need to initiate training programmes. Alternatively, they may be particularly attractive if labour attitudes are favourable and union activity is minimal.

Regarding productivity, large differences exist in the EC, between, for example, West Germany, Italy, and the United Kingdom. These in turn are affected by the quality of labour, which reflects contrasts in health, education, and housing. In the USA, labour quality favours the more northern states, whereas labour attitudes (in terms of absenteeism, turnover, and disputes) favour southern areas (Estall and Buchanan, 1980). Labour attitudes can be particularly important as entrepreneurs form preconceived ideas about certain regions or states and may seek to avoid those with higher turnover and absenteeism rates and/or well-organized and unionized labour (Watts, 1987). High turnover rates will reduce productivity and whilst spatial differences are unclear, rates would appear to decline with increasing unemployment. Similarly, absenteeism is known to vary between the northern and southern regions of the United Kingdom, being up to three times higher in the former than in the latter (Toyne, 1974). However, many people in peripheral areas are employed in less attractive jobs where higher levels of absenteeism can be expected (Watts, 1987).

Finally, there are spatial differences in labour disputes and strikes, although in the case of the United Kingdom this could be a reflection more of the size of plant than of area. In contrast, there are undoubtedly 'areas' in the USA where militancy is related to rates of union membership. The latter vary considerably, from less than 10 per cent of non-agricultural employees in the Carolinas to over 33 per cent in such states as New York, Pennsylvania, Michigan, and Washington (Fig. 4.6). Understandably, rates of union activity are highest in the older manufacturing areas. As if to counteract these 'areas', the right-to-work laws show an even more distinctive, but reverse, pattern to high union membership. The anti-union right-to-work laws outlaw compulsory union membership in a plant and are concentrated in the southern states, the west north-central region and the mountain region (Watts, 1987). With the contrasts portrayed in Fig. 4.6, it is not surprising that industry has been accused of 'running away' from labour unions (Bluestone, Harrison, and Baker, 1981); such avoidance is, however, difficult to prove. Similar contrasts in union activities have been identified in England and Wales by Massey and Miles (1984). Formerly concentrated in the industrial heartlands, membership is now more widely dispersed, although the authors noticed that anti-unionism was strong among the high status workers in the high-technology belt in southern and eastern England.

The cost of labour is, therefore, influenced by many factors, one of which is the type of labour and in particular the distinctions between full and part-time, male and female, and skilled and unskilled. These characteristics can affect the distribution of economic activity. In the tertiary sector, for example, the type of labour can have different locational effects on producer and consumer services. The former is information dependent and thus needs very specialized workers, who are most likely to be available in and around the largest conurbations (Daniels, 1985a). Less skilled workers, from a wider range of locations, can be recruited for the latter.

Indeed, the location of skilled workers still exerts an inertial influence on such craft industries as the potteries (Staffordshire), instrument specialities (Mohawk Valley, north-east USA), diamond quarters (Antwerp), and horticulture (Vale of Evesham, West Midlands). Despite this, technological change and the 'machine age' have increasingly permitted the use of cheaper semi-skilled and unskilled labour. This was a contributory factor in the movement of the car industry in the United Kingdom from Coventry and Birmingham to Oxford, Luton, and Dagenham in the 1960s (Estall and Buchanan, 1980). The modern

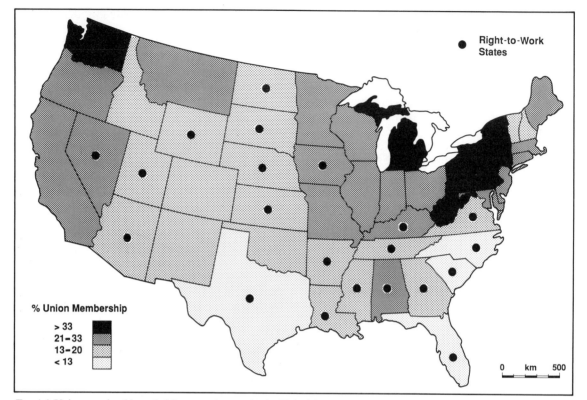

FIG 4.6 Union membership and right-to-work states in the United States, 1980 (*source*: Watts, 1987 p. 98)

trend is, indeed, towards an increasing division of labour, as mechanization makes many jobs more similar in nature. The need for reliable labour with high productivity is thus enhanced, encouraging global shifts in production to secure the right type of labour (cheap and non-unionized). Spatial differences in labour costs can, therefore, relate to the particular mix of skills available. Consequently, regional variations in skills create a *spatial division of labour* (Massey, 1984*b*). With individuals specializing in particular tasks, a spatial division of labour arises when these specialists are concentrated in certain regions, a situation which, in the case of the United Kingdom and the USA, developed a long time ago (although it has a modern-day equivalent in the concentration of high-technology industries in Silicon Valley in California, Silicon Glen in Scotland, and the M4 Corridor in England (see Chapter 6.2). The important point here is that the spatial division of labour has changed, from a division based on

type of industry to one based on type of occupation (Massey, 1979*b*).

A more recent phenomenon is the intra-sectoral division of labour by large firms (Watts, 1987), as head offices and R. & D. activities (in core areas) become spatially separated from mass production (in peripheral areas). The extent to which large corporate organizations exploit this situation is a matter of debate, although the development of dual labour markets would appear to support the idea. As competition in export markets increases, firms have to reduce costs and restructure their businesses (the restructuring thesis; see Massey, 1984*b*). The most economical way to achieve this is to exploit the secondary sector of the dual labour market and move the productive end of the operation to cheaper (peripheral) locations, where there is also less militancy and union membership.

Such temporal shifts in *labour processes* (the way in which labour is organized and controlled in production) have been interpreted as a characteristic feature of capitalist societies; four phases have been identified (Aglietta, 1979; Massey, 1984*b*; Chapters 2.1 and 6.1):

1. *Manufacture*, where previously independent workers are gathered together in a factory system, with its specialization in various production tasks.

2. *Machinofacture*, where mechanization and a division of labour are introduced to increase productivity.

3. *Scientific management and Fordism.* The former refers to where time and motion techniques are introduced to divide scientifically the work process into specific tasks. It is sometimes called *Taylorism*, after F. W. Taylor who introduced these techniques at the end of the nineteenth century. *Fordism*, which is closely associated with the use of scientific methods, refers to where assembly-line production techniques are introduced.

4. *Neo-Fordism*, where fragmentation and deskilling of the direct workforce are pushed further with the application of automated control systems in production. This development is particularly associated with the use of micro-processors.

Although these stages in the development of the production–labour process, or *regimes of capital accumulation* as they are sometimes called (Aglietta, 1979), have historically succeeded one another, they have been applied to different industrial sectors and regions at different points in time. Consequently, the stages overlap (Fig. 4.7).

The nature of each regime of accumulation has important implications for the development of spatial structures. Perrons (1981), for example, argues that the techniques introduced from the mid-sixteenth century to the early eighteenth century in the manufacture phase led, where they were adopted, to the concentration of production in factories in urban locations. In contrast, in the subsequent phases of Taylorism and Fordism, the principle of scientific management and 'flow-line' production ensured a division between control and execution and allowed the rise in the spatial separation of control and production. She goes on to assert that in the neo-Fordism stage, the adoption of micro-processor technology has enabled firms to move at least parts of the production process away from centres of industrially

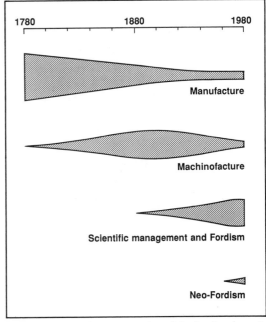

FIG 4.7 A schematic representation of the development of the labour process (*source*: Dunford and Perrons, 1983 p. 245)

experienced and trained workers to areas where labour can be obtained more cheaply (see also Chapter 7.3).

A final element to be considered in this section is the growth of part-time and female employment within the total labour force (J. Lewis, 1983 and 1984; McDowell and Massey, 1984; Henwood and Wyatt, 1986; Townsend, 1986). Using Census of Employment data, Townsend (1986) examines the increasing importance of part-time labour in Great Britain between 1971 and 1984. For the 1971–8 period in particular, part-time labour increased by 32.6 per cent, whilst full-time labour declined by 8.9 per cent; by 1981 21.0 per cent of all employees were part-time (< 30 hours). Part-time employment tended to grow in places where full-time employment was declining and the part-time market was dominated by women (80 per cent in 1981); by 1984, 46.4 per cent of all female employees were working part-time. Townsend examines the part-time share of total employment (PTS) in 1981 at three geographical scales: regional, county, and LLMAs. Variations in PTS values increased from 21 per cent for the regions to 50 per cent for the counties and 86 per cent for the LLMAs; the latter is mapped in Fig.

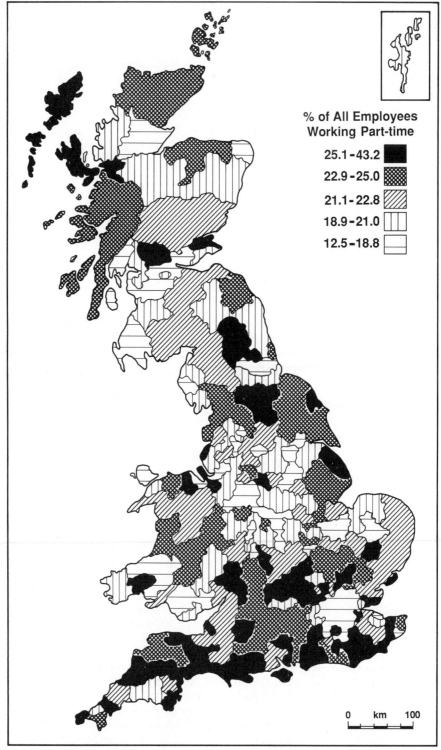

**% of All Employees
Working Part-time**

25.1 – 43.2

22.9 – 25.0

21.1 – 22.8

18.9 – 21.0

12.5 – 18.8

0   km   100

FIG 4.8 Part-time workers' share of total employees in Great Britain, 1981
(*source*: Townsend, 1986 p. 315)

4.8. The highest PTS values occurred in the South-East (outside Greater London) and in non-metropolitan Yorkshire and Humberside. Indeed, PTS was shown to be 'positively correlated with relative employment growth away from the conurbations and negatively correlated with the historic influence of heavy, male-employing industries in Scotland and Wales' (p. 316). When analysed in more detail, areas could be classified into three groups on the basis of spatial differences in the balance of part-time and full-time employment:

1. East Anglia and most southern counties, which experienced the highest full-time increases and only average part-time increases.
2. The conurbations plus the counties of Durham, Humberside, and South Glamorgan, which experienced below-average changes in both full-time and part-time employment.
3. Non-conurbation industrial areas lacking important regional service centres, which suffered a major loss of full-time jobs but an above-average increase in part-time employment. Wales and Scotland experienced poor performances for full-time work, but were second equal (behind the South-West) for part-time, with an increase of 45 per cent.

Townsend concludes that the increase in part-time employment was demand led, due to changes in population and the growth of specific (mainly service) industries, and was partly responsible for the convergence of lifestyles between the regions.

Some of these points formed the focus of interest in the examination by Lewis (1983) of female employment growth (by over three million) in Great Britain between 1951 and 1979. She confirms the concentration of women in the service sector, which in 1981 stood at 74 per cent (58 per cent for males), and highlights the decentralization of female employment away from metropolitan areas and towards non-metropolitan and peripheral regions to the north and west. In particular, the highest rates of growth occurred in both the older industrial regions, where male employment in secondary industries was formerly dominant, and the predominantly rural areas of East Anglia and the South-West. The rate of increase in female employment, therefore, has been greatest in those regions with traditionally low levels of female participation in the waged labour force.

It would appear from the analysis in this section that there is no general agreement on the current significance of labour as a factor affecting the location of, and locational change in, economic activity. On the one hand, mechanization has reduced its importance, whilst on the other, the need for high-tech skills may have enhanced its role. The above discussion has demonstrated that the supply, mobility, type, and cost of labour all vary spatially, leading to the conclusion that labour has played an important locational role in the restructuring of economic activity, especially at global but also at regional and local scales.

4.3 Capital

A key element in the production function of any farm, firm, or office, capital has often replaced land and labour in importance. The increasingly capital-intensive nature of economic activity demonstrates the importance of marketing skills in the deployment of capital. Indeed, it is rare for individual businesses to self-finance their development or expansion; exceptions are those small-scale owner-occupied farms, firms, and shops who are opposed to the idea of credit.

Generally speaking, therefore, access to and the cost of capital are vital considerations for the entrepreneur, which in turn are related to the type and mobility of capital. However, it is debatable whether they are powerful locating factors. For example, the cost of capital depends on interest rates which, with innovations in communications, should not vary significantly at regional and local levels. More important, probably, are spatial differences in the availability of capital and the willingness to finance the needs of entrepreneurs. Estall and Buchanan (1980) recognized this point and argued that the success of the USA car industry in the Mid-West was partly due to the greater willingness of local banks, especially in Detroit, to accommodate the unusual needs of the developing industry than eastern bankers.

Although evidence of geographical variations in the cost and availability of capital is speculative (Watts, 1987), there is no doubt that the growth of capital deployment in the different economic sectors and countries of the world has led to increased indebtedness. This is demonstrated quite clearly by the increasing debt crisis in such newly industrializing countries as Mexico and Brazil (see Chapter 14.3; Dicken, 1986). Similarly, in developed countries like the United Kingdom more capital is on loan to agriculture than any other business and in 1985 interest repayments on commercial debts other than for land purchase were equivalent to 25 per cent of farming income, compared with 10 per cent in the early 1970s (Marsden *et al.*, 1986*a*). In the USA, farm debts increased by 180 per cent in California alone during the 1970s.

There are two main types of capital:

1. *Physical*, including investment in land, buildings, and machinery; this is mainly immobile, although ownership can change.

2. *Money*, which has to be bought but tends to be more mobile.

The distinction between the two is important in showing that capital is not a perfectly mobile factor of production. Indeed, the geographical immobility of physical capital needs to be stressed and once established in an area is difficult to move. Consequently, the older industrial areas in Europe and North America accumulated stock and physical capital, thus encouraging industrial inertia. The occupational mobility of physical capital can be increased, however, if the buildings are used for different purposes, as in the conversion of textile factories into engineering plants. Elements of physical capital, in terms of buildings and machinery, have already been discussed in the sections on land and labour. Although more mobile, monetary capital can be fairly immobile at the macro scale, as its movement is restricted, not by distance but by such institutional barriers as national borders and trading blocs. Mobility can also be far from perfect within a nation, as demonstrated by Estall's (1972) study of the flow of investment funds in the USA, where certain impediments were identified:

1. Access to credit was related to the size of business. Large businesses experienced few problems of access to national funds from insurance companies, pension funds and similar bodies, whereas smaller businesses were dependent on local financial institutions, like banks. In the latter case, much depended on whether capital was actually available, together with close personal contacts and the attitudes of financiers.

2. Much new capital investment went towards supporting existing investments (incrementalism), which had become constrained by immobile physical capital. In the late 1960s, 80 per cent of new manufacturing investment went to support the expansion of existing sites, leaving relatively little for development in new, green-field sites.

3. Government policy (see Chapter 8.3) was actually promoting investment in development areas, showing the previous immobility of capital.

As already demonstrated in this chapter, the suppliers of capital—banks, insurance companies, pension funds, government agencies, special finance corporations, etc.—have increased in numbers considerably since the early 1960s. The spatial pattern of availability is, therefore, more and more dependent upon their policies and behaviour. Suppliers of capital will have a locational pattern of their own, which will not necessarily match the pattern of demand; movement of capital thus becomes necessary. The availability of capital seems to relate more to the size of business and the age and background of the borrower than to location; this suggests a fairly random pattern of availability. However, Ambrose and Colenutt (1975) stressed that financial capital invests only when and where demand and rents are rising, not where projects are needed. It is for this reason that investment in the United Kingdom has been concentrated in London and the South-East and on particular types of development like offices and shops.

Financial institutions have, for example, increasingly penetrated the agricultural industry. In the United Kingdom, credit from the clearing banks and the Agricultural Mortgage Corporation grew from 26 per cent of total credit in 1965 to 77 per cent in 1979, largely at the expense of private borrowing (Marsden *et al.*, 1986*a*). Their policies seem to favour the larger businesses, often run by younger, more educated farmers, and so capital tends to penetrate agriculture unevenly over space and time. As Marsden *et al.* (1986*a* p. 272) observe, 'some regions are highly resistant to new divisions of capital and labour due to their initial geographical endowments and the immobility or fixed nature of capital tied up in the production process.' Consequently, capital has penetrated some agricultural regions at the expense of others, intensifying the process of regional specialization (Bowler, 1985*a*).

When examining the availability of capital in

the secondary and tertiary sectors, it is important to distinguish between small and large corporate organizations (Chapter 7.1) and to assess, in relation to the former, the importance of *venture capital*. Small, market-system firms (Watts, 1987) borrow from banks and finance companies within their local area and, as outlined earlier, the attitudes and capabilities of such institutions will vary. It is in this context that venture capital has increased as a source of finance for smaller companies. Venture capital can be defined as 'medium- to long-term capital required to develop a new enterprise beyond its start-up phase, at a time when it begins to face more problems of competition, needs larger resources and more well-defined policies, and when the managerial deficiences of the entrepreneur begin to show' (Estall and Buchanan, 1980 p. 127). It is, therefore, capital loaned at great risk, on the assumption that the small number of successful ventures (as low as two out of every ten) will more than cover the cost of the larger number of failures. Venture capital is not equally available over space and, because close personal contact with the supported firms is needed, distance from the source of capital can act as a locational constraint. In the USA, venture capital has long been important in aiding the development of 'centres of innovations'. Estall (1972) outlines its importance in the emergence of R. & D. activities around Route 128 near Boston, where specialist finance institutions recognized the potential for new business and responded to the needs of innovative, but risky, science-based industries. In contrast, similar potential in Philadelphia was inhibited because of a more negative attitude by financial institutions. More recently, venture capital has been important in the development of a centre of high-tech business in Santa Clara county, California (Silicon Valley) (see Chapter 6.2; Oakey, 1984).

Indeed, three major centres of venture capital can be identified in the USA—California (San Francisco—Silicon Valley); New York; and New England (Massachusetts—Connecticut)—as well as three minor centres (Illinois (Chicago); Texas; and Minnesota). Venture capital firms in the USA tend to cluster in areas with high concentrations of financial institutions and technology-intensive enterprises (Florida and Kenney, 1988). It would appear that venture capital flows predominantly towards established high-technology areas (e.g.

Boston, Route 128) and where the pace of technological innovation and economic development accelerates considerably.

For many years it was difficult to raise venture capital in the United Kingdom generally and almost impossible in the peripheral regions. However, by 1986 there were 110 specialist venture capital groups, compared to just 19 in 1979; in 1985, the United Kingdom accounted for 41 per cent of the EC's risk capital (Mason, 1987a), although this was only equivalent to one-fifth of the total in the USA. Mason was able to demonstrate quite convincingly how the growth in venture capital had not penetrated all regions equally, but was heavily biased towards London and the South-East. Indeed, Greater London accounts for over one-third of venture capital investments by value and contains 23 per cent of the recipient companies; in addition, the rest of the South-East region claims a further 25 per cent of funds invested and 24 per cent of venture and capital-based companies (Table 4.5). In 1985, the South-East region in total obtained 60 per cent of the value of venture capital investments and 47 per cent of the benefiting companies.

Confirmation of this pattern of concentration was obtained by the same author in a survey of 24 members of the British Venture Capital Association (BVCA) in 1984 (56 per cent sample). The dominance of the South-East region in the

TABLE 4.5 Regional distribution of venture capital investments, in 1985 (%)

Region	Amount	Companies
South-East	60.1	47.1
(Greater London)	(35.5)	(23.2)
(Rest of South-East)	(24.6)	(23.9)
West-Midlands	7.8	6.8
South-West	6.7	7.3
Scotland	6.6	11.7
East-Anglia	6.4	5.7
Wales	3.9	8.6
Yorkshire/Humberside	3.2	3.7
East Midlands	2.1	3.7
North-West	1.6	2.2
North	1.4	2.0
Northern Ireland	0.2	1.2

Note: Figures exclude investments by Investors in Industry Group PLC.

Source: Mason (1987a p. 52).

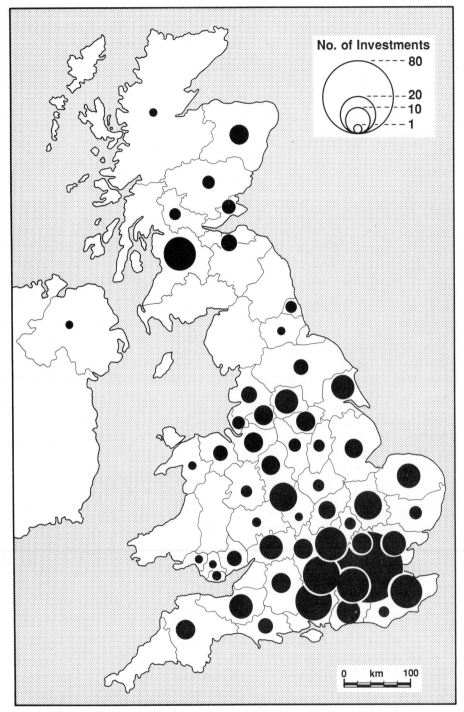

FIG 4.9 Number and distribution of venture capital investments of 24 companies in the United Kingdom (*source*: Mason, 1987*a* p. 55)

location of their total number of investments (52 per cent) is clearly shown in Fig. 4.9. In strict contrast, the peripheral regions of England (North, North-West, and Yorkshire and Humberside) attracted just 13 per cent of venture capital investments (despite having 21 per cent of all UK businesses) and Wales accounted for just 3 per cent (9 per cent of UK business stock). Mason (1987a) offers two possible explanations for such wide spatial differences in the availability of venture capital. First, it could reflect the lack of suitable investment opportunities in the peripheral regions. Support for this view comes from the higher rates of new firm formation in the South-East and East Anglia than elsewhere (Chapter 7.2), together with the disproportionate concentration of new technology-based enterprises in the South-East. In addition, independent firms in the peripheral regions have been shown to be less innovative than those in the South-East (Thwaites, 1982). This in turn is partly a function of the smaller number of independent firms requiring investment capital, due to the concentration of externally-owned branch plants in peripheral regions. Secondly, most venture capital funds operate from London; 70 per cent of the members of the BVCA in 1985 were based in London, with a further 8 per cent operating elsewhere in the South-East. No BVCA member operated from northern England or Northern Ireland, and the only representative for Wales was the government-backed Welsh Development Agency. A distance-decay effect would seem to exist, with investment opportunities in the peripheral regions being ignored. As Mason observes, it is impossible to obtain the empirical evidence to support such a hypothesis. However, geographical proximity between fund and client is desirable as venture capital firms require one of their executives to join the board of the investee company. This can only reduce the possibility of investment in peripheral areas.

The supply of capital is, of course, completely different in large corporate organizations that have opened subsidiaries or branches in locations spatially divorced from the head office. In such a situation, two questions affecting the spatial availability of capital need to be asked (Watts, 1987):

1. How much control over capital spending is exercised by the head office?

2. If funds are so controlled, is there any spatial bias in the way in which they are made available to particular plants?

Evidence suggests that plants do need to seek approval for investments over a certain, usually small, amount (Townroe, 1975). If the head office is also sensitive to distance constraints, plants in peripheral areas could be disadvantaged in terms of investment funds, especially if there are several plants producing the same product. However, the pattern of investment is more likely to depend upon the specific role of individual plants within the overall corporate strategy. Little, if any, empirical evidence is available to either support or refute such a claim.

It is quite clear from this discussion that capital markets in large corporate organizations are completely different from those for individual firms. In the former, attention needs to be directed towards the adopted company policies, whereas in the latter, the distribution and behaviour of specialized financial institutions seem to be the decisive factors.

4.4 Summary

This chapter has provided a wide-ranging investigation into the importance of the three main factors of production on the location of economic activity. The type, mobility, availability, and cost of each factor are often subject to spatial variations, although it is difficult to isolate and provide empirical evidence of their locational effects. Complexity is enhanced when it is recognized that the factors are interrelated and that their relative importance changes over time as well as space. Many of the issues raised in this chapter are, therefore, directly related to most of the other factors discussed in this book. However, the following summarizing points can be made:

- Although land is an immobile factor of production, the use to which it can be put is very flexible, depending on such characteristics as land quality, tenure, availability, and price. The land market is dynamic, with institutions and property developers increasingly affecting the location of, and locational change in, economic activity.

- Labour is a critical factor in geographical studies of economic activity. The supply, type, and cost of labour vary spatially and spatial differences in the cost of labour, for example, have contributed to the global shift in industry, away from developed and towards underdeveloped countries.
- Regional differences in labour skills have created a spatial division of labour, whereby individuals specializing in specific job tasks are concentrated in certain regions.
- Major temporal shifts in the production–labour process have occurred in capitalist societies, from manufacture to Neo-Fordism, with important implications for the distribution of land use and the location of economic activity.
- Capital is a fairly mobile factor of production, although its availability and cost depend not so much upon location but on the size of business, age of borrower, government policy, and the willingness of suppliers to finance the needs of entrepreneurs.
- Small firms in the secondary and tertiary sectors are becoming increasingly dependent on venture capital, which is spatially concentrated in high-tech areas, centres of innovation, and capital cities. In larger firms, the availability of capital depends more upon head office policies.

With improving technology, the 'friction' of distance to land, labour, and capital has been reduced (Chapter 5.2), providing entrepreneurs with more flexibility in their locational decisions. Despite this, factors of production will never be perfectly mobile and so will continue to exert an influence on the distribution of economic activity. It is to the context of demand, transport, and linkages that the next chapter turns.

5

Demand, Transport, and Linkages

This chapter is concerned with three closely related factors—demand, transport, and linkages—all of which influence where economic activity takes place and how the spatial pattern has evolved. Together they significantly modify the pattern which would be expected if the only location factors were the physical environment and the factors of production.

Demand is one of the fundamental factors affecting economic change and the spatial pattern of economic activity. This is because the level, character, and location of demand have a critical influence on the amount and nature of the goods and services produced in different places. The pattern of demand is geographically very uneven, reflecting variations in income and rates of economic growth at all spatial scales. One of the reasons why spatial variations in demand influence the location of economic activity and the pattern of land use is the cost of taking goods and services from the places where they are produced to the places where they are consumed.

Examining how the cost of overcoming distance influences the location of economic activity and land-use patterns has long been a traditional concern of Economic Geographers. The neoclassical models of von Thünen (Hall, 1966), Weber (1929), and Christaller (1966) all emphasize the importance of the cost of transport in determining the spatial patterns of economic activity that they model (Chapter 2.2). But developments in transport and communications technology have reduced the constraint of distance and led to an expansion of market and supply areas. Of all the variables considered in the part of this book concerned with the context of change, transport and communications have probably changed the most quickly and had the most profound consequences for the distribution of economic activity. Today there are only a limited number of economic activities in which transport costs are of

critical significance. As transport and communication innovations have been introduced, this has led to a dramatic restructuring of the economic landscape.

Innovations in transport and communications have also affected the nature of the linkage patterns between firms. It is through their material and information linkages that firms learn about changes in their environment, such as changes in demand. Linkages have an important influence on the location of economic activity and the way in which the pattern evolves. Most work has emphasized the role of local linkages in the formation and maintenance of agglomerations of economic activities. Recently attention has focused on examining the nature of linkages over whatever distance they occur and analysing linkages in the context of the way production is organized.

The main aim of this chapter is to examine the nature of demand, transport, and linkages and to assess their influence on the spatial pattern of economic activity. It begins by analysing the characteristics and geography of demand and assessing the effect that changes in demand have on the location of economic activity and land use. The effect of transport costs on the economic landscape is then reviewed before the nature of transport and communications innovations is examined and their impact on the spatial pattern of economic activity evaluated. The chapter finishes with an extended discussion of the relationship between location and linkage systems.

5.1 Demand

The nature and spatial impact of demand

The *level* of demand is closely related to the level of economic development and as a local or national economy grows the level of demand expands. The *structure* of demand patterns also alters, as an area becomes more prosperous with the proportion spent on luxury goods and services, such as consumer electronics and air travel, increasing and the proportion spent on basic goods and services, such as clothing and food, declining. In analysing demand patterns it is also important to identify different types of demand. For example, one distinction is that between *final demand* and *derived demand*. Whereas final demand refers to the amount bought by end users, for example the number of cars purchased by fleet companies; derived demand refers to the amount bought by intermediate users, for example the amount of steel purchased by car manufacturers.

Demand is influenced by both *cyclical* and *structural* factors. Various cycles in the level of economic activity are discussed in the economics literature, varying from *inventory cycles*, lasting anywhere between 18 to 40 months; *business* or *trade cycles*, typically of about nine years' duration; to *long cycles*, lasting about 50 years (Lipsey, 1983). The last of these have already been discussed in Chapter 2.1. Whereas inventory cycles are associated with lags in the impact of demand changes on the level of stocks held by retailers, wholesalers, and manufacturers, business cycles are associated with booms and recessions. The last major recession which affected most developed market economies occurred in the late 1970s and early 1980s. Many companies, particularly in the manufacturing sector, undertook major rationalization schemes leading to a massive loss of jobs and high levels of unemployment (Townsend, 1983).

The level of demand in an area for a particular product or service is also influenced by structural factors, including changes in the structure of the economy, shifts in the pattern of trade, and technological changes. For example, the demand for steel in developed market economies fell in the 1970s while demand in centrally planned and developing economies continued to rise. Dicken (1986 pp. 265–6) suggests that to account for this, structural factors as well as the cyclical effects of recession need to be considered.

Three kinds of structural influence seem to be especially important. First, in the mature industrial economies of Europe and the United States demand from the traditional heavy users of steel has been stagnating or even declining as these economies are becoming transformed into so-called 'postindustrial' economies. The new wave of information technology industries uses far less steel than the formerly dominant heavy manufacturing sectors. Second, part of this decline in demand also reflects the impact of imports of goods such as motor vehicles, ships and other steel-using manufactured goods. In this sense, the import of steel occurs in 'disguised' form and reduces the demand for domestically produced steel. Third, the steel-using industries have become far more parsimonious in their use of steel either because of design and technological changes in products and processes or because of substitution of other materials such as aluminium, plastics, glass and ceramics.

Changes in demand not only bring about economic changes, they also respond to changes in social and economic organization. For example, the shift from Fordist to neo-Fordist methods of organizing labour and production, already referred to in Chapters 2.1 and 4.2, is associated with changes from a system emphasizing mass consumption of standardized goods to one emphasizing increasingly differentiated and customized consumption patterns (see also Table 15.2). Markets which were previously supplied with standardized goods and services are increasingly being viewed as segmented, requiring differentiated goods and services often supplied by specialist outlets. This is clearly illustrated by changes occurring in retailing. One of the first large-scale examples in Britain was the Burton Group's development of Top Shop and Top Man chains. By 1988 it had nearly 1500 outlets under a dozen different names aimed at specific lifestyle and age-groups (see Table 7.2). Woolworths provides another example. In 1982 they had 1,095 stores in Britain under one fascia. By 1988 it operated three-quarters of its earlier units in a refocused format, with chains of DIY, drugstore, and electrical stores (Howard and Davies, 1988).

Changes in the nature of demand not only affect the type of goods and services produced and the character of the outlets through which they are sold, they also have an important influence on the spatial pattern of economic activity. For example, a change in the level of demand may result in the *threshold* required to support particular economic activities being passed. An illustration of this is the impact of the increasing demand for producer services. This has encouraged producer services to filter down the urban hierarchy where demand was not previously adequate to support them (Chapter 13.2). Another case where the demand threshold was critical was in the decision on where to locate an integrated iron and steel works in the United States following the Second World War. The availability of a significant regional market was a major reason why it was eventually sited not in New England but at Trenton, near Philadelphia. While New England was a desirable location in many respects, the extra transport costs to serve a wider market was an overriding objection (Estall and Buchanan, 1980).

Places vary in their responses to changes in the level and character of demand. An illustration of this is the leads and lags in the timing of the impact of business cycles on different local and national economies (Haggett, 1971). The variability in the spatial impact reflects, in part, differences in the inherited social and economic structures of different places. An example of this is the different capacities of tourist resorts to respond to major changes in demand. In the face of a decline in demand for traditional seaside holidays in Britain resorts with large numbers of high-quality hotels have been better able to develop a conference business (e.g. Brighton) than resorts with generally smaller hotels (e.g. Margate) where the process of conversion to homes for old people has been more significant (Buck, 1988). However, probably the most studied example of how a pre-existing structure affects the impact of a change in demand is that of industrial structure. Thus an area containing a large proportion of industries which are growing nationally would be expected to grow more rapidly than an area with a high proportion of industries for which demand is declining nationally.

The increased segmentation of markets and emphasis on providing more customized goods and services may also be having an impact on the economic landscape. The need for closer co-ordination between the producer and the customer, than was the case when a mass production of standardized items was more the norm, suggests that the importance of a market location is increasing. The supporting evidence for this proposition is not yet strong, though it has been suggested that it is a factor contributing to the return of some clothing production from the Third World to Europe (see Chapter 12.1) and the reagglomeration of some manufacturing and service activities in new locations (see Section 5.3).

However, it is difficult to separate the impact of changes in the character of demand from the effects of changes in technology and the organization of production, such as the increased use of micro-processors and just-in-time systems, which may also be contributing to these trends (Chapters 6 and 7).

Spatial patterns of demand

Demand patterns tend to be markedly uneven geographically, reflecting different levels of income and intensities of economic growth in different places. These spatial variations in demand can have a marked effect on spatial patterns of economic activity. The most fundamental differences are between the high incomes of the developed world and the low incomes of the developing world (see Fig. 14.1). One of the consequences is seen in the pattern of agricultural production. Whereas in the developed world a high proportion of farm income comes from livestock products, in the developing world the majority of farm income is derived from the sale of cereals and root crops. In explaining this difference Grigg (1984 p. 31) notes that:

In the latter the poverty of the mass of the population means that a very high proportion of the area in crops has to be devoted to cereals and root crops that give a cheap supply of energy. . . . Paradoxically, this does not mean that livestock are not numerous in these countries. Livestock are kept as a source of draught power on the farm, and their manure often forms the only supply of plant nutrients, although in some countries it is also used as a fuel. . . . In the developed countries high incomes means that livestock products provide a high proportion of farm income. . . . Yet this does not mean that cereals are unimportant in Europe and North America; a high proportion of cropland is in cereals but much of this is fed to livestock, while in addition Europe imports grain and other food crops.

The spatial pattern of demand which reflects the uneven distribution of the population and businesses which consume the goods and services, also affects the location of economic activity within countries. Spatial variations in demand reflect the uneven distribution of population and businesses which consume the goods and services. Consequently as the distribution of population and businesses alters it affects the level and character of demand in different places. For example, the suburbanization of the population is a major factor encouraging the decentralization of retailing (Chapter 13.1). It has also attracted offices and manufacturing industry to locate in the suburbs to be closer to the pool of labour they demand.

Of particular interest are those economic activities in which firms compete spatially for markets and/or supplies as the outcome of the competitive process has a direct impact on the spatial pattern of economic activity. The activities include some agricultural products, forest products, some food and drink industries, the extraction of sand and gravel, the cement industry, and several consumer services. These activities are generally characterized by a need to be in close proximity to the points of demand, because of relatively high transport costs (given the low value and bulk of many of the goods), the perishability of some food products, or the reluctance of consumers to travel far to purchase the items. Attempting to distinguish between *market* and *supply areas* is

not always helpful, because one firm's market area can be another's supply area, as for example in the case of a sugar-beet-farmer and a sugar-beet processor. Both involve aspects of demand, whether it be a food processor competing for the demands of suppliers or a retailer competing for the demands of consumers. The main features of market and supply areas are best illustrated by considering three specific examples, one from each of the primary, secondary, and tertiary sectors of the economy.

The first example examines the spatial patterns of demand associated with the growth of contract farming. Although sugar-beet contracts have been offered in the UK since the 1920s, the growth of the frozen food sector since the 1950s has encouraged food processors to offer contracts to farmers to produce for them. The consequence is that supply areas are defined in close proximity to the processing factories. The aim of the manufacturers is to ensure the highest possible quality

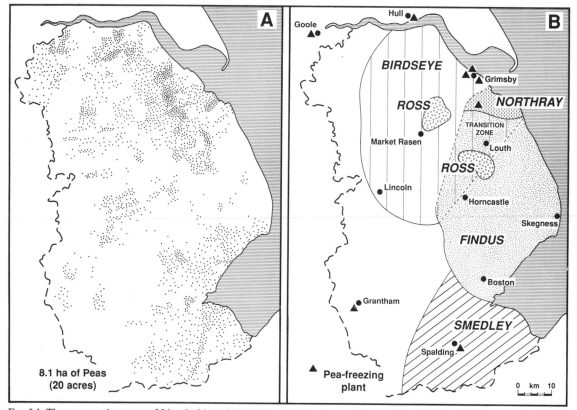

Fig 5.1 The pea-growing areas of Lincolnshire, 1969: (*a*) peas for freezing, canning, and dehydration; (*b*) supply areas of the main companies and location of pea-freezing plants (*source*: Dalton, 1971 pp. 135, 136)

by co-ordinating the harvesting with the processing. Contracting has been particularly important in fruit, vegetable, and poultry production. The growing of peas for freezing in eastern England provides a good illustration (Dalton, 1971).

Peas for freezing were first grown in Norfolk in the 1940s, using spare capacity at the Birdseye fish-packing factories in Great Yarmouth and Lowestoft. Demand soon outstripped supply, and pea-growing developed in Lincolnshire and North Humberside using spare fish-freezing capacity in the company's plants along Humberside. The problem with using coastal freezing centres is that half the potential supply area is in the sea and it is noticeable that new freezing capacity which developed in the 1970s was located inland at places like Grantham and Spalding. The pea-growing areas and the supply areas of the main companies in Lincolnshire are shown in Fig. 5.1. Smedley's factory is at the centre of the supply area, while Birdseye's is at the edge, and the processing plant run by Findus at Cleethorpes is actually outside its supply area. Birdseye draw most of their supplies from a 40 km radius of Grimsby, reflecting their early interest in the area. Findus have to transport peas over 80 km and this is only made possible by the establishment of chilling plants which are used in association with the vining machines used to harvest the crop.

The second example, from the manufacturing sector, examines the way in which firms competing for market areas behave under conditions of oligopolistic competition (i.e. markets dominated by a few companies). Watts (1978) makes a useful distinction between the role a firm plays in the interaction process and its behaviour within that role. He distinguishes two types of role—leader and satellite; and three types of behaviour—competitive, passive, and collusive. He proceeds to illustrate these with examples from the British brewing industry. This is an interesting case, because not only are market areas an important feature of the industry, but ownership is also concentrated in the hands of a few companies. Watts estimates that in 1971 the top seven companies controlled over 85 per cent of the market. In such an oligopolistic situation the behaviour of individual companies can have a marked effect on the spatial pattern of the industry as a whole. Another particular feature of the brewing industry is that because most beer is sold through tied outlets the only way in which companies can

expand their markets is to acquire other brewing companies or buy their outlets. The brewing companies exhibited different roles and behaviour patterns in the way they interacted during the period studied.

Watts suggests that Allied Breweries provides an example of a firm which in the 1950s and 1960s played the role of a *leader*, while Whitbread played the role of a *satellite* firm. Whereas Allied concentrated on taking over brewing firms based in large urban areas, Whitbread started to acquire companies rather later and was able only to acquire smaller plants. This difference in role helps to explain why in the early 1970s Allied had relatively few large breweries with a large average size, while Whitbread had many more breweries with a small average size (Fig 5.2). The emergence of United Breweries in the 1960s provides an example of *competitive* behaviour. The growth of United Breweries from a small base in Yorkshire represented the competitive strategy of Canadian Breweries to gain a foothold in the United Kingdom. This strategy led them to acquire ten firms in 1960–1, and a few years later they merged with other brewing firms to form Bass Charrington. This policy of rapid acquisition and merger reflects a deliberate attempt by the firm to obtain a widespread network of tied outlets. A *passive* policy may be illustrated by the case of Truman, Hanbury, Buxton. In 1968 this company had two breweries, one in Burton and another in London. Instead of expanding they sold off outlets in the North, because the cost of transport from Burton did not give them a sufficient return. Later they concentrated production in London to gain economies of scale and sold off outlets in the North and Midlands. By the early 1970s, apart from some outlets in Swansea, they were purely a South-East Company. In the mid-1970s they were absorbed by Watney Mann. *Collusive* behaviour unfortunately cannot be illustrated from this industry partly because the very nature of collusion means that agreements are rarely published. However, historical evidence of collusion over supply and market areas has been found in the sugar-beet industry in the 1920s (Watts, 1980b).

Whereas market areas are of significance to a limited number of manufacturing activities, their study in relation to retail centres has long been a preoccupation of geographers. Market areas are a fundamental feature of central place theory, with both Christaller (1966) and Losch (1954)

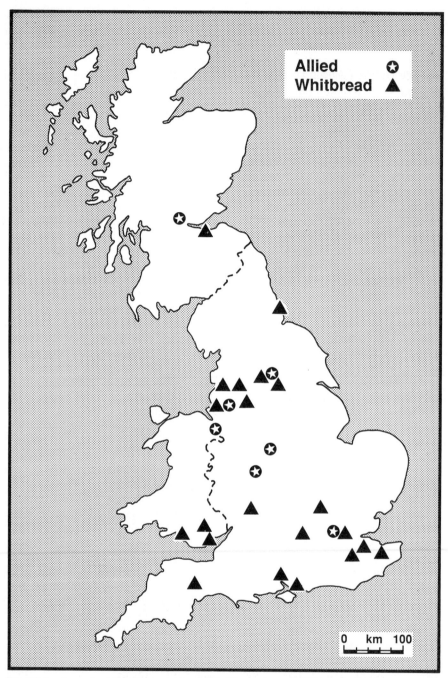

FIG 5.2 Leader and satellite firms: plants of Allied Breweries and Whitbread, 1971/2
(*source*: Watts, 1978 p. 222)

modelling their nature. In Christaller's model market areas are arranged in a *nested* pattern with the catchment area of lower-order goods packed within those of higher-order goods (Fig. 2.2). In Losch's model there is a much more complex web of interlocking market areas (Lewis, 1977). In attempting to estimate the size of market areas attention has focused on various applications of the gravity model. The simplest version was expounded by Reilly (1929). According to his *law of retail gravitation* a city will attract retail trade from a town in its hinterland in direct proportion to the population size of the city and in inverse proportion to the square of the distance from the city.

This may be represented formally in that city i will be attractive for retailing, A, to individuals in city j in direct proportion to the population P at i and in inverse proportion to the square of the distance from city i to city j, (d_{ij}^2)

$$A_i = \frac{P_i}{d_{ij}^2}$$

The break-point x between two settlements i and j can be worked out as follows:

$$d_{ix} = \frac{d_{ij}}{1 + \sqrt{P_j/P_i}}$$

For example, the break-point between Los Angeles (i), with a population of 9 m, and San Francisco (j), approximately 612 km away with a population of 5 m, is 350.7 km from Los Angeles.

$$d_{ix} = \frac{612}{1 + \sqrt{5/9}} = 350.7$$

The model predicts that at the break-point the same amount of retail trade will be attracted to Los Angeles as to San Francisco.

An important point, though not included by Reilly, is the possibility of calculating for any point between two centres the proportion of retail trade which will be attracted to each centre. It is possible to calculate and map probabilities as well as break-points (Haynes and Fotheringham, 1984). For example, Bakersfield (x) is approximately 450 km from San Francisco and 180 km from Los Angeles. The proportion of Bakersfield's retail expenditure going to Los Angeles and San Francisco will be in the ratio $A_i : A_j$ where

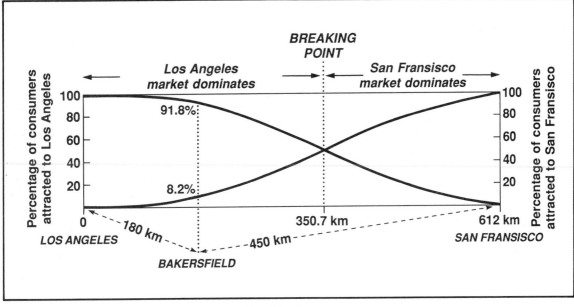

FIG 5.3 Retail market shares between Los Angeles and San Francisco

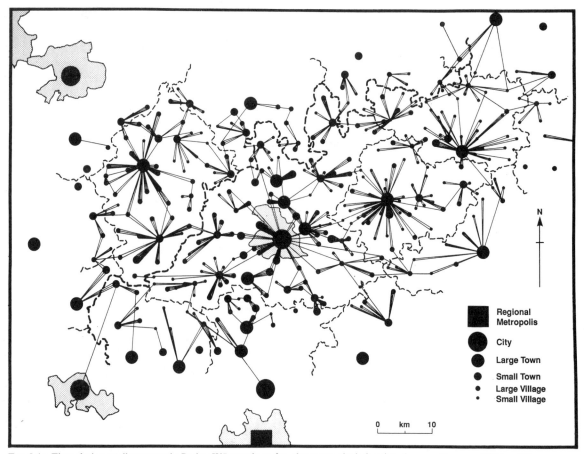

Fɪɢ 5.4*a* First-choice retail patterns in Baden-Württemberg for pharmaceutical chemists (*source*: Barnum, 1966 p. 60)

$$A_i = \frac{P_i}{d_{ix}^2} \quad \frac{9\,000\,000}{180^2} = 277.78$$

$$A_j = \frac{P_i}{d_{jx}^2} \quad \frac{5\,000\,000}{450^2} = 24.69$$

which gives the ratio $A_i : A_j = 277.78 : 24.69$ or 91.8 per cent to Los Angeles and 8.2 per cent to San Francisco (Fig 5.3).

In order to establish the nature of retail markets areas in the real world numerous studies have involved interviews with consumers to see which centres they patronize for various goods. These studies provide plenty of evidence of the nesting predicted by Christaller. For example, Fig. 5.4*a* shows the first-choice travel patterns for pharmacists in Baden-Württemberg. Although the dis-

tances travelled are small and not all consumers patronize their nearest centres, in general each centre draws on a local market area. In Fig. 5.4*b* the pattern for clothes shows that the main shopping centres of Heidelberg, Heilbronn, and Stuttgart dominate. The catchment area for the low-order pharmaceutical goods nests within the larger market area for the higher-order product clothes.

The implication of much of this analysis of market and supply areas and the spatial impact of changes in the location of demand is that the costs involved in transporting goods to the market and providing services where they are required may limit the locations in which it is economic for an activity to take place. This emphasizes the need to analyse the nature of transport costs.

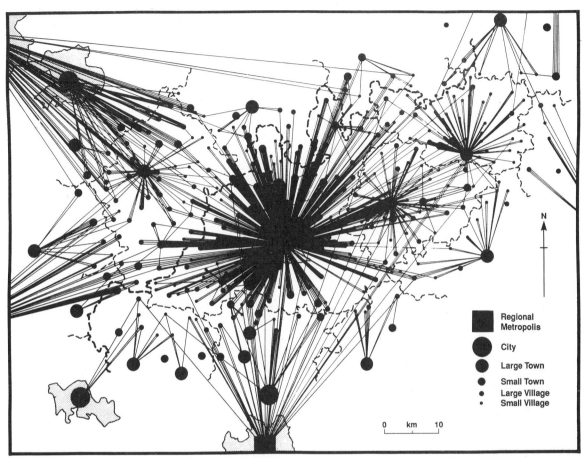

FIG 5.4b First-choice retail patterns in Baden-Württemberg for clothes (*source*: Barnum, 1966 p. 77)

5.2 Transport

Transport costs

Most of the neoclassical location models (see Chapter 2.2) begin with the assumption that transport costs are a function simply of the weight of goods and the distance over which they are moved (Fig. 5.5a). In reality, the structure of transport costs is much more complex. Their major characteristics are analysed in numerous texts (for example, Hoover, 1948; Lloyd and Dicken, 1977; White and Senior, 1983), hence only some of the main features will be summarized here.

Transport costs may be analysed both from the points of view of the *providers* and the *users* of the service. There are two elements in the cost struc-ture faced by the providers. These are (i) the *fixed costs*, which are incurred before any traffic moves, including the cost of infrastructure (e.g. terminal and route costs) and some staffing (e.g. administrators and terminal personnel); and (ii) the *variable costs*, which are incurred by the actual movement of traffic (Fig. 5.5b). The relative importance of the fixed and variable costs differs with the mode of transport. As a result, the various transport media offer advantages over different lengths of haul. For example, the cost of port and canal facilities is high, but the cost of transporting goods by water rises only slowly with distance. In contrast, with road transport variable costs tend to rise more steeply, whereas fixed costs tend to be lower (Fig. 5.5c). As a consequence water transport tends to be more competitive over longer distances than road

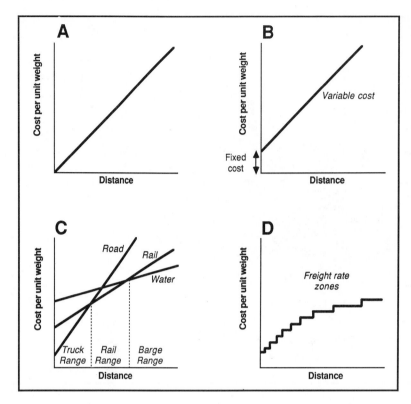

Fig 5.5 The structure of transport costs:
(*a*) assumed transport cost curve in neoclassical location models;
(*b*) fixed and variable transport costs;
(*c*) idealized transport cost curves for road, rail, and water;
(*d*) idealized transport rate charged to users

transport. The relative cost of railways tends to fall in between those for road and rail. These cost structures are not of course static, and over the last fifty years road transport has become competitive over increasing distances and has taken business away from both the waterways and the railways.

The transport cost to suppliers tends to increase regularly with distance. In contrast, the *rate charged to users* usually takes a different form. The structure of freight rates can be very complex, but they are often tapered. In other words, the costs are curvilinear as the *unit cost* (cost per tonne-km) falls as distance increases (Fig 5.5*d*). Freight rates also vary according to the characteristics of the commodity. Bulky goods, small shipments, fragile and perishable goods all tend to attract higher freight rates per unit weight; while high-value goods are often charged a higher rate because they are better able to bear them. Traffic characteristics can also affect freight rates. The rates tend to be lower where there is competition between transport media and where traffic densities are high. Low rates are also often charged where vehicles would otherwise have returned empty.

So far it has been assumed that the customer pays for the cost of transport from the point of origin. This is known as a *free-on-board pricing* system. In this system the further away the customer is from the supplier the higher the cost will be. Most pricing systems are, however, discriminatory in some form. A second basic type is *uniform delivered pricing* (sometimes referred to as cost, insurance, freight pricing). In this case the customer pays the same amount regardless of location. This has the advantage of simplicity for the buyer and seller. There are also several other pricing policies which combine various features of these two basic types. For example, in *zonal pricing* rates go up in steps and a uniform rate is charged within zones, while in *basing point pricing* all customers pay a free-on-board price from an identical basing point whether or not they buy from that point. The effect is that any one customer will be quoted an identical delivered price by all sellers, although this situation may be made more complex where multiple basing points are used. Such basing point systems used to be fairly common in the United States before they were declared illegal in 1948. They still operate in some industries in some countries, such as the cement industry in Britain (Moyes, 1980).

The relative importance of these various spatial pricing policies in the United States, Japan, and West Germany is shown in Table 5.1. Clearly no one system dominates among the firms in the survey, although the free-on-board pricing system is relatively more important in the United States, probably reflecting the greater spatial extent of the North American market. Other evidence from the United States suggests that uniform delivered prices are not only prevalent among consumer goods, especially those advertised nationally, but are also characteristic of a wide range of other commodities including rubber products, printing and publishing, and electrical generators (Chisholm, 1970).

The complexity of the transport rates charged in the real world affects the predictions of the neoclassical models which generally assume that transport costs are simply a function of weight and distance (Chapter 2.2). This can be illustrated both where a free-on-board pricing system operates and where a system of uniform delivered pricing is in use. Where transport costs are curvilinear, rather than linear, the effect is to increase the size of market and supply areas. For example, in von Thünen's model tapered location rent curves spread production zones, particularly the outer ones (Fig. 5.6a). Tapering rates also tend to encourage the least-cost location in Weber's model to occur either at the material source or the market, rather than somewhere in between (Fig.

5.6b). The main exception is at break-of-bulk points where goods are transhipped from one mode of transport to another. Such break-of-bulk points can be a low-cost location for production because one set of loading and unloading costs can be avoided as the supplies are transferred direct from one mode of transport into the factory and the goods are dispatched to market direct from the factory on to another mode of transport (Fig. 5.6c). Other assumptions about the nature of transport costs may also be relaxed. For instance, the effect of introducing different modes of transport and allowing for different degrees of competition along particular routes is that the boundaries of supply and market areas become highly irregular; while if transport prices are zoned, supply and market areas of different firms may overlap.

Where supplies are obtained at a uniform delivered price they are, in Weber's terms, *ubiquitous materials* and the costs of moving them has no influence on the location of production. On the other hand, where the goods are distributed at a uniform delivered price the optimum location for the manufacturer is at the geographic centre of the market, because the manufacturer still has to incur the actual cost of delivering goods to distant customers. Some supporting evidence for this comes from a study of the location of Coca-Cola's bottling plants in south-western Ontario. Osleeb and Cromley (1978) compared the optimal location pattern based on a combination of production and distribution costs with the actual pattern. No fewer than seven of Coca-Cola's eleven sites coincided with the predicted locations.

So far the discussion has been largely theoretical, showing the effects of relaxing the simplified assumptions made about transport costs in the neoclassical location models. Conventional

TABLE 5.1 Spatial pricing policies followed by firms in three nations

	% of firms with significant freight costs		
	Free-on-board	Uniform	Mixed
United States	33	21	46
Japan	18	27	55
West Germany	21	32	47

Source: Greenhut (1981 p. 79).

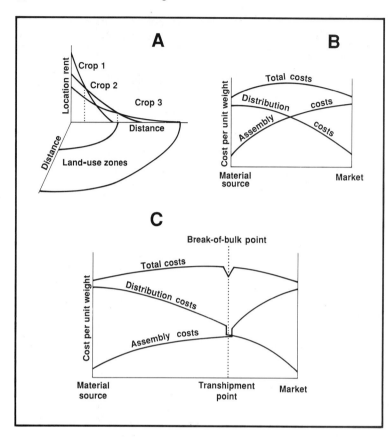

FIG 5.6 Transport and the location of economic activity: (*a*) effect of tapering freight rates on agricultural location rent curves and land-use zones; (*b*) effect of tapering freight rates on optimal location of manufacturing; (*c*) effect of break-of-bulk points between water and rail transport on optimal location of manufacturing

wisdom, however, suggests that transport costs are a small proportion of total costs. This assertion may be tested by examining some of the evidence on geographic variations in transport costs. Most studies of transport cost in manufacturing firms in Great Britain suggest that they account for less than 5 per cent of the value of gross output, with geographical variations between the highest- and lowest-cost regions being of the order of a maximum of 3 per cent of the value added by the manufacturing sector (Edwards, 1975; Gudgin, 1978). The findings that transport costs form a small proportion of the costs of firms have led some research workers to suggest that they play a relatively minor role in location decision-making (Lutterell, 1962). However, these studies were based on the existing location patterns of industry and may reflect past investment decisions designed to minimize their transport costs. Such *ex post facto* evaluations may thus underestimate the importance of transport costs in the investment decisions of firms.

An alternative methodology is to examine the transport costs of a typical firm setting up a manufacturing facility for the first time. Such an *ex-ante* perspective was adopted by Tyler and Kitson (1987). They found that the transport cost variation faced by a typical footloose manufacturing firm locating in Great Britain for the first time is of the order of 170 per cent. The lowest-cost locations are in the Midlands around Birmingham and the South-East around London. The Manchester area is also a low-cost location. Costs increase rapidly in all directions away from these places, so that Exeter has a cost disadvantage of nearly 100 per cent of the lowest-cost site, the North-East is about 60 per cent higher, Wales most typically about 70 per cent higher, and Scotland from 70 to 170 per cent higher (Fig 5.7).

The transport cost penalty incurred by a footloose firm in a peripheral location seems relatively large. However, since transport costs in such industries are generally less than 2 to 3 per cent of the value of gross output, the highest-cost areas will pay transport costs amounting to no more than about 5 to 8 per cent of total costs.

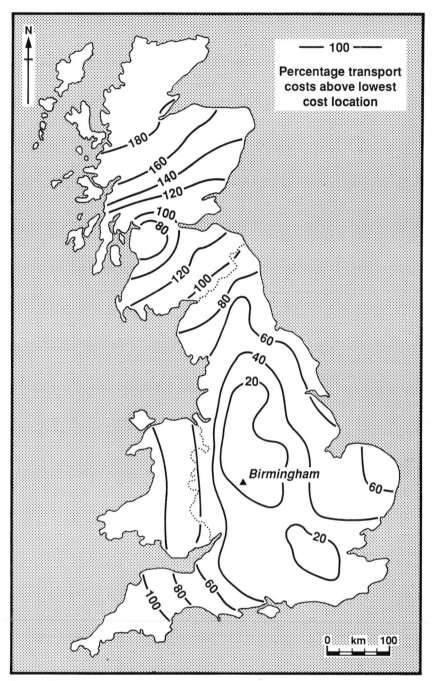

FIG 5.7 Transport cost variations for a footloose manufacturing firm considering a new location in Great Britain (*source*: based on data in Tyler and Kitson, 1978 p. 71)

Nevertheless, given the low level of profitability in British industry in recent years, such small items in the cost structure are important if a firm wishes to minimize costs and improve profitability.

Transport cost variations in North America are likely to be larger than in Britain, given its greater spatial extent. However, even in the motor vehicle industry, which experienced dispersal of assembly plants to reduce the cost of distributing finished cars to the market, regional assembly plants are becoming less significant (Chapter 12.4). This reflects, in part, the impact of changes in transport technology.

Transport and communications technology

Developments in transport and communications technology are reducing the friction of distance. Whereas it took twenty-four days to cross North America coast to coast by a combination of rail and stage coach in 1850, this was cut to four days using direct rail by 1900. The same journey today can be done in less than five hours by jet aeroplane (Haggett, 1983). Clearly in terms of time distance the world is 'shrinking'. The reduced effect of distance on communications is even more dramatic. Innovations in communications over the last 100 years—telegraph, telephone, telex, radio, cable, and satellite—have allowed almost instantaneous communication regardless of distance. Indeed with satellite communications the costs are the same, whether transmitting information 1000 km or 10 000 km.

This process of *time–space convergence* (Janelle, 1969), and *cost–space convergence* (Abler, 1971) is, however, uneven. Some places, usually the more prosperous and the larger centres, and some people, such as the better-off and those working for big business, benefit first. Some of the less important places and the poorer in society, on the other hand, are becoming relatively more remote and less well served. For them *time–space* and *time–cost divergence* is occurring.

Transport innovations have not only reduced the time and cost of linking places, they have also resulted in changes in the relative competitiveness of different modes of transport. For example, the relative shift of freight from rail to road over the last fifty years is, in part, accounted for by improvements to the road networks and the freight vehicles using them. In Britain, in 1958 rail moved

33 per cent of all tonne kilometres and road 43 per cent, while in 1986 the share moved by rail had fallen to 8 per cent and the proportion going by road had increased to 81 per cent (Palin, 1988). Other consequences of transport innovations are changes in the volume of goods carried, the number of movements, and the speed of loading and unloading. This can be illustrated with reference to the introduction of containerization in world shipping. It was estimated that in 1972, 80 per cent of the goods carried between Australia and England could be taken in 14 container ships, compared with over 100 conventional cargo ships which were required three or four years previously (Lloyd and Dicken, 1972). The use of pre-stowed containers has also meant a much more rapid turn round of ships with mammoth container cranes using fewer men than the traditional laborious method of loading by sling into the hold to be stowed by hand. The effect was that: 'one gang of 12 or 13 men could discharge a container ship in three to four days whereas a conventional ship carrying an equivalent cargo would have taken 100 men perhaps three weeks' (Cox 1984 p. 522).

The spatial implications of improvements in transport and communications are profound, though not always clear cut. Following the framework provided by Janelle (1969) in discussing the nature of *time–space* and *cost–space* convergence a number of impacts of transport and communication innovations may be suggested.

1. One argument is that these innovations have resulted in the location of economic activities becoming more *concentrated at the interregional scale*. It is suggested, for instance, that as market and supply areas have expanded the production and distribution units (farms, factories, offices, warehouses, shops) can be more concentrated. The same process may have contributed to an increase in the size of individual units.

2. A similar argument leads to the suggestion that telecommunications, rather than leading to the demise of cities, are *strengthening the economies of a handful of major world cities* by allowing once separate activities to become highly integrated functions (Moss, 1987). Support for this suggestion may be seen in the recent renaissance of some major metropolitan economies. New York and London are the prime examples where telecommunications have contributed to their growth as financial centres (Daniels, 1988).

3. At the same time, however, it is intimated that developments in transportation and communications have encouraged economic activities to *decentralize at the intraregional scale*. In particular, the spread of car ownership has allowed economic activities to be dispersed within city regions.

4. It is further suggested that innovations in transport and communications have *increased the spatial extent of production*. This was an important factor enabling the spread of commercial agriculture in the nineteenth century from Western Europe to continental North America and later South America and Australasia. One interpretation of this is that the increase in demand for food in Western Europe, fuelled by industrialization and the growth of population, and improvements in land and sea transport, particularly with the development of railways and steam ships, led to a reduction in the slope of von Thünen's location rent curves (Fig. 2.2a) and a spatial extension of the production zones (Peet, 1969). More recently the innovations in transport and the ability to transmit information over long distances at great speed have enabled production and marketing to be co-ordinated on a global scale (Chapter 7.2). For example, the Italian clothing company, Benetton, has a complex information network in its office at Villa Orba which will eventually be linked to a computerized cash till in every shop. This allows the company to respond quickly to trends in the market. So if a particular style is selling well in New York they can quickly arrange for more to be manufactured. This has the advantage that stocks can be kept low and the quantities manufactured can be kept small until sale trends are apparent (Withers and Fawcett, 1984, cited in Mitter, 1986).

5. Another suggestion is that developments in transport and communications have led to economic activities becoming *concentrated in areas of greatest comparative advantage*. As the proportion of total costs accounted for by transport costs has fallen, other location factors have become relatively more important. For example, production of many agricultural crops has become more concentrated in those areas where physical factors are favourable. For instance, witness the growth of market gardening in parts of Spain. The use of juggernaut vehicles to serve markets across Western Europe has allowed Spanish farmers to take advantage of their suitable climate to produce large quantities of cheap market garden produce.

Paradoxically, then, the reduction of spatial barriers has had the effect of greatly magnifying the significance of variations from place to place in such elements as resources, labour costs and skills, and government grants. In other words, the decrease in the tyranny of distance has increased the importance of geography. However, as with other aspects of technological change (Chapter 6) care needs to be taken in interpreting the consequences of transport and communication innovations. Improvements in transport and communication are essentially enabling technologies which allow spatial shifts in the location of economic activity to take place in response to other factors. They do not determine the changes in the space economy, although they may encourage locational adjustment to occur in certain directions rather than others. The possible variation in spatial outcomes is also apparent in the relationship between linkages and location.

5.3 Linkages and location

The discussion of market and supply areas has touched upon the nature of the linkage between producers and their customers and suppliers. Studying linkages is important because they show how establishments and firms are related to one another and to the wider environment in which they operate. It has been argued that firms learn about their environment through their linkage patterns and this may constrain and direct their subsequent locational behaviour (Taylor, 1975). Material linkages are also 'the mechanism whereby *changes* in demand are channelled through to the local economy' J. N. Marshall, 1987 p. 112). The geography of linkages is a topic in its own right. Here the interest is in examining the relationship between linkages and location. This relationship occurs in both directions in that the pattern of linkages influences the evolution of the spatial pattern of economic activity, just as the location of activities constrains the kind of linkage pattern which develops. In the account which follows particular emphasis is placed upon the relationship between linkages and agglomerations of economic activity and the need to interpret the relationship between linkages and location in the context of the way production is organized. These themes are illustrated with examples drawn mainly from the manufacturing and office sectors.

The nature of linkages

There are two main kinds of linkages: *material* flows and *information* flows. Associated with both there is usually a monetary flow and sometimes a movement of personnel as well. The main linkages of a manufacturing plant are shown in Fig. 5.8. They include raw materials, processed materials, equipment, service supplies, subcontracting links, and various marketing links. The inputs are sometimes referred to as *backward linkages*, while the outputs are referred to as *forward links*. *Subcontracting* often involves both backward and forward links for a plant, for example, as a product is sent out for processing (e.g. machining) before being returned for further manufacture. Other links, not shown in the figure, include meetings with central and local government personnel, trade-unionists, and business and trade organizations.

Information and material links to customers, suppliers, government personnel, and others are a key feature of the day-to-day running of all businesses. The need for close access, particularly to customers, is often mentioned in surveys of the factors influencing manufacturing and office loca-

tion decisions (Keeble, 1971; Alexander, 1979; Schmenner, 1982; see also Chapter 10.2). For example, in reviewing five surveys of factors which draw offices to a central location, Alexander (1979 p. 18) observes that 'the access or communications factor emerges as an important locational influence ... in all surveys.' There is also a growing debate over the role of relative regional accessibility in influencing the rate and nature of economic development in different regions (Keeble *et al.*, 1982*a*).

A commonly used measure of access to markets is that of *market potential*, though it is sometimes referred to as *economic potential*. Suitably modified the concept may also be used to measure *supply potential*, for example, for food processors using a spatially dispersed set of suppliers. A related idea, which attempts to measure access to information, is the concept of *contact potential*. These potential models give an indication of the pattern of material and information linkages which ought to occur given the assumptions behind the models.

A market potential surface describes the relative demand at particular locations in a given market area. The market potential calculation assumes that demand decreases as distance from the point of sale increases. This is most likely to apply where firms operate free-on-board pricing policies (see Section 5.2), but as Watts (1987

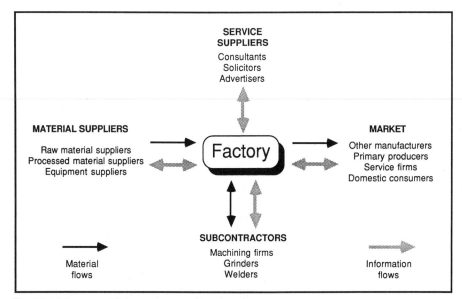

FIG 5.8 Main types of linkage of a manufacturing plant

p. 239) points out: 'this distance decay pattern applies quite widely.' The market potential for a given market (i) is calculated using the following formula:

$$MP_i = \frac{M_j}{D_{ij}^d}$$

where M_j measures the market (M) in a given part (j) of the total market, D_{ij} indicates the transport cost (D) from a point i to the market j, and d is an exponent which describes the friction of distance. The distance exponent is usually empirically defined, but given the lack of theoretical underpinning is often given a value of one. Various measures of the market may be used such as population, manufacturing employment, gross domestic product, or retail sales according to the purpose of the exercise. The index (MP_i) is, by itself, meaningless, but when calculated for

several points can be used to identify the point of maximum market potential and to construct a potential surface showing variations around that maximum potential location.

Figures 5.9a and b give an example of the use of market potential analysis to show change in accessibility to markets brought about by the expansion of the European Economic Community in 1973 from Six member states to Nine (Keeble *et al.*, 1982a). The maps isolate the effect of the removal of the tariff barrier had it been removed all at once rather than over a five-year transition period. As might have been expected, complete tariff removal in a single year, with the expansion of the Community to include Denmark, Ireland, and the United Kingdom, would have increased the relative accessibility to Community-wide economic activity of *all* regions. However, what is perhaps surprising is the scale of increase of the peripheral regions compared to

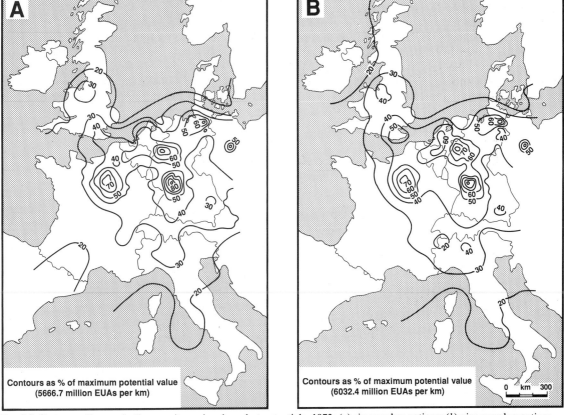

Contours as % of maximum potential value (5666.7 million EUAs per km)

Contours as % of maximum potential value (6032.4 million EUAs per km)

0   km   300

FIG 5.9 European Economic Community regional market potentials, 1973: (*a*) six member nations; (*b*) nine member nations (*source*: Keeble *et al.*, 1982a p. 427)

the increases recorded by the more central regions of the original six members. As Table 5.2 shows, potential values for the most peripheral regions of the United Kingdom, Ireland, and Denmark increased by between 40 and 76 per cent compared with increases in the central regions of the original Six members of between 6 and 11 per cent. Interestingly, the peripheral regions of the original Six members also gained more proportionally (14–17 per cent) than the central regions. However, this difference reflects small initial potential values in the peripheral regions of the Six and in absolute terms the expansion of the Community increased the disparities in accessibility to economic activity between the centre and periphery of the original six member states. Similar analyses could be performed to try to establish the impact of the 1992 Single European Market.

Examining changes in market potential brought about by particular events, such as an alteration in tariff barriers, is a useful way of attempting to isolate the effect of one variable. However, such an exercise is limited, because in the real world changes do not occur in isolation, but interact together to produce different outcomes in different places. This point is taken up in a review of attempts to use the method to assess the impact of the Channel Tunnel on the market

potential of various regions in north-west Europe (Clark et al., 1969; Keeble et al., 1982b). Vickerman (1987 pp. 190–1) notes that these studies are:

only indicative of what may happen to hypothetical levels of demand and how benefits would be distributed in the most neutral way, where no region has any structural or other advantage (other than its location) nor reacts in such a way as to gain any disproportionate advantage through regional policy measures.

Using market potential as a measure of access to markets is even more problematic. This is because the surrogates used to measure market potential may be picking up access to other things as well, such as access to labour supplies and to the localization and urbanization economies discussed later in this chapter. Further, as Watts (1987 p. 121) observes:

To argue that favourable levels of employment change in association with high scores on a market potential index reflects access to markets is a very dubious exercise, unless the market has been defined carefully in relation to the demand for the products supplied by the industries, firms or plants being considered.

Caution is also required in interpreting *contact potential* surfaces. This measure of potential information linkages was developed by Tornqvist (1973) in a study of the influence of information flows on regional development in Sweden. It

TABLE 5.2 Effect of European Economic Community expansion on market potential of selected regions, 1973

| | Millions of European Units of Account per km | | | |
| | Six-member nations | Nine-member nations | Change | |
			No.	%
Scotland	813	1233	+420	+40
Northern Ireland	1059	1583	+524	+49
Ireland	660	1050	+390	+59
Vest for Store Bælt	776	1378	+602	+76
Calabria	618	711	+93	+15
Puglia	839	962	+123	+15
Midi-Pyrénées	1085	1236	+151	+14
Bretagne	1442	1685	+243	+17
Rheinland-Pfalz	5667	6032	+365	+6
Düsseldorf	4730	5045	+315	+7
Île de France	4270	4570	+300	+7
Brabant	3323	3693	+370	+11

Source: Keeble et al. (1982a p. 427).

relates the accessibility of each region to potential contact sources in the remaining regions, such that

$$CP_i = (T_{ij} - D_{ij})K_j$$

where CP_i is the contact potential of region i; T_{ij} is the length of time in a single working day it is possible after a journey from region i, to remain in region j; D_{ij} is the travel time by the shortest route from i to j; and K_j is the total number of employees in j in contact-intensive job functions, weighted by the national average daily hours of contact for each job function.

In this way Tornqvist traces the development of the contact potential surface in Sweden and demonstrates the dominance of Stockholm, a position which would be reinforced if account was taken of access to potential international contacts. As Goddard (1975 p. 16) notes: 'It is both a cause and a consequence of such contact possibilities that organizations place their highest-level functions in the capital city.' The concept assumes that face-to-face contact is a key locational determinant. However, though spatial proximity is often emphasized as an important factor by office location decision-makers, it does not mean that 'such proximity is necessary, or that existing location patterns and trends are immutable' (Alexander, 1979 p. 13). The *quality* of potential information linkages is also as important as the *quantity* of the information obtained.

Potential models provide only an indirect measure of material and information linkages based on a set of assumptions as to the factors which determine their pattern. Direct measures of linkages are a better way to attempt to assess their impact on spatial patterns of economic activity although they are not without their problems. One way is to examine the linkages between industries by analysing which industries supply which other industries. Most of these studies are dependent on analysing *input–output tables*. These show the linkages between industries in a matrix form. On one axis of the matrix is the value of the purchases each industry obtains from each other industry, while on the other axis is the value of the sales made to each other industry. Although some attempts have been made to construct regional input–output tables, most input–output tables are available only at the national scale. A major use of them is to trace the impacts

of a change in demand for the products of an industry through the rest of the economy. A sector that has strong backward or forward linkages is known as a *growth pole* (see also Chapter 15.2). A key question is 'to what extent are linkages reflected in spatial concentrations of linked industries?' In other words, does a *growth pole* (an economic phenomenon) also act as a *growth centre* (a geographical phenomenon)?

The evidence is mixed. Attempts to correlate the extent of linkage with the degree of spatial association have generally found only a weak, or non-existent, relationship in national or regional studies (Hoare, 1985). On the other hand, studies of particular industrial complexes using data collected directly from the firms have found evidence of strong functional/spatial associations. A classic case is the linkages between the metal industries in the Black Country of the West Midlands (Florence, 1948; Taylor and Wood 1973), although there are indications that the association has declined in strength in recent years (Taylor, 1978). Such intense local linkage patterns suggest that the firms involved gain economically from agglomerating. However, Taylor and Wood (1973) show that strong local links were characteristic of small, privately-owned and technically unsophisticated firms. They argue that such linkage patterns reflect parochialism, and the advantages which accrue are more behavioural than economic in character, for example, through the reduction of uncertainty by retaining traditional suppliers and customers.

Strong linkage patterns have also been noted in office complexes. For example, in central Toronto, Gad (1979) has identified three groupings of activities based on an analysis of contact patterns. These office clusters were based on:

(i) banks, finance, mining, and law companies;
(ii) advertising and public relations companies and the media; and
(iii) architects, planners, real estate and engineering firms.

The seeming differences in the results of the national and regional studies and the local studies may, in part, reflect differences in the way in which linkages are measured in the two types of study. The tendency is to assume that the greater the total amount of the flow the stronger is the linkage. However, the *total* amount may not be the best indicator of linkage strength; for example, account needs also to be taken of the regularity and predictability of the linkage. Caution is also required in interpreting an observation of a spatial association between linked plants. Such an association is not necessarily causal, nor may spatial association be necessary to maintain the linkages.

Linkages and agglomerations

The last two examples illustrate that strong material and information linkages are often associated with agglomerations of economic activity, but to what extent linkages encourage agglomerations and how far linked firms need to be located in close proximity are more debatable questions. To begin to unravel the relationship between linkages and agglomerations it is first necessary to discuss the nature of *agglomeration economies*.

Agglomeration effects which arise from the clustering of activities and which are external to the firm are called *external economies of scale*. (Internal economies of scale are discussed in Chapter 6.1.) A common distinction is made between two types of external economy: *localization economies* and *urbanization economies*. Localization economies are cost-savings specific to the establishments of a particular industry, such as arise from spatial proximity to the units to which they are linked; while urbanization economies are cost-savings to *all* firms arising from location in an urban area, such as transport facilities, a range of industrial and office premises, or a pool of cheap labour. Not that it is always easy to distinguish between them in practice. For example, with a pool of skilled labour, the skilled element could be classified as a localization economy while the labour pool could be considered an urbanization economy. Urbanization economies are related to settlement size, the larger the settlement the greater the potential economies. Urbanization *diseconomies*, such as congestion, rising land prices, pollution, and escalating costs of providing public services, may also come into operation as the size of urban places increases, and have been suggested as an important factor contributing to the urban–rural shift of manufacturing employment which is a widespread phenomenon in developed market economies (Healey and Ilbery, 1985*b*). Many economic activities

continue to agglomerate, however, though not always in large metropolitan areas. The desire of linked activities to be located in close proximity may be part of the answer.

Linkages are an important aspect of localization economies. Their role in bringing about and maintaining agglomerations may be illustrated with reference to office location. In many office location studies emphasis is placed on the 'information-rich' agglomerations found in large metropolitan areas because of the concentration found there of organizational headquarters and other management and control functions. For example, Pred (1974) cites the case of Stockholm, Göteborg, and Malmö metropolitan areas, which together contained 31 per cent of Sweden's population in 1966, but accounted for more than 50 per cent of the nation's 'contact intensive' employment and 62 per cent of the 'highest level' administrative employees in public administration and other services. Another study, which examined Vancouver's corporate complex, found a dense system of inter-firm linkages within the metropolitan core. Ley and Hutton (1987) argue that the strength of the linkages between the head office operations and the producer services in central Vancouver suggests the behaviour of the classic growth pole.

Information linkages vary, however, in their effect on location. Thorngren (1970) makes a useful distinction between three types of information contact. First, there are *programmed contacts*, which are short, routine flows of information and are generally previously unarranged and usually conducted over the telephone. Secondly, there are *planning contacts* directed mainly towards R. & D. and using telephonic contact supplemented by occasional face-to-face meetings. *Orientation contacts* are the last category. They are generally longer, prearranged face-to-face meetings dealing with long-term actions.

Attempts have been made to ascertain the relative importance of these three types of contact by surveys in Stockholm and Central London using contact-diaries kept by office personnel (Thorngren, 1970; Goddard, 1973). The surveys showed that the majority of the contacts (*c.*70 per cent in Stockholm and *c.*80 per cent in London) were programmed, a smaller proportion (*c.*25 per cent in Stockholm and *c.*15 per cent in London) were orientation, and the remainder (*c.*5 per cent) were planned. These findings suggest that many functions do not require a location in a major metropolis. However, the need for internal co-ordination means that dividing office functions between different locations is a strategy which is followed infrequently, particularly by smaller firms. Perhaps more significantly, these surveys indicate that some types of office may be more suitable for dispersion than others. For example, Goddard identifies a group, including some finance offices, offices of primary industries, and commodity dealing offices, where orientation contacts form less than 10 per cent of total contacts. Such data could be used as an indicator of decentralization opportunities, although 'experience suggests that it is more appropriate to look at job characteristics than firm types in this regard' (Alexander, 1979 p. 24).

The argument for a relationship between link-ages and agglomerations is usually based on the cost savings that firms may accrue from local linkages. Although transport costs are an import-ant location factor for only a limited number of economic activities (Section 5.2), they are only one aspect of the effect of distance on costs. Distance also influences the cost of maintaining contact. This is especially important where non-standardized goods are being made and close contact between suppliers and producers is vital. There are also variations in the significance of transport costs between different sized firms. Small volumes attract relatively higher transport rates than large ones. Thus, as Scott (1983a p. 8) argues: 'industrial plants that produce unstandardized products on a small scale are likely to be considerably more limited in their range of locational options than plants that pro-duce highly standardized outputs on a large scale.'

A similar argument applies to office linkages. Information and service links which are unstand-ardized and changing are more costly than stand-ardized links which are stable. This is because more of the former are transacted by face-to-face contact, while the majority of the latter can be achieved by letter or over the telephone. As with manufacturing, the more that the links are unstandardized the greater the constraints on office location.

Clearly, as was suggested above, measuring the strength of linkages simply in terms of the amount of the flow is an inadquate indicator of their effects on location. Hoare (1985, pp. 75–6)

argues that: '*unpredictability*—breakdowns, surges in demand, fluctuating market conditions ... places far more of a premium on short dis-tance linkages than regular, predictable, mass movements of standardized inputs and products.' This suggests that small firms providing unstand-ardized products and services may be more de-pendent on the location of their large customers than their large customers are dependent upon the location of the small firms. This raises a key issue of unequal interdependence between dif-ferent sized firms which is examined further in Chapter 7.1.

A further reason why the relationship between linkages and agglomerations is not clear-cut is because linkages may be as much a consequence of the agglomeration of economic activity as a cause. Both manufacturing plants and offices have been found to be more tightly interlinked when spatially clustered than when dispersed. Some tendency has also been noted for plants and offices which decentralize to have more extensive linkages. For example, one study of manufactur-ing plants which had moved out of London to East Anglia or the North found that over half of them maintained their existing suppliers (Moseley and Townroe, 1973). Another study, of offices which had moved out of London, found that within a radius of 60 miles both telephone con-tacts and face-to-face meetings were concentrated on London (Goddard and Morris, 1976). Offices which had moved beyond that distance seemed to escape the shadow of London and began to establish contacts within the area into which they had moved.

This limited evidence on factories and offices which have moved suggests that spatial proximity is not a necessary requirement for the units to survive; although on Scott's argument selective migration seems probable, with the units which were least strongly tied to London being the most likely to have moved. Nevertheless, the potential for dispersion cannot be judged simply in terms of existing linkage patterns, because of the ability of the firms to adjust their linkages to a new loca-tion. Discussion of linkage adjustment following movement emphasizes the need to examine the dynamics of linkages and location.

The dynamics of linkages and location

Most linkage studies are static and cross-sectional, but to obtain a full understanding of the relationship between linkages and location it is important also to examine how the relationship evolves over time. This is well illustrated by J. N. Marshall (1987, p. 115), who found a great deal of volatility in manufacturing linkage patterns in Britain associated with industrial decline.

Firms search for new markets as an industry declines, and changes in production processes, designed to improve competitiveness, produce new component or material requirements, which can reduce local dependence. Frequently, industrial decline is associated with strong foreign competition, which encourages firms to restructure to gain access to growth markets abroad, which again reduces internal multipliers.

Whereas Marshall emphasizes the role of changes in demand, Scott (1983a) argues that the development of the relationship between location and linkages should be set in the context of the way production is organized.

The production process is the mechanism by which materials and equipment are combined with labour to produce commodities or services for sale. For some productive activities the characteristics of the final outputs restrict mechanization and encourage the proliferation of small, specialized, single-plant firms. This applies to many of the clothing and furniture industries and many business services, where rapidly changing products, sometimes with seasonal peaks, restrict firm size. In such small-scale, unstandardized, and labour-intensive forms of production the nature of the linkages is constantly changing and frequent face-to-face contact with suppliers and customers is usually necessary. Under these conditions there are strong pressures for linked firms to locate in clusters.

By contrast, where the productive activities involve large-scale, capital-intensive production of standardized outputs, linkages tend to be relatively stable and predictable, and the need for face-to-face contact is minimized. These circumstances allow dispersal of the factories and offices. There are many examples of this occurring in post-war Britain as branch plants of large companies, such as Courtaulds, were set up outside traditional agglomerations, and various government offices, such as the Driver Vehicle Licensing Centre, were dispersed from London.

There are some significant exceptions to this relationship between linkage type and location. For example, for activities which have restricted supply and/or market areas, such as some forest products and cement production (see Section 5.2), their locational choice is limited by their low-value, bulky, standardized inputs and/or outputs. Conversely there are some productive activities, such as international consultancies and the production of scientific instruments, which are characterized by small, unstandardized links which are virtually indifferent to linkage distance. In spite of these exceptions, Scott believes that an examination of the way in which production systems operate provides an important insight into conceptualizing the relationship between linkages and location.

There is, of course, a continuum of production types between the unstandardized, labour-intensive activities at one end, to the standardized, capital-intensive activities at the other. However, there does seem to have been an increase in the relative importance of large-scale, capital-intensive activities since the mid-nineteenth century, which, in part, reflects the growth of big business (see Chapter 7.1). This, in turn, has reduced the need for many activities to cluster together, especially when combined with new forms of production technology (see Chapter 6.1), and the greater ease and reduced costs of transportation and communication.

There is plenty of evidence of the break-up of existing agglomerations. For example, in the 1930s the radio industry in the United States was transformed from a small-scale labour-intensive industry, dependent on skilled labour and local subcontractors, into a highly standardized capital-intensive industry concentrated in a few large plants. This organizational change was accompanied by a shift in the location of the industry from New York to small towns in the Mid-West (Litchenburg, 1960, cited by Scott, 1983a).

In the office sector there are indications that the more capital-intensive, routine functions of firms, such as those engaged in accounting, data processing, payroll preparation, and the handling of sales orders, are decentralizing to suburban areas (Nelson, 1986; see also Chapter 13.2). The result of the changing organization of production and the accompanying spatial shifts is that a new spatial division of labour is developing. The tendency is for core regions to specialize increasingly in management and control functions, while peripheral areas concentrate on unskilled and semi-skilled branch plant activities.

Despite this relative decline in industrial agglomerations, new forms of small-scale unstandardized and labour-intensive production are creating new agglomerations. These agglomerations are associated with the development of flexible production systems (see Chapter 7.3). Examples of this selective reagglomeration of production include revitalized craft industries, such as furniture and clothing, in many inner areas of metropolitan regions; high-technology industry in suburban extensions of the same metropolitan regions, such as Route 128 to the west of Boston, and new agglomerations on the periphery and semi-periphery of the older industrial cores, such as the design-intensive, firms run by craftsmen in the north-east and centre of Italy (Scott, 1988). Even with the rapid improvements in transport and communications, new forms of production organization are creating 'powerful agglomerative tendencies at the regional level' for selected manufacturing and producer service activities (Storper and Christopherson, 1987 p. 115).

Production subcontracting

In this final section the relationship between location and linkages is illustrated with reference to one kind of linkage, which has recently received attention in the literature, that of *production subcontracting*. It is important to separate out for analysis different types of linkages because there are many studies where only limited insights have been obtained because the spatial characteristics of different types of linkage drawn from a wide range of different types of firms and industries have been indiscriminately grouped together in the analysis. Holmes (1986) argues that to understand a particular class of linkages it is necessary to examine the causal processes which have produced the linkages. He suggests that isolating one kind of linkage and focusing on the mechanisms which bring it about should make the concept of 'linkage' a little less of what Sayer (1982a) calls a *chaotic conception* (see also Chapter 2.2).

Subcontracting refers to a situation where the firm offering the subcontract requests another, legally independent, firm to carry out the processing of a material, component, part, or subassembly for it, according to specifications provided by the firm offering the subcontract (Watanabe, 1971). Subcontracting is thus an intermediate form of production between in-house production

(vertical integration) and buying in and assembling of components (vertical disintegration) (Rawlinson, 1989). There are indications of a general increase in subcontracting in Western economies (Imrie, 1986). In some cases subcontracting involves the farming out of overflow work which would normally be done in-house. This is usually referred to as *capacity* or *concurrent subcontracting*. In other cases the part or component is not produced in-house and it is referred to as *specialization* or *complementary subcontracting*. Holmes (1986) suggests that capacity subcontracting is far more common in West European countries, such as France and Italy, while specialization subcontracting is the predominant form of subcontracting in North America.

It has been argued that subcontracting relationships are based primarily on asymmetric power relations between large and small firms (Friedman, 1977; Taylor and Thrift, 1982a). However, this tends to conceptualize the small firm as a passive partner in the relationship and ignores the ability of some small firms to influence negotiations by virtue of their technical expertise, labour skills, and physical control of the work. As Imrie (1986 p. 957) observes: 'The problem with the literature which reduces all subcontractors to the category of a dependent firm is that it fails to recognise the rich and varied situations in which subcontracting takes place.' Given this variety it is not surprising that Holmes (1986) identifies different causal mechanisms to explain different types of subcontracting. He suggests that factors related to the nature of product markets, production technology, and labour markets combine to influence the extent and nature of subcontracting, with the outcome varying according to the specific historical experience of an industry or country.

The same argument leads Holmes to question whether it is possible to generalize about the spatial configuration of subcontracting relationships. In contrast, a number of general hypotheses have been proposed by Scott (1983b). Specifically, he argues that:

(i) 'networks of subcontracting relationships are likely to be more intimately and intensively developed where plants are clustered tightly together in geographical space' (pp. 242–3);

(ii) spatial concentration of production is common where the subcontracting connections are small in scale and where parent-subcontractor relationships are impermanent.

Notwithstanding the corroborating evidence for these relationships in the printed circuit board industry and the women's clothing industry of Los Angeles (Scott, 1983c; 1984), Holmes questions how far they can be generalized to other sectors and to other geographical scales and settings. To support his argument he points to the development of international subcontracting, particularly in the clothing and electronics industries, and to the operation of the Japanese 'just-in-time' production system pioneered by Toyota. In this system, despite the stability and magnitude of the linkages, the subcontractors are clustered around the parent plant because of the necessity to deliver parts to the assembly plant punctually (see also Chapter 7.3).

5.4 Summary

This chapter has focused on the role of demand, transport, and linkages in influencing the spatial pattern of economic activity and the evolution of the economic landscape.

- Demand is a fundamental factor affecting the operation of local and national economies. As the level of demand changes the impact varies from place to place. For example, the threshold required to support activities in different communities and regions may be passed. The inherited social and economic structure of places also influence the effect of demand changes, for instance, areas with favourable industrial structures are likely to grow faster than the national average. Changes in the character of demand may also have spatial impacts. A shift to neo-Fordist patterns of consumption, for example, may be associated with an increase in the significance of market locations.

- Demand also has a major influence on the spatial pattern of economic activity because it has an uneven geographical distribution reflecting variations in the level of income and economic growth from place to place. Further, there are a few economic activities, such as vegetables grown on contract for freezer firms, the manufacture of some food and drink products, and most retailing activities, in which firms compete spatially for markets and/or

supplies and close proximity to the points of demand is critical.

- Transport costs play a central role in neoclassical location theories. However, the effect of transport costs on the economic landscape differs from that assumed in these theories, because they fail to take account of the complexity of transport costs in the real world which vary according to, for example, the mode of transport, the characteristics of the commodity, the pricing policy of the provider, and the degree of competition along particular routes.

- More significantly, however, innovations in transport and communication technologies have reduced the importance of transport costs so that in most industries they form only a relatively small proportion of total costs. As these innovations have been introduced they have had a dramatic impact on the spatial pattern of economic activity, including encouraging concentration at the interregional scale; strengthening of the economies of a handful of major world cities; decentralization at the intraregional scale; an increase in the spatial extent of production; and a concentration of particular economic activities in areas of greatest comparative advantage. Paradoxically as distance has become less important, geographical variations in other factors have become more significant.

- Although transport costs have declined in significance, local material and information links to customers, suppliers, government personnel and others are still important in encouraging some economic activities to agglomerate. However, the legacy of neoclassical theory has encouraged their importance to be overemphasized, as is illustrated by the following quotations.

Opportunities are there for linkages to exist over greater distance than before, even if not all manufacturing firms want to take advantage of this, need so to do, or are able to exploit this potential (Hoare, 1985, p. 75).

While it is clear that contacts are an important ingredient in office location, their importance is easily exaggerated (Alexander 1979, p. 13).

- The relationship between location and linkages operates in both directions in that the pattern of linkages influences the evolution of the spatial pattern of economic activity, which in turn constrains the development of the linkage pattern. To understand the development of the relationship between location and linkages it helps to examine it in the context of the evolution of the organization of production.

- One argument is that in small-scale, unstandardized and labour-intensive forms of production the nature of the linkages is constantly changing and frequent face-to-face contact with suppliers and customers is usual. Under these conditions there are strong pressures for linked firms to agglomerate. As the relative importance of this type of production process changes so does the importance of the pressures to agglomerate. This helps to explain both the break-up of some agglomerations and the formation of new ones. Some of the new clusters of economic activity are associated with the development of high-technology industries and flexible production systems (Chapters 6 and 7). Another argument, illustrated by the case of production subcontracting, suggests that different types of subcontracting arise from the specific historical experience of particular industries and countries and hence it may not be possible to generalize about the spatial configuration of subcontracting relationships. Two of the factors which affect the conditions under which linkage systems develop are changes in technology and organizational structure. These are the topics of the next two chapters.

6

The Technological Context

Of all the factors influencing the evolution of spatial patterns of economic activity, technology is perhaps the single most important. This is because technology is concerned with what is produced, the way in which it is produced, and the scale of production at different places. New goods and services, such as cars, computers, and credit cards, have a fundamental effect on our material comfort and way of life, while changes in process technologies, such as mechanization and automation, have affected the nature of work in all sectors of the economy. Thus it is not surprising that there has been much discussion recently about the nature and impact of factory farming, automated factories, and electronic offices. Changing technologies moreover affect the economic size of farms, factories, and offices. The introduction of flow-line production methods, for example, led to an increase in the average size of establishments, while recent developments in micro-electronics and the use of flexible methods in the organization of production are encouraging a reduction in the economic size of units.

Technology is both an enabling and a constraining factor. As the type of technology used influences the material, land, labour, and capital requirements and the organizational structure of different industries, it allows changes to occur in the location of economic activity which might not otherwise have happened. Technology thus affects the relative importance of the other location factors. On the other hand, the use of outdated technologies may constrain the ability of organizations to adapt to changing economic conditions. Through these various impacts technology influences the relative competitiveness of firms and economies and is hence a major force in local, regional, and national economic development.

Technology is not, however, an independent force. It does not determine the location of economic activity and levels of employment and economic activity. Technology, as was argued in the discussion of Kondratieff waves in Chapter 2.1, is a social process. 'Society makes the choices, not technology, but the nature of technology at any given time strongly influences subsequent choices' (Dicken and Lloyd, 1981, p. 40). The search for new technologies and the rate of acceptance is closely tied to the nature of society. The demand for new technologies is in part a reflection of the problems faced by particular societies. For example, one of the reasons that the Japanese were among the first to adopt 'just-in-time' production methods, whereby materials and components arrive at the factory only as they are required, is the high cost of land in Japan, which makes stockholding expensive (Sayer, 1986b).

Technological change also has an impact on society. It can have economic, social, and ecological benefits and costs. For example, technological change can both create and reduce employment; it can lead to improvements in the quality of some jobs while deskilling others; it can result in pollution as well as help to prevent pollution; and it can lead to economic growth in some areas and economic decline elsewhere. The variety of impacts helps to emphasize that technology is linked to the nature of the society in which the technology is developed and applied. Consequently broad generalizations about the effects of technological change need to be treated cautiously.

Just as a change in technology can affect the location of economic activity, so location can influence the type of technology used. For example, it was pointed out in Chapter 1.1 that the same goods may be produced using labour-intensive technologies in a low labour cost area and capital-intensive technologies in a country where labour costs are high. In agriculture, a difference in the amount of land available is one of the factors which helps to explain differences in the technology used by farmers in Western Europe and European areas overseas. As Grigg (1984, p. 92) notes:

In densely populated countries land is costly and labour relatively abundant and cheap. The farmer will thus select those enterprises that give a high return per hectare, and will spend much on inputs that increase crop yields, such as fertilizers, pesticides and herbicides. In contrast, farmers with large areas of land at their disposal can gain large total incomes even if they practise enterprises with a low return per hectare. They concentrate on maximising output per capita, spend much on labour saving machinery and less on yield-increasing inputs.

The most economic type of technology varies between different parts of the world, because the conditions of production vary between different parts of the world.

Recently the media and policy-makers, as well as academics, have given much attention to *high technology*. Indeed there seems to be a view in many circles that 'high tech' is the universal panacea for economic development and regeneration.

In the countries of the advanced industrial world, it is hailed as the antidote to the decline of the smokestack industries of the 19th and early 20th centuries. In the newly industrializing countries of Latin America and East Asia, it is seen as the key to rapid economic catch-up. National political leaders commit their countries to it. Local elected officials seek to attract it. The new centers of high tech industry—California's Silicon Valley, Massachusetts' Highway 128, England's M4 Corridor, Scotland's Silicon Glen—exert an almost hypnotic hold over media people, and over their readers and viewers (Markusen *et al.*, 1986 p. 1).

Clearly, identifying high-technology industries and firms and the areas in which they are concentrated has become an important issue. Technology, however, is broader than just 'high technology' and technological change influences traditional economic activities as much as new ones.

The main aim of this chapter is to examine the characteristics of technology and technological change and to assess their influence on spatial patterns of economic activity. The greater part of the chapter is concerned with the origin, spread, and spatial impact of new technologies. The geography of technological change is analysed by examining, first, the spatial patterns of high tech-

nology, which Hall and Markusen (1985) aptly call 'silicon landscapes', and, secondly, discussing the spatial impact and diffusion of technology in different sectors of the economy. The chapter begins by considering the nature of technology and technological change.

6.1 Nature of technology and technological change

Technology is 'the "how?" and "what?" of production' (Perez, 1985 p. 442); while technological change may broadly be taken as involving an increase in the accumulated body of technical knowledge weighted by the number of firms or individuals who possess and use this knowledge (Goddard and Thwaites, 1987).

The process of technological change begins with inventions and innovations. According to Schumpeter (1939) *inventions* are the additions of new products and techniques to the existing stock of knowledge, whereas *innovations* are the commercial production and application of the inventions. This chapter is primarily concerned with innovations rather than inventions, though the dividing line between the two is not clear.

A potentially more useful distinction may be made between different kinds of technological innovation. Freeman (1986) suggests a threefold classification:

(i) *Incremental innovations.* These are relatively smooth continuous processes leading to a steady improvement in the range of existing products and services and the ways in which they are produced. The introduction of a new model of a dishwasher or a new word-processing package are examples.

(ii) *Radical innovations.* These refer to discontinuous events which may lead firms in a particular sector to make serious adjustments. Examples include the introduction of television or of an entirely new material in the textile industry.

(iii) *Technological revolutions.* These are changes leading to the emergence of a whole range of new product groups; they also have fundamental effects on many other branches of the economy by transforming their methods of production and their cost structures. The introduction of electric power or railways are examples of such transformations. These are the 'creative gales of destruction' which are at the heart of the Kondratieff–Schumpeter long wave theory (see Chapter 2.1).

Most attention has been given to *high-technology* innovations. Unfortunately high technology is 'as yet an ill-defined concept' (Harris and McArthur, 1985 p. 7). Nevertheless, examination of two commonly-used indices of high technology—expenditure on research and development (R. & D.) and the proportion of non-production staff, particularly technical and related staff, in the workforce (Thompson, 1988)—indicates that technological intensity varies markedly between industries and firms. Among the manufacturing industries which generally score highly when these kind of measures are applied are the aerospace, instrument engineering, electronic, and chemical industries (e.g. Markusen *et al.*, 1986; Keeble, 1987). As for firms, large companies are generally more technologically intensive than small ones; large firms can more easily afford the heavy investment involved in R. & D. and in the commercial application of the products of R. & D. None the less increased flexibility in production, associated with the micro-electronics revolution, is enabling small high-technology firms to compete effectively in several sectors, such as the manufacture of semi-conductors (Chapter 7.1).

Care needs to be taken in interpreting the findings of using surrogate measures to represent the innovativeness of industry because they give no indication of the nature or quality of the innovations. This is particularly important when assessing the impact of technological change because this varies with the kind of technology introduced; for example, whether it is currently widely diffusing, such as micro-electronics, or newly emerging, such as biotechnologies and composite materials (Harris and McArthur, 1985). A further problem is that many of the criteria used to define high-technology industry tend to identify the *producers* rather than the *users* of high technology. Yet the competitiveness of industry depends in part on the extent to which new technology is adopted.

Failure to conceptualize adequately what is meant by high technology can lead to confusions particularly in the policy field. Many discussions

of high-technology and 'sunrise' industries tend to imply that other 'low-technology' or 'sunset' industries are doomed to inevitable decline and extinction with all the implications this has for the communities in which they are located. Newson (1986) argues that this is an over-simplified view which ignores the fact that most innovations are incremental and arise in existing industries. New technology does not depend on destroying the old; more often, he suggests, it develops out of existing technology. The concept of 'sunset' industries also overlooks the potential of *technology transfer* and the regeneration of existing industries. The main outlet for much new technology lies in its application to the wide range of processes in existing industries and services; while M. Marshall (1987) notes that several industrial sectors in the British economy have experienced complex patterns of buoyancy and renewal in their development.

In this chapter two main types of technology are assessed, each of which has a critical effect on the location of economic activity: *product technology* and *process technology*. Transport technologies were examined in the last chapter, while discussion of a fourth type, concerned with innovations in management and organization, is considered in Chapter 7. These different types of technology are closely related. A firm *making* a new computer or a new machine tool, for instance, is manufacturing a new product, while a firm *using* the computer or machine tool is applying a new process. In other words, one firm's product innovation is another firm's process innovation. New forms of communications technology are also becoming increasingly integrated with other technologies. For example, the term *information technology* describes the interrelated applications of telecommunications, micro-electronics and computing.

Product technologies

The introduction of new products is an important characteristic of long-term economic growth. New products, such as plastics, artificial fibres, cars, and computers have a fundamental effect on standards of living. Most innovations occur in the manufacturing sector, but the service sector is not completely subordinate. Examples of recent important service innovations include electronic publishing, computer software, and auto banking. New goods and services are generally developed to attempt to give firms a competitive edge. So new models are frequently introduced, whether they be of cameras or screwdrivers, photocopiers or accountancy software packages. Freeman (1974) goes so far as to assert that large firms which do not innovate will not survive.

A key concept in understanding the nature and consequences of product innovations is that of the *product life cycle*. The essence of this concept is that products go through a life cycle of four main stages—early, growth, mature, and obsolescent (Fig. 6.1). Sales increase during the first two stages until they reach a ceiling during the third stage. Sales then decline as the product goes into old age. Not all products go through this cycle, indeed, many never get beyond the first stage, and there are indications that the rate the cycle proceeds is increasing (Dicken, 1986; Keeble, 1988).

Unfortunately there is little theoretical guidance as to what constitutes a 'new' product or a 'new' industry (Walker, 1985) and so it is perhaps not surprising that the product life cycle concept has been applied using a variety of levels of product aggregation. Generally, the greater the level of aggregation the longer the duration of the cycle. The product cycle, as developed by Vernon (1966), is of relatively short duration (often about six to eight years) and refers to a product in a fairly narrow sense, such as a new kind of machine tool or a particular model of a washing machine. More recently the concept has also been used in a wider sense, and with a longer timescale, to examine the development of whole industries, for instance, the steel industry or the automobile industry (Markusen *et al.*, 1986).

Much of this latter work has drawn on Kondratieff's theory of long waves of economic development (Chapter 2.1).

The appeal of the product life cycle model is its simplicity, but herein lies its greatest weakness. It focuses almost exclusively on technological change and the impact this has on investment decision-making. The model implies that for firms to grow and make profits they need to continue to innovate. Not all firms are, however, heavily involved in research and development. Some firms imitate successful enterprises, some act as subcontractors to large firms, while others serve a traditional, often highly localized market. Different firms have different roles in the space economy (Chapter 7.1). Markusen (1985) argues that the need to earn profits may be a better guide to the behaviour of firms than the need to innovate. She suggests that a *profit cycle model* gives a more realistic interpretation of corporate behaviour. Although a broader concept, Markusen's analysis shows that the profit cycle for a particular industrial sector is closely tied to the industry's product life cycle (see also Section 6.3, Chapter 15.2).

At a finer level of product disaggregation, the product life cycle model implies that inventions are introduced to the market in their final form, but many innovations are incremental and once products are created they are progressively altered and improved. As Taylor (1986 p. 754) observes: 'the product that begins a cycle may bear little resemblance to the one that eventually ends it.' Despite these and other limitations the model has had a significant impact on studies of industrial location and regional economic change (see Section 6.3 and Chapter 15.2).

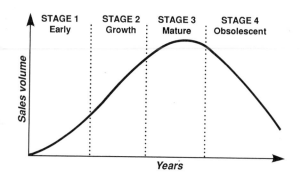

FIG 6.1 The product life cycle

Process technologies

Whereas product technologies are involved with *what* is produced, process technologies are concerned with *how* a product is manufactured or a service designed. Changes in process technologies are usually introduced to improve productivity and to reduce costs. Such changes may occur in all sectors of the economy. For example, in agriculture the post-1945 development of intensive livestock farming has changed the rearing of pigs, poultry, and veal calves from what were often ancillary enterprises integrated within a mixed farming system to large specialized enterprises in permanent indoor housing dependent on bought-in cereals.

The aim is to create an economically optimum environment by removing constraints upon the animal's energy metabolism which derive from the natural environment and especially from variations in temperature and humidity. The livestock are thus reared and fattened in an enclosed, stable thermal environment; fan ventilation is necessary to prevent the build-up of toxic gases and reduce outbreaks of disease among the densely housed stock. With the aim of reducing labour costs, straw bedding may be dispensed with and slatted floors introduced to allow natural drainage of slurry into underground storage tanks. Farrowing sows may be 'crated' to prevent accidental crushing of their young and dry sows tethered or confined in cubicles to restrain aggressive social behaviour in high density conditions (Symes and Marsden, 1985 p. 100).

Some of the most dramatic changes in the production process have occurred within manufacturing, where over several centuries of industrialization the production process, or more specifically the labour process (i.e. the way in which labour is organized and controlled in production), has gone through the four stages or *regimes of capitalist accumulation* discussed in Chapter 4.2—manufacture, machinofacture, scientific management and Fordism, and neo-Fordism (Fig. 4.7). According to this *regulationist* school of thought (e.g. Perrons, 1981) spatial patterns of economic activity are largely determined by the technological characteristics of production and labour processes. This contrast with the *institutionalists* (e.g. Piore and Sabel, 1984) who argue that the spatial outcomes of technological change are indeterminate (Meegan, 1988).

The nature of the production–labour process also has implications for the scale of production. The first three stages of capitalist accumulation are associated with an increase in *economies of large-scale production*. These are internal to a plant and should be distinguished from the external economies of scale discussed in the last chapter. Internal economies of scale arise from several sources. For example, as output increases specialist machines and labour may be employed, machines may be run for longer periods, production may be organized more efficiently, discounts may be obtained through bulk purchasing, and proportionally fewer spares may need to be stocked. Some of these economies may also be available to a large firm operating several small plants producing the same product, particularly where the plants are in close proximity. The extent to which these economies are available varies between industries. In iron castings and footwear, for instance, there are few savings from increasing the size of plants, while in the brewing and chemical industries the savings from building larger plants are quite considerable (Pratten, 1971). There are indications, however, that the increased flexibility associated with the diffusion of micro-processor technology in the neo-Fordism stage has led to a fall in the *minimum efficient size* of plants and contributed to the high rates of new firm formation witnessed in many developed countries since the late 1960s (Chapter 7.1). 'A flexible automation system can turn out a small batch or even a single copy of a product as efficiently as a production line designed to turn out a million identical items' (Bylinsky, 1983 p. 54, quoted in Dicken, 1986).

One reason why the scale of production varies between industries is because the type of industrial technology used may differ. There are three main kinds:

(i)   unit or batch production, for example, subcontracting work;

(ii) large batch or mass production, for example, motor vehicles; and

(iii) process production, for example, oil refining.

The labour, capital, and space requirements for production vary with these different technologies. For example, batch production tends to be labour-intensive, process production tends to be capital-intensive, and mass production usually demands a large amount of space. In addition the type of industrial technology affects linkage patterns and the need for spatial proximity between firms in the same industry. It was suggested in the last chapter that agglomerations were more likely with batch production than with mass production because of the unstandardized nature of the final product (Chapter 5.3).

The nature of the production process also varies according to the stage in the product life cycle. Each stage in the cycle tends to have certain production characteristics associated with technology, capital intensity, critical labour requirements, and industry structure (Dicken, 1986; Watts, 1987); these are summarized in Table 6.1. Different types of geographical location are also suitable for different stages of the product cycle (see Section 6.3).

In the early stage, while the product is being developed, production runs are short and techniques change rapidly. Consequently it is necessary to employ a high proportion of scientific, engineering, and technical workers. By extensive subcontracting the amount of fixed capital is kept low. This, in turn, helps to keep the barriers to entry low and allows many small, often specialist, firms to be established in the industry. Entry to the industry is based on 'know-how' rather than financial resources.

The characteristics of the production process are markedly different by the time the product reaches the growth stage of the cycle (assuming it does), when demand is increasing rapidly (Fig. 6.1). As the frequency of changes to techniques begins to slow down large-scale batch production occurs, gradually giving way to mass production. Capital intensity increases to allow production to expand and to replace plant and machinery made obsolescent by technical changes. Capital investment is also needed as companies begin to integrate vertically by bringing in-house production which was previously subcontracted. The growing market attracts more firms into the industry, but there is a high casualty rate and a few large firms begin to emerge, often through acquisition and merger. Managerial skills to plan and organize the growth of production and sales are at premium at this stage.

The product cycle model predicts that as production levels stabilize in the mature stage (Fig. 6.1) and significant technical changes are rare, long production runs using mass-production techniques become characteristic. This changes the labour requirements. Unskilled and semi-skilled labour able to perform routine, repetitive tasks is the prime need. High capital investment is required to establish the mass-production techniques, but labour costs are an increasingly significant element in the cost structure of the firms. Large financial resources are required to enter the industry and this entry barrier along with continued mergers and acquisitions reduces the number of firms in the industry.

This discussion of the production characteristics associated with the product life cycle model suggests a certain inevitability in the outcome. A similar point applies to the locational sequence associated with the model (Section 6.3). In practice there is a great deal more variety than is predicted by the model. This is in part because

different products ... have substantially different production methods with widely different potentials for standardisation, mechanisation and other means of rationalisation to raise productivity. The kind of continuous flow, automated processing possible in chemicals can only be dreamt of by the garment industry. Technology is quite specific to the physical processes involved (Storper and Walker, 1983 p. 25).

Nevertheless, despite the dangers of technological determinism implied in the product life cycle model, the effect that technology has on the relative importance of the factors of production is clearly illustrated. Moreover the discussion highlights the close relationship between product and process technologies, a feature which is also emphasized by research into the impact of technological change on employment.

Technology and employment

To understand the geography of technology and the relationship between technological change and the location of economic activity, it is important to appreciate the influence of technology on employment. For example, the number employed in agriculture in north-west Europe has been falling for over a century largely because of the introduction of labour-saving machinery. In the east and south of Europe, on the other hand, industrialization occurred later and employment decline only began in the 1950s (Grigg, 1984). The close association of technological change with employment has already been referred to in discussing how production and labour characteristics have had a tendency to vary over the last few hundred years with different regimes of

TABLE 6.1 Characteristics of the production process according to stage in the product life cycle

Production characteristics	Stage in product cycle		
	Early	Growth	Mature
Technology	Short runs Rapidly changing techniques Dependence on external economies	Mass production methods gradually introduced Variations in techniques still frequent	Long runs and stable technology Few innovations of importance
Capital intensity	Low	High, due to high obsolescence rate	High, due to large quantity of specialized equipment
Industry structure	Entry is 'know-how' determined Numerous firms	Growing numbers of firms, many casualties and mergers Growing vertical integration	Market position and financial resources affect entry Number of firms declining
Critical labour requirements	Scientific and engineering	Management	Unskilled and semi-skilled labour

Source: Hirsch (1967 p. 23).

accumulation and over shorter periods of time with different stages in the product life cycle. The short-term perspective is developed further here by examining the employment effects of new technology.

There has been much discussion over the last few years of the impact of new technology on employment. Views range from the creation of numerous new job opportunities to widespread job losses accompanied by a deskilling and casualization of much of the remaining labour force. Such a divergence of views is common in attempts to assess the results of applying new technologies, although there is a tendency towards optimism in times of economic growth and pessimism during periods of recession.

The different views in part reflect the difficulties inherent in assessing the impact of new technologies, particularly when a technological revolution transforms previous methods of production and relationships between capital and labour. A major difficulty is to attempt to isolate the effects of technological change from the impact of other factors on employment, such as demand for particular industries, shifts from full- to part-time work, or the condition of the national, regional, or local economy (Daniels, 1985a). A further complication is that the relative importance of the contribution of technological change to employment change alters over time. For instance, it has been suggested that the contribution to job loss of technological change in British manufacturing industry declined during the 1970s as rationalization in response to national and international recession became relatively more important (Massey and Meegan, 1983).

Despite the difficulties in assessing the impact of new technology on employment a few tentative observations may be made. It seems that employment loss is more likely to result from the application of process innovations than from the launch of new products (Goddard and Thwaites, 1980). The introduction of process innovations in developed market economies tends to increase levels of productivity enabling industries to produce the same output with fewer employees, whereas the development of new products and services may create market opportunities allowing an increase in the labour force to occur. Recent research suggests that major periods of job creation follow periods of product innovation bunching; in contrast succeeding periods of process innovation

lead first to stagnation, then to contraction of employment (Rothwell, 1982). New technology may be used to improve the quality of a product or service as much as to increase productivity. For example, although it has been estimated that with the advent of word processing productivity increases of over 100 per cent are obtainable by office workers (Sleigh *et al.*, 1979), the ease of revising typescripts means that reports may be redrafted more often.

The promotion of new process technology can provide a dilemma for policy-makers. Newson (1986 p. 23) suggests that 'not to adopt it is to lose jobs, through the closure of local companies, as they lose competitiveness, but exploiting the new technologies to the full may result in at best "jobless growth" and at worst a new wave of technological unemployment'. There is some confusion over the probable losses and benefits from the introduction of new technology. The potential trade-off between job losses and gains may be illustrated by an estimate in the early 1980s that 340 000 jobs could be lost in Britain between 1985 and 1990 as a direct result of micro-electronic innovation, but that 420 000 jobs would result from extra demand created by the reduced cost of goods and services (Institute for Employment Research, 1982).

The key to understanding the effects of technological change on employment is the broader social, economic, and institutional context within which the adoption of a new technology occurs. New technology introduced with the primary purpose of reducing production costs during a down-swing is likely to have different employment effects from a new technology associated with a web of complementary techniques and expanding product markets introduced during an up-swing (Harris and McArthur, 1985).

New technology not only affects the availability of jobs, it also has a marked impact on the nature of work (Finn, 1984). Again there is a wide range of views. Some argue that new technology is leading to a deskilling of the labour force as the new technologies facilitate an ever greater division and mechanization of labour (Massey and Meegan, 1983), thus continuing a general long-term trend apparent over several centuries of industrialization (Perrons, 1981; see Section 6.3). Others argue that the average level of skills will increase as the new technology takes over many of the tasks previously done by unskilled labour and the needs for a flexible labour force increase the basic level of training required (ACARD, 1979). These are not necessarily contradictory arguments, because what seems to be happening is a polarization of skills, with few skilled workers being demanded, a large pool of unemployed competing for a declining number of unskilled jobs, and an increase in demand for technologists, scientists, and technicians (Brady and Liff, 1983; Castells, 1985).

While skill level is a key element in the quality of working life, it is not the only one. There are many other dimensions ranging from hours of work and levels of pay through to safety and fringe benefits, all of which may be affected by the introduction of new technology. For example, the flexibility in the organization of work allowed by new technology has been associated with an increase in part-time, temporary, and home work (see also Chapter 4.2), which raises issues of employment rights, especially for women, who fill many of these jobs. New technology has also encouraged an increase in the employment of women in other areas, such as assembly-line work and keyboard operation.

The topic of the employment effects of technological change is one where there are many, often contrary, assertions and relatively little hard evidence. Much writing falls into the trap of technological determinism, but as Coombs and Green (1981, p. 20) note, 'there is no such thing as technological inevitability, technological change is an economic and a political process both in its causes and its effects.' This argument may also be applied to the spatial dimension. Both the spatial patterns and the spatial effects of technological change are variable, they are dependent on the social context in which the changes occur and are applied.

6.2 Silicon landscapes

A characteristic feature of new technology is that it occurs unevenly over space. Not only do technological innovations tend to be concentrated in particular areas, but the countries and regions in which different technological revolutions have occurred also differ. This section begins with a description of the spatial development of high-technology industries and research and development activities, and is followed by a discussion of various explanations of these so-called *silicon landscapes* and the implications of the analysis for policies devised to create technology clusters.

The geography of high-technology industry

Following the Kondratieff–Schumpeter framework (see Chapters 2.1 and 15.2), the high-technology industries of previous long waves have clearly occurred in different countries and regions (Hall, 1985). The first and second waves were concentrated in Great Britain, although Germany and the United States appeared on the stage during the second and they dominated the third. In the fourth wave the United States was predominant, with Japan beginning to emerge. Further, within Great Britain, the first wave was concentrated in Shropshire, the Black Country, and Lancashire; while regions such as South Wales and the North-East came to the fore in the second; and the West Midlands and South-East dominated in the third and fourth. According to Hall, the new industrial traditions develop in different places from the older ones. Some indication of the requirements for attracting innovative industries may be obtained by analysing the contemporary location of high-technology industry and research and development (R. & D.).

The world recession of the late 1970s and 1980s has helped to stimulate a great deal of interest in the location and development of 'high-tech' industries in many countries (see Section 6.1), including Canada (Britton, 1985; 1987), France (Pottier, 1987), Australia (Newton and O'Connor, 1987), and Japan (Nishioka and Takeuchi, 1987; Toda, 1987). Particularly interesting are two studies carried out in parallel in the United States and Great Britain, because they allow a comparison of the findings (Markusen *et al.*, 1986; Breheny and McQuaid, 1987; Hall *et al.*, 1987; Hall, 1987*b*). However, caution is required in interpreting similarities and differences in the geography of high technology in the two countries because of the very different size of the United States and Great Britain.

Both studies defined high technology using occupational profiles so as to include all manufacturing industries in which the percentage of scientific and technological occupations were above the average for all industry. Such an approach gives, they argue, a precise and objective definition, but it does result in the inclusion of a wide variety of industries. In the British study most of the analysis was restricted to a 'core' set of seven industries which, in addition, had relatively high R. & D. expenditures: pharmaceutical chemicals and preparations; telegraph and telephone apparatus and equipment; radio and electronics components; broadcast receiving and some reproducing equipment; electronic computers; radio, radar, and electronic capital goods; and aerospace equipment manufacture and repair. The American study, on the other hand, was broader and was based on twenty-nine sectors, including not only similar industries to the British study, but also other industries, such as printing ink, nitrogenous fertilizer, and soap and other detergents.

One of the most notable contrasts between the high-technology industries in the two countries is in their employment performance. Whereas Great Britain lost over 75 000 high-technology jobs in the 1970s, in the equivalent industries the American economy gained over 600 000. Nevertheless,

in both countries the high-technology sector performed relatively better than all manufacturing taken together. In Great Britain employment in the seven high-technology industries declined by 11 per cent between 1971 and 1981, while manufacturing industry as a whole lost 25 per cent. In the United States the equivalent ten industries grew by 30 per cent between 1972 and 1981, while all manufacturing grew by 6.5 per cent.

In both countries the location of high-technology industry is heavily concentrated. In Great Britain no less than 49 per cent of high-technology employment in 1981 was located in three areas, including just eleven counties (Table 6.2). The London Western Crescent alone in Great Britain had one-third of high-technology employment; two counties in north-west England had a further 9 per cent and the 'Silicon Glen' of central Scotland—despite its media reputation—had only 6 per cent. In the United States five major areas, involving ten states, accounted for 42 per cent of all high-technology employment in 1977

TABLE 6.2 Employment change in major concentrations of high-technology industry in Great Britain by county groupings, 1975–1981

	Employment 1981	Employment change 1975–81 (%)	Location quotient
1. *London Western Crescent*			
Greater London	91 400	−15.7	0.85
Hertfordshire	45 100	+15.1	3.60
Hampshire	33 800	+6.8	2.00
Berkshire	19 700	+62.2	2.04
Buckinghamshire	6 900	n.a.	1.15
Surrey	18 200	+11.1	1.79
TOTAL	215 100		
2. *North-West England*			
Greater Manchester	27 300	n.a.	0.86
Lancashire	30 000	+4.8	2.01
TOTAL	57 300		
3. *'Silicon Glen' (central Scotland)*			
Strathclyde	23 600	−14.0	0.88
Lothians	9 000	+19.3	0.93
Fife	8 100	n.a.	2.24
TOTAL	40 700		
GRAND TOTAL (3 areas)	313 100		
GREAT BRITAIN	640 900	−6.2	

Sources: Breheny and McQuaid (1985 p. 10); Hall (1987*b* p. 145).

(Table 6.3). The Pacific South-West, principally California, had the largest concentration with close on 700 000 high-technology employees. The Western Gulf states, Old New England, and the Lower Great Lakes area each recorded between 350 000 and 400 000 high-technology jobs; while the Chesapeake/Delaware River area added a further 280 000 jobs.

These concentrations of course partly reflect the general concentration of employment. Relative concentrations, as measured by location quotients, give a rather different picture. The counties of Hertfordshire, Avon, and Fife in Great Britain had the highest relative concentrations, while Greater London, Greater Manchester, Strathclyde, and Lothians had less high-technology employment than would be expected from their share of all manufacturing employment (i.e. loca-

tion quotients below 1), and are excluded from Fig. 6.2. Similarly, in the United States several states with high absolute employment totals had weak relative concentrations as measured by the location quotient. Thus states like New York, Ohio, and Pennsylvania, all of which had around 300 000 high-technology jobs in 1977, had location quotients below 1 and are not included in either Table 6.3 or Fig. 6.3. The highest relative concentrations of high-technology employment in the United States are in the States of Arizona, Connecticut, Kansas, Maryland, and Colorado. The data suggest that concentrations in Great Britain were more pronounced than in the USA, with Hertfordshire having a location quotient twice the value of that for Arizona, although this may reflect differences in the size of the reporting unit. Hall *et al.* (1987) suggest that federal politics

TABLE 6.3 Employment change in major concentrations of high-technology industry in the United States by state groupings, 1972–1977

	Employment 1977	Employment change 1972–7 (%)	Location quotient
1. *Pacific South-West*			
California	641 300	+ 17.9	1.49
Arizona	45 900	+ 26.1	1.80
TOTAL	687 200		
2. *Western Gulf*			
Texas	285 700	+ 20.9	1.33
Louisiana	56 400	+ 10.6	1.22
Oklahoma	53 900	+ 34.4	1.38
TOTAL	396 000		
3. *Chesapeake/Delaware River*			
New Jersey	232 300	− 1.2	1.23
Maryland	48 400	− 7.6	1.60
TOTAL	280 700		
4. *Old New England*			
Massachusetts	204 600	+ 12.1	1.43
Connecticut	160 000	+ 1.7	1.65
TOTAL	364 600		
5. *Lower Great Lakes*			
Illinois	360 300	+ 1.1	1.15
TOTAL	360 300		
GRAND TOTAL (5 areas)	2 099 200	+ 11.0	
USA	4 760 100	+ 8.7	

Source: Markusen *et al.* (1986 pp. 101, 107-9).

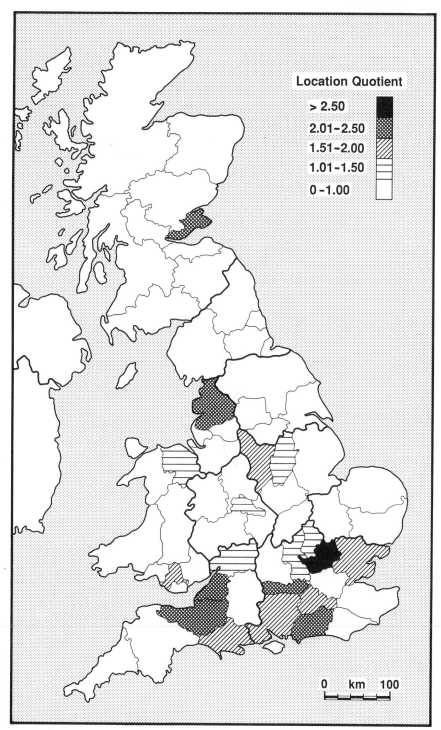

FIG 6.2 The relative concentration of high-technology employment in Great Britain, 1981
(*source*: based on data in Hall *et al.*, 1987 p. 32)

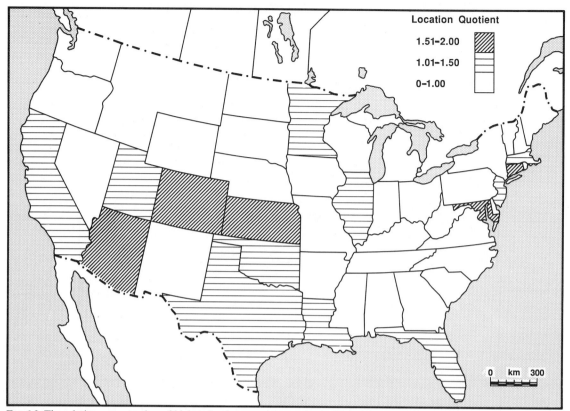

FIG 6.3 The relative concentration of high-technology employment in the United States, 1977 (*source*: based on data in Markusen *et al.*, 1987 p. 100)

in the United States ensure a more even distribution of high-technology benefits.

The places where high-technology industries are concentrated are not necessarily the areas in which they are growing the fastest. Of the five major American cores shown in Table 6.3, those in the 'Frostbelt', with the exception of Massachusetts, grew less rapidly than those in the 'Sunbelt' during the 1970s (see also Chapter 16.1). Looking more closely at the pattern of change there is evidence that the five major cores, with the exception of the Chesapeake/Delaware River area, were decentralizing locally outwards into neighbouring states. Thus California grew less rapidly than Nevada or Arizona; Texas less rapidly than Arkansas or Oklahoma; Massachusetts less rapidly than New Hampshire or Vermont. In Britain a similar pattern of decentralization has occurred with the urban cores of Greater London, Greater Manchester, and Strathclyde all losing high-technology jobs, while surrounding counties gained (Table 6.2). By far the largest growth of high-technology employment in the late 1970s took place in Berkshire, which gained 7600 jobs, an increase of 63 per cent. This does not of course necessarily mean that firms were moving from the high-technology cores to the fringes; growth may well have come from elsewhere (see also Keeble, 1988).

The geography of research and development

Most new technologies today originate through the deliberate expenditure of time and effort in R. & D. activity. The majority of R. & D. is directed towards the improvement and development of new products (Malecki, 1985). Hence a critical ingredient in explaining the origin of high-technology clusters may lie in the location of the R. & D. function, although recent work in the USA found no significant correlation between the intensity of R. & D. (as measured by all federal funding to universities) and high-technology location and growth at the Standard Metropolitan Statistical Area level (Markusen *et al.*, 1986).

Malecki's work (1979; 1980; 1981; 1982; 1985) in the United States shows that there is a fundamental distinction between R. & D. funded by private industry and R. & D. funded by government (see also Chapter 8.3). Although 70 per cent of federal R. & D. is carried out by private companies, its location is quite different from that done by corporations on their own account. Private industry R. & D., which accounted for 67 per cent of all R. & D. expenditure in 1977 (Malecki, 1985), is largely conducted in the older industrial cities, particularly in the traditional manufacturing belt, and many of the cities are the headquarters of the corporations involved. The rapidly growing Sunbelt cities, such as Houston, have been markedly unsuccessful in attracting their share of corporate R. & D. Almost 94 per cent of total R. & D. spending of the top 500 companies in 1975 was attributable to firms with headquarters outside the Sunbelt (Cohen, 1977). Federal R. & D., on the other hand, is located in quite different places, most of them university cities (e.g. Lincoln, Nebraska; Austin, Texas) or centres of federal government research (e.g. Huntsville, Alabama; Washington DC), mainly outside the manufacturing belt. The difference in location in the two kinds of R. & D. is underlined by the finding that of 41 metropolitan areas with location quotients of over 1.0, for either kind of R. & D., only 11 scored on both lists (Malecki, 1980).

Of the two kinds of R. & D., that funded by the United States government is probably more innovatory in the sense that it is likely to generate new industries. No less than 78 per cent of all federal support to industry goes to just two industrial sectors, aerospace and electronics, and 58 per cent comes from the Department of Defence. It is also highly concentrated geographically; no fewer than 61 per cent of all aerospace R. & D. laboratories are in the Los Angeles area, while five metropolitan areas (Boston, New York, Philadelphia, San Francisco, and Los Angeles) account for much of the electronics research (Malecki, 1981; see also Chapter 8.3).

Similarly, work in Britain shows that R. & D. is highly concentrated in south-east England, particularly the Western Crescent, where it is associated with the location of government research laboratories and defence establishments (Buswell and Lewis, 1970; Howells, 1984; Buswell *et al.*, 1985). In 1981, 53 per cent of all UK employment in separate R. & D. units was in the South-East region (Keeble, 1987). The significance of the South-East for innovation is also emphasized by other work, which shows that plants in the South-East were more innovative than those located in other regions (Oakey *et al.*, 1980) and introduced a significantly higher proportion of new and improved products than plants in Development Areas (Thwaites, 1982).

Explaining the geography of high-technology innovation

Seeking an explanation of the location of high-technology industry and R. & D. is a complex task. Indeed, some research workers have argued that 'high technology', at least, is too broad and imprecise a term and should be disaggregated into more meaningful industrial sectors, such as computers or semiconductors, before attempting any explanation (Harris and McArthur, 1985). These conceptual problems have not, however, prevented numerous attempts to analyse and explain the location of high-technology industries.

One method has been to examine in detail the origin and development of particular 'technology-oriented complexes' (Steed and DeGenova, 1983). Among the complexes (Fig. 6.4) which have been analysed in this way are: Silicon Valley, Santa Clara County, south of San Francisco (Saxenian, 1983; Rogers and Larsen, 1984); Orange County, south of Los Angeles (Scott, 1986); Route 128 out of Boston (Dorfman, 1983); Silicon Valley North, Ottawa (Steed and DeGenova, 1983); Cambridge (Segal Quince and Partners, 1985; Keeble, 1989*b*); the M4 Corridor (Boddy *et al.*, 1986; Macgregor *et al.*, 1986; Hall *et al.*, 1987); and Silicon Glen in central Scotland (Haug, 1986). It is clear from this rapidly burgeoning research that the different technology-orientated complexes vary in their nature, origin, and development (Aydalot, 1988; Keeble, 1988). For example, whereas Silicon Valley initially relied on university–industry partnership and government spending on R. & D., and developed particularly with the aid of military contracts; Silicon Glen originated as an attractive production site for US multinationals serving the

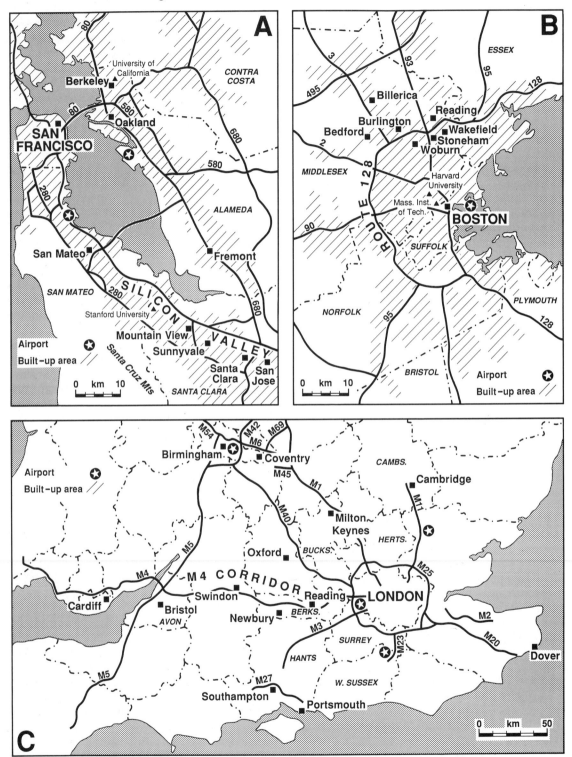

FIG 6.4. Silicon landscapes: (*a*) Silicon Valley; (*b*) Route 128; (*c*) M4 Corridor

British and European markets. Only later did competitive pressures, product complexity and market demands compel the American multi-nationals to allocate R. & D. and engineering operations to their Scottish plants and develop links with local universities (Haug, 1986).

Drawing on this and other work, several research workers have attempted to explain the location and development of high-technology industries and to account, to a greater or lesser degree, for the variety apparent in the patterns of 'high-tech' development. Although virtually all writers seem to agree that the locational decisions of high-technology firms are not determined by the costs of moving materials, products, or people across space, there is less agreement over which factors are important (Castells, 1985; Kelly, 1987). Most work has tended to adopt one or other of two main explanatory approaches. The first stresses *location factors* which are presumed favourable to the growth of high-technology production; while the other emphasizes a *structuralist perspective* examining historical changes in the organization of high-technology capitalist enterprises (Gordon and Kimball, 1987).

According to Hall (1985), who adopts the first approach, one important attribute an area should have to attract high-technology industry is a negative one, the lack of very old-established industrial traditions. Hall cites the case of ship-building in Glasgow as a good example of the potential inhibiting effect of a previous cycle of industrial development. He suggests that earlier success in building ships blinded the Glaswegians from the need to build them in new ways and to develop new industries. Checkland (1975) calls this *'the upas tree effect'*, after the Pacific tree which spreads so far that it prevents new vegetation growing in its shade. Similarly for the USA, Markusen (1985) argues that oligopolistic domination of local resource markets explains the relatively poor growth performance of cities such as Pittsburgh (steel) and Detroit (vehicles). However, there are exceptions where a pre-existing industrial environment is restructured as, for example, happened with the regeneration of industry in the Swiss Jura when the production of mechanical watches was replaced by the production of electronic components (Aydalot, 1988).

Lack of an inhibiting industrial tradition may nevertheless often be a necessary condition for the development of new industries, but it is not a sufficient one. Most non-industrialized areas do not attract new industries. Thus, according to the *location factor* or *local environment-based* approach, as Aydalot and Keeble (1988) call it, there must be some other favourable factor or factors which encourage new industries to locate and prosper in particular places. A variety of factors has been suggested which may meet this requirement, including a pleasant residential environment to attract the entrepreneurs, skilled technicians and scientists needed to establish and work in the high-technology firms and R. & D. departments (e.g. Keeble, 1987); the availability of venture capital (e.g. Oakey, 1984) and business services (e.g. Markusen *et al.*, 1986); a developed transport infrastructure including motorways and international airports (e.g. Hall *et al.*, 1987); the presence of science-based universities and government research establishments which generate a local pool of highly qualified manpower and provide many of the entrepreneurs establishing new high-technology firms (e.g. Steed and De-Genova, 1983); and the receipt of defence contracts (e.g. Markusen and Bloch, 1985; Breheny, 1988). However, it is not so much the existence of a particular attribute as the interaction of these factors in combination which is critical. This point is made clearly by Keeble and Kelly (1986, p. 80), who describe technology-oriented complexes as:

highly localised clusters of new high technology firms which exhibit dynamic growth through a process of 'synergy', or intense interaction, between new firms and entrepreneurs, research institutions, local banks and finance agencies, and business service organisations. . . . underpinning if not initiating this dynamism in most documented cases is the impact of existing major scientific research institutions, such as large science-based universities or government research facilities, together with a high-quality local residential environment which attracts and retains the crucially important but intrinsically highly mobile research scientists and entrepreneurs whose activities create the complex.

A similar point is made by Breheny and McQuaid (1987, p. 330) when they describe the 'layers of cumulative advantage' which have characterized the development of high-technology industry in the Western Crescent of the United Kingdom.

In the *location factor* approach, the variety in the nature, origin, and development of technology-oriented complexes is accounted for by differences in the relative importance of the factors present in an area. This method is criticized by research workers favouring a *structuralist approach* to explaining the location of high-technology industry. For example, Scott and Storper (1987 p. 220) argue that 'these factors turn out to be little more than *ad hoc* lists ... the cloth (of which) can be (and is) cut to suit every possible circumstance'. They suggest, following Aglietta (1979), that a more meaningful theoretical generalization may be obtained by examining the different regimes of accumulation which emerge at different moments in the history of capitalist development, although they seem to recognize a greater variety in spatial outcomes than some others of the *regulationist school* (see Section 6.1 and Chapters 2.1, 4.2, and 15.2). According to Scott and Storper the latest regime, based on high-technology industry, has been associated with 'a series of major and largely unforeseen geographical shifts' (p. 216).

In interpreting the development of high-technology industry in the United States, Scott and Storper suggest that 'a window of locational opportunity' opened in the 1950s with the emergence of some novel advanced technologies and products (e.g. in the semiconductor and communications industries). Wishing to avoid locating in regions with unionized and politicized workforces, many firms sought locations in the South and West. Other firms, which were tied by agglomeration economies to a pre-existing electronics industry in the North-East, managed to evade the traditional male working class by hiring skilled technical labour on the one hand, and unskilled, ethnic, and female labour on the other.

At this early stage numerous centres of high-technology industry emerged. Some of these areas, including Santa Clara County and Orange County, and to a much lesser extent, Phoenix and Dallas-Fort Worth, were then transformed in the course of time into self-reinforcing foci of growth and development. The key process at this stage, suggest Scott and Storper, was the development of agglomeration economies. Both localization economies, via the linkage structures of the complex, and urbanization economies, with increasing efficiencies in infrastructure provision, might be expected to lead to a fall in the costs of production within each centre (Chapter 5.3). This leads to the window of locational opportunity closing around a limited number of locations which 'crystallize out as dominant production regions' (Scott and Storper, 1987 p. 227) for the new regime of accumulation. These centres tend to grow further through processes of innovation and new entrepreneurial activity.

Clearly neither approach to analysing the location of high-technology industry has a monopoly on explanation. Whereas the structuralist approach emphasizes the need to examine spatial patterns of economic activity as a historical process in which changes in the technology and organization of production interact with the existing geographical pattern of production opportunities to produce unique outcomes in specific places, the location factor approach stresses the range of different factors which in combination constrain the locational opportunities available for profitable production. Interestingly, both approaches emphasize the importance of agglomeration economies and the labour characteristics of the high-technology complexes. However, neither approach has yet adequately explained why, for example, although Texas Instruments began semiconductor manufacture in Dallas, and Motorolla started production in Phoenix, at more or less the same time that Schockley Laboratories began in Santa Clara County in the 1950s; in neither case did the local area attract as many semiconductor manufacturers as the Santa Clara area. How and why some places develop expanding industrial complexes, while others develop differently or are stillborn is, as Scott and Storper (1987, p. 227) observe, 'largely an unresolved puzzle in contemporary economic geography'. A satisfactory understanding of the development of high-technology industry may require a synthesis of both approaches.

Creating high-technology clusters

The policy implications of this analysis are relatively bleak for many of the attempts to mimic the example of Silicon Valley and Route 128 elsewhere in North America, Europe, Australia, and Japan (Gordon and Kimball, 1987; Glasmeier, 1988).

Silicon Valley and Route 128 both grew out of a historically unique confluence of political, economic, and institutional circumstances. The origins of these seedbeds of technology-based industry lie in World War II, in the spending priorities of the Cold War, and in the development of close links between federal funding sources, local academic institutions, and local

FIG 6.5 The location of science parks in the United Kingdom, 1988 (*source*: Rowe, 1988 p. iv)

industry. It is unlikely that this particular combination of circumstance will be repeated (Saxenian, 1985 p. 99).

This illustrates again that the relationship between technology and society is a two-way one. Technology may encourage economic development but the nature of technology and the form it takes is affected by the nature of society.

Silicon Valley grew out of Stanford University Industrial Park established in the early 1950s, while the growth of high-technology industry along Route 128 was closely associated with MIT and to a lesser extent with Harvard (Dorfman, 1983). In Britain the idea of developing *science parks* to link industry to higher education research blossomed in the 1980s. By 1988 there were 36 Science Parks in existence or under construction in the UK, only two of which opened before the 1980s (Monck *et al.*, 1988). It seems unlikely that all these can prosper (Fig. 6.5). The first, and arguably the most successful, was established by Cambridge University in the early 1970s. By 1986 there were 68 firms employing some 1900 people at Cambridge Park. Interestingly, Cambridge and the M11 Corridor is one of the few areas in Britain where Hall *et al.* (1987) believe that the high-technology growth of the eastern M4 corridor might be replicated. Indeed in the early 1980s Cambridgeshire experienced the highest increase in high-technology employment of any county in Great Britain (Keeble, 1989*b*). Yet even Cambridge Park is small by North American standards. For example, Research Triangle Park, which was established in the late 1950s by three universities in North Carolina, employed 27 000 people in the mid-1980s, and was estimated to have room for 60 000 at full occupancy (Pizzano, 1985, cited by Monck *et al.*, 1988). Policy-makers may not wish, however, to mimic all aspects of the economic success of Silicon Valley and Route 128. In both areas there are major problems of congestion, overcrowding, and a rising cost of living, leading to calls for a halt to these high-technology centres. Indeed some firms faced with these rising costs have begun to reorganize functionally and spatially by dispersing the more routine production and administrative tasks while retaining managerial and developmental activities at the 'right addresses' (Saxenian, 1985).

6.3 Spatial diffusion and the impact of new technology

New technologies are mainly produced in the manufacturing sector, but the application of new processes and the use of new products occur throughout the economic system. The diffusion and impact of new technologies occur unevenly over space. This section begins with an examination of examples of the spatial diffusion of innovations from the manufacturing and agricultural sectors, and ends with an analysis of the spatial impact of the introduction of information technology primarily in the service sector.

Diffusion of product innovations

In discussing the development of high-technology industries in the last section the account focused primarily on the location of technology-oriented complexes, where the flexible, often customized, forms of production encourage agglomeration. It has been suggested that such agglomeration tendencies characterize the entire life cycles of many high-technology products because these are often of no more than five years duration and omit a prolonged standardization or mature phase (Oakey, 1984). Nevertheless, *some* of the component production processes of the complexes undergo routinization and standardization of parts. Where this occurs, for example, with the assembly of semiconductors, it enables production units to be decentralized, often in the form of branch plants, to peripheral regions and Third World countries (Sayer, 1986*a*; Henderson and Scott, 1987; Scott, 1987*a*; Scott and Angel, 1987). The decentralization of product technologies may be seen as an example of the spatial diffusion of product innovations.

The product life cycle framework has been widely used for examining the spatial diffusion of innovations in manufacturing industry. The a-spatial characteristics of this concept were discussed in Section 6.1 where it was asserted that each stage of the cycle has different production requirements. Places vary in their ability to meet these requirements, so the location of production may be expected to shift as products and industries proceed through the cycle. Attempts have been made to apply the concept at both international and intranational scales.

Vernon (1966) has suggested that the early and growth stages of the product life cycle are located in the developed world, attracted by the access to technical knowledge, specialized information, and a network of subcontractors. In the mature stage, with mass production, product standardization, and competitive pressures to reduce costs, manufacture is shifted to developing economies, attracted by low cost, semi-skilled, and unskilled labour. This cycle also has implications for understanding international trade, because it predicts that in the early stages the developed country where the innovation has occurred will export the product to the rest of the world, while in later stages, as production is shifted, the country will eventually become a net importer of the product. An application of this idea to the USA is shown in Fig. 6.6. This describes the post-war expansion of large American enterprises, first into Europe to serve the large market, and then into Less Developed Countries (LDCs) to exploit cheap labour resources. Interestingly, the shift to the Third World in search of cheap labour supplies is what Weber would predict from his theory of industrial location (Dicken, 1977), although at the time Vernon suggested this sequence (mid-

1960s) there was little evidence of LDCs serving as a production base for markets in the United States and Europe. However, the beginnings of a trend towards production returning to the developed world, in for example electronics (Chapter 7.3) and clothing (Chapter 12.1), associated with the need for closer co-ordination of production in the face of changing technology and demand patterns, raises doubts about the logic and predictions of the product cycle model (see also Chapters 1.2 and 14.1).

At the intranational scale the product life cycle concept is more commonly referred to as *filter-down theory*. The idea has been applied to the diffusion of new products from urban to rural areas, from large towns to small towns and from core regions to peripheral regions (Watts, 1987). This suggestion, that innovations 'trickle down' the hierarchies of both regions and cities, is also associated with growth pole theory (Chapter 15.2). However, the supporting evidence at the intranational scale is weak. Some of the findings of studies in non-metropolitan areas of the United States are in line with the filter-down concept. For example, there is a tendency for plants in these areas to be involved in the

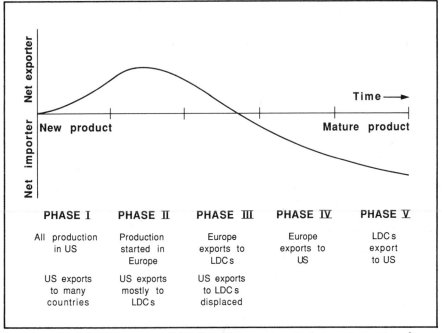

FIG 6.6 A schematic representation of the effects of the product life cycle on the location of United States production and trade (*source*: Wells, 1972 p. 15)

assembly of standardized products. Further, the management of the plants emphasize the attraction of a pool of unskilled labour and make little reference to advantages of external economies (Erickson and Leinbach, 1979). In the United Kingdom, on the other hand, a study of the pharmaceutical industry found no significant bias towards new products in larger settlements, more urbanized areas, or within more centrally located regions (Howells, 1983).

Several criticisms may be made of the locational interpretation of the product life cycle model, in addition to the more general limitations discussed in Section 6.1. In later work, Vernon (1971 p. 108) himself recognizes that it 'was beginning in some respects to be inadequate as a way of looking at the U.S.-controlled multinational' and shifted the emphasis to examining the oligopolistic behaviour of transnational corporations (TNCs) (Vernon, 1974; Chapter 7.2). One reason why the model may be less relevant today is that leading multinationals have developed global networks, and innovations may originate and go into production at any point in the network and not just spread out from the home country. Similarly at the intranational scale the concept seems to apply best to interpreting the behaviour of firms as they expand spatially and is not as relevant to understanding the behaviour of firms which have already established national manufacturing systems. The model is also not very helpful for interpreting the major flow of international investment between advanced industrialized countries. Moreover, nothing is said about the rate at which the sequence operates, or when transition between one phase and the next will occur. Nevertheless,

there is some general value in such ideal-type models in emphasizing the dynamic nature of the major processes involved and in pointing to possible interrelationships between key elements. But their actual application to real-world circumstances must be time and place specific. In the case of the product life cycle model of the locational evolution of TNCs its specific context was that of the postwar expansion of large United States enterprises. Its current relevance to TNCs in general is quite limited to the explanation of *some*—though not all—types of international production (Dicken, 1986 p. 132).

The need to be aware of the danger of over-generalization applies equally to studies of spatial diffusion of agricultural innovations.

Diffusion of agricultural innovations

There is a large body of literature on the diffusion of agricultural innovations, which is well summarized by Ilbery (1985a) and G. Clark (1986), while Shaw (1987) provides a useful review of agricultural innovation diffusion and its consequences in the Third World. Three main perspectives are apparent in this work—adoption, diffusion agency, and society—which have varied in significance over time.

The adoption perspective

The traditional approach to diffusion studies focuses upon the process by which adoption occurs. This is essentially a demand-based approach in which the emphasis is placed on the role of communications in the adoption process and the farmer as a decision-maker (Blaikie, 1978). It is well represented by the seminal study by Hagerstrand (1967), originally published in Swedish in 1953, which modelled the diffusion of various agricultural innovations, such as bovine tuberculosis control and subsidies for the improvement of grazing, in an area of central Sweden. An important feature of the model was the inclusion of a random element to allow for non-rational, non-economic behaviour.

The work of Hagerstrand and others identified a number of empirical regularities in the diffusion process concerned with spatial patterns, rates of adoption, and the characteristics of adopters. Hagerstrand saw the principal spatial pattern of diffusion as a *contagious* or *neighbourhood* process in which an innovation spreads out from the point of origin in a wave-like fashion, strongly constrained by the friction of distance. Later work showed that some types of innovation diffusion are better described as a *hierarchical* pattern in which an innovation tends to be adopted at the top end of a hierarchy of places before working its way down to less important places. For example, hybrid corn was first adopted in the principal maize-growing areas of the USA, and only later was accepted in areas which were less suited to the crop (Griliches, 1957). Agricultural innovations also often cascade down the farm size hierarchy, as they tend to be adopted first on large farms. If the different farm sizes are randomly distributed over space this form of innovation diffusion will also appear to be spatially random.

A further regularity in the diffusion of innovations is the cumulative rate of adoption curve, which typically has a logistic, or 'S' shaped form. When the number of adopters are plotted over time the curve takes on the form of a normal distribution (Fig. 6.7). A number of categories of adopters are usually recognized, ranging from innovators to laggards, depending on when they accept an innovation. A summary of the characteristics of different groups of adopters arising from studies of the diffusion of agricultural innovations is shown in Table 6.4. It is clear that not only do the personal characteristics of adopters vary at different stages in the diffusion cycle, but so do the sources of information about the innovations. It is suggested that *innovators* tend to be of high social status, are often young and well educated, and run large specialized farms. For information they have close contacts with scientific information sources and other innovators. At the other end of the adoption cycle are the *late adopters* and *laggards* who as a group tend to be of low social status, are often aged, have low incomes, and run small farms. Their main sources of information are friends, neigh-

bours, and relatives. The use of such pejorative term as 'laggard' is unfortunate, because the late adopters will include people for whom the innovation is only marginally suited in terms of its capabilities and costs (Yapa and Mayfield, 1978). Indeed followers of the society perspective emphasize that many farmers are not so much laggards as constrained by lack of resources, especially capital.

The diffusion agency perspective

One of the assumptions of the adoption perspective is that an innovation is simultaneously available to the whole population, while its rate of acceptance is influenced by factors such as the characteristics of individuals, the distance the area is from the origin point, and the position of the area within a hierarchy of places. However, this ignores the possibility that the diffusion pattern is affected by the strategies of the propagating agencies. The way in which innovations are distributed, or supplied, is particularly emphasized by Brown (1975, 1981). He suggests that the diffusion pattern will differ according to whether the organization concerned has a centralized or decentralized structure. In the former case, criteria such as profitability or sales potential will determine the choice of areas in which to market a new product first; while a decentralized structure (e.g. a franchise system of marketing a service like machinery maintenance) will lead to a more random pattern of supply.

An illustration of the importance of agencies comes from a study of the spatial diffusion of the broiler industry in the East Midlands. In a survey of the reasons why plant owners decided to start intensively rearing young chickens, the most important influence was the information provided by representatives of feed sales or processor firms (White and Watts, 1977). The importance of such 'self-interested propagators' of innovations is also emphasized in a study of agrarian change in north-west Portugal. Unwin (1988) examined the pattern of adoption of new agricultural equipment and chemicals by analysing the activities of the Ministry of Agriculture, co-operatives and companies selling tractors, chemicals, and agricultural machinery. He concluded that the most significant influence on recent change has been the activity of the companies involved in propagating that change, but that the roles of the Ministry of Agriculture and the co-operatives

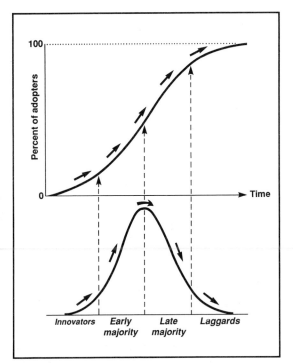

FIG 6.7 Diffusion through time: logistic curve and categories of adopters (*source*: Abler, Adams, and Gould, 1971 p. 405)

TABLE 6.4 Characteristics of farmers in the five adoption categories

Adopter category	Personal characteristics	Salient values and social relationships	Communication behaviour
Innovators	Highest social status; largest and most specialized operations; wealthy; often young; well educated; often experience in non-farming environment	'Venturesome'; willing to accept risks; some opinion leadership; cosmopolite	Closest contact with scientific information sources; interaction with other innovators; relatively greatest use of impersonal channels of information
Early adopters	High social status; often large and specialized operations	'Respected'; regarded by many others in the community as a model and as influential; greatest opinion leadership of any adopter category in most communities	Greatest contact with local change agents (including extension or advisory services, commercial technical advisers, etc.); competent users of mass media
Early majority	Above-average social status; average-sized operations	'Deliberate'; willing to consider new ideas only after peers have adopted; some opinion leadership	Considerable contact with change agents and early adopters; receive mass media
Late majority	Below-average social status; small operations; little specialization; relatively low income	'Sceptical'; overwhelming pressure from peers needed before adoption occurs; little opinion leadership	Interaction with peers who are mainly early or late majority; less use of mass media
Laggards	Little specialization; lowest social status; smallest operations; lowest income; often oldest	'Traditional'; oriented towards the past; avoid risks; little if any opinion leadership; almost isolated socially	Neighbours, friends, and relatives with similar values are main information source; suspicious of change agents

Source: Jones (1975 p. 42).

could be particularly important in limiting the adverse effects of developments, such as the accession to the European Community, on the poorest farmers in the region.

The adoption and diffusion agency perspectives are concerned with the adoption of innovations by *individuals* and what affects the demand for them and their supply. The two approaches are complementary and many studies include aspects of both (Brown, 1981; Unwin, 1988). The third, and most recent, approach focuses upon the relationship between agricultural innovations and *society*.

The society perspective
This perspective emphasizes that the relationship operates in both directions. The nature of the society affects the kinds of innovation which are developed and the rates of acceptance; while the pattern of innovation diffusion has important

social, economic and environmental consequences.

Central to influencing the kinds of innovation developed is the control of funding for agricultural research. G. Clark (1986 p. 85), in reviewing research in the USA on alternative agriculture, notes that:

The kinds of developments that are fostered are usually those which commercial companies support because profits can be foreseen from their sale. Sales potential is equated with usefulness. Developments in husbandry which favour small, mixed farms or which dispense with machinery or agrochemicals are less often funded.

Political factors may also constrain the pattern of innovations. Freeman (1985), for instance, emphasizes the importance of political lobbying by early adopters to restrict the spread of new ideas which might undermine their competitive advantage. It is further claimed that the structure of society makes it easier for some groups than for others to adopt innovations. The opportunities for adoption are unequally distributed. For example, in agriculture, farm size is an important structural variable. Large farms, because of their higher incomes, social prestige, economic power, and links with political authorities at the local and national levels, generally enjoy a more assured supply of modern inputs, and the credit necessary to utilize the new agricultural technology (Shaw, 1987).

Such structural constraints also affect the consequences of the diffusion of agricultural innovations. The impact of the introduction in developing countries of high-yielding cereal varieties (HYVs) in the 1960s—the *Green Revolution*— provides an excellent illustration. One consequence of the Green Revolution has been to alter the crops grown and the farming methods employed. Increasing yields have made wheat and rice more profitable for farmers than some other crops, leading to an expansion of the area given over to the cultivation of these two crops. The HYVs have also resulted in an expansion of irrigation and multiple cropping in many countries (Hazell and Anderson, 1986). However, the consequences are unevenly felt between areas and income groups because of the institutional and structural constraints. A study of the effects of the Green Revolution in the Indian Punjab and Gujarat, found that the former benefited most because of its relative advantage over the latter in terms of access to seed and fertilizer, irrigation and credit (Nicholson, 1984). Most research suggests that: 'Although farms of all sizes and different agroclimatic conditions have adopted high yielding varieties, the resultant gains have been concentrated primarily in irrigated areas, often among large-size farmers' (Shaw, 1987, p. 11). The Green Revolution has also had major ecological impacts. For example, Shaw (1987) cites examples where the increased use of agricultural chemicals has contributed to micro-nutrient deficiencies in the soil and chemical residues in food. There is evidence that the latter has led directly to human intoxification and a number of deaths (see also Chapter 17.2).

The society perspective emphasizes that the causes and consequences of agricultural innovation diffusion vary over time, and differ between and within societies. However, for a fuller explanation of the diffusion of agricultural innova-

tions the insights of the society perspective need to be integrated with the understanding of the diffusion process derived from the adoption and agency perspectives.

Spatial impacts of information technology

The discussion of the diffusion of innovations in the agricultural and manufacturing sectors has focused particularly on the spread of product innovations. To provide some balance this last section analyses the spatial impact of a process innovation, the application of information technology (IT), primarily on the service sector. It complements the discussion of the impact of transport and communication innovations in Chapter 5. Indeed, in theory IT can substitute for the movement of goods, materials, and persons. By making co-ordination more efficient the movement of goods may be reduced, while telecommunications may substitute for face-to-face meetings. It is argued that the effect of this *telecommunication–transportation trade-off*, or *T3*, as it has been called (Jussawalla *et al.*, 1978; Nilles *et al.*, 1976), is to make industry and people locationally more footloose. However, the limited evidence available suggests that telecommunications complement rather than substitute for the movement of people (Mandeville, 1983). Indeed, by increasing the opportunities for interaction in society the use of telecommunications can generate more travel than it replaces (Goddard, 1980).

It is increasingly being suggested that the current convergence of electronics, computing, and telecommunications into a composite information technology has the potential to generate an enormous growth in service activities, particularly where they are supported by computer network applications, such as teleworking, telebanking, teleshopping, and so on, which are capable of transmitting large volumes of information instantaneously over great distances (Barras, 1985; Hepworth, 1987).

The spatial impact of IT is an area where there are many assertions, but little hard evidence (see also Chapter 13.2). The main difficulty, as in other areas (see for example the diffusion of the effect of technological change on employment in Section 6.1), lies in separating out the technological effect from that of other factors. One view is that the application of IT is reducing the importance of agglomeration economies for activities primarily concerned with the handling of information. Nilles *et al.* (1976), for example, suggest that organizations which largely handle information evolve in four stages (Fig. 6.8):

1. Centralization—the current stage for most information using industries.
2. Decentralization—involving relocation of units such as accountancy departments and branches of banks.
3. Dispersion—in which employees report only to that part of the organization which is nearest to their home. Work is distributed,

supervised, and collected largely by computer networks and extensive use of telecommunications.

4. Diffusion—in which employees work from home.

It is, perhaps, doubtful that such radical changes in the organization and location of work will happen across the board. There is 'a vast difference between technological possibility and economic feasibility' (Mandeville, 1983 p. 67). In the *long run*, change along these lines is likely for *some* economic activities. As yet, however, there

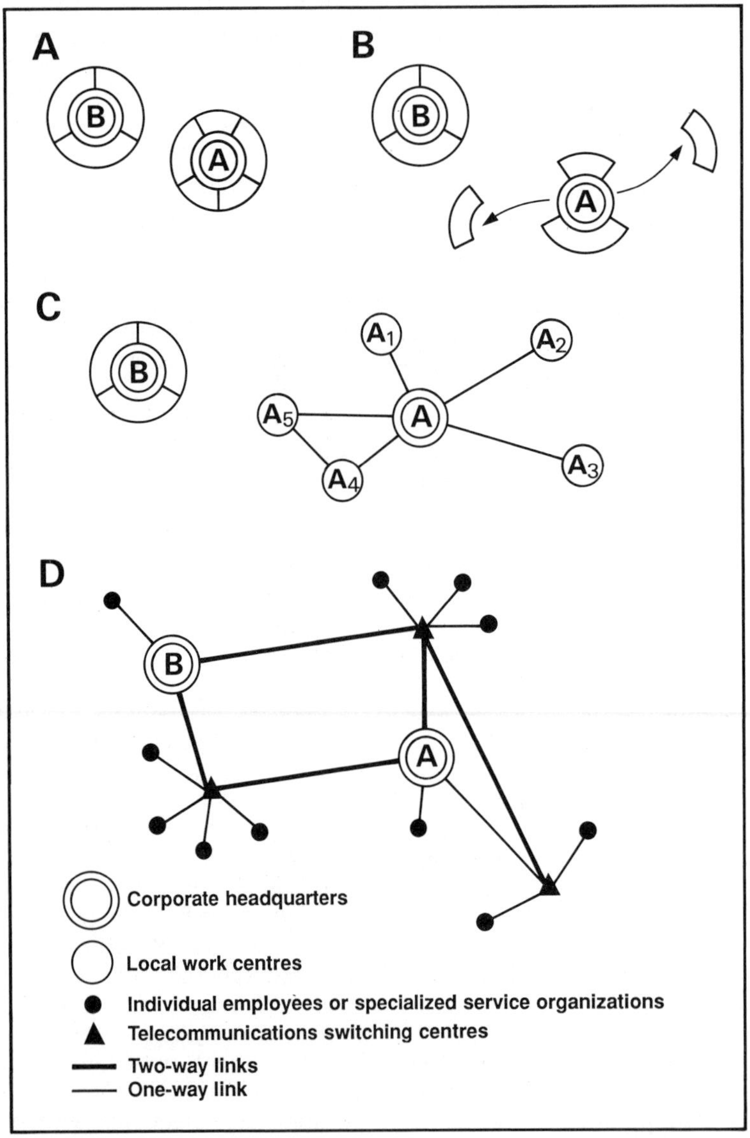

Fig 6.8 Evolution of the spatial structure of an organization utilizing innovations in telecommunications (*source*: Nilles *et al.*, 1976 p. 12)

have only been a few serious attempts to introduce home working or satellite office teleworking arrangements in the USA, Sweden, France, West Germany, and the United Kingdom. One recent estimate suggested only some 3500 employees were so far involved in these schemes, in posts ranging from managers to typists (Jaeger and Durrenberger, 1987, cited by Daniels, 1988).

Moss (1986) goes further and argues that new communications technologies have not led to the decline of cities, but rather enhanced the importance of a handful of cities which are at the hubs of the information networks. He suggests (p. 38) that:

Although many so called futurists argue that the electronic cottage will replace the office building and that teleconferencing will replace the in-person meeting, such speculation merely demonstrates a poor understanding of urban functions, a willingness to assume that technological feasibility is equivalent to technological acceptability, and a disregard for the incremental and evolutionary process of technological innovation in organizations. . . . The 'wired city' has arrived, but it is orientated to the office, not the home.

There are, nevertheless, suggestions that the information revolution is leading to an increased in social and regional inequalities, dividing classes and regions into a dualistic society of the 'information rich' and the 'information poor'. For example, peripherality on both national and European scales is strongly associated with low levels of up-take of business telecommunications equipment (Gillespie and Hepworth, 1988).

A specific example of the spatial impact of information technology is in the organization of physical distribution by retailers. The use of electronic point of sale (EPOS) computer systems to link laser-scanning cash tills reading bar-coded products to the central administration and warehouse/distribution network have become commonplace in large stores.

With a full EPOS system, as goods are purchased by the consumer, within-store stock levels are adjusted, orders for deliveries are made automatically, goods are made ready for despatch from automated warehouses, fresh supplies to the warehouses are requested, and invoices are matched and paid by an automated accounting system. Moreover, up-to-date sales information is available on-line to management, and sales can be analysed line by line, store by store, region by region, and informed decisions regarding shelf allocation, stocking policy, product promotion, new store

location strategy etc, can be taken (Wrigley, 1988 p. 18).

The improved level of information such systems provide reduce the amount of stock which needs to be kept in the stores. For example, Tesco keeps only 24 hours' stock for some products. Purpose-built warehouses on industrial estates are a cheaper and more labour-efficient proposition than a multiplicity of stock points at retail outlets (Sparks, 1986).

Nevertheless, technological development, as Goddard (1980 p. 97) notes, 'is a necessary, though not sufficient, condition for locational change'. This is because there are major social and infrastructural constraints on the application of information technology. There are many social factors constraining the acceptance of new innovations. The uncertainty as to the number and kind of jobs and the conditions of work associated with the introduction of new technology can slow down the acceptance of information technology (Mandeville, 1983). For example, a switch to working from home would demand considerable adjustment for many employees and employers. For some, going to work is a source of social well-being as well as economic value. The nature of the urban infrastructure is another important factor limiting the speed with which new technologies diffuse. The investment in buildings, homes, and the physical transport system cannot be abandoned overnight. Many offices, for example, built in the last twenty years were not designed to take the amount of wiring, heat, and noise insulation required to use the modern technology (Bateman, 1985). The consequence of ignoring these social and infrastructural constraints is that 'the speed of diffusion of new technologies is often grossly overestimated' (Goddard, 1980 p. 103).

Even ignoring the rate of change there is far from general agreement over the nature of the spatial consequences of introducing IT. For example, a study of the United Kingdom banking sector found that it was becoming spatially more concentrated as a result of using information technology (Marshall and Bachter, 1984). However, the study suggested that the prospects are for a more dispersed location pattern as new technologies such as electronic funds transfer, autobanking, and point of sale facilities become more widespread. The difficulty of generalizing about spatial outcomes is also emphasized in a Canadian study of the impact of innovations in computer networks. Hepworth (1986) shows that these innovations can lead to both centralized and decentralized patterns of direct production and office activity. Indeed, Marshall (1984) shows that information technology can be used to support either the centralization or decentralization of office work. He shows how in Unilever, a decentralized organization, information technology has encouraged the decentralization of routine functions, while in the more tightly controlled Ford, the mechanization of accounts has been associated with the centralization of administration at key sites. This spatial indeterminancy in the impact of technological change tends to support the arguments of the institutionalists rather than the regulationists (see Section 6.1).

6.4 Summary

- New technologies, in the form of product and process innovations, have the capability to revolutionize the manner in which businesses and governments operate, create new goods and services, and change the everyday basis of work, leisure, and consumption. However, the origin, spread, and impact of new technologies are spatially uneven and the use of outdated technologies may constrain the ability of organizations to adapt to changed economic conditions.
- The product life cycle model illustrates the typical stages many products go through and the nature of the associated production processes, but the application of the model to interpreting the international and intranational locational evolution of businesses is more problematic and limited.
- Attempts have also been made to relate spatial patterns of economic activity to the regimes of capitalist accumulation, which describe the development of the production–labour process over several centuries of industrialization, but others argue that the spatial outcomes of technological change are indeterminate.
- Technology is a permissive factor. It facilitates changes in the spatial pattern of economic activity and the level and nature of employment, but it does not determine them. The key to understanding the effects of technological

changes is the broader social, economic, and institutional context in which the adoption of a new technology occurs.
- Both high-technology industries and R. & D. activities have concentrated location patterns, though there are significant variations in the way different technologically-oriented complexes have originated and developed. The *location factors approach* to explaining the location and evolution of high-technology industry emphasizes that there are only a few places where the combination of factors favourable to the growth of high technology production are found; whereas the *structuralist* approach argues that it is necessary to examine historically how changes in the technology and organization of production have interacted with the existing geographical pattern of production opportunities to produce unique outcomes in specific places.
- There are also different approaches to examining the spread of technological innovations in agriculture. The *adoption perspective* is a demand-based approach which lays stress on the personal characteristics of individuals that affect their propensity to adopt new ideas; whereas the *diffusion agency perspective* focuses on the role of different agencies in promoting or restricting the spread of innovations. In contrast the *society perspective* emphasizes the relationship between agricultural innovations and society. The nature of the society affects the kinds of innovations which are developed and the rates of acceptance; while the pattern of innovation diffusion has important social, economic, and environmental consequences.
- The social and infrastructural constraints on the spread of new technologies are well illustrated by examining the spatial impact of information technology. The speed of implementation of IT is affected for example by the social acceptability of the new ideas and the ability of office buildings to take the necessary wiring and insulation. The limited evidence available on the spatial consequences of IT suggests that they are probably both centralizing and decentralizing.

This difficulty in generalizing about spatial outcomes gives a further illustration of a major theme of this chapter that technological change is a social process, both in its causes and its effects.

'The determining factor is not the technology but how we choose to use the technology' (Mandeville, 1983 p. 70). An important factor influencing the way that technology is used is the organizational context in which it is introduced. This is the subject of the next chapter.

7

The Organizational Context

Major changes in the organizational structure of businesses and industries have been occurring in recent years which have profound implications for the spatial pattern of economic activity. Prime among these changes has been the growth of 'big business'. The increased concentration of economic activities in the hands of large multi-establishment, often multinational corporations, some of which have a spending power larger than significant nation states, means that their investment and disinvestment decisions may have critical impacts on communities hundreds or thousands of kilometres distant from the board room in which the decisions are made. However, despite the growing dominance of big business, many developed market economies have also witnessed a resurgence in small businesses in the last two decades. The rate at which new firms are formed varies significantly from place to place.

Associated with these changes in the size of organizations are important changes in the way in which production is organized, which have far-reaching implications for the location of economic activity and land-use patterns. As companies grow many become vertically integrated as more of the different stages of production are incorporated within the same enterprise. More recently, a counter trend towards disintegration is becoming apparent in some companies as they divest activities which are seen as marginal to the main business of the company, or they subcontract selected specialized activities. This trend towards disintegration is often linked to the development of flexible production methods. Several authorities have suggested that whereas vertical integration has contributed to the spatial dispersion of economic activities, vertical disintegration and flexible production is encouraging the reagglomeration of selected economic activities, sometimes in new locations. However, as with the impact of technological change (Chapter 6), cau-

tion is needed in generalizing about the spatial effects of organizational changes. Both need to be interpreted in the context of the changing social, economic, and political situation which may stimulate or constrain the implementation of technological and organizational changes.

Examining the nature of organizations is important because different types of organization often tend to exhibit different types of locational behaviour. In Chapter 5 it was suggested that firms producing small-scale, unstandardized outputs are more likely to agglomerate with related activities than other types of organization; while in the last chapter it was observed that in studies of the spatial diffusion of agricultural innovations farmers who were innovators had different personal characteristics from those who were late in adopting new innovations. However, the relationship between the organization of businesses and industries and the location of economic activity does not operate only in one direction. Indeed, where a business or industry is located can have a significant influence on the way in which it is organized. For example, branch plants in remote areas tend to be larger and more autonomous than those in more accessible areas (Watts, 1981). Vertical integration may also be encouraged by relative remoteness. For instance, Scott (1987b) notes a tendency for branch plants in peripheral areas and the Third World to be more vertically integrated than branch plants elsewhere.

The main aims of this chapter are, first, to outline the ways in which businesses and industries are organized and have evolved over the last few decades; secondly, to examine the main features of the spatial patterns of organizations; and thirdly, to assess the implications of the way businesses and industries are organized and have evolved for the location of economic activity. Discussion of location and land-use decision-making is left until Chapter 10.

7.1 The changing organization of businesses and industries

The organizations which are responsible for making location and land-use decisions vary from owner-manager firms to giant multinationals and from privately run businesses to government-owned organizations. Interest in the *geography of enterprise* began in the late 1950s and early 1960s (McNee, 1960; Krumme, 1969) and continues to be an important focus for research (Hayter and Watts, 1983; Healey and Watts, 1987). More recently a parallel interest has developed in the geographical consequences of the organization of economic activity with analyses of topics such as segmented economies, vertical integration and disintegration, and flexible methods of organizing production. This section outlines the main a-spatial characteristics of the changing organization of businesses and industries which are needed to understand the following discussion of the economic geography of organizations and organizational change.

Big business

Probably the most significant feature of the organization of businesses in the twentieth century is the dominance of large companies. The twenty largest industrial groupings in the world in 1986 listed in Table 7.1 had sales larger than the gross national product of many significant nation states, such as New Zealand, Ireland, Kuwait, and Portugal. The top three industrial groupings in the world in the late 1980s—Mitsui & Co, Mitsubishi, and C. Itoh—are all Japanese general trading companies, or *sogo shosha*, which own thousands of commercial, financial, and industrial businesses across the globe. Large business organizations differ in their nature from small organizations in three main ways (Watts, 1980a). First, they tend to be impersonal, hierarchically organized bureaucracies in which ownership is separated from control. Secondly, many are also multi-site organizations, often with facilities in more than one country. The third difference is that many large businesses are involved in several different industries.

Big businesses have grown and come to dominate all the main sectors of developed market economies. They are the 'prime movers' (Lloyd and Reeve, 1982) in local and national economies. For example, in 1909 it took more than 2000 firms to produce half the manufacturing output in the United Kingdom; by 1970 it took 140 firms (Prais, 1976). There are indications, however, that the trend towards an increase in the concentration of output in the top 100 manufacturing firms ceased in the mid-1970s in both the United Kingdom and the USA (Prais, 1976; Shutt and Whittington, 1987; Watts, 1987). Big business also dominates much of the service sector. As a result of mergers and acquisitions the multiple retail chains now have a commanding lead over other kinds of retail outlet, particularly in Britain (Dawson and Kirby, 1980). Though not immediately obvious, many of the familiar High Street shops are owned by a handful of companies (Table 7.2). The market share of the multiples in the United Kingdom has doubled in the past twenty-five years; while their share of the retail grocery sector rose from 22 per cent in 1950 to 63 per cent in 1981 (Sheffield City Council, 1987).

Large businesses also seem to be increasing in importance in agriculture, although the topic requires more research. In the late 1970s Smith (1980) identified almost 800 primarily agricultural businesses in the United States with annual sales of more than a million dollars. Several of these 'superfarms' had sales of over $100 million dollars. For example, G. Boswell Co., based in Los Angeles, controlled 155 000 acres (62 753 ha). Their principal activities involved general crop farms, cotton ginning, wholesaling cotton, general livestock farms, crop harvesting, manufacturing cotton seed oil, and cattle feeding and ranching. The development of *agribusinesses*, in which agriculture is being incorporated into sectors which deal with both the provision of farm inputs (e.g. chemicals, feedstuffs, and machinery) and the processing and marketing of agricultural produce (Healey and Ilbery, 1985a), suggests that there are significant economies to be achieved through vertical integration.

An important feature of large businesses is that they operate more or less as integrated corporate systems. This suggests that how an organization is structured may be a key factor influencing not only the flow of information within a business, but also the ways in which it can change and adjust the location of its activities (Chandler, 1963; Watts, 1980a; Chapman and Walker, 1987). Smaller companies are often organized on

TABLE 7.1 The world's twenty largest business organizations by turnover ranked against the largest countries by gross national product, 1986

Rank	Country/company	$US billion	Rank	Country/company	$US billion
1	United States	4 223	31	Argentina	73
2	Japan	1 560	32	Nigeria	66
3	Germany, Federal Republic	736	33 =	Norway	65
			33 =	Nissho Iwai (Japan)[a]	65
4	France	594	35	Denmark	64
5	United Kingdom	503	36	Ford Motor (USA)	63
6	Italy	489	37 =	Finland	60
7	Canada	361	37 =	South Africa	60
8	China	316	39	Algeria	58
9	Brazil	251	40	Turkey	57
10	India	227	41	British Petroleum (UK)	55
11	Australia	191	42	Yugoslavia	54
12	Spain	188	43	Venezuela	52
13	Mexico	149	44	International Business Machines (USA)	51
14	Netherlands	146			
15	Mitsui & Co (Japan)[a]	123	45	Toyota Motor (Japan)	45
16	Mitsubishi (Japan)[a]	116	46	Sears Roebuck (USA)	44
17	Switzerland	115	47	Thailand	43
18	Sweden	111	48	Mobil (USA)	42
19	C. Itoh (Japan)[a]	108	49	ENI-Ente Nazionale Idrocarburi (Italy)	41
20	General Motors (USA)	103			
21 =	Korea	98	50	Egypt	38
21 =	Sunitomo (Japan)[a]	98	51 =	Hong Kong	37
23	Belgium	91	51 =	Greece	37
24	'Shell' Transport & Trading/Royal Dutch Petroleum (UK/Netherlands)	89	53 =	Daimler-Benz (West Germany)[a]	36
25	Saudi Arabia	83	53 =	Columbia	36
26	Indonesia	82	55 =	General Electric (USA)	35
27	Marubeni (Japan)[a]	81	55 =	Toyo Menka Kaisha (Japan)[a]	35
28	Poland	78	55 =	Pakistan	35
29	Austria	76	55 =	Nippon Telegraph Q Telephone (Japan)	35
30	Exxon (USA)	75			

[a] A *sogo shosha* is an umbrella organization providing integrated marketing, financing, transport, and information services for their member companies.
Sources: Based on *Times 1000 1987/8* p. 7 and World Bank (1988 pp. 222–3).

TABLE 7.2 Two large retail groups in the United Kingdom

A SEARS HOLDINGS	
(i) *Retailing*	(iii) *Footwear retailing*:
Olympic Sports	British Shoe Corporation
Mappin & Webb	Freeman Hardy & Willis
Wallis	Saxone
Fosters	Lilley & Skinner
Selfridges	Trueform
Dormie	Curtess
Miss Selfridges	Dolcis
Garrard	Roland Cartier
The New Lewis's	Manfield
Supra Sports	Shoe City
Miss Erika	Tiptoe
Adams	
Millets	
Esquires	
(ii) *Betting offices*:	(iv) *Motor sales*:
William Hill	SMT
	Shaw & Kilburn
	Gilbert Rice

B   BURTON GROUP
Peter Robinson
Principles
Principles for Men
Evans Collection
Dorothy Perkins
Topman/Fenton/Studio
Top Shop
Burton Retailer
Jackson
Collier
Chapman

Debenhams Group:
Debenhams
Harvey Nicholls

Sources: *Who owns whom 1988*; company annual reports.

functional lines with, for example, separate production, marketing, and financial departments (Fig. 7.1*a*), while larger, more diversified companies may have separate divisions for each of their main activities (Fig. 7.1*b*). Many multinational companies operate territorial divisions, for example, Ford of Europe (Fig. 7.1*c*), while a company which has several unrelated businesses (a conglomerate) may choose a holding company structure (Fig. 7.1*d*). Many larger companies adopt a combination of these organizational types. Despite the complexity, a tendency towards one type of organizational structure rather than another may have important spatial implications.

For example, a structure based on territorial divisions may result in solutions to spatial problems being sought within the region for which the division is responsible, whereas with a division based on products a solution may be sought on an interregional basis (Watts, 1980*a*; Section 7.3).

'Small is beautiful'?

Despite the dominance of big business there has been a revival of interest in the small firm sector in recent years from politicians, policy-makers, and academics. The main reason for the growth of interest in small firms has been an apparent

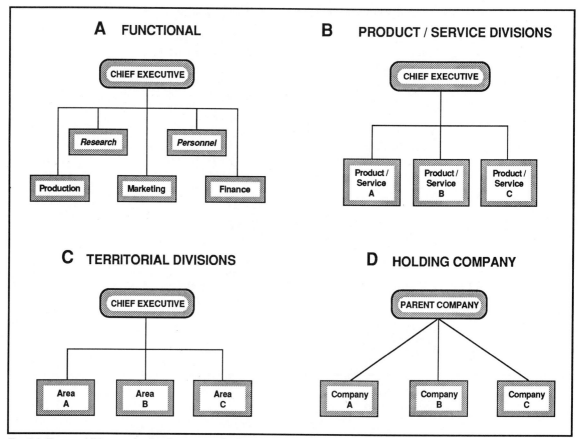

Fig 7.1 Four possible organizational structures for large businesses

revival in this sector of the economy in both Europe and North America (Birch, 1979; Keeble and Wever, 1986*a*). For example, the number of small manufacturing firms in the United Kingdom fell sharply between 1930 and 1960 (Fig. 7.2), but the decline ceased in the 1960s, and between 1970 and 1980 there was an increase of over 50 per cent in the number of manufacturing plants employing ten or less employees (Keeble, 1987). This reflects not only the contraction of establishments previously employing more than ten people, but also an increase in the rate of new firm formation. For instance, between 1974 and 1984 the number of new company registrations in all sectors of the British economy more than doubled (Mason, 1987*b*).

Keeble and Wever (1986*b*) identify three main groups of theories which they argue together provide a convincing explanation for the resurgence of new and small firms in Europe. The first is the *recession push* theory. This suggests that the increase in redundancies and unemployment and, probably more significantly, the increase in the perception of job instability and poor career prospects brought on by the deepening recession is the prime factor influencing the new firm revival (Gudgin, 1984). Large firm rationalization may also be related to this explanation, because their withdrawal from less profitable peripheral activities may have created market niches which could be taken over by small more flexible firms with lower overheads. The second explanation Keeble and Wever call the *income growth* theory. According to this explanation the substantial increase in household incomes since the mid-1960s has led to a significant demand for more varied and customized goods; a market which small firms can serve efficiently (Brusco, 1982; 1986). This is related to the third explanation, which involves *technological change* theory, because the changing pattern

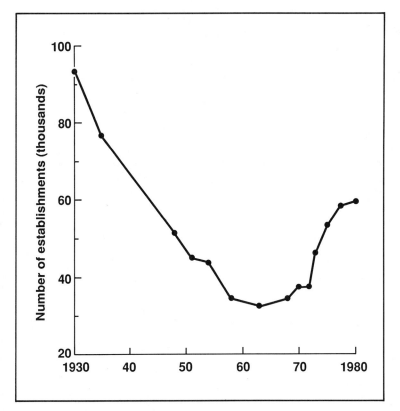

FIG 7.2 Small manufacturing establishments (ten employees or less) in the United Kingdom, 1930–80 (*source*: Keeble, 1987 p. 8)

of demand has encouraged the adoption of neo-Fordist flexible technologies. These, it is asserted, are particularly suitable for small firms, because they enable them to respond quickly to changing market demands and to fill small market niches economically (Piore and Sabel, 1984). Equally it may be argued that the development of microelectronic technologies, associated with the fifth Kondratieff cycle (Chapter 2.1), is 'creating a host of new product, process and market opportunities which are particularly suited to exploitation by small firms set up by skilled or research-based entrepreneurs' (Keeble and Wever, 1986b pp. 13–14).

Despite the recent revival of small firms in the manufacturing sector small businesses are much more significant in the agricultural and service sectors. In the former, family farms, most of which are small, continue to be the most important business units, despite some doubts about their ability to survive (Wallace, 1985). There are a variety of reasons for the continued importance of small farms, including government support measures and agricultural reform policies, as well

as the lack of alternative employment in more isolated regions and the importance farmers place on independence and the farming 'way of life' (Ilbery, 1985a). Many small farms are run on a part-time basis (Mage, 1982; Gasson, 1988). In Europe an important group of part-time farmers are the *worker-peasants* who commute to urban industrial jobs, yet still manage to run their farms in the evenings and at weekends (Franklin, 1971). Although the number of these 'five o'clock' farmers is on the wane, there has been a general increase in part-time farming in Western Europe (Ilbery, 1986). For example, in the United Kingdom the percentage of part-time farmers rose from 23 to 27 per cent between 1971 and 1979 (Gasson, 1982). Part-time farming has also been increasing in the United States. In 1940, only 15 per cent of farm operators had 100 or more days of off-farm employment. By 1978, 44 per cent of farmers worked off the farm for 100 or more days and 92 per cent of farm families had some type of non-farm income in 1979 (Albrecht and Murdock, 1984). Interestingly, the growth of part-time farming is not, with the exception of hobby farming (Layton, 1979; T. L. Daniels, 1986), due to people entering the industry, but the result of farmers who previously worked full-time finding alternative jobs to supplement their income (Healey and Ilbery, 1985b).

The majority of new and small businesses are in the service sector. For example, data on new firm formation in the United Kingdom show that over 70 per cent of new businesses registering for value added tax (VAT) between 1980 and 1983 were in services (Ganguly, 1984). There is, nevertheless, considerable inter-industry variation in the significance of small firms. One study found that the largest 232 hairdressing establishments in the United Kingdom accounted for only 5.5 per cent of total turnover, while the 10 largest firms in television rental accounted for 80 per cent of the rental business (Aaronovitch and Sawyer, 1975). This variation is emphasized by a more recent study which showed that the turnover of small firms as a percentage of all firms in the sector varied between 63 per cent for catering and 2 per cent for finance (Mendham and Barnock, 1982, cited by Howells and Green, 1986). Not all service industries have, however, participated in the small firm revival. Retailing stands out as one activity in which both the number of small businesses in the United Kingdom and their share of total sales have continued to decrease in the face of rising concentration (Mason, 1987b).

The segmented economy

The dominance of large companies and the revival of small businesses has led to an interest in segmented economies 'characterised by a variety of firms ranging from large multinational organisations to the small back-street workshop' (Watts, 1987 p. 52). Several authorities have drawn a distinction between the handful of large firms and the mass of small firms operating in an economy. Averitt (1968), for example, distinguishes between *centre* and *periphery* firms, while Galbraith (1967) identifies *planning system* and *market system* firms. An application of this idea of a dual economy to the British brewing industry is shown in Figure 7.3. In agriculture large and small (often part-time) farming businesses are surviving at the expense of the 'disappearing middle', which is characterized by increasing indebtedness (Healey and Ilbery, 1985b). The dual-economy model is, nevertheless,

a simplification and it is perhaps best to think of businesses being ranked along a size continuum with the large and small businesses positioned at opposite ends.

Large businesses have several advantages over small ones (Pratten, 1986). Economies of scale are the most important. Although the plant scale economies have reduced in significance with the development of flexible methods of organizing production, the company scale economies have increased in significance as businesses have grown to serve the enlarged markets which have arisen as barriers to trade have shrunken and transport and communications have improved. Large companies are also better able to meet the costs of product development and improvement than small ones, and may have access to more information about technology, markets, and strategies of rivals when deciding whether to adopt a project. Moreover they have advantages in risk-taking and may be able to obtain finance at a lower cost. In addition to the economies of scale there are also *economies of growth*. For example, Penrose (1959) argues that firms need to make use of their productive resources, particularly management. Hence once a project is completed it makes sense for the management which is released to be used to develop other projects which are perceived to be profitable. The economies of growth may encourage firms to grow beyond the point that releases any further economies of scale.

Despite the advantages of large businesses many small firms prosper, either because large firms benefit from their existence or because they operate in markets in which small firms can compete effectively. An important feature of the dual economy model is the *unequal interdependence* which exists between many large and small firms (Taylor and Thrift, 1982a; 1982b; 1983). One of the most striking elements of this interdependence lies in the material and information flows between the two systems. Many small firms are dependent on large firms for their markets or source of supplies, or because they act as subcontractors or franchisees (see Chapter 5.3). However, there are 'independent' small firms as well as 'dependent' ones (Tarling, 1981). Some independent firms serve small local or specialized markets, such as plumbers and hairdressers, or are able to exploit a new or unique product or process, such as in some aspects of computing and microelectronics; while others in, for example, furni-

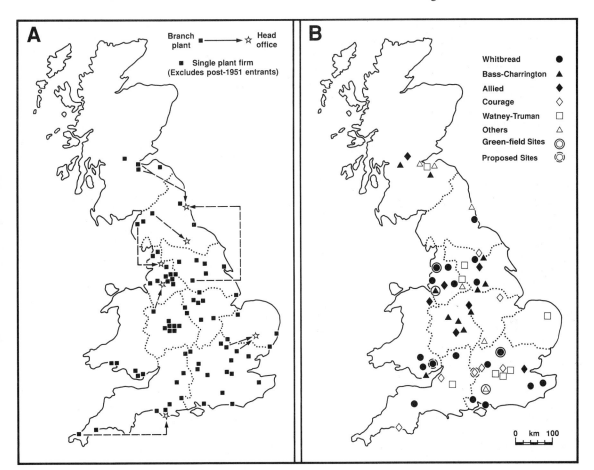

FIG 7.3 Dual economy in the British brewing industry, 1976: (*a*) market system firms; (*b*) planning system firms (*source*: Watts, 1980 pp. 173, 176)

ture, clothing, and printing, compete with large firms by paying low wages and using often old equipment.

Large and small businesses vary, of course, in more than their unequal interdependence. In US agriculture, for example, larger farming businesses rely less on off-farm income, have a greater proportion of their production under contract, receive more money from the federal government for support of agricultural commodities, and are more capital intensive. Larger farming businesses also have higher debts, rely more heavily on cash-wage labour, have higher fixed costs, and are more bureaucratic in their organization (Vogeler, 1981).

These distinctions between different types of business help to stress that firms play different roles in the creation of the geography of economic activity. However, businesses not only vary in their size and in the roles they play, they also vary in the degree to which activities are integrated within companies and in the extent to which flexible methods of organizing production are used.

Vertical integration and disintegration

The extent to which different stages of production are integrated within the same organization varies from fully internal at one end, to free market transactions at the other, with subcontracting falling in between (Holmes, 1986). Whereas in agriculture some farms are becoming more integrated into the food chain as they are taken over by, or receive exclusive contracts from, food producers (Healey and Ilbery, 1985*a*); in manufacturing and some service industries there are indications that some large firms are becoming less integrated as they subcontract out more of their activities (Storper and Christopherson, 1987). The complexity of industrial organization is emphasized by the fact that in some sectors integration and disintegration are proceeding simultaneously. For example, the growth of speciality crop production in the Salinas Valley in California has led to many of the previously independent farmers becoming subcontractors for the larger firms and shippers. However, at the same time, services, which previously the farmers undertook for themselves, such as soil testing, pest and weed control, well drilling, and irrigation system development and maintenance, are increasingly being taken over by more efficient specialized producer service subcontractors (FitzSimmons, 1986).

The economies of vertical integration, or the *internal economies of scope* as they are sometimes called, are such that: 'A firm will tend to expand until the costs of organizing an extra transaction within the firm become equal to the costs of carrying out the same transaction by means of an exchange on the open market' (Coase, 1937 p. 395; quoted by Scott, 1987*b* p. 219). For example, many steel companies are integrated, with rolling mills and steel furnaces on the same sites, because it is cheaper to use molten steel than steel ingots. Sometimes there are also significant managerial economies with vertical integration. Quality control, for instance, may be easier where related activities are under the same managerial supervision (Scott, 1983*b*). The converse of this argument suggests that *vertical disintegration* will occur where it is cheaper to buy in a product or service than it is to produce it in-house. This is likely to apply where markets are competitive. For instance, law firms typically use outside printing services, because the open markets in printing services are usually very efficient (Scott, 1987*b*).

Several research workers have suggested that disintegration of production is increasing in importance (Bagnasco, 1981; FitzSimmons, 1986; Storper and Christopherson, 1987; Scott, 1988). Some of them see it as part of a broader trend towards *production decentralization* (Murray, 1983; Cooke and Rosa Pires, 1985), or *fragmentation*, which Shutt and Whittington (1987) suggest is becoming more important among large firms. One of the most frequent reasons for this is

to reduce the risks of fluctuating demand, and is a strategy followed by large motor vehicle firms and by large speciality crop farms which cope with cyclical demand by subcontracting (Friedman, 1977; FitzSimmons, 1986; see also Chapter 5.3).

The fragmentation of large companies into separate ownership units may also result from *horizontal disintegration*, where the specialized firms are involved in the same activities as the integrated companies. This is common where dual labour markets exist (see Chapter 4.3), because it can pay large unionized firms using expensive 'primary' labour to subcontract work to firms using cheaper 'secondary' labour. This situation is frequent in the clothing industry (Chapter 12.2) and is widespread among several industries in parts of Italy, particularly in areas of the 'Third Italy', such as Emilia-Romagna, around Bologna (Brusco, 1982). Large firm policies which encourage franchising and management buy-outs also contribute to disintegration (Mason and Harrison, 1985; Wright *et al.*, 1984; Lovejoy, 1988). However, Keeble and Wever (1986*b*) suggest that the deliberate fragmentation of large companies is a minor factor accounting for the increase in the number of small firms and they point to evidence from surveys of new firms which show that a minority are dependent on large firms for their markets.

It has often been suggested that the development of co-operatives might reduce the influence of big business in local economies. However, co-operative ventures have not flourished, at least in manufacturing, with the notable exception of Mondragon in the Basque area of Spain. By 1980 the complex had 80 industrial co-operatives employing 18 000 members (Bradley and Gelb, 1983). The success of this venture has been attributed to the cultural environment of this part of Spain, in particular the strong sense of identity among the minority Basques (Thomas and Logan, 1982).

Flexible production

One factor which has made disintegration easier and, as has already been argued, has helped small firms to prosper, is the growth in importance of flexible methods of organizing production. This topic has received much attention recently both in the popular and academic press, but as with the phenomenon of high technology, discussed in the last chapter, there is disagreement over its nature and consequences and some exaggeration of its extent. Gertler (1988) suggests that there are a variety of uses of the term 'flexible', which span a range of scales from the individual machine on the shop (or office) floor to the way that an economy and society is organized.

1. *Flexible machines.* These significantly reduce the cost penalty for short production runs and batches, because flexible machines, such as robots and computer numerically controlled (CNC) machine tools, can be quickly reprogrammed to produce a variety of new products.

2. *Flexible manufacturing systems (FMS).* These result where a number of flexible machines are linked together. They often integrate various phases of the production process, including design (using computer-aided design or (CAD)), manufacture (using computer-aided manufacture or (CAM)) and distribution. The latter may include the use of *just-in-time* delivery systems, which reduce both the size of the parts inventory held by the assembling firm and the length of time that inventory is held, though just-in-time systems may be introduced independently of FMS (Sayer, 1986*b*).

3. *Flexible specialization and integration.* This describes the ability of firms to respond to fluctuations in market demand and to adopt new products quickly (Piore and Sabel, 1984). This is in part dependent on their use of flexible machines and FMS, but is also a function of the flexible use of labour. The latter involves both workers performing a greater variety of tasks and firms making greater use of overtime, part-time employment, and temporary workers.

4. *Flexible accumulation.* This, following Aglietta (1979), refers to a new regime of capitalist accumulation with a shift from Fordist to neo-Fordist methods (Chapter 2.1 and 4.3). As well as the intrafirm changes referred to above, it includes the increased use of subcontracting (see Chapter 5.3) and the formation of flexible strategic alliances (Cooke, 1988).

Clearly the *flexible hierarchy* covers both specific technologies and more general methods of organization and emphasizes the close links between much of the material covered in this chapter and the previous one on technological change.

Gertler (1988) argues that these recent changes in the way production is organized represent the intensification and development of historical trends established long ago. This view sees flexible forms of production coexisting with, rather than replacing, mass-production-based Fordism. According to Gertler, the adoption of these organizational forms is not as widespread or as easy to implement as is sometimes implied (see also Meegan, 1988). Indeed he suggests that the clearest examples are concentrated in a single industry—motor vehicles—and even in this industry he cites a Canadian study (Fertey *et al.*, 1986), which, though it found evidence of the adoption of many specific flexible technologies in isolation, as well as extensive use of just-in-time, could find no successful applications of full-scale FMS technology.

Nevertheless, despite Gertler and Meegan's salutary warnings about exaggerating the extent to which flexible production methods are being applied, it does seem that the relative importance of Fordist and neo-Fordist methods of production organization is beginning to shift towards the latter (see also Chapter 15.2). Intriguingly, several research workers have suggested that the disintegration of production and the adoption of flexible production is encouraging the spatial reconcentration of economic activity, although the necessity for this has also been questioned (Section 7.3). Before turning to the effects of these, and other organizational forms on the location of economic activity, some of the spatial patterns of the organizations themselves are examined.

7.2 Spatial patterns of organizations

This section follows the structure used at the beginning of the last one by examining selected examples of the spatial patterns of both large and small businesses. The large business section begins with some comments on the geography of agribusiness; goes on to examine how the spatial organization of large companies tend to be organized in locational hierarchies; and ends with a discussion of the geography of what is probably the most significant organizational form of the twentieth century, the multinational corporation. The discussion of the geography of small firms focuses on spatial variations in the formation of new businesses and their subsequent performance. The section concentrates on new and small firms in the manufacturing and, to a lesser extent, service sectors. The geography of small and part-time farms is well reviewed elsewhere (Mage, 1982; Ilbery, 1985a; Gasson, 1988).

Agribusinesses

Spatial variations are apparent in the distribution of agribusinesses at both the international and intranational scales (Healey and Ilbery, 1985b). For example, the growth of agribusinesses is more developed in the USA than in the United Kingdom (Smith, 1980; Wallace and Smith, 1985). Large American companies, like Tenneco and Taggares, are involved in most of the stages in the food chain, from the production of seeds, the farming of the land, and the processing, storage, packaging, and marketing of produce, to the distribution and retailing of food. In the United Kingdom, by contrast, food processors are rarely directly involved in farming the land. The lower levels of agribusiness development in the United Kingdom reflect the higher cost of land, the difficulty of obtaining significant economies of scale in farming (Bowers, 1985; Bowler, 1985b; Symes and Marsden, 1985) and the fact that developments in food processing and marketing occurred when a highly commercialized farming class was already well established (Newby and Utting, 1981). Nevertheless, though the level of direct *ownership* of farms by food processing companies is less in Britain, there is a trend towards increased *control* of agricultural production by the food processing firms contracting farmers to produce exclusively for them (Chapter 5.1).

The evidence for spatial variations in agribusinesses within countries is less clear, although it would be reasonable to assume that as agribusinesses are more frequently involved in some agricultural enterprises (such as broilers, sugar beet, vegetables for processing, and seed crops) than others (such as field crops), their distribution will to an extent reflect spatial variations in the patterns of these enterprises. Some support for the uneven distribution of agribusinesses is given by research into the industrialization of agriculture in the United States by Gregor (1982). Using a composite index of industrialization based on scale (size of the operation) and intensity (measures of input, e.g. capital, labour, and energy) he found that the pattern of agricultural industrialization was a concentrated one. It

reached its highest levels in the Middle West, around the metropolitan core in the North-East, the valleys in the Pacific North-West, southern Florida, portions of the Mississippi alluvial valley, parts of the Mid-South, the Snake River farming area of Idaho and the west Texas High Plains.

Locational hierarchies

The different functions of large business organizations, such as administration, R. & D., and production, are often located in different places, reflecting the varying locational requirements of the different activities. Although such *locational hierarchies* are apparent in some agribusinesses they are most developed in large organizations in the mining, manufacturing, and service sectors. Figure 7.4 shows the distribution of employment in Cadbury Schweppes in the United Kingdom in 1984. It had its head office in central London, a separate R. & D. unit in Reading, and 32 main manufacturing units in a variety of divisions scattered around the country, the largest of which was the Bournville complex in Birmingham. The ability of organizations to operate successfully at several separate locations, some of which may be in different countries, has been made easier by recent improvements in transportation and communications (Chapter 5.2).

Simon (1960, p. 40) refers to the structure of modern business organizations as 'a three layered cake', where the bottom layer consists of the basic work processes, the middle layer involves day-to-day administration, and the top layer is where the control and top-level decisions are located (Fig. 7.5). The top two layers have much the same locational requirements, whether the organization is a heavy engineering firm or a retail company. The top layer typically requires an information-rich environment where frequent face-to-face contact outside the organization is possible, while the second layer, though not needing frequent face-to-face contact, usually requires good access to communications facilities and a pool of 'white-collar' workers to employ as clerks, secretaries, typists, and so forth. On the other hand, the bottom layer varies in its locational requirements, depending on the kind of product or service being provided. For example, whereas a manufacturer of 'hi-fi' equipment may emphasize access to a pool of cheap, semi-skilled labour

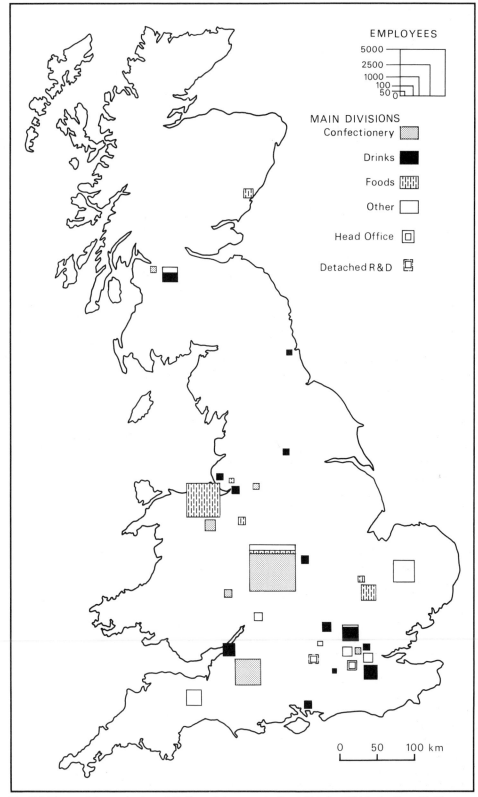

FIG 7.4 The spatial organization of Cadbury Schweppes in Great Britain, 1984 (only sites with 50 or more employees shown) (*source*: Healey and Watts, 1987 p. 152)

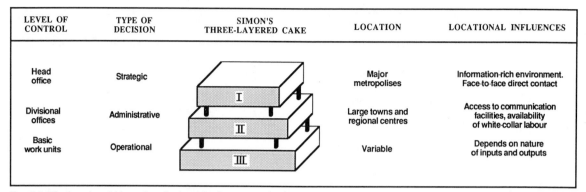

FIG 7.5 The locational hierarchy of a large business organization

(Chapter 4.3), an insurance broker establishing a chain of offices is likely to consider the potential number of customers for each office (Chapter 5.3), and a company establishing a R. & D. unit may choose a site close to a residentially attractive area for scientists and technicians in reasonable proximity to its head office (Chapter 6.2).

The aggregate effect of these locational hierarchies is to produce distinctive types of *spatial division of labour*—i.e. where different activities and types of jobs are located (Chapter 4.3). For example, within countries there is a tendency for top-level decisions to concentrate at *control centres*, such as London, New York, Toronto, and Tokyo. However, not all activities have the same control centres, for instance, Hartford, Connecticut is an important centre for life insurance companies in the USA, while Detroit is an important location for the head offices of major manufacturing companies (Dicken and Lloyd, 1981). A similar spatial division of labour is also apparent at the international scale. Hymer (1979)

argues that whereas production activities are found throughout the world, the lower-level administration is concentrated in large cities, and the long-term strategic planning functions are concentrated in the metropolises. Although there is clearly some validity in Hymer's model, it oversimplifies the complexity of the modern global organization of economic activity. Different types of geographical area contain different mixes of corporate units (Fig. 7.6). Major metropolises, like London, New York, and Tokyo, do not only contain the major corporate headquarters but are also the location for many lower-level control functions and production units (Dicken, 1986).

Multinationals

The spread of multinational enterprise is unquestionably one of the most important recent developments in the geography of the world economy. They are so important that Holland (1976*a*) coined the term *mesoeconomic* sector to

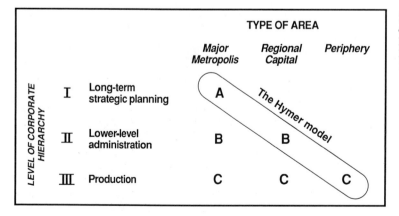

FIG 7.6 Relationships between corporate and geographical hierarchies in a spatial division of labour (*source*: Morgan and Sayer, 1983*b* p. 6)

describe their significance between the micro- and macro-sectors of the economy. Between 20 and 25 per cent of total world production outside the centrally planned economies is accounted for by multinationals, or transnational corporations as they are also called. Their share of world trade is even higher. For example, almost one-third of all United Kingdom exports in 1980 went to 'related concerns', while almost half of all United States imports in 1977 were from establishments 'related by ownership'. Most *foreign direct investment* (FDI) is in manufacturing and extractive industries, but paralleling this has been an internationalization of many business services such as advertising agencies, banks, insurance firms, car rental chains, and hotel groups (Dicken, 1986; Daniels, 1985a; see also Chapter 13.2).

Multinational investment, contrary to some popular thought, is concentrated in developed countries and this dominance is increasing. In 1967, 31 per cent of the world's FDI was located in the developing countries; by 1975 this share had fallen to 26 per cent. By the late 1970s not only was three-quarters of FDI in the developed market economies it was also highly concentrated in a few countries (Dicken, 1986). In 1975 44 per cent of total world FDI was in four countries—Canada, USA, United Kingdom, and West Germany. Not surprisingly, the main source countries are also in the developed world. The USA continues to dominate, but along with the United Kingdom is declining relatively, while West Germany and Japan are increasingly important sources of FDI. There are indications, however, that a new wave of investment may be starting with the emergence of multinationals based in developing market economies, such as Hong Kong, South Korea, Brazil, and Mexico (Chapter 14). Nearly 10 per cent of the top 500 non-US-based corporations in the world are based in developed countries (Thrift, 1986). State-owned enterprises from the USSR and Eastern Europe are also beginning to invest abroad, though as yet only in relatively small amounts (McMillan, 1987).

Three main types of overseas investment by firms may be recognized (Dicken, 1986):

1. *Market-oriented investments.* These are the most important type of FDI for manufacturing and service industries.
2. *Supply-oriented investments.* These have a long history, indeed many of the early overseas investments by British, continental European, and American firms in the late nineteenth and early twentieth centuries were to ensure raw material supplies.
3. *Cost-oriented investments.* These are a relatively recent phenomena which seek to reduce the costs of production by, for example, locating in low-wage regions.

Given the variety in the nature, patterns, and motives for FDI it is, perhaps, unreasonable to expect a general theory to explain all FDI. For example, in the last Chapter (Section 6.3), the discussion of the application of the product life cycle to understanding the spread of manufacturing production overseas from developed countries concluded that, though useful, the concept could not explain all types of international production. Dunning (1979; 1980) attempts to get round this problem of explaining the diversity of FDI by drawing on several different theories—the theory of the firm, organizational theory, trade theory, and location theory—to provide a framework within which specific cases can be examined. According to Dunning, a firm will engage in international production when three conditions are present:

1. A firm possesses certain specific advantages not possessed by competing firms of other nationalities, such as R. & D. capacity, or production or marketing expertise.
2. It must be more profitable for the firm to exploit its assets in overseas, rather than domestic locations. This may be, for example, because of access to markets, government restrictions on imports, or lower production costs, particularly labour costs.
3. Such advantages are most suitably exploited by the firm itself, rather than by selling or leasing them to other firms, because, for instance, the firm is vertically integrated.

These three conditions—ownership-specific advantages, location-specific advantages, and internalization advantages—combine together to influence different types of international production as illustrated in Table 7.3.

Another aspect of the diversity of multinational behaviour lies in the spatial patterns of their investments. Multinationals from different source countries tend to favour different parts of the

TABLE 7.3 Types of international production and their major determinants

Types of international production	Ownership advantages	Location advantages	Internalization advantages	Illustration of types of activity which favour MNEs
1. Resource-based	Capital, technology, access to markets	Possession of resources	To ensure stability of supply at right price. Control of markets	Oil, copper, tin, zinc, bauxite, bananas, pineapples, cocoa, tea
2. Import substituting manufacturing	Capital, technology, management and organizational skills; surplus R. & D. and other capacity, economies of scale; Trade marks	Material & labour costs, markets, government policy (with respect to barrier to imports, investment incentives, etc.)	Wish to exploit technology advantages, high transaction or information costs, buyer uncertainty, etc.	Computers, pharmaceuticals, motor vehicles, cigarettes
3. Export platform manufacturing	As above, but also access to markets	Low labour costs. Incentives to local production by host governments	The economies of vertical integration	Consumer electronics, textiles and clothing, cameras, etc.
4. Trade and distribution	Products to distribute	Local markets. Need to be near customers. After-sales servicing, etc.	Need to ensure sales outlets and to protect company's name	A variety of goods—particularly those requiring close consumer contact
5. Ancillary services	Access to markets (in the case of other foreign investors)	Markets	Broadly as for 2/4	Insurance, banking, and consultancy services
6. Miscellaneous	Variety—but include geographical diversification (airlines and hotels)	Markets	Various (see above)	Various kinds (a) Portfolio investment—properties (b) Where spatial linkages essential (airlines and hotels)

Source: Dunning (1980 p. 13).

world in which to locate their facilities. For example, whereas multinationals based in the United States, Germany, and the United Kingdom had about 70–80 per cent of all their investments in developed countries in 1971, Japanese multinationals had over 80 per cent of their investments in developing countries. The most important destinations for firms based in the United States were Canada and Mexico; United Kingdom-based firms favoured Australia, New Zealand, and South Africa; German companies tended to locate elsewhere in the European Community; while Japanese companies concentrated on Asia. Not that these patterns are static, for instance, the major growth areas for both British and Japanese companies are Western Europe and the United States (A. D. Morgan, 1978; Dicken, 1988). Watts (1987) suggests that these differences may be explained by a combination of factors, including spatial proximity, size of market, tariff barriers, production costs, and cultural affinity.

Interestingly, multinationals from different source countries often locate in different areas within the same countries. Thus in the United States, Japanese firms have favoured the West Coast, while British companies have placed most emphasis on the manufacturing belt of the North-East (McConnell, 1983); while in Britain, European companies have invested in East Anglia more than American companies (Watts, 1980c). Similar contrasts have also been found at the intraregional scale. For example, in Ireland, one study found that American firms were concentrated in development areas, industrial estates, and peripheral areas (although all of these reflected the success of one development—the Shannon Industrial Estate), while West German firms favoured locations in the small remote towns of south-western Ireland (Blackbourn, 1972).

There is also evidence that multinationals are sometimes located in different areas of the host countries compared to indigenous firms. Much multinational investment goes to the more developed core areas, such as the manufacturing belt of the United States, or the 'Golden Triangle' in north-west Europe (Hamilton, 1976; Holland, 1976b; Blackbourn, 1982; McConnell, 1983). The United Kingdom is in some ways an exception, as although there is some concentration in the South-East and East Anglia, three other regions—Wales, Scotland, and Northern Ireland—also have a greater share of employment in foreign establishments than would be expected from their share of all manufacturing employment (Watts, 1980a). The difference in the location of FDI in the United Kingdom may, in part, reflect the operation of regional policy in the 1960s, which encouraged many multinationals investing in Britain to establish their manufacturing plants in the development areas concentrated in the periphery of the country (Law, 1980). The areas favoured by multinationals may, however, change over time. For example, there are indications in the United States that during the 1970s foreign corporations were belatedly beginning to follow the decentralization pattern which was already well established by indigenous firms (McConnell, 1980; Chapter 16.1).

A second type of location in which multinationals are often concentrated is in areas just over the border from the source country. Thus a high proportion of United States FDI in Mexico and Canada is located close to the United States border, while West German investment in France is concentrated just over the border in the Alsace region, and Belgian investment is focused on adjoining Nord. There are exceptions, for example Canadian investment in the United States favours the South to the manufacturing belt, while Dutch companies are more likely to locate in the Paris region than along the Belgian border (Blackbourn, 1982). Nevertheless, it seems reasonable to conclude that the locational behaviour of multinationals in many countries may 'contribute to regional disequilibria' (Blackbourn, 1978 p. 125).

Small businesses

Whereas the effect of the growth of multi-plant and multinational businesses on economic development attracted the interest of research workers in the 1970s (see, for example, the review by Watts (1981) of branch plant economies), the realization in the 1980s of the resurgence of small firms (Section 7.1) shifted some attention towards an examination of their role in regional development (e.g. Keeble and Wever, 1986a; Storey and Johnson, 1987a). The precise impact of small firms on economic development varies from place to place because of marked spatial variations both in the rate at which new businesses are formed and in their subsequent performance.

However, the evidence for this is only partial because most of the research has concentrated on the geography of new firms in the manufacturing sector, particularly in the United Kingdom and to a lesser extent in Europe and North America. The amount of research on spatial variations in small firm performance, the geography of small firms in services, and in other parts of the world, is more limited (Mason and Harrison, 1985).

Unfortunately, the definition of both new and small firms is not clear-cut or unambiguous (Mason, 1983; 1987b). The main problems in identifying new firms involve establishing the start-up date and distinguishing new firms from branch plants. Moreover, the small size of most new firms means that their existence is sometimes overlooked in both official and academic surveys. The definition of a 'small' business also varies. The Bolton Committee, for instance, defined a small firm in manufacturing as one employing 200 or less, while a figure of 25 employees or less was used in considering construction and mining and quarrying, and varying limits based on turnover were used in most other sectors (Bolton, 1971).

Despite these difficulties, it is still possible to identify some important variations in the significance of small firms and in new firm formation rates at various spatial scales. For example, at the international scale the proportion of total manufacturing employment in small businesses (i.e. establishments employing less than 200 people) in the late 1970s in Japan (68 per cent) and Spain (64 per cent) was almost twice that in the United States (39 per cent), Austria (35 per cent) or the United Kingdom (30 per cent) (Ganguly and Povey, 1983). The spatial variations in new business start-ups may be illustrated by United Kingdom VAT registration statistics, which show that over the period 1980–6 the highest rates for all industries occurred in the South-East and the lowest rates were found in some of the peripheral regions—notably Scotland, Wales, and Northern Ireland (Table 7.4). There is also evidence from the East Midlands (Fothergill and Gudgin, 1982) and East Anglia (Gould and Keeble, 1984), that point to higher rates of new manufacturing firm formation in rural areas than in large towns and cities.

For most new enterprises the question of location is not explicitly considered. This is substantiated by a survey of over 300 new firms in the English East Midlands, which found that 81 per

TABLE 7.4 Regional distribution of new business registrations in the United Kingdom, 1980–1986

Region	New firm formation rate annual average, 1980–6
South-East	16.1
North-West	13.5
West Midlands	13.2
East Midlands	12.5
Yorkshire and Humberside	12.5
South-West	12.2
North	12.1
East Anglia	12.0
Scotland	11.4
Wales	10.7
Northern Ireland	8.2
United Kingdom	13.4

Source: Derived from *Regional Trends 1988* p. 135.

cent of the entrepreneurs had strong associations with the areas in which their firms were founded (Gudgin, 1978). The choice of the local area makes good economic sense, because local knowledge of potential suppliers, markets, premises, and employees reduces uncertainty. Also as many start in business on a part-time basis a location close to home is often essential. Moreover, the costs of establishing a new business means that few can afford at this critical stage to move to another area.

As most entrepreneurs establish their businesses locally, spatial variations in the formation of new firms are likely to be a reflection mainly of differences in the *supply of potential entrepreneurs* and the extent to which the *local environment* is conducive to starting new businesses. Neither of these elements is readily separated (Watts, 1987) and each is composed of several interrelated influences (Table 7.5).

A. *Supply of potential entrepreneurs*
1. *Industrial structure.* This is important for two reasons. First, most entrepreneurs have had previous contact with the industry in which they start their business; for example, in the East Midlands survey, Gudgin (1978) found that 85 per cent of entrepreneurs had previous experience of the same trade. Secondly, differences in barriers to entry, production technology, and market growth affect the propensity for new firm formation in different industries (Keeble and Wever, 1986b). In

TABLE 7.5 Factors influencing the rate of new firm formation

Factor	High rate of new firm formation
A *Supply of potential entrepreneurs*	
Industrial structure	Low entry barriers
Firm structure	Small firms
Occupational structure	High proportion non-manual occupations
Educational achievements	Highly qualified
B *Local environment*	
Access to capital	High level of owner-occupation
Access to markets	High regional income and industrial prosperity
Premises	Small premises available
Government policies	Awareness and good delivery
Attitude towards small business and self-employment	Favourable attitude to entrepreneurship; tradition of self-employment

both the East Midlands and Ireland the four manufacturing industries with the highest entry rates were wood, cork, brushes; furniture; printing; and plastics (O'Farrell and Crouchley, 1984) all of which have low barriers to entry.

2. *Firm size structure.* According to several surveys this has a more important influence on new firm formation than industrial structure, although firm size structure is, of course, related to the local industrial structure (Fothergill and Gudgin, 1982; Storey, 1982; Lloyd and Mason, 1984). These and other surveys have found that the rate at which new businesses are started is highest in areas dominated by small firms. This is because small firms provide a better training ground for potential entrepreneurs than large firms with their more hierarchical and occupationally segmented structures.

3. *Occupational structure and educational achievements.* The significance of these is less clear-cut. High rates of new firm formation have been found to be associated with regions with a high proportion of non-manual occupations (Whittington, 1984); while a study in East Anglia found that the high rate of new firm formation, especially in Cambridgeshire, reflected an unusually large proportion of highly qualified and educated entrepreneurs (Keeble and Gould, 1985). However, another study found no relationship between occupational structure and new firm formation in the East Midlands and the counties

of Tyne and Wear, Durham, and Cleveland (Gudgin and Fothergill, 1984). Doubt has also been expressed about the significance of educational qualifications outside the more modern and technologically sophisticated industries and especially in the non-manufacturing sectors (Storey, 1982).

B. *Local environment*

1. *Access to capital.* For some firms, access to venture capital may be an important influence on their formation and early success (see Chapter 4.4). Another, and perhaps more important factor, at least in the United Kingdom, is the regional variation in house prices, because many entrepreneurs use their homes as security against which to borrow money (Storey, 1982). High house prices in the South-East may make a contribution towards the high rate of new firm formation in that region. Supporting evidence is provided by Whittington (1984), who has shown that the rate of new firm formation in all sectors is related to the level of owner-occupation.

2. *Access to markets.* The size and growth of the local market is likely to be most important in the service sector, although the majority of surveys of new firms in manufacturing show that, at least initially, they also have a high degree of dependence on local markets (Keeble and Wever, 1986b). Within the United Kingdom the distribution of wealth and industrial prosperity again

favours new firm starting in the South-East (Storey, 1982; Mason, 1987*b*).

3. *Premises*. The evidence on the availability of premises suggests that the extent to which it is a constraining factor varies widely from, for example, 7 per cent of entrepreneurs who mentioned it as a problem in Manchester and Merseyside, to 70 per cent in the more prosperous area of south Hampshire (Lloyd and Mason, 1984).

4. *Government policies*. Several initiatives have been introduced in the United Kingdom in the last few years to promote the small firm sector, including the Loan Guarantee Scheme, the Business Expansion Scheme, the Small Engineering Firms Investment Scheme, and the Enterprise Allowance Scheme. Mason and Harrison (1985) show that firms in the South-East and East Anglia obtained more than their 'fair share' of the expenditure on each of these schemes. This, they suggest, reflects not only the greater degree of business dynamism in these regions, but also other factors, such as a greater local awareness and better delivery of the schemes.

5. *Attitude towards small business and self-employment*. This may help to account for both some international and some regional differences in business start-up rates (Keeble and Wever, 1986*b*). For example, Britain, where historically attitudes to entrepreneurship have been less favourable than in many other countries, has a low new firm formation rate (Gudgin, 1978). Some agriculturally based regions in Denmark (Illeris, 1986) and Italy (Brusco, 1986), which have a tradition of self-employment, are characterized by a high rate of new business start-ups; whereas South Wales, which, according to Morgan and Sayer (1985) is lacking an indigenous 'business class' of owners, managers, and entrepreneurs, has a low rate of formation of new firms.

Clearly there are a wide variety of factors influencing the geography of new firm formation. Despite the large number of new businesses which come into existence, only a very small proportion grow rapidly and many do not survive more than a few years. Drawing on work in the Northern region of the United Kingdom, Storey and Johnson (1987*b* p. 34) state that it appears that:

Out of every 100 manufacturing businesses which begin, 30 cease to trade within 2–3 years. A further 30 cease to trade over the next 7–8 years so that after a

decade only 40 businesses will survive. Of these 40 businesses, 4 will provide half the jobs.

This suggests that the spatial distribution of the few 'successful' firms is a more important contributor to regional welfare than spatial variations in new firm formation. As yet little work has been done on this topic, although in the United Kingdom there are indications, from examining small firm competition winners and companies on the Unlisted Securities Market, that they may be concentrated in southern England, particularly the South-East (Mason, 1985). This view is supported by evidence that small firms in the South-East have a much higher level of product innovation than their counterparts in peripheral regions (Thwaites, 1982; Oakey *et al.*, 1982), and, according to Hitchens and O'Farrell (1987), make products which are more price competitive, of higher quality, and more modern design than similar firms in Northern Ireland.

7.3 The changing organization of businesses and industries and the location of economic activity

It is clear from the discussion in the last section that spatial variations in the potential for establishing new businesses, the mixture of small and large businesses, and the kind of functions undertaken by different units within large organizations inevitably have an important impact on the location of economic activity. In this section the relationship between the organization of businesses and industries and the location of economic activity is explored in more detail through a selective examination of two topics: the spatial behaviour of multi-establishment enterprises and the impact of flexible production and vertical disintegration on the geography of economic activity. Other material relevant to the theme of this section may be found in Chapter 2.2, where some aspects of the restructuring of agriculture is discussed.

The spatial behaviour of multi-establishment enterprises

Large firms generally have a greater degree of locational freedom than small firms. There is evidence from several studies that material linkages (Lever, 1974; Cadden, 1975; Taylor, 1978) and service linkages (Britton, 1974) take place over longer distances in plants belonging to multi-plant enterprises than in single plant enterprises. Such plants are likely to be less influenced by their local environment than single-plant businesses. Many of the external economies which single-plant enterprises derive from locating in an industrial agglomeration are thus relatively unimportant to the plants of multi-plant concerns where they are internalized within the organization (Gilmour, 1974). Courtaulds, for example, was one of the first major textile companies to locate branches outside the traditional British textile areas, when it opened mills in the North and Northern Ireland in the 1950s and 1960s. This later led to a 'follow the leader effect' as other companies followed suit.

An important factor that a multi-establishment company has to take account of in deciding on the location of investments and disinvestments is how they fit into the spatial organization of the company as a whole. So, for instance, a unit which provides a key component or performs an essential service may be kept open even though it is making a loss. Conversely a profitable establishment may be closed or sold if it is perceived to be marginal to the company's main activities. Neither of these strategies is available to a single establishment enterprise (Healey and Watts, 1987).

It is indisputable that the behaviour and performance of any single unit of a multi-plant enterprise has to be seen within the context of that enterprise as a whole, and that decisions affecting the unit's activities may well be made on non-local criteria (Dicken, 1976 p. 404).

Significantly, a multi-establishment enterprise has the potential both to reorganize its product/service locations between establishments and to select particular units for adjustment, choices which are denied the single-establishment business (Healey, 1981a).

A useful concept for examining the spatial rationalization of large businesses is that of *activity locations*. For a manufacturing company this refers to the location of each product, or each stage of production which it is feasible to locate separately (Healey, 1984). For example, the enterprise in Figure 7.7a has two single-product plants and two plants each manufacturing two products,

making six activity locations. This pattern may be altered in various ways by adopting different spatial rationalization policies. The pursuance of a policy of specialization (Fig. 7.7b), with the advantage of longer production runs and the reduction of costs through economies of scale, reduces the number of acitivity locations to four. Plant closure also usually results in a fall in the number of activity locations, as most transfers of production following closures are to plants already engaged in those activities. In the two cases illustrated in Figure 7.7, concentrating production at an existing site (Fig. 7.7c) leads to the number of activity locations being reduced from six to four, while following a policy of concentration at a new site (Fig. 7.7d) reduces the number to three. The advantages of concentrating production at one of the existing sites and closing the other units, include economies of scale in production, savings in administration, services, and inter-plant linkage costs, and the sale of abandoned sites. Whereas concentrating production at a green-field site releases the other sites for alternative uses, and enables construction to proceed without disturbing the production capacity of the existing units. Mixes of these policies may also occur (Fig. 7.7e), and sometimes products may be exchanged between plants.

The spatial rationalization policy adopted varies from firm to firm, often depending on the existing spatial structure of the organization. For example, a policy of spatial specialization is only an option for companies with multi-activity units. One study of multi-plant enterprises in the United Kingdom textile and clothing industry found that the most common policy followed during the late 1960s and early 1970s was concentration of production at an existing site (Fig. 7.7c). This was followed, either on its own or as part of a mixed strategy, by almost 90 per cent of the enterprises which rationalized the location of their production (Healey, 1984).

Several studies have suggested that differences in the way businesses and their establishments are organized may have an important influence on whether or not a spatial rationalization policy is adopted and the form it takes (e.g. Watts, 1974; 1980a; Healey, 1982; 1984; Townsend and Peck, 1985a). However, where the idea has been tested the results vary. For example, Watts (1980a) suggests, on the basis of case study evidence, that when in the late 1960s three British brewing

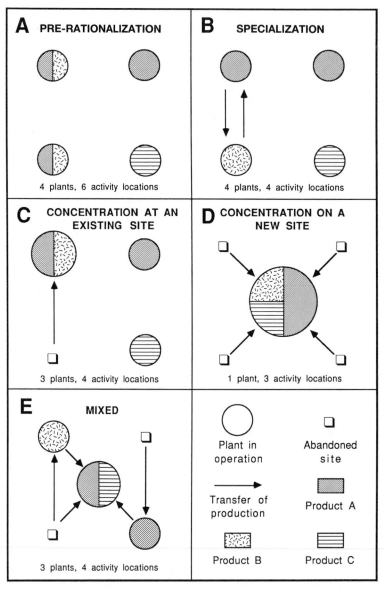

FIG 7.7 Spatial rationalization policies and activity locations in a hypothetical multi-plant enterprise (*source*: Healey, 1984 p. 137)

companies changed from a primarily territorial-based organizational structure to a divisional one (Fig. 7.1), it made it easier for company-wide reviews of their production facilities to be undertaken, which led to some sites being expanded and others abandoned (Fig. 7.7c). On the other hand, a larger survey of 64 multi-plant enterprises found no significant relationship between organizational structure and the frequency of closures, plant-size changes, or product changes (Healey, 1979; 1981b; 1982). As for the impact of organizational differences between establishments, some studies have found that in the manufacturing sector remote plants have a higher probability of being closed than centrally located plants (Keeble, 1968; Loasby, 1967), while others have cast doubt on the existence of such a relationship (Leigh and North, 1978; Healey, 1982). More generalized evidence suggests that the peripheral regions of the United Kingdom were the *first* to be affected by large corporations closing their plants in the late 1970s and early 1980s (Townsend and Peck, 1985b); while, in the context of the restructuring of ICI's world-wide paints division, Clarke (1985) found that plants which were peripheral, in an organizational as well as a geographic sense, were the least likely to survive.

There are a variety of reasons why the findings on the influence of organizational factors on the spatial rationalization and closure of economic acitivties seem unclear. On the one hand, the different results may reflect methodological difficulties in separating the influence of one factor from that of all the other influences on spatial rationalization (Watts, 1981). If this is where the problem lies, one way round it may be to use a matched pairs research design, such as that which Hitchens and O'Farrell (1987) used to compare the performance of small firms in the South-East and Northern Ireland (see Section 7.2). On the other hand, the differences in the findings may reflect more fundamental conceptual difficulties, in that most of the studies have attempted to divorce the examination of the spatial outcomes of rationalization from the analysis of the reasons which brought about the rationalization. This suggests that to understand locational behaviour it needs to be set within the context of the wider forces bringing about investment and disinvestment (Massey and Meegan, 1982; Lloyd and Shutt, 1985). This view is expanded in Chapter 10.2 as part of a wider discussion of the factors influencing closure decisions.

Flexible production, vertical disintegration, and the geography of economic activity

Recently several authorities have suggested that the development of flexible methods of organizing production and the trend towards vertical disintegration of businesses to which it is often linked (Section 7.1; Chapter 15.2) are encouraging the spatial concentration of economic activity (e.g. Estall, 1985; Sayer, 1986b; Scott, 1987b; Storper and Christopherson, 1987). The logic of the argument revolves around the alterations in the speed, frequency, and variability of the transactions which the organizational changes generate. The changes to linkage patterns apply both within firms and between firms and their suppliers and customers (Gertler, 1988). In the case of the first, the adoption of flexible manufacturing systems helps to emphasize the need for 'tighter co-ordination of all phases of the manufacturing process from design and engineering through final assembly' (Schoenberger, 1987 p. 204).

According to Schoenberger, failure to bring these functions together spatially may lead to serious problems in the implementation of new product and design ideas. As for changes to the pattern of inter-firm linkages, those associated with the introduction of just-in-time systems and vertical disintegration seem the most likely to increase the pressures for spatial concentration.

A key feature of the just-in-time system which encourages spatial concentration is the use of low inventories by which manufacturers reduce their stockholding of parts to a minimum (Estall, 1985). For the system to work efficiently suppliers and subcontractors need to be in close proximity to the manufacturer to respond quickly to changes in demand and to be able to deliver parts frequently, *as they are required*, sometimes several times a day (Sayer, 1986b). The most extreme example of such a localized complex is Toyota City, on the outskirts of Nagoya, where almost all Toyota's 3 million vehicles per annum are manufactured (Sheard, 1983; Chapter 5.3). There is some tentative evidence that where just-in-time systems are introduced locational adjustments take place both at the regional and international scales. For example, it has been suggested that the adoption of just-in-time systems in the American motor vehicle industry is leading to some recentralization of the industry in the Mid-West, although associated changes in labour practices have tended to lead firms to select green-field sites outside the traditional automobile centres (Chapter 12.4). There are also indications that the introduction of just-in-time systems is leading to some international recentralization of production as some multinationals open capital-intensive plants in their home countries, rather than locating in the Third World. For instance, Sayer (1986b) cites the case of Apple, the computer manufacturer, which decided to assemble its Mackintosh personal computer in a highly automated just-in-time factory in Fremont, California, instead of shipping components out to Singapore for assembly, which, despite lower labour costs, was expensive on inventories, inflexible, and difficult to co-ordinate. This and similar cases raise further doubts about the logic of the locational sequence predicted by the product cycle model discussed in the last chapter, which ends with mature industries characterized by mass production in low labour cost locations.

A further perspective on the tendency towards

spatial concentration is provided by the literature on vertical disintegration (Scott, 1987*b*; 1988; Scott and Storper, 1987; Storper and Christopherson, 1987). Scott (1987*b*) suggests that vertical disintegration and the agglomeration of economic activity are mutually reinforcing trends. Vertical disintegration (and horizontal disintegration for that matter) increases the level of external transactions. This, in turn, encourages those producers with specially intense and costly linkages to one another to cluster together. The resulting savings in external economies from locating in such agglomerations stimulates more firms to disintegrate vertically. It was argued in Chapter 5.3 that firms which provide frequently changing, unstandardized products or services on a small scale are the most likely to cluster together. The growth of such firms, stimulated by an increased demand for specialized goods and services and increased use of methods of flexible production, has led, so the argument goes, to a 'massive though selective reagglomeration of production' (Scott, 1988 p. 178).

Thus increasing levels of vertical disintegration and the development of flexible manufacturing methods have, according to Scott (1988), brought into existence a series of 'new industrial spaces' in North America and Western Europe. He distinguishes between enclaves in older industrial areas and developments in formerly non-industrialized areas peripheral to the main concentrations of industry. Several examples of new high-technology agglomerations were discussed in the last chapter. Route 128 and Silicon Valley illustrate respectively Scott's first and second categories. However, the new industrial spaces are not confined to high-technology industries. The revitalization of craft industries, such as leather, jewellery, and clothing, in inner-city locations, and the expansion of localized production complexes in the so called 'Third Italy' provide other examples. A particularly interesting case, involving both the manufacturing and service sectors, is the development of the film industry in Los Angeles.

Examining the United States motion picture industry is informative because it has changed from a vertically integrated industry to a vertically disintegrated one in a little over two decades. It therefore provides a good historical record from whch to explore the locational implications of disintegration and flexible production (Christ-

opherson and Storper, 1986; Storper and Christopherson, 1987). The share of the major studios (Paramount, Universal, Twentieth-Century Fox, MGM, Warner Brothers) in film *production* fell between 1960 and 1980 from 66 per cent to 31 per cent. This disintegration of the industry, which began in the 1950s, reflects a combination of factors which encouraged the large studios to reduce significantly their in-house production schedules. These factors included falling levels of profitability; changes in technology which allowed the production process to be split; a demand for a more differentiated product; and government antitrust legislation.

Associated with the vertical disintegration of the industry has been an increase in the concentration of both establishments and employment in California, particularly in Los Angeles, where Hollywood alone accounts for 65 per cent of the establishments in the industry (excluding the major studios). According to Storper and Christopherson the increased concentration of establishments in Los Angeles reflects the growth in the number of subcontracting firms, most of which are attracted to the city, despite high land and labour costs and inflexible labour relations, because:

1. By locating in the centre of the motion picture industry they increase their opportunities to obtain contracts and to negotiate details of contracted work. The specialized nature of their services and the ever-changing nature of their product requires frequent, non-standardized, contact with other firms. Indeed, the specialized production firms often combine and recombine with each other in flexible alliances to work on various projects.

2. Many subcontracting firms specialize in particular activities (e.g. special effects, recording) which are marketed not only to motion picture companies, but are also required by other entertainment industries (e.g. television, video, theatre) which are similarly concentrated in southern California.

3. Location at the centre of the industry gives them access to a large, highly specialized and skilled labour force, most of whom work on short contracts.

Storper and Christopherson (1987) argue that the reasons for the reconcentration of employment and establishments in the motion picture industry apply generally to flexibly specialized manufacturing and producer service industries. If this is accepted, then flexible specialization may have a dramatic impact on urbanization, regional development, and trade patterns and may, they suggest, help to account for the resurgence of metropolitan growth that has taken place in the United States in the 1980s. However, such views need to be treated cautiously, because the trend towards flexible production and vertical disintegration are, as yet, too tentative and the evidence for spatial reconcentration too limited to reach a firm conclusion (Gertler, 1988; Meegan, 1988). Indeed, other studies have emphasized that these trends may encourage dispersion as well as centralization (e.g. Oberhauser, 1987; Schoenberger, 1987).

7.4 Summary

- Significant changes have occurred over the last few decades in the organization of businesses and industries which have far-reaching implications on the location of economic activities and the uses to which land is put. Examining the nature of organizations is important because different types of organization often tend to exhibit different types of locational behaviour.
- The growing dominance of big business accompanied by a recent revival of small businesses has led several authorities to discuss the idea of segmented economies. Both large business organizations and small have distinctive geographies which are spatially uneven and contribute to regional disequilibria.
- An important distinction between large and small businesses is that the former are usually multi-establishment and often multi-divisional and multinational as well. One consequence of this is that locational hierarchies develop within large businesses, reflecting the varying locational requirements of different functions, such as administration, R. & D., and production. Another is that unlike single-establishment companies large businesses are able to rationalize the spatial organization of their activities. Further, whereas spatial variations in the formation of new firms are likely to be

influenced mainly by the local supply of potential entrepreneurs and the extent to which the local environment is conducive to starting new businesses, the behaviour of units of a multi-establishment organization have to be seen within the context of the enterprise as a whole and are often influenced by non-local criteria.
- Linked to the changes in size of companies are changes in the organization of industries. As businesses have grown in size many have become vertically integrated. Recently, associated with the development of flexible production methods, a counter-trend towards disintegration is apparent among some companies. Several research workers have suggested that whereas vertical integration has enabled the spatial dispersion of economic activities to occur, the trend towards disintegration is associated with the reagglomeration of selected economic activities, often in new places.

However, caution is needed in examining the effects of organizational changes and differences in organizational structure. There is a need to evaluate them in the context of the wider forces bringing about investment and disinvestment. As with the assessment of the spatial impacts of technological change (Chapter 6) there is a danger of creating what Sayer (1985) calls 'spatial stereotypes'. Specific social and economic changes do not necessarily lead to particular spatial outcomes. As two recent commentators have put it:

The new technologies and organizational methods may alter the locational possibilities and constraints faced by the firm, but they in no sense dictate the outcome (Schoenberger, 1987, p. 211).

Capital accumulation has never led to a single, universal type of spatial outcome, and there is no reason to believe that future capital accumulation will be any different, though non-random changes will surely be discernible (Sayer, 1986b p. 66).

This chapter has focused upon the spatial outcomes of the different and changing ways that businesses and industries are organized. Two important factors which influence this process are the activities of government and the social and cultural context in which the changes are introduced. The nature of these factors, and their effects on the location of economic activity and land use patterns, are the subjects of the next two chapters.

8

The Political Context

Patterns of economic activity are shaped by a dynamic set of interrelated factors. One of the factors that was ignored in traditional location theory is government intervention. It is impossible to ignore the political context as all governments intervene in the operation of their economies. As Dicken (1986 p. 136) remarks, 'political factors can create, alter or destroy the bases of comparative advantage.'

In line with the general objectives of this section of the book, this chapter seeks to examine the effects of government policy on the location, and changing distribution, of economic activity. This will be achieved by analysing government intervention at three different geographical scales—international, interregional, and urban and rural. Emphasis will be placed on changes in policy over time, drawing a distinction between, and examining the consequences of, specific spatial and aspatial policies. Such is the breadth of the subject-matter that only selected examples can be drawn from each geographical scale. However, a range of examples from the three main economic sectors is incorporated into the overall discussion. Before embarking on this, it is first necessary to briefly outline the reasons for, and levels of, government intervention.

8.1 Nature of government intervention

Many reasons can be advanced as to why governments intervene in the economic development of their countries. In agriculture, for example, Grigg (1984) lists four reasons:

1. To secure certain levels of self-sufficiency, especially during war time.
2. To prevent farm incomes from falling further behind those of other sectors (especially as agriculture is of declining import-

ance in employment terms in developed market economies).
3. To stabilize prices of products and 'even out' fluctuations in the supply of agricultural produce caused by such uncertain conditions as climate and disease.
4. To encourage technological developments in agriculture and the adoption of new farming methods.

To this list can be added three additional reasons (Ilbery, 1985a):

5. To further the contribution of agriculture to the balance of trade and gross national product; in New Zealand, for example, agriculture continues to be a vital source of export income.
6. To provide food at reasonable prices, a stated objective of the Common Agricultural Policy (CAP) for example, but one that has not been successfully ascertained.
7. To help prevent rural depopulation and maintain services and social stability in the more remote rural areas.

Reasons for government intervention in the secondary and tertiary sectors are similar, including employment creation, maintaining the balance of trade, assisting industries against foreign competition, and sustaining strategically important industries. However, policies are often more deliberately spatial in nature, aimed at reducing regional and local disparities in economic development (Chapter 16.4). Under free market conditions, there is a tendency for industry and services to become concentrated in prosperous cities and regions. Ironically, such congestion, which increases the cost of land, rent, and wages, could have been encouraged by national (aspatial) government policies for such things as defence and mergers.

The actual level of government intervention varies over time and between the different types of economic system and sectors of an economy. The obvious contrast in economic systems is between the centrally planned (socialist) economies of, for example, COMECON (Council for Mutual Economic Assistance), where all major economic decisions are made by the state, and developed market (capitalist) economies, where the level of intervention in an essentially market process depends upon the political party in power. For example, the Democratic and Labour parties in the USA and the United Kingdom respectively are more interventionist than the Republican and Conservative parties, which attempt to reduce the amount of state interference and encourage private enterprise and free market conditions.

Two important points regarding spatial differences in levels of government intervention need to be made (Dicken, 1986). First, whilst the amount of centralized control in market economies tended to increase up until the 1980s, there has been some relaxation of such control in planned economies. Although the state continues to make the major decisions and set the overall objectives in socialist economies, greater autonomy has been afforded to individual enterprises. This relates to the realization that a policy of self-sufficiency, based on the development of such heavy industrial staples as iron and steel and coal in each COMECON member, has created considerable duplication but not permitted total economic independence (see Chapter 10.2); indeed, trade between individual COMECON and Western European countries in particular has increased considerably in recent years (Mellor, 1975; Turnock, 1984). Hungary has for some time argued that production should relate more to market demand and not simply to central instructions. The country has encouraged the development of export-oriented industries and thus trade, both within and outside COMECON. Secondly, countries that have industrialized most recently, the Newly Industrialized Countries (NICs), have pursued the strongest national policies; for example, they have been much more restrictive than developed market economies in their policies towards foreign investment (see Chapter 14.3). Government policy in the NICs is beyond the scope of this discussion and the interested reader is referred to such texts as W. Morgan (1978), Kemp (1983), and Simpson (1987).

Levels of government intervention also vary significantly between the different economic sectors. Within the primary sector, for example, agriculture has long been 'protected' by a suite of policy measures, whereas service industries have received little support and only recently have become subjected to direct government influences. This lack of apparent interest is related to the view that services have been 'unproductive' (Daniels, 1985a). The manufacturing industries of the secondary sector occupy a position somewhere in the middle of this continuum of extremes, although they too have experienced increasing intervention since the Second World War. Within each economic sector, government policies have tended to favour certain types of farming, industry, and services at the expense of others (see below), demonstrating the complex role of government policy in the distribution of economic activities.

A diverse and exhaustive set of measures, of a spatial and non-spatial nature, have been used by different governments. They have undoubtedly had spatial ramifications, although it is very difficult to 'isolate' the effect of government policy on the location of economic activity from the many other influences. One can never be sure that changes in location subsequent upon specific policy measures would not have occurred anyway.

An apparent paradox would appear to exist, whereby deliberate *spatial* policies have been introduced to help overcome the problems created in part by *aspatial* measures. Part of this anomaly reflects the different scales at which policies are introduced. Policies are often implemented in a hierarchical structure (from national to regional and local), with the amount of political power declining as the scale of analysis is reduced. This of course varies according to the type of economic system, with a federal system for example, as operated in countries like West Germany and Austria, having greater regional autonomy than a centralized government system, as found in say France and the United Kingdom. Clearly, any particular national (aspatial) policy could have spatial consequences at lower scales of analysis (see section 8.3), just as aspatial policies introduced by individual local authorities will create spatial differences at the regional level.

Watts (1987 p. 127) simplifies the confusion between spatial and aspatial policies by classifying government measures within a nation into three interrelated types:

1. *Implicit spatial policies*, which involve national policies not normally thought of as having a spatial outcome; for example, merger policy, defence policy, and trade agreements.

2. *Derived spatial policies*, which involve lower-tier governments pursuing different policies, where for example 'one authority may take an active attitude to industrial development whereas another may discourage it.'

3. *Explicit spatial policies*, which are 'targeted' at specific geographical areas, such as different regions (regional policy), cities (urban policy), and rural communities (rural policy).

The distinction betwen spatial and aspatial policies is, therefore, scale dependent. For example, implicit spatial policies introduced by individual countries could, at the global scale, be classified as derived spatial policies. In the following insights into government policy at different geographical scales, discussion is, for reasons of space, restricted almost exclusively to implicit and explicit spatial policies. Discussion of the justification and limitations of area-based policies is left to Chapter 16.4.

8.2 The international dimension

The need to develop a global perspective when examining the distribution of economic activities, where a change in any one component (or area) of the world's economic system can have repercussions for the rest of the system, has already been discussed in Chapter 1.2. However, its importance needs to be highlighted once again because government policies introduced in any one area (e.g. the EC) will have an impact on countries outside the 'union', as well as on individual members (Hay, 1985; Dicken, 1986). A very good example of this would be trade policies, which have to be examined within an international institutional context. There are two major elements to this international structure: first, the General Agreement on Tariffs and Trade (GATT), which was formed after the Second World War and is primarily concerned with trade between developed nations; and secondly, the United Nations Conference on Trade and Development (UNCTAD), formed in 1964 to promote the trading interests of developing nations. Nations do not necessarily abide by the rules of GATT and UNCTAD, but international pressures are placed upon national governments as they pursue their trade policies.

With a reduction in import tarrifs in the world economy and an increased interest in export policies, particular groups of countries have formed trading blocs. By 1960, for example, most countries of Europe belonged to one of three trading groups: the EC (formed originally under the European Economic Community in 1957), COMECON (1949) or EFTA (European Free Trade Association, 1960). More recently, similar international groups have emerged in Latin America (Latin American Free Trade Association–LAFTA), Asia (Association of South East Asian Countries—ASEAN), and Africa (West African blocs). The pattern of world trade and economic activity is, therefore, being increasingly affected by government policies, especially as trading arrangements are developing between the different blocs. Trading blocs are discriminatory and thus go against the ethos of GATT in so far as enlarged internal markets are protected from outside influences by tariff and non-tariff barriers. The most powerful of the trading blocs is the EC, which has gradually increased its number of members from six in 1957 to twelve in 1986. It is having a dominant effect on world trade patterns and has, through the Lomé Convention for example, developed preferential trading agreements with groups of developing countries. Lomé I was an agreement signed in 1975 between the EC and 57 African, Caribbean, and Pacific (ACP) countries, which, as well as permitting the free entry of ACP manufactured goods into the EC, made development aid available to ACP members (Ilbery, 1986). The signing of Lomé III in 1984 also gave ACP countries (which had risen to 66 by 1985) access to surplus EC farm produce.

Agriculture and the EC can, in fact, be used to further demonstrate the effect of international government policies, of both a spatially implicit and explicit nature. The *Common Agricultural Policy* (CAP) represents the most important (and successful when compared with other common policies) spheres of government intervention in Western Europe and possibly the world. Its development and geographical consequences have been examined by numerous authors (see for example B. E. Hill, 1984; Bowler, 1985a; 1986;

Ilbery, 1986; and Winchester and Ilbery, 1988). For convenience, three temporal stages in its evolution can be identified, in which the balance between aspatial and spatial policies has altered:

Implicit spatial policies, 1957–1974

The Treaty of Rome (1957) singled out agriculture for special consideration and Article 39 laid down five objectives of a common agricultural policy:

(i) To increase agricultural productivity through technical progress and rational development.

(ii) To ensure a fair standard of living for the agricultural community.

(iii) To stabilize markets.

(iv) To assure the availability of supplies.

(v) To ensure that supplies reach consumers at reasonable prices.

The formation of the *European Agricultural Guidance and Guarantee Fund* (EAGGF) in 1962 represented the beginnings of the CAP. The guarantee section of this financial body was to become responsible for providing guaranteed prices for products when market prices fell below accepted fixed levels. A system of price support, therefore, dominated the early phases of CAP. Support prices, for a majority of products, were fixed well above world market prices and an intervention system was introduced whereby the EC bought directly in the market place, at the support price, in order to keep prices high and 'remove' any

surplus production. This naturally raised the cost of food to the consumer, which ran counter to Article 39, and the excess food generated by the system had to be either stored (at great cost), exported at highly subsidized prices (often to Eastern European countries), or destroyed; this continues to create considerable public hostility.

The non-spatial price support system created a secure and risk-free economic environment for inefficient as well as efficient farmers, both sets of which responded by intensifying production and specializing in fewer products. In increasing food supply, policy proved more than successful; indeed, the EC had become self-sufficient in no less than 17 agricultural products by the early 1980s (Table 8.1). Surplus production is a recurrent problem and the EC has become infamous for its butter and beef 'mountains', wine and milk 'lakes', and currant 'hills'.

Unfortunately, the price support system also had some adverse spatial consequences for agriculture in the EC. As long as required quality standards are reached, farmers receive guaranteed prices for as much as they can produce. Consequently, policy has favoured larger farms in the northern parts of the EC. The small farm structures in 'southern' areas have effectively been penalized, especially as 'northern' products like beef, milk, and cereals receive higher levels of price support than products from southern Mediterranean regions. The CAP has, therefore, exacerbated rather than reduced regional disparities in farm incomes, creating a distinct core (rich) and periphery (poor) pattern (Fig. 8.1a). Even

TABLE 8.1 Self-sufficiency in agricultural products in the European Community 'Ten', 1985

Exceeding 100%		Around 100%		Below 100%	
Whole-milk powder	396	Oats	105	Maize	88
Concentrated milk	161	Potatoes	103	Fresh fruit	82
Wheat	145	Eggs	102	Sheepmeat	74
Skimmed milk powder	143	Fresh milk products	101	Rice	67
Barley	133	Pigmeat	101	Citrus fruit	46
Sugar	132	Fresh vegetables	101	Veg. oils/fats	24
Butter	129	Wine	97		
Rye	124				
Beef and veal	111				
Cheese	108				
Poultrymeat	107				

Source: Eurostat—Basic Statistics of the Community, 1987.

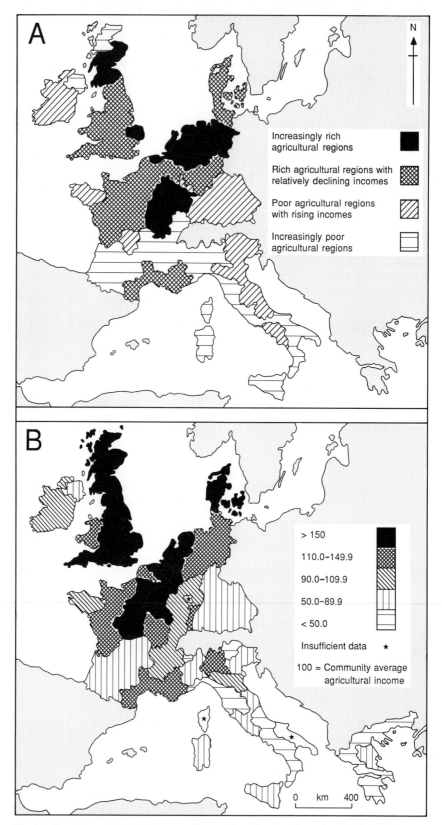

FIG 8.1 Farm incomes in the European Community: (*a*) regional trends, 1968/9–1976/7; (*b*) regional variations in 1983 (*source*: (*a*) based on Henry, 1981; (*b*) based on Green Europe, 1985)

when examined for one point in time (1982) the contrasts between 'northern' and 'southern' regions are readily apparent (Fig. 8.1b).

With the need to practise a mixed system of farming being reduced, price support policies have helped to intensify the trend towards a greater regional specialization of farming within the EC. Two-thirds of the census regions of the EC 'Nine' became more specialized between 1960 and 1977 (Bowler, 1986). Some regions have become more specialized in cereals, oils and fats, beef and veal, and wine, whilst others have actually reduced their specialization. For example, intensive livestock (pigs and poultry) has become a less intensive element within Ireland, the United Kingdom, and Denmark. The overall pattern of changing regional specialization in agriculture is fairly complex (Fig. 8.2), although as a broad generalization specialization has increased in those regions where a product was already an important element of the agricultural system. Guaranteed prices have effectively encouraged farming to become increasingly differentiated on the basis of physical criteria.

Explicit spatial policies, 1974–1983

Although price support continued to totally dominate the financial budgets of EAGGF, a change in policy direction could be detected by the number of structural measures that were introduced from 1974 to tackle problems associated with the small farm sector. In particular, deliberate spatial policies were used from 1975 onwards, in an attempt to reduce the regional disparities in agriculture intensified by existing aspatial policies.

The CAP became more geographically sensitive with its adoption of the *Less Favoured Areas Directive* (LFAD) in 1975. This was designed to 'maintain rural population densities, conserve and manage the landscape, and safeguard agricultural activities in regions with physical handicaps to production' (Winchester and Ilbery, 1988, p. 22). Recognizing that farm income problems are created by the nature of the areas and not necessarily by farm size, areas requiring priority aid from EAGGF were identified on the basis of three criteria: first, an above Community average employment in agriculture; secondly, a per capita gross domestic product below the Community average; and thirdly, a below-average number of

workers in manufacturing employment. The boundaries of three types of problem area were delimited (Fig. 8.3):

1. Areas with mountain and hill farming, where production is restricted by slopes, altitude, and soil type.
2. Areas with low population densities and severe depopulation.
3. Areas with specific problems, such as poor infrastructure or the need to maintain agriculture to either protect the countryside or preserve tourist potential.

As demonstrated in Figure 8.3, extensive areas were identified, including much of Ireland and Italy, upland Scotland, and the southern parts of West Germany, Belgium, and France. Within these peripherally located priority zones, an annual compensatory allowance is available to cover the increased costs of production. This is paid in terms of a grant per hectare (ha) or per head of livestock on a farm. Favourable rates are also available for both structural modernization and investment in non-agricultural enterprises. By 1984, over 600 000 farmers were benefiting from the scheme, mainly in the United Kingdom, Ireland, France, and West Germany; Italy only began to apply the LFAD in 1978. In 1985, the problem areas were further extended. Although little research has been conducted into the LFAD, it would appear that the social objectives of the scheme are not being fulfilled as disproportionately high payments are being made to large and not small farms.

As a result of the minimal effect of the LFAD in southern regions, further explicitly spatial measures, in the form of the *Mediterranean Package* and *Integrated Rural Development Programmes*, were introduced in 1978 and 1979 respectively. The former provided Mediterranean farmers with financial help for specific types of structural change, such as irrigation measures in the Mezzogiorno, flood protection in the Herault Valley of southern France, afforestation and improvement of rural infrastructure in the upland areas of southern Italy and southern France, and co-operative projects (Clout, 1984; Clout et al., 1985). With the latter, the CAP combined with both the regional and social funds of the EC (see Ilbery, 1986) to promote a mixture of agricultural and non-agricultural projects in three selected areas—the Western Isles of Scotland, the *départe-*

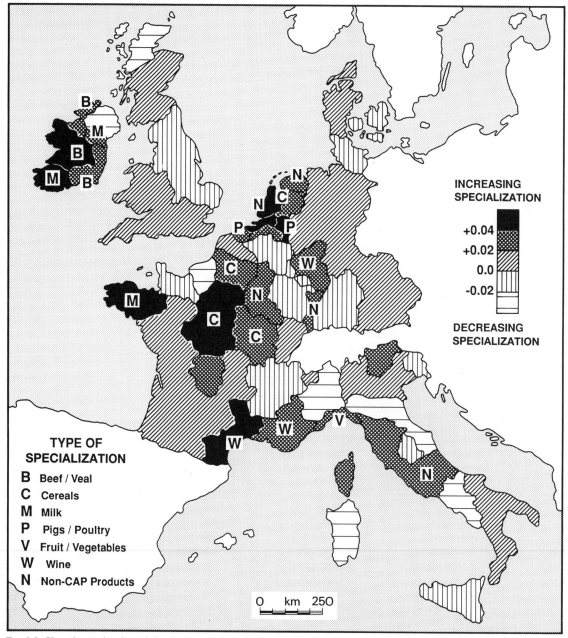

FIG 8.2 Changing regional specialization in agriculture in the European Community, 1964–77 (*source*: Bowler, 1986 p. 21)

ment of Lozère in France, and the province of Luxembourg in south-west Belgium.

Yet again, a change in policy direction could be detected as it was at last recognized that the problems of the countryside could not be solved by structural programmes in agriculture alone. Nevertheless, it is doubtful whether the explicit spatial measures introduced between 1974 and 1983 will be successful in reducing the imbalance in farm structures and incomes between northern and southern regions. The main reason for such scepticism is the continued dominance of price support policies for agriculture in the EC.

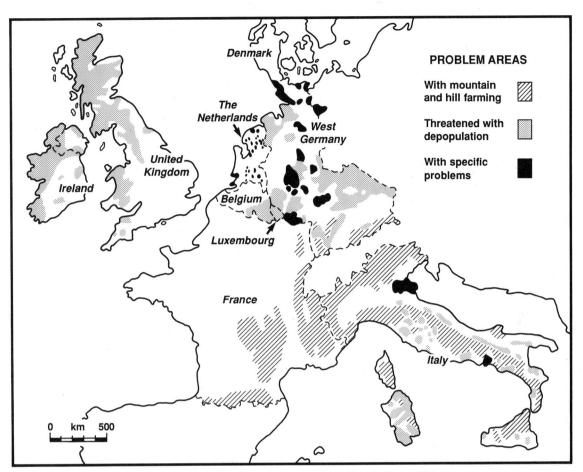

FIG 8.3 Agricultural problem areas of the European Community (*source:* Ilbery, 1985*a* p. 108)

Implicit and explicit spatial policies, 1983 to date

With the accession of Greece to the EC in 1981 and the more recent acquisition of Portugal and Spain in 1986, specific measures for southern regions have continued to form an important component of CAP policy throughout the 1980s. This was demonstrated when the European Commission announced an integrated plan for the Mediterranean regions in 1983. This is an explicitly spatial six-year programme, which began in 1985 and is designed to raise income levels and improve job opportunities in strongly rural areas. Twenty-nine *Integrated Mediterranean Programmes* (IMPs) were outlined for the Mezzogiorno, parts of central Italy, the whole of Greece except Greater Athens, and the six southernmost regions of France.

Between £6 and £7 million have been budgeted for the six-year programme, with 60 per cent coming from all EC members and 40 per cent from the three beneficiaries. In more detail, the money has been allocated as follows: 40 per cent for agricultural projects; 33 per cent for tourism and off-farm employment in small and medium-sized industries and craft activities; and 27 per cent for afforestation, fishing, and training schemes. Although it is too early to assess a scheme that has hardly started in some of the IMPs, concern has already been expressed by environmentalists, who are 'alarmed that the way IMPs are operating could produce significant damage to the traditional landscapes and wildlife habitat of the Mediterranean' (Smyth, 1988 p. 19). For further discussion of the environmental impacts of such government policies see Chapter 17.2.

Schemes aimed at specific geographical areas will achieve success only if simultaneous controls on price support are introduced. This message has, at last, managed to 'get through' to Ministers, as demonstrated in a policy statement from the European Commission (1986 p. 8): 'European agriculture has to accept economic realities and learn to produce for the market, to adapt to commercial demands and to continue to modernise.' The old model, whereby higher farm incomes can be achieved by increasing output at high guaranteed prices, has to be changed. However, this will have to be a slow process, for if the price support measures were abolished immediately one-third of British farmers, among the most efficient in Europe, would become bankrupt (Harvey et al., 1986).

In 1984, a series of decisions concerned with a 'restrictive price policy' were announced by the European Commission. Various measures were introduced, the most far-reaching being the sudden imposition of milk quotas. New production limits and prices were set for member states (Table 8.2) and price guarantees were restricted to 99.5 million tonnes of output, when 109 million tonnes were being produced and only 88 million tonnes consumed. Quotas were not imposed equally on members and whilst Ireland, Greece, and Luxembourg gained quite considerably from the new arrangements, remaining members (apart from Italy) had their quotas reduced by between 2 and 6.7 per cent. This has caused considerable hardship and unrest, especially among those farming communities that had, under the price support measures, been encouraged to specialize in milk production (see Fig. 8.2). Nevertheless, quotas have proved effective in lowering the butter 'mountain' (Erlichman, 1988).

Further agreements on the production of milk

and beef were reached in 1986, the year in which the EC introduced the idea of *Environmentally Sensitive Areas* (ESAs). Concern over the environmental consequences of agricultural modernization (see Chapter 17) led to the designation of specific geographical areas in which farmers would be compensated for agreeing to adopt farming practices which help to safeguard characteristic landscape, wildlife, and archaeological features. In the United Kingdom, for example, the scheme began in 1987 and by February 1988, 19 ESAs had been designated: 12 in England and Wales, 5 in Scotland, and 2 in Northern Ireland (Fig. 8.4). Farmers in the ESAs are being paid to maintain a low level of inputs, particularly of fertilizers; they are also being compensated for every ha of cereal land that reverts to pasture and for leaving six-metre strips of uncropped land at the edge of arable fields, to allow natural regeneration and encourage wildlife. In the North Peak ESA, heather moorland conservation is also being encouraged. A total of 750 000 ha is now covered by the ESA scheme in the United Kingdom.

Possibly the most determined measure aimed at balancing agricultural supply and demand is *Regulation 1094/88*: the set-aside of arable land and the extensification and conversion of production. Under this 1988 Regulation, which is compulsory for member countries but not individual farmers, producers will be paid either to take out of production at least 20 per cent of their arable land or to reduce production of specified products by the same percentage figure for a period of five years (see Ilbery, 1990a for details). Rates of compensation will vary from 100 to 600 ECU (European Unit of Account: in 1988 one ECU was 68 pence) per ha and the Community will contribute 50 per cent of the first 200 ECU, 25 per

TABLE 8.2 Milk production quotas and prices in the European Community, 1984

	1	2		1	2
West Germany	−6.7	−0.6	Luxembourg	+3.5	+ 2.8
France	−2.0	+5.0	Britain	−6.5	− 0.6
Italy	nil	+6.4	Ireland	+4.6	+ 2.7
Netherlands	−6.2	−0.5	Denmark	−5.7	+ 1.5
Belgium	−3.0	+2.7	Greece	+7.2	+17.6

1: % change in the 10 states of milk production quotas.
2: % change in the 10 states of prices expressed in national currencies.

Source: Ilbery (1985a p. 137).

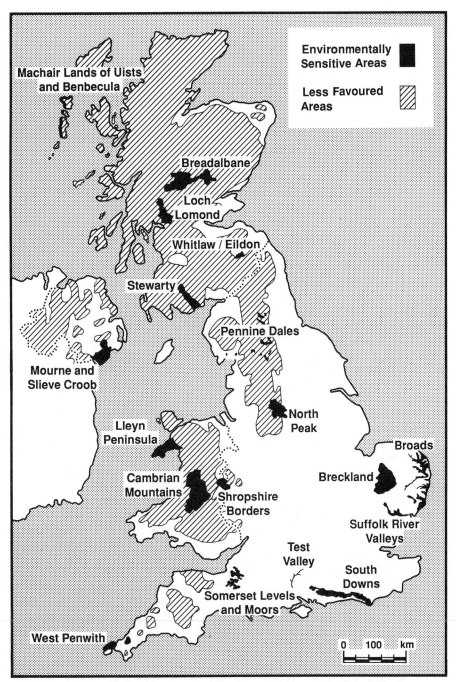

Fɪɢ 8.4 Environmentally Sensitive Areas and Less Favoured Areas in the United Kingdom

cent of the next 200 to 400 ECU, and 15 per cent of the remaining 400 to 600 ECU. In the United Kingdom, for example, a maximum figure of £200 per ha has been agreed (£180 in LFAs), which compares unfavourably with West Germany's £400 per ha. The Ministry of Agriculture, Fisheries, and Food has estimated the cost of the scheme in Britain to be £16.5 million in the first year (1989), £22 million in the second year, and no limit thereafter. Spatially, regional exemptions to compulsory application are allowed, the most logical being those problem areas qualifying for aid from the LFAD. Indeed, the set-aside scheme is aimed primarily at traditional lowland grassland areas that 'came under the plough' in response to favourable support prices for cereals. The initial uptake has been rather disappointing, with only 2000 farmers (offering just 61 000 ha) participating in the scheme in 1989, although there is some evidence that uptake has been highest in marginal cereal areas (Ilbery, 1990b).

Clearly, the pace of change in the CAP has intensified since 1983, comprising a combination of implicit and explicit spatial policies. Their effects are as yet uncertain and rates of uptake need careful monitoring and detailed examination. In contrast to the CAP, the EC does not have a common policy for either industry or the service sector. However, following the Davignon Plan of 1977 the EC developed a common policy for the steel industry which, like agriculture, has suffered from excess capacity and overproduction. Consequently, compulsory quotas were introduced in 1980 to remove 27 million tonnes of steel, before being removed in 1988. Similarly, the EC has operated a *European Regional Development Fund* (ERDF) since 1975 in the 'economic' problem areas of the Community. Space does not permit discussion of regional policy in the EC and detailed accounts can be found in Clout *et al.*, (1985), Ilbery (1986), and Clout (1987).

8.3 The interregional dimension

At this level, policies are implemented by national governments and specially created regional bodies, such as the Welsh and Scottish Development Agencies. Although regional/federal governments may apply uniform policies throughout their areas of jurisdiction, these could be of different types and so create spatial con-

trasts nationally (derived spatial policies). This section concentrates upon implicit and explicit spatial policies, with particular reference to the USA, the United Kingdom, and France.

(a) Implicit spatial policies in the USA and United Kingdom

Both countries have applied national policies for agriculture and industry that have had spatial consequences. However, this section will use national defence as its main example of implicit spatial policies. Although uniformly available in the USA, government defence and high-technology contracts have distinct spatial expressions (Rees and Weinstein, 1983; Malecki, 1984; see Chapter 6.2). Nearly one-third of defence expenditure is spent on military prime supply contracts, 70 per cent of which are concentrated in just 10 to 15 states. Contracts awarded by the Defence Department also tend to go to large firms, like Boeing, McDonnell Douglas, General Dynamics, and Lockheed. Between 1960 and 1967, 100 corporations received two-thirds of all prime military contracts awarded and in 1980, the 10 largest suppliers to the military accounted for 30 per cent of the value of contracts (Malecki, 1984). This degree of concentration has remained fairly constant since the 1950s and actually rises when the defence industry is disaggregated according to the individual services (Army, Navy, Air Force) and to such military products as bombers, missiles, and fighter planes. As Malecki (1984 p. 34) comments, 'each service tends to buy from only a subset of defence firms, and very few firms receive large contracts from more than one service.' Likewise, the degree of concentration in Research, Development, Testing, and Evaluation contracts (RDT and E) has remained high since the 1960s; again, large firms are dominant. Nearly three-quarters of RDT and E contracts are accounted for by three high-technology categories—aircraft, missile and space systems, and electronics and communication equipment.

As defence contracts favour a few large firms, government policy is spatially selective towards the location of these firms. Not surprisingly, therefore, a relatively small number of states have continued to receive the bulk of prime contracts since the 1950s. In 1960, the list was dominated by California, a 'contract' state with over 20 per cent of total awards (Table 8.3); the top 10 states (with

TABLE 8.3 Top states of the USA in receipt of prime contracts 1959–1980

Fiscal year 1959–60		Fiscal year 1980	
State	USA total (%)	State	USA total (%)
California	24.0	California	20.4
New York	11.4	New York	8.3
Texas	5.8	Texas	8.0
Massachusetts	5.3	Connecticut	5.7
New Jersey	5.0	Massachusetts	5.5
Ohio	4.4	Virginia	4.9
Connecticut	4.2	Missouri	4.8
Washington	4.0	Washington	3.4
Michigan	3.3	Pennsylvania	3.3
Pennsylvania	3.2	Florida	3.0

Source: Malecki (1984 p. 36).

49 per cent of the population) had 70.6 per cent of all contracts. By 1980, 67.3 per cent of all contracts were still awarded to the top 10 states (with 44 per cent of the population), although Missouri, Florida, and Virginia had replaced New Jersey, Ohio, and Michigan in the list (the latter three remained in the top 15 states). Once established, the pattern of defence contracts remains fairly constant, as the government tends to reallocate contracts to the same people (incrementalism). The only major spatial change occurred when there was a movement away from automotive products (tanks, armoured vehicles) in the Mid-West to missiles and aircraft systems in the West and South-West (Watts, 1987).

RDT and E contracts are even more spatially concentrated, with the top 10 states (41 per cent of population) accounting for just over three-quarters of the US total. Fourteen states have above-average levels of RDT and E; indeed, they tend to have high percentages of their total defence contracting in RDT and E. Spatially, they are clustered into six areas (Fig. 8.5): the Pacific coast (California and Washington), the Mountain West (Colorado, New Mexico, and Arizona), Missouri and Kansas, Florida, New England (Massachusetts and Connecticut), and the Washington DC region (Maryland, Virginia, and the District of Columbia). Possibly of greater significance is the relegation, from a position of some importance for prime contracts, of such industrial states as New York, Ohio, Texas, Michigan, and Pennyslvania. Although very difficult to prove, this could indicate that policy is biased against the industrial states of the North-East and towards the home states of government ministers (pork-barrel effect) (see also Chapter 16.1).

As much as, or over, 50 per cent of defence contracts may be subcontracted out to other firms. In theory, this could help to disperse the pattern of concentration. However, in practice subcontracting is more spatially concentrated than prime contracts, leading to a greater overall concentration within the defence industry. This can be explained by the fact that 'the same firms that are common prime contractors are most often the largest subcontractors on other systems' (Malecki, 1984 pp. 38–9). Subcontracting, therefore, tends to occur locally or go to other prime contract firms elsewhere. In contrast to RDT and E and prime contracts, the manufacturing belt (especially Ohio, New Jersey, and Vermont) is a major location for subcontracted work, often from Florida and Texas.

A picture of spatial concentration also emerges if similar analyses are applied to the defence industry in the United Kingdom (Short, 1981; Law, 1983; Boddy and Lovering, 1986). In terms of defence employment, the South-East, South-West, East Anglia, and Northern Ireland have a higher figure than their share of the total population would suggest. Similarly with research activities, all but one (in Dunfermline) of the 32 Ministry of Defence R. & D. laboratories are located in southern England, just as private sector defence research (mainly in aerospace and electronics) is heavily concentrated in the 'sunrise' belt along the M4 Corridor, the M25 motorway,

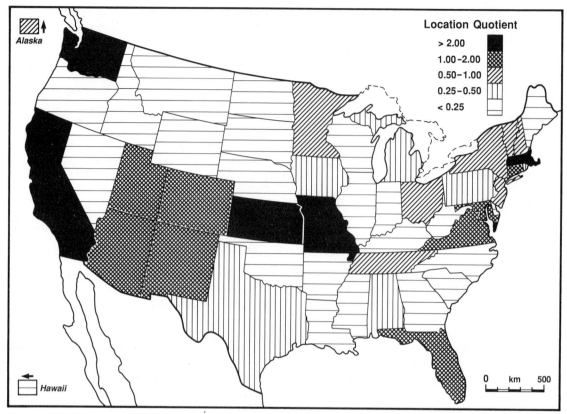

FIG 8.5 Distribution of defence research, development, testing, and evaluation contracts in states of the United States, 1980 (*source*: based on data in Malecki, 1984 p. 38)

and the Cambridge district (see Chapter 6.2). Many small firms are subcontracting from major government establishments in the area (Chapter 5.3). However, there has been some movement from the South-East to more northern and western areas, which Law (1983) explains in terms of the product life cycle, whereby defence products are pioneered in the South-East and later passed to factories in more peripheral regions.

In terms of defence expenditure, Short (1981) calculated that the South-West received £232 per head of population over the 1974–8 period, which was considerably higher than the other 'above-average' regions of the South-East (151.7), East Anglia (121.6), Northern Ireland (113.8), and the East Midlands (113.5). The South-West, and the Bristol area in particular, has a high concentration of service personnel and aerospace industries. An important feature has been the lack of defence spending in the 'assisted areas' of the United Kingdom (see below). The government's

stated policy of giving priority to firms in areas of high unemployment when seeking tenders for, and awarding, contracts appears not to be acted upon as only 0.6, 1.0, 1.0, and 0.6 per cent of contracts placed in the assisted areas between 1974 and 1978 were the result of the Special Preference Scheme, where producers are allowed to retender for contracts (Short, 1981).

Clearly, therefore, implicit spatial policies in the USA and the United Kingdom have led to concentrations of defence contracts in certain favoured areas. Such regions tend to attract other forms of economic activity, leading to increased spatial disparities in economic development. This is one reason why governments introduce explicit spatial policies, in an attempt to achieve a more equitable distribution of 'economic health' (see Chapter 16.4).

(b) Explicit spatial policies in France and the United Kingdom

This section concentrates upon explicit spatial policies in the secondary and tertiary sectors. Such policies have been applied in both France and the United Kingdom, as well as in many other countries, although only in recent years has it been realized that services can play an important role in regional policy initiatives. Levels of intervention in regional policy have varied over time, reflecting different government philosophies; for example, the present Conservative government in the United Kingdom has reduced its commitment to regional policy since 1979, whilst the Socialist government in France has increased its interest since 1981 in the redistribution of 'economic health'.

Explicit spatial policies can conveniently be subdivided into two groups:

1. *Negative measures*, or policies of constraint aimed at discouraging growth in congested (often city) regions.
2. *Positive measures*, or incentives to relocate in less developed and often peripheral areas.

The two have often been applied jointly, in the hope that poorer regions will 'catch up' with richer ones. Negative measures have been used in an attempt to reduce the dominance of both the Paris region (Île de France) and London and the South-East. In both countries, the most commonly used type of constraint has been to force businesses over a defined minimum size to seek permission to locate or expand within certain restricted areas. This has taken the form of *Industrial Development Certificates* (IDCs) and *Office Development Permits* (ODPs) in the United Kingdom, and *Occupation Permits* (*agréments*) in France.

IDCs were introduced under the Town and Country Planning Act of 1947 and survived for just over thirty years before being abolished by the Conservative government in 1979. Firms in non-assisted areas (see below) wishing to erect a new plant or extension of over 5000 square feet (later raised to 15 000 and then 50 000 square feet) were required, by law, to apply for and obtain an IDC before planning permission would be granted. The scheme was able to restrict growth in specific areas in three ways (Watts, 1987): first, through outright refusal of an IDC; secondly,

through informal advice by government officials, to the effect that an IDC might not be granted (and so no application was made); and thirdly, through firms believing that it was not possible to obtain an IDC and thus not applying or seeking advice. IDCs were initially successful as little industrial development occurred in London, for example, during the first three years of the scheme. However, refusal rates varied over time, peaking in the mid-1960s at a time of significant economic growth, before 'tailing off' quite dramatically until their abolition in 1979. Indeed, it proved difficult to operate IDC policy at a time of rising unemployment, especially as the 'targeted' South-East region was itself experiencing an increasing rate of unemployment. Watts (1987) also demonstrates how larger firms sometimes managed to circumvent IDC policy. He gives the examples of Ford, who were allowed to expand in the South-East on the condition that further expansion would take place in government-assisted areas (see below), and Courtaulds, who were granted IDCs in return for an agreement to expand one of its existing plants in an assisted area. Consequently, only a relatively small percentage of industrial movement was due to IDC policy, which needed to be combined with positive measures in order to entice firms to locate in peripheral 'development areas'.

ODPs were introduced later in the United Kingdom, in 1965, and managed to survive for fourteen years. Initially introduced in Greater London, where developers had to obtain an ODP for developing over 280 square metres of office space, the scheme was quickly extended to include South-East England, East Anglia, the home counties, and the Midlands by 1966 (Fig. 8.6). However, it was soon realized that offices would rather remain the same size or move into existing larger premises than have to move long distances from London and the South-East in order to expand. Consequently, controls in East Anglia and the Midlands were removed in 1969 and 1970 (Daniels, 1982). In some years, no ODPs were granted in Central London, although for the 1965–77 period some 1400 were issued for that area (Alexander, 1979). Despite achieving some success, ODPs have been criticized on numerous grounds (Ambrose and Colenutt, 1975; Alexander, 1979; Daniels, 1982 and 1985a):

1. They created an artificial shortage of office

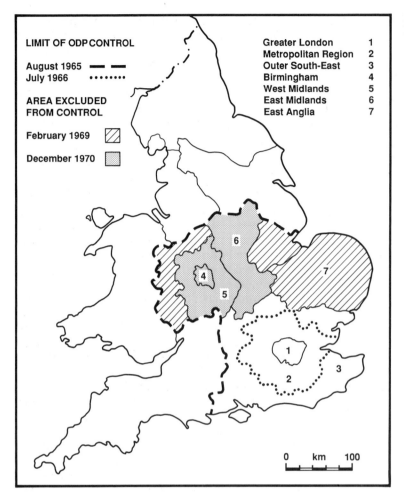

FIG 8.6 Areas covered by Office Development Permits in England, 1965–79 (*source*: Daniels, 1982, p. 83)

accommodation, especially in London. With demand exceeding supply, rents for new office space increased quite dramatically in central London, from £35 per square metre in 1967 to £212 in 1973, the benefits of which went to the property developers. Consequently, London and the South-East became more, not less attractive for property investment. Indeed, London became the most expensive European location for office-based services, forcing many multinationals to choose other European cities as a base.

2. They were granted only to those office activities that could demonstrate a need for a central location. Yet, no criteria for assessing need were established.

3. ODPs applied to the developer and not the occupier of the premises and so the former had a vested interest in proving his prospective tenant's need for a central location.

4. Controls on office development appeared to operate in an arbitrary manner, as shown in (2) above, and there was no guarantee that those forced to relocate (in order to expand) were the best suited to decentralization.

5. Those who were refused ODPs could still stay, either by attempting to obtain an ODP later or by moving into existing premises.

6. ODP legislation did not limit the use to which space vacated by decentralizing office firms could be put; as a result it was readily acquired by either expanding indigenous firms or in-migrants like foreign banks.

7. The low threshold size of 280 square metres adversely affected small firm development. Although this had been raised to 2800 square metres by 1977, congestion was by then no longer the major problem and had been replaced by rising unemployment. Consequently, ODPs were

thought inappropriate and were abandoned in 1979.

In France, controls on industry failed to halt the growth of Paris, which was due mainly to developments in the tertiary sector. To counteract this, occupiers proposing to move into office accommodation in excess of 3000 square metres were, from 1967, required to obtain permission from a 'decentralization' committee (Bateman, 1985). This had little real effect and in 1969 a system of occupation permits (*agréments*) was introduced for all office activities requiring over 10 000 square metres of new accommodation in Paris. Again, the effect was minimal, as a majority of new developments were below the threshold size (Flockton, 1982). Demand for office space in Paris was increasing substantially and whilst the French government was aware of the continued over-dominance of Paris, it was also keen to maintain its position in Europe's urban hierarchy. Consequently, the demand for offices in Paris was being acceded to at an increasing rate, from 325 000 square metres worth of approvals in 1967 to 1.4 million in 1971.

In 1974, policy became more restrictive and a ceiling of 900 000 square metres per annum was fixed for the entire Paris region, of which only 8 per cent could be in the *département* of Paris itself. Three years later, the *Schema Directeur* introduced a very restrictive policy for office development in the commercial and financial districts of central Paris. Although existing offices could be modernized or replaced, there was to be no increase in employment densities. Elsewhere in the Paris region, particularly in the eastern districts of the city itself and in the new towns and suburban growth poles, office development was actively encouraged. This led to such major office developments as La Defense in the immediate western suburbs (Burtenshaw *et al.*, 1981; Bateman, 1985). Described as one of 'the most innovative office development projects in Europe' (Bateman, 1985 p. 108), La Defense was planned to provide 1.55 million square metres of office floorspace by 1990. It has become an area of high-density tower blocks which, as well as attempting to attract city-centre offices, houses such international companies as IBM and Rank Xerox. Overall, policy appeared to be more successful than in the late 1960s and an analysis of the *agréments* given in 1981 shows that central Paris obtained just 5.5 per

cent of the total space approved, compared with 32.2 per cent for La Defense, 30.1 per cent for the new towns, and 32.2 per cent for the rest of the Paris region (Bateman, 1985).

Another type of negative measure employed in the Paris region has taken the form of a building development tax (*redevance*). This has been imposed, since 1960, on new industrial and office development. As with the *agréments*, the *redevance* became spatially selective (in 1971), favouring the eastern and peripheral areas of the Paris region and penalizing western and central districts (Burtenshaw *et al.*, 1981). However, this 'once only' payment appears to have had less effect on office and industrial development than spatial differences in land costs within the Paris region. A similar conclusion can be drawn regarding the transport tax (2 per cent of pay role) imposed on businesses in the Paris region.

Positive measures, or incentives, have an even longer and probably more successful history in France and the United Kingdom. Various types of incentive have been used to encourage first industry and more recently services to relocate, or begin, in designated 'zones'.

In France, such measures began with the *programmes for regional action* introduced by the central government after 1955; until 1963, the objective was to 'even out spatial imbalances in national life, using industrial relocation policy as the main mechanism' (Clout, 1987 p. 171). However, in 1964, as part of the fourth National Plan, eight *métropoles d'équilibre* (balancing metropolitan areas) were designated in an attempt to counterbalance the dominance of the Paris region (Fig. 8.7). These ranged from the large linked *métropole* of Lyon/Saint Étienne/Grenoble (nearly two million inhabitants) to the free-standing city of Strasbourg (356 000). The selected centres were considered to be logical places for the generation of economic growth in their respective regions. Besides helping to regenerate old industrial areas, the *métropoles* were designed to 'help the prosperous industrial areas and support the poor hill farming areas' (Ilbery, 1986 p. 172). Financial assistance for the centres came mainly in the form of infrastructure investment, subsidies for the relocation of research, administration, and banking, grants of up to 25 per cent towards the costs of construction of office and similar developments, tax benefits, and staff removal costs.

Concern over the potential negative effect of

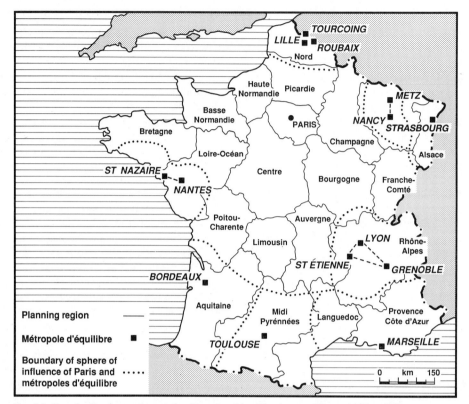

FIG 8.7 French planning regions and *métropoles d'équilibre* (*source*: Ilbery, 1986 p. 173)

the *métropoles* on the future of smaller towns led, in 1967, to the selection of a further seven centres to receive financial help for attracting tertiary employment: Besançon, Clermont-Ferrand, Dijon, Rennes, Limoges, Montpellier, and Poitiers. Four years later, the virtues of small and medium-sized towns (*villes moyennes*), ranging from 20 000 to 200 000 inhabitants, were recognized and finance was obtained from the state for improving housing, transport, job provision, and cultural facilities. Elsewhere, finance was made available in such 'problem areas' as coalfields, textile-producing towns, backward rural zones, and old manufacturing regions. The government also relocated some of its own tertiary activities, including higher education, branches of the Civil Service, and some research units (Clout, 1987).

Since positive and negative measures have been introduced in France, there has been a slight reduction in the dominance of the Paris region. However, it is not clear whether this is the result of government policy or whether it would have occurred anyway. Continuous changes in policy,

from large to small growth centres for example, have made it very difficult to assess the effectiveness of French regional economic policy.

Regional policy in the United Kingdom began in 1934 with the designation of four *Special Areas*, primarily in coalfield districts, under the Special Areas Act. In 1945, these were replaced by *Development Areas* (DAs) which, together with *Special Development Areas* (SDAs, from 1967) and *Intermediate Areas* (IAs, from 1969), continued to expand geographically until 1979 (Fig. 8.8). Policy was most active between 1963 and 1977 and primarily concerned with manufacturing location. A wide range of incentives were available to firms willing to relocate or begin business in 'assisted' areas. These are summarized by Watts (1987) and include grants (especially the Regional Development Grant established by the 1972 Industry Act), loans, tax allowance, equity investments (where the government purchases shares in a firm to allow the latter to raise extra funds), industrial infrastructure (as in the provision of advance factories), general infrastructure,

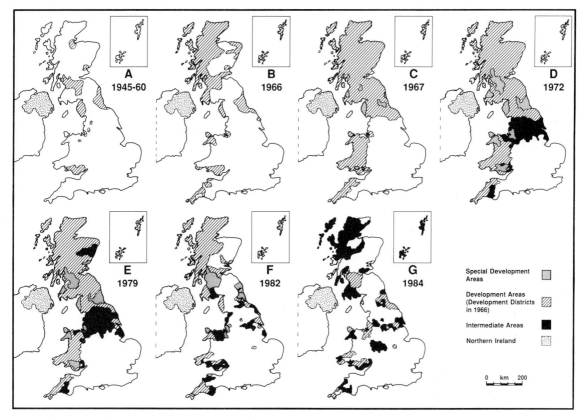

FIG 8.8 Regional policy assisted areas in the United Kingdom, 1945–88

and labour subsidies (e.g. the Regional Employment Premium which firms received for each new job created). Aid was highest in the SDAs, lower in the DAs and lowest of all in the IAs.

Incentives for service industries did not begin until 1973 when the Service Industry Grant Scheme encouraged the growth of office and service employment in the assisted areas. This changed its name to the *Office and Service Industry Scheme* (OSIS), which provided special grants for activities like administration offices, R. & D. laboratories and central training establishments that create additional employment in assisted areas. Three types of grant were available (Daniels, 1985a):

1. A negotiable grant to employers of up to £8000 for each job created in the assisted area.
2. A fixed grant up to £2000 for essential employees moving with their work (up to a maximum of 30 per cent of the jobs being created).

3. A contribution towards the cost of studies determining the feasibility of a particular activity in the assisted areas.

Response to the scheme was poor. Between 1972 and 1983, the cumulative number of offers of assistance finally accepted under the OSIS scheme was less than 7 per cent of the total and only 28 615 new service jobs were created, out of a total for all industries of over 420 000 (Table 8.4). The North-West and Yorkshire and Humberside have together accounted for nearly one-half of new service jobs, which in turn have been more popular in the IAs than in either the DAs or the SDAs. The OSIS was abolished in 1984 when the *Regional Selective Assistance Scheme* (see below) began to cover both manufacturing and service projects.

The government itself encouraged decentralization by relocating some of its own offices: for example, the Department of Employment to Runcorn, the Passport Office to Newport and Peterborough, the Driving and Vehicle Licensing

TABLE 8.4 Offers of Office and Service Industry Scheme assistance accepted, by regions and assisted areas of Britain, 1972–1983

	No. of grants	%	Value (£m)	%	Estimated new employment	%
REGIONS						
Scotland	57	3.6	7 882	3.4	2 646	2.4
Wales	89	7.9	9 471	8.1	4 350	7.0
North-East	80	7.9	10 293	8.2	4 490	7.8
North-West	171	8.2	14 257	7.7	8.514	9.0
Yorkshire and Humberside	94	7.0	8 146	11.4	6 174	9.6
South-West	16	5.1	419	2.2	383	3.1
East and West Midlands	22	5.3	7 500	3.4	2 058	10.6
ASSISTED AREAS						
Special Development Areas	180	6.9	23 402	5.8	8 795	5.2
Development Areas	139	7.1	19 874	11.3	7 435	7.2
Intermediate Areas	210	6.4	14 693	7.6	12 385	8.5
TOTALS	529	6.7	57 969	6.9	28 615	6.8

Source: Daniels (1985a p. 242).

Centre to Morriston (Swansea), the Department of Health and Social Security to Newcastle upon Tyne, and the Royal Mint to Llantrisant. It also established the Location of Offices Bureau (LOB) in 1963, a promotion agency designed to help in the decentralization process. Between 1963 and 1977, over 4000 firms consulted LOB, but less than one-half eventually relocated all or part of their operation, of which 82 per cent moved only within the South-East (Daniels, 1985a). Consequently, in 1977 LOB's terms of reference changed, away from decentralization and towards promoting a better distribution of offices in England and Wales. However, it was soon realized that the inner cities were declining (see below) and, in complete contrast to its earlier role, LOB attempted to encourage inner-city office development in London (but not in the City) and provincial cities. With such a chequered history, it was not surprising that the agency was terminated in 1979.

Indeed, the inappropriateness of many regional policy measures in the United Kingdom to the recession period of the late 1970s was recognized (Townsend, 1987). Full employment had come to an end, investment in new plants was declining and new 'problem areas', like the West Midlands and the inner cities, began to emerge. Regional policy was still primarily related to manufacturing, which no longer represented the expanding sector of the economy. It was against this back-

ground that the new Conservative party announced major cuts in regional aid in 1979. By 1982, assisted areas had been reduced substantially and in 1984 SDAs were abolished, leaving just DAs and IAs (see Fig. 8.8). In the 1984 changes, IAs were increased (to cover 20 per cent of the working population) and, for the first time, included the West Midlands; at the same time, the old SDAs had been relegated to the status of DAs (now covering 15 per cent of the working population) and many original DAs had either become IAs or lost assisted status altogether. Such manœuvres led to both a saving of approximately £300 million per year and a shift in balance away from the standard Regional Development Grant (available in DAs but not IAs) and towards Regional Selective Assistance (available on a competitive (discretionary) basis in both DAs and IAs). Additional service industries became eligible for aid for the first time in 1984, but just for Regional Development Grants and thus only in DAs. Both DAs and IAs are eligible for maximum assistance under the EC's ERDF (Ilbery, 1986).

Much debate exists on the 'efficiency' of regional policy initiatives in the United Kingdom, although work by Moore and Rhodes (1973) and Moore, Rhodes, and Tyler (1977; 1986) suggests some success. In particular, their latest report (1986) estimates that regional policy generated 450 000 net manufacturing jobs (those generated by regional policy and surviving to the end of the period being evaluated) in the DAs between 1960 and 1981; a further 154 000 jobs had been generated but were lost before 1981. These estimates excluded any secondary or multiplier effects on employment in service industries in the DAs, which could have resulted in up to a further 180 000 jobs. If this figure is added to the 450 000, a total of surviving regional policy jobs stood at 630 000 in 1981. To quote Moore *et al.* (1986 p. 9), 'this is a real and substantial achievement.'

Further investigation by Moore *et al.* (1986) demonstrates that there was an almost equal division in the generation of the 450 000 manufacturing jobs between the 1960s and the 1970s: thus 'regional policy continued to be effective in the 1970s' (p. 10). Even between 1976 and 1981, when the economic recession was at its most severe, 12 000 net manufacturing jobs per year were generated. Moore *et al.* continued to show that:

1. Individual industries responded to regional policy very differently, with chemicals and steel, for example, receiving large amounts of grant and creating very few extra jobs, and industries like clothing, vehicles, and electrical engineering receiving relatively little grant but creating a relatively large number of jobs.
2. The urban parts of the DAs failed to secure the share of policy jobs that their existing manufacturing employment would have suggested.
3. Each new job created by regional policy cost about £40 000 (at 1982 prices).

This last point raises the question of the cost-effectiveness of regional policy, especially as regional differences in economic health have not been reduced significantly (see Chapter 16.2). Knox and Agnew (1989 p. 363) see regional policy as 'both an expensive luxury and an increasing liability', a view shared increasingly by the USA and the United Kingdom Conservative Governments. This relates to the fairly rapid globalization of the world economy (Chapters 1.2 and 14.3), in which firms no longer confine their choice of site(s) to one country; national competitiveness is now more important than regional competitiveness. Massey (1979*b* and 1984*b*) also suggests that there is not really a 'regional problem' in the old sense, but a localized pattern of spatial inequality and restructuring (Chapter 9.2 and 15.1). Indeed, local and especially urban problems had become very important by the late

1970s, causing Keeble (1977) to argue that spatial policy in Britain should be less regional-based and more urban-based. It is to urban and rural policies that this chapter now turns.

8.4 The urban and rural dimension

With the efficacy of explicit regional policy measures being questioned, attention in the United Kingdom became focused on more locally-based policies, especially for the inner cities but also for many rural areas (both inside and outside assisted areas). Considerable central–local government conflict emerged as the former began to encroach upon small-firm and small-area initiatives introduced by agencies like local authorities. Indeed, local authority expenditure has been reduced at a time of increasing national support for local-area/inner-city policies. Whether or not national policy has been undermining local democracy, urban policy has itself undergone considerable change, from a system of planned decentralization to a programme of support for inner cities.

Between 1978 and 1988, a complex set of measures was introduced to finance inner-city development; these are too numerous to discuss in detail and are summarized in Table 8.5. The Inner Urban Areas Act of 1978 gave additional powers to 'designated' inner-city authorities (those with severe levels of deprivation, according to the 1971 census). Three tiers of deprived inner-city areas were designated. First, seven inner-city *partnerships* (between central and local governments) were created in those areas with the worst deprivation (Liverpool, Birmingham, Lambeth, London's Dockland, Manchester/Salford, Newcastle/Gateshead, and Hackney/Islington); these became eligible for additional revenue in the form of a 75 per cent government grant. Secondly, 15 inner-city *programmes*, with fewer powers and lower levels of support, were defined. Finally, 13 designated *districts* were provided with enhanced powers but no government grants (Lever, 1987*b*). Designated area authorities were, therefore, given special powers to declare improvement areas, provide advance factory buildings and assist small firms. By 1981, the number of partnerships had risen to nine, the number of programmes to 23 and the number of districts to 16 (Fig. 8.9*a*).

In 1981 the first *Urban Development*

TABLE 8.5 Inner-city policies in the United Kingdom, 1978–1988

Date	Policy	Details
1978	Inner Urban Areas Act	7 Partnership Areas 15 Programme Areas 13 Designated Districts
1981	Enterprise Zones (EZs)	11 Zones designated
	Urban Development Corporations (UDCs)	London's Docklands and Merseyside
	Merseyside Task Force	Toxteth
	Urban Development Grant Programme	Minimum public sector money to encourage private sector investment
	Inner City Enterprise	Property development company: inner-city projects with private sector funding
	Extension of Inner Urban Areas Act	9 Partnership Areas 23 Programme Areas 16 Designated Districts
1982	More EZs designated	Total reaches 25 by 1984
1984	Free Port Zones (FPZs)	6 designated at ports and airports
1985	City Action Teams (CATs)	5 agencies, spanning different government departments, to aid inner-city recovery
1987	Extension of UDCs	9 now designated
1988	Action for Cities	Includes: New UDC for Sheffield, extension of Merseyside UDC, 2 new CATs for Leeds and Nottingham, creation of Land Register, city grant for private sector development

Corporations (UDCs) were established in the Docklands of London and Merseyside. UDCs are independent bodies that are 100 per cent Department of the Environment financed and have powers superseding those of local authorities. They are answerable directly to central government and were, according to Hudson and Williams (1986), introduced as a reaction to the 'slowness' of local government policies. In 1981–2, the two UDCs received £82 million of government funding, of which £65 million were allocated to London's Dockland (which compares favourably with the £18 million that the largest inner-city partnership—Liverpool—received) (Lever, 1987b). The number of UDCs was later (1987) increased to six with the introduction of Teesside, Trafford Park (Manchester), Tyne and Wear, and the Black Country; these were followed in the next year by 'mini' UDCs in Bristol, Leeds, Wolverhampton, and central Manchester (and subsequently Sheffield) (Hetherington, 1988).

Such urban policies met with limited success and the inner-city partnerships, for example, failed to develop the anticipated 'integrated approach to policy formulation and implementation' (Hudson and Williams, 1986 p. 144). Indeed, Parkinson and Wilks (1985) comment upon the 'failure' of the Liverpool partnership. Fuelled by inner-city riots, further policy initiatives were introduced in 1981, including the Urban Development Grant Programme (UDGP), the Inner City Enterprise (ICE), the Merseyside Task Force and Enterprise Zones (Table 8.5).

The most discussed, and criticized, policy has been the designation of *Enterprise Zones* (EZs); 11 were announced in 1981 and by 1984 the number had been extended to 25 (Fig. 8.9b). EZs represent an attempt to create 'an urban economic policy to assist those cities that had experienced particularly acute employment difficulties' (Hudson and Williams, 1986 p. 115). In more detail, the benefits of EZ status over a ten-year period are (Hasluck, 1987 p. 165):

1. Exemption from general rates on industrial and commercial property (reimbursed to the local authority by the Treasury).
2. 100 per cent allowance from corporation and income tax for capital expenditure on industrial and commercial property.
3. Exemption from development land tax.
4. Priority to be given to applications from firms for certain customs facilities.
5. Exemption from industrial training levies.
6. Speedier administration of any controls remaining in force.
7. Reduced requests for statistical information.

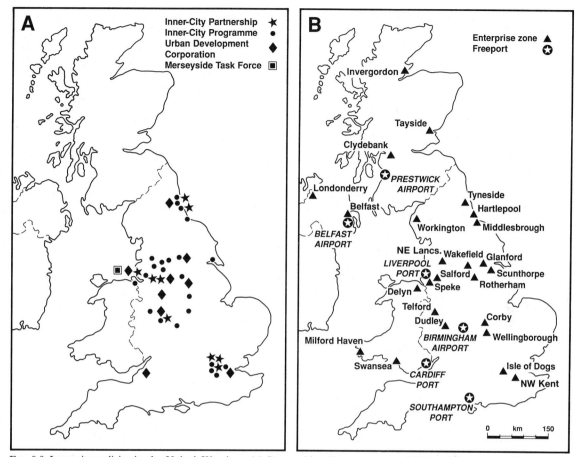

FIG 8.9 Inner-city policies in the United Kingdom: (*a*) Partnerships, Programmes, and Urban Development Corporations; (*b*) Enterprise Zones and Free Port Zones

EZ policy is administered by the local authorities in which they are located and it should be stressed that they are not all inner-city based, with some being located in suburban (e.g. Speke) and rural (e.g. Invergorden) areas. Early years of the scheme suggested a certain amount of success, with up to a quarter of derelict land/buildings being brought into productive use and over 700 firms (start-ups and transfers) established and more than 8000 new jobs created in the original 11 EZs between 1981 and 1983 (Lever, 1987*b*). However, success varied spatially, with Clydeside, Swansea, and Corby each accounting for more than 1000 new jobs (Bromley and Morgan, 1985; Lever, 1987*b*), compared to less than 100 each in Belfast and Gateshead. Branch plants of major companies or transport, distribution, and service industries were the main types of industry involved; the latter were attractive to female and

part-time workers but not to unemployed males. Indeed, inner cities are no longer the most attractive location for industry (see Chapter 4.1).

Despite some success, EZ policy has received considerable criticism (Norcliffe and Hoare, 1982; Anderson, 1983; Bromley and Morgan, 1985; Hasluck, 1987), with Massey (1982) suggesting that they represent another way in which the national government can create a 'political' space to attack local government and local services. In more detail, EZs have:

1. Created a boundary effect, whereby firms from just outside the designated area have relocated within the EZ to benefit from the financial benefits listed above. A negative shadow effect exists outside the zone, where the demand for, and rents of, buildings in adjacent areas have been falling (Norcliffe and Hoare, 1982). In

Clydeside for example, one of the most successful EZs, 66 per cent of the 1800 jobs created by 1984 came from short-distance transfers, with only 29 per cent from new start-ups and 5 per cent from firms already in the EZ before designation (Lever, 1987b). Between 1981 and 1983, 40 per cent of firms relocated from other areas to the original 11 EZs, of which 86 per cent had moved from within the same county (Hasluck, 1987). The number of new jobs created is, therefore, less than 10 per cent of the overall gross effect.

2. Failed to attract dynamic, innovative, small (sunrise) firms that would generate growth. Reflecting the boundary effect, EZs have simply attracted the traditional enterprises of their respective regions.

3. Offered few benefits to labour, despite recognizing that unemployment is the crucial inner-city problem. Instead the scheme favours entrepreneurs and the use of capital and space inputs (Norcliffe and Hoare, 1982).

4. Been very expensive. With over £130 million spent on EZs between 1981 and 1983 for example, this 'works out' at nearly £17 000 per gross job created or nearly £168 000 if the net effect (less than 10 per cent of all new jobs in EZs) is used (Hasluck, 1987).

5. Provided a 'fig leaf' to the government's desire to solve the problem of rising unemployment (Anderson, 1983 p. 341) and presented 'old style regional policy dressed up in a modern guise' (Hasluck, 1987 p. 167).

6. Reduced the power of the local authorities and increased central–local government conflict. In particular, Shutt (1984) argued that the financial incentives inside the EZs were used as a lever to make adjacent (Labour) councils reduce their business rates.

The growing conflict between central and local government initiatives is clearly demonstrated in Merseyside. Aware of its poor 'image', Liverpool City Council embarked upon a policy to stimulate the local market and create a better 'business climate' than other local authorities (derived spatial policy). As well as providing space and buildings, the council offered rent guarantees and financial support to attract advance office building, and agreed not to levy taxes on new office space until it was leased (Daniels, 1985a). The scheme led to an upsurge in office development before increasing national control— in the form

of the Inner City Partnership, Urban Development Corporation, Merseyside Task Force, City Action Team (see below), Enterprise Zone, and Freeport—created conflict, resentment and a reduced local commitment (Lindley, 1985; Parkinson and Wilks, 1985).

EZs were originally conceived to be 'free ports' and six *Free Port Zones* (FPZs) were duly announced in 1984 (Fig. 8.9b). These are intended to act as entrepôt zones for the processing of imported materials which, if re-exported, are exempt from customs duties and VAT. Apart from the financial savings of locating with an FPZ, other advantages (in theory) include reduced paperwork and bureaucratic regulations, agglomeration economies, increased employment opportunities and (because FPZs are policed and monitored by customs authorities) a safe and secure 'environment' for firms. Although too early to judge their relative success, FPZs have already been the subject of criticism, notably from Balasubramanyan and Rothschild (1985). As with EZs, FPZs may create a negative shadow effect in adjacent areas and encourage relocation rather than generate new investments. More worryingly, 'they appear to be FPZs in spirit, but not in substance' (Balasubramanyan and Rothschild, 1985 p. 23). Unlike the classic export-processing zones of Hong Kong, Singapore, and South Korea (Chapter 14.3), existing legislation on planning, health and safety, and employment (e.g. wages and welfare) will continue to apply in the United Kingdom's FPZs, and there will be no relief from taxation other than that pertaining to custom duties. Moreover, as all intra-EC trade is exempt from duties, FPZs in the United Kingdom will be unattractive to firms from other EC countries.

Inner-city policies continued in 1985 with the designation of five *City Action Teams* (CATs) for Birmingham, Liverpool, Merseyside/Salford, London (Hackney, Islington, and Lambeth), and Newcastle/Gateshead. These are small agencies embracing the Departments of Employment, Environment, and Trade and Industry; their introduction 'signals an increased orientation towards job creation and the use of the Urban Programme as a means to reduce inner city unemployment' (Hasluck, 1987 p. 164). More resources can be directed into the inner cities by the CATs, again bypassing the local authorities. The aim is to bring together those civil servants most responsible for business and preparing people for work, and to help break down departmental barriers.

Clearly, urban policy in the United Kingdom is 'much more confused than regional policy' (Lever, 1987b p. 256), being implemented by bodies that may be in direct conflict (e.g. national/ local government). For this reason, and others, an *Action For Cities* programme was announced in 1988, involving six government departments— Environment, Home Office, Employment, Education, Trade and Industry, and Transport. The 'plan' is effectively a repackaging of existing schemes, with some new money, and relies heavily on the Conservative party's belief of encouraging private sector initiatives and an entrepreneur culture. In more detail, 'Action For Cities' suggested a new UDC for the lower Don Valley, Sheffield; a doubling of the area covered by the Merseyside UDC; two new CATs, for Leeds and Nottingham; a simplified City Grant to encourage private-sector development in the inner city; two new road schemes, for London and the Black Country; the creation of a Land Register; the compulsory sale of large tracts of unused local-authority land; and extra provision of premises for new businesses in run-down inner cities. It is too early to judge whether 'Action For Cities' will have more success than some of its predecessors. However, it is clear that the government is determined to continue exerting increasing national control on the inner cities of the United Kingdom.

Turning attention away from the inner cities and towards government initiatives for rural areas, certain policies (mainly in relation to the United Kingdom's 'assisted' areas and the EC's Less Favoured Areas) have already been outlined in this chapter. Space does not permit a discussion of planning measures concerned with such 'protected' areas as National Parks, Areas of Outstanding Natural Beauty, Heritage Coasts, and Green Belts. However, the essentially explicit spatial policies of different government agencies need to be examined briefly. Three state agencies dominate rural development policies in the United Kingdom: the Rural Development Commission (simply the Development Commission until 1988); Mid-Wales Development; and the Highland and Islands Development Board (Fig. 8.10).

Formed in 1909, the Development Commission has been the subject of recent research (see Wil-

liams, 1984; Tricker and Martin, 1984; Chisholm, 1984 and 1985). The Commission operated throughout Great Britain until the Scottish and Welsh Development Agencies were formed in 1975 and 1976 respectively. Since the mid-1970s, the main task of the now *Rural Development Commission* has been to carry out a programme of work concerned with the creation of employment opportunities in the *Special Investment Areas* of England. In 1984, these were replaced by slightly less extensive *Rural Development Areas* (RDAs, see Fig. 8.10). The RDAs cover 'those parts of rural England which have the most severe problems—of unemployment, access to jobs, sparsity of population, and loss of population' (Chisholm, 1985 p. 282). Through the provision of factory premises, jobs are created in three ways: first, by building new factory and workshop units in the RDAs and meeting the whole cost; secondly, by contributing 25 per cent of the cost of converting redundant buildings in RDAs (on projects up to £50 000); and thirdly, by collaborating with local authorities throughout rural England, sharing the cost on a fifty–fifty basis. Each of these will be outlined briefly.

The Rural Development Commission uses approximately 50 per cent of its funds for the construction of small advance factories and workshops in England. Initially, these were constructed by English Estates in the Special Investment Areas and by the Council for Small Industries in Rural Areas (COSIRA) elsewhere. However, since 1981 English Estates has taken over the whole programme of factory and workshop construction, leaving COSIRA to concentrate, until its incorporation into the Rural Development Commission in 1988, upon its other duties (see below). Between 1974 and 1983, 930 workshops and 1 980 000 feet of floorspace were completed (Williams, 1984; Chisholm, 1985). Most of the premises are located in small settlements (less than 10 000 inhabitants), in the remoter and upland parts of England. As with the other rural agencies, spatially concentrated investment within the rural areas has been favoured. The limited evidence available (Chisholm, 1985) suggests that up to three-quarters of the jobs created by the programme are either in entirely new firms or attributable to expansion following relocation; this compares favourably with the achievements of the EZs for example.

The *conversion of redundant buildings pro-*

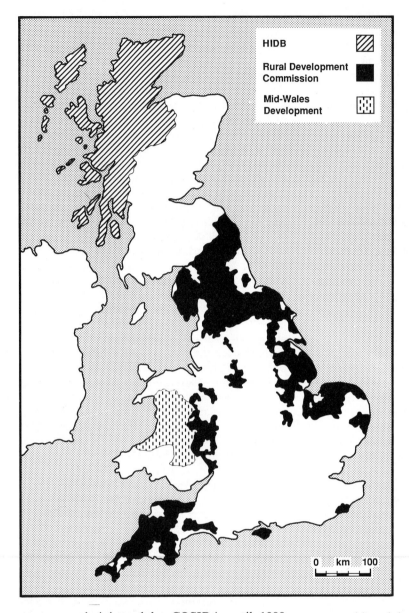

FIG 8.10 Rural Development Agencies in Great Britain (*source*: based on Chisholm, 1985 p. 281 and Hudson and Williams, 1986 p. 173)

gramme, administered by COSIRA until 1988, has experienced similar interest since its full introduction in 1983. Between 1983 and 1984, 222 schemes were approved, costing the Development Commission £450 000 in grants. Since 1984, over 300 schemes per annum have received support, leading to approximately 1500 employment opportunities, at between £750 and £1000 per job. COSIRA was a fully funded agency of the Development Commission, although it was only a lender of the last resort. Its primary function was

to provide advice and training for small businesses in rural England. Consequently, COSIRA played an important role in the Conservative government's policy of encouraging small business ventures in the United Kingdom.

Introduced in 1981, the *partnership workshop scheme* involves the Rural Development Commission matching local authority expenditure on suitable workshop projects identified by the authorities. Responsibility for the design, letting, and management of workshops rests with the relevant local authority, but the scheme provides an opportunity for the Rural Development Commission to meet local needs. Although much smaller than the factory and workshop programme (in terms of expenditure and floorspace), the scheme helped to provide over 1000 jobs by March 1984 (Chisholm, 1985). One of the main problems, however, is that expenditure by local authorities is controlled by central government, representing yet another example of increasing national control over local government policies. Indeed, local-authority reactions to the government's aim of encouraging the development of small businesses in rural areas (Circular 22/80) have been very varied (Tricker and Bozeat, 1983). Such derived spatial policy has seen some local authorities respond positively, by providing grants and loans for 'rural' projects, and others to make few, if any, changes in policy.

Similar central control is exercised over *Mid-Wales Development*, which replaced the Development Board for Rural Wales in 1977 and is directly responsible to the Secretary of State. With a very limited budget, of just £10 million in 1984 for example (Williams, 1984), the agency has adopted a policy of concentrated investment. Besides overseeing and spending about 50 per cent of its annual budget on the growth and development of Newtown in Powys, four 'tiers' of factory provision form the basis of the overall strategy. First, loans, grants, and equity capital are available for factory developments of over 10 000 feet in five growth centres; secondly, similar incentives for workshops of less than 5000 feet are provided in nine special towns; thirdly, a range of small factories and workshops are encouraged in eight key towns; and finally, an experimental programme of initiatives has been undertaken in 25 villages. Not surprisingly, therefore, Mid-Wales Development has been criticized for ignoring the remoter rural areas. However, it had helped to provide more than 7000 jobs in 360 units by 1983 (Planning Exchange, 1985). About 40 to 60 per cent of the agency's budget is usually spent on manufacturing and service industries (Williams, 1984) and, unlike the Development Commission, most factories are built to the needs of specific firms (Fothergill *et al.*, 1987).

Finally, in this chapter, the *Highland and Islands Development Board* (HIDB) was established in 1965 to promote 'an overall strategy of regional development in the north of Scotland'

(Hudson and Williams, 1986 p. 174). In contrast to its English and Welsh counterparts, it has adopted a more broadly-based policy, relying less on the provision of industrial premises and instead spending around 30 and 20 per cent of its budget on tourism and fishery projects respectively. However, the HIDB favours concentrated development, in three major areas (Fort William, Inverness, and Caithness) and 27 rural development, or growth, points (Hudson and Williams, 1986). Despite this, the Board has more recently diverted some attention to the remoter rural areas and actively promoted community co-operatives; by 1983, for example, it had provided funds for 14 such initiatives, creating jobs for 40 full-time and 150 part-time employees in horticulture, fisheries, manufacturing, and other projects (Williams, 1984). As with the Rural Development Commission and Mid-Wales Development, the HIDB is seriously constrained by a lack of financial resources.

8.5 Summary

This chapter has outlined and briefly assessed the effects of a wide range of government policies on economic location and change. Attention has been concentrated upon implicit and explicit spatial policies. The distinction between different types of policy is scale dependent and for this reason three scales of analysis formed the focus of attention. There can be little doubt that, as with other factors examined in the 'context of change' section of this book, government policy has played an important role in shaping temporal and spatial changes in the distribution of economic activities.

Governments intervene in the process of economic development for many reasons, but the level of intervention varies between different types of economic system and sectors of an economy. However, it should be clear that:

● Government policy affects the location of economic activity both directly and indirectly, as well as affecting other factors of change (e.g. labour cost relations, transport costs—by deregulation, and the organization of businesses—by merger policy).

● The distinction between implicit and explicit spatial policies raises the issue of whether the problems of particular areas should be addressed by spatial or aspatial policies (see Chapter 16.2). An element of uncertainty will always exist as to whether economic change is due to government policy or whether it would have occurred anyway.

- A large number of policy initiatives have been introduced since the early 1980s, but their effects upon economic location and change are for the most part still to be assessed.
- The Common Agricultural Policy is an excellent example of government intervention in the primary sector because the balance between implicit and explicit spatial policies has continued to change since the early 1960s. Present policy is attempting to deal with such problems as food surpluses and environmental degradation that were in part created by earlier policies.
- National defence policies in the USA and the United Kingdom have had a spatially varied impact, with prime military and high-technology contracts being concentrated in such states as California and New York and in southern England respectively.

- A range of explicit spatial policies, of both a negative and positive nature, have been used in France and the United Kingdom in an attempt to reduce the dominance of the Paris and London regions and to generate employment in the more peripheral areas.
- A plethora of policies now exist for the urban and rural areas of the United Kingdom; these will require close monitoring. Many of these have been introduced by central rather than local governments, creating a source of conflict that could reduce the level of success in solving urban and rural problems.

Government policy is, therefore, an important factor shaping patterns of economic location and change. However, it is only one of many influencing factors. Attention in the next chapter turns away from economic factors and examines the effect of social and cultural factors on the changing distribution of land use and economic activity.

9

The Social and Cultural Context

Economic systems are created and continuously modified within particular social and cultural settings. This relatively simple statement needs emphasizing, for the distribution of economic activities cannot be explained without considering the role of social and cultural factors (Massey, 1984b). Yet in their explanations of spatial patterns, economic geographers have examined how economic processes operate unevenly over space; they have not really investigated the importance of social and cultural processes in the distribution of economic activities. Social relations (interactions between social groups in society e.g. class, gender, race), however, have an important spatial dimension, for as Massey (1985 p. 12) remarks, 'social relations are constructed over space' and 'it is not just that the spatial is socially constructed; the social is spatially constructed too' (Massey, 1984a p. 6). Different societies evolve in different localities; this creates varied local/regional responses to national processes of economic change and leads to uneven economic development (see Chapters 15 and 16).

Three general points need to be made at the outset. First, societies evolve over time within different cultural contexts. In turn, different societies and cultures encourage contrasting spatial patterns of economic activity (see below). If society changes so too will the nature of its economic activities. This leads to an important early conclusion: it is possible to understand the nature of an economic system only within the context of its specific social setting, both spatially and temporally. Time and geographical specificity is a dominant feature of the structuralist approach to explaining uneven economic development (Chapter 2.2). This approach advocates the adoption of a historical perspective; for example, the spatial dimension of agricultural and industrial change in the United Kingdom can be understood only be considering the nature of

specific 'regions' in the past (Massey, 1984b; Marsden et al., 1986b). Local areas experience changes that are unique to their locality, reflecting local culture, history, and personalities. Massey (1983) sees local economies as the product of a 'combination of layers', built up in response to successive rounds of structural change and investment. Each new layer interacts with existing layers and, in theory, brings about a new economic basis for social organization.

Secondly, economic systems change in response to changes in the many other factors examined in this book, such as technology, factors of production, markets, and government policy. However, it needs to be stressed that these factors are, in turn, shaped and conditioned by social and cultural influences, causing each to have a varied spatial impact. For example, at the macro scale the diffusion of new agricultural technology and crops varies over space according to the distribution of different cultural traits like religion and race (see below).

Thirdly, a two-way relationship appears to exist between space and society. Although social and cultural factors help to 'determine' the spatial nature of economic change, the latter in turn affects social relations. A region that originally developed on the basis of a particular type of industry will have a specific set of social relations and class structures (Massey, 1983). It is these relations that help to shape the nature of economic change in that region and, of course, the future social structure (see Section 9.2).

The study of economic location and change, therefore, cannot be isolated from the more general study of socio-spatial structures. As Dicken and Lloyd (1981 p. 12) state, 'in order to understand how and why economic activity is arranged spatially we need to understand the ways in which society operates.' It should be impressed upon students of social science that the processes creating spatial inequalities and change in economic activity are not necessarily spatial in origin; instead they arise from processes operating in the social, economic, political, and cultural spheres. There are no purely spatial processes, but neither are there non-spatial social processes (Massey, 1984b). Society does not operate on the head of a pin; it functions in a spatial environment in which movement, distance, perception of the environment, and differences between places have an important influence on the character of a society. Whilst geographers have to draw upon the work of other social scientists, the latter need also to appreciate the value of economic geography (see also Chapter 1.1).

With these points in mind, this chapter is devoted to two main themes:

1. The role of social and particularly cultural factors in influencing the changing distribution of economic activity, in relation to agriculture.
2. The relationship between social organization and the restructuring of economic activity, in relation to industry.

Together, the two themes help to demonstrate the two-way relationship between location and social and cultural factors. The first theme examines the effect that spatial differences and changes in social and cultural factors have on patterns of economic activity, taking agricultural land use as an example, whereas the second demonstrates how the changing distribution of economic activity (in this case industry) can influence local societies and class structures. Society, culture, and location are, therefore, highly interrelated and the local economic impact of national processes of change, for example, are mediated by the social character of locality.

9.1 Social and cultural factors in agriculture

Two general points regarding the effect of social and cultural factors on agricultural land use and change needs to be made at the outset. First, as with other forms of economic activity, the importance of social and cultural factors is scale dependent. At the individual farm level, socio-personal factors, such as age and education, can have a significant influence on decision-making behaviour, whereas cultural factors, such as language and religion, may be more important at the group level. Secondly, economic change and modernization may have reduced the significance of such factors as religion and traditional beliefs in agriculture. Nevertheless, they continue to exert more than a passing effect on the agricultural geography of different areas, especially in developing countries but also in developed economies. It is mainly to the latter that this section is addressed.

Research has highlighted the importance of socio-personal influences in agricultural decision-making (see Ilbery, 1978 and Chapter 10.2). Although agriculture has become increasingly industrialized since the 1960s (Healey and Ilbery, 1985a), it is still essentially a family business (Gasson et al., 1988), where prestige and status are sought by most landowners. For many, pride of ownership is more important than the use to which the land is put (Mather, 1986). Consequently, psychological characteristics and non-economic motives help to account for low levels of production and traditional farming systems. Indeed, with rising land values it would be more 'economic' for some farmers to sell their holdings and invest the capital elsewhere. However, most are dissuaded from this course of action by such factors as a personal preference for working the land, being independent, enjoying a challenging occupation, and social inertia. The latter was shown to be particularly important in the traditional but declining hop-farming region in Hereford and Worcestershire (see Chapter 11.2) and horticultural production in the Vale of Evesham (Ilbery, 1985b).

Psychological characteristics and motives in farming are in turn related to the age and education of the farmer. Both 'variables' are known to affect the adoption of agricultural innovations for example (see Chapter 6.3). Younger farmers tend to be better educated than their older counterparts and are more likely to seek information, be innovative and have a more positive attitude towards government loans and grants, the borrowing of capital and the taking of risk. These differences have important implications for the spatial incidence of farming systems and reflect the contrasting values held by farmers. In a study of the values of hop-farmers in the West Midlands (Ilbery, 1983*d*), important differences emerged on the basis of their age. Younger hop-farmers (under forty-five years) placed more emphasis on meeting a challenge, making maximum income, and expanding the business than those over forty-five, who stressed the importance of independence.

In a case study of the Norfolk tobacco belt in southern Ontario, Fotheringham and Reeds (1979) asked a sample of tobacco-growers to name their choice of substitute crop(s) if the demand for tobacco was to fall. Of the four variables affecting the farmers' choice (area of land owned, amount of local labour, age of the farmer, and amount of expansion already undertaken on the farm), age emerged as the most important. The older farmers chose wheat as the main substitute, a crop with an assured yield and market and one that would provide a return within the first year of production. In contrast, the younger farmers selected strawberries and in some cases livestock. These are riskier enterprises, with uncertain but potentially higher long-term yields and returns. Clearly, the latter group was prepared to gamble and experiment with new crops, whereas the older farmers were satisficers and not interested in 'risky' crops.

The premier importance of age in the development of the farm business is confirmed by Hine and Houston (1973). However, age is closely related to the family development cycle (Gasson *et al.*, 1988), which is particularly relevant to larger family farm businesses with likely successors. Younger farmers with children are often attracted to innovations needing technical knowledge and strive to increase the total value of their assets. At a later stage in the development cycle, when children have either left home or are established in a farm business, the farmer becomes more interested in security and consolidation.

At larger scales of analysis, cultural factors (like religion, language, and race) have played an important role in shaping patterns of agricultural change. Religion, for example, affects global patterns of farming in both negative and positive ways (Grigg, 1984). Religious beliefs help to explain the almost complete absence of pig-farming in Moslem areas of the world (Central Asia, India, Malaysia, and Indonesia) and the high density of cattle in India. While Moslems consider the pig to be an unclean animal, Hindus and Buddhists believe that it is wrong to kill animals (especially cattle); indeed, in some Indian states it is illegal to slaughter cattle.

More positively, there has been a connection, since the earliest records, between wine production and religion (Stanislawski, 1975) and Dickenson and Salt (1982 p. 163) argue that 'much of the present spatial pattern of wine production can be explained by the diffusion of viticulture in association with conquest, religion and trade.' The spread of the vine can be related to the emergence and spread of Western civilization. For example, the Phoenicians and Greeks were responsible for diffusing the vine and wine around the Mediterranean, to Italy, southern France, Spain, and North Africa, and viticulture became part of the Mediterranean 'triad' (wheat, olives, and vines). The Romans then aided the diffusion process northwards into Europe, as part of their campaign of conquest and occupation. They established a pattern of viticulture in Europe that largely survives today. By the sixteenth century, the vine had been taken overseas by the Spanish and, with the exception of Australia and South Africa, the main producing areas outside Europe (Argentina, California, Chile) are of Spanish origin (Grigg, 1984).

With quite sharp cultural differences often occurring between nation states, it is possible to hypothesize that farming will differ on either side of international boundaries. This topic has received scant attention in the literature, not least because it is very difficult to 'isolate' the effect of any one factor on agricultural land-use patterns. However, Reitsma (1971; 1986) has examined agricultural differences on either side of the USA/Canadian border. In a detailed case study of the Okanagan Valley region, one of the reasons given for the more intensive and diversified system of farming on the Canadian side was that of cultural background. Boosted by tourism and retirement, the smaller farms in Canada produced more small fruits, grapes, and vegetables than on the American side and often marketed them direct to the public. Many of the Canadian farms were run by first-generation immigrants, largely of south-east European origin, with a cultural heritage in fruit and vegetable production. The farm operation was a committed family business, where the wife and children provided much of the farm labour and the husband often engaged in off-farm work. As Reitsma (1986) demonstrates, the immigrants have been more willing than the indigenous farmers to work harder and accept a lower standard of material well-being; they are more self-sufficient, less commercialized and have an 'old world' outlook on life.

Even within national boundaries, geographers have long reported on what Kollmorgen (1941 and 1943) called 'cultural islands' of agricultural activity that are 'out of line' with the general structure and spatial organization of farming in a region. Indeed, different cultural interpretations of the resource base explain in great part the rather anomalous juxtaposition of two different patterns of land use, which often persist in a relatively homogeneous physical setting (Pigram, 1972). Studies of such contrasts fall into two categories: first, those that emphasize the farming systems of particular ethnic groups; and secondly, those that concentrate upon specific and often specialized crops, again cultivated by immigrant groups.

Within the first group, the successful farming systems of the Mennonite immigrants in Canada and the USA have attracted considerable attention (Todd and Brierley, 1977; McQuillan, 1978; De Lisle, 1982). Todd and Brierley demonstrate how the different ethnic groups in southern Manitoba responded in a variety of ways to the prevailing physical and economic environments; each group had different cultural appraisals of the natural resource. In particular, the German-speaking Mennonites, who came from the Ukraine in 1874, were already familiar with prairie-like farming conditions and were the first farmers to cultivate the prairie properly. They are very progressive, innovative, and successful, and run highly mechanized farms on a four-year rotation and an infield–outfield system (system of more intensively cultivated crops near the village and less intensive farming in fields further removed) (De Lisle, 1982). However, they still uphold traditions and are closely related to their past, particularly in terms of social and cultural values and religious beliefs. In complete contrast,

the Slavonic farmers in the area have lower education levels and much poorer farming systems; their response to economic change has been introspective and whilst this helps to preserve their ethnic identity, it means that they have not integrated into the wider agricultural community.

Similar contrasts are drawn by McQuillan (1978) in a historical study of three immigrant groups of farmers in central Kansas (the Mennonites, French-Canadians, and the Swedish), each of which represented a cultural island of farming. In terms of farm size differences, the Swedish immigrants could be said to be the most successful (Table 9.1). However, this takes no account of land-use intensity and in this respect McQuillan shows that the Mennonites were clearly the most successful. Their intensive, mainly wheat and dairy, farms were a reflection of 'hard work, frugal habits, community co-operation, and the re-investment of capital in agriculture' (p. 63); this contrasted with the 'slovenly, lazy and spendthrift' (p. 64) attitude of the French-Canadian farmers who tended to produce corn (maize) using poor husbandry, primitive methods, and antiquated machinery.

Tobacco provides a good example of a specialist crop grown by migrating ethnic groups. For example, the diffusion of tobacco in the USA has been related to religion and the nationality of farmers; in particular, the social network in ethnic neighbourhoods acts as an interpersonal communication channel for the spread of tobacco culture (Raitz and Mather, 1971; Raitz, 1973; Buchanan, 1975). In Wisconsin, the distribution of tobacco is related not to physical factors, markets, labour, or economic inertia, but to the distribution of ethnic groups and Norwegians in particular (Fig. 9.1). As Raitz and Mather (1971 p. 688) hypothesize, 'the social and cultural variable might provide the best explanation for the distribution of tobacco in western Wisconsin.' When Norwegians began entering the USA in the late 1830s they were very poor and knew nothing about

TABLE 9.1 Farm size differences between three immigrant groups in central Kansas, 1875–1925

	1875	1885	1895	1905	1915	1925
Swedes	160	184	193	251	240	276
Mennonites	185	142	141	161	172	196
French-Canadians	164	153	175	184	177	214

Source: McQuillan (1978 p. 60).

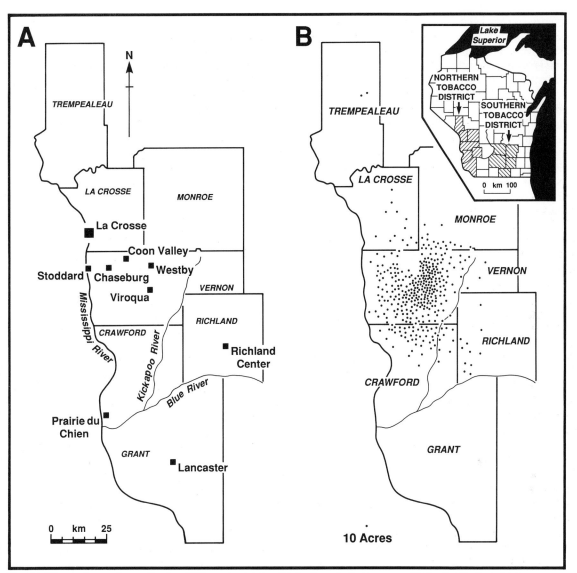

FIG 9.1 The northern tobacco district of Wisconsin: (*a*) the distribution of ethnic groups; (*b*) the distribution of tobacco (*source*: Raitz and Mather, 1971 p. 693)

tobacco. Those establishing their home in Wisconsin saw tobacco-farming as a source of income; its labour-intensive nature and low return per hour was similar to small-scale farming systems in Norway. The best way to gain knowledge of tobacco culture was to become a sharecropper, whereby a landowner provided rent-free accommodation and the major fixed costs (e.g. land, buildings, and equipment) for growing tobacco, in return for a proportion (30–50 per cent) of the gross return from the final crop.

From these beginnings, the tobacco crop soon diffused through a community strongly united by religion, occupation, and a common social and cultural background. Work exchange groups, church membership, and farmer co-operatives helped to reinforce the cohesion of the Norwegian community and spread the tobacco culture (Raitz, 1973). Tobacco became a family affair, with women and children working the fields. Such a commitment contrasted with the indigenous farmers, who were more interested in less labour-intensive crops with higher net incomes. In a 25 per cent sample of tobacco-growers from western Wisconsin in the late 1960s, Raitz and Mather (1971) found that 70 per cent were Norwegian and 80 per cent had Norwegian wives. The latter was explained by intermarriage between ethnic groups, especially between Germans and Norwegians. Religion provided an important link between these two groups, as over 90 per cent of the Norwegian growers and 50 per cent of the Germans were Lutheran. Although not advocating a deterministic approach to tobacco production in Wisconsin (not all Norwegians produce tobacco), Raitz and Mather (1971 p. 696) conclude that 'the direct and indirect association of Norwegian ethnic stock and tobacco production in this region is remarkably pronounced.'

Similar conclusions are drawn by Buchanan (1975) for the association between south European immigrants and tobacco-growing in the Australian states of Queensland and New South Wales. Two areas of tobacco production exist— inland and coastal. The former has a long history, dominated by a system of sharecropping (where landowners receive between 20 and 30 per cent of the gross return for tobacco), and the latter is relatively new, with many previous immigrant 'inland' sharecroppers buying their own farms (Fig. 9.2). The south Europeans formed a close-knit community, where the extended family idea was highly suited to the labour-intensive tobacco industry. Usually, more than one sharecropping family worked on the same farm and the immigrants tended not to integrate with their land-owning counterparts. However, upward social mobility was sought and after learning the complexities of the tobacco culture as sharecroppers, many immigrants saved enough money to purchase their own holdings in the coastal areas. The cohesive nature of the immigrant community ensured concentrated pockets of tobacco production.

In theory, such cultural islands of agricultural activity may fade over time, either because the cultural group becomes incorporated into the general agricultural system of the area or because the local farmers begin practising similar types of farming to the immigrants. The latter has happened in the Namoi Valley of New South Wales for example, where local farmers ventured into cotton-growing after Californian immigrants had produced it successfully (Pigram, 1972). How-

ever, the evidence presented in this section suggests that immigrant ethnic groups continue to maintain close-knit and spatially concentrated neighbourhoods, and develop their own type of farming systems. What is clear is that social and cultural factors can affect agricultural land-use patterns and play an important role in the process of agricultural change.

9.2 Social organization and the restructuring of industry

A characteristic feature of societies with a substantial division of labour is their hierarchical organization. People become stratified into social groups according to their 'position' in society, which is related to the degree of power or influence held over resources. Three types of social-class groupings can be defined (Dicken and Lloyd, 1981):

1. *Economic*, depending upon the way money is earned.
2. *Social*, depending upon styles of living.
3. *Political*, depending upon the way in which power is allocated in society.

The three types are interrelated and important in understanding the process of structural change in industry (restructuring). Social relations are constituted geographically and most people live their lives locally, with their consciousness formed in a distinct place (Massey, 1984b). Different localities have different histories, class structures, and social characteristics, and respond in different ways to national economic changes and the emerging wider spatial divisions of labour (see Chapters 14.3, 15.2, and 16). Massey (1984b p. 195) summarizes the situation well: 'what we see are national processes in combination with and embedded in particular conditions producing the uniqueness of local economic and social structures.'

Industrial restructuring encourages social and class restructuring, with changes in national processes being moulded by existing conditions in local areas. This is the main thrust of work undertaken by Massey (1983 and 1984b), McDowell and Massey (1984), and Dunford and Perrons (1986) on the restructuring of the UK economy. The restructuring process is not, of

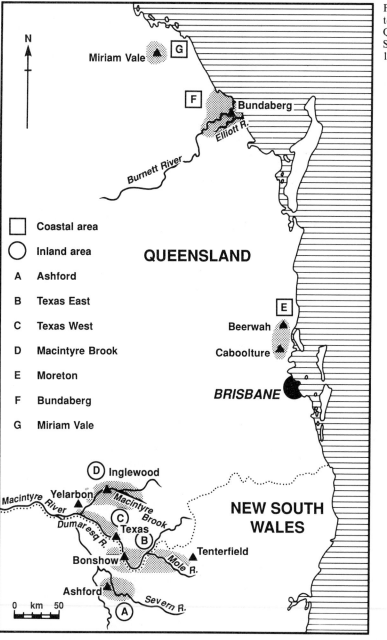

FIG 9.2 Inland and coastal tobacco-growing areas of southern Queensland and northern New South Wales (*source*: Buchanan, 1975 p. 183)

course, confined to the United Kingdom and analogies of the case studies developed in this section can be drawn from, for example, the traditional industrial regions of the USA and the West European coalfield areas.

Massey (1983) and McDowell and Massey (1984) examined social organization and economic change in five different areas and especially the role of women in the workplace (see Chapter 4.2):

1. Coal-mining areas of north-east England, South Wales and central Scotland.
2. Factory work in the cotton towns of Lancashire.

3. Sweated labour of the inner-London cloth-ing industry.
4. Agricultural gang workers of the Fens.
5. Cornwall.

Attention in this section focuses on both the coalfield areas (especially South Wales) and Cornwall, with brief reference to the other areas. How does social organization influence patterns of economic change? What has been the effect of industrial change on social change and class structure in these areas? What impact has the decentralization of jobs for women had on the different areas? Interest centres on the social and economic evolution of particular places, with the importance of both local characteristics and the changing role an area plays in the wider national/international economy being stressed. In order to understand economic changes in an area, therefore, it is necessary to take account of the way the social and economic characteristics of that area combine historically and how its changing position in the wider world economy leads to a series of layers of investment and disinvestment (see discussion in Chapter 15.2). No attempt was made by Massey (1983 and 1984) to provide a complete explanation of local class character-istics, as this requires consideration of many factors other than industrial change.

The influx of new industries into the mining areas of Britain since the late 1960s has led to quite major social and economic changes and helped to break down the strong sense of coher-ence and homogeneity. As the result of a depend-ence on coal-mining, the valleys of South Wales and other districts developed a very specific set of economic and social relations. This revolved around the dominance of the working class and the lack of a social hierarchical structure. The working class in turn was relatively undifferen-tiated, providing a basis for solidarity and polit-ical unity. Trade union membership, overwhelm-ingly in the same union, was high and worker resistance was greater than in less tightly-knit communities (especially as there was often only one employer to fight). This economic militancy was a male-dominated affair and reflected, in part, the lack of paid employment for women. Within this type of social organization, other social classes were of relative insignificance. How-ever, there had been 'quite a significant and fairly long-lasting old petty bourgeoisie' (Massey 1983

p. 77), providing locally-owned services in the fairly isolated mining communities. The relatively small market demand generated in the coal-mining areas discouraged the entry of national retailing chain stores (until the influx of new industries—see below) and this influenced the nature of economic change.

The coherence of the mining communities was not based solely on economic factors, but was aided by the following social and political pro-cesses:

1. The lack of paid work for women. Humphrys (1972 p. 30) summarizes the male attitude toward female employment: 'their place was seen as being in the home looking after the bread-winner.'
2. An active policy, by the then National Coal Board for example, to reduce alternative employment opportunities for men within the coal-mining areas.
3. The lack of competition from locally de-veloped firms for the male coal-miner.

These closely-knit and predominantly working-class mining communities were transformed, socially and economically, by the process of industrial restructuring. This took various forms. First, the incoming (often multinational) firms were attracted by the availability of cheap female labour, the quality and quantity of infrastructural facilities provided by the state, and the availabil-ity of 'assisted area' grants (Dunford and Perrons, 1986). Their entry coincided with the time when increasing redundancies in the coal-mining indus-try reduced the bargaining power of the male worker. The managerial personnel of the incom-ing industries did not seek prominent positions in local political and civic affairs. This can be explained in terms of many factors, including the greater diversity of incoming industries, the lack of senior management in the production-oriented branch plants, and the fact that individual managers saw the region and their present posi-tion as a temporary phase in their career develop-ment.

Secondly, the incoming industries were organ-izationally different from locally-based firms. They were often larger and exhibited an advanced division of labour, characterized by longer hier-archies of administration and control. Indeed, control and production had become spatially separated and only the middle and lower management were 'sent' to the coal-mining areas; the top managers and R. & D. activities remained at the headquarters of the multinational companies in London and the prosperous South-East (Chapter 7.2). Such spatial separation meant that the coalfield areas had become subjected to increasing external control. Moreover, the branch plants developed few links with the local/regional economy.

Thirdly, local entrepreneurs and services were being pushed out of the market place by the influx of national retail firms. As Massey (1983 p. 79) remarks, 'the old petty bourgeoisie can no longer reproduce itself as a class and . . . is being replaced by the wage labour of chain stores.' Fourthly, the changing nature of the industrial base in the mining areas had a dramatic effect upon the structure and organization of the working class. Its strength and coherence were being undermined as it declined in size. The increase in female activity rates, in low-paid clerical and service work, coincided with the continued retreat of basic industries and the exclusion of older men from the workforce. This in turn created conflicts within the working class, between the traditional bread-winners and women; the role of the latter was still perceived (by the men) to be at home. Finally, the increase in long-term male unemployment, the 'deskilling' of miners to cope with flow-line and routine assembly work, and the increase in female, often part-time, employment have all contributed to both a change in attitude to work and a decline in the basis of union organization. High turnover rates and greater absenteeism are part of the dismantling of the solidarity which characterized the coal-mining areas and with women not having the experience of union membership, no real basis of union organization exists.

Cornwall has also been affected by the spatial restructuring of industry in Britain. However, 'the social structure into which the new industries have been implanted could hardly be more of a contrast with the coalfields' (Massey, 1983 p. 83). This is because Cornwall has had a completely different history, dominated by employment in agriculture, mining, and tourism. The area has been characterized not by one large-scale industry but by a significant number of small industries and self-employment. Consequently, a highly organized and relatively well-paid working class has never existed.

Like the coal-mining areas, Cornwall has historically been characterized by a low female activity rate. Yet, the reasons for this are different and the attitude towards women is not the same. Cornwall County Council (1976, cited in Massey, 1983) advocated four reasons for the low rate of female participation in the full-time labour force:

1. The lack of work opportunities.
2. The availability of seasonal work during the summer.
3. The fairly high overall level of unemployment.
4. The geographical nature of the county and in particular the distribution of the population in relatively small towns and villages. This increases 'journey-to-work' distances and especially affects women without access to the family car.

In response to the last factor in particular, women tended to stay at home and either help out on the farm or become involved in the summer tourist industry by providing accommodation and food. Many married women, therefore, were neither just a wife nor fully integrated into the labour process (with union membership). A tradition of self-sufficiency and independence characterized the low-wage Cornish economy. Indeed, self-employed people are over twice as important in Cornwall as nationally.

The influx of industry into Cornwall, from the mid-1960s onwards, was similar to that experienced in the coalfield areas in two respects: first, it was dominated by branch plants providing low-paid semi-skilled and unskilled employment; and secondly, it was heavily biased towards female labour. However, the effect of this industrial restructuring on social and class relations has been quite different. In particular, there has been a less dramatic effect on, and conflict within, the working class. Wages have not been lowered relatively and trade union power has not been undermined (simply because labour has never been strongly organized). Another feature which distinguishes Cornwall from the coalfield areas is that part of the new in-migrating industry is small scale and run by middle-class entrepreneurs, attracted by the 'perceived environment' of the area rather than the desire to maximize profits. Indeed, it has been suggested that something of a semi-retirement culture prevails in Cornwall, comprising redundant and disenchanted executives from larger corporations (Perry, 1979).

McDowell and Massey (1984) conducted similar explorations into the effects of industrial change on social forms of production in different areas, with the role of women again emphasized. For example, the cotton towns of Lancashire, in contrast to the coalfield areas and Cornwall, have a long history of women working, joining unions, and being fairly well paid and independent. It is partly for these reasons, together with the lack of 'development area' status, that new industries chose not to move to the area (even though the decline of the cotton industry meant that female labour was available). In yet another contrast, the clothing industry in Hackney was long dominated by non-unionized and cheap female labour, working mainly from home and thus isolated from fellow workers. With decentralization of the industry from London and competition from cheap imports, survival of the industry has been possible only by intensifying labour inputs. This has often been through the extended family idea of ethnic groups. As a lack of alternative employment exists in the area, the poorly-paid rag trade remains the only option for women who are tied to their home.

From this discussion, it should be clear that it is very difficult to make empirical generalizations about the effects of industrial restructuring (in this case in the different regions of the United Kingdom). Each locality is unique, causing the national process of industrial decentralization to be locally varied in its operation and effects. This is because the social characteristics of different areas, themselves a reflection of traditional industrial structures, have 'created the preconditions for the new roles that they are coming to play' (Massey, 1983 p. 86).

9.3 Summary

This chapter has attempted to highlight the two-way relationship that exists between economic location and change on the one hand and social and cultural factors on the other. Spatial variations, and changes, in social and cultural factors affect the distribution of economic activity, as demonstrated in the case of agriculture. However, economic change (in response to national processes) varies between different localities according to the nature of local social relations. Some of the important points to emerge from this chapter are as follows:

- It is impossible to explain the nature of, and changes in, a local economic system without consideration of its specific social setting. A full understanding of economic location and change, therefore, can be obtained only be examining the history, culture, and personalities of particular localities.
- The effect of social and cultural factors on the distribution of economic activity differs according to the scale of analysis; social factors increase in significance with a reduction in scale to the level of the individual farm, firm, or office, whereas cultural factors become more important at more aggregate scales.
- Farmers' motives (and hence decisions and patterns of land use—see Chapter 10.2) are affected by such socio-personal factors as age, stage in family life cycle, and level of education.
- Cultural factors like religion and language help to create cultural islands of agricultural activity and continue to affect the pattern of agricultural change at the regional level.
- Economic change varies between localities and national processes of industrial change (e.g. decentralization) affect the nature of social change in these areas. For example, the influx of new industry had a far greater social impact on the mining communities of South Wales than it did on Cornwall.

The last seven chapters of this book have examined the effects of spatial variations in a wide range of factors on economic location and change. However, it is difficult to isolate the effects of any one factor because the decisions made by entrepreneurs are often affected by a complex interaction of factors. Some of these complexities are discussed in the next chapter.

10

Location and Land-Use Decision-Making

Many factors affecting the distribution and changing location of economic activities have been examined separately within the 'context of change' section of this book. The objective of this chapter is to examine the decision-making process and the relative importance of the factors involved. Interest in the way individuals and/or groups make location and land-use decisions emerged in the late 1960s, partly in response to the inadequacies of neoclassical location theory with its unreal assumptions of complete knowledge and full ability to use that knowledge (see Chapter 2). The term *location decision* refers to changes in the number, location, and size of establishments, and to the nature of activities occurring within them. It is, therefore, most applicable to decision-making in the secondary and tertiary sectors (involving, for example, factories and offices), although it is also relevant in the primary sector (e.g. mines). In contrast, *land-use decision* refers to changes in the number and size of units (e.g. farms, forests) and types of land use occurring on them; location tends to be fixed, a characteristic of most activities in the primary sector (e.g. agricultural land use). Inevitably, there is overlap between the ideas of location and land-use decisions; for example, the decisions of where to plant a forest is a location rather than land-use decision, just as the decision of what to manufacture at a given factory is a land-use rather than location decision.

Decision-making processes are usually quite complex and a considerable body of literature has emerged, in relation to both the different theories and methodologies developed in economic geography and the different sectors of an economy. Consequently, this chapter can only hope to be representative of these two 'elements' and select aspects for discussion. This will be achieved in two distinct stages: first, by briefly reviewing the different theoretical approaches to decision-mak-

ing in economic geography; and secondly, by examining location and land-use decision-making processes in practice, with reference to both developed market economies and centrally planned (socialist) economies.

10.1 Location and land-use decision-making in theory

The different theoretical perspectives on economic geography were considered at length in Chapter 2.2, where the emphasis was placed on philosophical and methodological issues and on the disadvantages of different approaches. Here, the intention is to consider briefly the nature of location and land-use decision-making from neoclassical, structuralist, and behavioural perspectives and to stress the importance of different factors.

Neoclassical approach

In traditional approaches to economic location, the decision-maker is assumed to be economically rational (economic man), with the ultimate goal of maximizing profitability (optimizer). This necessitates complete knowledge and a remarkable range of information regarding such factors as the costs of transporting products from the factory/farm to the market, labour costs, and the desirability of producing one product/crop *vis-à-vis* others. Profit maximization can be phrased in terms of finding the least-cost site (e.g. Weber) or the point of maximum demand (e.g. Losch). Weber, for example, assumed perfect competition in his analysis of a single firm reacting optimally to locational factors, with the ultimate aim of cost minimization.

Although the limitations of neoclassical models

are now widely recognized, they do retain a 'capacity to solve practical problems where the objective is to locate a single unit of production at the point of least operating costs' (Smith, 1979 p. 38). This may apply where the production unit operates in isolation from others, as in the Mexican steel industry (Kennelly, 1954–5); such situations are, however, rare, although a firm setting up a distribution system may well use this kind of approach.

To counter the problems surrounding economic rationality and profit maximization, extensions to neoclassical theory have been proposed. The concept of *spatial margins to profitability*, for example, was developed by Rawstron (1958) and Smith (1966). This demonstrates how both costs and revenues vary over space (Fig. 10.1), causing total cost and total revenue curves to intersect and enclose an area in which it is possible for a firm to make some profit, although not necessarily the maximum profit. The point of minimum costs is still the optimum location (unless revenue is higher at somewhere other than the least-cost point), but at every point within the spatial margins some profit is earned. The concept helps in the interpretation of patterns but it has received little attention outside geography; two factors have limited its practical application: first, the difficulty of empirical identification; and secondly, its limited value as an explanatory device (Smith, 1979).

Lack of suitable data have made it difficult to identify the spatial margins to profitability and the few studies undertaken suggest that the area can be very large and markedly unstable over time. For example, Taylor (1970) found that the spatial margins to profitability for the UK iron foundry industry covered most of Great Britain. Similarly, McDermott (1973) identified spatial margins for five industries in New Zealand and whilst the margins for the leather goods industry covered the whole country, smaller areas were enclosed for basic metal, sheetmetal, wire-working, and stationery. The margins were shown to shift substantially over time; for example, the margin for the basic metal industry contracted considerably between 1963 and 1969. It was for this reason, together with the fact that transport to the market was the only spatially variable cost assumed to be operating, that McDermott dismissed the spatial margins to profitability as being of limited value.

The concept of spatial margins to profitability also has limited explanatory power because it cannot explain the choice of final location within the margins; however, it remains useful for demonstrating how certain areas may be more profitable than others for certain industries and plants (Watts, 1987). Behavioural and structuralist approaches (see below) have attempted to overcome this deficiency by respectively concentrating upon the decision-making behaviour of individuals and the broader economic structures within which the entrepreneurs operate.

The concept of *psychic income* is another proposed extension to neoclassical theory (Greenhut, 1956). This attempted to overcome the problems surrounding the idea of 'complete knowledge' by incorporating non-economic motives into locational and land-use decision-making. The wish to live in one area rather than another or to practise a particular type of farming may be incorporated into the calculation of total costs and revenues, although it is difficult to actually measure the psychic income element. The concept provides a link between the neoclassical and behavioural approaches; however, by assuming that individuals are still attempting to maximize total income (monetary and psychic), it is firmly in the neoclassical tradition.

Further extensions to neoclassical theory have been outlined by Smith (1977 and 1979), in terms of the spatial aspects of welfare economics and territorial-production complexes. The optimal location for a new hospital or airport, for example, can be calculated using cost-benefit analyses (if costs and revenues can be redefined in broad social terms), where 'externalities' (see Chapter 17.1) like noise and pollution can be quantified and incorporated into the calculations. As with the spatial margins to profitability, an area is identified where benefits exceed costs and where well-being is increased; beyond the margins the net contribution of the facility is negative. As Smith (1979 p. 52) comments, 'who suffers where is socially determined as the location decision is made.' Yet again, however, such extensions are based on a single facility in isolation, which is unlikely in reality. This kind of *welfare approach* is still in the normative tradition of neoclassical theory because it is concerned with what *ought* to be there, based on a set of assumptions, rather than with an explanation of what *is* there.

In summary, location and land-use decisions

1. LEAST–COST MODEL

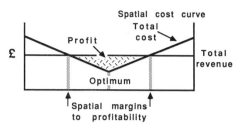

FIG 10.1 Spatial margins to
profitability

2. MAXIMUM SALES MODEL

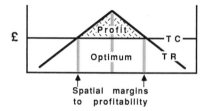

3. MAXIMUM PROFIT MODEL

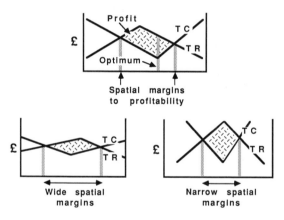

are, according to neoclassical theory (and its extensions), a response to a search for profits. It should be stressed that the models used (e.g. von Thünen, Weber, Christaller) are normative and concerned with what ought to occur rather than with what actually does occur.

Structuralist approach

In parallel with neoclassical theories, the search for profits is central to the structuralist approach. However, the similarities end there as the latter is concerned with describing and explaining real world behaviour, rather than with predicting behaviour on the basis of various assumptions. Indeed, structuralists interpret decision-making behaviour as a product of the system (e.g. capitalist/socialist) in which the individual business is set, and of its place within that structure (Massey, 1979a). Consequently, they argue that neoclassical and behavioural theories (see below) of economic location cannot explain spatial

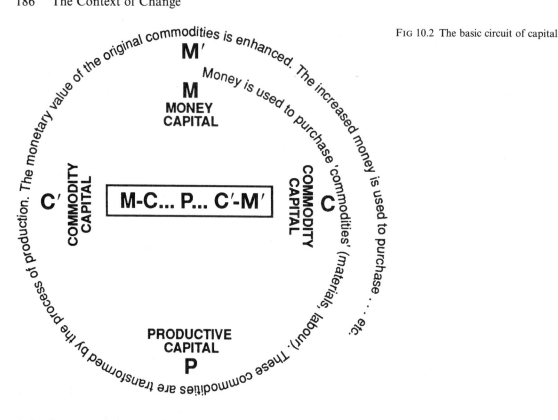

FIG 10.2 The basic circuit of capital

behaviour, or account for changes in such behaviour. This is because the major decision-making processes are not contained within the patterns themselves (the superstructure), but in the processes (infrastructure)—see Chapter 2.2 for details. The infrastructure cannot be observed, but its nature can be theorized and compared with its output in the superstructure (Johnston, 1987).

Central to the structuralist approach is the view that investment in a capitalist economy is an attempt to increase profits and accumulate capital. Farmers and industrialists, for example, are becoming increasingly dependent on wider *circuits of capital* (see below). Indeed, agriculture has been penetrated by industrial capital; this penetration has itself been uneven over space and time, as demonstrated for example by the increased regional specialization of agriculture in the EC (Bowler, 1985a). Such structural changes affect decision-making behaviour, causing farmers to adapt in a variety of ways to the changing nature of capitalism and to the different sources of capital available to them (Harvey, 1982; Marsden *et al.*, 1986b). New ways to main-

tain the same levels of capital accumulation are continuously being sought by farmers, with consequent effects upon the structure and spatial organization of farm businesses.

The notion of the *circuit of capital* is important in this context (Fig. 10.2). In the circuit, money (*M*) is used to purchase commodities (*C*) like materials and labour. These in turn are transformed by the process of production (*P*) and thus acquire increased value (*C'*). When exchanged for money (*M'*) this increased value can be used to purchase more inputs for the production process and so the circuit continues. If one firm, farm, or company is able to improve its efficiency, find cheaper sources of inputs (i.e. materials and labour), or make a better commodity than its competitors, then the difference between *C* and *C'* will increase and profits will be enlarged. In a capitalist economy, this will threaten the profits of competitors, who are forced to respond and produce more *C'*, but in so far as they are successful this will in turn force competitors to do the same. The structuralist approach argues that this continuous process is necessary for businesses to maintain their profits, let alone increase them.

The attempt to accumulate capital is in fact a condition of survival (Sayer, 1985; Marsden *et al.*, 1986*b*).

Within the structuralist approach, therefore, location and land-use decisions are one way in which businesses can attempt to maintain their profits by seeking out either lower-cost places or locations where they can sell more (or, in the case of agriculture, alternative on-farm and off-farm enterprises). Similarly, disinvestment in one location or type of farming would occur when a greater return on capital is possible elsewhere in the organization or in a new activity.

As an extension to, or modification of, the structuralist approach, *realism* recognizes that individuals make decisions within the constraints set by economic processes (Sayer, 1984). In contrast to neoclassical and behavioural approaches to economic geography, which are characterized by *extensive* research programmes concerned with discovering common properties and general patterns in a population as a whole, the study of causation in a realist context also involves *intensive* research programmes which attempt to explore in detail how causal processes work out in specific areas (Sayer and Morgan, 1985). Intensive research, therefore, works on the basis that a national cause (e.g. changing interest rates, government industrial/agricultural policies) can produce very different effects in different areas because of the way in which the factor in question is articulated in those locations in relation to other factors (Massey and Meegan, 1985*b*).

In order to understand how real causal processes affect location and land-use decision-making, a distinction has to be made between *necessary* (internal) and *contingent* (external) *relations* (Sayer, 1984). A necessary relationship is a dependent relationship. For example, the capitalist mode of production depends upon land, labour, and privately-owned capital interacting in a specific way. If any necessary relations are broken (e.g. land is removed from production), the structure will no longer exist and the system would cease to be capitalist. A necessary relationship may also be asymmetric, where one is dependent on the other but not vice versa; good examples would include the relationships between company and branch plant and landlord and tenant. Contingent relationships, by way of contrast, are not necessary for the reproduction of a structure (e.g. the capitalist mode of production).

For example, capitalism can exist irrespective of whether the labour involved is male or female, black or white, Christian or Muslim, etc.

Extensive research has ignored the distinction between necessary and contingent relations, resulting in 'chaotic conceptions' (Sayer, 1984). A good example of such a conception in industrial geography would be a components of change classification based on *outcomes* (e.g. closures, openings, *in situ* contraction) rather than *processes* (e.g. rationalization, intensification, and investment and technical change—see Chapter 2.2 and Section 10.2). Realists suggest that if the objective is a search for causes it is necessary to use a classification based on processes. What is required in intensive research, therefore, is a separation of contingent and necessary relations within the overall structure of, for example, an industrial sector (see example of fletton brick industry in section 10.2), nation, or international economy.

Behavioural approach

Whereas neoclassical and structuralist approaches assume that location and land-use decisions are determined by the need for profitability, the behavioural approach suggests that entrepreneurs have other goals than just profit maximization (Found, 1971; Gasson, 1973; Hamilton, 1974; Ilbery, 1978). For example, in a large firm where management is separated from ownership a production manager put in charge of searching for a new location would tend to emphasize a low-cost site, while a sales manager charged with the same task would probably emphasize a location which would facilitate high sales. Stability, security, pride of ownership, and independence are often advocated by decision-makers above the making of maximum profits. Indeed, decisions about location and land use may not be made with careful deliberation, but may simply reflect a 'hunch', 'convenience', or proximity to the owner's home (Watts, 1987). For small-scale industrialists and farmers, for example, the choice of location is often a non-issue: it is fixed and the main question to be answered is 'given the location, what and how much shall he produce' (Hamilton, 1974 p. 7). This helps to illustrate the overlap between land-use and location decisions outlined at the beginning of this chapter.

Most work adopting a behavioural approach in economic geography has examined various aspects of the locational behaviour of individuals or groups and attempted to see whether there is any systematic variation in their behaviour. An important aspect of this work has been to investigate how individuals/firms make location and land-use decisions and the factors which influence them (see Section 10.2). Individual and group decision-making takes place within an environment of uncertainty; all decision-makers are faced with this, but the actual decisions made will vary because individuals have different goals, different levels of knowledge, and they vary in their aversion to risk and uncertainty (Wolpert, 1964). In the light of this uncertainty, entrepreneurs attempt to make satisfactory decisions and the *satisficer concept* has been put forward as a more realistic alternative to optimizing behaviour. The term satisficing is rather ambiguous (see Chapter 2.2) but is, perhaps, best taken to mean the level of profit which an entrepreneur can reasonably expect given his or her knowledge level and ability (Lloyd and Dicken, 1977).

The attraction of the satisficer concept is clear, as the decision-maker lists the various alternatives in his/her 'subjective environment' according to whether or not their expected incomes are satisfactory.

If the elements of the set of satisfactory outcomes can be ranked, then the least satisfactory outcome of that set may be referred to as the level-of-aspiration adopted by the decision maker for that problem. The theory suggests that aspiration levels tend to adjust to the attainable, to past achievement levels, and to levels achieved by other individuals with whom he compares himself (Wolpert, 1964 p. 545).

The satisficer concept recognizes the limitations placed on the entrepreneur as a decision-maker, whose attitudes to his/her task will be constrained by age, education, size and profitability of business, experience of the world outside their business socio-economic background, personal traits, personal ambitions, attitudes, belief and interests, as well as the realities of the world in which he/she exists (Blunden, 1977; Ilbery, 1978; Healey, 1981a).

Uncertainty and the making of satisfactory decisions are in turn conditioned by the amount of information available to decision-makers and their ability to use it. The former will reflect such characteristics as age, education, size of business, available resources, and subjective perceptions of different places/land uses. With the information collected, an entrepreneur has then to decide upon a course of action and the final decision made will reflect his or her ability to use that information. Variations in ability will again reflect differences in education and experience, with the more able individual making better decisions than the less educated. Similarly aspiration levels will vary between individuals, reflecting past experiences. As Daniels (1985a p. 113) notes, 'decisions are essentially the product of the way information is sought, received and used by individual entrepreneurs, corporate decision makers and central government agencies.'

Watts (1980b) gives an interesting example from the British sugar industry, where variations in information and ability of two major companies resulted in different types of location decision. The Anglo-Scottish group, with little experience in the sugar industry and thus limited ability to assess the information collected, decided to build five relatively small beet-sugar plants widely dispersed over the arable area of central and eastern England. In contrast, the Anglo-Dutch group, with its experience in the Dutch sugar industry built four larger plants, spatially concentrated in the main beet-growing area of East Anglia. Whilst the Anglo-Dutch group was soon reporting profits on its British plants, the less well-informed and less able Anglo-Scottish group was recording a loss.

One of the few attempts to express information levels and the decision-making ability of individuals in a theoretical framework was Pred's (1967 and 1969) behavioural matrix (see Chapter 2.2 for details). Each individual can be allocated to a cell in the matrix according to the amount of information they have and their ability to use it (the two axes of the matrix—see Fig. 2.3). Only the theoretical economic man (with maximum information and ability) can occupy the cell in the bottom right-hand corner of the matrix. Although there is a tendency for better location and land-use decisions to be made the nearer an entrepreneur is to this cell, uncertainty may lead to a poor choice; similarly, an entrepreneur with limited information and ability may choose a near optimal location or land-use pattern by chance. Pred's model remains virtually untested in the real world (for an exception see Selby, 1987), mainly

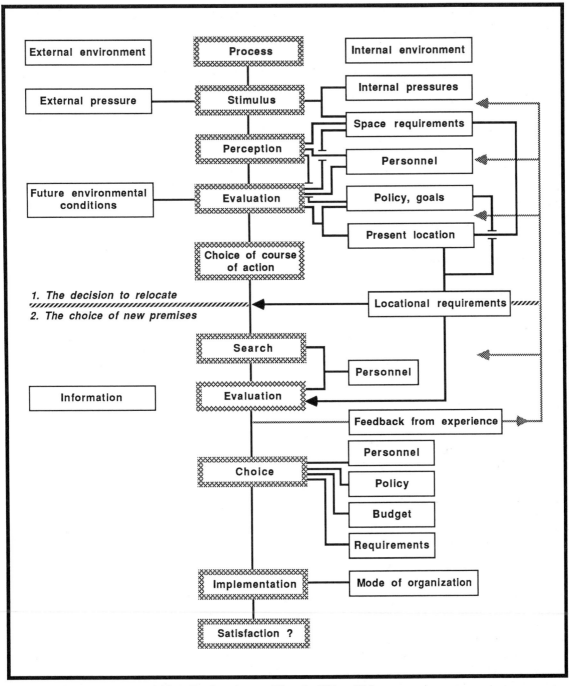

FIG 10.3 A decision process model for office firms (*source*: Edwards, 1983 p. 1334)

because of the difficulty of measuring the two axes of the matrix for a decision-maker or a firm, plus the problem that the two axes are not independent of one another. Consequently, it is a useful conceptual device, but of little value in explaining actual location and land-use decisions.

Many other attempts have been made to produce general models of the location/land-use decision-making process in the different economic sectors (e.g. Found, 1971; North, 1974; Ilbery, 1978; Edwards, 1983; Mather, 1986; Watts, 1987). Most tend to include a number of distinct stages, including the stimulus, search, evaluation, and choice, and to recognize that firms, farms, and offices are influenced by internal and external pressures and constraints. Internal pressures and constraints include changes in organizational structure, marketing, and policy, whilst external ones include the cost of inputs such as labour and materials, and competition. Edwards (1983) developed such a model for office firms (Fig. 10.3), where the location decision process is divided into two stages: first, the decision to relocate; and secondly, the choice of new premises. For new offices starting up for the first time, stage one is ignored and the second component is immediately utilized. Stage one in the decision-making process is initiated by 'a mismatch of the requirements of an establishment and its relationship with the environment in order to fulfil these requirements' (Edwards, 1983 p. 1333). Once initiated, the firm has to assess the best way to respond to the mismatch, which in turn will be affected 'by attitudes and perceptions of the personnel involved, the ways in which they interpret the policies and goals of the organization, and how these are translated into space needs, types of premises, or the limitations of the existing location' (Daniels, 1985a p. 118). If, after evaluation, the course of action is to relocate (or for a new office to find their first premises) then the sequence of search, evaluation, choice, and implementation (in stage two) begins. This sequence will again be influenced by the personnel involved and their ability to use the information that is available, as well as by company policy and resource constraints.

The objective of this section has not been to review the advantages and disadvantages of the different theoretical approaches to location and land-use decision-making; this can be found in Chapter 2.2. Rather, the intention has been to show how the approaches emphasize the importance of different factors in the decision-making process. Consequently, they can be viewed as complementary rather than conflicting. This is aptly demonstrated by Watts and Stafford (1986 p. 208) in their review of the decision-making process surrounding plant closures. They note that 'in terms of the explanation of the geography of plant closures it seems that the structuralists tend to blame the economic system, the behaviouralists point the finger at firms and the neoclassical work tends to blame the plant or its environment.'

10.2 Location and land-use decision-making in practice

The objective of this section is to examine, briefly, empirical case study work on the decision-making process. This incorporates both developed market and centrally planned economies, with the former concentrating on examples from agriculture and manufacturing and the latter on socialist principles of location and the iron and steel industry.

Decision-making in developed market economies

Agriculture
Studies of agricultural decision-making have helped to highlight the inadequacies of neoclassical approaches to agricultural location, with their assumptions of complete knowledge and economic rationality. A range of decision-making models and techniques, stressing the satisficing nature of economic behaviour, have been developed (see Ilbery, 1985a for details). Mather (1986) has schematically portrayed some of the factors which consciously or unconsciously affect land-use decision-making (Fig. 10.4). As with similar models developed for the secondary and tertiary sectors, these factors can be of an internal or external nature, ranging from the age, ability, and personality of the farmer to the nature of the land unit and its wider cultural setting. Processes and objectives form the remaining components of Mather's model. Processes are depicted in a manner similar to Pred's behavioural matrix, with decisions ranging from conscious, rational ones to habitual, non-rational ones. As Mather (1986 p. 32) suggests:

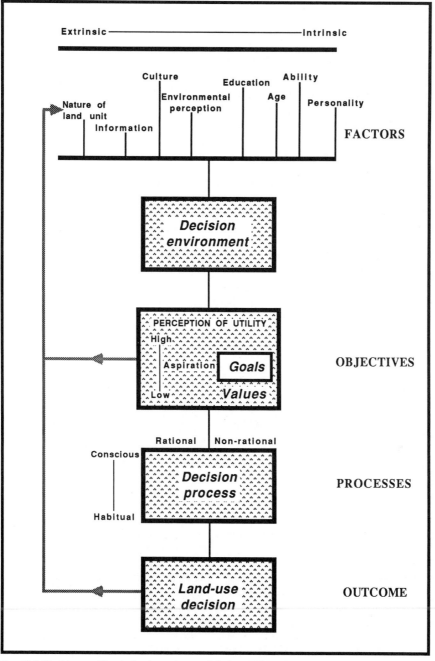

FIG 10.4 Decision-making in land use (*source*: Mather, 1986 p. 27)

having made a conscious decision initially and having found that the outcome was satisfactory, the decision maker simply implements the same decision again without conscious evaluation or consideration of the alternatives. This tendency towards routine or habitual behaviour is readily understandable.

A considerable body of evidence has developed in relation to objectives in agricultural decision-making; this has been especially critical of the assumption that the sole objective of farming is profit maximization. Farmers are more likely to maximize utility and satisfy a hierarchy of goals and values. Utility can be defined as 'that property in any object, whereby it tends to produce benefit, advantage, pleasure, good or happiness ... to the party whose interest is considered' (Mather, 1986 p. 33). Non-material benefits and personal elements are thus incorporated into a concept that means different things to different people. Similarly, goals and values are concerned with farmers' motivations, where the emphasis is placed on why rather than the way decisions are made. Gasson (1973) classified a set of values that might apply in a broad range of farming situations into four major groups (Table 10.1):

1. *Instrumental*, where farming is viewed as a means of obtaining income and security, in pleasant working conditions.
2. *Social*, where farming is practised for the sake of interpersonal relationships in work.
3. *Expressive*, where farming is a means of self-expression and personal fulfilment.
4. *Intrinsic*, where farming is valued as an activity in its own right.

It is the ordering of these groups relative to one another that influences farmers' decisions in situations of choice. After pilot studies in eastern England, where farmers were asked to attach a degree of importance to each of twenty values, it was revealed that farmers had a predominantly intrinsic orientation towards work, valuing the way of life, independence, and performance of work tasks above expressive, instrumental, and social aspects of farming (Gasson, 1973). The importance of non-economic motives in farming and hence the satisficer concept had seemingly been confirmed. Gasson also demonstrated how the importance of values varied according to the size of farm business, with 'smaller' farmers valuing intrinsic aspects of farming more highly than 'larger' ones, who placed more emphasis on

TABLE 10.1 Dominant values in farming

Intrinsic
Independence
Doing the work you like
Leading a healthy, outdoor life
Purposeful activity, value in hard work
Control in a variety of situations

Expressive
Meeting a challenge
Being creative
Pride of ownership
Self-respect for doing a worthwhile job
Exercising special abilities and aptitudes

Instrumental
Making maximum income
Making a satisfactory income
Safeguarding income for the future
Expanding the business
Being able to arrange hours of work

Social
Belonging to the farming community
Gaining recognition, prestige as a farmer
Continuing the family tradition
Earning respect of workers
Working close to family and home

Source: Gasson (1973 p. 527).

instrumental and social aspects. However, it was not shown whether values varied with the type of farming practised or the socio-personal characteristics of the farmers. This led to further work in different parts of England and Ireland (Ilbery, 1983*d* and 1985*b*; Gillmor, 1986). A study of hop-farming in the West Midlands (see Chapter 11.2) confirmed the dominance of intrinsic values, above expressive and instrumental values, with social values having the lowest priority of all (Ilbery, 1983*d*). A significant correlation was found between the ranking of values by hop-farmers and by farmers in East Anglia. The same order of priority was later reported for horticultural growers in the Vale of Evesham (Ilbery, 1985*b*).

Gillmor (1986) compared the values of English hop-farmers with samples of farmers in the counties of Meath and Leitrim in Ireland. Statistically significant similarities were found between the two groups of Irish farmers and between the English hop-farmers and Meath farmers; however, the value orientations of the Leitrim sample were at variance with the hop-farmers. Table 10.2

TABLE 10.2 Goals and values of farmers in England and Ireland

Goals and values	Rank order		
	English hop farmers	Meath farmers	Leitrim farmers
Intrinsic			
Doing the work you like	1	2	1
Independence	2	3	6
Healthy, outdoor life	7	6	5
Control in varied situations	8	9	9
Value of hard work	14	18	17
Expressive			
Self-respect in worthwhile job	5	14	13
Meeting a challenge	6	10	14
Using special abilities	11	11	15
Being creative	12	17	19
Pride of ownership	15	12	11
Instrumental			
Making satisfactory income	3	1	3
Safeguarding income for future	9	3	10
Making maximum income	10	5	12
Expanding the business	17	14	16
Able to arrange work hours	18	13	7
Social			
Earning respect of workers	4	20	20
Working close to family and home	13	7	2
Belonging to farming community	16	16	8
Continuing the family tradition	19	8	4
Recognition and prestige	20	19	18
	% of total points		
Intrinsic	28.07	27.44	27.91
Expressive	25.88	23.05	21.76
Instrumental	24.48	28.16	26.29
Social	21.58	21.35	24.04

Sources: Ilbery (1983*d* p. 333) and Gillmor (1986 p. 24).

confirms that income maximization is not the leading goal of farmers, reaching a highest rank of just the fifth most important value in Meath (tenth and twelfth in English hops and Leitrim respectively). In contrast, making a satisfactory income was of considerable importance in all areas. Whilst intrinsic values are dominant among Leitrim farmers, the greater economic orientation of Meath farmers forces them into second place, just behind instrumental values. The top-ranking value in the three case studies was 'doing the work I like' which, after 'satisfactory income', was followed by 'independence' and 'healthy, outdoor life'. This confirms the strength of intrinsic values as the principal category of values and the strong preferential attachment to agricultural work. In contrast to Gasson's findings, no significant differences occurred in these studies between value orientations and farm size, type of farming or farmer characteristics. Clearly, systematic variations do exist in the attitudes and motivations of farmers, but these are not necessarily related to factors within the farms themselves.

As the reported studies are not representative of all farming situations, more research, in different types of agricultural area, is needed. However, studies of decision-making processes in agriculture are hampered by various problems. First, many of the factors affecting farmers' decisions are interrelated, increasing the difficulty of isolating or measuring the importance of individual factors, especially at the aggregate level. Secondly, a degree of circumspection is required in the interpretation of questionnaire surveys which subjectively measure attitudes and motives. For example, Gasson (1973) and Ilbery (1985a) warn of the existence of different layers of values, ranging from those that are admitted by an individual only to himself or herself, to the 'outer skin' which comprises values upheld by society and publicly expressed (Gillmor, 1986). It is not clear whether the layer examined in surveys is the same as the one used for productive decision-making. This could represent the difference between attitudes and actual behaviour, a major criticism levelled at behavioural studies (Bunting and Guelke, 1979). However, all values are socially learned and those expressed tend to become internalized over time and influence an individual's motivations. As Gasson (1973 p. 526) comments, 'superficial answers are still meaningful and individual variations in what is thought to be socially acceptable can be highly revealing.' Thirdly, it is difficult to examine the role of past decisions, although it is recognized that 'the past has left a legacy of existing land use and perhaps equipment and buildings as well as experience' (Mather, 1986 p. 63). Indeed, the relationship between the past and present influences agricultural decision-making, especially as farmers tend to perpetuate family and area tradition. Historical and geographical specificity are important in studies of agricultural land use and farmers in different areas have been shown to emphasize the importance of different decision-making factors (Ilbery, 1985a).

It is, therefore, very difficult to investigate the decision-making behaviour of farmers. However, the fact remains that 'the use of land reflects human decisions ... and an understanding of land use patterns requires an understanding of these decisions' (Mather, 1986 p. 63). Although most research has concentrated on the point of production itself (the farm), structuralist approaches emphasize that relations external to the farm are of equal significance in agricultural decision-making (Marsden et al., 1986a and b). Such work has concentrated upon the restructuring process in agriculture and the extent to which

farm households in different areas have sought alternative sources of income/capital in the light of declining farm incomes and the price-cost squeeze. The ways in which farmers attempt to accumulate capital have an important influence upon the organization of the farm business and land-use patterns.

Farmers in three localities (the urban fringe of London, east Bedfordshire and west Dorset), with contrasting agricultural traditions, have provided the focus of research interest in the work of Marsden et al (1986a and b). Their urban fringe study produced an important new typology of farm businesses, based on the financial importance of farm-based income to the family household. Apart from full-time farm businesses, three main types of farm household were identified:

1. *Hobby and part-time* businesses, which have no farm debts and are not reliant on agriculture for income.

2. *Survivors*, where farmers remain in business through either relying on pensions and savings (and so reducing personal consumption) or by diversifying their activities into non-agricultural (farm and off-farm) sources of income.

3. *Accumulators*, where capital generated from farm or off-farm businesses is being invested in off-farm and farm businesses respectively. This group consists of large family farms and corporate businesses; in the latter, farming forms only a small part of the overall business.

The predominantly structuralist approach developed by Marsden et al. emphasizes the need to examine the strategies different farm businesses adopt as they respond to the changing context of agricultural production (external factors). In particular, the ways in which farmers make decisions and adapt to the increasing penetration of financial and industrial capital need to be examined; the farm should no longer be treated as a unit narrowly focused on agricultural production alone.

Industry
Considerable conceptual and empirical research has been conducted into the nature of locational decision-making among different types of industry, at different geographical scales and points in a firm's development history. Much of this work has examined spatial changes in industry in terms of different types of location decision: the birth in

an area of entirely new firms, the contraction, the expansion, the death, or the emigration of an area's firms, and the immigration to an area of existing firms from elsewhere (Keeble, 1976). Space does not permit an examination of each of these and discussion will concentrate upon movement and plant closure decisions.

Movement decisions
Research undertaken in North America and the United Kingdom in the 1960s and 1970s demonstrated that different types of location decision are made in response to different stimuli and stress factors (e.g. North, 1974; Rees, 1974; Stafford, 1974). For example, in a study of the locational behaviour of 100 firms in the UK plastics industry in the 1960s, North (1974) identifies ten types of stress and the most frequent type of locational decision associated with each one (Table 10.3). The table demonstrates that extensions were the usual response to the planned growth of existing production lines, while branch plants were the normal method of developing regional markets. Similarly, transfers were the most frequent response to externally generated stresses and the unplanned growth of existing production lines. Take-overs were common

TABLE 10.3 Stresses leading to locational decisions in firms in the United Kingdom plastics industry

Stresses	Most frequent location decision
1. Planned growth of existing product lines	Extensions
2. Development of regional markets	Branch plants
3. Unplanned growth of existing product lines	Transfers
4. Diversification into new product lines	Acquisitions
5. Vertical integration	Acquisitions
6. Horizontal integration	Acquisitions
7. Externally generated	Transfers
8. Stress imposed by pattern of market distribution	n.s.
9. Decision imposed by parent company	n.s.
10. Rationalization of operations	Closure

n.s.: not specified

Source: based on North (1974 pp. 228–31).

among firms wishing to diversify or to integrate horizontally or vertically.

In more detail, North found that firms making different kinds of location decision had distinctive characteristics. For example, relocating firms tended to be younger and smaller than those making other types of location decision; they also tended to have high growth rates and be private companies. The search for a suitable site was often undertaken quickly, without specified requirements, and restricted to a ten-mile radius of the present site. This enabled labour, customers, and business contacts to be retained and meant that executives did not have to move house. Only for the large relocating firms was a wider sphere of influence incorporated into their search process, but this was also still within the same region. Firms that opened branch plants were often older, larger, and more profitable; 75 per cent were either subsidiaries of public companies or themselves publicly owned and run by professional managers. Of the twenty branch plant moves in the plastics industry in North's study, nine established new factories close to their existing ones, for similar reasons to relocating firms. A further seven conducted an unsophisticated search within a new, but specified, region, with the final site being determined by such factors as the time and cost of transport, labour availability, and industrial infrastructure. Only four firms carried out systematic cost analyses of different regions, including the advantages of Development Area benefits; however, for three of these 'personal considerations in the end had an overriding influence' (North, 1974 p. 235).

Other studies of industrial movement in Britain have supported the view that different factors are important at different scales (Keeble, 1971; Townroe, 1971). Keeble demonstrated that movement consists of a dual population comprising short-distance movement of small plants, dominated by transfers, and long-distance movement of larger plants, dominated by branch plants. Reporting on various micro-level studies, Keeble (1971) suggests that long-distance moves to the peripheral areas of Britain were influenced by four main factors:

1. Labour availability.
2. Government inducements.
3. Access to regional markets.
4. Distance from a given area of origin.

In contrast, the main factor influencing short-distance overspill moves, especially from London, was proximity to the conurbation. The final choice of location in such a situation was constrained by four factors:

1. Labour availability.
2. Residential desirability.
3. Planning controls and influences.
4. The tendency for radial movement within the same compass sector as the original factory.

An interesting omission from both lists are the traditional cost factors espoused by neoclassical theories. This is at variance with the three-stage model of industrial movement proposed by Stafford (1972) for firms in America. Here the search process consisted of:

1. Delimitation of a region based on market demand.
2. Selection of a finite number of production sites, based on the principle of least cost.
3. Final site slection, using judgement as to the best site to maximize 'psychic' income.

Stafford's model suggests that the ideas of maximizing demand (Losch), minimizing costs (Weber), and including non-monetary income (Greenhut) may be complementary principles operating at different spatial scales. These views were partially confirmed in a detailed study of the locational behaviour of six firms in south-east Ohio (Stafford, 1974). Eight location decisions were involved (six new plants, including two relocations, and two *in situ* expansions), of which seven were non-headquarters branch plants of multi-plant firms. Applying content analysis to the long, open-ended interviews (with minimum interviewer interference). fourteen factors affecting the location decision were identified (Table 10.4). These included such traditional economic influences as labour, markets and supplies accessibility, infrastructure (facilities and utilities), and taxes. However, personal co-operation, contacts, and information emerged as the most important factors, with executive convenience and internal dispersal tendencies (factors rarely considered in traditional industrial location theory) also figuring prominently. When the results were disaggregated according to four spatial scales (Table

TABLE 10.4 Factors affecting the locational behaviour of six firms in south-east Ohio (evaluated responses)

Factors	Total no. of counts	Spatial scales			
		1	2	3	4
Personal contacts	117	1	23	27	66
Labour productivity	108	18	25	27	38
Labour availability	50	2	8	19	21
Local amenities	49	0	2	15	32
Transport facilities	42	4	14	18	6
Labour rates	39	4	6	18	11
Dispersion tendencies	28	2	14	4	8
Executive convenience	27	1	4	12	10
Facilities and utilities	25	5	2	8	10
Corporate communications	20	0	3	9	8
Supplies accessibility	17	1	5	7	4
Induced amenities	13	0	0	7	6
Market accessibility	12	3	5	1	3
Taxes	1	0	1	0	0
TOTALS	548	41	112	172	223

1: National.
2: Sub-national.
3: Regional.
4: Local.

Source: based on Stafford (1974 pp. 174, 177).

10.4), the local amenities and personal contact factors became more important as the scale of analysis decreased; in contrast, market accessibility showed a major downward shift with decreasing regional scale. With these differences noted, a fair degree of stability in the rankings existed across the scales.

The importance of labour as a location factor (in terms of a favourable labour climate—see Chapter 4.2) was noted in a study of sixty plants established in North Carolina by firms based outside the state (Moriarty, 1983). Such factors as community attitudes towards industry, the suitability of highways and access roads, and room for expansion (in less constrained sites) were also important. However, in contrast to Stafford's (1974) study, little emphasis was placed on personal influences. This is a reflection of the different methodologies adopted by Stafford and Moriarty, especially as the latter presented managers with a pre-selected list of possible location factors, to which a degree of importance had to be attached. Such an approach will only include factors thought to be important by the investigator, unlike the less structured method used by Stafford. A further problem with Moriarty's study is that no account was taken of the relative importance of factors at different spatial scales.

This last point was accommodated by Schmenner (1982) who examined, at both regional and site levels, the reasons given for branch plant moves by 410 major manufacturers in the USA (Table 10.5). At the regional scale, labour climate again emerged as a major location factor, followed by access to markets; community attitudes were not important. However, at the site level emphasis was placed on transport facilities and utilities, with both urban and rural sites being favoured (depending on the type of branch plant involved).

Geographical variations in labour markets, therefore, appear to represent a major factor in explaining regional patterns of industrial movement, although at local scales of analysis personal contacts and community attitudes become just as, or more, important.

Closure decisions
Cost factors may play an important role in the relative success of companies in their chosen locations. Some indication of this comes from

TABLE 10.5 Location factors for branch plants for 410 major United States manufacturers in the 1970s

A. REGIONAL/STATE LEVEL

Location factor	Plant openings citing at least one factor (%)
Favourable labour climate	76
Near market	55
Attractive place for engineers/managers to live	35
Near supplies and resources	31
Low labour rates	30
Near existing company facilities	25
Environmental permits	17
Others	6
Community attitude	0

B. SITE LEVEL

Location factor	Plant openings citing at least one factor (%)
Rail service	47
On expressway	42
Special provision of utilities	34
Rural area	27
Environmental permits	23
Within metropolitan area	21
On water	16
Available land/building	8
Others	7

Source: based on Schmenner (1982 p. 150).

studies examining the factors affecting plant closures. Summary lists of such factors have been produced by Townsend and Peck (1985a) and Watts and Stafford (1986). The latter classified factors influencing plant closures in multi-plant firms in two ways: first, according to the categories found in traditional studies of industrial location; and secondly, following Massey and Meegan's (1982) division of closure factors, according to plant and area levels (Table 10.6). An important omission from the list is a consideration of profits and costs. This reflects a lack of data on the costs/profits of individual plants within a firm. Despite this, a key feature of the table is the way in which the vast majority of factors mentioned in the literature

TABLE 10.6 A classification of factors affecting plant closures in multi-plant firms[a]

Category	Plant level	Area level
Access to markets	(1) Links with region $(-)$ (2) Links with firms $(-)$	(1) Accessibility to markets $(-)$
Access to supplies	(3) Links with region $(-)$ (4) Links with firm $(-)$	(2) Acessibility to material inputs $(-)$ (3) Acessibility to business services $(-)$ (4) Acessibility to head office $(-)$
Land		(5) Site value/rent $(+)$ (6) Space for expansion $(-)$
Capital	(5) Capital intensity $(-)$ (6) Machinery valuation $(-)$ (7) Age of machinery $(+)$ (8) Age of buildings $(+)$ (9) Size of plant $(-)$	
Labour	(10) % female labour $(+)$ (11) Labour productivity $(-)$ (12) Labour intensity $(+)$	(7) Wage rates $(+)$ (8) Labour relations $(-)$ (9) Unionization of labour force $(+)$
Organization	(13) Managerial autonomy $(-)$ (14) Length of ownership $(-)$ (15) Management expertise $(-)$	(10) Coporate interaction $(+)$
Technology	(16) Flexibility of operations $(-)$ (17) Appropriateness of technology $(-)$	
Policy environment		(11) Regional policy environment $(-)$ (12) Local policy environment $(-)$ (13) Local taxes $(+)$ (14) Environmental regulations $(+)$
Personal	(18) Personal attachments $(-)$	(15) Residential amenities $(-)$ (16) Community dependence upon plant $(-)$

[a]The probability of a plant being selected for closure increases as the predictive variable increases $(+)$ or decreases $(-)$.
Source: Watts and Stafford (1986 p. 221).

can be classified to categories recognised in traditional work in industrial location such as land, labour, capital and access to supplies and markets. This would suggest that investigators have been drawing implicitly and explicitly upon the existing body of location theory (Watts and Stafford, 1986 p. 220).

The distinction between plant and area variables is also important: although most plant level variables can be manipulated by the firm, area variables are often outside their control (see below).

Few detailed analyses of selective closures in multi-plant firms have been undertaken. However, case studies by Healey (1982) and Peck and Townsend (1984) have outlined both the characteristics of closed plants and the reasons why they were selected for closure. In a survey of sixty-four multi-plant firms in the clothing and textile indus-

try, Healey (1982) demonstrates how plant closures were more likely to occur in:

1. small plants;
2. plants with little room for expansion;
3. plants with low degrees of managerial autonomy;
4. acquired plants, especially after five years and as part of a horizontal acquisition.

However, age of plant and distance from head office were not significantly related to plant closure. Interesting though these results are, they do not explain the spatial pattern of plant closures and, in contrast to studies of industrial movement, there is less attempt to examine decision-making processes surrounding closures. This is because the choice of plants to close is restricted to existing plants and thus fairly straightforward for management without detailed analysis. Far more important is whether or not to close and when. A similar lack of examination of decision-making processes occurs in Peck and Townsend's (1984) study of plant closures in three large firms—British Shipbuilders, Plessey, and Metal Box. Their work suggests that the likelihood of closure is related to five factors: a recent history of labour difficulties; the age of equipment; unsuitable buildings to accommodate modern technology; the loss of markets to rival firms; and the restructuring of a site for expansion.

The geography of job loss

The above studies have concentrated on why particular plants have been selected for closure (the *selection* question—Watts and Stafford, 1986). However, before being able to answer this question it is, according to the structuralist approach, important to ask why it is necessary to close a plant in the first place (the *motivation* question). This necessitates an analysis of the broader topic of employment decline or job loss (*in situ* decline and closure) (Massey and Meegan, 1982). Such an approach is initially concerned with the different forms of productive reorganization, so that the causes of employment decline can be unravelled. It is only 'by examining the causes and mechanisms of employment decline ... that a greater understanding of its geography ... can really be explained' (Massey and Meegan, 1982

p. 13). In other words, the reason why, and the process by which, jobs are being lost must be understood before the location dimension can be incorporated. The geography of job loss cannot be explained simply in terms of the characteristics of different areas or the different firms and plants involved.

Three processes leading to job loss are identified by Massey and Meegan (1982):

1. *Intensification*, including changes designed to increase the productivity of labour, but without major new investment or substantial reorganization of production technique. The decline in employment is associated primarily with this reorganization of production and labour within existing plants.

2. *Rationalization*, involving a simple reduction in total capacity, arising from the lack of profitability in sectors with excess capacity. Plants may be closed as part of the rationalization process.

3. *Investment and technical change*, where job losses occur in the context of significant investment, often related to the introduction of new technologies which reduce costs. Investment in specific sites may occur as other sites are closed.

Applying these processes to thirty-one industries in the United Kingdom, the authors were able to indicate their likely spatial implications (Table 10.7). The major point to emerge from the

TABLE 10.7 Spatial implications of the different forms of production reorganization

Forms of production reorganization	Output change		
	Falling	Stable average growth	Rising
Intensification	Employment losses *in situ*		—
Rationalization	Employment losses *in situ* Plant closure Possibility of relatively small local gains as a result of concentration of capacity No new locations		—
Technical change	Employment cuts *in situ* *or* New locations (some local gains) and closures	Any combination of *in situ* employment losses, new locations, and plant closures to meet capacity requirements	

Source: Massey and Meegan (1982 p. 127)

table is that each kind of production reorganization has different geographical ramifications. This is best explained in terms of 'potentially mobile employment', which 'relates to the possibility that different forms of production reorganisation offer for individual regions/locations to secure employment gains even though the aggregate sectoral content in which these occur is one of decline' (Massey and Meegan, 1982 p. 124). In terms of intensification, there will be no potentially mobile employment as its impact is confined to the existing distribution of plants in the sectors concerned; job losses will, therefore, occur *in situ* only. Rationalization similarly involves no new locations, but it may generate potentially mobile employment if a redistribution of production between sites occurs as part of the general reduction in employment. It may also involve the complete closure of plants in individual locations. Spatial rationalization strategies are further examined in Chapter 7.3. Finally and in complete contrast, technical change always involves the generation of potentially mobile employment as it includes investment in new production capacity. The different geographical consequences resulting from investment and technical change are listed in Table 10.7 and range from *in situ* employment losses and plant closures to new locations. Case studies, relating each of the three processes to a particular industry, were given by Massey and Meegan. In terms of technical change, for example, job loss in the fletton brick industry was examined.

The United Kingdom fletton brick industry in the late 1960s and early 1970s was dominated by the London Brick Company (LBC), which purchased Marston Valley in 1965, the second major producer, all the fletton interests of Redland in 1971 and a works from the National Coal Board in 1973. Indeed, by 1973 the LBC accounted for all fletton brick production and was in a strong position to provide necessary capital for new investment. The downturn in house building in the late 1960s in the United Kingdom provided an opportunity to cut costs and embark upon 'a different form of production reorganisation: that of major capital investment embodying labour-saving technical change' (Massey and Meegan, 1982 p. 82). Within the overall experience of employment decline in the industry, three distinct processes were apparent:

1. The location of new investment in two huge works at New Saxon and Kings Dyke in 1968. These were expanded in 1973 in order to achieve an increase in labour productivity. The decision to locate both plants in the traditional area of Peterborough was determined by such factors as good access to established markets in the South and expanding ones in the North, proximity to existing production, which enabled half-made bricks to be transported to other kilns in the area, the existence of land owned by the company, and the availability of the necessary raw material (Oxford clay). Locationally, the LBC was thus restricted to this area and could not move to another area to benefit from cheaper and more abundant labour; this problem was overcome by increasing the use of immigrant labour.

2. The closure of some works to compensate for the new investment. Initially, the rationalization process was based solely on internal production costs and productivity and not locational characteristics. Closures included two Marston works in 1969 and the Yardley works in 1972. However, later, older, and less efficient works were closed and the pattern of closures was increasingly influenced by such factors as the cost of transporting the output to the market, the availability of labour (if the existing workforce was dispersed), and the quality of clay (which varied between sites).

3. On-site cut-backs to improve productivity at the remaining sites. This involved mechanization of many of the works, the standardization of bricks in general and between the main company and those it had acquired, and the intensification of the work process.

The pattern of job loss in the fletton brick industry was, therefore, the net result of three components of change: new plants, closures, and on-site cut-backs. Technical change dominated the first and second and combined with intensification in the third. In all three, the importance of location factors varied, from being very important in the siting of new investment to being relatively insignificant in on-site cut-backs.

Although examination of such processes helps to explain why employment decline takes place, the methodology provides 'only a limited understanding as to why decline is concentrated in specific areas' (Watts, 1987 p. 188). Lloyd and

Shutt (1985), in a research project on industrial decline in the north-western region of England from the mid-1970s to the early 1980s, propose a two-stage methodology for studying job loss. The first involves an examination of the decision behaviour of the 'prime movers' in the area (the major agencies of job loss), whilst the second investigates the broader forces leading to change (beyond the behaviour of individual corporations). With the latter, they argue that the causes of job loss in the North-West lie in the underlying mechanisms of capitalism; consequently, explanation of regional events comes from the circulatory flows of corporate structure at national and international levels.

Fifty-four prime movers were identified in the North-West. They were categorized into three types: foreign multinationals, UK multinationals/nationals controlled from outside the North-West, and locally controlled UK multinationals/nationals. Despite this, evidence was presented to show that the process of internationalization was important to each group. For example, such locally controlled companies as Renold, Pilkington, and Tootal have been involved in the international reconfiguration of their operations. The authors demonstrate how Tootal, a world manufacturer of thread, textiles, and clothing, has restructured its business since the recession in 1979 to become a fully international concern. In this process, eleven operations were reduced to four, with a total shedding of 8818 jobs in the United Kingdom and a corresponding growth in employment overseas of 8578. Within the North-West region specifically, Tootal had shed 46 per cent of its 1975 labour force by 1984 and then decided to transfer the headquarters of its thread division from Manchester to the USA. The explanation for such wholesale disinvestment in the North-West, therefore, cannot be found solely from within the characteristics of the region itself. Lloyd and Shutt reported similar events for externally controlled companies like Dunlop, Plessey, ICI, and GEC, all of which were increasing their activities abroad, and for such foreign multinationals as Ford and General Motors (both with key plants in the North-West), who are 'currently locked into a corporate strategy to develop the "world car" and "world truck" as a means of achieving greater economies of scale and reducing R and D costs and marketing dupli-

cation' (Lloyd and Shutt, 1985 p. 42; see also Chapter 12.3).

Attempts to explain plant closure and job loss decisions in particular regions like the North-West are, therefore, incomplete unless they are set in a global context within which prime movers articulate their operations. This contrasts markedly with the 'components of change' approach to examining locational decisions surrounding movement and closures, which to researchers like Massey and Meegan (1982) and Lloyd and Shutt (1985) can only describe, rather than explain, decision-making behaviour.

It should be clear from this brief review of plant closures and employment decline that different approaches to the location decision problem have been developed. The structuralists highlight the importance of higher-level processes which cause firms to reduce jobs and close plants, whereas the behavioural approach, based more at the firm level, attempts to understand why one plant rather than another is closed. This division led Watts and Stafford (1986 pp. 223–4) to call for a more eclectic approach to plant closures, where

the structuralist approach can stress the wider context within which selective closures occur and can emphasise the motivation for selective closures ... and ... the neoclassical and behavioural approaches will focus attention on the specific geographies of plant closure.

Decision-making in planned economies

In a planned economy, the state both owns the factories, resources, and the infrastructure, and controls prices, profits, and wages. Centralized decision-making is, therefore, characteristic of planned economies although, as indicated in Chapter 8, such economies now operate through 'increasing polycentric decision-making within a controlled, but more market-mechanistic environment of more flexible, though not free, prices' (Hamilton, 1970 p. 84). This is in contrast to the increasingly centralized decision-making behaviour of market economies. In theory, location decision-making in such planned economies as Eastern Europe and the USSR should be simpler than elsewhere because Lenin and the Soviet Communist Party established a set of 'laws of socialist location' to guide decision-makers. These were intended to relate to industry, on the basis that this sector was the 'springboard' to economic development and prosperity. The ten laws, or principles, have been outlined and examined by Hamilton (1970; 1971*a*) and state that activities should be located:

1. Close to the resources or inputs they use.
2. Close to the market they supply.
3. Interregionally to develop maximum regional specialization of production.
4. Between regions to achieve maximum regional self-sufficiency.
5. As evenly as possible to exploit regionally or locally under-utilized resources.
6. In a dispersed fashion throughout the countryside to create 'proletarian bastions of socialism'.
7. Preferentially in backward, national minority, or underdeveloped regions.
8. To eliminate cultural, economic and social differences between town and country.
9. As strategically as possible to meet war eventualities.
10. To achieve international and intrabloc division of labour and optimum trade flows within COMECON.

Socialist ideology, therefore, seeks equality of opportunity and living standards, a dispersed rather than concentrated pattern of economic activity, and elimination of differences between town and country. In practice, location decision-making is far from simple and there is disagreement as to whether the principles have created a specific, socialist, type of landscape. One school of thought supports the view that socialism has had particular effects on the landscape (Hamilton, 1971*b*; French and Hamilton, 1979; Rugg, 1985), whereas the other feels that the economic geography of Eastern Europe has few intrinsically 'socialist' characteristics (Turnock, 1978 and 1984). Indeed, the latter argues that discussions of socialist location principles have revealed little that is not reconcilable with approaches adopted in market economies.

The complexity of the decision-making process in planned economies relates to the conflicting and overlapping nature of the ten principles and the hierarchical manner in which they are applied. This has caused their application to vary over space and time and between the different economic sectors. Principles 1 to 4 and 10 are primarily economic in nature and can conflict with the essentially military and political nature of principles 5 to 9. Similarly, in spatial terms, pairs of principles overlap, especially 1 and 3, 2 and 4, 1 and 5, 5 and 6, 5 and 7, 6 and 8, and 3 and 10 (Hamilton, 1970). This creates additional problems when the principles are applied in practice. Application results from a complex interaction between decision-makers and different interest groups. Many people are involved and, with the exception of the decentralized system in Yugoslavia, the power structure takes the form of a pyramid, with a few party executives at the top (with the greatest influence on locational decisions), a broad base of local government authorities and other vested interests at the bottom, and the planners at the centre (Fig. 10.5). As indicated in the diagram, a complex series of interactions occur, between the planners themselves, between the other participants themselves, and between the planners and other participants. Some groups are more powerful than others; likewise preference is given to industry over agriculture, to heavy industry over light, and to production over services. With services lagging behind the development of production, the pressure to increase the latter in existing centres is increased.

The likelihood of an optimal location being chosen for a particular industry is not enhanced by the 'laws of socialist location'. Indeed, the decision-making search is likely to be similar to that outlined in earlier sections of this chapter. Much depends on the amount of information available and the ability of planners to use it. Consequently, there is a tendency to choose the first location that either satisfies a socialist location principle or indicates economic efficiency (Hamilton, 1970). Little evidence exists to suggest that the search process proceeds in a systematic manner and the chance of the 'best' location being selected decreases as decision-making becomes more centralized. Many poor location decisions have been made as a result (see below). Hamilton (1971*a*) outlines three conflicting factors which influence the locational search process;

1. The acute pressure on planners' time suggests that the theory of least effort is highly relevant to their search behaviour.
2. Many planners (and the other interest groups pressurizing planners) retain a strong sense of territorial identity with their

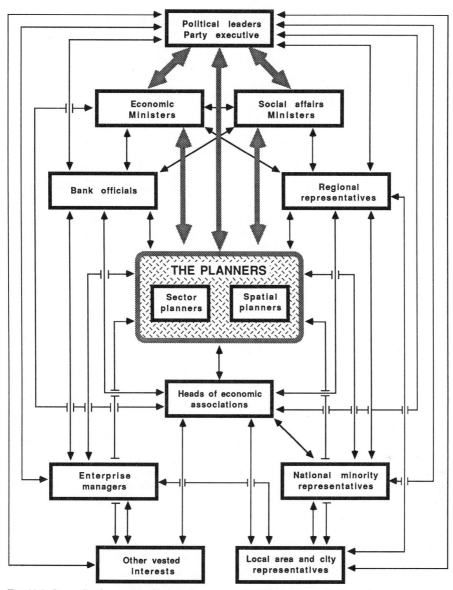

FIG 10.5 Generalized patterns of interaction among decision-makers in a planned economy (*source*: Hamilton, 1970 p. 87)

home area and are in a position to channel investment there.

3. As the number of interest groups in the planning process broadened, the planners became subjected to more interactions and thus a greater range of possible locations.

As a consequence, the application of the laws of socialist location varied spatially according to different ideological, information, and economic 'environments'. Hamilton (1970) summarizes, for the period up to the late 1960s, the extent to which the ten principles influenced decision-making in Eastern Europe, the Union of Soviet Socialist Republics, and China (Table 10.8). Countries frequently applying a principle were awarded a score of 1 in the binary matrix, whereas a 0 was recorded where principles infrequently influenced decision-making. Certain interesting features emerge from the matrix. First, location near

TABLE 10.8 Matrix indicating the importance or unimportance of socialist location principles by countries

Countries	Location Principles[a]									
	1	2	3	4	5	6	7	8	9	10
Bulgaria	1	0	1	0	1	1	0	1	1	0
China	1	1	1	1	1	1	0	1	1	0
Czechoslovakia	1	0	1	0	1	0	1	0	0	1
East Germany	1	1	1	0	1	0	0	0	0	0
Hungary	1	1	0	0	1	1	0	0	0	0
Poland	1	1	1	0	1	1	0	0	1	1
Romania	1	0	1	0	1	1	0	1	0	0
Soviet Union	1	1	1	1	1	1	1	0	1	0
Yugoslavia	1	0	1	0	1	1	1	0	1	0
RANKING	1	5	3	9	2	4	7	8	6	10

[a]The location principles numbered 1 to 10 are as in the text.

Source: Hamilton (1970 p. 103).

natural resources and an even geographical distribution of economic activity were the most important principles and the only two to be applied in all countries. Secondly, regional specialization and the desire to disperse socialism throughout the countryside were the next ranked principles; these were applied in all countries except Hungary, and Czechoslovakia and East Germany respectively. Thirdly, proximity to markets and strategic factors were only of average importance, in part reflecting the small size of many East European countries. These principles were most important in China, the USSR, and Poland, but neither were influential in Romania and Czechoslovakia. Fourthly, the elimination of rural–urban differences and advancement of national minority groups were only really applied in three (different) countries each (Bulgaria, China, and Romania for the former and Czechoslovakia, Yugoslavia, and the USSR for the latter). The cases of Czechoslovakia and Yugoslavia are interesting in that they are the only states in Eastern Europe to have 'federal systems of government that represent attempts to handle multinational situations' (Rugg, 1985 pp. 304–5). Finally, the principles of lowest rank were self-sufficiency and the achievement of an international division of labour within COMECON. Regional self-sufficiency was encouraged in China and the USSR, a reflection of their size and the desire to reduce transport costs.

It would appear, therefore, that the laws of socialist location have been only partially applied, with characteristic variations between countries. Indeed, Pallot and Shaw (1981) are very cynical about the value of these laws altogether. Over time, attitudes and decision-making behaviour have also changed, especially in terms of their relationship with socialist ideology. Rugg (1985) outlines three periods in socialist planning, with each emphasizing the importance of different principles:

1. *Self-sufficiency and the command economy.* The Soviet model of self-sufficiency, based primarily on heavy industry, dominated planning in the early years after the Second World War. Centralized and ideological decision-making attempted to encourage modernization and economic development by establishing heavy industry in all parts of a country, but especially in backward regions. Dispersal of industry into new areas represented an attempt to utilize labour and unexploited resources. However, full appraisals of the latter were not always available (see below) and policy often led to high investment in inefficient locations and over-diversification of economies. As Rugg (1985 p. 266) explained, 'perhaps the primary weakness . . . was that under an autarkic sysem countries found difficulty in specialising in those products for which they had a comparative advantage.' The application of ideological-strategic principles was strongly supported by planners in the early years. Indeed, the military exercised considerable influence over location decisions until 1954, especially in terms

of industrial dispersal into inaccessible (safe) areas (Hamilton, 1971a).

2. *Regional specialization and economic efficiency*. The inadequacies of economic self-sufficiency (autarky) were readily apparent by the mid-1950s and after 1957 greater emphasis was placed upon the division of labour between countries and hence regional specialization and trade. Economic efficiency began to replace purely ideological principles, stimulating interest in 'better' location decisions. The inclusion of more interest groups (including ministers and managers of larger industrial enterprises) in the increasingly decentralized decision-making process, encouraged a greater spatial concentration of industry by arguing for the expansion of existing plants, or the location of new plants, in already industrialized regions. This reflected an increasing desire to reduce investment, operating, and marketing costs. Within the pattern of concentration, however, policy favoured dispersal towards the edge of existing agglomerations. Throughout this period towards a more decentralized economy, the state continued to command total control, although not all 'members' were happy with the plan to develop international patterns of regional specialization. For example, Romania was not pleased with its role as provider of raw materials to other members of COMECON, as this restricted its own development prospects. Consequently, the country has embarked upon a more independent application of socialism.

3. *Economic reform and external trade*. Since the late 1960s, COMECON members have exerted increasing pressure for more decentralized management, greater autonomy for individual enterprises to make their own decisions, and the importation of Western technology. Indeed, in July 1988, COMECON and the EC signed a trade agreement which enabled the two organizations to trade with each other for the first time. Trade negotiations between the EC and individual Eastern Bloc countries are already underway. In many ways, these developments followed the early lead of Yugoslavia, a non-member of COMECON, with its policy of decentralized economic development. Hungary has probably progressed further than any other country in this direction (Enyedi, 1976) (although at the time of writing most East European countries were experiencing notable change) and producers are directly involved in the decision-making process of running an efficient and economic enterprise. However, all economic decisions still have to be made within the constraints of a centrally controlled political system. Economic efficiency thus outweighs ideological considerations and factories are rarely located in isolated areas. The trend is towards larger industrial–agricultural complexes, which are replacing the earlier agro-industrial complexes in an attempt to obtain scale economies and encourage a more efficient use of capital.

The East European iron and steel industry

Spatial and temporal dimensions of socialist location principles are clearly portrayed in the East European iron and steel industry (Hamilton, 1964; Rugg, 1985; Ilbery, 1986). Before the Second World War, production was heavily concentrated in such areas as Upper Silesia (Poland), the Ostrava district (Czechoslovakia), and Slovenia (Yugoslavia). However, the introduction of economic self-sufficiency and a policy of heavy investment in heavy industry led to an expansion of production in existing centres and new iron and steel plants in relatively underdeveloped regions. Ideological and strategic reasons governed this policy of dispersal, rather than such traditional economic factors as raw materials, transport costs, labour, and markets; the result was often unfruitful investments (white elephants) in areas with small potential markets. Good examples of such investments include Košice (Czechoslovakia), Eisenhüttenstadt (East Germany), Nowa Huta (Poland), Dunaujváros (Hungary), and Nikšić (Yugoslavia), none of which possessed the necessary combination of iron-ore, coal, infrastructure (power, transport, and water supply), and skilled labour (Hamilton, 1971a and b) (Fig. 10.6). All five depended upon costly hauls of materials from distant or foreign regions. For example, the Košice iron and steel works was based on unrealistic appraisals of iron-ore reserves in the local area and so resulted in high transport costs for iron-ore (from the Soviet Union) and coking coal (from the Moravian coalfield). Similarly, resources for the Nikšić integrated plant came from over 150 miles away. Indeed, Nikšić (Montenegro) and Skopje (Macedonia) were early attempts in Yugoslavia to develop 'bastions of socialism in the underdeveloped republics' (Rugg, 1985 p. 301). The

FIG 10.6 Major iron and steel plants in Eastern Europe

iron and steel works at Skopje used very low-grade iron-ore and brown coal—bituminous coal mixes; this soon created various technical difficulties.

Rugg (1985) argues that many of the new iron and steel plants were located in backward areas for military–strategic reasons rather than ideological ones. Plants at Eisenhüttenstadt, Nowa Huta, Košice, and Galati (Romania) were all built in the eastern part of their respective countries to afford closer proximity to the Soviet Union, upon whom they often depended for their raw materials. However, this was not always the case, for plants at Dunaujváros (Hungary) and

Kremikovtsi (Bulgaria) were sited in western regions (although they still depended upon the Soviet Union), just as plants in Yugoslavia and Albania were not influenced by COMECON policy.

The failure of economic self-sufficiency led, after 1956, to a wider application of economic criteria in the East European iron and steel industry. Greater spatial concentration and regional specialization was encouraged, by Ministers, sector planners, and the managers of large industrial enterprises, and trade between COMECON members initiated. Countries with a reasonable resource endowment and well-equipped iron and steel plants (e.g. Poland and Czechoslovakia) were to expand production, whilst other members could either provide raw materials or concentrate on the later stages of production and supply specialized products. As a consequence, a national pattern of spatial segregation began to emerge, with the less-developed countries (like Romania and Bulgaria) supplying materials, Poland and Czechoslovakia concentrating on mass production, and Hungary and East Germany producing sheet iron and higher-grade steels respectively. Outside COMECON, Yugoslavia attempted to increase output and overcome financial losses incurred at plants like Nikšić by considering more favourable economic sites on the Dalmatian coast (e.g. at Split).

Not all members of COMECON were happy with the policy of specialization and trade. In particular, Romania thought it would restrict its own development opportunities. Consequently, the country built a large integrated iron and steel works at Galati, on the bank of the Danube, in the 1960s, at a time when it should have been supplying raw materials to other COMECON members. This represents a delayed attempt at applying the principles of economic self-sufficiency.

Iron and steel production in Eastern Europe continued to follow economic rather than ideological considerations throughout the 1960s and 1970s. As in Western Europe, the industry was adversely affected by world economic recession, although production continued to increase into the 1980s. The modern trend is towards more decentralized management and greater trade links with the EC.

10.3 Summary

This chapter has attempted to demonstrate the complexity of the decision-making process and its importance to an understanding of patterns of land use and locational change in economic activity. Various theoretical and methodological approaches have been developed in order to study decision-making behaviour in different types of political and economic system. It is important to remember that:

- Neoclassical approaches to land-use and locational decision-making are based on the assumptions of profit maximization and complete knowledge, although such concepts as spatial margins to profitability, psychic income, and welfare economics have added more flexibility.

- Structuralist approaches argue that decision-making behaviour is constrained by the structure (e.g. capitalism) in which decisions are made, although realism recognizes that individuals do make decisions within the constraints set by economic processes.

- Behavioural approaches suggest that decisions are made within an environment of risk and uncertainty and so place more emphasis on individual goals other than profit maximization.

- Studies of agricultural decision-making have highlighted the importance of intrinsic and expressive values above income oriented and social values. However, it is recognized that as the context of agriculture changes, the decisions of farmers are increasingly being affected by factors external to the farm.

- The decision to move or close an industrial plant is affected by a cross-section of factors from each of the theoretical perspectives outlined in this chapter. A proper understanding of industrial decline, for example, requires an examination of higher-level processes and an understanding of why one plant rather than another is closed.

- In centrally planned economies the decision-making process is different. For example, ten principles of socialist location guide decision-makers in Eastern Europe and the Soviet Union. However, adherence to the principles has led to many uneconomic locations being selected (e.g. in the iron and steel industry) and there is debate as to whether a specific socialist landscape has been created. Indeed, there are also similarities with decision-making behaviour in developed market economies, including stages in the decision-making process, the influence of perception, and the importance of uncertainty.

The many factors considered in the 'context of change' section of this book are interrelated and combine to govern the nature of decision-making in economic geography. The importance of these factors is highlighted in the next section of the book, which applies the analysis of land use and locational change to the primary, manufacturing, and service sectors.

III Applications

11

Primary Industries

This chapter seeks to apply the concepts and principles developed in earlier sections of the book to an understanding of land use and locational change in the primary sector. As primary activities tend to be extensive users of space, it is less easy, although not impossible, to talk in terms of spatial shifts in location (as in the secondary and tertiary sectors). Indeed, the location of agricultural land, minerals, and natural forests is essentially fixed, although their economic value varies over time and space in accordance with the changing relative importance of such influencing factors as transport costs, technology, organizational structure, government policy, and market trends.

Using forestry and hop-farming as two examples of primary industries, global trends and patterns are initially described. Detailed case studies, at national and regional scales, then follow. Emphasis is placed upon the 'context of change', demonstrating the need to examine a wide range of factors, at different geographical scales, from the global to the local, when accounting for spatial and temporal trends.

11.1 Forestry

Global Trends

Deforestation and afforestation
Estimates of the world's forested area vary from 3 to 5 million hectares (ha), or 23 to 38 per cent of the earth's surface (Mather, 1987). This wide range reflects the inadequacies and conflicting nature of available data sources. Despite this, there is general agreement that both the closed forest area (forest with a dense, continuous tree canopy, which excludes sunlight and thus limits the amount of ground vegetation) and the total

area of forest and woodland are declining, especially in the tropical areas of developing countries (Barney, 1980; Allen and Barnes, 1985; Mather, 1987). In association with an increasing population base, this means that the area of forest and woodland has declined from two ha per person in the 1930s to less than one ha in the late 1980s; the figure could be as low as 0.5 by the year 2000. Annual rates of deforestation are not really known and estimates range from nearly 20 million ha (Barney, 1980; Myers, 1980) to 10 million (Food and Agricultural Organization (FAO) Yearbooks). Whilst the latter may represent an underestimation, the projection of nearly 20 million ha in the Global 2000 report (Barney, 1980) cannot be substantiated. Rates of removal have, however, been the subject of mounting concern, regarding such environmental effects as erosion, flooding, and the loss of ecological diversity (see Chapter 17.2).

Based on conservative FAO estimates, 31 per cent of the earth's surface is covered by forests and woodland (including shrub, open woodland, and closed forest). The pattern of distribution is far from uniform (Fig. 11.1*a*) and four groups of countries can be identified (Mather, 1987):

1. The tropical countries of Latin America, Central Africa, and South-East Asia, where over 50 per cent of the land area is covered by forests and woodland; in some countries the figure rises above 75 per cent (e.g. Gabon 78 per cent, Guyana 83, Surinam 97).

2. The small group of countries outside the tropics that can boast a figure of over 50 per cent of forest cover—Finland, Sweden, Japan, and the Koreas.

3. Several countries in such climatically marginal areas as North Africa, Greenland, and Iceland (too dry or cold), where less than 10 per cent of the land surface is given over to woodland.

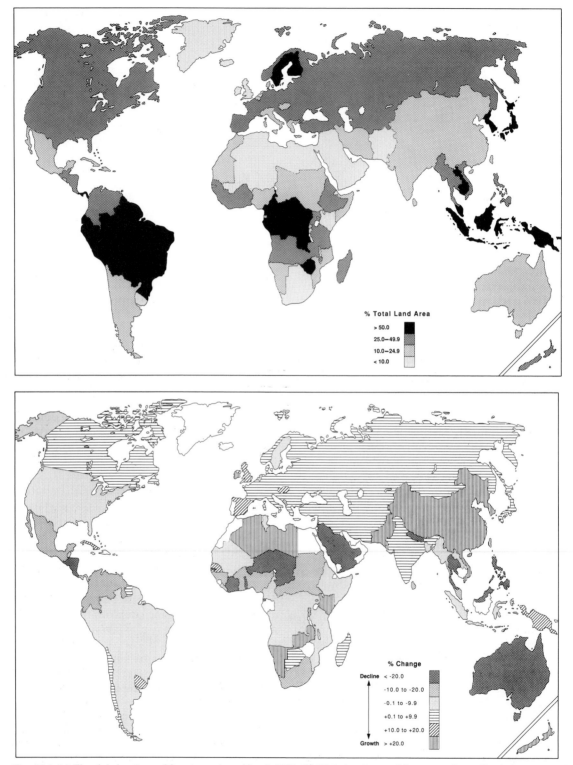

FIG 11.1 (*a*) The global pattern of forestry and woodland, 1984; (*b*) Global patterns of forestry and woodland change, 1970–84 (*source:* based on data in *FAO production yearbook* various years)

4. The countries of north-western Europe, which are now poorly endowed with forest resources; this especially applies to the United Kingdom (9 per cent), the Netherlands (9), Ireland (5), and Denmark (12).

Over one hundred million ha of forest and woodland, or 3 per cent of the total area, have been lost since 1970. Two major temporal trends can be identified: first, fairly large-scale *deforestation* in such well-endowed areas as Central America, West Africa, and South-East Asia; and secondly, substantial rates of *afforestation*, often in countries with small areas of woodland like China, India, parts of North Africa, and much of Europe. This is, of course, an oversimplification and the patterns of change are far more complex (Fig. 11.1b).

Research has indicated that changes in the distribution of forests and woodlands relate to such factors as agricultural expansion, population growth, the demand for fuel and commercialization. Whilst per capita GNP is not positively related to changes in forest area, the latter appears to be inversely related to changes in the amount of land devoted to arable farming (Allen and Barnes, 1985). In many African and Latin American countries, for example, the decline in forestry has been linked to both an increase in arable activities and high population growth, whereas the more recent afforestation in the low population growth countries of Europe has taken place at the expense of previous arable land. Very few countries have experienced an increase in both forestry and arable area since 1970; China is one of the major exceptions.

Allen and Barnes (1985) show that deforestation in the developing world has, in the short-term, been encouraged by population growth and agricultural expansion and, in the longer term, aggravated by the harvesting of wood for fuel and export. Commercial logging is of minor significance in the short term, although it has assumed considerable importance in certain areas, especially Malaysia, the Philippines, and the Ivory Coast. The latter has one of the world's highest rates of clearance, at 50 per cent since 1970 (Mather, 1987). The growth in commercial farming, as in cattle ranches in Brazil for example, is another relevant factor, together with the rising importance of plantation forestry. Occupying approximately 3 per cent of the closed forest area, over 90 per cent of plantations are concentrated in developed and centrally planned countries. However, expansion in the tropics has been rapid since the 1960s, with Brazil showing a growth of 3.2 million ha in fourteen years, from 0.5 million ha in 1966 to 3.7 million in 1979 (Evans, 1982). A probable explanation for this is the higher productivity rate (3 to 7 times) and shorter rotation period (20 compared to over 60 years) than elsewhere. Little consideration has yet been given to the potential problems associated with intensive timber production, such as soil exhaustion, pest attacks (with less species diversity), and ecological sustainability.

It would appear from these explanations that deforestation and afforestation trends can be related to different stages in the economic development process. In the initial stages (hunting and gathering), the area of natural woodland tends to decline, whereas the movement to a more advanced 'farming' stage is associated with increasing rates of timber production per unit area and a corresponding fall in the destruction of woodland. At still higher stages of economic development, increasing technology and larger organizational structures reduce the demand for agricultural land and active programmes of afforestation can be undertaken. Such a model suggests that the present destruction of tropical forests is a temporary and not permanent feature of the landscape and so should be treated with caution.

Patterns of roundwood production

On a global scale, there is no shortage of timber for industrial and commercial purposes and a reasonable balance between supply and demand exists. However, as with food production, a major imbalance exists between patterns of supply and demand and some areas are very short of timber. This necessitates trade agreements with more favourably endowed countries and can be illustrated best by a brief analysis of roundwood production figures (Table 11.1). Roundwood is used almost equally for fuelwood and industrial/constructional purposes. Nine countries have continued to account for about 60 per cent of roundwood production since the early 1960s; indeed, nearly one-half comes from just five countries: the USA, the USSR, India, China, and Brazil. Nevertheless, important locational changes have occurred during the past twenty-five

TABLE 11.1 World roundwood production, 1961–1983 (million cubic metres)

	1961	%	1971	%	1981	%	1983	%
USA	302	15.3	334	13.2	419	14.1	438	14.4
USSR	367	18.6	385	15.2	358	12.1	356	11.7
India	*	*	179	7.1	224	7.6	233	7.7
China	132	6.7	175	6.9	224	7.6	232	7.6
Brazil	138	7.0	145	5.7	213	7.2	220	7.2
Canada	99	5.0	122	4.8	145	4.9	142	4.7
Indonesia	86	4.4	107	4.2	126	4.3	122	4.0
Nigeria	41	2.1	57	2.2	81	2.7	86	2.8
Sweden	47	2.4	65	2.6	50	1.7	53	1.7
WORLD	1974		2534		2963		3042	

*No data

Source: United Nations Statistical Yearbook, various years.

years. First, the USSR has continued to produce a declining proportion of the world's total, from 18.6 per cent in 1961 to 12.1 per cent in 1982. Secondly, Europe's share of the total has also fallen, but only since the 1970s (as shown in the case of Sweden). Thirdly, a group of countries including India, China, and Brazil have, for different reasons, consistently increased their output of roundwood. No simple core–periphery pattern is apparent among the major producers.

The main consumers of roundwood and forest products are the industrialized nations, including countries where forestry itself is often unimportant. An international system of trade, controlled by government agreements between different countries, is the result. Within Europe, for example, Scandinavian and Alpine countries supply those with fewer resources. The latter also receive timber from the USSR, Canada, and the USA. Patterns become more complex when it is realized that the USA in turn imports from Canada, as does Japan, which also obtains timber from South-East Asia.

Patterns of production are complicated by two further problems. First, only 30 per cent of the world's forests are considered productive enough to warrant exploitation, of which two-thirds are relatively inaccessible. Secondly, the 'best' forests, in terms of productivity and accessibility, have already been destroyed. These were located in such highly populated and/or industrialized areas as Western Europe, the US Mid-West, and much of China and India. Early patterns of exploitation, therefore, exhibited a distance-decay rela-

tionship, based upon cost/weight loss considerations and proximity to the market.

Over time, patterns of production change and formerly inaccessible resources may become economically accessible. This relates to a wide range of factors, including an increasing demand (reflecting population growth and a rise in affluence), new technologies in the growing and harvesting of timber, a relative decline in transport costs with improving modes of transport, a growth in the size of operation units (multiproduct operations and vertical integration), and government policies, in the form of different grants and incentives. As a consequence, forestry activities have, through a process of land-use competition, become increasingly concentrated on land unsuited to agriculture. This land is usually beyond the physical margins of agricultural cultivation and so forestry often becomes a frontier activity. However, with surplus food production in many Western economies the situation could change and the pressure on forestry to replace farming on higher-quality (and lowland) land is increasing.

Various factors have been shown to be relevant to a discussion of global trends in forestry. Some of these, and especially the role of organizational structures and governmental policies, will be stressed in two contrasting case studies of the forest product sector: first, from Canada, the sixth ranked producer of roundwood; and secondly, from the United Kingdom, where 90 per cent of timber requirements are imported and where an active policy of afforestation has been pursued. In both examples, changes over space and time are emphasized.

The Canadian forest product sector

Canada is one of the world's major producers of roundwood, with output continuously rising, from 99 million cubic metres in 1961 to 142 million in 1983 (Table 11.1). Throughout the twentieth century, timber, pulp, and newsprint have been among Canada's top six export earners and even in the 1980s such products continue to account for 20 per cent of the export trade. Over 300 000 people are employed in forestry and related industries, which are vital to the Canadian economy and dominant in such areas as British Columbia (Hayter, 1981), Quebec (Bradbury, 1982), and the Atlantic provinces. In some towns, the forest product sector is virtually the only form of economic activity (Hayter, 1985).

The pattern of exports has varied over time, from the early specialized links with the United Kingdom in the eighteenth and nineteenth centuries, to the rapid increase in trade with the USA in the twentieth century (which has outstripped that of the United Kingdom since 1950) and recent growth with Japan (which now exceeds that with Europe). Such temporal shifts can be related to the changing patterns of foreign investment and Hayter (1985) identifies and explains five distinct phases in the development of the Canadian forest product sector:

1. *Pre-1860*, when exploitation of Canadian forests was dominated by British interests and demands. This mainly comprised the export of logs and squared timber, taken from the more accessible valleys (to the British) in eastern Canada; little felling took place in western regions. British entrepreneurs and merchants were centrally involved and often invested in forest product operations. As Hayter established, however, British ownership could not, at that time, be described as foreign.

2. *1860–1910*, when American capital and family-based concerns increased their involvement in Canadian logging and lumber activities. Aware of this 'intrusion', the Canadian government increased the export duty on logs, in an attempt to force US companies to establish sawmills in Canada. The flow of American capital continued to be dominated by family-owned businesses and by the end of the nineteenth century a pulp and paper industry was beginning to develop.

3. *1910–1945*, when American investment in pulp and paper continued to expand, but more in the form of corporate rather than family interests. The period was characterized by a northward movement of the newsprint industry, in response to two developments: first, the prohibition of pulp wood exports by both provincial governments and the national government on federally owned crown lands; and secondly, the removal of the US tariff on newsprint in 1911. Rather than acquiring existing pulp and paper mills, US investment took the form of developing new mills and by 1933 American-owned mills controlled 51 per cent of newsprint production. Whilst corporate interests were concentrated in the more eastern parts of Canada, foreign capital from private families and individuals continued to dominate the lumber industry, especially on the west coast. The latter was more susceptible to Canadian take-over and control (Hayter, 1985), although it could be argued that US capital provided essential managerial and technological know-how, which was not locally available, as well as finance and markets.

4. *1945–1975*, when family-based investment had largely disappeared and most aspects of the Canadian forest product sector were dominated by foreign multinational companies, mainly based in the USA. American firms began to acquire existing indigenous firms and the process of horizontal and vertical integration was intensified. This was spatially selective, concentrating initially upon British Columbia and later on the Prairies and Atlantic Canada. Towards the end of this period foreign 'penetration' was substantial, especially as European and Japanese investments had also increased; however, this tended to take the form of joint ventures with locally-based firms.

5. *1975 to date*, which has been characterized by increasing 'Canadianization' of the forest product sector, with some large foreign-controlled mills being 'taken over' by Canadian interests. The ensuing world economic recession began to encourage a global restructuring of the forestry industry, with many operations becoming part of more diversified conglomerates. 'Canadianization' has not, therefore, simply been a function of national government policies.

Most commentators are of the opinion that the long period of foreign investment 'truncated' the forest product sector in Canada, with for example imported technology restricting the development of local R. & D. activities. Clearly, an understanding of the development of the forestry industry in Canada can be achieved only through an analysis of both the behaviour of investing companies and the operation of wider processes leading to the restructuring of world forestry. This, by definition, necessitates the adoption of behavioural and structuralist perspectives to the study of Canadian forestry, elements of which have emerged in more detailed regional studies (Hayter, 1981; Bradbury, 1982).

Hayter (1981) related the impressive growth of British Columbia's forest product economy to such factors as a favourable resource base, technology, demand, competition, and above all else political conditions. The latter promoted forestry through 'the establishment of economic infrastructure, appropriate resource utilisation and tenure laws, and a climate attractive for foreign investment' (Hayter, 1981 p. 103). A similar process of foreign penetration and integration as previously outlined occurred in British Columbia and this undoubtedly aided the growth of the forest sector, by providing locally scarce financial and managerial inputs, access to international markets, and a growth 'mentality', and lessening the uncertainties of investments in new facilities. However, foreign capital did permit the penetration of domestic markets, reduce local R. & D. and prevent opportunities in high-level scientific and managerial occupations; truncation of British Columbia's forest sector was the inevitable result.

The role of the state has also been emphasized in the recent development of the forestry sector in Quebec (Bradbury, 1982). For example, the Société de Récuperation Forestière d'Exploitation et de Developpement Forestières du Quebec (REXFOR) was created in 1971 to invest in infrastructure and rationalize the production of inputs and outputs in the province's sawmill and pulpmill industry. In particular, the corporation attempted to stimulate the forest industry in a number of declining, backward, and older lumber and pulp regions by providing funds for new mills and the updating of existing ones. In essence, REXFOR 'advocated support for small private firms in isolated areas, encouraged the location of large externally owned pulp mills, and provided

funds for the regional integration of backward and forward linkages' (Bradbury, 1982 p. 52). Similar state involvement, in association with industrial capital and a pulp and paper union, occurred in the forestry related TEMPEC co-operative (Témiscaming–Quebec Forest Products). With the help of REXFOR, the co-operative has helped to provide employment and maintain the local economy within a region experiencing decline after the construction phase of a series of HEP dams. In Quebec, therefore, the state has played a prominent and stabilizing role in the forestry sector since 1970, especially in rural and backward areas.

In an examination of the locational decision-making process of selected pulp and paper industries in British Columbia, Hayter (1978) identified a two-stage search process, which was constrained by both time and cost: the first stage was concerned with identifying the 'best' region, whilst the second involved choosing the most suitable site(s) within the selected region (see also Chapter 10.2). It became clear that firms did not evaluate all available locational alternatives. For example, both Northwood Pulp and Timber (NPT) and British Columbia Forest Products (BCFP) considered one region—Prince George and Mackenzie respectively—whereas Prince George Pulp and Paper (PGPP) investigated north-western Alberta as well as Prince George. Similarly, the number of specific sites examined varied fromt two (BCFP) to seven (PGPP). Most companies had established a list of between six and eight factors thought to affect site selection—including the availability of housing, taxation levels, the availability and quality of labour, and the effects of air pollution—and whilst senior executives of NPT undertook the necessary research, PGPP employed consultants. Air pollution was the decisive influence on the choice of site for PGPP, although local taxes were also an important issue for both NPT and PGPP. The final choice of site was not 'optimal', in neoclassical terms, and most companies admitted to being able to improve on site selection.

The Canadian forest product sector, therefore, has developed in a number of distinct stages in response to changing patterns of foreign investment and multinational company behaviour. Government involvement has increased over time, particularly in the major regional centres of the forestry industry, but a proper understanding of the location of pulp and paper industries for example can be obtained only by examining the decision-making behaviour of the individual entrepreneurs.

Afforestation in the United Kingdom

The United Kingdom is one of Europe's least-wooded countries. Years of exploitation and deforestation had reduced the forested area to just 5 per cent of the total land surface by the end of the First World War. Since then, a deliberate policy of afforestation has enabled forests and woodlands to recover considerably and by the mid-1980s they were occupying over 9 per cent of the total land area. Indeed, the area of forest plantations and woodland has doubled since 1920 and now stands at over 2.25 million ha. Change has been even more dramatic than implied by these figures, for many of the woods which existed in 1919 (when the Forestry Commission was formed) have been replanted with different species (Lowe *et al.*, 1986). Coniferous plantations have replaced large areas of ancient and semi-natural woodlands, with a concomitant loss in ecological diversity.

The revival of forestry can be related mainly to the increasing level of state involvement through the Forestry Commission, which owns half of the country's woodland. The Commission was established, primarily for strategic reasons, after the First World War in an attempt to restore timber supplies. Its work was soon disrupted by the Second World War, after which an afforestation policy established a target of two million ha of productive forests by the year 2010. This is unlikely to be met because of subsequent shifts in policy objectives (see below), although the recent concern over surplus agricultural land has already led to a renewed interest in woodland. The Commission can purchase land on the open market, afforest it, and sell the timber. Whilst its main objective is the production of timber, it has, since 1967, had a special responsibility to cater for rural recreation, enhance the rural landscape, and provide rural employment.

Post-war forestry has been characterized by three features: first, spatial and temporal variations in the rates of afforestation; secondly, differences between state (public) and private sectors; and thirdly, variations in the influence of such 'external' factors as the performance of other land uses in marginal upland areas and changing economic and fiscal conditions. Distinct phases in Britain's afforestation programme can be identified (Mather, 1978):

1. 1945–1957

A White Paper on post-war policy was published in 1943 and advocated a vigorous programme of expansion over a fifty-year period. The target was set at two million ha, comprising 1.2 million ha of new forests and considerable replanting and upgrading of the existing 0.8 million ha of woodland. Defence strategy was the main objective, in the event of future wars and naval blockades, and although the policy was initially successful problems soon became apparent. First, a scarcity of suitable land led to a decline in the rate of afforestation after 1955. Whilst the compulsory purchasing of land was possible, the Forestry Commission did not use these powers. Secondly, an improvement in hill and upland agriculture, as a response to the Hill Farming Act (1946), encouraged an expansion in agricultural production in marginal areas. This compounded the problems associated with land scarcity. Thirdly, there was a shortage of labour in the more remote rural areas, stemming in part from a lack of housing. Although the Forestry Commission implemented a house-building programme, this became delayed by a lack of materials and the high costs of construction in isolated areas.

The White Paper also introduced a Dedication Scheme, to encourage the rehabilitation of existing woodlands by the private sector. This involved the provision of grant aid for planting and management, in return for a commitment by the owner to manage his/her woodland for productive forestry. Private planting did increase steadily and by 1955 the target area had been exceeded. This, in part, reflected the greater availability of land as private landowners, unlike the state sector, could transfer agricultural land into forest use without the agreement of the agricultural ministry.

Spatially, the early years of the afforestation programme were confined to areas of rough grazing (physically marginal for agriculture). One-half of the plantable area was allocated to Scotland, while the remaining half was divided on a two-third/one-third basis between England and Wales respectively. Although the pattern of afforestation did reflect the distribution of rough grazing, it was complicated by different factors. One of these was the harsh environment in some of the areas perceived to be plantable, especially in the Highland region of Scotland. Another was the varying structure of land holdings which led to different propensities to sell land for afforestation. For example, Mather (1978) demonstrated that much of southern Scotland was held in relatively small hill sheep farms, in contrast to the larger estates in the northern areas. Similarly in Wales, large areas of plantable land were unavailable for afforestation as they coincided with common land, which was open to public access and thus retained rough grazing.

One objective of early policy was to develop large forest regions that would be able to support wood-using industries. However, the shortage of available land led to a rather random pattern of acquisitions, reducing the extent of spatial concentration. It took longer than anticipated, therefore, for forestry to develop a comparative advantage (see Chapter 3.2) over hill farming and for extensively afforested areas, as in south-west Scotland and Argyll, to be formed.

2. 1958–1965

A decline in planting after 1954, together with the increasing inappropriateness of growing trees for strategic reasons, led to a policy statement in 1958, which established a planting programme for the next two five-year periods. A target of 120 000 ha was set for the 1958–63 period, with a lower total of 95 000 ha for the years 1964 to 1968. The Forestry Commission achieved 80 per cent of the first target, despite continued problems over land acquisition. In the 1958 policy statement, emphasis was placed on the regional dimension of afforestation, especially in the upland areas of Scotland and Wales. Important perceived spin-offs of such a spatially concentrated policy were social benefits and the diversification of employment opportunities. The level of Dedication Grants was also increased, to encourage the development of private forestry. A number of private investment syndicates did enter the forestry industry and operated on a small scale in England and Wales.

A further report in 1963 suggested a ten-year planting programme of 180 000 ha and confirmed the policy of concentrating land acquisitions in those upland areas of Scotland and Wales suffering from depopulation.

3. 1965–1972

The election of a Labour government in 1964 heralded radical changes in forestry policy, including large-scale expansion and stronger spatial and social dimensions. The Scottish programme was especially pronounced, with a target of 20 000 ha per year being set in 1967 for a nine-year period. Similarly, at least 80 per cent of the overall planting programme in Britain (24 000 ha/ year) was to be through new planting. Such a policy of rapid afforestation was to benefit in the late 1960s from the poor state of hill sheep-farming, where farmers were now more willing to sell land for forestry purposes. However, much of the available land was acquired by private forestry investment groups because of fiscal advantages related to estate duty. Indeed, private afforestation rates increased dramatically and in some instances exceeded the efforts of the Forestry Commission. Spatially, the activities of public and private sectors become segregated. Whilst the emphasis of state policy was on increased planting in northern and western areas, especially in the crofting counties of the Scottish Highlands (for social as well as economic reasons), the private sector's attention was concentrated in southern Scotland, where higher tree growth rates offered better financial returns.

4. 1972–1977

The early 1970s saw yet another change in the fortunes of afforestation, characterized by reduced activities. This was related first to a further shortage of land, due to an improvement in hill sheep-farming; secondly, to the unknown prospects of entering the European Community in 1973; and thirdly, to a dramatic increase in venison prices in 1969 and 1970 (Mather, 1978). Previously established afforestation targets could not be met and the newly elected Conservative government issued a policy document, in which a reduced Forestry Commission target of 22 000 ha per year was set. Social objectives remained important, but not regardless of cost, and while the crofting counties were not specifically emphasized, activities were still to be confined to upland areas.

The private sector experienced even greater problems, through the complex interplay of three main factors:

1. Uncertainty over the desirability of long-

term investments in forestry at a time of low general investment confidence.

2. Suspension of the Dedication Scheme. A new scheme was introduced in 1973, but this offered less financial support.

3. The advent of capital transfer tax, replacing the favourable estate duty. Some relief for investment in woodland came in the 1975 Finance Act, but this was too late.

A further influence and constraint upon afforestation patterns was the requirement, from 1972, that both the state and private sectors had to seek approval from agricultural ministries and local planning authorities over proposed acquisitions. This reflected the increasing concern surrounding potential environmental problems from continued afforestation.

5. 1977 onwards

A Forestry Commission report in the late 1970s advocated a major expansion of forestry, to around 36 000 ha per year. However, its budget was successively squeezed and in 1981 the Forestry Act effectively transferred to the minister the right to sell land in the Commission's ownership and pass the profits to the Treasury. The Dedication Scheme was replaced by a Forestry Grant Scheme in the same year, further weakening the Commission's influence over the management of grant-aided plantations. Special restrictions were, therefore, placed on expansion in the public sector. At the same time, the private sector was encouraged to increase its rates of planting. The decisive factor here was the concessions on income, capital transfer, and capital gains taxation. This received considerable media coverage regarding well-known personalities investing in forestry as a tax shelter and the 'loop-hole' was closed in 1988.

Although afforestation remains focused upon upland areas, the mounting concern over agricultural surpluses and the introduction of land set-aside schemes have led to considerable interest in lowland forestry. The government's ALURE package (Alternative Land Uses for the Rural Economy) of 1987 earmarked three and ten million pounds per year for traditional forestry and farm woodland respectively. Similarly, the 1988 Farm Woodlands Scheme permits an annual payment to farmers of between £100 and £190 per ha, for up to thiry years, to grow trees. However, only

arable and improved grassland areas (and not physically marginal areas) are eligible for the maximum payment. A lowland arable farmer, for example, is able to claim for up to 40 ha of trees and receive £7600 per year from the Treasury. This continues for a thirty-year period, if a mixture of broadleaved and coniferous trees are planted, or for twenty years, if just conifers are grown. In addition, farmers can obtain a grant from the Forestry Commission towards the cost of the trees themselves. The stated objective is to plant an extra 30 million trees each year, mainly in lowland areas.

Forestry and farm woodlands are, therefore, in a state of flux. Development of the industry has varied over space and time and between public and private sectors. The main process at work has been government policy, which has itself changed according to political ideologies, the availability of land, the state of hill farming, the need to provide rural employment, environmental conditions, and private investment syndicates.

11.2 Hop-Farming

Hops are a specialized industrial crop, grown exclusively for processing and concentrated in relatively few areas. Globally, less than 100 000 ha of land are devoted to hops, but the demands of the brewing industry ensure that it is a crop of considerable economic importance. Hop-farming is both labour- and capital-intensive and demonstrates well many of the factors examined in the 'context of change' section of this book.

Global trends

The area under hops increased from 49 000 ha in 1950 to an all-time world peak of 88 000 ha in 1981. However, in response to overproduction the total had fallen back to 82 000 ha by 1985. Europe accounts for over 60 per cent of the total area, with the USA and the USSR contributing a further one-third. Production is, therefore, highly spatially concentrated (Fig. 11.2a), with the five leading producers (West Germany, USSR, Czechoslovakia, USA, and the United Kingdom) providing nearly 80 per cent of the total area (Fig. 11.3). The actual output of hops peaked a little later, in 1983/4, although there are considerable

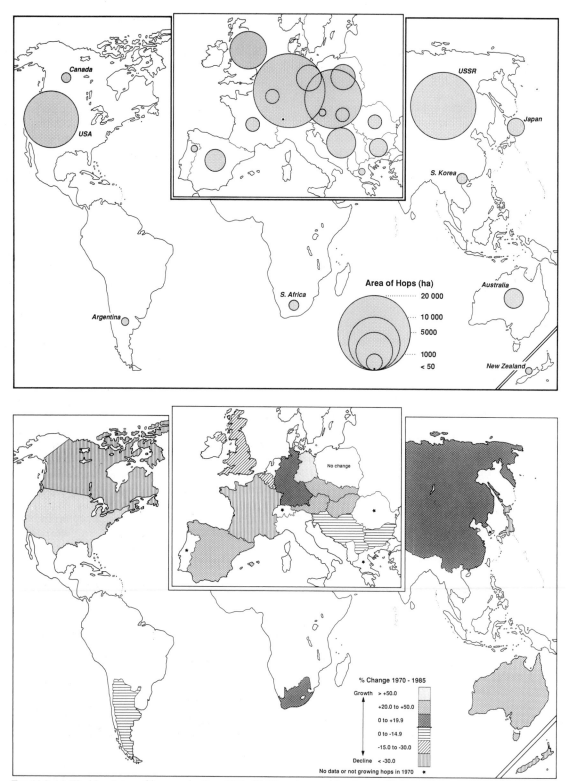

FIG 11.2 (*a*) World patterns of hop production, 1985; (*b*) Changing world patterns of hop production, 1970–85 (*source:* based on data in *FAO production yearbook*, various issues)

differences in yields between producers, from over 2000 kg/ha in the USA to less than 700 in the USSR.

The brewing industry has been characterized by a process of rationalization and mergers, leading to fewer and larger organizational units (e.g. Watts, 1977). However, it has not undergone the same global shifts as many manufacturing industries, which have tended to move from 'developed' to 'developing' economies and from 'core' to 'periphery'. Hops are, because of cultural influences (a lack of demand for beer), still virtually absent from Third World countries. Nevertheless, considerable change has occurred in the relative importance of producing countries during the post-war period (Figs. 11.2*b* and 11.3). In 1950, the USA was the main producer, accounting for nearly one-third of the world's hop area, with the United Kingdom in second place (18.4 per cent), and Czechoslovakia in third (16.3 per cent). By the end of the 1950s, two major changes had occurred: first, the decline of the United Kingdom, from second to fifth producer and with just 12.6 per cent of the total area by 1960; and secondly, the sudden expansion of the USSR which, with 18.7 per cent of the world's area, joined the USA as the leading producer. This was, however, only in terms of area, as poor yields kept output well below the American total.

The 1960s witnessed further changes, dominated by the emergence of West Germany as the leading producer (in areal terms) and the relative decline of the USA, into third place. With an increased area and higher yields per ha, signs of world overproduction were becoming apparent by 1970, a situation aggravated by continued expansion in West Germany and the USSR. The former maintained its dominant position and reached a peak of 20 200 ha of hops in 1975, although the USA continued to produce a higher overall output until the early 1980s. Since 1980, West Germany's hop area has declined to between 18 000 and 19 500 ha, but this still keeps her ahead of the USSR (second in terms of area but only fifth in yield). Czechoslovakia's steady, but continuously, upward trend throughout the 1970s and 1980s has taken her into third position in both area (behind West Germany and the USSR) and output (behind West Germany and the USA).

If the patterns of change for the more recent 1970 to 1985 period are examined, a fairly complex picture emerges, involving some unpredictable trends (Fig. 11.2*b*). Within Europe, for example, countries like France, Belgium, and to a lesser extent Yugoslavia have experienced a similar percentage reduction in area to Britain, although they are far less important producers of hops. In contrast, it is not only the major producers like West Germany and Czechoslovakia

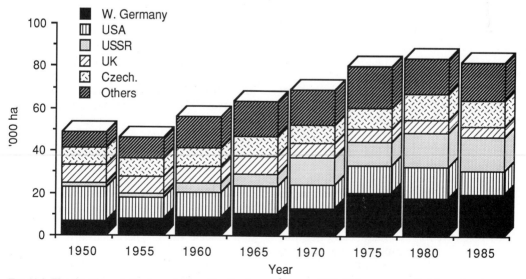

FIG 11.3 The changing relative importance of leading hop-producers, 1950–85 (*source*: compiled from data in *FAO production yearbook*, various issues)

that have made substantial gains in area; countries like Austria, Spain, and Hungary have witnessed a growth rate of between 29 and 44 per cent, although admittedly from a very low base in 1970. Outside Europe, considerable growth has been recorded in Australia and South Africa (again from low bases), but they are completely overshadowed by the phenomenal increase in area, of 196 per cent, in the USSR. These gains were counterbalanced by reductions of over 30 per cent in such insignificant producers as Canada, Japan, and New Zealand.

Over the whole 1950 to 1985 period, therefore, four main trends have been apparent:

1. The dramatic rise in importance of the USSR, especially in the 1950s and mid-1970s. This has been partly offset by consistently poor yields.
2. The fluctuating fortunes of the USA, where the 1950 area of hops was not repeated until 1980, since when it has again fallen back.
3. The continuous decline of the United Kingdom, from a prominent position before and during the 1950s to a state of crisis by 1985.
4. The almost continuous upward trend of West Germany until the early 1980s, interrupted only by an EC planting ban in 1977–9, and the steady growth in importance of Czechoslovakia as a hop-producer.

The deterioration of the United Kingdom's hop industry will be examined in detail in the next section, but it is worth noting some of the reasons suggested for the prominent position of West Germany as a hop-producer. Scott (1977) attributes success to three major factors: first, an increase in the consumption of lager, which is produced from seedless hops, the main type of hop grown in West Germany but not the United Kingdom; secondly, favourable government policy which tended not to rigorously apply the full EC ban on the planting of new hop areas; and thirdly, a family labour tradition on comparatively small and often part-time hop farms. Children, parents, and grandparents combine to produce a labour-intensive commitment that is unbeatable anywhere else in the world. It is an amalgam of positive internal factors and negative factors elsewhere (especially in the United Kingdom) that has elevated West Germany to its lofty position.

Despite an almost uninterrupted upward trend

in beer consumption, the fears of world overproduction became a reality in the 1970s, when West Germany, the USSR, and the USA continued to increase their hop areas in a seemingly unconstrained way. This became the focus of interest of the International Hop Growers Convention (IHGC), whose twelve members held their first meeting in England in 1954. By the time of the 1982 meeting in Belgium, the need to solve the severely depressed state of the hop market, caused by oversupply, was recognized. Members were in general agreement as to the need for some international arrangement. However, the IHGC has no statutory powers and thus total participation is required for success. Consequently, the 1982 conference could only recommend that first, member countries should keep their area of hops 'reasonable' and secondly, growers should not sell hops below the costs of production. Without formal controls, world competition will continue to encourage a spatial restructuring of the industry, whereby West Germany, the USSR, and to a smaller extent the USA and Czechoslovakia will dominate over less important producers and the United Kingdom, whose position is becoming increasingly untenable. It is to the latter that the rest of this chapter now turns.

The declining hop industry in the United Kingdom

In the early nineteenth century, hops were grown in at least forty counties in Britain (Pocock, 1957). By the end of the century, however, they had become concentrated into two main areas: Kent and the West Midlands. Although physical factors were of some importance in the process of change, such regional specialization reflected the proximity of the two districts to major metropolitan areas. The latter provided a ready supply of both workers, for the labour-intensive crop, and waste, for spreading on the hop yards and gardens, as well as acting as a major market for the finished product—beer.

Market/distance relationships have for a long time been central to an understanding of agricultural location and were crucial to Harvey's (1963) classic explanation of the pattern of hop expansion in Kent during the nineteenth century. Harvey demonstrated the tendency for the density of hop production to decrease with distance from a core area based on Wateringbury as its centre. Whilst this core was closely defined by the excellence of soils, elsewhere there was little relationship between density of production and soil quality. Consequently, the pattern of decreasing hop density with distance was attributed to the interaction of three economic processes:

1. *Agglomeration economies*, which declined in importance with increasing distance from Wateringbury. External economies of scale, rather than those internal to the farm, aided the pattern of concentration. For example, specialized financial facilities, provided by local country bankers, hop factors, and merchants, made access to capital easier in established locations. Similarly, expansion in the central area was encouraged by a skilled labour supply, special woodland management for locally produced hop poles, local trades in manure and fertilizer, and parish reputation.

2. *Cumulative change.* The development of hops in an area led to further expansion through a self-sustaining process of cumulative causation.

Harvey showed the importance of this in relation to rents and wages. Since hops were a high-return crop, rents in an area renowned for hop production would be increased, irrespective of whether or not a farmer grew hops. A similar process led to higher labour costs. These higher costs provided the necessary incentive to produce hops and so the process of cumulative change encouraged spatial concentration by eliminating alternative forms of land use with cost diseconomies.

3. *Diminishing returns*, which helped to explain the spatial limits, or margins, to hop production. Harvey interpreted the outward spread of hops from the core as the centrifugal effects of diminishing returns from an optimum area density. With improving economic conditions, diminishing returns would lead to the spread of hops into areas possessing no other inherent advantage except proximity to the core. This principle assumed there was some optimum economic level for hop density.

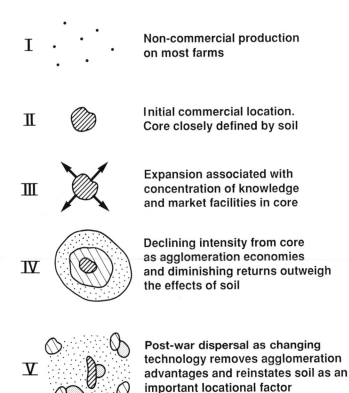

I — Non-commercial production on most farms

II — Initial commercial location. Core closely defined by soil

III — Expansion associated with concentration of knowledge and market facilities in core

IV — Declining intensity from core as agglomeration economies and diminishing returns outweigh the effects of soil

V — Post-war dispersal as changing technology removes agglomeration advantages and reinstates soil as an important locational factor

FIG 11.4 A five-stage model of location change in the hop industry (*source*: Ilbery, 1983*a*, p. 118)

Harvey differentiated, therefore, between the initial reasons for location, such as the physical factor of soil, and those which perpetuated the pattern of concentration, which were mainly economic. These ideas can be used to develop a five-stage model of locational change in hop production (Ilbery, 1983a). The first four stages closely follow Harvey's principles (Fig. 11.4). However, the fifth stage relates specifically to the pattern of post-war decline and suggests a more dispersed pattern, with soil again playing an important locational role as disease and changing technology remove many of the advantages of agglomeration. This point will be further developed in the next section.

Hop production in the United Kingdom has experienced a general process of decay since reaching a peak of 28 000 ha in 1886 (Scott, 1977). Kent has suffered most from the downward trend and its area of hops was reduced by 58 per cent between 1878 and 1915 alone (Pocock, 1957). In contrast, decline in Herefordshire and Worcestershire has been more gradual, due to the area's early adoption of high-quality hops, greater attention to the cultivation and drying of hops, and the ability to produce cheaper hops because of lower land values (Pocock, 1957).

Signs of real trouble in the hop industry appeared when brewers drastically cut production during the First World War. The ensuing problem of overproduction was intensified by the lack of a marketing organization for hops. It was for this reason that the English Hop Growers cooperative was formed in 1925, but this was soon abandoned in 1928 because non-members continued to expand production. Between 1929 and 1931, the price of hops fell below the costs of production, forcing many growers out of business. In 1932, the Hops Marketing Board (HMB) was formed and offered much-needed stability to the industry by controlling production through a quota system. Quotas (based on quantity and not area) were allocated to farms and not farmers, helping to fossilize the pattern of hop-farming in the two major production areas. The amount of quota was determined annually at a meeting between the HMB and the Brewers Society and it was by regulating supply and demand that prices were controlled (Ilbery, 1984a). However, the policies of the HMB inadvertently helped to perpetuate the decline of the British hop industry (see below).

Three trends have characterized post-war hop-farming in Britain:

1. A reduction in the total area under hops, from 9000 ha in 1950 to 4800 ha in 1985.
2. A substantial fall in the number of growers from 954 in 1950 to less than 350 in 1985, leading to a corresponding increase in the average size of hop unit, from 9.4 ha in 1950 to over 16 ha in 1985.
3. A significant change into new varieties of 'high alpha' hops, leading to a much higher yield of brewing value per ha. Encouraged by a HMB incentive scheme, considerable replanting took place between 1972 and 1976, at the end of which 60 per cent of the hop area was devoted to high alpha varieties.

According to Scott (1977 p. 174) 'the explanation for the decline in the English hop industry is that, prior to the United Kingdom entering the EC, it had become a protected and insular industry.' Although highlighting an important contributory factor, this is an oversimplification of a complex set of factors that perpetuated the process of decline. At least five groups of interrelated factors can be recognized (Ilbery, 1983b), which have been schematically portrayed in Figure 11.5. Uncertainty and world competition are central elements, which in turn have influenced the other major factors:

1. Institutional factors
Hop-farming in Britain has been largely controlled by institutional factors since the formation of the HMB in 1932 and these have, in no small way, contributed to its decline. The HMB was the first of various marketing boards created in the 1930s to both provide stability in those products in which the nation was mainly self-sufficient and to protect home production from foreign competition. All growers had to be registered with the statutory HMB and few complained because it assured them of a profit, protected them from competition, and removed uncertainty in the market place.

The HMB was soon part of the tradition of British hop-growing, but it became solely oriented to the demands of the home brewer; little attempt was made, over forty years, to explore the export potential of British hops or to examine the trends developing elsewhere in the world. Fur-

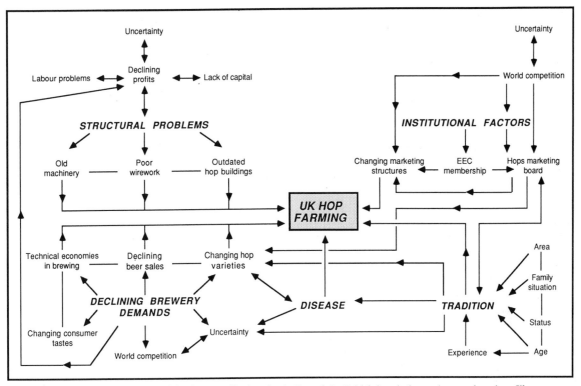

FIG 11.5 Schematic flow diagram of the factors affecting the decline of the British hop industry (*source:* based on Ilbery, 1983*b*, p. 122)

thermore, the rigid quota system aided the inefficient hop-grower and hampered the progressive ones and the whole industry appeared to be run for the benefit of the average grower. Hop-farming in Britain had become insular and protected from external competition by heavy duties and strict quotas. Unfortunately, internal factors did not remain constant and declining brewery demand (see below) caused the home market for hops to fall throughout the 1960s. This culminated in a quota redemption scheme, introduced by the HMB in 1968 in an attempt to redress the imbalance between supply and demand. With an incentive of £1000 for every acre (0.4 ha) of hops grubbed, over 400 ha went out of production. However, the aim of encouraging small-scale, traditional growers to grub up their hops failed, as many large growers accepted the golden handshake.

Britain's entry into the EC in 1973 led to the removal of import restrictions and, at a time of world overproduction, hop-growers were exposed to the full rigours of international competition, primarily from an EC partner, West Germany. The defects of the rigid producer-controlled statutes of the HMB were soon clear, as the EC introduced a ban on new hop-planting between 1977 and 1979 and a different system of hop marketing. Quota arrangements were replaced by a system of three-year forward contracts. Numerous pools were established, in a hierarchical structure according to quality and demand; the higher the pool the higher the price a farmer received for his hops. The system was quite complex and many traditional growers took this as a signal to abandon their association with hops. In addition, the EC considered the HMB to be a monopoly, which ran counter to the Treaty of Rome (Griffin, 1982). After prolonged resistance, the HMB succumbed to increasing pressure and became a producer group (the HMB Limited, until 1985, when it became English Hops Ltd.), with voluntary membership, in 1982. The full effects of this major change in status have not been examined, but it did provide brewers with an opportunity to 'seek out' progressive growers and discuss possible contract arrangements. This in turn could lead to further rationalization in the industry and a continued fall in the number of growers.

Once initiated, therefore, the pattern of decay became cumulative, with institutional factors playing a leading role. The HMB was responsible for the uncompetitive nature of British hops, which were expensive and unattractive in export markets. Indeed, the export potential remains low because the hops are of the seeded variety, whereas world trade is primarily in seedless hops.

2. Declining brewery demands

The relationship between brewer and grower is crucial to an understanding of trends in the British hop industry. Growers have been at the mercy of the brewers and forced to reduce output in accordance with declining demands, despite a continuous increase in beer consumption between 1950 and 1980. Figure 11.5 highlights the reasons for this. First, the brewers' increasing desire for the high-yielding alpha hops had a profound effect on the area devoted to the crop, as the same amount of alpha acid could be produced from fewer hectares. For example, the traditional aroma 'fuggle' hop has only 68.5 kilos of alpha acid per ha, compared with 144 kg/ha for modern 'northdown' or 'target' varieties (Neve, 1977). Secondly, changing consumer tastes, away from traditional bitter beer and towards the blander lager with its lower hop requirements, have led to fewer British hops being required. Lager's share of beer sales increased from 6 to over 30 per cent between 1969 and 1984, due to such factors as package holidays abroad, the (relatively) hot summers of 1975 and 1976, and the changing attitude towards women drinking. Most lagers made in Britain are under the licence of foreign brewers, who insist that imported seedless hops are used in the production process, even though lager can just as easily be made from seeded hops. The effect of this on the demand for British hops has been quite dramatic. Thirdly, economies and improved technology in the brewing industry have led to a steady, but continuous, decline in the amount of hops needed to brew beer. The advent of hop extracts, pellets, and powders has enabled brewers to preserve the bittering compounds more easily and the increased efficiency associated with such modern brewing equipment as whirlpool separators and conical fermenters has had a consequent effect upon hop demand.

Finally, the economic recession of the late 1970s and early 1980s caused beer sales to fall significantly for the first time and led to a further squeeze on hop production.

3. Structural problems

The once highly profitable hop enterprise has been deteriorating since the 1950s because of declining demand and price–cost squeeze, whereby the price of hop inputs (e.g. fertilizers, chemicals, and labour) has increased at a much greater rate than the increase in product prices. Reduced profits lead to uncertainty and a lack of capital for reinvestment, which in turn creates structural problems for the growers of the capital and labour-intensive hop crop. The major structural problems are worn-out hop-picking machines, poor wirework in the hop yards, and outdated oast-houses and hop kilns. Many growers continue to rely upon their first and only hop-picking machine, now over thirty years old and in need of replacement. However, it would cost in excess of £100 000 to completely modernize the hop enterprise, which most growers could not afford. Not surprisingly, therefore, very few new growers have entered the industry over the past thirty years; those that have are usually funded by industrial companies, who welcome the opportunity to diversify. Major injections of capital are urgently required to prevent further decline and a survey of growers that had grubbed up their hops altogether listed capital outlay as the joint main factor, with the uncertain future in the industry, affecting their final decision (Ilbery, 1982).

4. Area and family tradition

The decline in hop area has coincided with a breakdown in area and especially family tradition. Hop-farming in the United Kingdom is controlled by two types of grower: first, the older, traditional grower with his small, owner-occupied farm and hop unit; and secondly, the younger, innovative grower with his large, often tenanted, farm and expanding hop unit. The former still dominates the industry, although it is this group that is in decline. Many of these growers abandon hops because of uncertainty, age and/or poor health, and most importantly because they have son(s) who are not interested in an intensive enterprise that is inefficient and non-profitable. Indeed, the rate of decline would have been greater but for 'social inertia'; farmers are often reluctant to abandon a crop which has been in the family for generations. A number of traditional growers similarly resisted the change to high alpha hops and continued to produce unwanted varieties, for which they received lower prices. Eventually, they had little option but to grub up their hops.

Area tradition also now exerts less influence and many of the acquired advantages that accompanied regional agglomeration have been removed with improved communications and changing technology. In fact, area tradition and localized production can be an active disadvantage, as demonstrated with the ease in which disease spreads in a concentrated area of hop production, forcing many growers out of production.

5. Disease

British growers have been plagued by two hop diseases since the 1920s—downy mildew and verticillium wilt. The latter can be particularly devastating and was responsible for eliminating large areas of traditional hops in mid-Kent. Wilt has still to penetrate the West Midlands on such a scale, but the threat has often been sufficient to encourage growers to 'get out' before they are affected. Considerable progress has been made towards producing disease-resistant varieties of hops and scientists at Wye College have managed to combine wilt resistance with high alpha (e.g. 'target' variety), although they will have to be grown seedless if they are to have a major effect in Britain. The spread of wilt has also been reduced by the adoption of no-cultivation techniques (where the soil is undisturbed), so that less-contaminated soil is carried by cultivation machinery. This, in turn, has encouraged downy mildew, although the disease is more easily controlled than wilt by chemicals.

The British hop industry has declined steadily throughout the twentieth century due to a combination of factors external and internal to the farm. Institutional factors, in the form of the HMB and EC policy, have been particularly influential in the process of decline, but disease, structural problems, and the breakdown of area and family tradition have also played an important role. The industry is no longer competitive in international markets and major changes—like the move to seedless hops—are required. Yet, with a change in attitude Britain has a favourable farm structure (compared to West Germany for example) and the hop scientists and growers needed to make the necessary adjustments.

A regional case study: hop-farming in the West Midlands

The objective of this final section is to outline briefly some of the findings of a detailed research project on the changing relative importance of physical, economic, and socio-personal factors in the pattern of hop-farming in Herefordshire and Worcestershire (Ilbery, 1982; 1983a, c, and d; and 1984b). Hop-farming in the West Midlands has been characterized by the three main trends listed above. In the early part of the twentieth century, hops were grown widely in Herefordshire and Worcestershire, covering 132 parishes in 1913. The highest density of production was concentrated on the favourable soils of the Frome Valley, with an outlier of secondary production in the Teme Valley to the north (Fig. 11.6a). A core area could be identified, as found by Harvey (1963) in Kent, and was centred on the parishes of Castle Frome, Munsley, and Dormington. Hop production appeared to decline with distance from the core, gradually to the north-west and more abruptly to the south-east and south-west. A secondary and much smaller core occurred in the north-east, based on the parish of Lindridge.

From this pre-First World War situation, the number of hop-growing parishes had declined to just 69 by 1978 (Table 11.2); this process of decline has continued throughout the 1980s. The data in Table 11.2 are arranged to show the pattern of decline with distance from Castle Frome, which had established itself as the central core of production by the 1930s. Of the 33 hop-growing parishes within 10 km of Castle Frome in 1913, only 12 per cent had gone out of production by 1978; this is in complete contrast to the 60 and 87 per cent reductions in hop-growing parishes between 10 and 20 km and over 30 km away from Castle Frome respectively. It would appear, therefore, that a pattern of increasing concentration has occurred as the industry has declined, with distance an important variable helping to shape the pattern of spatial variation around Castle Frome. In examining the effect of distance further by means of regression analysis (which measures statistically the effect of one

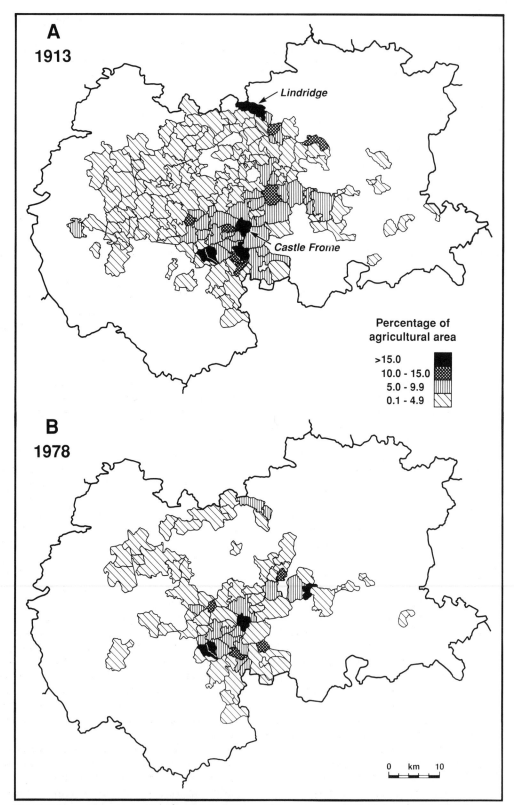

FIG 11.6 The spatial retreat of hops in Herefordshire and Worcestershire, 1913–78 (*source:* Modified from Ilbery, 1983*a* p. 115–16)

TABLE 11.2 The changing location of hop-growing parishes with distance from Castle Frome, 1913–1978

	1913	1930	1950	1960	1969	1978	decline 1913–78 (%)
< 10 km	33	32	32	30	30	29	12.1
10–19	57	41	36	34	29	23	59.6
20–30	34	29	28	26	21	16	52.9
> 30	8	2	4	4	1	1	87.5
TOTAL	132	104	100	94	81	69	47.7

Source: Ilbery (1983*a* p. 115).

(independent) variable on another (dependent) variable), two points emerged: first, a significant inverse relationship existed between hop density and distance from Castle Frome for each of three separate dates; and secondly, distance became more important in the pattern of concentration between 1930 and 1978. In 1930, the variation in distance accounted for 20.6 per cent of the variation in hop density; by 1978 this had increased to 32.8 per cent. However, over two-thirds of the variance in hop density remained unexplained and the mapping of the regression residuals suggested that parishes with more hops than expected coincided with favourable physical conditions (especially soils), just as those with less hops than expected were located in areas of poor land quality.

Consequently, the relationship between physical factors and the distribution of hops was investigated for both the 280 farms with hops in 1960 and the 164 in 1980, together with the 116 that had grubbed the crop between the two years. In each case, the observed distribution of hop farms was compared with an expected distribution, calculated according to the percentage of area devoted to different types of geology, soils, and land-use capability (Table 11.3). The differences were all statistically significant (using the chi-square test), illustrating the important role played by environmental factors in the distribution of hops in the West Midlands. However, not all of the grubbed hop farms, for example, were located in areas of inferior conditions; indeed, more than expected were found on land with only minor limitations and highly suitable argillic brown earth soils (Table 11.3). One can hypothesize from this, therefore, that factors other than those of a physical nature have also played a part

in the pattern of locational change. In fact, a survey of 40 of the 116 grubbed hop farms indicated that declining soil fertility and distance from the core of hop production were not important factors affecting the decision to abandon the crop. For 25 per cent, the fundamental reason was the HMB's quota redemption scheme; among the remainder, economic factors were dominant, especially the lack of capital and the cost and availability of labour. Disease, the need to change hop varieties, and the degree of risk and uncertainty in hop-farming were other important considerations.

Technological change in the hop industry, together with the decline in brewery demands and the policies of the HMB (where all growers received information on new techniques and varieties and were charged a standard cost for transporting dried hops to the nearest warehouse) have rendered Harvey's economic principles for an expanding hop industry less relevant to one that is in decline. Many agglomeration advantages have been removed. For example, most inputs (chemicals, sprays, wire-work, and fertilizers) are supplied by general agricultural distributors that are not concentrated in or near the core of production. Similarly, hop-picking machines have reduced the demand for local skilled labour and allowed casual student labour to increase. With improvements in transportation, the increased mobility of factors of production, and a decline in the importance of agglomeration economies and cumulative change, hop production would appear to be coming more locally specialized in those parts of Herefordshire and Worcestershire that are better physically endowed. A recurrence of factors over time can be seen: soil played an important initial role in determining the core

TABLE 11.3 The relationship between hops and environmental factors

	Number of hop-farms						Decline 1960–80 (%)
	1960 (280)		1980 (164)		Grubbed (116)		
	Obs.	(Exp.)	Obs.	(Exp.)	Obs.	(Exp.)	
Geology	$X^2 = 121.5$		$X^2 = 113.7$		$X^2 = 29.9$		
Middle ORS[a]	39	61.6	23	36.1	16	25.2	41.0
Lower ORS	171	88.5	114	51.8	57	36.7	33.3
Keuper Marl	36	56.0	18	32.8	18	23.3	50.0
Lias Clay	3	32.3	2	18.9	1	13.3	33.3
Others[b]	31	41.7	7	24.4	24	17.3	77.4
Soils	$X^2 = 91.7$		$X^2 = 60.6$		$X^2 = 33.1$		
Argillic Brown Earths	224	156.3	135	91.5	89	64.7	39.7
Brown Earths	17	78.4	10	45.9	7	32.5	41.4
Stagnogley	6	17.6	1	9.8	5	7.2	83.3
Brown Alluvial Soils	8	12.1	4	7.1	4	5.1	50.0
Alluvial Gleys	25	15.8	14	9.2	11	6.5	44.0
Land-use capability[c] Land with:	$X^2 = 55.6$		$X^2 = 56.5$		$X^2 = 14.1$		
Very severe limitations	0	1.4	0	0.8	0	0.6	—
Moderately severe limitations	48	36.1	22	21.2	26	15.0	54.2
Moderate limitations	64	125.7	33	73.6	31	48.4	48.4
Minor limitations	168	116.8	109	68.4	59	52.0	35.1

Note: All X^2 values significant at 0.01 level.

[a] Old Red Sandstone.

[b] Silurian, Keuper Sandstone, and Bunter Sandstone.

[c] Categories 1 and 2 amalgamated for X^2 calculations.

Source: Ilbery (1983a p. 121).

area; economic factors then helped to explain the pattern of expansion away from the core; and finally environmental factors have reinforced their dominance as the hop area has contracted. The importance of natural and acquired advantages has, therefore, varied through time with changing technological and economic conditions.

Although physical factors, and especially soils, are once again of increasing importance, they do not determine spatial patterns of hop production and a full understanding can be obtained only by examining the relative importance of physical, economic, and socio-personal factors in the decision behaviour of hop farmers. This necessitates a behavioural approach to explaining patterns of change, where emphasis is placed on the satisfic-

ing behaviour and the motives of farmers (see Chapter 10.2). A questionnaire survey of 127 hop-farmers isolated those factors which were perceived to be important in hop-growing. The results are presented in Table 11.4 and clearly demonstrate the importance of economic and not physical factors, with four of the first six ranked factors being economic in nature. Specialized buildings and machinery and a stable market demand were thought to be the most important and many farmers stated that it would be impossible to begin a hop enterprise without having the necessary facilities already provided on the farm. Many growers thought they would grub up their hops once the buildings and/or machinery became inadequate and needed replacing. The

TABLE 11.4 Perceived rank order of decision-making factors in hop farming

Rank	Factor	Score	%A	%T	%I
1.	Buildings/machinery	440	100	86.6	86.6
2.	Stable market/demand	423	100	83.3	83.3
3.	Drainage	416	100	81.9	81.9
4.	Soil type	396	100	80.0	80.0
5.	Labour supply	387	100	76.2	76.2
6.	Capital availability	386	100	76.0	76.0
7.	Experience	362	99.2	71.3	71.8
8.	Regular income	356	100	70.1	70.1
9.	Verticillium wilt	341	98.4	67.1	68.2
10.	Shelter	337	99.2	66.3	66.9
11.	Personal preference	330	99.2	65.0	65.5
12.	25–35″ rainfall	287	100	56.5	56.5
13.	Height of water table	286	98.4	56.3	57.2
14.	Vol./supply of water	285	96.9	56.1	57.9
15.	Temperature	284	99.2	55.9	56.3
16.	Area tradition	247	94.5	48.6	51.3
17.	Level land	190	96.9	37.4	38.6
18.	Family tradition	182	82.7	35.8	43.3
19.	Frequency of frosts	172	96.9	33.9	34.7
20.	Agricultural training	172	90.6	33.9	37.4
21.	Size of farm	53	32.3	10.4	32.3
22.	Free time	45	25.2	8.9	35.2
23.	Low levels of risk	31	15.0	6.1	40.8
24.	Distance from HMB	20	13.4	3.9	29.4

%A: The number of cases where the factor applied, as a % of the total number of cases.
%T: The total score, as a % of the maximum possible score for all cases investigated.
%I: The total score, as a % of the maximum possible score for all those cases where the factor was applicable.
Source: Ilbery (1983c p. 451).

role of the HMB has already been discussed, but most growers emphasized the need for a stable demand and were in favour of the Board (although the survey was undertaken before it became a producer group with voluntary membership). This reflects two factors: first, many growers could remember or were told by their fathers of the 'free-for-all' days before the HMB was formed; and secondly, the instability and uncertainty of the 1970s, caused by EC membership, the need to change hop varieties and world overproduction, led to a desire for more stable conditions. The previously discussed importance of labour and capital, and soils and drainage, is also confirmed in Table 11.4.

Experience (7th) and personal preference (11th) were the most important socio-personal factors, being ranked more highly than either agricultural training (20th) or area (16th) and family tradition (18th). The poor ranking of the latter was initially puzzling and, with over 60 per cent of the farmers having fathers who grew hops, needs to be treated with a degree of circumspection. This appears to be a case of farmers not admitting to its importance or simply taking it for granted. An examination of the farmers' motives, by means of their goals and values (see Chapter 10.2 and Table 10.1) helped to account for the apparent anomaly. Intrinsic values (doing the work you like, being independent, and leading a healthy outdoor life) were emphasized above expressive (e.g. meeting a challenge, pride of ownership), instrumental (e.g. making maximum income, expanding the business), and especially social values (e.g. continuing the family tradition, belonging to the farming community). Factors of a personal and intrinsic nature do, therefore, affect the decision behaviour of the West Midlands' hop-growers. The placing of 'low levels of risk' near the bottom of the list of decision-making factors helps to confirm this, implying that hops are a high risk crop.

The adopted behavioural approach (see

Chapter 2.2 and 10.1) helps to demonstrate that spatial and temporal trends in hop-farming are related to two concepts: *opportunity cost* and *social inertia*. The former can be defined as the value of alternatives which have to be foregone in order to achieve a particular thing. It is necessary, therefore, to consider the alternative options available to a farmer before understanding why he/she continues to grow hops. These alternatives will vary between farmers, according to such factors as farm size and status. Despite small profit margins, hops are grown on some farms because they are an integral part of the adopted farm system and can, for example, help to make use of casual labour at different times of the year. Alternatively, hops are the main source of income on many small farms and cannot easily be replaced by other intensive crops, which would be either less profitable or unsuited to the existing physical conditions. Hops may be grown, therefore, not because they are ideally suited to the soils but because no other crop will provide the same returns.

Although hops may now be an inefficient enterprise on many of the smaller, owner-occupied farms, growers are often reluctant to abandon the crop because of a long family tradition, or social inertia. Many growers fear that, with the high level of capital investment involved, there would be no way of getting back into the industry once they had grubbed up their hop yard. The decision to grub is a definite and final one, causing many growers to carry on a little longer. Social inertia relates to such personal factors as tradition, inheritance, enjoyment, satisfaction and a fascination with hops, and without such commitment the decline of hop-growing in Herefordshire and Worcestershire would have been far more rapid than that actually experienced.

An attempt has been made in the second half of this chapter to demonstrate that, in the case of hop-farming (as in many other forms of economic activity), it is the interplay of physical, political, economic, and socio–personal factors that influences patterns of production. Structural factors (e.g. level of demand, interest rates), which constrain the decisions of hop-growers, are also significant even though they have not been considered in this section. Factors affecting locational change in the hop industry actually change in importance over time and as the scale of analysis is reduced from international to regional and

local levels. The 'decision environment' is a complex one and a proper explanation of the distribution of hops cannot be sought merely with regard to one factor. In the final analysis, the decision to abandon or continue with hop-farming is a personal one, influenced by a farmer's values, motives and perceptions.

11.3 Summary

Although employing a relatively small and declining proportion of the working population, primary industries remain important and include some major extensive users of space. These have experienced considerable change over space and time as the factors affecting their distribution have also changed. In particular, this chapter has emphasized that

- The relative importance of factors affecting the location and the changing distribution of primary activities varies as the scale of analysis changes from the local to the global. As the scale increases, factors external to the individual farm, mine or forest become more significant.

- The situation is further complicated inasmuch as the influencing factors also vary in importance over time.

- Deforestation and afforestation have dominated global trends in forestry, although the former has occurred on a much larger scale than the latter. Patterns of timber production have changed over time in response to such factors as land-use competition, technological developments, declining transport costs, vertical integration, and government policies. However, a spatial mismatch between the major suppliers and users of timber has led to the development of an international system of trade, controlled by bilateral government agreements.

- In Canada, the forest product sector has developed in distinct phases according to changing patterns of foreign investment and increased levels of state involvement. The latter has also varied in importance over time in the afforestation of the more marginal upland areas of the United Kingdom.

- Although the world's hop area continued to increase until the early 1980s, the relative importance of producing countries changed considerably, with major growth in West Germany and the USSR, stagnation in the USA, and decline in the United Kingdom.

- Technological change, declining brewery demands and policies of the HMB combined to reduce the significance of agglomeration economies and cumulative change in regional patterns of hop production in the United Kingdom. However, at the local level, factors of a more social and intrinsic nature are important in the decision-making behaviour of hop growers.

Clearly, a wide range of factors needs to be considered when examining economic location and change in primary industries, a statement that equally applies to manufacturing and service industries.

12

Manufacturing Industries

The aim of this chapter is to apply the concepts and factors discussed in Parts I and II of this book to help to understand recent changes in the location of manufacturing industries. Two contrasting case studies—the clothing and motor vehicle industries—are examined. The analysis shows that the relative importance of location factors varies both between and within the two industries according to the scale of analysis and the time period being examined. An eclectic approach to analysing recent locational trends in the two industries is adopted, emphasizing, for example, not only cost factors, but also the international and national economic context and the strategies of different groups of firms. Various ideas from the neoclassical, structuralist, and behavioural approaches are used where they help to understand the locational trends being examined. The chapter focuses upon recent changes in the international and intranational location of the two industries.

12.1 International trends in the clothing industry

The clothing industry is very widespread geographically. The largest concentrations of employment are in the USSR, USA, and Japan. However, Western Europe remains very important, with major clothing industries in the United Kingdom, West Germany, France, and Italy. Apart from the USSR, Poland and Czechoslovakia are the largest producers of clothing in the centrally planned economies of Eastern Europe. Hong Kong, South Korea, and the Phillipines are the largest centres in the developing economies (Fig. 12.1). However, the pattern was very different thirty to forty years ago. In 1953, less than 10 per cent of clothing production and one-third of employment was found in developing countries. By 1980 this had increased, so that a quarter of production and over 60 per cent of employment were found in these parts of the world (Table 12.1). During the 1970s some of the largest losses of clothing employment were recorded by West Germany and the United Kingdom, while rapid increases occurred in Hong Kong and South Korea. Malta, Cyprus, the Phillipines, and Greece also experienced large increases in employment (Dicken, 1986).

These trends in the location of production have been paralleled by changes in trade patterns. The rise in exports from developing area countries is matched by a rise in imports into developed countries. Shepherd (1981, p. 138) suggests that 'international sub-contracting in clothing has probably been the single most important external stimulant to developing country exports'. He goes on to make a useful distinction between 'overspill' exporters, such as India and Mexico, exporting on the basis of processed domestic raw materials or a large domestic market, and 'export oriented' countries, for example, in East Asia and Southern Europe, which export as part of a deliberate strategy to exploit their comparative advantages to meet world demand. A further interesting group is the 'dependent' exporters which have developed clothing export industries largely as a result of the initiatives taken by manufacturers and importers in nearby industrialized countries. Malta and Morocco, for instance, are very dependent on exporting to the European Community, while many Caribbean countries rely on the United States market. Nevertheless, despite the growth of exporting by newly industrializing countries (Chapter 14.3), it is worth emphasizing that the bulk of the world's clothing trade still occurs between the industrialized countries (Dicken, 1986).

A combination of factors helps to account for

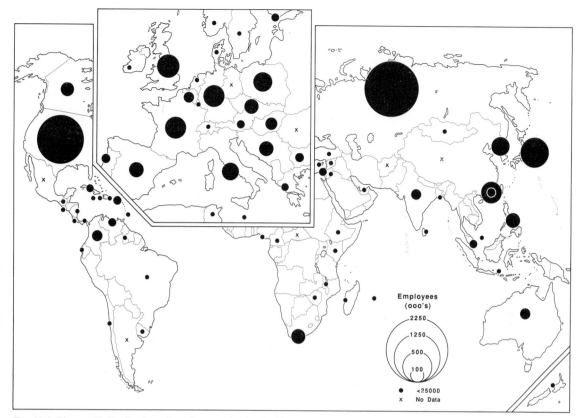

FIG 12.1 The world distribution of employment in the clothing industry, 1981 (*source:* Dicken, 1986 p. 231)

TABLE 12.1 The share of employment and production in clothing in developed and developing countries, 1953 and 1980

	Employment		Production	
	1953	1980	1953	1980
Developed countries	67	39	92	75
North America	23	14	59	33
Japan	2	6	1	8
Western Europe	40	16	29	30
EC (9)	35	15	25	26
Developing countries	33	61	8	25
Southern Europe	6	8	2	8
Asia	19	40	3	8
Latin America	7	8	3	7
Africa	1	—	—	—
ALL MARKET ECONOMIES	100	100	100	100

Source: Silbertson (1984 p. 8).

these international trends. They can be classified into three main groups: technological changes and production costs, the pattern of demand and the organizational context, and government policies.

Technological changes and production costs

The making of clothes consists of a series of manual operations. Although some firms, primarily in developed countries, have introduced some automation into the production process this has been mainly at the design, pattern-making, and cutting stages. The assembly stage, however, which accounts for about 80 per cent of labour costs, is still dependent on the sewing machine, which has not changed dramatically in design during the last fifty years. The making of clothes, therefore, remains a very labour-intensive industry, particularly in developing countries.

Technological change is important in two ways. First, improvements in transport and communications have made it feasible to shift some production to developing countries. Secondly, the relatively low level of technical sophistication and change in the production process has meant that not only is production easy to establish, but countries well endowed with supplies of low-cost labour can develop an advantage in the production of several clothing items. Over the last three decades developing countries have competed most successfully in the type of clothing products which are standard items, such as men's shirts, and/or the low- to medium-quality products which have reached the mature or mass-production stage of the product cycle. A recent report concluded that 'major technological developments that would make the industry in high wage countries cost competitive with supplies from low wage countries, are not at present available' (OECD, 1988, p. 143). Innovations which allow for the automatic handling of limp materials will be required to change this cost difference.

Labour costs are the most important element in production costs, accounting for about 60 per cent of the costs of production. Marked spatial variations in wage costs and a more intensive use of equipment have given developing countries a *comparative advantage* over the developed world when competitiveness is measured solely in terms of price (Steed, 1981). For example, if an hourly wage it taken to be 100 in France, it is 73 in

Britain, 19 in Hong Kong, 9 in South Korea, and 2 in India and Sri Lanka (Conseil Économique et Social 1982, cited by Morokvasic *et al.*, 1986). Given these kind of differentials, it is perhaps surprising that not more of the clothing industry has shifted to developing countries. The fact that this has not occurred may in part be accounted for by the pattern of demand and the organizational context of the industry.

Pattern of demand and organizational context

The spatial pattern of demand for clothing is markedly uneven. It is in part related to the pattern of incomes. Hence the main demand comes from the developed market economies. However, as incomes increase the *proportion* spent on clothing declines. To attempt to counter this tendency and the effects of recent sluggish demand, retailers and manufacturers in developed countries have increasingly encouraged fashion changes. This kind of product differentiation, which demands close contact between the manufacturer and the retailer in the fashion segment of the market, is a major reason for the survival of the clothing industry in Western Europe.

The concentration of clothing sales among a few large retailers means that they are the dominant partners in the relationship with manufacturers. In the United Kingdom, for example, it is estimated that 40 per cent of total sales in the British clothing market is accounted for by the ten largest clothing retailers, including Marks & Spencer, British Home Stores, Littlewoods, C & A Modes, Debenhams, and Burton (Allen and Brown, 1984). Some large retailers, such as Marks & Spencer, encourage their suppliers to invest in new technology. Others, such as Benetton, act as both retailers and manufacturers. However, although Benetton has strong central control of marketing (see Chapter 5.2), only a limited number of employees are directly engaged in production and much is subcontracted to small firms (Gibbs, 1986*b*).

Some retailers encourage the use of domestic manufacturers. A notable example is the policy of Marks & Spencer to 'buy British' (Allen and Brown, 1984). Other retailers obtain their supplies direct from Third World countries. Still others place orders with domestic agents and manufacturers who subcontract some of their orders to suppliers in developing countries. A few large manufacturers have production plants overseas. For example, among American companies making jeans, Levi-Strauss has 31 overseas plants and Blue Bell (Wrangler) has 27 plants (Clairmonte and Cavanagh, 1981).

Corporate strategies are particularly apparent in the operation of international subcontracting and licensing arrangements between firms. These are the main ways in which production from developing countries finds its way into the markets of developed countries. Overseas sourcing is more important in some countries, such as West Germany and the United States, than it is in others, such as the United Kingdom and France, where more reliance has been put on using the domestic subcontracting system, especially among ethnic businesses (Morokvasic *et al.*, 1986). Plant (1981) claims that in West Germany 56 per cent of textile and clothing manufacturers were using overseas production facilities in 1974, while 38 per cent of all clothing production in the Netherlands had undergone some processing abroad. Often only the assembly stage takes place overseas, with design and cutting remaining in the developed country. Reference has already been made to some of the strong geographical biases in the pattern of international subcontracting. In West Germany, for example, over 80 per cent of clothing imports manufactured under subcontracting arrangements in the 1970s came from Bulgaria, East Germany, Hungary, Poland, Romania, and Yugoslavia (Frobel *et al.*, 1980).

Despite the rapid increase in international sourcing in the last two decades, imports are not the main cause of the fall in clothing employment in developed economies. Productivity increases are far more significant. For example, in the United Kingdom it has been estimated that the employment effects of productivity increases are approximately 2.5 times the effects of imports (Cable, 1983). However, caution is needed in interpreting estimates of this kind because these two factors are not independent. Rises in imports, particularly from low-cost producers, encourage increases in productivity. An important influence on the nature and pattern of clothing imports lies in the varying policies of governments.

Government policies

One way in which governments have had a major impact on the international pattern of clothing production is through their trade policies. The textile and clothing industries are unique in the extent to which international trade is regulated through the Multi-Fibre Arrangement (MFA) (Chapter 14.4). The first MFA came into effect in 1974, replacing earlier long-term agreements between particular countries; MFA IV was negotiated in 1986. The aim of the MFAs is to provide an 'orderly' development of trade in textiles and clothing. The main mechanism used to achieve this is to slow down the rate of growth of developing country exports by establishing quotas. This has occurred to an extent, though the operation of the MFAs has also had unintended consequences, such as an increase in trade among developed countries (Dicken, 1986), and 'quota hopping' by producers. The latter occurs when producers based in countries which have reached their quotas set up clothing factories in states which have a more liberal access to developed country markets. Hong Kong is the leading 'quota hopping' nation and is responsible for much of the export-oriented investments in Sri Lanka and Mauritius, two of the newest suppliers (Shepherd, 1981).

Nevertheless, while the MFAs have given some degree of protection to clothing industries in developed countries, the trade policies of some of the industrialised countries, notably the United States, the Netherlands, and West Germany in the 1970s, also encouraged the international subcontracting of clothing production. This is because many of the tariffs they applied required duty to be paid only on the value added content of an import, which tends to be small because of the low wages paid in the countries to which production is subcontracted. In West Germany, for instance, Shepherd (1981, p. 143) notes that:

Foreign investment and outward processing have been supported by the government in the form of special outward-processing arrangements, additional to normal clothing quotas, a concession available only to clothing manufacturers; thus manufacturers have been able to cross-subsidize domestic production, including exports, from imports. ... The Federal Republic of Germany has also administered the growth of its quotas to favour its Eastern and Southern European economic hinterland (importers of German fibres and textiles), at the expense of the East Asian NICs (importers of Japanese and American fibres and textiles). The relatively liberal growth of imports from developed countries appears, however, to be coming to an end: recession and employment decline have prompted strong pressure for protectionism and the government have acquiesced, in spite of its publicly announced distaste for them, in the EEC's new restrictive MFA quotas.

A second way in which governments have influenced the location of the industry is by giving subsidies and incentives to clothing firms. For example, it has been estimated that Italy and the Netherlands in the mid-1970s gave subsidies totalling over $300 per head to the clothing industry, while in Britain the figure was $200 (Farrands, 1982). These subsidies were to aid restructuring of the industry and encourage investment. Some developing countries have also given incentives for clothing firms to establish production facilities in their countries.

Although the main recent trend in the global distribution of the clothing industry has been for a relative shift to developing countries there are indications that the international division of labour established over the last thirty years may be changing. The price competition of the 1970s is shifting to competition based on high-quality production serving particular sectors of the market. The development of the 'Next Phenomenon' of specialized outlets requires greater control over production. This trend, together with the operation of the MFA, is encouraging an increase in sourcing closer to the point of sale, either from domestic suppliers or nearby countries. The 1990s are likely to see a growth of clothing production in, for example, low-cost Southern European countries, particularly Spain and Portugal with their accession to the EC.

At the same time that international shifts in the location of clothing production have been occurring there have also been significant changes taking place in the spatial pattern of the industry within the industrialized countries. This may be illustrated by examining a case study of recent changes in the geography of the British clothing industry.

12.2 Recent changes in the location of the clothing industry in Great Britain

Two main trends are discernible in the changing location of the British clothing industry over the last thirty years, combining decentralization with dispersion. First, there has been an urban–rural shift in the location of the clothing industry. In 1959, 51 per cent of employment in clothing was in London, West Yorkshire, and Manchester. By 1971 this had fallen to 39 per cent (Keeble, 1976). The main growth areas during this period were in peripheral and rural areas, principally in Wales, Scotland, the North, the South-West, and parts of East Anglia (Fig. 12.2a). This trend continued to an extent in the following decade with the largest falls in employment between 1971 and 1981 occurring in Greater London, West Yorkshire, and Greater Manchester and the largest gains occurring in Buckinghamshire, the Central Region of Scotland, and Powys in Wales (Fig. 12.2b).

A second and slightly contradictory trend, which has become apparent since the mid-1970s, is the development of the clothing industry in cities in the Midlands (Fig. 12.2c). Some, such as the Birmingham/Black Country conurbation and Coventry, were not previously associated with the industry (Leigh and North, 1983; Healey et al., 1987; see also Chapter 16.3), while others, such as Nottingham and Leicester, were more associated with hosiery and knitwear than with clothing. Often the clothing industry is the only manufacturing industry in these cities to show growth in employment. The change largely reflects the growth of businesses within the immigrant community. For example, the West Midlands region experienced a 32 per cent growth in employment in clothing between 1981 and 1984, higher than for any other region, and this during a period when the industry lost 8 per cent of its employment nationally. This new industry is dominated by Asian-owned clothing firms located in the inner-city areas of Birmingham and Coventry. Ethnic minority clothing businesses have also become relatively more significant in the traditional clothing centres, particularly London. In 1984, the only counties to have more than 7000 employees in the clothing industry were Greater London, Greater Manchester, West Yorkshire, Strathclyde, Nottinghamshire, Leicestershire, Derbyshire, and the West Midlands (Fig. 12.2d). Together they accounted for 52 per cent of clothing employment in Great Britain. However, whereas the first four counties experienced the highest employment *losses* in the clothing industry between 1981 and 1984, the last four experienced the highest *gains* (Fig. 12.2c).

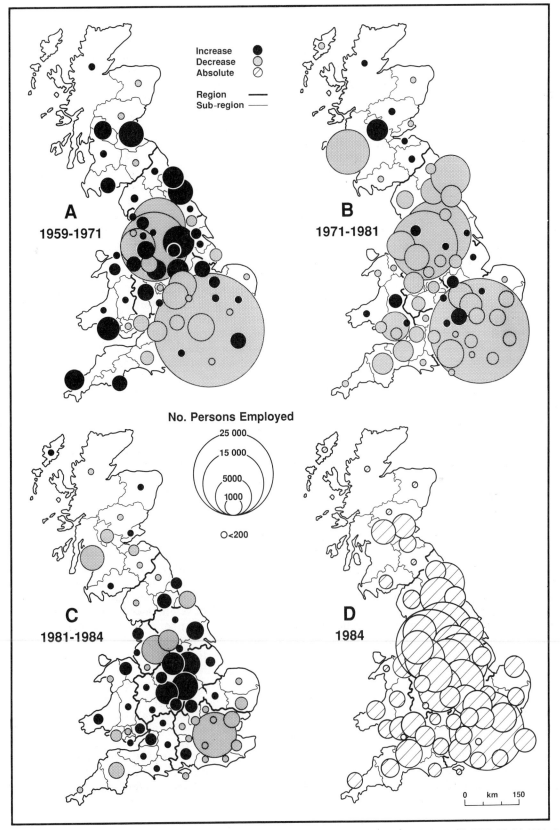

FIG 12.2 Sub-regional employment change in clothing manufacturing in Great Britain: (*a*) 1959–71; (*b*) 1971–81; (*c*) 1981–4; (*d*) 1984 (*source:* (*a*) Keeble, 1976 p. 175; (*b*), (*c*), and (*d*) based on unpublished Department of Employment statistics)

Various approaches to understanding the shifts in the location of the British clothing industry may be used. Here a mainly structuralist one is examined. Some features of this approach are discussed in Chapters 2.2 and 10.1. According to the structuralist approach, to understand the recent shifts in the location of the British clothing industry it is necessary to examine recent changes in both the economic conditions, which affect the requirements of production of the industry, and its geographical environment (Fig. 2.4).

Changes in economic conditions and production requirements

The main changes in the economic conditions affecting the British clothing industry over the last thirty years have been an increase in imports and a decline in growth of the home market, although these trends have slowed down recently with the shift by some retailers to 'buy British'. These changes have led to pressures to decrease costs to remain competitive. Two of the main ways of reducing costs are to increase labour productivity through *technical change* and to search for *cheap labour* or methods of reducing the cost of labour (Massey, 1981). The extent to which these different strategies have been adopted varies between sectors and different firms within the industry. The two strategies are not however independent because technical change can alter the nature of the labour requirements.

One of the problems for the clothing industry is that, as was noted in the last section, the opportunities to mechanize are restricted. Until recently only where the production processes are relatively simple and standardization and mass production have been possible, such as with the manufacture of shirts and jeans, has much mechanization occurred. Such technical changes reduce the levels of skill needed in the workforce and hence enable firms to seek sources of lower-cost labour. More recently, however, the increased flexibility made possible by the introduction of micro-processor technology has also allowed firms in sectors where there are rapid fashion changes to benefit from technical changes. For example, a recent survey found that the new technology has allowed one large firm making women's outerwear to produce up to 200 new sample designs a week for its customers to choose from, any one of which can go into full production within two weeks of

an order being placed (Phizaclea, 1986). Computer-aided design is ideally suited to firms where a large number of short runs predominate. The introduction of micro-electronic innovations is continuing the trend towards the subdivision of tasks and the deskilling of labour. In some companies this has a marked spatial dimension. For instance, one company, S. R. Gent, has centralized its cutting and distribution functions in Barnsley, has a computer-aided design studio in London, and eighteen 'satellite' sewing factories in Yorkshire (Zeitlin, 1985, cited by D. Gibbs, 1987).

The opportunities to introduce technical changes also vary by size of firm, because generally only the larger firms can afford the investment involved. Smaller companies are limited to introducing various small gadgets such as automatic needle-threaders which speed up the work process. Massey and Meegan (1983) refer to this as *intensification* as against *technical change and investment*, in which the larger firms may be involved. For most firms, however, the main strategy for remaining competitive is to keep labour costs down. This has encouraged an increase in the employment of married women and members of the ethnic communities. It has also led to a greater use of homeworkers and an increase in subcontracting to small firms with lower overheads. Such groups have relatively little bargaining power and have thus enabled the main employers to hold down wages and overall costs.

A consequence of the varying abilities of different sized firms to introduce new technology and to hold down labour costs has been that middle-sized firms have increasingly been squeezed out, leaving a dual economy based on a few large multi-plant clothing companies supplying the major retailers and mail-order companies and a large number of small businesses acting as subcontractors to the larger companies or supplying more downmarket sectors such as market traders. This polarization in the size structure of clothing companies also has a spatial dimension. For example, in the North-West of England large manufacturers have increasingly relocated out of the centre of the Manchester conurbation into the surrounding fringes of Cheshire and Lancashire, while the small manufacturers remain in the poor condition of the inner city (Gibbs, 1988).

A further element in the economic environment

affecting clothing companies has been the changing pattern of demand from the large retailers which dominate the British clothing market. Major retailers in search of growth have increasingly emphasized market segmentation, greater design, and better quality garments. They have also introduced four to six seasons a year resulting in manufacturers facing shorter but more frequent production runs. Such changes in the strategies of retailers have encouraged the 'return' of clothing production to Britain as the need to supervise and co-ordinate design and manufacture locally has strengthened. However, there are indications that some of the benefits are going to manufacturers in other member countries of the European Community who are increasingly being considered as domestic suppliers by British retailers (D. Gibbs, 1987; 1988).

Changes in the geographical environment

At the same time that clothing firms have been seeking to reduce costs and meet the new demands of retailers, there have also been changes in the locational opportunities available to the industry. These reflect long-term changes in the geography of female employment (Massey 1981, 1984b). The increase in the employment of women in the economy in general has reduced the availability of female labour for the clothing industry in the traditional centres. This was brought about by the growth of alternative sources of employment, particularly secretarial and clerical jobs, the relative decline of female wage rates in the clothing industries since the mid-1960s compared with the national average wages for women in manufacturing, and the 'sweatshop' image of the clothing sector. Together these factors made employment in the clothing sector appear relatively unattractive in the major centres of the industry, especially in London.

Simultaneously, however, the increased desire of women to enter the labour market brought about a potential reserve of female labour in the more rural and peripheral areas where there were relatively few jobs available for women. A good example is the coalfield areas where female activity rates were low in the 1960s. The collapse of male employment in these areas made it both more possible and more necessary for women to go out to work (see also Chapter 9.2). A further factor reducing costs in many of the peripheral areas from the mid-1960s was the availability of grants and subsidies resulting from the operation of government regional policy.

Just as large and small firms responded differently to the changes in economic conditions, so the reaction to changes in the geographical environment also varied with the size of company. Most small firms lacked the resources to move and many were tied to the fashion market in London. Faced with increased competition for labour, they had to make adjustments at their existing locations to cut costs in the ways outlined above. Many, however, did not survive. Large firms, on the other hand, had greater resources and geographical flexibility. A few of the largest firms shifted production to Third World countries and hence contributed to the problem of increased imports. More common were moves to small towns and the Assisted Areas within Britain, where lower cost, non-unionized, female labour was available and often a virtual monopoly over the labour force could be established by a single firm. For example, one manufacturer of men's clothing had a strategy of opening branch plants in the late 1960s in small towns in the 10 000–18 000 population range in Assisted Areas within a day's return journey of their main factory in Leeds. They believed that the labour force tended to be less militant in small towns and the company could become part of the community. In each case, the company chose a town which was not highly industrialized and where there was no large employer of female labour (Healey, 1979).

The different strategies followed by many large firms to overcome shortages of female and male labour provides an interesting example of the gender division of labour. Shortages of machinists (predominantly female) were reduced by a geographical shift, while shortages of pattern-makers and cutters (predominantly male) were reduced by automation.

Locational responses

These changes in the requirements of production and the geographical environment led in the 1960s and early 1970s, as indicated earlier, to a large decline in clothing employment in the traditional conurbations, and a net increase in jobs in several rural and peripheral areas, though the gain was mainly in lower paid and lesser skilled jobs. Since then a new trend has become discernible with the growth of the clothing industry in some non-traditional cities and conurbations. This development reflects the growth of indigenous ethnic businesses in immigrant communities established in the 1950s and 1960s. Several of the new businesses are dependent on the subcontracting of work from firms in the traditional centres. Subcontracting to lower-cost firms is another strategy used by the established firms to overcome labour shortages and reduce costs. Some of the new firms, however, are involved in the complete manufacturing process and compete directly with firms in the main clothing centres.

The growth of minority clothing businesses reflects the desire from members of the ethnic community to establish businesses, the ease of setting up firms in the clothing sector, and the competitive advantage enjoyed by ethnic minority businesses. There is evidence of the existence of an enterprise culture among some immigrant groups, particularly among these organized on patriarchal lines such as most of those from the Indian subcontinent, which encourages male members of the society to establish their own businesses (Ward and Jenkins, 1984). The difficulties faced by minority groups in obtaining satisfying and rewarding jobs within the host community is another spur to self-employment. The rag trade is a relatively easy sector in which to establish businesses. The capital needed to buy a few second-hand sewing machines is low and the management skills required to carry out subcontract work are not extensive. The consequence is that the clothing sector can attract entrepreneurs with no previous experience in the trade. For example, a survey of the clothing industry in Coventry found that just over half of the 91 entrepreneurs responsible for setting up 57 new clothing firms in the city between 1974 and 1987 had not worked before in the industry, either in manufacturing or retailing (Healey et al., 1987). Ethnic minority businesses in the clothing sector have several competitive advantages over other firms in the industry (Ward et al., 1986). The most important of these is a ready access to a low-cost labour force, which has relatively few alternative employment opportunities, members of which often wish to work for people from the same ethnic group and are consequently in a weak bargaining position. Minority businesses may also receive support from other businesses in the same ethnic group and the minority community in the form of, for example, supplies, orders, advice, and financial help.

In many ways, structuralist explanations of recent changes in the location of the British clothing industry differ from other explanations only in a matter of emphasis. Traditional (neo-classical) explanations emphasize geographic variations in the cost and availability of labour and government incentives, while behavioural approaches emphasize the variety of responses of different types of firms to these geographic variations. Structuralist approaches attempt to put these factors in a broader context. They emphasize that changed economic conditions have increased the need for firms to respond to variations in the geographic environment and in order to remain profitable they have to reduce their costs (the dynamics of capitalism). They also argue that firms vary in the ways in which they can reduce costs and that the options available to them are constrained, particularly by the size of the firms and the characteristics of the sector in which they produce. This suggests that the neoclassical, behavioural, and structuralist approaches are complementary and there is a need to take account of a broad range of factors in seeking explanations for changes in industrial location. A similar argument applies when attempting to understand geographic shifts in the motor industry.

12.3 International trends in the motor vehicle assembly industry

In contrast to the clothing industry, the motor vehicle industry is a capital-intensive, high-technology industry dominated by large companies operating large plants. It is also an assembly industry dependent on bringing together thousands of different parts. There are several stages in the production sequence before final assembly, including the manufacture of bodies, engines, transmissions, and components. There is considerable flexibility in where these different processes may be located and the extent to which the vehicle manufacturers undertake the tasks themselves. Generally, however, they tend to 'buy in' between 40 and 60 per cent of the value of the vehicle. This account focuses, for the most part, on recent trends in the location of the final assembly plants. After an examination of recent shifts in the location and nature of motor assembly plants at the international scale, recent trends in the North American motor industry are discussed.

Between 1960 and 1985, world production of passenger cars increased almost two and a half times. Output reached 32 m vehicles in 1978, then fell back and this figure was only reached again in 1985. The *production* of automobiles is, for the most part, concentrated in the developed world. Those developing world countries with a motor vehicle industry concentrate mainly on *assembly* (Fig. 12.3). The developed market economies accounted for 97 per cent of world output in 1960 and 89 per cent in 1984. The core group of countries for the production of motor vehicles are Western Europe (principally West Germany, France, Italy, and the United Kingdom), Japan, and North America. However, there were very large variations in the relative performance of different countries within this group over the period from 1960 to 1984. Whereas production in the EC countries fell from 40 to 30 per cent of world output and in the USA from 51 to 25 per cent, it increased dramatically in Japan from 1 to 23 per cent. The United Kingdom's share fell over the same period from 10 to 3 per cent. In 1984 both Spain and Canada produced more cars than the United Kingdom (Table 12.2).

There are only two significant concentrations outside the core group. The CMEA (COMECON) group (notably USSR, Poland, East Germany, and Czechoslovakia) accounted for 7 per cent of world output in 1984. Latin America (principally Brazil, Mexico, and Argentina) accounted for a further 3 per cent. Most of the car industry in the rest of the developing world is based on assembly from kits. An exception is South Korea which is developing an independent motor vehicle industry.

Clearly the location of motor car production has altered in the last quarter of a century, although the shift to the developing world has

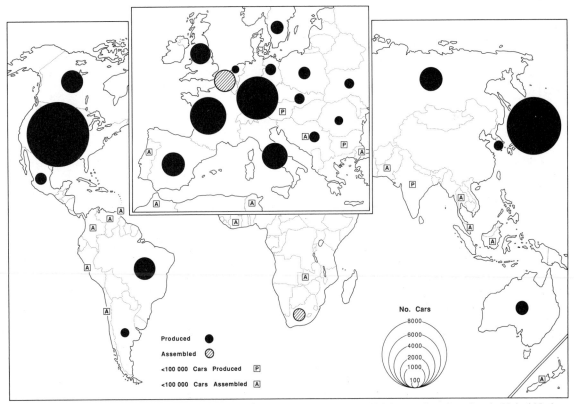

FIG 12.3 The world distribution of production and assembly of passenger cars, 1984 (*source:* based on data in United Nations (1986) *Yearbook of industrial statistics, 1984* (United Nations, New York))

TABLE 12.2 Growth of passenger car output by major producing countries, 1960–1984

Country	1960		1984		Percentage change in production
	Production (000s units)	World Share (%)	Production (000s units)	World Share (%)	
EEC	5 155	39.7	9 146	30.1	+ 77.4
Belgium	194	1.5	109	0.4	− 43.8
France	1 175	9.0	2 909	1.0	+ 147.6
West Germany	1 817	14.0	3 783	12.4	+ 108.2
Italy	596	4.6	1 436	4.7	+ 140.9
United Kingdom	1 353	10.4	909	3.0	− 32.8
Spain	43	0.3	1 174	3.9	+ 2 630.2
Sweden	108	0.8	378	1.2	+ 250.0
North America	6 998	53.8	8 655	28.5	+ 23.7
United States	6 675	51.4	7 622	25.1	+ 14.2
Canada	323	2.5	1 033	3.4	+ 219.8
Japan	165	1.3	7 073	23.3	+ 4 186.7
Australia	125	1.0	341	1.1	+ 172.8
CMEA	264	2.0	2 127	7.0	+ 705.7
USSR	139	1.1	1 327	4.4	+ 854.7
Czechoslovakia	—	—	180	0.6	—
Poland	—	—	278	0.9	—
Latin America	133	1.0	1 053	3.5	+ 691.7
Argentina	30	0.2	143	0.5	+ 376.7
Brazil	38	0.3	666	2.2	+ 1 652.6
Mexico	28	0.2	244	0.8	+ 771.4
WORLD	12 999	100.0	30 406	100.0	+ 133.9

Sources: 1960 data Dicken (1986 p. 283); 1984 data based on United Nations (1986) *Yearbook of industrial statistics, 1984* (United Nations, New York).

been far less than for the clothing industry. During its history three major transformations have shaped the motor industry.

Each arose from a creative breakthrough by a particular set of producers in technology and on the organization of the industry that facilitated a rapid growth of demand and led to a powerful export threat to producers in the rest of the world. The first of these transformations was the breakthrough by American producers, around 1910, from a custom-building to a mass-volume industry. The second occurred in Western Europe from the late 1950s when European producers combined mass production with an emphasis on product innovation and differentiation to challenge American based production for the first time. The third commenced in Japan in the late 1960s, when Japanese producers made dramatic breakthroughs in production organization that soon yielded a lower cost product of far greater manufacturing accuracy (Jones and Womack, 1985 p. 397).

The same classification of factors which was used for explaining global shifts in the clothing industry may be used to discuss the international trends in the motor vehicle industry, although, of course, the relative importance of the factors differs.

Technological changes and production costs

Just as with the clothing industry, improvements in the ease of transportation and communications have allowed the large motor companies to organise their production systems internationally. Significant technological changes have also occurred in the way in which cars are made and in product innovations, both of which have locational implications (Bloomfield, 1978).

One of the most important features of car production is the time and cost involved in designing new models. For instance, the Ford Escort project cost $3 billion and over four years were spent in designing, manufacturing, and marketing the new model. Consequently, manufacturers faced with these resource commitments are concerned to produce large quantities in order to recover their costs. There are also significant economies to be made by producing in volume. For instance, in the late 1960s the cost per car of producing 1 m cars was 70 per cent of the cost of making 100 000 cars (Dicken, 1986). The economies of scale vary, however, for different processes (Table 12.3). The minimum efficient scale for body panel pressing is 1–2 m units, while for final assembly the minimum efficient scale is between 200 000 and 250 000 units. The importance of plant size is, however, beginning to lessen with the introduction of flexible manufacturing systems which have markedly increased the efficiency and productivity of motor vehicle plants.

A further way in which some manufacturers are attempting to reduce their costs is to introduce the Japanese 'Kanban' or 'just-in-time' production system (Sheard, 1983). Under this system, suppliers are required to deliver the goods 'just-in-time' for their use on the factory floor (Chapter 7.3). The savings are made in reducing stocks. It has been calculated that the savings in interest charges and other costs of stockholding may amount to about a quarter of the cost price of the stocks (Firth, 1976). Ford has calculated that the streamlined working practices and more efficient production methods employed by Nissan in north-east England gives it a cost advantage of about £250 per car (Leadbeater, 1987). The system also means that there is pressure on suppliers

TABLE 12.3 The world league table of motor car manufacturers, 1985

Rank	Company	Country of origin	Passenger car production	Share of world total (%)
1.	General Motors	USA	7 090 664	22.0
2.	Ford Motors	USA	3 813 031	11.8
3.	Toyota	Japan	2 619 599	8.1
4.	Volkswagen	West Germany	2 126 998	6.6
5.	Nissan	Japan	2 005 020	6.2
6.	Renault	France	1 607 609	5.0
7.	Peugeot-Citroen	France	1 545 762	4.8
8.	Chrysler	USA	1 305 100	4.0
9.	Fiat	Italy	1 230 308	3.8
10.	Honda	Japan	1 101 747	3.4
11.	Mazda	Japan	815 074	2.5
12.	Uaz	USSR	785 000	2.4
13.	Mitsubishi	Japan	570 865	1.8
14.	Daimler-Benz	West Germany	537 909	1.7
15.	British Leyland	UK	485 104	1.5
16.	BMW	West Germany	431 085	1.3
17.	Volvo	Sweden	407 098	1.3
18.	Seat	Spain	304 753	0.9
19.	Fuji	Japan	259 673	0.8
20.	Polski	Poland	259 245	0.8
Total 20 manufacturers			29 301 719	
Others			2 931 509	
Total production			32 233 228	
Summary of World Production				
North American Companies			12 330 030	
Japanese Companies			7 982 787	
Western European Companies			8 549 508	
Eastern European Companies			1 811 448	

Source: *Financial Times*, 22 Oct. 1987.

to be located in close proximity to the assembly plants—in Japan the distance rarely exceeds 100 km (Estall, 1985). This is a factor militating against the recent trend towards international sourcing, though there are still powerful forces encouraging firms to operate on an international basis.

Perhaps, however, the major effect of introducing this system in Western countries will be to maintain the motor industry in the developed world. The predictions of the product cycle model (Chapter 6.3) and the new international division of labour thesis (Chapter 14.3; Hill, 1987) that mature products utilizing standardized technology will shift to the Third World to take advantage of low labour costs seem to have little relevance to current trends in the automobile industry. Indeed, Jones and Womack (1985) suggest that the industry is now undergoing a fourth transition involving flexible automation and new materials which, when combined with the Japanese advances in production organization, are continuing to reduce dramatically the number of person hours required to build a car. They argue that all the major elements of competitiveness in the industry are in a state of great flux and change; the product, the market, the production equipment, and the way the industry is organized are no longer mature. As a result of this dematurity, they do not foresee a great shift of production out of the developed world and they suggest that the bulk of Third World production will be to supply domestic market needs. They further point out that even some of the most promising Third World production sites, such as South Korea, have substantially higher production costs than the Japanese and the requirements of 'just-in-time' delivery are leading to the relocation back to the OECD countries of some of the component processes previously shifted to developing countries. These views are well summarized in a report to which Jones and Womack contributed:

The new production technologies mean that the shift to low wage locations will not occur on the scale once expected. The markets of the developed countries are demanding precise, high quality production. Flexible manufacturing in combination with the redesign of products to gain its full benefits can provide this while sharply increasing labour productivity. These innovations have shifted the focus of thought about the future geography of production location from the less developed countries to the concentrated production of most components near the point of final assembly in the developed countries (Altshuler et al., 1984 p. 249).

Investing in new technology is one strategy for European and American firms facing falling profits. Another is to try to reduce labour costs and improve labour relations. Labour costs are not as significant as in the clothing industry. For the motor vehicle industry as a whole, labour costs may account for between one-quarter and one-third of total production costs (Dicken, 1986). Profitability has also been shown in one study to be inversely related to labour militancy and the strength of organized labour (Glyn and Sutcliffe, 1972). Faced with these pressures companies have tended to adopt two types of strategy: either to establish plants in areas where labour costs and militancy are less; and/or change the nature of the labour force at their existing plants. Ford of Europe illustrates both strategies. The search for lower labour cost locations was one of the factors which led Ford to establish production plants in Spain and Portugal, and by hiring a greater number of immigrants and members of ethnic minority groups they have reduced some of the pressure on labour costs and militancy in their existing centres of production. In the mid- to late-1970s over a third of Ford workers in Germany were *Gastarbeiter*, while a quarter of their workers in the United Kingdom were Asian or West Indian. A slightly different strategy was followed in the United Kingdom at their Halewood plant on Merseyside, where one commentator noted that 'Ford attempted to recruit mainly young workers with families. ... Men under twenty years of age were barred and dockers and building workers were avoided' (Ward, 1982 p. 449).

New techniques of production are, of course, changing both the demand for labour and the kind of skills required. A number of motor car companies, such as Nissan, are now operating 'lights out' manufacturing (all-night production without supervision) of major components (Griffiths, 1987). Flexible working practices have also been introduced to accompany the introduction of new technology. For example, in Britain Ford reached agreement with the unions to reduce the number of job demarcations from 500 to 58. Similarly, demarcations between skilled workers have gradually been eroded. Most companies now operate two or three types of skilled crafts-men, with complete mobility within a skill. The growing importance of multi-skilled, flexible, more capable shop-floor workers has had other consequences. For instance, most companies have made moves to harmonize the conditions of white collar and blue-collar workers (Leadbeater, 1987).

The combination of changes in technology and production cost variations has affected interna-tional competitiveness and helps to account for the very rapid rate of growth of the Japanese industry, which by 1980 had a 20 to 30 per cent cost advantage over European and North Amer-ican firms at the point of import. 'This was due mainly to low labour costs, harmonious labour relations, a well-educated workforce, a high level of process automation, advanced quality control, and a flexible relationship between car firms and component suppliers' (Jones, 1983, p. 117). Ulti-mately, of course, the potential to gain from production cost advantages depends on the size of the market and, increasingly, the ability of the firms to organize production and marketing on an international basis.

Pattern of demand and organizational context

Motor vehicle production is strongly market-oriented at the national scale and historically has been concentrated in the developed market economies. However, the pattern of demand has changed in two main ways since the 1960s. First, the rate of growth of demand in developed mar-ket economies has been falling since the 1960s. In the 1980s, the market in Western Europe and North America, which is largely replacement de-mand, has approached saturation. The highest rates of growth in demand are coming from developing countries, although a significant in-crease in total demand depends on the growth of personal income. Secondly, there has been an integration of world markets. This has been encouraged by the recession which followed the oil price rises in 1973 and 1979, and the shift in demand to smaller, fuel-efficient cars. The former has meant that to maintain their output manufac-turers have been forced to extend the geograph-ical distribution of their markets; while the latter has enabled producers of these cars, particularly the Japanese, and to a lesser extent the Euro-peans, to penetrate the North American market.

A major feature of the motor vehicle industry is its increasing domination by multinational com-panies. For example, there were twenty major car manufacturers in Europe in the early 1960s, by 1980 this had fallen to twelve. The world league table in 1985 is shown in Table 12.3. Of the top twenty companies three are American, six are Japanese, nine are Western European, and two are Eastern European; together they accounted for 91 per cent of world car production. The concentration of ownership means that the strat-egies followed by the largest companies have a major impact on the behaviour of every other company. For example, 'it is no coincidence that 1986, when GM stopped chasing volume and concentrated more on profit, was the first year in a decade that the European volume car com-panies made a combined net profit of about $1.2 bn' (Gooding, 1987).

Faced with the changing pattern of demand, manufacturers have tended to adopt one of two production strategies. At one end of the spectrum some of the major manufacturers, such as Ford and GM, began to develop 'world cars', like the Escort and the Cavalier, in which production is integrated on a world basis. Although this strategy has generally been found to be over-ambitious, indeed both the Escort and Cavalier were redesigned for the US market, most of the large manufacturers have gone some way along the road to international integration on a re-gional, if not a world basis. At the other end of the spectrum some manufacturers, such as Daimler Benz, Jaguar (taken over by Ford in 1989) and BMW, have specialized in high-quality cars which are produced, often exclusively, in the home country. Significantly, both strategies depend on selling cars in regional or world mar-kets; national markets are too small to support motor vehicle manufacturers (Dicken, 1986).

One of the most important developments of recent years is that most of the world's car manufacturers are increasingly involved in com-plex transnational sourcing arrangements for components and in collaborative agreements with other manufacturers (Dicken, 1986). This increas-ing international integration has resulted in the emergence of Spain, Brazil, and Mexico as poten-tially significant newly industrializing countries exporting cars and components as part of the strategy of multinationals. Examples of new strategic alliances include Ford and Nissan in

Australia, Rover and Honda in the United Kingdom, and Daimler Benz and Mitsubishi in Western Europe. Probably the most significant collaboration though is that between Ford and VW in setting up Autolatina to merge their production operations in Brazil and Argentina. This joint venture enables VW and Ford to stay in Latin America but limit their losses until that time when the potential market in South America may be realized (Gooding, 1987).

Companies vary widely in the extent of their transnational activities. Whereas over a third of GM's production and over 60 per cent of Ford's production takes place outside the home country, the Japanese car companies are somewhat exceptional in that they are involved in mass production, but predominantly, at least until the mid-1980s, from a domestic base. However, this is beginning to change as the strengthening of the Yen against other currencies in the late 1980s has reduced the cost advantage of exporting from Japan. A further factor has been pressures from North American and European governments for the Japanese to establish manufacturing bases in their countries.

Government policies

Government policies concerned with trade, investment incentives, restructuring and vehicle regulations have all had effects on the location of production.

1. *Trade*. Restrictions on imports have been used by many countries at various times to protect their domestic industries. In 1960 both the United Kingdom and France had a 30 per cent import tariff and Japan had a 40 per cent tariff. Duties in Taiwan at one time exceeded 100 per cent. The common European Community tariff is at present 11 per cent, the United States has a 3 per cent tariff and Japan now has no import duty, though significant non-tariff barriers still impede the ability of countries trying to export to Japan. Several Western European countries and the United States have also negotiated voluntary export restraints with Japan. These barriers have encouraged firms such as Nissan and Toyota in the United Kingdom and Ford in Spain to set up production facilities within the tariff barriers. A major reason for the United States auto-investments in developing countries in the 1960s was to obtain access to their markets, reinforced by a high degree of oligopolistic reaction on the part of major producers. International integration to cover costs only came later (Schoenberger, 1987).

A common practice, particularly among developing countries, is to negotiate minimum local content clauses with multinationals setting up production facilities. For example, at one time these were set at 55 per cent in Spain and 75 per cent in Mexico. More recently the emphasis has shifted to specifying a minimum proportion of the company's output which must be exported. In return for these agreements the multinationals negotiate other concessions. For example, when Ford set up in Spain the government were so keen to attract them that they waived the legislation that any company should be at least 50 per cent Spanish, reduced the local content requirement and cut import duties on components from 39 per cent to 5 per cent (Ward, 1982).

2. *Investment incentives*. The significance of the motor industry has meant that many governments are prepared to give large financial incentives to attract motor plants. When Ford was persuaded to set up their engine plant in the United Kingdom (at Bridgend in South Wales) rather than in West Germany (in West Berlin) by the offer of a £148 m grant towards development costs (estimated at almost two-thirds of total development costs) (Reeves, 1980).

3. *Restructuring aid*. Falling levels of profitability and recession conditions have meant that several motor vehicle companies have fallen into financial difficulty and governments have stepped in with financial help. For example, both the United States government and various European governments gave financial aid to Chrysler in the 1970s to prevent it going bankrupt. Earlier BL went into public ownership. Several companies though, such as Jaguar, Rover, Alpha Romeo, and Seat of Spain, have returned to private ownership.

4. *Vehicle regulations*. The imposition of these by governments have influenced trade patterns and hence the relative competitiveness of the vehicle industries of different nations. For instance, the stringent safety, fuel economy, and emission regulations applied in the United States and Japan have restricted the import of foreign cars into their markets and given a degree of protection, particularly in the case of Japan, to their domestic car industries.

Locational shifts in motor vehicle production have not only occurred at the international scale. There have also been major changes in the location and organization of production within countries. This can be illustrated by examining recent changes in the geography of the North American motor vehicle industry, which remains a major centre of production despite a rapid decline in its share of world output in the last twenty-five years.

12.4 Recent changes in the location and organization of the North American motor vehicle assembly industry

The North American motor vehicle industry, which for the purposes of this account is taken to be that of the US and Canada, has undergone a dramatic change in the last few decades. Its share of world production fell from over half in 1960 to slightly over a quarter in the mid-1980s (Table 12.2). The consequent rationalization has been accompanied by major changes in production organization and techniques. There has also been a tendency for the earlier trend of decentralization of production to be replaced by one of recentralization in the Mid-West, although in new locations. This most recent trend may be described as one of *dispersed concentration* (Fig. 12.4).

During the history of the motor assembly industry in North America its locational pattern has alternated between concentration and dispersal. The industry began in the mid-1890s with factories dispersed throughout the North-East. In the next decade, it concentrated in southern Michigan. From 1914 to the mid-1960s it decentralized to many other parts of North America and Canada. Since then there has been renewed interest in the Mid-West. Between 1965 and 1986, all fifteen sites for new automobile assembly in the United States were in the Mid-West, while nine out of the thirteen plants closed in this period were outside the Mid-West (Boas, 1961; Rubenstein, 1986). There has also been a trend since the

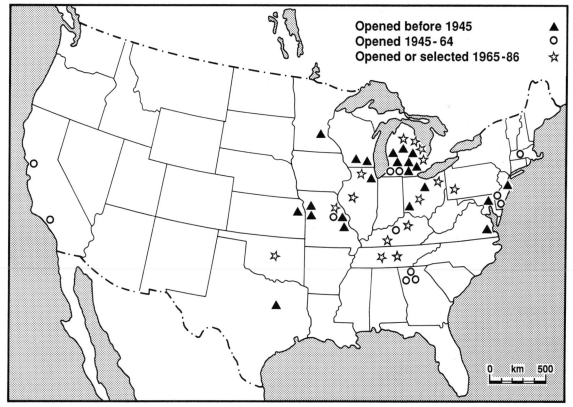

FIG 12.4 Automobile assembly plants in the United States, 1986 (*source:* based on Rubenstein, 1986 p. 290)

early 1970s for the Canadian plants of American manufacturers to perform better in employment terms than plants in the United States, being hit relatively more mildly in times of recession and afterwards recovering more rapidly (Holmes, 1987).

To understand the locational shifts and the technical and organizational adjustments made to existing complexes, it is important to view them within the context of the responses of American manufacturers to the changing pattern of demand and increasing international competition referred to in the last section. As with the clothing industry, to obtain a full understanding of these changes it is insufficient to analyse only changes in the relative importance of location factors, it is also necessary to examine the recent *international and national pressures to rationalize* and the *corporate locational and organizational responses* they have encouraged. As Holmes (1983, p. 252) notes: 'pressures to restructure and reorganize production lead to changes in production and labor processes which invariably have an impact on the locational structure of the industry.'

Rationalization pressures

The pressures to rationalize are apparent both at an international scale and within the North American motor industry (Holmes, 1983; 1987). The main international pressures to reorganize production have come from the rises in oil prices in the 1970s and increased international competition. The two are linked, as the oil crises led to an increase in demand for smaller cars, where foreign producers have the greatest competitive advantage. By the early 1980s it has been estimated, for example, that Japanese motor manufacturers had a cost advantage of between £1500 and £2200 per car over domestic producers (G. L. Clark, 1986).

The increased competition, in combination with the general recession in the American economy in the late 1970s and early 1980s, led to overcapacity in the industry. To remain competitive manufacturers attempted to increase productivity by introducing more automation. They also tried to integrate production on an international scale so that each plant could operate at near to optimal capacity. The ultimate outcome of this tendency was the concept of the 'world car' referred to earlier—a small, energy-efficient vehicle with standardized, interchangeable com-

ponents, designed to be manufactured and marketed throughout the world (R. C. Hill, 1984).

Pressures to integrate production within North America were felt earlier. Prior to 1963 the auto industries of Canada and the USA, while dominated by the same three companies (General Motors, Ford, and Chrysler), were organized separately. As a consequence many models were produced on both sides of the border, there was little trade between the two countries, and the limited domestic market prevented the Canadian plants operating efficiently. In the following three years tariff barriers on assembled cars and original equipment parts were removed, culminating in the Canada–US Automotive Products Trade Agreement (the Auto Pact). This paved the way for integration of the North American car industry on a continental basis.

Other internal pressures to reorganize production included labour disputes in the major car plants, particularly in the late 1960s, and a slowing down in the rate of productivity growth. Whether or not these were linked, as some authorities have argued, the result was a rise in labour costs per unit of output and a decline in profitability.

Corporate responses

In the face of the various national and international pressures to rationalize production, the companies attempted to restore profitability in various ways. These inevitably had impacts on the location and organization of production. Among the impacts were the decentralization of production within the United States; the emergence of new spatial divisions of labour; and the introduction of new process technologies. The first two trends were prevalent particularly in the post-war period up to the 1960s, but in the 1980s there were signs that they were being modified by technical changes and alterations in competitive strategies.

Decentralization of production
Decentralization of the motor industry has been occurring for many years in the United States. It has mainly affected the final assembly plants and only to a limited extent the manufacturers of parts. However, the reasons for and the geographical scale at which decentralization has occurred have changed over time. In the early post-war years, a major reason for *national*

decentralization was to obtain better access to regional markets which were expensive to serve direct from the Mid-West. This led to assembly plants being opened as far afield as California, Georgia, Texas, New Jersey, and Massachusetts. Access to regional markets became less important in the 1960s with changes in transport technology. The development of new three-tiered car-carrying wagons reduced the cost of distributing finished cars and made the cost advantage of branch assembly plants, with the possible exception of those on the West coast, insignificant (Estall and Buchanan, 1980). The need for branch plants to serve regional markets also fell as the number of models increased from 216 in 1955 to 370 in 1967 and manufacturers converted regional assembly plants to specialized factories that produced one or two models for nationwide distribution (Rubenstein, 1986).

As the relative importance of access to regional markets declined, the desire to establish assembly plants where the labour climate was perceived to be more favourable than in the traditional locations in the Mid-West increased in significance. This led to several plants being located in rural areas and in adjoining southern states. This trend towards *regional decentralization or dispersed concentration* goes back to the 1950s when the major companies adopted policies of parallel production and multi-sourcing to reduce the power of organized labour and the potential disruptive effects of strikes or production breakdowns, but has continued as the trend towards greater plant specialization was introduced. For example, between 1975 and 1980 GM opened fourteen plants in the deep South. Nine of these were in right-to-work states (Bluestone and Harrison, 1982).

Spatial divisions of labour

The attempts by manufacturers to integrate production have led to the emergence of new spatial divisions of labour (i.e. what types of job are done where—see Chapters 4.2 and 15.2) both internationally and within North America. On the one hand, the trend towards the internationalization of production has resulted not only in American companies setting up plants in other countries, particularly in Western Europe, South America, and Mexico, but also to foreign companies establishing plants in North America. An early example of the latter was VW's decision in the 1970s

to open a factory at New Stanton, Pennsylvania (Krumme, 1981), though it has since been closed. More recently, the Japanese have begun to change their policy of serving the North American market from Japan and are rapidly commissioning plants on the North American mainland. By the late 1980s at least eleven such plants were operational (Fig. 12.5). All but one of these *transplants* (the jointly owned Toyota/GM New United Manufacturing Plant at Fremont, California), is located in the Mid-West or just over the border in Ontario. Production at these plants is planned to reach 2 million units by 1991. At 150 yen to the dollar it is calculated that cars can be built in the United States as cheaply as in Japan, once the $500 per car transport costs are taken into account. A significant proportion of these cars will be exported to Europe and Japan as 'American' cars (Gooding, 1987; Robertson, 1987).

Earlier attempts at integration affected the relative location and character of the motor industry between the United States and Canada. Following the Auto Pact in 1965, there has been a tendency for manufacturers to concentrate their research and design facilities and the key production planning decision-making in the United States, while locating their more labour-intensive processes in Canada. The latter reflects the lower labour costs in the Canadian motor industry, which were approximately 30 per cent lower at the time the Auto-Pact was signed. This cost difference also helps to explain why the manufacturers cut back relatively more harshly in the USA than in Canada in the recession of the early 1980s (Holmes, 1983).

Technological changes

A further response to the pressures to rationalize is for firms to introduce new process technologies. During the late 1970s and 1980s, the North American motor industry has been in a state of transition as it has changed from Fordist to neo-Fordist techniques of production (see also Chapters 4.2, 6.1, 7.3, and 15.2). This change-over has had significant effects both on the location and organization of production (Holmes, 1987; Schoenberger, 1987). Under Fordism, a common response to falling profitability was to cut unit costs of production through automation, product standardization and the seeking of economies of large-scale production. The same

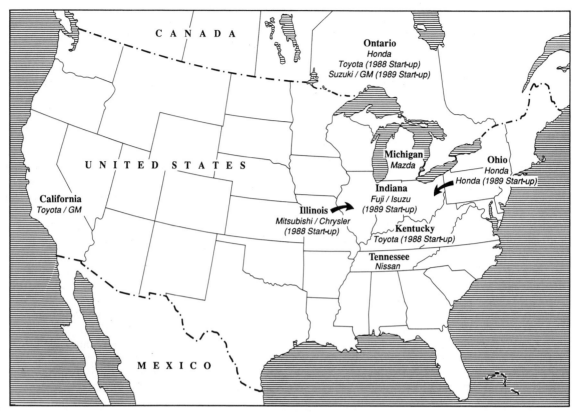

FIG 12.5 Japanese motor plants in North America in the late 1980s (*source:* Gooding, 1987)

principle indicated a shift to low-cost locations and the development of the 'world car'. However, with the emphasis on market segmentation, the introduction of flexible manufacturing systems, and Japanese methods of working, the link between lowering production costs and long production runs based on economies of scale was severed and the desire to produce the 'world car' was lost. Further, there has been a tendency to shift the emphasis from dispersion to low-cost locations to concentration in production complexes where most components are made in close proximity to the point of final assembly.

There are also pressures for the highly differentiated spatial division of labour associated with Fordism and described in the last section to be modified. The Japanese methods of work involve an increase in the range of skills and tasks performed by individuals and encourage a reintegration of design and engineering skills with those of the programmers and operators of equipment in existing and new production complexes. The changing locational tendencies which arise from

the close relationships between competitive strategies, technology, and the organization of production are summarized in Fig. 12.6.

A good example of these interrelationships is given by GM's new Saturn car plant at Spring Hill, a small town near Nashville, Tennessee (Meyer, 1986a; 1986b). When the plans were announced in 1985, it was estimated that it would cost $5 billion, produce 500 000 small cars per annum (since altered to 250 000 mid-range cars per annum (Glasmeier and McCluskey, 1987)), and provide jobs for 6000 United Auto Workers (UAW) laid off at other plants of the company. Such an investment of over $830 000 per worker is considerably above the average for US manufacturing of about $75 000 per employee. Much of this investment is in the flexible equipment which can produce different products in the same factory, using computer-controlled retooling. GM are using the Saturn plant as a showpiece for their software system, known as 'manufacturing automation protocol' (MAP), which enables the computerized equipment of different manufacturers in

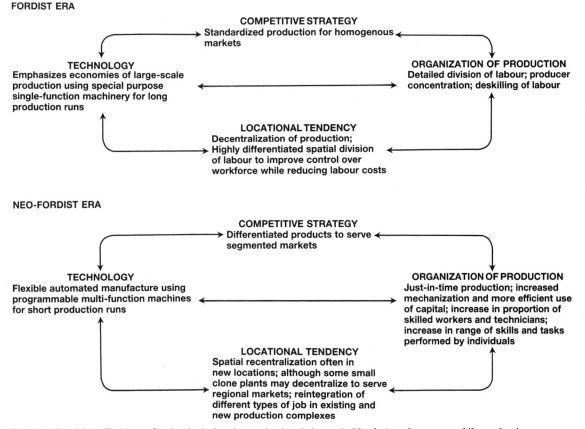

FIG 12.6 Spatial implications of technological and organizational change in North American automobile production (*source:* based in part on information in Holmes, 1987 and Schoenberger, 1987)

a plant to communicate with each other and be centrally co-ordinated. The plant also incorporates 'just-in-time' inventory-free production and discrete work-groups, or quality circles, which will control much of the production process.

The choice of Spring Hill, which has a population of only 1095, continues GM's recent policy of favouring rural sites. Not only is space available for the large facility, but rural areas seem to be perceived as having lower operating costs and a more acquiescent labour force. Although the workers will be members of the UAW and many may come from other plants, Meyer (1986a, p. 210) suggests that 'they know and accept beforehand the new work rules and production organization associated with their new jobs'. A further attraction of locating in Tenessee may have been 'to increase the likelihood of unionizing the nearby Nissan plant, benefiting both the UAW (through extending the reach of the union) and

GM (by forcing its Japanese competition to play by the same rules)' (Schoenberger, 1987 p. 206).

The locational effects of the introduction of new process technologies are varied and may be contradictory. On the one hand, the smaller plants, allowed by the MAP flexibility, may disperse to be closer to the location of final consumers. On the other hand, the adoption of 'just-in-time' procedures may encourage a contraction in the geographic spread of manufacturers of original equipment, as more emphasis is placed on locating near to their markets. With the change in emphasis to single sourcing, the market for many suppliers will often be a single plant. If this trend prevails it could see the re-creation of local specializations, though based on vertically integrated concentrations rather than the horizontally integrated concentrations which were more common in the past. Which outcome prevails will depend, in part, on whether the automobile assemblers decide to centralize production or take advantage of the MAP flexibility to operate several identical branch plants. This gives a good illustration of the argument developed in Chapters 6 and 7 that the introduction of new technologies may result in either spatial dispersion or concentration. Technological and organizational changes do not determine spatial outcomes; rather they provide a set of possibilities from which society may choose.

12.5 Summary

This chapter has attempted to illustrate the use and operation of the concepts and factors discussed earlier in the book to interpret international and intranational shifts in the location of two manufacturing industries—clothing and motor vehicles.

- There are major differences between the clothing and motor vehicle industries in terms of technology, ownership, and capital/labour ratios. Nevertheless, at an international scale the main locational trend in both industries has been a relative shift in production to the newly industrializing countries (NICs) although it has occurred to a much lesser extent in the case of motor vehicles, where the growth of production in Japan and the relative decline in the importance of North America is a much more significant trend. Within the motor industry, this shift has been accomplished mostly by international integration of production within individual multinational motor corporations. In contrast, in the clothing sector international subcontracting of production has been more common.

- Some of this shift has been to serve the domestic markets of the NICs. This has been the main strategy in the car industry although, for instance, Brazil, Mexico, and Spain export cars; this occurs within a multinational company framework and only South Korea has recently developed an independent export strategy for cars. In the clothing industry, in contrast, although an important domestic market has developed in many Third World countries, the main strategy, especially in South-East Asia, has been to develop export-oriented production.

- Some developed market countries are attempting to adjust to the changed circumstances of the last two to three decades. While others are emphasizing protection rather than adjustment. At one end of the spectrum West Germany, in both clothing and vehicles, has opted for up-market specialization and the transfer of some production abroad. On the other hand the United Kingdom has emphasized protection for both industries. Yet different again, the United States, France, and Italy have emphasized protectionism in clothing, while encouraging direct competition in cars. Perhaps the most interesting paradox is Italy where the dominant strategy in clothing is based on low wages and small-scale production, while in cars it is based on advanced automation and internationalization (Shepherd, 1981).

- Nevertheless, there are indications in both industries that, contrary to the predictions of the product cycle and the new international division of labour thesis the shift of production to the Third World may have largely ceased and in some sectors reversed. The reasons are, however, different in the two industries. In the clothing industry, it reflects changes in the pattern of demand, as competition is based more on quality than price and more frequent style changes necessitate short production runs and encourages sourcing closer to the points of sale. In the motor industry, it is based more on technological and organizational changes. The introduction of robotics and flexible manufacturing systems is offsetting high labour costs in developed countries and the need for closer co-ordination of production is encouraging greater spatial concentration.

- Some tentative similarities may also be noted about the recent locational changes experienced by the British clothing industry and the North American motor industry. Both seem to have undergone a trend towards concentrated dispersal with traditional locations experiencing losses of employment, while employment gains have occurred in selected new locations.

- In response to the pressure to rationalize and to changes in the geographical environments faced by firms, new spatial divisions of labour have emerged in both industries. In the North American motor industry, international integration of production has occurred both within North America and overseas. One consequence has been that the research and design and high-level decision-making departments have become concentrated in the United States, while there has been some shift of the more labour-intensive processes to Canada. Moreover, the proliferation of models from domestic and foreign-owned firms and the introduction of flexible production methods have encouraged a reconcentration of automobile assembly in the Mid-West. Manufacturers are, however, avoiding the communities traditionally associated with the industry preferring rural sites adjacent to metropolitan areas. In the British clothing industry, there has been a tendency to shift to low-cost labour locations, where female labour is available, and to extend the subcon-

tracting system to ethnic businesses, located in both traditional and new centres.

Clearly, a wide range of factors needs to be considered in seeking to explain locational shifts in manufacturing activity. Spatial variations in costs and government activities, the variety of responses by different firms, and changes in the international economy all need to be taken into account. This supports the general argument made in several places in this book that the neoclassical, behavioural, and structuralist approaches to explaining locational shifts in economic activity are complementary rather than competing. A wide range of factors also needs to be examined when explaining locational changes in service industries.

13

Service Industries

The evolution of service economies is associated, according to Toffler (1980), with 'the Third Wave', which followed the development of agriculture as the first wave and the industrial revolution as the second wave. This is analogous to the Fisher–Clark thesis that there is a natural history of industrialization, with, first, primary industry, secondly, manufacturing industry, and, thirdly, service industry becoming in turn the leading and the most sizeable employment sector (see Chapter 1.3). Most developed market economies have now undergone the third sectoral transformation in which service industries become the dominant employment sector (Kellerman, 1985a). For example, by 1983 the service sector accounted for almost 70 per cent of employment in the United States, almost two thirds of employment in the United Kingdom, and over half of all employment in West Germany and Japan (Hall, 1987a). Services are also the most rapidly growing sector in employment terms in these countries. Between 1963 and 1983, service employment in the United Kingdom, for instance, grew by 22 per cent compared with a fall in manufacturing employment of 36 per cent; while in the United States over the same period, whereas manufacturing employment grew by 10 per cent, service employment grew by 58 per cent.

Given the significance of the service sector, it is somewhat surprising that its treatment in the geographical literature is rather fragmented. The analysis of retailing has a long history within the discipline, while several studies of the geography of both offices and tourism have appeared recently; most other service industries have not received the attention they deserve. Indeed the first textbooks on services only appeared in the 1980s (Daniels, 1982; 1985a; Price and Blair, 1989).

Services may be defined as 'those activities which do not produce or modify physical objects (commodities or products) and purchases which are immaterial, transient and produced mainly by people' (Howells and Green, 1986 p. 89). They have traditionally been viewed as a passive sector which follows trends in population and manufacturing. However, this idea is increasingly being questioned and some authorities have argued that the location of several service industries can influence trends in the location of manufacturing and population as well as respond to them (Marshall, 1982; Daniels, 1983; see also Chapter 1.3). Despite the realization of the interdependence between services and other sectors, Daniels (1985b) has argued that the service sector should be studied separately. He suggests that the locational, physical, and transactional characteristics of services makes them a distinct sector. Nevertheless it is important to recognize that service industries are extremely diverse. Indeed, it has been suggested that 'failure to distinguish among major types of services . . . has obstructed intelligent discussion of trends in service growth' (Stanback, 1979 p. 1).

Common distinctions are made between:

1. *goods-related* services (e.g. retailing, wholesaling, and freight transport), *information-processing* services (e.g. finance, education, and marketing), and *personnel support* services (e.g. welfare services and hotel and catering);
2. *public* services (e.g. local and central government) and *private* services (e.g. retailing and banking);
3. *basic* services which are mainly exported outside the local area (e.g. tourism and freight transport) and *non-basic* services which serve primarily local consumer needs (e.g. retailing);
4. *producer* (or intermediate) services which serve other industries (e.g. research and de-

velopment and market research), and *consumer* services which provide output going directly to consumers or households (e.g. leisure services and education).

A combination of these different classifications is often desirable, although in devising them it is necessary to take account of the availability of data and the conceptual basis of the classifications used (Allen, 1988*a*). Two slightly different classifications which were devised taking account of the limitations of the official employment statistics available in the United States and Great Britain are shown in Table 13.1.

The classifications may be used to examine recent employment trends in the service sector in the two countries (Tables 13.2 and 13.3). The data for the United States cover a thirty year period from 1947 to 1977, while that for Great Britain cover the decade 1971 to 1981. Despite the different lengths of time examined the producer sector shows a consistent and significant increase in relative importance in both countries, while wholesaling and transportation account for a decreasing share of service employment in both. In the United States, the other main growth sector has been health and education, while em-

ployment in government services grew rapidly in the 1950s and 1960s, but its share of service employment declined in the 1970s. Retailing grew more or less in step with the overall economy and consumer services declined, largely because of reductions in private household services. In Britain, the welfare services exhibited a sharp increase in their share of employment in services during the 1970s, while private and public consumer services more or less held their own.

These shifts in the relative significance of different service industries are important, but they are only one way in which change has affected the service sector. There have also been significant alterations in the nature and quality of the services provided, in the amount and kind of labour inputs, in the extent to which new technologies have been introduced, and in who provides the services and where they are located. Urry (1987) identifies no less than eleven different forms of service sector restructuring, which are summarized in Table 13.4. Some of these changes are illustrated in the two case studies of service industries which are the main concern of this chapter.

The aim of the case studies is to apply the concepts and factors discussed in Parts I and II of this book to help explain recent changes in the

TABLE 13.1 Two classifications of service industries

Revised Singleman classification	Lancaster Regionalism Group
Producer services, e.g. finance, insurance, real estate, legal, social services	Privately-owned managerial producer services, e.g. insurance, banking, legal, research and development
Distributive services, e.g. transportation, wholesale	Privately-owned distributional producer services, e.g. wholesale, dealing
Retail services	Circulation services, e.g. rail, road, sea, and air transport
Mainly consumer services, e.g. hotels, personal services, garages, recreation services	Privately-owned consumer services, e.g. retail, hotel, motor repairers, personal services
Government and government enterprises	Publicly-owned consumer services, e.g. health, education, local and central government
Non profit services, e.g. health, education	Privately-owned welfare services, e.g. religious organizations, welfare and charitable services

Sources: Based on Noyelle and Stanback (1984 p. 9); Bagguley (1986 pp. 66–8).

TABLE 13.2 Service sector employment in the United States, 1947, 1969, 1977

	Full-time equivalent employment (%)		
	1947	1969	1977
Producer services	10.7	15.5	17.5
Distributive services	23.9	16.9	16.6
Retail services	22.2	20.0	20.7
Mainly consumer services	13.5	8.9	7.3
Government and government enterprises	25.0	31.6	28.6
Non profit services	4.6	7.2	9.3
ALL SERVICES	100.0	100.0	100.0

Source: Derived from Noyelle and Stanback (1984 p. 15).

TABLE 13.3 Service sector employment in Great Britain, 1971, 1981

	Employment (%)	
	1971	1981
Private managerial services	11.8	13.8
Private distribution services	7.9	7.4
Circulation services	13.6	10.8
Private consumer services	28.3	27.8
Public consumer services	35.0	35.1
Private welfare services	3.3	5.1
ALL SERVICES	100.0	100.0

Source: Bagguley (1986 pp. 69–74).

spatial pattern of two service industries, retailing and producer services, which both make a major contribution to the economic landscape of mature industrial economies. Retailing and producer services provide two contrasting case studies in that they have distinct spatial patterns and may best be explained using different theoretical frameworks. For example, retailing, like most consumer services, tends to be located in relation to the distribution of population and may be amenable to analysis using ideas from central place theory. Producer services, on the other hand, are spatially more concentrated and many may be better understood in terms of information diffusion theory or contact theory which emphasize

access to specialized information and the attraction of an information rich environment (Daniels, 1982). The recent changes in retailing and producer services are examined at both the inter-regional and intraregional scales, although in the case of retailing most attention is given to the latter.

13.1 Recent changes in the nature and location of retailing

Retailing has been going through a revolution in terms of its organization, methods of selling, use of technology, and location. Undoubtedly one of the most visible impacts of this revolution has been the development of planned shopping centres or malls. Although these centres have a long history, they have only become widespread since the 1950s in North America and since the 1960s in Europe. With the largest providing not only shops, but also restaurants and entertainment facilities, spending time in them is rapidly becoming part of the way of life for a large number of people. According to a recent television documentary, 78 per cent of Americans went to an enclosed mall at least once a month. In 1960 the average visit lasted 20 minutes, in 1970 it lasted 1.5 hours and now it lasts 4 hours (Durlacher, 1987). Development of these planned shopping centres has contributed, especially in North America, to the decentralization of retailing. The relative shift out of the centre of towns and cities is the major locational trend affecting retail patterns in developed market economies, and most space in this section is given over to an analysis of the reasons behind it.

Shopping centre developments

A planned shopping *centre* is 'a group of commercial establishments which have been designed, planned, developed, owned, marketed and managed as a unit' (Dawson and Lord, 1985 p. 1). It is distinct from a shopping *district*, which is a concentration of shops and other commercial establishments each in individual ownership and on individual sites. Control and management are the key features distinguishing shopping centres and shopping districts. Within the United States over half of total retail sales now pass through shopping centres; in Britain it is probably less

TABLE 13.4 Forms of service sector restructuring

1. *Partial self-provisioning* of the service function.
   Self-service in retail distribution.
   Self-servicing of the entertainment function through the development of televisions, hi-fi, videos, etc.

2. *Intensification*: increases in labour productivity through managerial or organizational changes with little or no investment or major loss of capacity.
   Higher education, for example, degrees and diplomas produced per member of staff in universities increased 2.5% per annum 1972–82.
   Health sector, especially in the provision of ancillary services in hospitals.

3. *Investment and technical change*: heavy capital investment within new forms of production and, as a result, considerable job loss, often highly unequally distributed.
   Private managerial producer services, particularly through the development of the electronic office.
   Growth of the Open University at the expense of conventional universities—made possible by the use of existing household equipment (television and video) for the service delivery.
   Point-of-sale computer terminals in retailing in supermarkets and superstores.

4. *Rationalization*: closure of capacity with little or no new investment or new technology.
   Closure of cinemas, mostly because of intense competition from household investment in televisions.
   Cut-backs in circulation services.

5. *Subcontracting* parts of the service sector to specialized companies, particularly of producer services.
   Privatization of cleaning, laundry, catering, etc. functions in the health service to specialist private companies.
   Growth of private managerial producer services.

6. *Replacement of existing labour input* with part-time female, or non-white labour.
   Marked growth in part-time female labour in retailing.
   General growth of part-time work in all services, but especially in private consumer services.
   Increased use of temporary workers especially amongst larger, faster growing firms in the 1980s.

7. *Enhancement of quality* of the service function through increased labour input (that is, more labour, higher skills, better training).
   In some parts of private consumer services, especially hotels and restaurants there is a shift away from cheap 'family labour'.

8. *Materialization* of the service function so that the service takes the form of a material product that can be bought, sold, transported, stored, etc.
   Circulation services partly replaced with privately owned cars or vans.
   Entertainment from videos or television rather than from 'live' theatre, cinema, sport.

9. *Spatial relocation*: movement into areas with cheaper rents because much service work is labour-intensive and hence requires extensive space. Movement of offices from central London to surrounding satellite towns.

10. *Domestication*: that is, the partial relocation of the provision of the function within forms of household or family labour.
    Community care programmes in the health service which involve some relocation from public consumer services to privately owned welfare services (private houses) and to women's domestic labour.

11. *Centralization*: the spatial centralization of services in larger units and the closure or reduction of the number or scale of smaller units.
    The reorganization of general practitioners into group practices with reduced levels of accessibility.
    The reorganization of hospital provision into larger units and the running down of smaller units.

Source: Urry (1987 p. 17).

than half this figure (Dawson and Lord, 1985). Sales in shopping centres are growing more rapidly than retailing generally.

The first shopping centre was a fifty-shop, three-level enclosed shopping arcade in Providence, Rhode Island, opened in 1829 (Dawson, 1983a). However, the idea did not catch on and it was not until 1907 that the next was established at Roland Park, Baltimore. The first truly suburban centre was the Country Club Plaza, built on the outskirts of Kansas City in 1923 (Davies, 1976). It was not until the 1950s that regional shopping centres began to be developed and the early 1970s that the super-regional centre emerged (Sternleib and Hughes, 1981). In the 1950s they were concentrated in the industrial north-east of the USA. From there they spread out westwards and southwards usually first to the largest or second largest city within a state (Cohen, 1972). By 1984 there were close on 25 000 planned shopping centres in the USA (Lord, 1987a).

A fourfold hierarchical classification of centres is frequently used (Table 13.5). At the top of the heirarchy are the super-regional centres, such as Eaton Center (Toronto), Beverly Center (Los Angeles), and Metro Centre (Gateshead, England) each with over 100 000 sq m of covered shopping space. They have at least 100 units and include restaurants and entertainment facilities. Such super-regional malls aim to provide attractions for all the family in a secure and controlled environment. Currently the largest centre in the world is the West Edmonton Mall in Alberta. Its 480 000 sq m of gross leasable space provides room for over 800 stores and more than 100 restaurants. Among its major tenants are Eaton's, The Bay, Sears, Woodwards, and Zellers. It also has 19 theatres or cinemas, a hotel, a 'Fantasyland' amusement park, an ice rink, and a waterpark (Fig. 13.1). The scale of this shopping centre suggests that it has crossed the threshold into the *mega*-regional category (Johnson, 1987). Lower down the hierarchy are the regional, community, and neighbourhood shopping centres; they have fewer shops and services and a smaller catchment population. Nevertheless, the smaller centres, with less than 20 000 sq m, accounted for over half of total sales and 85 per cent of the outlets in the USA in 1980 (Rogers, 1983).

This hierarchical classification is based on the experience of the development of free-standing shopping centres in North America. Kivell and Shaw (1980, p. 139) suggest that such a typology 'has little relevance for Britain, where the pace and scale of development has been entirely different'. However, by 1986 there were 299 planned shopping schemes in the United Kingdom of at least 10 764 sq m (100 000 sq ft) of gross leasable area (URPI, 1987). They are spread widely, although there are notable concentrations around Greater London, the West Midlands, Lancashire and Yorkshire, the North-East, and Clydeside (Fig. 13.2). The first large managed shopping scheme to open in the United Kingdom was the

TABLE 13.5 A classification of free-standing shopping centres

Type	Location	Size (sq m)	Character
Super-regional	Major metropolises middle to high income areas	100 000 +	100 + units; 3 + department stores; entertainment facilities, e.g. cinema, ice rink
Regional	Adjacent to major highway intersections	40 000–100 000	Catchment area of 100 000 + population; 1–3 anchor stores; parking for 4000 + cars
Community	Highway intersections and large new residential areas	10 000–40 000	Catchment area of 25 000–100 000 population; parking for 1000–1500 vehicles; anchored by discount department store or catalogue showroom
Neighbourhood	Local highway intersections in residential areas	3 000–10 000	Catchment of 8000–20 000 population; anchored by supermarket and/or drugstore; often associated with primary school, health centre and/or district library

Sources: Based on information in Dawson (1983a); Rogers (1983) and Daniels (1985a).

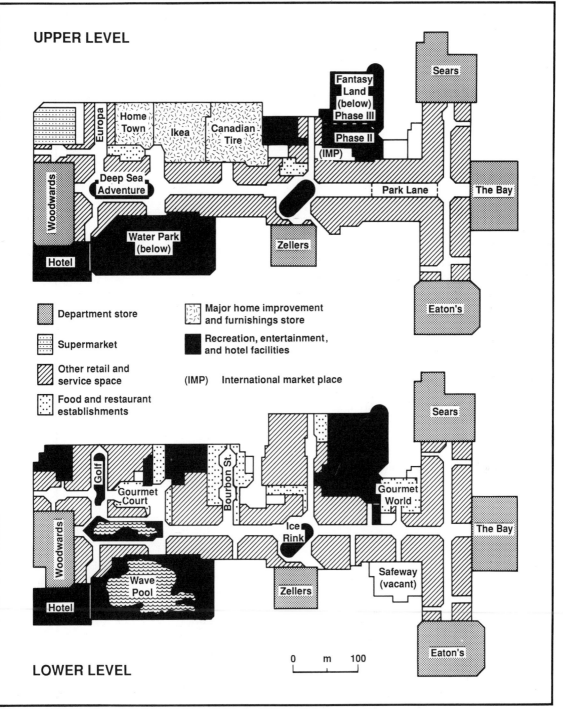

UPPER LEVEL

Sears

Fantasy Land (below) Phase III

Phase II

(IMP)

Home Town

Ikea

Canadian Tire

Europa

Woodwards

Deep Sea Adventure

Park Lane

The Bay

Water Park (below)

Zellers

Hotel

Eaton's

Department store

Major home improvement and furnishings store

Supermarket

Recreation, entertainment, and hotel facilities

Other retail and service space

Food and restaurant establishments

(IMP)   International market place

Sears

Golf

Bourbon St.

Gourmet Court

Gourmet World

Woodwards

Ice Rink

The Bay

Wave Pool

Zellers

Safeway (vacant)

Hotel

Eaton's

0   m   100

LOWER LEVEL

FIG 13.1 West Edmonton Mall, Alberta (*source:* Johnson, 1987 p. 56)

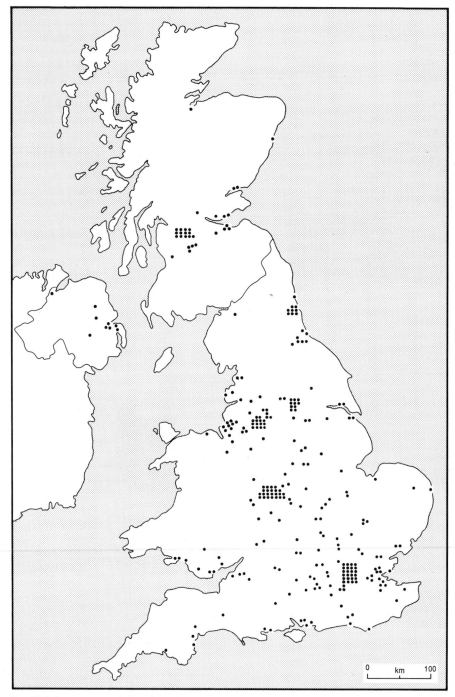

FIG 13.2 Large managed shopping schemes in the United Kingdom, January 1986
(*source:* based on data in URPI, 1987 pp. 327–34)

TABLE 13.6 The ten largest planned shopping schemes in the United Kingdom, January 1986

Name of scheme	Town	Gross leasable area (sq m)	Year opened
1. Arndale Centre	Manchester	109 907	1976
2. Central Milton Keynes	Milton Keynes	98 602	1979
3. Town Square	Basildon	74 694	1958
4. Eldon Square	Newcastle	72 222	1976
5. Brent Cross	London, Hendon	71 037	1976
6. Arndale Centre	Luton	64 815	1972
7. Kingfisher Centre	Redditch	62 583	1973
8. Telford Shopping Centre	Telford	60 185	1973
9. Queensgate Centre	Peterborough	60 185	1982
10. Cwmbran Shopping Centre	Cwmbran	59 546	1961

Source: URPI (1987 p. 3).

Queensway/Town Square development in Billingham, which opened in 1954. Prior to 1967 most schemes were built in or around Greater London (Bennison and Davies, 1980). The late 1960s and early 1970s witnessed the peak in numbers of new schemes opening. Three-quarters of them are located in the traditional town/city centre, only 22 per cent are free standing. The ten largest schemes at the beginning of 1986 are listed in Table 13.6. The majority of these were very large schemes opened in the 1970s. Of these ten, seven are located within part of the traditional town/city centre and no less than six have been built in New Towns.

There are indications that dramatic changes have occurred in retail developments in Britain in the second half of the 1980s. A recent authoritive review of shopping centre development (Dawson, 1983a) stated that there is only one strictly 'regional' shopping centre in Britain, opened in 1976 at Brent Cross in north-west London. Yet within three years of the publication of this book, Howard (1986) noted the existence of 35 regional out-of-town centre proposals, several of which are large enough to warrant the description 'super-regional', not that all of them will receive planning permission. The first of this new wave of shopping developments, which began trading in 1986, is the Metro Centre on the Gateshead enterprise zone. With 160 000 sq m of space, it is the largest shopping centre in Western Europe. It includes the largest Marks & Spencer branch in the country, and its first out-of town store; the first out-of-town venture for BHS and Littlewood, the first new style House of Fraser store, a

Carrefour store, a ten-screen cinema and Metro Land entertainment for children based on 'The Enchanted Land of King Wiz'.

The character of shopping centres differs by more than just size and location; they also vary in the way they have developed and the kind of store used to anchor the development. In France, for instance, Burt (1987) identifies three types of shopping centre development:

1. *Hypermarket focused centres*. These are particularly common in France having evolved from 'stand alone' hypermarkets. The developer is usually the company operating the hypermarket. There were 629 of them in 1986. A good example is Valentin at Besançon which is based on a Carrefour hypermarket with 36 other units and cafés.

2. *Regional shopping centres*. They developed in France earlier than in the United Kingdom. Most opened between 1971 and 1975. Some are in traditional town centres (e.g. Forum in the centre of Paris); others are in new towns or in out of town/peripheral locations. Most of the latter are in the Paris region. Many are being renovated. Although originally focused on department stores many have changed their anchor store to food hypermarkets. This change reflects both the poor performance of many department stores and the planning restrictions on new hypermarkets, which means that hypermarket companies are increasingly looking for outlets within existing centres.

3. *Factory outlets and off-price centres*. These are the latest shopping centre developments in France. The first factory outlet, A L'Usine in

Roubaix, selling cheaply at production prices, opened in 1983. By 1987 there were 17 of them. Most of them sell end-of-the-range textile products. The first off-price centre in Europe, '-X%', opened in 1985 at Île-St-Denis in Paris. It specializes in selling goods at a discount.

The development of planned shopping centres has contributed to the trend towards retail decentralization, although the extent varies between countries. For example, in North America planned shopping centres are predominantly found in the suburbs or sometimes on major highways between towns, while in Britain and, to a lesser extent, France they are more common in the central areas of towns and cities.

Decentralization of retailing

A major feature of post-war retail change in developed market economies has been the relative decline of the central area as the locus of retailing activity and the relative growth of retailing in suburban and out of town locations. Decentralization is not a new trend. It dates from at least the 1890s in North America (Vance, 1962), while as long ago as 1609 retailers in central London were bitterly opposed to the construction of an out-of-town shopping centre in the then suburban location of The Strand (Davis, 1966). Nevertheless, the trend accelerated after the Second World War and nowhere more so than in North America, where decentralization has been a feature of the development of towns and cities of all sizes.

In the United States, for instance, the proportion of retail sales in suburban major retail centres surpassed that attributable to the central business districts (CBDs) in 1962 (Fig. 13.3). The intersection percentage is relatively low (14 per cent) because the CBDs had been declining in significance for several years, while the rapid growth of the main retail centres reflects the widespread diffusion of planned shopping centres in the 1950s (Kellerman, 1985b). In several North American and Australian cities the CBD is no longer the largest shopping centre. For instance, Atlanta City has three suburban centres which have larger retail sales than the CBD, while the Woden Centre in the southern suburbs of Canberra has greater retail power and sales than the city centre. The decline of the CBD has gone so far in Detroit that it no longer has a single department store in the central area. Lord (1987a) suggests that New York and Chicago are probably the only two cities in the United States where the CBD is likely to remain, in the foreseeable future, the largest retail centre in the metropolitan area.

In contrast to North American experience, the decline of the CBD has been much less marked in Europe, but even in Britain decline has occurred (Dawson and Kirby, 1980). Indeed, Schiller (1986) has identified three overlapping *waves of decentralization* which have occurred in post-war Britain. The first, which commenced in the 1960s and reached its peak in the late 1970s, centred upon the food-based superstore. The second wave, which reached its height in the late 1980s, involves discount retail warehouses selling non-

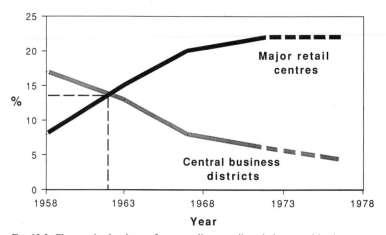

FIG 13.3 Changes in the share of metropolitan retail trade in central business districts and major retail centres (*source:* Kellerman, 1985b p. 21)

food bulky goods like flat pack furniture, carpets, DIY, and electrical equipment. The third, and most recent, wave of retail decentralization comprises the opening of regional shopping centres selling the traditional mainstays of High Street retailing—clothing, jewellery, shoes, and so on, such as the Metro Centre, Gateshead.

The reasons for the suburbanization of retailing may be analysed under five headings—demand changes, organizational changes, land and labour, technological changes, and planning policies. Differences in the relative importance of the five groups of factors help to account for the dispersed pattern of retail trade found in North America and Australia compared with the more concentrated pattern found in Europe, particularly Britain.

Demand changes

Shopping habits have changed in the post-war period. There has been a reduction in the frequency of short, daily shopping trips for small quantities of convenience goods and an increase in weekly bulk purchase trips. This reflects increased personal mobility, the growth of female employment, and the increased use of freezers. These changes have encouraged the growth of family weekend and evening shopping and increased demand for one-stop shopping centres. Demographic and life style changes have also encouraged marketing organizations to move away from the uni-dimensional view of consumers to one which recognizes highly specific consumer groups. This has resulted in the development of stores carefully designed to appeal to particular market segments.

More fundamental in accounting for retail decentralization, however, has been the shift in the population to the suburbs. Indeed, Dawson (1974 p. 156) has argued that 'the primary factor responsible for the growth of suburban retail activity is the decentralization of the demand'. The move of the younger, better off, and more mobile sections of society to the suburbs created a large source of demand which was under-served by retailing outlets. For example, in Nottingham the suburban population grew by a third between 1951 and 1968, while the number of retail outlets provided grew by only a tenth (Giggs, 1972). The severe under-provision of retailing in many suburbs has also been suggested as an important

influence on retail decentralization in France and Germany (Law et al., 1988).

Nevertheless, it is not entirely clear whether the suburbanization of retailing is primarily a response to changing patterns of demand or whether demand is being shaped by the locational strategies of retailers. The latter is becoming a distinct possibility with the organizational changes which have affected retailing over the last thirty years.

Organizational changes

The methods and organization of retailing have changed dramatically in the period following the Second World War. These have included the wide-scale adoption of self-service, the development of cash and carry wholesalers, the emergence of superstores and discount stores, and the growth of mail-order companies. Collectively, these changes have blurred the traditional distinction between wholesaling and retailing and reduced the dependency of retail establishments on the wholesaling facilities which were once concentrated in and around the central area.

Associated with these changes in the method and organization of retailing has been a change in the scale of retailing organizations. Economies of bulk purchasing have encouraged the growth of multiples or chain stores; while the development of superstores, hypermarkets, and retail warehouses has encouraged decentralization from high-cost crowded city centres (Dawson, 1984; Jones, 1984). The distinction between these types of units is largely based on a combination of size, function, and type of building (TEST, 1989). Superstores usually have a net floorspace of at least 2500 sq m (smaller units are referred to as supermarkets) and sell predominantly convenience goods. British examples include larger units of Sainsbury, Tesco, and ASDA. Hypermarkets, on the other hand, usually have a minimum net floorspace of 5000 sq m divided between grocery and durable goods. The first in Britain was a Carrefour hypermarket in Caerphilly, South Wales, while a more recent development in the chain of SavaCentres in which originally Sainsbury and BHS shared the same selling space in one building. Retail warehouses are usually of a similar size to superstores (2500 + sq m), but are occupied predominantly by furniture, carpet, and DIY retailers, such as MFI, Allied Carpet, and Texas Homecare. Initially many occupied converted factories or garages frequently are on industrial estates, but they are increasingly using purpose-built units on retail parks, such as in the Lower Swansea Valley (Thomas and Bromley, 1987).

The corollary of these changes seems at first to have been the decline in the number of small units, particularly corner shops. For example, the number of independent shops, most of which are small, declined in the United Kingdom from 450 000 in 1951 to 230 000 in 1981 (Dawson, 1983a). However, more recently there seems to have been a revival of small convenience units, although most are franchised rather than independent. The net outcome of these changes is that large retail companies have increased in significance so that by 1984 large companies controlling over 100 retail outlets accounted for 42 per cent of retail turnover compared with 33 per cent in 1976 (Howard and Davies, 1988).

The increased concentration of ownership has meant that the locational strategies of major retail groups can have a significant influence on the pattern of retail provision. For example, ASDA stores were founded in 1965 when Associated Dairies, a Leeds-based dairy group, combined with a local supermarket. Within fifteen years they had moved out of their West Yorkshire base and opened over 70 stores as far afield as Aberdeen, Chelmsford, and Plymouth. By 1987 it operated 15 stores and 99 superstores. In searching for likely sites the investigators examine the population of the area, the location of likely competitors, and the road network in the area. On average ASDA superstores have 120 000 people within a three-mile radius (Jones, 1981). Although some of the early stores were opened in high street locations, more recent ones have tended to locate in a variety of usually suburban places including edge of town locations (e.g. Merthyr Tydfil), in new urban areas (e.g. outskirts of Aberdeen) or in redeveloped areas (e.g. Crewe). Many of the locations chosen are areas previously poorly served by retail provision, although competitors have sometimes followed their lead. For instance, ASDA opened a superstore on the edge of Lincoln in 1970, since then Woolco, Tesco, Sainsbury, and Hillards (later taken over by Tesco) have all opened large stores in and around the city (Jones, 1981).

The trend towards fewer but larger stores is, to an extent, counterbalanced by a renaissance of

the small shop sector. The geographical dispersal of hypermarket style operations provides an opportunity for the growth of convenience stores situated in easily accessible locations, usually in the suburbs, and providing a wide range but limited assortment of fast-moving merchandise. Such small shops complement rather than compete with the large stores in that they provide 'essential "emergency" and topping-up facilities for one-stop shoppers and cater for those unwilling or unable to patronise the larger, bulk order-orientated outlets' (Brown, 1987a p. 158). A good illustration of the growth of convenience stores is shown by the development of 7-Eleven stores. From 2000 stores in the United States in 1960 the chain grew to 20 000 in 1973 and 30 000 in 1977. Much of this growth has been in the residential suburbs of large and medium-sized cities. The Southland Corporation owns around 60 per cent of the stores and franchises the rest. 'The art of the 7-Eleven contractual and corporate chain is the replication of a total retail service in every store in the chain. The atmosphere, the layout of goods, the location, the total retail experience is the same in suburban Baltimore as in ... suburban Oakland' (Dawson and Kirby, 1980 pp. 122–3). The Southland Corporation has also franchised 7-Eleven stores in many other countries including Australia, Japan, and Britain.

The growing polarity in operating scale in retailing is paralleled by polarity in the range of merchandise provided and the extent to which a sales policy is based on price or service (Table 13.7). It is suggested that developments at one end of the retail spectrum induce activity at the other end (Brown 1987a, 1987b). In contemporary Britain the balance

appears to be tipping towards the positions occupied by the rapidly growing numbers of small specialists (Next, Benetton, Principles and so on) and convenience stores (Cullens, 7-Eleven, Martins etc) and away from that held by departmental and variety stores and, to some extent, superstores and hypermarkets ... The multi-polarisation model, in short, contends that inventory diversification inspires specialisation, large outlets beget small and a high level of service gives rise to no-frills retail operations (Brown, 1987a p. 160).

Although the model attempts to account only for changes in the nature of retailing rather than locational trends, it could be suggested that attempts to protect city-centre retailing only increase the pressures for retail decentralization,

TABLE 13.7 The polarization of retail institutional formats

Merchandise assortment	Sales policy	Establishment size	Institutional type	Examples
Broad	Price	Large	Superstore, hypermarket	Asda, Tesco
Broad	Price	Small	Catalogue showroom	Argos, Littlewoods Catalogue Shop
Broad	Service	Large	Department store	John Lewis, Debenhams
Broad	Service	Small	Convenience store	7-Eleven, Cullens
Narrow	Price	Large	Retail warehouse	Toys 'R' Us, Texstyle World
Narrow	Price	Small	Limited line discount store	Kwik Save, Victor Value
Narrow	Service	Large	'Super' specialist	Ultimate, Hamleys
Narrow	Service	Small	Specialist	Next, Tie Rack

Source: Brown (1987a p. 159).

while excessive decentralization might possibly encourage some return to the city centre, particularly if at the same time there is a revitalization of small retail units.

Land and labour

One of the major factors encouraging decentralization has been the high cost of land in city centres, which has made it very expensive for the major land users, such as the large grocery and furniture stores, to maintain their city-centre sites. As the average size of store has increased, so the demands for more space are increasingly difficult to meet in the city centres. The push away from the central areas is matched by the pull asserted by the developers of the out-of-centre shopping schemes. In order to fill their retail developments, the managers of the shopping centres need to make them attractive to the retailers. It is critically important for them to attract the large stores which because of their anticipated power to draw customers will 'anchor' the development.

A further factor encouraging decentralization is access to labour. The suburbanization of the population has not only shifted the locus of demand away from the city centre, it has also moved the labour force. Retailing is becoming increasingly dependent on a part-time female labour force. For example, two-thirds of the workforce of Sainsbury and Marks & Spencer work less than 16 hours, while the figure for ASDA is 84 per cent (Gavin, 1988). The ease of access to this primarily suburban labour pool benefits many out-of-centre shopping complexes.

Technological changes

Technological changes are an important influence on suburbanization because they have affected both the spatial pattern of demand and the locational behaviour of the retailers. Perhaps the most important technological change permitting the decentralization of retailing has been the increased availability of motor cars. However, the impact has had a differential social effect. Whereas higher income groups have been able to take advantage of the new suburban retail opportunities, lower income groups, dependent on public transport, have continued to rely largely on local and central shops which are relatively, and sometimes absolutely, declining in number, range, and quality. Technological changes in transportation and organization have also contributed to the trend towards fewer, larger units and the growth in the importance of multiple retailers referred to in the last section.

There has been much discussion in recent years on the potential impact of information technology (IT) on retailing. A recent review noted that IT is mainly used as a labour-saving device which will further reduce the quantity and quality of employment in retailing (Guy, 1985a). For example, the increased use of electronic point-of-sale (EPOS) scanning equipment is having a major effect on store efficiency and stock control (Chapter 6.3 and Table 13.4). Another innovation, which may slow down the rate of suburbanization, is teleshopping.

Remote shopping using the telecommunication network is particularly interesting because it has the potential to reduce the number of shopping trips, to make the consumer's choice of retail outlet independent of his or her distance from the firm's nearest suitable shop and to replace some retail stores by retail warehouses. There is considerable disagreement in the literature about the extent to which the choice and ordering of goods using viewdata or cable television will be a substitute for other forms of shopping. It has the potential for helping consumers who have problems of access to shops, as witnessed by the successful experiment in Gateshead in remote shopping, which was aimed specifically at the disadvantaged (Davies, 1985). However, American experience suggests that the likely users of viewdata are 'under 45 years of age, in households with two working adults, and are concerned about organising sufficient information to shop efficiently' (Howard, 1985 p. 149). North American developments in teleshopping are more numerous than in the United Kingdom, but with the more rapid spread of cable television in Britain, along with a greater national penetration of multiple stores and the more compact market, Britain may have a greater potential for the growth of teleshopping than North America.

Experience to date suggests that the impact of teleshopping will be gradual, limited, and selective.

Viewdata shopping will probably have the greatest competitive impact on existing methods of 'nonstore retailing' (for example, mail order) and unconventional retailing (for example, catalogue sales). The main locational implications are, first, accelerated rates of change in the use of retail and service premises within city centres, and, secondly, some reduction in recent rates of increase in the use of retail and surburban 'retail warehouses' (Guy, 1985b p. 193).

Growth in the demand for showroom facilities in city centres, combined with some decrease in the importance of free-standing centres in the suburbs, amounts to a slowing down of the trend towards suburbanization of retailing activity. Guy (1985b p. 207) goes as far as to suggest that 'speculation about a reversal of this trend, because of increasing costs of personal transport, as much as from the effects of viewdata and other technological advances, may be justified.' It may be premature, however, to suggest an end to the well-established trend of retail decentralization.

Planning policies
There is a marked difference between the attitude of local authorities to retail development in North America and Western Europe. A major reason for the more extensive suburbanization of retailing in North America is that there has been little planning controls over this decentralization. In contrast, the most stringent planning controls over retailing in the Western world operate in the United Kingdom. Further, the control over the decentralization of retailing has been more stringent than over either manufacturing or office activities, although there are indications that the degree of control has weakened in recent years. The debate over decentralization in Britain has revolved around three main issues (Davies, 1976, 1978):

1. *Economic issues.* These concern the extent to which public and private investment in the central area needs protection from the greater competitive advantage that large stores have in suburbs. Most local authorities have policies in their structure plans which aim to maintain the status quo in respect of the trading relationships amongst shopping districts within their authority (Burt et al., 1983). However, the potential deterimental effect of suburban and out-of-town superstore and hypermarket developments seems to have been exaggerated in the past. Most research suggests that the impact on employment and sales in competing centres and stores tends to be widely diffused, rather than concentrated (Howard and Davies, 1988). An indication that the effect on the city centre is not very great is that many of the chain stores maintain their city-centre branches after setting up units in the suburbs. For instance, a study of a suburban unplanned retail park, located in the Swansea Enterprise Zone about 7 km from the city centre, found that the mixture of superstores and retail warehouses did not constitute a strong competitive threat to the city centre, but did have a stronger competitive relationship with the nearby middle-order shopping centres (Thomas and Bromley, 1987).

2. *Social issues.* It is sometimes argued that allowing major suburban retail development produces inequity in retailing provision between the middle-class, car-oriented suburban centres and the traditional shopping centres which may become more impoverished and run down. Again the case is often exaggerated. Inequity already exists in the retail system and Davies (1976 p. 176) argues that 'although attention needs to be given to the requirements of minority groups, there is

no reason why the majority should be deprived of a greater choice'.

3. *Environmental issues.* Planners in Britain are cautious of any developments which may contribute to urban sprawl. So edge-of-town and out-of-town applications for retail development are looked at critically for their effects on the green belt. This is one reason why the out-of-town superstore common in North America is usually an in-town development in the United Kingdom. On the other hand, the arguments for maintaining retailing in the centre have recently beenturned on their heads. Many town centres suffer from too much traffic, not enough car parking, and development demands which conflict with conservation policies which may be relieved by building out-of-centre (Howard and Davies, 1988).

Not surprisingly local authorities have varied in their responses to these three issues. This may be illustrated by examining the distribution of retail warehouses in London (A. Gibbs, 1987). Considerable variation exists between boroughs in both inner and outer London (Fig. 13.4). In outer London, for instance, Merton and Brent (296 sq m and 259 sq m of retail warehouse floorspace per 1000 people in 1986) both have quite flexible attitudes towards the development of retail warehouses, while in neighbouring Sutton and Richmond, which each have levels of provision below the *inner* London average (25 sq m per thousand people), restrictive policies have been strictly enforced.

One of the reasons for the restrictions imposed in many European countries on the

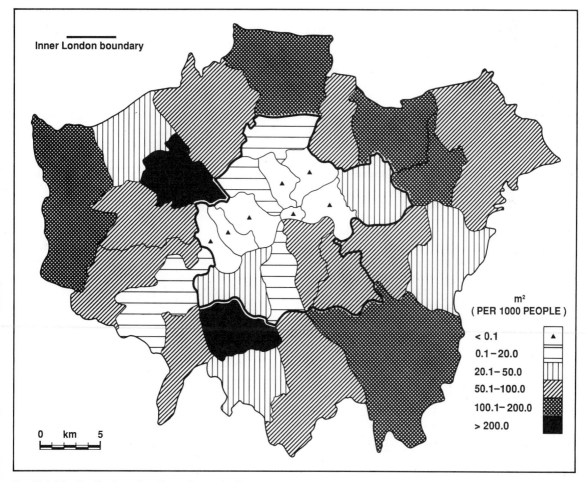

Inner London boundary

m²
(PER 1000 PEOPLE)

< 0.1
0.1 – 20.0
20.1 – 50.0
50.1 – 100.0
100.1 – 200.0
> 200.0

0   km   5

FIG 13.4 The distribution of retail warehouses in Greater London, 1986 (*source:* based on data in A. Gibbs, 1987 p. 596)

decentralization of retailing has been the desire to protect the retailing provision in city centres. In Britain, the modernization of retailing has usually occurred as part of a wider programme of re-development involving all types of land use. Some attempts have also been made to revitalize retailing in the central area of North American cities. However, although particular central area schemes, such as the Gallery in Philadelphia and Nicollet Mall in Minneapolis, have been successful, the early optimism has gradually given way to pessimism as physical deterioration has occurred in the modernized stores and decline of the city centre has set in again (Gross, 1978). Although there are examples of this cycle in European cities, it seems less prevalent than in North America.

As the process of decentralization of retailing continues and the relative accessibility of suburban centres improves, the city centres, particularly in North America, are losing their metropolitan shoppers. Nevertheless, they still have a captive market of city-centre employees and residents and visitors to the central area and an increasing number of revitalization schemes in the central area are being oriented towards these more diverse markets. Many are small-scale specialist projects, such as the craft centre at The Rocks, a renovated historical building by Sydney Harbour bridge, but complete redevelopment of large areas, such as Fisherman's Wharf in San Francisco and Quince Market/Faneuil Hall in Boston, have also taken place.

Many trends in retailing are cyclical, such as institutional formats, advertising styles, shop hours. Some writers have suggested that the same may be true of locational trends. They point to trends in the United States with retail activity 'originally focused in the city centre, massive decentralization and subsequent recovery of the urban core' (Brown, 1987a p. 161). However, the trend towards further decentralization in the United States still continues (Lord 1987a; Robertson, 1983). In Britain also, though the extent of suburbanization has been much less and the investment in redevelopment of central areas far more, the trend towards decentralization is unmistakable (Dawson, 1988). The prime factor influencing the suburbanization of retail activity is the decentralization of demand, and until this changes it is unlikely that there will be a reversal of retail location trends.

13.2 Recent changes in the location of producer services

The change from an industrial to a post-industrial economic system is now well under way in developed market economies (Chapter 1.3). This involves a gradual shift of emphasis from goods-producing to information-handling activities which are predominantly concentrated among service rather than manufacturing industries. Prime among the information-handling activities are the producer service industries, sometimes also referred to as business services. Producer service firms provide their output to other firms. They include insurance, banking, finance, other business services such as advertising and market research, and professional and scientific services such as accountancy, legal services, and research and development (Howells and Green, 1986). Some authorities also include in this category the distribution and storage of goods, office cleaning, and security services (Daniels, 1985a; Marshall et al., 1988).

Producer services make an important contribution to the economies of developed nations and many cities in particular. In the United States, for example, Stanback et al. (1981) estimate that producer services contributed more than 25 per cent of GNP in the late 1970s, thereby accounting for more value added than the manufacturing sector; while a study of the Central Puget Sound economy in Washington State found that half of the region's exports were coming from services (Beyers et al., 1986). It has further been suggested that the relative shortage of business services in peripheral areas is a major handicap which impedes the ability of their manufacturing sectors to grow and prosper (Marshall, 1985).

Identifying the true significance of producer services is not, however, easy in practice, for two main reasons. First, a large proportion of employment classified as manufacturing is not directly concerned with production (e.g. market researchers, accountants, security staff)—Gudgin et al. (1979) suggests about a third in the United Kingdom—and many in manufacturing are doing similar, and in theory interchangeable, jobs to those working for specialist producer service firms. Secondly, many services, such as insurance, banking, and transport, serve both a business and a consumer market. Attempts have been made to reduce the latter problem by estimating the proportion of jobs in each service industry which belong to the producer category. For example, Greenfield (1966) suggests that the proportion of all employment in the United States which was producer oriented grew from 12.5 per cent in 1950 to 13.2 per cent in 1960. An indication that this growth trend has continued comes from the estimate by P. W. Daniels (1986) that producer services accounted for almost 22 per cent of total employment in Britain in 1980, or one in three jobs within the service sector.

The spatial distribution of producer services is more uneven than that of consumer services such as retailing (Marquand, 1983). Producer services are concentrated in the city centres, large city regions, and in particular areas, such as the South-East of the United Kingdom and the North-East of the United States (Noyelle and Stanback, 1984; P. W. Daniels, 1986). Recent locational changes in producer services in developed market economies are therefore starting from a locational pattern which is already markedly uneven. Some of the recent locational shifts are reducing the disparities in the distribution of producer service industries, while others are widening them. However, the effect varies between countries. For example, at the interregional scale there is a shift towards the more prosperous regions. In Britain, this is leading to an increasing concentration in the South, while in the USA it is leading to a spread of producer service industries to the South and West. At the interurban scale the trend is less clear, the large metropolitan areas remain attractive (i.e. *metropolitanization*) although there is some indication of *downfiltering* occurring away from the largest metropolitan centres, but this tendency towards dispersion is to an extent countered by the opposite tendency for the relative share of producer service employment in smaller centres to be declining. The clearest and most consistent trend is happening within metropolitan areas where *decentralization* is leading to a more widespread distribution of producer services (Alexander, 1979; Stanback *et al.*, 1981; Gillespie and Green, 1987; Kirn, 1987).

Not all producer service industries, however, exhibit a similar locational behaviour. R. & D., in the United Kingdom for instance, while concentrated in the core-areas, shows a preference for location in small non-industrialized market towns within metropolitan spheres of influence (Chapter 6.2; Gillespie and Green, 1987). Banking in the United States provides another exception, in that it increased its concentration in large metropolitan areas whereas the proportion of most business studies located in the large metropolitan areas declined (Kirn, 1987).

The dominance of large metropolitan centres can be seen clearly by examining the location of 'corporate activities' (i.e. head offices, divisional offices, and business services) in the United States. Both in 1959 and 1976, only centres with a population of over one million had location quotients of over one (i.e. they had a higher proportion of employment in corporate activities than would be expected on the basis of their share of all employment). The trend, however, shows that it is the centres with between 0.5 and 2 million population which have gained relatively at the expense of both the largest and smallest metropolitan centres (Table 13.8). Nevertheless, Stanback *et al.*, (1981, p. 108) conclude their analysis of the transformation of the American urban system by noting that 'the most innovative dimensions of the transformation at work—which features the development of new services and the birth of new service based firms—have been and will remain strongly restricted to those metropolitan centres that are already well established as part of the service economy.'

A similar pattern of concentration and 'downfiltering' is apparent in Britain. Howells and Green (1986) found that 34 per cent of all employment in producer services in 1981 was located in London. London also had the highest relative concentration of producer service employment in the country with a location quotient of 1.85. The extent of this concentration is, however, decreasing. In 1971, for instance, London accounted for 40 per cent of producer service employment in Great Britain. Over the same decade there was a slight shift in favour of the other metropolitan regions, while in national core–periphery terms the domination of the South was maintained and slightly reinforced (Table 13.9).

A more dramatic spatial trend than inter-urban downfiltering of producer service employment has been decentralization within regions. In Britain, for example, the deconcentration within metropolitan regions has led to growth frequently spilling over into free-standing cities and towns which surround them in both the North and

TABLE 13.8 Employment in corporate activity complexes by size of Standard Metropolitan Statistical Area (SMSA) in the United States

Population size: range of SMSA	Location quotient		Share of all employment	
	1959	1976	1959	1976
More than 2 million	1.41	1.36	14.4	20.0
1 to 2 million	1.10	1.13	11.2	16.6
0.5 to 1 million	0.94	0.99	9.6	14.6
0.25 to 0.5 million	0.88	0.84	9.0	12.4
Less than 0.25 million	0.61	0.59	6.3	8.7
TOTAL US	1.00	1.00	10.2	14.7

Source: Based on Stanback *et al.* (1981 pp. 92, 94–5).

South of the country (Gillespie and Green, 1987). In the United States the decentralization trend has gone even further. A recent feature has been the development of office parks in the suburbs. In Morris County, New Jersey, for instance, about 30 km from downtown Manhattan, there were at least 15 office parks established by the early 1980s, most of which were developed since the late 1970s (Daniels, 1985a). Among the attractions of the area are the lowest county tax rate in New Jersey, modern interstate highways, a 'good' labour pool and educational facilities, and proximity to the centre of New York.

A model of the evolution of office-based pro-

TABLE 13.9 Change in producer service employment in local labour market areas (LLMAs) in Britain, 1971–1981

LLMA class	Example	Location quotient		Employment share	
		1971	1981	1971	1981
London	London	2.04	1.85	40.3	34.1
Conurbation dominants	Manchester	1.04	1.07	13.1	12.0
Provincial dominants	Edinburgh	0.92	0.99	6.4	6.9
Sub-regional dominants	Portsmouth	0.68	0.84	6.6	4.3
London subdominant cities	Southend	1.17	1.21	3.1	3.6
London subdominant towns	Maidenhead	0.99	1.05	4.2	5.0
Conurbation subdominant cities	Motherwell	0.44	0.58	2.6	3.1
Conburbation subdominant towns	Northwich	0.55	0.69	2.2	2.8
Smaller northern subdominants	Rugby	0.35	0.40	1.7	2.0
Southern free-standing cities	Norwich	0.84	0.94	5.6	7.0
Northern free-standing cities	Derby	0.59	0.63	4.2	4.5
Southern service towns	Canterbury	0.82	0.84	2.9	3.4
Southern commercial towns	Trowbridge	0.78	0.78	2.2	2.5
Southern manufacturing towns	Wellingborough	0.61	0.77	1.1	1.6
Northern service towns	Llandudno	0.75	0.67	1.4	1.4
Northern commercial towns	Hereford	0.48	0.50	1.7	1.8
Northern manufacturing towns	Scunthorpe	0.39	0.45	1.1	1.2
Southern rural areas	Penzance	0.72	0.89	1.0	1.4
Northern rural areas	Penrith	0.72	0.63	1.6	1.6
GREAT BRITAIN	—	1.00	1.00	100.0	100.0

Sources: Howells and Green (1986 p. 113); Gillespie and Green (1987 pp. 403, 405).

ducer service location within metropolitan areas has been suggested by Daniels (1985a, p. 225). It has four phases (Fig. 13.5). Prior to 1960 it assumes a highly centralized location pattern focused on the central business district (CBD). The 1960s see the beginnings of dispersion with random locations being chosen by individual companies, while the 1970s see the beginnings of suburban clusters of offices at the intersections of highways or, in Europe, at interchanges of public and private transport. Finally, in the 1980s further concentration occurs in selected suburban

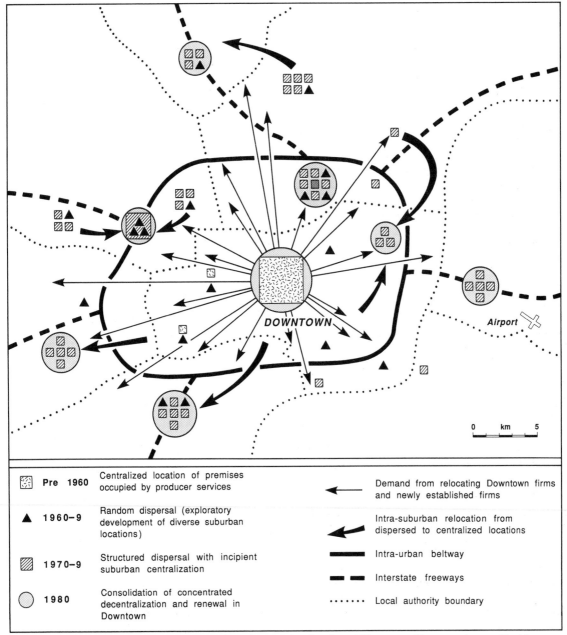

FIG 13.5 A model of the evolution of office-based producer services location within metropolitan areas (*source:* Daniels, 1985a, p. 225)

locations as firms seek the kind of agglomeration advantages they originally found in the CBD.

The pattern of concentrated dispersal of producer services so far described relates to all employment. However, the pattern is rather different if the quality of the jobs is taken into account. What evidence is available suggests that the spatial trends have tended to polarize, with the higher status jobs becoming concentrated and the lower status jobs more dispersed. This trend seems to apply at both the interregional and intraregional scales. In Britain, for example, the evidence suggests an increasing concentration of higher status jobs in London and the South, while lower status jobs are becoming more evenly distributed across the regions (Howells and Green, 1986). There are also indications that while higher status jobs are remaining concentrated in central areas of cities, many lower status jobs are being decentralized (Marquand, 1979).

This decentralization of lower status producer service jobs (and indeed in offices more generally) reflects an emerging spatial division of labour, based on the growth of 'back offices'. According to Nelson (1986, p. 149) a back office is 'a consolidation of corporate internal services that require little face-to-face contact with either the corporate personnel they support or with the extra-corporate world.' Examples of such internal services are computer operations, accounting, payroll, billing, and certain office-based (i.e. non-laboratory) technical or research activities. Back offices are highly automated and employ a high proportion of low paid clerical labour. Nelson notes that in the San Francisco Bay Area during the late 1970s and 1980s there was an accelerating trend for corporations to separate their back-office functions from their headquarters, divisional offices and other 'front-office' activities and to relocate them away from the central area. In the Bay Area this has led to a major concentration in one particular area, the sub-region along Interstate 680, particularly in central Contra Costa.

Clearly the producer service sector has recently experienced a variety of different spatial trends within developed market economies. The remainder of this section examines the factors which may help to explain this variety. The factors are discussed under similar headings—demand changes; organizational changes; land and labour; technological changes; and government—to those used

earlier in the chapter in examining the decentralization of retailing.

Demand changes

Changes in demand are significant in affecting both the growth and the spatial patterns of producer services. The changing demand for producer services reflects five main influences (Gillespie and Green, 1987; Marshall et al., 1988).

1. The growth of large organizations has increased the demand for existing producer services, including design, R. & D., marketing and advertising, and created a demand for new services, such as information systems and data-processing services. This, in part, reflects the increasing administrative overheads which accompany the growing scale of organizations, particularly in the areas of co-ordination and integration (Stanback et al., 1981).

2. The increased complexity of regulations and technological changes has encouraged the growth of services such as training and consultancy. As Marshall et al. (1985, p. 24) note:

The pace and complexity of economic and technical change have necessitated greater utilisation of more specialised services by the production sector, for example in research, design and development, marketing, training, finance and investment. Essentially competition in the modern industrial system requires firms to be adaptive and responsive, depending upon elaborate intelligence gathering and the ability to process and act upon specialist information effectively.

3. Structural changes within services have also led to a decline in demand for some services and an increase in demand for others. Some physical distribution services, for instance, have been affected by the contraction in manufacturing industry; while the demand for other producer services, such as management consultancy and accountancy, has increased. Demand for new services, many associated with information technology, such as the provision of on-line data bases, has also been growing very rapidly.

4. A further source of demand for producer services is an increase in the extent to which firms subcontract out services. In some cases this has been encouraged by recession. For example, in an attempt to remain competitive some large manufacturing firms have introduced flexible working schemes involving the subcontracting of routine services. In the United Kingdom, cut-backs in

public expenditure and the preference of the Conservative government for the private sector have also encouraged the externalization of services such as cleaning, catering, and maintenance (Howells and Green, 1986).

5. Increased competition is also encouraging a growth in producer services as more companies enter the market place. This is, in part, related to the internationalization of services such as banking, finance, management consultancy, and advertising. In Britain it also reflects the trend towards the privatization of services, such as telecommunications, and the deregulation of financial services, which has removed restrictions on firms trading in the City.

These changes in the pattern of demand have had significant, though often contrasting, spatial effects. For example, on the one hand, the growth in demand is encouraging 'downfiltering' as thresholds for specific services are reached at lower levels of the urban hierarchy where demand had previously been inadequate to support high-order services (Kirn, 1987). On the other hand, the trend towards increased externalization of services is favouring the continued centralization of business services by encouraging the expansion of national service companies located in major metropolitan areas. Such companies tend to provide services either centrally, as with computer services; or, where frequent physical contact is required, as with cleaning, maintenance, and security services, through low-order branches of the national, centrally located, service company (Howells and Green, 1986). It has also been suggested that, because specialization and diversification of economic activities tend to be greater in more urbanized locations, the tendency to subcontract services will increase with city size (Stanback et al., 1981), and thus contribute to the metropolitanization of producer services. A further example of the impact of demand changes on the location of producer services arises from the decentralization of population and other economic activities. For instance, the decentralization of retailing has encouraged the growth of the distribution of food and drink in the suburbs and out-of-town locations.

Organizational changes
As with the manufacturing sector, a major trend in the last forty years among service industries has been the growth of large companies. The small firm sector, however, has also prospered. This suggests that a dual economy may be developing in the service sector, leading to a squeezing out of medium-sized firms. Supporting evidence for this proposition has been found in the United Kingdom computer services industry and more generally in the British and European services sector (Howells and Green, 1986; Howells, 1987).

The level of employment concentration in large firms varies widely within the producer service sector. The financial sector, such as banking, is highly concentrated, while most professional services, such as solicitors, are highly fragmented. The general trend is for an increase in concentration. Associated with this has been the recent growth of international service companies. For example, Coopers and Lybrand, the accountancy and management consultancy firm, has over 2000 partners and 400 offices world-wide; while Saatchi and Saatchi, the largest business service company and fifth largest advertiser in the world, has 150 offices. The trend towards internationalization reflects not only the search for profitable opportunities, but also the fact that many of their clients have become international and to provide a full service they need to match their customers locational networks. A further recent phenomenon involving large companies has been that of diversification. Some manufacturing companies have diversified into services; for example, British American Tobacco (BAT) moved into insurance in 1984 with the take-over of the Eagle Star Group. Many service companies are also diversifying within services; for instance, several British estate agents (real estate) were taken over in the late 1980s by banks and insurance companies (Howells and Green, 1986; Marshall et al., 1988).

The increasing concentration of economic activity in large corporations has important implications for the location of producer services and helps to account for the trend towards spatial concentration in metropolitan areas. This is because large companies tend to locate their high-order service functions, such as financial and planning activities, at their head offices which are concentrated in large metropolitan areas. Indeed, there are indications that the head offices of service companies in general are more concentrated than their manufacturing counterparts (Goddard and Smith, 1978). Large companies also internalize a large proportion of their service activities and those which are subcontracted tend to go to firms in close proximity to their head offices. The growth in the number of 'back offices' may be seen as another example of the effect of the increasing importance of locational hierarchies among large corporations (Chapter 7.2).

The process by which large firms grow also contributes to concentration in particular regions, especially where this occurs through the acquisition of other companies. In the United Kingdom, many of these mergers involve companies based in the South-East taking over companies located in the provinces. The rationalization which usually follows mergers frequently leads to the centralization of service functions in the South-East and a reduced demand in the provinces (Leigh and North, 1978). The effects of external control on business service linkages may be illustrated by a study in the Northern region of Great Britain. Among business service firms in the North, almost 70 per cent of the major service suppliers to branch offices were from outside the Northern region, compared with less than a quarter for independent firms (Marshall, 1982). External dependence for service linkages can be a major constraint on the economic development of the regions involved. A similar observation is made by Noyelle and Stanback (1983) in interpreting spatial variations in the growth of producer services in the United States. They conclude that places classified as production centres (e.g. Buffalo) and functional-nodal centres (e.g. Detroit) are not sharing in the expansion of the producer services, in large part because their economies are dominated by industrial activity that is controlled or managed from elsewhere, thereby failing to create local demand for the producer services.

A further factor which seems to be contributing to the spatial concentration of the producer service sector is the beginning of internationalization. Although there is a lack of evidence in this area, Howells and Green (1986) suggest that it is highly likely that United Kingdom multinational service organizations will be particularly concentrated around the City of London and other centres in the London metropolitan region, such as Croydon. The concentration of foreign-owned service firms is probably even higher. One study of 261 United States owned business service firms operating in the United Kingdom found that as many as 82 per cent were located in central London and a further 13 per cent were elsewhere in London. This left only 5 per cent in the rest of the country, most of which were located elsewhere in the South-East (Dunning and Norman, 1983).

Despite the growth of large service firms, small firms remain very important in the service sector. Some, such as computer service firms, have resulted as a spin-off of the growth of large companies. Many new innovative firms have been formed by staff from large firms leaving to establish their own businesses. Given the location of computer staff in large organizations, it is likely that new service organizations in the United Kingdom will be highly concentrated in the main metropolitan areas of southern Britain. A further encouragement to the growth in the number of the small firms in the British producer services sector was the tendency during the recessionary 1970s of large service companies to specialize on their core functions and discard their peripheral activities. Thus, as Marshall et al. (1988, p. 194) note:

High levels of new firm formation and the growth of small firms in producer services need to be understood in the context of the role such firms play in servicing the corporate sector, whether as subcontractors with a reservoir of spare capacity, as a source of innovation or in providing a competitive sector in which the price of services may be kept down.

Some indication of the spatial effects of the development of the small firm sector in Britain comes from data on new firm formation rates. This shows that in the service sector regions with the highest rates of new firm formation are the South-East and South-West (Ganguly, 1984).

Small firms also sometimes work in unison, for example, by providing construction, design, and financing services on particular projects. This provides an example of the flexible formation of strategic alliances referred to in Chapter 7.1. Beyers et al. (1986), for example, found many firms operating in concert with other types of service firms to undertake projects for common clients in their study of producer service firms in the Central Puget Sound Region. This suggests that producer service firms located in agglomerations with other service firms have a commercial advantage; this is a further encouragement to the trend towards the metropolitanization of producer services.

Land and labour

High rents in the centre of cities is one of the main factors emphasized by firms as a push factor encouraging them to decentralize offices (Alexander, 1979). Such dispersal usually remains within the metropolitan region. The main reason for this is suggested by research in the United Kingdom which found that the savings in rent, rates, and salaries of office dispersal from London tend to level out at approximately 130 km from the centre of London, while the costs of maintaining communications with the capital continue to increase (Goddard and Pye, 1977).

High space costs may not, however, deter the concentration of producer service firms in large cities if they are compensated for by savings in other costs. This is well illustrated by the case of London which has some of the highest site costs in the world. The high rents, in part, reflect the importance of the City as an international financial centre and the high profits to be made from investment in the development of office property in central London in most years since the early 1960s (Bateman, 1985; Massey, 1986). But they also reflect the fact that office labour costs are much lower than in other European or American cities. For example, in 1977 prime rental costs in the City were between two and three times those in Amsterdam, Brussels, and Geneva, and one-third to one-half higher than those in Dusseldorf and Paris. Yet salary costs for secretarial, clerical, and managerial grades in London were between one-half and one-third of those in the other European cities. It is estimated that the combined labour and floorspace costs for the six cities meant that the costs of a central London location were around half of those in Paris, Dusseldorf, and Geneva and at least 50 per cent cheaper than those in Amsterdam and Brussels (Economist's Advisory Group, 1979).

Patterns of labour availability have also had marked effects on locational trends. At the regional scale access to a well-educated pool of labour is increasingly important. The occupational statistics clearly show that there is a rising demand for managerial, professional, and technical staff both in absolute terms and as a relative share of the workforce. For many company head offices, R. & D., engineering, and related services, proximity to a university appears to be a factor (Stanback, 1985). This is clearly seen in the rapid development of many high-technology complexes (Chapter 6.2). The quality and quantity of education also affects the number of entrepreneurs and potential entrepreneurs there is in a population. In their study of the growth of producer services in the Central Puget Sound Region, Beyers et al. (1986) found that the entrepreneurs who had established the 400 firms in the survey had impressive educational qualifications. Over three-quarters of them had bachelor's degrees; a third had advanced degrees; and one in thirty-three had a doctorate. They also had strong ties to higher education; two in three reported a link to colleges and universities.

At the intrametropolitan scale, the residential preferences of professional and technical staff can influence locational patterns. In the United Kingdom this helps to explain the preference of R. & D. for small non-industrialized market towns within the London metropolitan region (Crum et al., 1979; Massey, 1984b). However, it is access to clerical labour which is the critical locational constraint at the intrametropolitan scale because, in constrast to the managerial, technical, and professional staff, clerical workers are restricted to short journeys to work. Given the major suburbanization which has taken place in residential populations, non-central city locations are increasingly favoured in terms of labour supply. There is also evidence that absenteeism is lower and productivity higher in non-central offices (Marquand, 1979). The relative concentration of a well-educated, predominantly white suburban female workforce seeking second incomes in central Contra Costa is one of the major reasons that Nelson (1986) gives for back office relocation to the I-680 corridor in the San Francisco Bay Area. She suggests that:

To the managers of offices employing large numbers of low-wage clerical workers, a female labor supply associated with areas of growing single-family housing represents a significant lowering of labor costs through reduced turnover, lowered training time, increased productivity, a longer working day, and a reduced chance of unionisation (Nelson, 1986 p. 165).

Technological changes

One of the factors enabling back offices to relocate to take advantage of the availability of a suitable labour force has been changes in technology. Whereas previously back offices were limited to batch operations, whose product then had to be physically transported to other offices, the introduction of on-line transmission of information has allowed work to progress interactively over space. Office work which needs checking without face-to-face meetings by personnel in the front office, such as the preparation of documents, can now be consolidated and relocated in back offices.

The introduction of new technology has also allowed producer service offices to remain competitive in city-centre locations by improving labour productivity. For example, in London the combination of shortages of clerical labour and increased competition for markets in the 1960s and 1970s put considerable pressure on companies to reduce labour inputs. Some firms decentralized to find sufficient labour, but the main response to these pressures was to introduce new technology (Marshall et al., 1988).

The spatial impacts of new technology have thus been varied and sometimes contrary. Some companies such as Rank Xerox and ICL have introduced distance home working. The need for face-to-face contact at the main office at least once a week means, however, that the employment effects are restricted to a localized intraregional scale. One study of the United States insurance industry found evidence of both centralization and decentralization responses to the introduction of computer technology (Baran, 1985 cited by Howells and Green, 1986). The study found that at first the tendency was to centralize data processing in large single units serving all the branches, while more recently the technology has been used to decentralize at least the data entry function back to the branch offices. In effect while direction, control, and decision-making is being highly centralized, data entry is being dispersed. In the United Kingdom insurance and banking industry, the introduction of computer data processing has also affected branch reorganization. Data processing has been concentrated in key area offices and branches have been organized around larger general purpose offices. Both sectors have increased their concentration in metropolitan areas and this has been accompanied by the withdrawal of employment from rural areas, where some branches have been closed because they served small markets and were less economic. Although some decentralization of employment from city centres

has occurred this has been retained within the metropolitan hinterlands (Marshall et al., 1988).

The application of new technology has influenced both the number and kinds of jobs in the producer service sector (see also Table 13.4 and Chapter 6.1). Improvements in productivity have replaced some jobs, but expansion in demand has more than outweighed these losses, leading to a net increase in employment in many producer services. Furthermore, many new technologies, such as word processing and desk-top publishing, have been used to improve the quality of the output as much as to increase productivity. An important feature of the effects of new technology on employment is that its impacts are uneven by firm size and type of job. Process innovations, involving for instance sophisticated data processing, are more commonly introduced in large firms and therefore job losses are more likely to be found in them. On the other hand, many innovations in terms of the introduction of new services, such as management consultancy and computer services, frequently occur in small specialist firms. As for the impact on the type of jobs there is evidence for both deskilling and reskilling. Technology has reskilled some managerial and secretarial work, while in data-processing 'factories' it has continued the subdivision and routinization of clerical and junior administrative office tasks (Marshall et al., 1988).

Finally, it is important to recognize the strategic role of telecommunications. Efficient high-volume data transmission requires electronic digital switching equipment and the linking of computer hardware and terminals through fibre optic cable, microwave radio, or coaxial cable. Although a number of very large companies, such as Lloyds Bank International and Sears, have invested enormous sums in linking their establishments in national or international systems, for most small users and those without extensive requirements the basic telecommunication system for data processing is the telephone system. For them the facilities of the local telephone system may be the limiting factor. For example, in the United states electronic switching is available for well under 50 per cent of the national network. This will limit the use of sophisticated data processing systems in many of the smaller places for some years to come (Stanback, 1985). As the most advanced telecommunications systems are usually first installed where traffic is heaviest, this re-inforces the comparative advantage of those places, such as New York, London, Tokyo, and Brussels, which are already national service centres. Conversely, as Howells and Green (1986 p. 170) have noted: 'the peripheral, less favoured regions ... are trapped in a closed loop of con-straint—low demand for new services inhibits the infrastructure necessary to supply them, which in turn constrains new service activities appearing in such areas.' This suggests that government inter-vention may be needed to enhance the ability of peripheral areas to attract producer service activ-ities.

Government
The policies of both local and central govern-ments have had an important influence on trends in the location of producer service activity. As with retailing (Section 13.1), differences in plan-ning policies between nations have had a major effect on the more extensive decentralization of producer services which has occurred in North American cities compared with European metro-politan areas. Not that this has prevented major suburban office complexes being developed in European cities as witnessed, for example, by City-Nord in Hamburg and La Défense in Paris (Bateman, 1988).

Several governments of developed Western nations have also attempted to reduce the disad-vantage of peripheral areas by encouraging both selected units of their own and private sector producer service firms to relocate there. However, the effect of these *explicit* spatial policies are often more than countered by the impact of their *im-plicit* spatial policies, manifested through, for example, their expenditure patterns and their industrial policies, which in many cases further foster the existing prosperous areas. The opera-tion of office location policies and the effects of defence expenditure on the location of R. & D. have already been discussed in Chapter 8. Here attention is focused on the impact on the location of producer services of American and British government policies towards competition and pri-vatization.

Although the United States government is often portrayed as being less interventionist than most European governments, there are many cases where it has deliberately restricted competi-tion and significant spatial consequences for the location of economic activity have resulted. Such policies have not only been designed to protect domestic companies from foreign competition, but have also operated within the United States. An example of this has occurred in the banking industry, which, until recently, has been an intra-state activity, controlled by federal and state laws which have restricted the geographic areas in which banks can operate (Daniels, 1985a; Holly, 1987). Interstate banking through the establish-ment of branches has been prohibited since the McFadden Act of 1927. Many states followed suit by limiting banks opening branches to the coun-ties in which their head offices were located, and in some cases to adjacent counties, or prohibiting branching altogether. States in the latter category are referred to as Unit Banking states (Fig. 13.6). The effect of these limitations is that banking in the United States of America is diverse and decentralized with almost 14 500 commercial banks in the early 1980s compared with Canada which had only eleven. At that time the largest five banks in the United States only held some 19 per cent of all deposits, set against 78 per cent in Canada and 76 per cent in France. Until the early 1980s the rationalization of banking services in the United States and the opportunities to take advantage of economies of scale were severely limited. Since then some of the restrictions on interstate banking have been lifted by individual states. A spate of acquisitions has followed this legislation, leading to geographic shifts in the corporate control of banking. This has resulted in the expansion of the regional banking function of cities such as Atlanta, Charlotte, Boston, and Los Angeles (Lord, 1987b).

Restraints on competition among producer ser-vice firms have also been relaxed in Britain. Since 1979 there have been some fundamental changes in the regulatory environment and level of state ownership and intervention under the *laissez-faire* Conservative government (Howells and Green, 1986). First, a policy of deregulation has been followed with the aim of increasing competition and the reduction of state intervention and con-trols. There have been three main areas within the producer services sector where deregulation has occurred: telecommunications, transport, and the financial sector. Each has had spatial impli-cations. For example, the restructuring of the

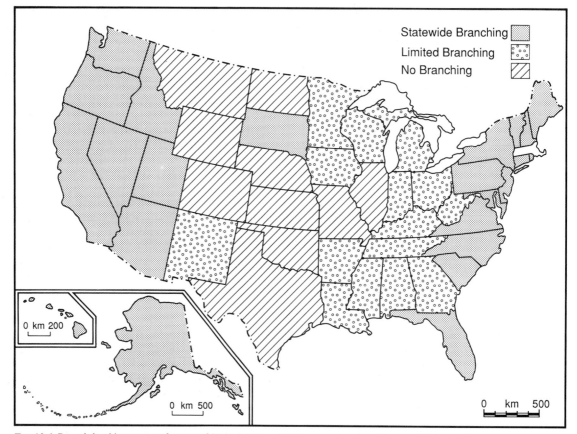

FIG 13.6 Branch banking status of states of United States, 1983 (*source:* Lord and Lynds, 1984 p. 147)

financial markets led to the opening up of the stock exchange in London to more competition. This increased the attraction of central London as a world financial centre. The consequence was that in preparation for the 'Big Bang' of 1986 there was a massive increase in office floorspace in the City. Close on 800 000 sq m of office space was built in the first five years of the 1980s, almost as much as the whole amount built in any previous decade (Lenon, 1987). More than a further one million sq m of office space is currrently being built at Canary Wharf in London's Docklands to help meet the increased demand from the financial services in the City (Bateman, 1988).

The same political philosophy of increasing competition and reducing state intervention has been behind the policy of privatization. Among the companies affected, which are involved in providing services, are BT, Associated British Ports, and the National Freight Corporation.

Distinguishing the spatial impacts of privatization is difficult, because privatization is usually accompanied by a degree of deregulation. Howells and Green (1986 p. 159) suggest that, as far as services based on networks (telecommunications and transport) are concerned, privatization and deregulation have had two different effects:

On lines or routes carrying the heaviest traffic, costs are reduced and competition, in terms of efficiency and innovation, is increased as market entrants concentrate on these lucrative market segments. By contrast unprofitable lines or subsystems in low density, peripheral areas attract few if any entrants, whilst previous monopolies in response to deregulation and increased competition in key markets try to reduce their peripheral network commitments.

The final elements of the Conservative government's *laissez-faire* policy has been the strong pressure put on public bodies to contract out services such as catering, cleaning, and cleansing

(Table 13.4). Howells and Green (1986) expect that most contracts will continue to go to large national companies based in the South of England, such as Waste Management Ltd and Pritchard and Exclusive in cleaning, whose aim is to expand their network of branches further across the country. They suggest that some local authorities may give preference to local companies when they come to contract out services, but this has since become illegal under the Local Government Act of 1988.

13.3 Summary

The service sector comprises a heterogeneous group of economic activities, some are concerned with handling goods, some with handling information, and others with supporting personnel. The study of the geography of services has not yet received the attention it deserves. Considering that the majority of the working population in developed market economies earn their living in the service sector, this is a somewhat surprising state of affairs. This chapter has attempted to apply some of the insights derived from Parts I and II of the book to interpreting recent shifts in the location of retailing and producer services within developed market economies. Retailing geography is a relatively mature sub-discipline, whereas the analysis of the nature and location of the producer service sector is only just beginning.

- Planned shopping centres have become a major feature in the economic landscape. They are most common in North America where they are usually located in the suburbs or sometimes out-of-town on major highways. In Europe, particularly Britain, they are more frequently sited in the central areas of towns and cities.
- Decentralization within urban regions is the major locational trend affecting retailing. Overlapping waves of decentralization have affected different retailing activities at different periods. The prime factor accounting for retail decentralization has been the changing pattern of demand, particularly its suburbanization. Organizational and technological changes have enabled the shift to occur, although some developments, such as teleshopping, may in the future slow down the rate of decentralization.

High city-centre land costs have encouraged large land users to move out of the centre and access to a suburban labour force has acted as a pull factor. Differences in planning policies between North America and Europe are a major factor explaining the more extensive suburbanization of retailing in the former.

- Producer services include a great variety of activities, such as insurance and banking, legal services and R. & D., and the distribution and storage of goods. It is therefore perhaps not surprising that in comparison with retailing the intranational spatial trends are more diverse. In addition to decentralization occurring within metropolitan regions there are indications of producer services being attracted to the major metropolitan areas, filtering down the metropolitan heirarchy and shifting to more prosperous regions. Some of these trends are leading to a more widespread distribution of producer services, others are contributing to an increase in the already high degree of spatial concentration exhibited by many producer services, although the impact varies between countries.
- It is also difficult to generalize about the factors influencing the shifts in the location of producer services because their impact is often variable. The shift to the more prosperous areas largely reflects the growth in demand which these areas are generating, while the continued attraction of the large metropolitan areas is influenced, in part, by the growth of large business service organizations and the increase in the buying-in of services. Both of these trends have been further encouraged by government policies of privatization and deregulation. The location of the most advanced telecommunications facilities in the major metropolitan areas also contributes to their attraction as does the ease of face-to-face contact with customers, suppliers and other organizations.
- One of the main factors encouraging downfiltering is the increase in demand for producer services, as this has allowed smaller metropolitan areas to generate the demand thresholds to support high-level services. As for the decentralization which is occurring within metropolitan regions, this has been affected by several factors, including the high cost of office space in the centre of cities, the attraction of a suburban

labour force and the encouragement given by some central and local governments to firms to move out of the central areas of some large cities. Both downfiltering and decentralization have also been made easier by the development of locational hierarchies in large businesses and the improvements in telecommunications which have enabled the more standardized work processes which requires little face-to-face contact to be relocated in smaller settlements and suburban areas.

- Finally, caution is needed in seeking generalizations about the spatial outcomes of the changes in the internal and external environments affecting producer services, not only because different activities are influenced in different ways, but also because the same activity may exhibit different spatial trends which vary between places, time periods, and types of organization.

IV The Geography of Economic Change

14

International Economic Change

The aim of this chapter is to examine patterns of economic activity and change at the international scale. The world is characterized by spatial inequalities and all countries are linked together in some way in a world system. Few people would deny that the well-being of the world's poor countries depends largely upon the policies adopted by the rich countries (Gilbert, 1985). The relationship between the two groups of countries is often considered to be an exploitative one, whereby the rich develop at the expense of the poor. Poor countries are thus seen as dependent on the rich and the emergence of an unequal world reflects the penetration of poor countries by 'Western' ideas and capital. It follows, therefore, that the causes (and remedies) of world poverty, for example, can be found only by developing a global scale of analysis.

Global thinking is not new (see Johnston and Taylor, 1986) and geographers have long classified the countries of the world into such categories as First (developed/industrialized/Western), Second, (socialist/Communist/planned) and Third (underdeveloped/developing) Worlds, North and South, and Core and Periphery. However, until recently they have tended to view change as a state-level process, with outside influences allowed only a minor role. In reality, the relationship between core and periphery is more complex than a simple situation whereby the developing economies are dependent on the developed economies; it is characterized by a whole series of dependencies and interdependencies operating in both directions (Sewell, 1979; Section 14.1). Change in developed market economies can be understood only within a holistic framework, where global processes are examined. As Brookfield (1975, p. 189) commented, 'the interconnection of the world economy . . . has brought into existence a set of processes which have operated, albeit in radically different ways,

on all parts and peoples touched by the interdependent system.'

Since it is not possible to understand developed market economies without viewing them in the context of the rest of the world economy, a global perspective is necessary. Knox and Agnew (1989) advocate two reasons for working at the world scale: first, the rapidly increasing interdependence within the world economy, where economic change within countries, regions, and local communities depends more and more on interrelations at the global scale; and secondly, the need to combine traditional approaches to economic geography (mainly concerned with developed economies) with those adopted in the geography of development (mainly concerned with developing economies).

This chapter falls into four distinct parts. In the first, international patterns of economic inequality and change are examined briefly and in the second, some theoretical explanations for the contrasts are offered. The third section concentrates on the development of the world economy and in particular the emergence of a new international division of labour (NIDL) and newly industrializing countries (NICs). Finally, some of the adjustments made by the older developed countries to the new world economy are considered.

14.1 Patterns of economic change

Geographical inequalities in the world economy are endemic. Academics have often classified the economic world into two interdependent but highly unequal parts, commonly referred to as *core* (or centre) and *periphery*. The former includes rich, market-type economies that play an active role in world trade and control the international movement of capital, whilst the latter comprises either subsistence or market-type economies that play a passive role in world trade and depend upon the core for imports and capital and as a destination for their exports (Knox and Agnew, 1989).

In 1980, the deep gulf dividing rich and poor nations was cast in terms of *'North'* and *'South'* (Brandt, 1980). The North includes Europe (including the USSR), North America, Australia, New Zealand, and Japan, which together account for 90 per cent of the world's manufacturing. In contrast, the South—China and all countries in Latin America, Africa, the Middle East, Southern Asia, and South-East Asia (see Fig. 14.1)—contains three-quarters of the world's population but just one-fifth of its income. Clearly, northern countries dominate the international economic system and institutions of trade, money, and finance, and it is this economic (and political) power difference which is at the heart of the contemporary north–south relationship. The key feature of the international pattern of economic development, therefore, is that it is one of *unequal interdependence*. Indeed, the Brandt Commission argues that policies needed to be developed to protect the weaker partners in this relationship. The report also suggests, more controversially, that it is in the interest of the North to help the less-developed countries, on the basis that all countries benefit from an increase in world trade and economic growth.

Prior to the publication of the Brandt Report, a different division of the world economy was advocated by Wallerstein (1974) in his world-system theory (see Chapter 2.1 and Taylor, 1986; 1988). This views the modern world as consisting of a single entity, the capitalist world economy, which evolved from about 1500 to encompass the whole world by around 1900. The world economy is divided into a core, periphery, and semi-periphery and countries can 'move' from core to periphery, periphery to semi-periphery, and so on. Core, periphery, and semi-periphery thus refer to types of area in which different processes may be operating. For example, the core is characterized by high wages, advanced technology, and a diversified production mix. Quite the opposite is true of the periphery (low wages, little

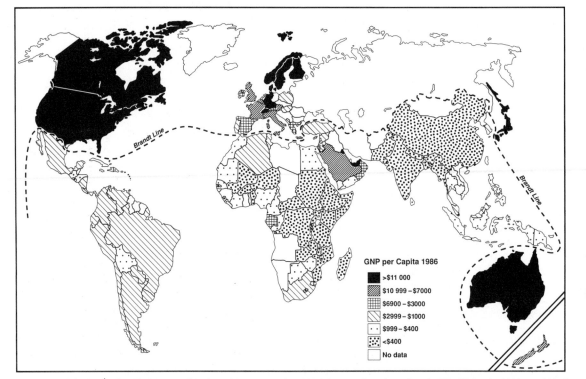

GNP per Capita 1986

■ >$11 000
▨ $10 999 – $7000
▦ $6900 – $3000
▨ $2999 – $1000
· · $999 – $400
▨ <$400
□ No data

Fig 14.1 Global variations in gross national product per capita, 1986 (*source:* based on data in World Bank, 1988 pp. 223–4)

technology, and a narrow economic base), whereas countries in the semi-periphery have a combination of both sets of characteristics; they exploit peripheral countries and are exploited by core countries (Knox and Agnew, 1989).

Such divisions have much appeal. In particular, the north–south categorization helps to emphasize that many of today's prosperous nations were colonial powers which controlled large areas of what now constitute poor countries. It is also suggested that most key decisions at a world scale are made by governments and institutions, such as multinationals, which are based in the rich countries. However, these divisions are extremely crude and hide many important differences. A more detailed classification is the one developed by the World Bank, which identifies five main groups of countries based on a mixture of economic and political criteria:

1. *Low-income developing countries*, with a 1986 Gross National Product (GNP) per capita of $425 or less and including most of south and east Asia, China, and sub-Saharan Africa.

2. *Middle-income developing countries*, with a GNP per capita of between $460 and $7410 and including the rest of Africa and Asia, virtually the whole of Central and Southern America, and a few European countries such as Greece, Portugal, and Yugoslavia.

3. *High-income oil exporters*, including Saudi Arabia, Kuwait, Bahrain, Brunei, Qatar, Libya, and the United Arab Emirates.

4. *Industrial market economies*, including all members of the Organization for Economic Cooperation and Development (OECD) except Greece, Portugal, and Turkey (included in group 2).

5. *Non-reporting non-market economies*, including the Union of Soviet Socialist Republics, Mongolia, Democratic People's Republic of Korea, East Germany, Czechoslovakia, Cuba, Bulgaria, Angola, and Albania.

The GNP per capita is a widely-used international indicator of economic development (GNP is the value of the total output of goods and services—at home and overseas—accruing to the residents of a country). Figure 14.1 highlights some of the core–periphery and north–south contrasts previously described. In particular, the strong geographical concentration of countries with high per capita GNP levels either side of the

North Atlantic stands out. Similarly in the Pacific Basin, Australia and New Zealand have a high GNP per capita, although the value in the latter is $4460 below the former. Kuwait and the United Arab Emirates are also among the countries with a high income level. The enormous disparity between rich and poor nations is the central feature of Figure 14.1; the difference between the lowest ranking country (Ethiopia, $120) and the highest (Switzerland, $17 680) is in the ratio of 147 : 1! However, some caution is needed in using GNP per capita as an indicator of levels of economic development (Wilson and Woods, 1982). For example, comparisons are made on the basis of a single currency (US dollars), and conversions into this currency can cause distortions due to exchange rates. Similarly, some countries will dispose of more of their GNP than others simply because they are larger (e.g. more is spent on transport and communications) or colder (more on clothing, shelter, and heating). Inequalities within countries are also 'hidden' by such national indicators, yet it is clear that large sections of a country's population have little access to the goods and services.

The economies of all countries have changed over time. However, rates of change have varied between developed and developing countries and within each group. Of real significance is the fact that the gap between developed and developing nations has widened (Forbes, 1984), especially in the 1960–70 period. Since 1970, GNP per capita has often increased at a greater percentage rate in developing countries, but there has been no real 'catching up' because large percentage increases from a low base can be very misleading. A second important feature is that the inequalities between countries of the developing world have increased. Whilst the GNP for the low-income countries increased by 4.2 per cent between 1960 and 1970 and 4.0 per cent between 1970 and 1980, it increased by a larger amount in the middle-income countries. Some countries in this category experienced impressive growth between 1960 and 1981, especially such newly industrializing countries (NICs) as South Korea (annual per capita growth in GNP of 6.9 per cent), Brazil (5.1) and Singapore (7.4) (Gilbert, 1985). It is the middle-income countries, rather than all developing countries, that have narrowed the 'economic' gap with the developed world. Forbes (1984) notes two other features about inequalities in the distribution of wealth. First, income is concentrated in the hands of few people in most developing countries; for example, in Zambia 61 per cent of the wealth in 1976 was in the hands of 20 per cent of the population. Secondly, variations in the patterns of inequality are quite marked, with the average income in urban areas being considerably higher than in rural areas.

One important trend characterizing economic change in the world economy has been the global shift in manufacturing (Dicken, 1986). Changes have occurred both between and within core and peripheral countries. Developed market economies decreased their share of world manufacturing output from 72 to 65 per cent between 1953 and 1975, whereas peripheral countries nearly doubled their share, from 4.8 to 9 per cent over the same time period. The most noticeable feature of change within the core countries has been the decline in importance of the USA, from producing 40 per cent of the world's manufactured goods in 1963 to 24 per cent in 1983, and the rapid rise in importance of Japan, from 5.5 to 16 per cent over the same twenty years.

Whilst the developing world has increased its share of manufacturing output, this growth has been unevenly distributed. It has occurred primarily in the middle-income countries and especially the NICs (in the semi-periphery). Details

of the growth of manufacturing production for the ten major NICs, mainly for the 1960–80 period of growth, are provided in Table 14.1. Although Spain and Brazil were the most important in terms of manufacturing output, the highest growth rates occurred in the Asian 'gang of four' (Hong Kong, Singapore, South Korea, and Taiwan), especially in South Korea and Taiwan. Indeed, rates of growth in the NICs remained high throughout the 1970s, unlike the poor performance in most developed economies; however, even the NICs have experienced major problems since the mid-1980s (see Section 14.3).

Economic change at the international scale is, therefore, more complex than that depicted by such terms as core/periphery and north/south. As Dicken (1986 p. 390) remarks, 'the world is more a mosaic of unevenness in a continual state of flux than a simple dichotomous structure of core and periphery.' Economic change occurs along a continuum and does not fit into discrete categories.

14.2 Explaining international economic change

Theoretical explanations of economic growth and change at the international level fall into three

TABLE 14.1 The growth of manufacturing production in the leading newly industrializing countries, 1960–1986

	Share of world manufacturing output (%)			Average annual growth in manufacturing (%)		
	1963	1970	1980	1960–70	1970–81	1980–86
Hong Kong	0.08	0.15	0.27	—	10.1	—
Singapore	0.05	0.06	0.16	13.0	9.7	2.2
South Korea	0.11	0.22	0.66	17.6	15.6	9.8
Taiwan	0.11	0.23	0.46[a]	15.5[b]	11.5[c]	—
Brazil	1.57	1.73	3.01	—	8.7	1.2
Mexico	1.04	1.27	1.95	9.4	7.1	0.0
Spain	0.88	1.18	2.24	—	6.0[d]	0.3
Portugal	0.23	0.27	0.40	8.9	4.5	1.4
Greece	0.19	0.25	0.31	10.2	5.5	0.2
Yugoslavia	1.14	1.25	0.89	5.7	7.1	1.1
Total (10 NICs)	5.40	6.61	10.54			

[a]1977 [b]1961–70 [c]1971–8 [d]1970–80

Sources: Dicken (1986 p. 30) and World Bank (1988).

broad schools of thought. The first is *modernization theory* which dominated academic thinking in the 1960s and advocates that, under free market conditions, *all* countries pass through various 'stages' of economic growth during the development process. The second is *dependency theory* which was popular in the 1970s and suggests that development (or more accurately underdevelopment) in peripheral countries is dependent on core countries—indeed peripheral countries will not develop so long as links are maintained with developed countries in a world economy (Gilbert, 1985). The third, *world system theory*, advocates a more historical approach and involves examining the historical phases in the development of the

world economy and the macro-economic activities of states; this approach has been popular in the 1980s and will be discussed in Section 14.3.

The main architect of modernization theory was Rostow (1960), who suggested that development of a country would occur by means of 'linear stages of economic growth'. Based on data for fifteen countries only (plus outline information for others), Rostow maintained that all societies in the world would progress along a continuum in five main stages, which he referred to as traditional society, preconditions for take-off, take-off into self-sustained growth, drive to maturity, and age of high mass consumption (Fig. 14.2). The critical phase in the model was the

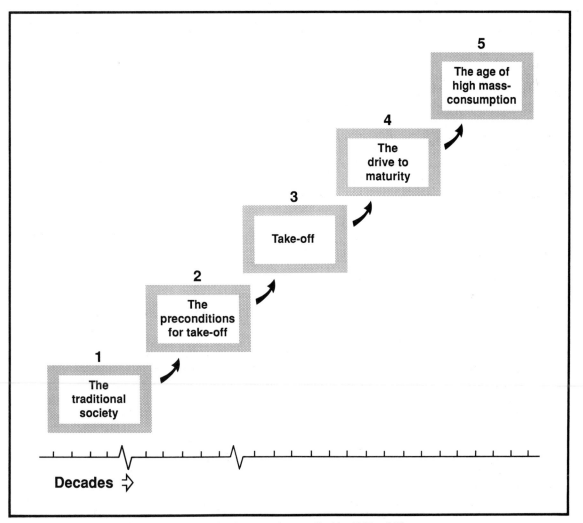

FIG 14.2 Rostow's stages theory of economic development (*source:* Keeble, 1967 p. 250)

decade or so when a country began to experience self-sustaining growth. Brookfield (1975) summarizes the three main features of this 'take off':

1. The rate of productive investment rises from about 5 per cent of national income to over 10 per cent.
2. One or more substantial manufacturing sectors emerge to become 'leading sectors' in growth.
3. The political and social framework is modified to exploit the impulses in the modern sector, and thus give growth its self-sustaining character.

How these conditions are achieved is not outlined and it is never questioned whether such a development path is appropriate or desirable. However, as Brookfield (1975) notes, Rostow's writings were extraordinarily persuasive. At a time when economic growth dominated policy, his model seemed to give every country an equal chance; it 'explained' the advantage of the developed countries; it offered a clear path to progress; and it identified the requirements for advance with the virtues of the West. Rostow's concepts of 'take-off' and 'sustained growth' became part of the established language of economic development.

In an excellent review of modernization and dependency theories, Foster-Carter (1985) identifies four inter-linked characteristics of the Rostow model. First, it is *evolutionist* and sees socioeconomic change as unfolding through a fixed set of stages. Secondly, it is *unilinear* as all countries must pass by the same route, in the same order; there are no short cuts. Thirdly, it is *internalist* as the crucial dimensions of change are internally generated within each society; external influences are relegated to a position of insignificance. Fourthly, it is *recapitulationist* in the sense that developing countries today have to follow precisely the same path as did the developed countries.

Rostow's model was criticized in each of these 'areas', not least by the emerging 'dependency' school of thought (Frank, 1967 and 1969). In particular, the model seems to 'fall down' in terms of empirical validity, theoretical reasoning, and policy effectiveness (Foster-Carter, 1985). Frank (1969) argues that a number of countries in Latin America never had a traditional stage at all, either because there were no pre-existing societies or because they were destroyed by European conquest, and they still remain underdeveloped. Sim-

ilarly, there is little empirical evidence to confirm that an increase in investment characterizes 'take-off'. On a theoretical note, there is no reason why countries that are developing today have to follow the same stages that countries like the USA and the United Kingdom passed through. Rostow clearly underplays the importance of external relationships in the development process, especially in the sense that later developing countries can use techniques developed by earlier developing countries and thus possibly 'leap' over a stage or two in Rostow's model. Indeed, the situation for developing countries today is completely different from that when the major core countries developed because they have to try to develop within a highly integrated world economy dominated by a few very powerful countries. In terms of policy, take-off can only be identified after it has happened, which is of little use to planners. More significantly, progress through Rostow's five stages is assumed to occur without state help, yet government policy plays an increasingly important role and is a major factor in the 'context of change' of economic activity (Chapter 8).

Dissatisfaction with the 'stages' approach to economic development led to increasing acceptance of more left-wing (structuralist) interpretations of development. A major early advocate of dependency theory was Frank (1967), who feels that modernization will not overcome poverty. Instead, he views national economies as structural elements in a global capitalist system, where prosperity in the 'core' is based on underdevelopment in the 'periphery'.

Frank derived a simple model, based on a hierarchical structure of metropolises and satellites, to explain how developing countries are dependent on developed economies. A process of exploitation occurs, whereby small towns in the 'periphery' expropriate any surplus capital from the local rural areas, only for this surplus to be successively expropriated by large cities in the periphery and then by the metropolis in the 'core'. Frank envisages a world metropolis (based on the USA) at the top of the international hierarchy. Beneath this level are major cities in the periphery like Sao Paulo, which act as both an international satellite (to the USA) and a metropolis (to areas within Brazil). Such surplus capital extraction within the hierarchy is made possible by unequal trade arrangements, dominated by the metropolis. Consequently, surplus capital accumulates in the hands of the metropolitan powers who are effectively controlling the world economy.

In a similar manner to the way he examined Rostow's model, Foster-Carter (1985) outlines four main features of Frank's theoretical model. First, it is *externalist* as change in developing countries is initiated by outside forces. Secondly, it is *bilinear* in so far as the metropolis and satellites pursue totally different paths from the beginning, determined by their different structural roles in the system. Thirdly, it is *stagnationist* in the sense that the structure (metropolis and satellites) remains the same. Fourthly, it is *discontinuist* because developing countries have to make a radical break with the entire system if they ever want to develop.

In support of these theoretical notions of dependency, there is considerable empirical evidence of dependent relationships. Dependence means a 'lack of autonomy and a weakening of national controls over the economic future' (Gilbert, 1985 p. 27). The same author identifies four dimensions of this dependency relationship:

1. *The trade relationship.* Two features are significant here. First, most developing countries export 'primary' products in exchange for manufactured goods. Secondly, the trading relationship is unbalanced, in so far as poor countries depend more on rich countries to buy their primary products than developed countries depend on less-developed countries to buy their manufactured goods. Put simply, poor countries have most to lose in a trade dispute with rich countries, especially as the demand for primary products has declined (Chapter 1.2) and their price varies from year to year.

2. *The technology relationship.* Most innovations and technologies originate in institutions in developed countries. These can be imported by developing countries, but only at a cost and by increasing their dependence on trade with the developed world. Imported technology may also be inappropriate (e.g. labour-saving in an area of surplus labour) and benefit the new manufacturing class only, thereby increasing income disparities within the economy.

3. *Cultural dependence.* Many people in power in developing countries (e.g. politicians, administrators, and managers) were trained in the developed world and continue to adopt their life styles and traditions on their return home. This not only leads to a rejection of local traditions, products, and techniques, but also to an increasing trade and technological dependence.

4. *Capital dependence.* It is very difficult to accumulate capital in countries where much of the economy is at a subsistence level, population growth is high, and the balance of payments is in deficit. Many developing countries, therefore, depend on external capital, either in the form of concessional aid (thereby increasing their dependence) from such institutions as the World Bank or the International Monetary Fund (IMF) or borrowing from major commercial banks.

Clearly, less-developed countries are dependent on developed countries in a variety of ways. However, the relationship is not always straightforward. For example, some countries are more able than others to adapt to the problems of dependence. It is suggested that South Korea and Taiwan, both NICs, have escaped some of the constraints of dependence through hard work and an excessively authoritarian government (Gilbert, 1985; Section 14.3). Similarly, some forms of dependence are less constraining than others. Kuwait is a good example of a country whose dependence has been lessened by being a major oil producer.

It is not surprising, in view of comments like these, that dependency theory has also been the subject of criticism. The very fact that Frank's model suggests development in the periphery or South is impossible under capitalism seems inconsistent with the growth that has occurred in the NICs. Part of the weakness lies in the almost total disregard of internal conditions in different countries. With the emphasis on external factors, there is no room for the operation of specific historical, cultural, and political forces (Dicken, 1986); yet it is the interplay between internal and external processes that 'determines' the nature of development in individual countries. Forbes (1984) emphasizes the importance of this two-way relationship in the development process, rather than assuming that development in one area can occur only at the expense of another. The developing world can and does affect economic growth in the developed world, as was graphically illustrated in a decision by the Organization of Petroleum Exporting Countries (OPEC) to increase the price of oil fourfold in 1973/4. Third World countries have some autonomy and dependency theory does not properly consider such socio-economic features as internal class structures, government policy, and the role of the state. Similarly, Reitsma (1982) criticizes dependency theory for being one-sided and failing to consider dependency relations involving socialist countries. Finally, the processes at work are mechanistic, inevitably producing underdevelopment and offering no escape from it.

In response to such criticisms, there has been a trend in economic geography towards a more historical approach to understanding the main processes which give rise to patterns of development. Effectively, there has been a move towards examining the 'historical geography of economic development based upon the historical phases of the world economy and the macro-economic activities of states' (Knox and Agnew, 1989 p. 63). It is to the development of the world economy that this chapter now turns.

14.3 The development of the world economy

The generalized core–periphery or north–south pattern of uneven development that exists in the world today has evolved over several centuries. However, the pattern of evolution is complex with different countries developing at different paces and at different times. Consequently, the best way of trying to understand these events is to trace how the form of interdependence has changed over time and to look at which countries were involved at what periods. Such a historical approach should help to explain how and why an uneven geographical pattern of global development emerged. This approach is adopted by Wallerstein (1974) in his world system theory (see Chapter 2.1). The theory represents a version of dependency theory that can cope with the apparent inconsistency noted in Section 14.2 of developing countries turning into NICs. The capitalist world, rather than individual countries, is the main object of analysis, where the fluctuating relationships between core, periphery, and semi-periphery create 'an ever changing dynamic system' (Taylor, 1988 p. 259).

There are three main periods in the evolving

pattern of uneven development (Crow and Thomas, 1982):

1. *The Pre-Age of discovery*. Before European domination of the world, there was a very different pattern of empires, social structures and trade. Among the Third World civilizations which existed in the period when the Europeans set out on their discoveries were the Ming of China; the Maya, Inca, and Aztec in the Americas; the Mogul in India; and the great civilizations of Africa, especially the Zimbabwe. Development was largely independent of territorial states except for the emergence of certain trading centres as politically independent 'city-states', and the early world economy was essentially *transnational*.

2. *European expansion and the emergence of capitalism*. The expansion of European control over the world began in earnest around 1500. The next 450 years or so witnessed the development of the *old international division of labour* (OIDL), whereby certain areas began to specialize in particular types of economic activity (a process of regional/national specialization). On a global basis, this meant a broad division between non-industrial countries (which supplied raw materials and agricultural products to the 'North') and industrialized countries (which produced manufactured goods and exported some of them to the 'South'). Effectively, colonial powers were extracting various resources from their foreign enclaves and in return traded manufactured goods. Taxes were imposed on the indigenous population, to encourage them to work in the plantations or mines, and slaves were imported if the local population was too small (Norcliffe, 1985). World trade was dominated by this two-way pattern of unequal interdependence between advanced industrialized countries and backward primary producers. Much of this OIDL survives today, reflecting the large consumption of resources by developed countries, although ownership is often in the form of foreign corporations.

Knox and Agnew (1989) emphasize that, unlike the Pre-Age of discovery, this phase in the development of the world economy consisted of different developed 'national' economies penetrating the underdeveloped world. Economic flows aided capital accumulation at the *national* rather than transnational scale and the division of labour was organized within national economies. The gap between developed and developing economies widened considerably during this period. This reflected different forms of interdependence (Crow and Thomas, 1982). First, Europe's plunder of the Third World saw the accumulation of resources, goods, and/or labour with little or no exchange. For example, it is estimated that almost ten million Africans were shipped—during the slave trade—to the Americas between the sixteenth and nineteenth centuries. The wealth accumulated from such plunder was part of the condition for the industrial revolution and the emergence of European capitalism; it provided the necessary basis for the development of the OIDL. Secondly, Europe increased its control of production world-wide, in both agriculture and manufacturing. Under the OIDL, Europe specialized in the production of manufactured goods. Some of these were exported to the Third World, but this had the effect of undermining local handicraft industries and thus increasing dependence. For example, India's cotton-spinning and hand-loom-weaving industry was severely pruned in the early nineteenth century because of competition from cheaper European cotton goods manufactured in steam-powered factories.

Thirdly, once factories had been established in Europe, their owners campaigned for free trade to buy raw materials wherever they were most cheaply produced and to open up the whole of the world for their wares. This was the beginning of the world economy. From the late eighteenth century to the end of the period of European expansion (around 1950), two major changes occurred in this world economy: first, there was a dramatic growth in world trade, much of which was centred on London; and secondly, the wealth generated was invested—by Britain—in railways, canals, cotton mills, and plantations overseas, so as to further extend its control over the Third World. Finally, the increasing economic interdependence between Europe and the Third World led to an extension of European political control, through the colonization of South and Central America, Asia and Africa. This situation basically remained up until the Second World War.

3. *Multinationals and the rise of newly industrializing countries (NICs).* Since 1950 and especially the late 1960s, a *new international division of labour* (NIDL) has emerged and been superimposed on the old division (Frobel *et al.*, 1980). This effectively means a change in the geographical pattern of specialization at the global scale (Dicken, 1986). Based on the international spread of manufacturing, trade flows have become more complex and involve subsidiaries or joint ventures of global corporations producing goods in different parts of the world. New centres of industrial production emerged (NICs) as production became fragmented and relocated on a global scale. The NIDL, therefore, is a system of production on a world scale, where a greater number of people have been integrated into the activities conducted by large international producers of goods (multinationals) and by the international firms which service these producers (Thrift, 1986; Chapter 1.2). As Knox and Agnew (1989 p. 91) observe, 'the world economy has entered a third stage of development in which there has been a re-emergence of the *transnational* element in its operation.'

There are two fundamental features of this NIDL. First, a wider range and quantity of manufacturing goods is being produced in more and different countries than before; much of this is the result of direct investment overseas by multinationals. Secondly, the relationship between the developed and newly industrializing countries is changing. Many of the NICs are exporting manufactured goods to the developed world, which is facing severe competition in the production of some goods. For example, even the Japanese can no longer compete with the Koreans in shipbuilding as their costs are higher.

It is possible to explore the characteristics of the NIDL by examining the relationship between developed and developing countries. A prime motive affecting the changing role of developed countries in the NIDL is the pursuit of profit by capitalist (often multinational) enterprises (see Chapter 7.2). Such organizations have sought profitable new locations, especially if profits from Fordist-like production in older locations have been declining. This has led to a global shift in production (Section 14.1), which in turn has been encouraged by new technologies in transport and communications, incentives from certain host countries, and developments in the technologies of production and business organization. These conditions have permitted the geographical separation of production processes, especially labour-intensive ones which can take advantage of low-cost labour in selected Third World countries. This outflow of production and thus jobs from developed countries has important implications for their economies (see Section 14.4). However, most overseas investment has gone to other advanced economies and often been compensated by an inflow of capital and production (e.g. by the Nissan motor car company in Britain).

Within the developing world, only a few countries have so far justified the term NIC. In the late 1970s, the OECD (1979) identified ten NICs (two in the Americas—Brazil and Mexico, four in South-East Asia—Hong Kong, Singapore, South Korea, and Taiwan, and four in Europe—Spain, Portugal, Greece, and Yugoslavia, see Table 14.1), although by the mid-1980s these were being challenged by a 'new wave', including Indonesia, Malaysia, Thailand, and China (OECD, 1988). For the majority of developing countries, therefore, their relationship with developed countries has not changed significantly under the NIDL, except that with decolonization most countries are not ruled directly by other powers.

Two main kinds of industrialization strategy have been followed by NICs: first, import substitution industrialization, where the manufacture of goods which would otherwise be imported is encouraged; and secondly, export-oriented industrialization, where export industries are encouraged to establish within a country, often in special export-processing zones (EPZs). The first strategy was followed by Latin American NICs, with the intention of protecting their infant industry, diversifying their economic base, and reducing their dependence on foreign technology and capital (Schmitz, 1984; Harris, 1986). Sustained industrial growth was to be obtained by first reducing the level of dependence on imported consumer goods, before producing intermediate and capital goods internally. In reality, progress beyond the domestic production of consumer goods proved difficult and it was soon realized that import substitution could not lead to full industrialization. This was because production usually required imported intermediate and capital goods and sustained industrial growth depended on the expansion of exports, to provide the necessary foreign exchange. Import substitution, therefore, led to substantial inefficiency and foreign exchange problems; it was unsuitable with the NIDL. A switch to export-oriented industrial-

ization was the key to sustained economic growth. Indeed, this was the main strategy followed by the Far East NICs of Taiwan, Singapore, Hong Kong, and South Korea (the gang of four).

The objective of export-oriented industrialization is to create a specialized role in the world economy. Its growth in importance was aided by the rapid development of world trade in the 1960s, the 'shrinkage' of geographical distance (through developments in transport and communications), and the global spread of multi-national companies (Dicken, 1986). Industrialization takes place mainly in EPZs, which are small geographically separated areas within countries designed to attract export-oriented industries. This is achieved by offering favourable investment and trade conditions as compared with the rest of the host country. Incentives include the provision of infrastructure and services for manufacturing, the waiving of excise duties on components, tax 'holidays', reduced pollution control, and constraints on labour organizations (e.g. strikes are banned). EPZs are, therefore, export enclaves set up for the processing and assembly of export products from mainly imported materials and components. From a total of just two before 1966 (in India and Puerto Rico), the number of EPZs increased rapidly and by 1984 there were 68 in 40 developing countries (Thrift, 1986); over 50 per cent are concentrated in Asia and Central America (including the Caribbean).

Production taking place in EPZs is mainly in textiles, clothing, micro-electronics, and the assembly of cars and bicycles (labour-intensive stages of production); over 60 per cent of the employment in Asian EPZs is in electronics (Knox and Agnew, 1989). Much of the foreign investment is owned by multinationals, which are often attracted by the cheap and non-unionized labour, as well as the other incentives listed. There would appear to be few benefits to the local economy outside the EPZs. However, it would be wrong to assume that industrialization in the NICs is the result of external forces only. Indeed, there is tremendous variation within NICs, with the nature of industrialization varying according to the way in which specific internal conditions interact with external factors (Dicken, 1987). In particular, Dicken highlighted the importance of political forces and the different roles of the state in the industrialization of Hong Kong and

Singapore. Although growth was spectacular throughout the 1960s and 1970s, the dynamic nature of the world economy was demonstrated when the NICs were faced with substantial problems in the mid-1980s. In the case of Hong Kong, for example, gross domestic product grew by just 0.8 per cent in 1985, compared with 9.6 per cent in 1984. Similarly for Singapore, a growth in gross domestic product of 8.2 per cent in 1984 was turned into a decline of −1.8 per cent in 1985. Dicken lists five main factors involved in this sudden downturn:

1. The falling demand for and protection against imported goods in the USA (their main market for manufactured exports) and Western Europe.
2. The sensitivity of the major industrial sectors in Hong Kong and Singapore (textiles, clothing, electronics, and oil refining) to fluctuations in the world economy.
3. The slump in the construction industry of Singapore, used deliberately to offset the cyclical downturn in the economy.
4. The major collapse of the property industry in Singapore, leaving an overcapacity of office and hotel accommodation.
5. The uncertainty in Hong Kong (especially after the crushing of the student revolution in China in 1989), of the pending reversion of the colony to China in 1997.

An important point to emerge from this discussion, in the overall context of this book, is that different parts of the world have reacted in quite distinctive ways to the expansion of the world economy; local systems either resist or adapt to outside influences as the process of development is mediated culturally and regionally (Knox and Agnew, 1989). Developed market economies, for example, have had to adjust to increased competition from the NICs and developments in the world economy. These adjustments are briefly outlined in the last section of this chapter.

14.4 Adjustments made by the older developed countries to the new world economy

The NIDL and industrialization of the NICs have affected the economies of the older developed countries (ODCs), especially those in Europe. High unemployment and job losses in manufacturing have been major problems in the 1980s; the latter have not been compensated sufficiently by job gains in service industries (see Chapter 1.3). This is in contrast to the major growth in producer services in the USA and Japan.

Faced with increasing competition from the new world economy and the NICs and Japan in particular, the ODCs need to adjust. However, there have been marked differences in the extent to which firms in the various developed countries have been able to adjust. For example, much depends on the types of industry involved and the extent to which process and product innovations (Chapter 6.1) are able to succeed in revitalizing threatened industrial activities. Textile technology (process innovation) is a good example of an innovation that diffuses rapidly throughout the world, thus removing long-term competitiveness and permitting adjustment. In contrast, there is less scope for adjustment in heavy industries (e.g. steel) if they are characterized by world overcapacity and limited opportunity for product diversification.

A major factor affecting the adjustment process is government policy and here again differences in approach are apparent. The USA, for example, has financed economic growth through running a large budget deficit (hence job creation rather than job loss), whereas countries like the United Kingdom and West Germany have adopted strong deflationary policies, including major cuts in public expenditure and tight monetary restrictions (hence the higher unemployment). Attempts have been made to reduce the power of trade unions (an 'inefficiency' in the labour market for employers—Dicken, 1986) and encourage labour mobility (Chapter 4.2). Japan represents yet another, more holistic, approach to adjustment, within a framework of long-term forecasts; this is achieved by 'deploying an array of instruments aimed, in various sectors, at restructuring and modernisation, reduction of excess capacity and reorientation of activities' (OECD, 1988, p. 77).

A popular government response to the upswing in the NICs and the exporting policies of Japan has been to restrict imports of manufactured goods in one way or another—the so-called *protectionist fix* (Dicken, 1986). As the OECD (1988 p. 73) observe, 'the rapid structural changes in the world economy have been such as to warrant protection in some cases so as to prevent large-scale employment dislocations and to provide breathing space for adjustment.' The main problem has not been the volume of NIC imports, but their very rapid growth at a time of deep recession in the ODCs; this has been compounded by the fact that the major growth in imports has occurred in industries that are particularly sensitive in the developed countries (Dicken, 1986). Discriminating trade restrictions, mainly on Japan and the Asian NICs, have included import quotas, surcharges, and licences, and take the form of 'orderly marketing agreements' or 'voluntary export restrictions'. Many of these agreements are bilateral, although the Multi-Fibre Agreement (MFA), operative since 1974, is an excellent example of a more comprehensive agreement (see Chapter 12.1). The MFA represents an attempt to regulate imports of Third World textiles and clothing, with the objective of benefiting both developed and developing countries. However, the agreement has been dominated by European and North American interests to protect the disruption of their domestic markets. Effectively, the ODCs have lost their comparative advantage in certain run-down industries to the NICs and are claiming unfair competition.

The protectionist fix is rather contentious. It can have adverse effects on economic development in the less-developed countries, as well as raising costs to the consumer in the developed countries. It is not, therefore, a solution in itself. A more positive response by the ODCs would be to look upon developments in the NICs as providing new opportunities for partnership relations of benefit to both parties. There is considerable interdependence in trade between the NICs and the OECD for example; the NICs require capital goods and high-tech imports from the OECD nations, which remain the main customer for NIC exports.

Dicken (1986) refers to three other 'fixes' or types of adjustment that the ODCs can make to the new world economy. The first is the *foreign investment fix*, which primarily takes the form of encouraging multinationals to locate new investment in ODCs. Europe and the USA have been attempting to entice Japanese investment in particular, and the United Kingdom has been especially successful in attracting Japanese multinational motor vehicle companies (Toyota, Nissan, and Honda have all invested in locations in

the United Kingdom since the mid-1980s). Japan clearly sees the United Kingdom, with its relatively cheap labour costs, as an ideal base to 'exploit' the European car market. However, it is less clear whether or not there will be long-term benefits for the host country, in terms of job creation, impacts on indigenous motor car firms, and technological developments (see also Chapter 12.3).

The two remaining fixes are the development of new technologies and the promotion of small firms (for details see Chapters 6 and 7). With the *technological fix*, where sophisticated components, computers, and information technology are perceived to be the salvation of the ODCs, there is considerable debate over whether jobs are actually created or destroyed (Chapter 6). Assuming that jobs are created, there is still the problem that they will require different skills and this means that firms are likely to locate (or relocate) in different areas (because the traditional centres of industry have inappropriate skills). There is some general agreement that reindustrialization in the ODCs is due in part to the *small firm fix* (Keeble, 1989a) and small batch production and flexible specialization in particular (Chapter 1.3). Yet again though, it is doubtful whether the promotion of small firms can have a major effect on unemployment, especially as thousands of small firms would be required to offset the losses resulting from the restructuring and rationalization of large firms. Also, most small firms depend on large firms for their markets and the failure rate of small firms is high.

Adjustments by the ODCs to the new world economy take on different forms and it seems clear that any one particular 'fix' will, on its own, be inadequate to encourage employment and economic growth. The situation is well summarized by Dicken (1986, p. 408):

The problems facing the older industrialised countries are both the *general* ones of economic recession and stagnation and the *particular* ones facing individual countries and particular segments of their populations. Within the overall context of recession some countries face greater problems of adjustment to change than others ... Within individual nations, too, there is a strong geographical dimension to these problems. Regions of decline are contrasted with regions of growth ... Adjustment to change has a distinctive geographical face. Above all, the problem is one of unemployment.

It is to the nature of economic change within countries that the next two chapters turn.

14.5 Summary

The world is characterized by marked spatial inequalities in economic change and development, typified in the contrasts between 'North' and 'South' and 'core' and 'periphery'. These spatial disparities are dynamic and can be understood only by adopting a global perspective and examining macro processes of change. The world economy is an interdependent system and change in one area (e.g. the core) affects and is affected by change in another area (e.g. the periphery). This chapter has highlighted some of these complex relationships and drawn attention to the following key points:

- The development of the world economy is not based on a simple dependency relationship between developed and developing countries. The relationship is one of unequal interdependence.
- Changes in developed market economies, the main focus of this book, need to be examined in the context of the world economy.
- Within the world economy, economic change has occurred in both developed and developing countries. For example, there has been a global shift in manufacturing, from the USA and Western Europe to Japan and the Newly Industrializing Countries (NICs). The emergence of the NICs has led to increasing disparities within the Third World.
- Attempts to explain economic change at the international level include modernization theory (e.g. Rostow), dependency theory (e.g. Frank) and a more historical approach based on world systems theory (e.g. Wallerstein).
- The development of the new world economy has been characterized by a change from an Old International Division of Labour (pattern of international specialization where the developing countries exported raw materials to and imported manufactured goods from the developed countries) to a New International Division of Labour (more complex pattern of trade flows between developed and developing countries, including the export of manufactured goods from the latter to the former).
- The NICs have followed two industrialization strategies: import substitution and export processing. The latter has been the more successful and involves the creation of Export Processing Zones, which attempt to develop a specialized role in the world economy in such products as textiles, clothing, and electronics.
- Changes in the world economy, notably the global shift in manufacturing and the development of the NICs, has necessitated adjustments in the Older Developed Countries (ODCs). Various 'fixes' have been introduced to overcome the fluctuating problem of unemployment and to adjust to the changing pattern of competition, ranging from protectionist policies to the encouragement of foreign investment, technological developments and small firm generation.
- The adjustment process has varied both between and within the ODCs and includes a very strong regional dimension. Regional differences in 'economic health' are examined in the next two chapters.

15

Regional Economic Change, I: Nature and Theories

'Dramatic long-run regional economic change is a normal product of capitalist development dynamics' (Markusen, 1985 p. 11). Regional economic change tends to favour some areas more than others. Competitive economic struggles cannot have winners without also having losers, although the absolute level of regional development may rise over a long historical period.

The study of regional economic changes is important because such changes have an impact on the incomes and social well-being of people living in different areas and on the job opportunities available in different places. The nature and extent of these spatial variations in economic and social health and the way the disparities change over time, in particular whether they are increasing or decreasing, are key issues for policymaking. However, whereas the main features of regional economic change are generally not widely disputed, there is far less agreement about their interpretation and explanation.

This chapter and the following one concentrate on analysing patterns of economic change *between* and *within* regions of developed market economies. Gore (1984) and Hollier (1988) provide useful discussions of regional development issues in the Third World, while Kuklinski (1982) and Demko (1984) discuss aspects of regional development in centrally planned economies. This first chapter begins with a discussion of the nature of recent regional economic changes, before concentrating on an assessment of some general theories of regional economic change. The next chapter illustrates the nature of regional economic change and its explanation through three case studies chosen to give examples of economic change at different spatial scales. The chapter ends with a discussion of the justification and effectiveness of regional economic policies.

15.1 The nature of regional economic change

The nature of regional economic inequalities in developed market economies has changed dramatically during the twentieth century and particularly in the period since the Second World War. Not only has the relative importance of the different types of problem area changed, but so also has the pattern and form of uneven development.

Types of problem area

Various types of problem area have been identified by different research workers. For example, Stohr (1987, p. 189) suggests that in the last twenty years there has been a shift from a 'bipolar to a tri-polar situation in regional development'. He argues that up to the 1970s the regional problem dimension in almost all countries was based on a centre–periphery contrast, with an over-concentration of population and economic activity and high levels of development in the centre and low population densities, a lack of industrialization and low levels of development in peripheral areas. However, after the 'world economic crisis' of the 1970s he goes on to suggest (p. 189) that the regional problem dimension in most industrialized countries has been characterized by three polar types, based mainly on spatial differences in innovation:

(i) *highly innovative regions*: certain urban areas, environmentally attractive 'sunbelt' or 'mountainbelt' areas, regions around technology complexes or science parks, etc, based mainly on endogenous high-technology development;

(ii) *'old' industrial areas* stemming usually from the

period of the first industrial regions ... frequently mineral resource or staple product-orientated and dominated by what today are often called smoke-stack industries; and

(iii) *underdeveloped regions* which are usually rural, sometimes with infrequent industrialization mainly of a branch-plant type dependent on exogenous, low-technology production.

On the other hand, several British research workers had already used a threefold classification of problem regions in the 1960s and 70s which distinguished pressurized regions, depressed industrialized regions and underdeveloped areas (e.g. Glasson, 1978). Stohr's main contribution is to emphasize the role of technology.

These simple regional classifications intuitively make sense, but there is no explicit reference to the economic processes which have shaped them. A potentially more useful classification has been suggested by Lewis (1984). He distinguishes between *regions of rapid accumulation* and *regions of slow accumulation*. These may be further subdivided according to the type of accumulation process. Rapid accumulation regions include metropolitan areas, with concentrations of ownership and control of capital, and newly emergent zones of accumulation, such as planned economic complexes and areas of dispersed economic growth. Slow accumulation regions are those characterized by obsolete capital (especially in mining or specialized declining industrial sectors) or by pre-capitalist production (in agricul-

ture). An application of this classification to economic regions in Europe is shown in Table 15.1. The classification is useful, because as Williams (1987 p. 249) notes: 'Economic change has different requirements and poses different challenges in each of these regional types. This has led to distinctive political reactions to the process of economic adjustment and to different types of economic policy responses.'

There have also been suggestions that the spatial scale of problem regions has changed with a shift in emphasis from interregional to intraregional variations in economic well-being (e.g. Keeble, 1977). By the late 1970s, it was realized that inner-city areas had become one of the main types of problem region in the United States and the United Kingdom, and there were indications that other industrialized countries were beginning to experience similar trends (Hall, 1981b). In the United Kingdom, studies in the mid-1970s showed that all large cities in both prosperous and declining areas were affected, and unemployment levels in inner-Birmingham and inner-London exceeded levels in some government assisted areas (Chapman and Walker, 1987). This contributed to a weakening of British regional policy and the development of urban-based policies (Damesick, 1987).

The increased significance of inner-city problems should not, however, detract attention away from broader regional disparities, many of which are also increasing in importance. For example, Martin (1988b, p. 390), in writing about the British situation, notes that:

TABLE 15.1 A general classification of economic regions in Western Europe

(a) RAPID ACCUMULATION

Metropolitan
Examples: London, Paris, Frankfurt, Randstadt, Milan-Turin, Athens

Newly-emergent zones of accumulation
Examples: north-eastern and central Italy, parts of southern Italy, western Portugal, western France, eastern Ireland, southern Norway, East Anglia, much of Switzerland and Denmark

(b) SLOW ACCUMULATION

Obsolete capital
Examples: Ruhr, Saar, southern Belgium, UK coalfields, north-east France, Luneburg (Netherlands), Basque country

Rural regions, less articulated with capitalist development
Examples: interior of Spain and Portugal, northern Scandinavia, Greece (excepting Athens and Thessaloníki), western Ireland

Source: Williams (1987 p. 250).

Intra-regional disparities are not new. ... as is well known, the degree of spatial inequality in the socio-economy is scale-dependent, with a tendency to increase as the geographical coverage of the areal divisions employed decreases. The debate is not just over the existence or significance of local disparities, which can be found everywhere: the issue is also that these local disparities map out and form part of a broader 'north–south' geography of socio-economic inequality, and that this regional divide has become an increasingly prominent feature of British society.

This twofold division into 'north' and 'south' suggests that elements of a core–periphery dimension to regional problems still exist within the United Kingdom.

Patterns of uneven development

The pattern of regional economic inequalities changes dramatically with time, so that over a period of perhaps a century the pattern of prosperity and decline may alter almost beyond recognition. For example, when Canada became a Confederation in 1867, the Maritime Provinces were prosperous and highly industrialized; today they have some of the lowest income levels and highest unemployment rates in the country (Phillips, 1982). The Canadian space-economy at Confederation had the classic centre–periphery structure with Central Canada and the Maritimes at one end of the spectrum and the West and peripheral regions of the Canadian Shield at the other. By 1979, the resource-rich British Columbia and Alberta had not only caught up with Ontario, but had also overtaken it, at least in terms of per capita incomes.

An uneven, though changing, spatial pattern of development seems to be a general feature of the economic history of all countries. Britain provides a further illustration. For much of the nineteenth century, the most prosperous parts of Britain were in the North and West, while much of the South was in the grip of an agricultural depression. In the 1920s and 1930s this situation was reversed (Massey, 1986). It was the industrial regions of the North and West which had the highest rates of unemployment, while the newer industries were growing in the South-East and the West Midlands. In 1914 London and the South-East region had the highest unemployment rates, while in the depths of the recession in 1932 they had the lowest (Meegan, 1985). Since the mid-

1960s, new areas of high unemployment have become apparent, notably in the West Midlands and the inner cities, while high-status, high-paid jobs are becoming concentrated in the so called 'British sunbelt'; this period also saw the emergence of the 'north–south' divide (Town and Country Planning Association, 1987; Green, 1988; Martin, 1988b).

Forms of uneven development

Some forms of regional development are resistant to change, while others may alter significantly over the period of a few decades. For instance, in Canada the main basis of regional disparities remains differences in natural resources and fluctuating foreign demand. This is well illustrated by developments in the Prairies. The boom in the 1970s in Alberta, and to a lesser extent Saskatchewan, was based largely on the demand for the oil, gas, and mineral deposits found in these states. Relative to its two neighbours Manitoba has an inferior resource base. As a consequence, while both Saskatchewan and Alberta showed a marked relative improvement in per capita income over the period 1969–79, Manitoba did not show any improvement (Phillips, 1982).

On the other hand, in many advanced industrialized countries the significance of regional differences in industrial structure has generally lessened over the last fifty or so years, while the importance of occupational differences has increased. For example, in Britain in the nineteenth century the difference between the prosperous North and West and the poor South was largely based on the concentration of the new manufacturing industries in the former and the dependence of the latter on a depressed agricultural sector. In the inter-war period the situation was reversed, with new manufacturing industries locating in the South and Midlands, while the older manufacturing industries in the North and West took the brunt of the depression. By the 1970s and 1980s, the form of the spatial inequality had changed radically and the prosperity of the South had become based more on the type of job located there than the type of industry. Today it is the concentration of white-collar occupations in the South which distinguishes it from the rest of the country. In other words, the earlier dominant *sectoral* spatial division of labour has been replaced by an *occupational* division (Massey,

1979*b*; 1984*b*; Chapter 4.2). There are signs, however, of a re-emergence of an element of sectoral division between North and South with the concentration of financial, technical, and professional services in the South (Massey, 1988*a*; Chapter 13.3). The fact that employment in these sectors is composed largely of white-collar jobs shows that sectoral and occupational spatial divisions of labour may overlap.

A major factor underlying this change in the spatial division of labour is the development of locational hierarchies by multi-establishment and multinational enterprises (Chapter 7.2; Healey and Watts, 1987). The potential regional development implications of the geographical separation of control and production are profound. On the negative side, branch plant regions may suffer from an outflow of profits, a shortage of high status and skilled jobs, a low level of local provision of materials and business services, a concentration of products at the mature stage of the product cycle, a dampening down of entrepreneurial initiative, and an insensitivity to local circumstances by decision-makers located at a distance. Against these disadvantages are the possibility that the plants belonging to multi-region firms may well benefit the regions in which they are located by allowing access to the financial resources and markets of the parent firms and by permitting access to any technological and administrative innovations adopted by the parent firms. The implications of the development of *branch plant economies* has generated a wealth of research (Watts, 1981); however, difficulties in separating out the effect of external control from other variables means that much of the evidence is not clear-cut (see also Chapter 7.3).

A high level of external control of the industries of an area may become an important national issue. For example, in Canada, which has been described as 'a branch-plant, down-sized economy using borrowed technology' (Phillips, 1982 p. 119), over half of manufacturing production is foreign owned (principally by firms based in the USA), as are many of the natural resources. The Canadian economy is 'truncated' in that much of the decision-making and research and development functions are missing from the foreign-owned plants (Chapter 11.1; Hayter, 1982). This argument is persuasively developed by Britton and Gilmour (1978), who suggest that foreign-owned branch plants limit local autonomy over

investment decision-making, increase dependency on imported technology, goods, and services by substituting corporate for local linkages, and inhibit export potential in secondary manufacturing. Others, in contrast, maintain that foreign direct investment stimulates competition and innovation and fosters growth and efficiency by providing scarce managerial, technical, marketing, and financial resources (e.g. Daly, 1979, Safarian, 1979).

It is clear from this brief review of the nature of regional economic change in developed market economies that it is a dynamic process in which the type of problem area and the pattern and form of uneven development can change dramatically within a few decades. For a theory of regional economic change to be adequate it needs to account for this dynamism.

15.2 Theories of regional economic change

There is a wide variety of theories concerned with regional economic change which are well summarized in the standard texts (e.g. Richardson, 1978; Armstrong and Taylor, 1985; Rees and Stafford, 1986; Allen and Massey, 1988). Aspects of most of the theories of regional economic change have been discussed at various points in this book (see Chapter 2 for discussion of theories of economic change and location). Some theories emphasize spatial variations in resources, markets, or factors of production (Chapters 3–5), while others concentrate on regional differences in technological innovations (Chapter 6) or the organization of labour and production (Chapters 4.2 and 7). Factors internal to the regions are emphasized by some approaches, while others focus on the interaction between local and external factors. Indeed, it is increasingly being suggested that patterns of regional development within a nation are closely associated with the international patterns discussed in Chapter 14 (Massey, 1986; Thrift, 1985; 1986). Here attention is focused on those theories which are concerned with *long-term* regional economic changes and which emphasize one of four groups of factors— the export base, the mobility of capital and labour, technological change, and changes in the organization of labour.

Export base theory

The main idea of export base theory, or economic base theory as it is sometimes called, is that regional economic change depends on the proportion of the economic activities in a region which produce goods or services for export. Most work has concentrated on applying the theory to understanding the growth of regions, although it has been applied also at both the urban (urban economic base) and national scales. The theory divides economic activities in a region into:

(i) basic or export activities which export outside the region; and

(ii) non-basic or service activities which produce goods and services for internal consumption.

According to the theory, the fortunes of a region are dependent on changes in the amount of basic activity within the region. Generally the larger the region the higher the proportion of its activities which are basic. A growth in basic activities will increase the flow of labour into the region, increasing the demand for goods and services within it and bring about a corresponding increase in the amount of non-basic activities. A fall in the demand for the products of a region will have the reverse effect.

The attractiveness of export base theory lies in its simplicity, although technical and conceptual problems concerned with measuring the size of the basic sector and the choice of study area limit its effectiveness. Glasson (1978) suggests that these limitations are least severe when dealing with small regions with a high level of dependence on specialized export activities. Supporters of the theory argue that it stands up to a variety of real-life situations. Brook and Hay (1984) have used it, for example, to interpret economic growth in the Pacific North-West, industrial decline in North-East England and economic stagnation in Western Ireland. However, as they stress, such illustrations of the theory 'cannot be called proof of these ideas' (p. 68). Nevertheless the theory provides one interpretation of events.

The Pacific North-West is a classic case study in the literature on export base theory because its development has been associated with the growth of a succession of export staples (e.g. North, 1955). The first major resource to be exploited was timber. To begin with it was exported to

California by sea, but with the building of the transcontinental railway in the 1880s and the exhaustion of other timber resources elsewhere in the United States, it was able to build up its timber trade so that in the first half of the twentieth century it consistently contributed about 40 per cent of exports by value. From the 1890s timber exports were joined by wheat and, later, fruit. This was followed by the rapid development of hydro-electric power (HEP) from the 1930s to the 1950s, which indirectly contributed to the export base by attracting metallurgical and smelting industries to the region. Like the previous export staples, HEP is a natural resource and has largely reached the limits of its expansion. The last export staple, passenger and jet planes from the Boeing Aircraft Company, differs from the previous ones in that it was established independently of natural resources or locational advantage. By the late 1960s Boeing employed 80 000 in the Seattle area. Although the dependence of the region on the success of one company brings about its own problems of instability, the area is at least no longer dependent on an export which has natural resource constraints (Brook and Hay, 1974).

Export base theory is an aggregate theory and it is highly unlikely that a change in employment in every basic activity will have the same influence on non-basic employment. The theory further assumes that export activities are the only factor bringing about regional change. It ignores, for example, the changes in the comparative advantage of the region *vis-à-vis* other regions with respect to such elements as land, labour, and transfer costs. Change may also occur through the exhaustion of a natural resource or the discovery of a new one. Other factors which the theory neglects include the influence of the amount of imports, the consequences of government expenditure and the effect of the adoption of innovations on regional development. A further important point is that export base theory suggests that the level of development in an area depends on its ability to generate wealth through exporting, but there is no indication as to whether it is the regions which are initially prosperous or poor which are most likely to increase their exports. Thus the theory does not shed any light on whether regional imbalances in economic health are likely to increase or decrease. To explore this question, it is necessary to examine theories which emphasize the flow of capital and labour between regions.

Theories based on the interregional movement of capital and labour

Within this group, there are two main types of theory which predict different outcomes. On the one hand, the *neoclassical* models of regional growth suggest that economic systems tend towards equilibrium. Initial differences based on, for example, the pattern of resources, will tend to reduce as labour is attracted to high-wage areas and capital is attracted to low-wage areas. For example, the low wages in the southern states of the USA attracted capital from the northern states in the 1970s (Wheaton, 1979). On the other hand, another group of models based on *cumulat-*

ive causation suggest that once disparities come into existence a self-reinforcing process comes into operation which, in the absence of catastrophic events, maintains the status of the growing areas. The operation of this process is illustrated in Fig. 15.1, which shows how an area which attracts a new industry is likely to continue to attract more. A similar process is implied in the Brandt Commission report on north–south differences on an international scale (Chapter 14.1).

Although the predictions are different, both models depend on a ready (or instantaneous in the case of the neoclassical models) movement of capital and labour in response to the regional variations in wage levels or growth potential. However, this ignores the constraints on the mobility of these factors of production, such as the major investment in fixed capital in the case of

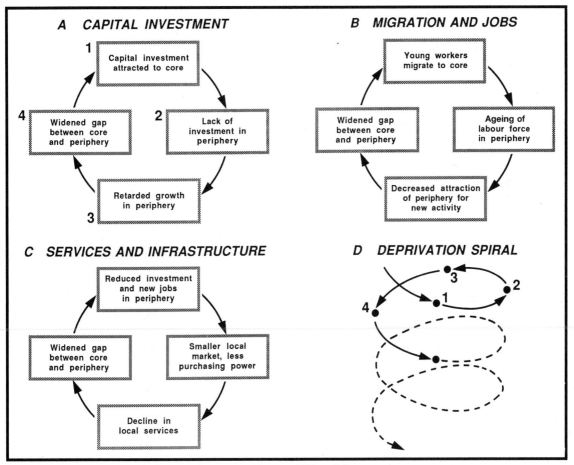

FIG 15.1 The process of cumulative causation (*source:* Haggett, 1983 p. 524)

industry, and differences in house prices and difficulties in obtaining council (public) housing in the case of labour (Chapter 4). It also neglects the large number of different factors which influence the location decisions of industrialists and individuals (Chapter 10).

Moreover, they both ignore the possibility that countervailing trends may be more powerful. The neoclassical models are essentially static and do not allow for a dynamic situation in which things are changing at different rates and at different times. For example, changes in technology or the resource base may be more important in bringing about or reinforcing regional disparities than the tendency to move towards the state of equilibrium predicted by the theory. The cumulative causation model, on the other hand, although it emphasizes the process of change, focuses only on what Myrdal (1957) called the *backwash effect* (i.e. the self-reinforcing process). However, development may be transferred to other regions through a *spread* or *trickle down* effect. Sometimes the diffusion process is strong enough for a new process of cumulative causation to start in these regions, although this tends to happen only in the late stages of development and may require strong government intervention (Hirschman, 1958). For example, Rees and Stafford (1986 p. 27) note that in the case of the USA:

The predominance of military bases set up in the South and West, first associated with World War II . . . had an appreciable influence on net migration flows. Between 1965 and 1970 military personnel accounted for 14 percent of interregional migrants, a testimony to the role that government policy can play in spread effects.

Other examples of government intervention to aid the South include the massive public investments since the 1930s in the Tennessee Valley Authority, the Area Redevelopment Administration, and the Appalachian Regional Commission (Weinstein and Firestine, 1978).

Another example of the process of cumulative causation can be seen in a rather mechanistic interpretation of the *Marxist theory of uneven development* which stems from the operation of the capitalist system. According to this argument, for individual enterprises to survive they have to accumulate capital. This brings about a tendency to concentrate production in large units and centralize control in large companies. This, according to the theory, inevitably has a spatial outcome with both production units and control units tending to locate in groups to gain economies of agglomeration (Meegan, 1985). The theory suggests that both capital and labour flow into the rapidly growing areas. Like other models based on cumulative causation, this deterministic version of the Marxist theory of uneven development is embarrassed by evidence of spatial disparities reducing, for example through the urban–rural shift of manufacturing.

The main features of the neoclassical model and the various theories emphasizing the principle of cumulative causation are summarized in Table 15.2. Whereas the neoclassical model predicts convergence in the long-term level of economic health between regions, most of the theories emphasizing cumulative causation suggest that divergence in the fortunes of regions is the most probable outcome. An exception to this is the late stage of the theory by Hirschman, which suggests that other factors such as government intervention may bring about convergence. A major weakness of these theories based on the interregional flow of capital and labour is their

TABLE 15.2 Models of regional economic growth

Model	Characteristics of fast-growing regions			Interregional growth
	Level of income	Capital flow	Labour flow	
Neoclassical	Low	In	Out	Convergence
Myrdal	High[a]	In	In	Divergence
Hirschman—Early	High[a]	In	In	Divergence
Late	Low	In	In	Convergence
Marxist	High[a]	In	In	Divergence

[a]Not specified at beginning of process. Stimulus may start in low income area. However, divergence implies growing regions will eventually have higher incomes.

failure to make the role of technological change explicit. This deficiency is overcome in the following group of theories of regional economic change.

Theories based on technological change

'Technological change is arguably one of the single most important ... influences on regional change' (Malecki, 1983 p. 89). Several theories which emphasize the importance of technological change in regional development have been discussed at various stages in this book. The main features of three of these are summarized here.

1. Growth pole theory

This was briefly mentioned in Chapter 5.3 in connection with the discussion of linkages. The origin of growth pole theory is usually credited to Francois Perroux, a French economist who first used the term in 1955. Perroux's conception referred to leading industries and propulsive firms acting as *growth poles*, which through a multiplier process would stimulate other industries and businesses. The spatial dimension was added later by regional planners under the term *growth centre* (Darwent, 1969; Hansen, 1972). According to Perroux, leading industries are characterized by their newness, high technology, and strong linkages with other sectors, while propulsive firms are usually relatively large, belong to a growth industry and have a high ability to innovate and generate growth. Sectoral polarization does not necessarily imply geographical clustering. However, it is generally recognized that the multiplier process often encourages spatial polarization (Lloyd and Dicken, 1977), thus further enhancing the position of the initially advantaged region.

Growth pole theory, therefore, gives a more explicit recognition to the link between innovation, technological change, and regional economic growth than the other theories reviewed so far. The process may be illustrated by the development of the American urban system. At the end of the nineteenth century:

New or enlarged industries and their 'multiplier' effects created the employment opportunities that successively attracted 'active' and 'passive' migrants to the infant metropolises, and eventually led to additional manufacturing growth by directly or indirectly enhancing the possibility of invention and innovation (Pred, 1966 p. 39).

This implies that entrepreneurial skill and innovation potential were at this time concentrated in large urban areas. However, in the latter half of the twentieth century the revitalization of non-metropolitan areas and the more rapid growth of small and medium centres suggest that powerful agglomerating tendencies are also at work in these smaller centres. This led Rees and Stafford (1986 pp. 29–30) to argue that:

The next round of high-tech growth poles may well be away from the large agglomerations of Boston, San Francisco, New York, Dallas and Phoenix, and toward medium-sized growth centers, places like Austin, Texas, Albuquerque, New Mexico, Colorado Springs, Colorado, Portland, Oregon, or Lowell, Massachusetts. These are generally urban places small enough to offer a good life while still being large enough to provide necessary services and accessibility (see also Chapter 6.2).

2. Product life and profit cycles

The explicit recognition of the role of technological change in growth pole theory was taken a stage further by regional research workers in the 1970s with the application of product life cycle ideas to examining regional economic change (Thomas, 1980; see also Chapters 6.1, 6.3, and 16.1). The model suggests that locational shifts occur as products go through a life cycle from innovation to growth, maturity, and eventual obsolescence, because each stage has distinct locational requirements. Thus the innovation phase, which usually entails a large amount of R. & D., tends to be carried out either in areas where there is already a concentration of technical and scientific labour or in areas where this labour can be attracted. On the other hand, the mature phase of production tends to favour low-cost locations, typically peripheral areas where labour costs are cheap and unionization levels are low. However, some of these 'peripheral' locations may, through the development of external economies and new firm formation, develop into new growth centres in their own right, such as the Dallas–Fort Worth area. This implies that 'over time regions can change their roles from being recipients of innovation (branch plants) to become generators of innovation through indigenous growth' (Rees and Stafford, 1986 p. 33). A similar process has been suggested to have been in operation in 'Silicon Glen' in central Scotland (Haug, 1986). However, this shift of innovative capacity into the periphery seems to go beyond the predictions of the product life cycle and is not as Rees (1979) suggests a locational implication of the cycle.

More recent work has shifted the emphasis from studying product life cycles to examining industrial profit cycles and the role of oligopolies. According to Markusen (1985, p. 27) the profit cycle has five stages:

1. *Zero profit*: corresponding to the initial birth and design stage of an industry.
2. *Super profit*: corresponding to the era of excess profit from temporary monopoly and innovative edge.
3. *Normal profit*: corresponding to the stage of open entry, movement towards market saturation, and absence of substantial market power.
4. *Normal-plus or Normal-minus profit*: corresponding to the post-saturation stage, where either successful oligopolization boosts profits again, or predatory and excessive competition squeezes profit.
5. *Negative profit*: corresponding to the obsolescence stage of the sector.

She goes on to suggest that the development of oligopolies early in the evolution of an industry may have detrimental effects on both potentially competitive regions and the host regions. In the innovative era, oligopolistic industry structures tend to retard decentralization of production, leading to the underdevelopment of peripheral areas, while later in a profit squeeze during the mature stage the switching of production to low-cost locations can result in large job losses in the host communities. A region which acts as a host to the core of an oligopoly may appear to enjoy a long period of prosperity, but it may evolve as a relatively non-diversified local economy with great vulnerability to the inevitable restructuring of the oligopolistic sector. Economic change in twentieth-century Coventry provides a clear illustration of this process (see Chapter 16.3). The success of the large motor and engineering industry firms in the city during the first half of the twentieth century provided boom conditions, while the restructuring of these same firms during the 1970s and early 1980s created a major recession in the local economy. Regions which host the branch plants of an oligopolistic sector may find their own capacity underdeveloped, particularly with respect to supplier industries. For example, when Rootes established a branch plant at Lin-wood near Glasgow in the early 1960s, few motor component firms were attracted to Scotland to serve the new motor assembly plant (Simms and Wood, 1984).

3. Long wave theories

Whereas product life and profit cycle ideas are usually applied to specific products and industries, long wave theory relates changes in technology to changes in the economy as a whole. The main features of long wave theory were outlined in Chapter 2.1. The theory, originally developed by Kondratieff, suggests that economic cycles lasting about fifty years, from the beginning of an up-swing to the end of a down-swing, are related to the clustering of innovations in the recession phase of the previous cycle and the speed with which the innovations are diffused (Fig. 2.1). Much of the debate has focused on whether the causes of long waves of economic activity are internal or external to the capitalist system. Explanations which emphasize the automatic internal regulation of the system are deterministic in their predictions, while explanations which emphasize the social, economic, and political relationships in which particular forms of technology are developed and diffused allow a greater possibility of intervention to attempt to steer the course and nature of economic cycles. A similar debate has arisen over the relationship of long waves to regional economic change.

Hall (1981a, 1985) suggests that key innovations are bunched in space as well as in time and the locus of innovation shifts from one cycle to the next. Thus in Britain the first Kondratieff wave was concentrated in Shropshire, the Black Country, and Lancashire; while regions such as South Wales and the North-East came to the fore in the second; and the West Midlands and the South-East dominated in the third and fourth. The fifth Kondratieff cycle, which is just beginning, is hypothesized to be focused on non-industrialized areas associated with scientific research, such as Cambridge and the M4 Corridor (Chapter 6.2). According to Hall, new industrial traditions take root in places different from the older ones. His theory is also sectoral in that the 'sunrise' industries of today will be the 'sunset' industries of tomorrow. Hall suggests a certain inevitability in these trends and he advocates policies which foster and facilitate them.

Others, such as Freeman *et al.* (1982), Rothwell

(1982), and M. Marshall (1987), break away somewhat from this deterministic interpretation of long wave theory by emphasizing the social, economic, and political context in which particular regions come to the fore, and hence open up the possibility that 'in spite of all the observable regularities the shape of the future is mouldable, is ours to create' (Massey, 1988b p. 88). Significantly, Marshall questions the inevitability of 'sunrise' and 'sunset' industries (see also Chapter 6.1) and emphasizes that new technology involves process technologies as well as product technologies and new processes can equally be applied to traditional industries as to new ones. By explicitly incorporating changes in the way that production is organized into his explanation, Marshall provides a bridge between theories of regional economic change based on technological change and those emphasizing changes in the organization of labour.

Theories based on changes in the organization of labour

Earlier sections of this book have touched upon two groups of theories which emphasize changes in the organization of labour. One group of theories, based on the spatial division of labour, suggests that uneven development is related to the continuous restructuring of society, which leads to changes in where different kinds of jobs and activities occur (Chapter 4.2). The other group, concerned with regulationist theories, suggests that regional economic change in a capitalist country reflects 'the dominant regime of accumulation' which characterizes the particular phase of development the economy has reached. The different regimes of accumulation—manufacture, machinofacture, scientific management and Fordism, and neo-Fordism—are usually described in terms of the way labour is organized and controlled in the production process (Chapters 2.1; 4.2; and 6.1). The spatial division of labour and regulationist schools are related and to an extent different regimes of accumulation are characterized by different spatial divisions of labour. But regulationist approaches suggest that changes in the organization of labour are concentrated in particular periods and are also related to changes in the role of the state and the nature of consumption patterns.

1. Spatial division of labour

The degree to which the spatial division of labour leads to regional inequalities depends on the extent to which the division of labour in society is itself unequal (e.g. by class, occupation, and gender) and the way in which that inequality is organized over space (Massey, 1984a, 1988a, 1988b). For example, in Britain there are major divisions between management and shop-floor workers, between scientific/professional and manual workers and between sectors. This division of labour is also quite highly structured over space. Thus managerial and control jobs are concentrated in the South-East, particularly Greater London, while many of the scientific and technical professions are located in towns and semi-rural locations in the outer South-East. In contrast, direct production jobs, whether in manufacturing or services, form a relatively high proportion of the labour force in the 'North'.

A key feature of the spatial division of labour concept is that it 'attempts to clarify the way in which spatial inequality is both *produced and used* by firms in their search for conditions favourable for profitable production and continued capital accumulation' (Meegan, 1985 p. 14). Thus current patterns of regional inequality are produced in part by past patterns of investment and disinvestment by firms. Firms in turn use existing patterns of uneven development to their advantage. Thus, according to this view, the decentralization of industry in Britain in the late 1960s and early 1970s (Chapter 16.2) can be interpreted as firms responding to the pattern of inequality to improve their competitiveness.

It was the legacy of the previous form of uneven development based in the sectoral spatial division of labour (high levels of unemployment from previously dominant sectors which had overwhelmingly employed men) which provided the conditions (regional policy grants, a 'green', female labour force anxious for paid employment) which attracted in this new form of economic activity and laid down a new form of uneven development (Massey, 1988b p. 79).

This argument suggests that uneven development is necessary to the origins and survival of capitalism (cf. Browett, 1984 and Smith, 1986).

Central to the spatial division of labour view is the idea of *layers of investment and disinvestment*. Investment is attracted to areas where there are profitable opportunities, while disinvestment occurs in areas where the profitable opportunities have been exhausted. Contrary to neoclassical theories, processes of cumulative causation, and the more deterministic versions of the Marxist theory of uneven development, change is not thought to be irreversible. The spatial division of labour approach assumes that the 'pattern of geographical differentiation will itself be continually transformed as successive rounds of investment and disinvestment interact with the changing geography of profitable production' (Meegan, 1985 p. 15).

Hence the development of a particular region is a result of a combination of its changing role in the wider national and international economy and the distinctive history of the region itself. In other words, the character of a place results from the interaction of external factors (the national and international context) and local factors (such as the available material resources and factors of production, industrial structure, and social composition of the area). The external framework in

which regional inequalities develop is particularly emphasized by the regulationist theories.

2. Regulationist theories

This group of theories suggest that capitalist economies have developed through a series of regimes of accumulation, each exhibiting a degree of stability in the structure of national and international regulation, the organization of labour in the production process and spatial form (Lipietz, 1986). Of critical importance are the transition periods between phases which are characterized by crises and intense restructuring, often leading to the accelerated decline of highly industrialized regions from the previous phase of accumulation and the emergence elsewhere of newly industrializing or reindustrializing regions which match the requirements of the next phase (Soja, 1985).

It is suggested by proponents of this approach that since about the early to mid-1970s capitalist economies have been in a transition phase

TABLE 15.3 Key features of Fordist and neo-Fordist regimes in Britain

Characteristic	Fordist: the post war expansionary regime, late 1940s to early 1970	Neo-Fordist: the emergent regime of flexible accumulation, mid-1970s onwards
Accumulation regime	*Monopolistic*	*Flexible*
Industry	Monopolistic; increasing concentration of capital; steady growth of output and productivity, especially in new consumer durable goods sectors; secular expansion of private and especially public services	Rationalization and modernization of established sectors to restore profitability and improve competitiveness; growth of high-tech and producer service activities, and small firm sector
Employment	Full employment; growth of manufacturing jobs up to mid-1960s; progressive expansion of service employment; growth of female work; marked skill divisions of labour	Persistent mass unemployment; generalized contraction of manufacturing employment, growth of private service sector jobs; partial de-feminization (in manufacturing); flexibilization of labour utilization; large part-time and temporary segment
Consumption	Rise and spread of mass-consumption norms for standardized household durables (especially electrical goods) and motor vehicles	Increasingly differentiated (customized) consumption patterns for new goods (especially electronics) and household services
Production	Economies of scale; volume, mechanized (Fordist-type) production processes; functional decentralization and multinationalization of production	Growing importance of economies of scope; use of post-Fordist flexible automation; small batch specialization; organizational fragmentation combined with internationalization of production

TABLE 15.3 (*Cont.*)

Characteristic	Fordist: the post war expansionary regime, late 1940s to early 1970	Neo-Fordist: the emergent regime of flexible accumulation, mid-1970s onwards
Socio-institutional structure	*Collectivistic*	*Competitive-individualist*
Labour market	Collectivistic; segmented by skill increasingly institutionalized and unionized; spread of collective wage-bargaining; employment protection	Competitive; de-unionization and de-rigidification; increasing dualism between core and peripheral workers; less collective, more localized wage determination.
Social structure	Organized mainly by occupation, but tendency towards homogenization. Income distribution slowly convergent	Trichotomous and increasingly hierarchical; income distribution divergent
Politics	Closely aligned with occupation and organized labour; working-class politics important; regionalist	De-alignment from socio-economic class; marked decline of working-class politics; rise of conservative individualism; localist
State intervention	Keynesian-liberal collectivist; regulation of markets; maintenance of demand; expansion of welfare state; corporatist; nationalization of capital for the state	Keynesianism replaced by free-market Conservatism; monetary and supply-side intervention rather than demand stabilization; de-regulation of markets; constraints on welfare; self-help ideology; privatizing the state for capital
Space-economy	Convergent; inherited regional sectoral specialization (both old and new industries) overlaid by new spatial division of labour based on functional decentralization and specialization; regional unemployment disparities relatively stable	Divergent; decline of industrial areas (pre- and post-war); rise of new high-tech and producer services complexes; increasingly polarized spatial division of labour; widening of regional and local unemployment disparities

Source: Martin (1988*b* pp. 213, 219).

between Fordism and neo-Fordism. Among the characteristics of Fordism are mass production, mass consumption, state intervention in the management of the economy, and collective bargaining. This contrasts with neo-Fordism, which is characterized by flexible specialization, customized consumption patterns, and individualism (see Chapter 2.1). A more detailed outline of the main features of the two phases as applied to Britain is given in Table 15.3.

Significantly, it is suggested that each phase has its own geography. Thus Fordism in Britain is dominated by large plants making consumer goods and is associated principally with the West Midlands and the South-East. In contrast, the northern industrial regions were dominated by older industries producing intermediate goods which had been the basis of earlier expansion. The spatial decentralization of industry from the mid 1960s, stimulated by both government regional policy and by the search for sources of cheaper labour, encouraged the convergence of industrial structure across the regions. It also led to a new spatial division of labour with a shift of the lower-skilled assembly and final production activities to the North, while increasing the concentration of corporate head offices, research and development units, and similar high-order functions in the South.

In contrast to the pattern and form of economic change associated with Fordism, Martin (1988*a*) suggests that the transition to neo-

Fordism has been characterized by divergence in fortunes at both regional and local levels. At the regional scale a widening in the divide between the 'North' and 'South' of Britain has occurred, particularly in the 1980s. There is an inverse relationship between deindustrialization and tertiarization. For example, those regions which experienced the highest rates of job loss in manufacturing between 1978 and 1988 gained least from the expansion of jobs within the service sector (Fig.16.3). This Martin explains in terms of the advantages of the 'South', including the existence of a more diverse, more flexible and more technical labour force; the long-established concentration of corporate, financial and political power in the South-East; and the clustering of private and government research establishments and defence-related industry.

The shift to neo-Fordism has also been associated with an increase in inequality at the local scale:

There are several areas in the 'south' with problems of economic decline and unemployment comparable to any of those found in the most depressed northern localities. Equally, within the 'north' there are numerous localities where industrial renewal, high-technology development and expansion of provincial financial centres and consumer services (including new, giant shopping complexes) are forming the basis of an economic renaissance. ... There are now sharp divisions between 'newly industrializing' rural zones and economically stagnant urban areas; between buoyant service-based localities and depressed manufacturing towns; between the deprived and unemployed population entrapped in the inner cities and an increasingly affluent, securely employed and successful new middle class living in suburbia or in 'gentrified' and 'yuppified' metropolitan areas; between those in peripheral occupations and low-paid service employment (Martin, 1988a p. 226).

The application of the regulationist approach to regional economic change has not, however, gone unchallenged. Two of the main debates have revolved around, first, the extent to which the different regimes of accumulation have replaced each other; and secondly, the nature of the geography associated with each phase. Several research workers have questioned the applicability of regulationist ideas. Hudson (1988), for example, is sceptical of conceptualizing national social and economic change in terms of regimes of accumulation such as Fordism and neo-Fordism, and is even more critical over their use in regional analysis. In examining older industrial regions,

Hudson argues that Fordism has never established more than a tenuous hold in many of these regions. For instance, many of the branch plants opened in the 1950s and 1960s, which introduced Fordist techniques to the older industrial regions of Britain, shed labour or closed completely in the 1970s. He further suggests that many of the changes currently taking place in these areas in the organization of production constitute a selective reworking which reproduces, in modified form, pre-Fordist and Fordist methods of production, rather than a transition to neo-Fordist flexibility. New methods of production have to be integrated with existing methods, as Sayer (1989 p. 305) asks rhetorically: 'Wouldn't it be extraordinary if the future just happened to be the opposite of the past?' (original in italics).

Others have questioned the spatial trends associated with different phases of accumulation. For example, Meegan (1988, p. 181) warns of associating particular spatial patterns with particular regimes: 'There is a danger of assuming that new flexible production systems, or older inflexible ones for that matter, have a necessary geography. Care has to be taken to avoid creating spatial stereotypes.' The dangers of assuming that particular changes always have the same spatial outcome have been emphasized at several points in this book (e.g. Chapters 5.3; 6.3; and 7.3), although some outcomes may be more probable than others.

Both the spatial division of labour and regulationist theories draw heavily on structuralist ideas, which argue that to understand spatial patterns of economic activity and inequality it is necessary to examine the structure of the society in which they are produced (Chapter 2.2). According to this school of thought, as the structure of society changes so does the pattern and form of regional inequality. However, whereas the spatial division of labour approach emphasizes that change is continuous as local factors interact with external factors, the regulationist theories argue that major restructuring is concentrated in periods of transition between phases of capitalist accumulation.

15.3 Summary

This chapter has brought together several of the arguments introduced elsewhere in the book on the relative merits of different approaches to explaining economic location and change both between and within regions of developed market economies. The main points covered include the following:

- A variety of types of problem area have been identified including underdeveloped, depressed industrial, and pressurized regions. A potentially more useful classification is based on the type of accumulation process and distinguishes between regions of slow and rapid accumulation. Intraregional variations have also been given more emphasis recently particularly with the recognition of inner-city problems.

- Not only have the types of problem area changed, but so have the pattern and form of uneven development. Many regions have experienced complete reversals in their fortunes over a matter of a few decades, while in many countries the dominant *sectoral* spatial division of labour of fifty or so years ago has been replaced largely by an *occupational* spatial division of labour.

- Different theories stress different factors affecting long-term regional economic change. Recently there has been a shift in emphasis from theories which stress the supply of resources and factors of production to those emphasizing the role of technology and the changing organization of labour. There has also been a shift of emphasis from theories stressing the characteristics of areas to theories which stress the combination of the historical development of regions with their changing role in the wider world. These shifts may in part reflect the better ability of the latter theories to account for changes and reversals of trends in the pattern and form of regional economic change.

- Export base theory suggests that the fortunes of a region are dependent on changes in the volume of basic or export activities within the region. It is a simple idea which has been used to help understand the development of areas such as the Pacific North-West. However, it is an aggregate theory which gives no indication of whether it is the initially prosperous or poor regions which are likely to increase their exports.

- Two groups of theories emphasize the mobility of capital and labour between regions. Neoclassical theory suggests that labour will be attracted to high-wage areas whereas capital will move in the reverse direction, thus leading to regional convergence. Cumulative causation theory, on the other hand, argues that capital and labour will both be drawn to rapidly growing areas, thus leading to regional divergence, although government intervention in the latter stages may cause the benefits of growth to be spread more widely.

- A further group of theories emphasize the role of technology. Growth pole theory and its spatial derivative, growth centre theory, suggest that leading firms and industries, particularly those in high-technology sectors, encourage the growth of linked industries often in close spatial proximity. This is taken a stage further by product life and profit cycle ideas which suggest that although the early stages of production tend to agglomerate, usually where there is already a concentration of technical and scientific labour, later stages tend to favour low-cost labour locations. The development of oligopolies early in the evolution of an industry may, however, slow down the decentralization of production and encourage the development of a non-diversified economy in the core area, which is vulnerable to later restructuring. Long wave theory moves the debate over the regional impact of technological change to the level of the economy as a whole. Some research workers (e.g. Hall, 1985) imply that the process of replacement of 'sunset' industries by 'sunrise' industries is almost inevitable; others (e.g. M. Marshall, 1987), by emphasizing the social, political, and institutional context of technological change, argue that it is possible to intervene to steer the course and nature of economic cycles and their associated patterns of regional development.

- This move away from deterministic outcomes is further developed in the final group of theories considered, which emphasize the role of changes in the organization of labour. The spatial division of labour approach, in particular, stresses that the pattern of regional development is continually changing as local factors interact with national and international factors. Regulationist theories, on the other hand, argue that major restructuring is concentrated in periods of transition between phases of capitalist accumulation. However, the extent to which the different regimes of accumulation have replaced each other has been questioned and care has to be taken to avoid assuming each phase is associated with a particular geographic pattern of economic activity.

In the following chapter the emphasis shifts from a discussion of the general features of regional economic change and the theories which have been developed to try to understand it to a detailed analysis of specific examples. It examines three case studies which illustrate the nature of regional economic change in developed market economies at different spatial scales and allows the discussion of different explanatory frameworks applied to particular examples.

16

Regional Economic Change, II: Case Studies and Policies

To explore further the nature of regional economic changes in developed market economies and their explanation, both of which were discussed in general terms in the preceding chapter, this chapter examines three detailed case studies chosen to illustrate regional economic change at different spatial scales. The first analyses the different rates of employment growth experienced in the core and periphery of the United States; this is followed by an analysis of the spatial dimensions of deindustrialization in Britain; while the third examines some of the features of local economic development, through a case study of industrial change in one local economy, that of Coventry, England. Thus one example analyses economic change within a country of almost continental proportions, in which there are no language or political barriers; the second case study examines economic change within a country which is smaller in area than many of the individual states of the USA; while the third considers change at the scale of the local economy.

In each of the examples different explanations of the patterns are highlighted, and the insights provided by some of the theories and perspectives discussed in Parts I and II of this book, as well as the last chapter, are examined. The emphasis of some of these theories on the role of the structure of society in influencing the nature of regional economic change raises questions about the effectiveness of policies which attempt to reduce the regional inequalities by redistributing resources between areas. The final part of this chapter examines this debate by discussing the justification and limitations of regional economic policies.

One of the fascinations about discussing regional economic changes and policies is that it raises many of the controversies currently being debated in the social sciences about what constitutes an adequate explanation and whether policy can be devised independently of the theories and methods used in the analysis (Massey and Meegan, 1985; Allen and Massey, 1988).

16.1 Regional economic change in the United States

Some dramatic changes have occurred in the economic well-being of different regions within the United States over the last fifty years. In the first half of the twentieth century the Manufacturing Belt in the North-East was the core of the economy. However, the rates of employment growth experienced by the South and West began to accelerate during the 1950s. The difference between the 'North' and the 'South' became clearer after 1969 when the decline of the Manufacturing Belt became absolute in character, while the periphery continued to grow. This led several academics, journalists, and politicians to use a number of evocative terms to describe what a *Business Week* article in May 1976 called 'the second war between the States'. For example, the term 'Sunbelt' was first used by Phillips (1968), who identified what he saw as a fundamental change in the political and cultural geography of the Florida-Texas-Southern California Sunbelt at the end of the 1960s. The concept of the 'Sunbelt' required an oppositional idea, and terms such as 'Snowbelt', 'Frostbelt', and 'Rustbelt' were coined to emphasize the apparent contrasts between the growing 'South' and the stagnant 'North' (Bradshaw, 1988). Such descriptions, though oversimplifying the differences and ignoring the fact that many locations in the Frostbelt retained their long-run viability while many areas within the Sunbelt (e.g. Mississippi) remained impoverished, did serve to put regional disparities on the political agenda.

Unfortunately, although the term 'Sunbelt' is widely used in the literature, it is neither a distinct and homogeneous unit nor is it applied consistently; for example, it sometimes refers to the warmer parts of the country in the South and South-West, while on other occasions it is used as a residual category, which includes the Mountain and Pacific states such as Idaho, Washington, and Alaska. The division of the United States into core (i.e. the Manufacturing Belt) and periphery (i.e. the remainder, though for many purposes further subdivision is appropriate) is still perhaps the simplest and most useful territorial classification for examining employment changes. However, as Browning and Gesler (1979 p. 74) note:

We may quarrel with the delimitation of the Sun Belt, question its homogeneity, and caution against the often misleading impression the term conveys, but no matter, it is a notion whose time has come. The Sun Belt has become fixed firmly in the minds of many Americans; the image is the reality.

Nevertheless, no sooner had public awareness of Sunbelt versus Frostbelt differences increased, than the pattern of regional inequality began to change again. So, by the end of the 1980s commentators were talking about the development of a fragmented core (Agnew, 1987), the resurgence of New England (Hall, 1988) and the shrinking of the Sunbelt to only a very few 'Sunspots' (Weinstein and Gross, 1988).

The changing trends in regional employment between 1960 and 1985 are illustrated in Table 16.1 and Fig. 16.1. The main trend over the period is the decentralization of employment from the *Manufacturing Belt*. Whereas 51 per cent of non-agricultural employment was found in the three regions comprising the Belt in 1960, this had fallen to just under 40 per cent by 1985. All six regions in the *Periphery* performed better in terms of employment growth during the 1960s and 1970s than any of the three regions in the Manufacturing Belt. However, during the first half of the 1980s a distinction needs to be made between the *Rural Middle*, which suffered a net loss of employment, and the *Sunbelt* regions (used as a residual category), all of which continued to experience above-average employment growth

TABLE 16.1 Regional non-agricultural employment change in the United States, 1960–1985

Regions	1960 (000s)	% change in employment			1985 (000s)
		1960–70	1970–80	1980–5[a]	
MANUFACTURING BELT	27 271.3	+22.0	+12.1	+1.0	37 545.9
New England	3 697.7	+23.0	+20.3	+9.3	5 917.8
Middle Atlantic	11 914.4	+18.5	+6.3	+2.9	15 456.3
East North Central	11 659.2	+25.3	+15.2	−3.4	16 171.8
PERIPHERY	25 788.3	+43.5	+44.5	+5.7	56 433.1
Rural Middle[b]	6 003.7	+53.1	+30.9	−0.7	11 966.7
West North Central	3 244.3	+65.3	+28.7	−0.5	6 873.5
East South Central	2 759.4	+38.9	+33.9	−0.9	5 093.2
Sunbelt	19 784.6	+40.6	+49.1	+7.6	44 466.4
South Atlantic	7 179.2	+40.2	+45.3	+7.1	15 479.3
West South Central	4 267.2	+39.6	+56.3	+6.9	9 952.8
Mountain	1 874.2	+42.2	+67.6	+9.6	4 932.7
Pacific	6 463.8	+41.1	+43.1	+7.8	14 101.6
UNITED STATES	53 059.6	+32.5	+29.2	+3.8	93 979.0

[a]Based on 1980 employment figures in Hall (1988) which differ slightly from those in Weinstein *et al.* (1985).
[b]In some classifications West North Central is amalgamated with the regions of the Manufacturing Belt to form the 'Frostbelt' or 'Snowbelt', while East South Central is included with the 'Sunbelt'.

Sources: based on data in Weinstein *et al.* (1985 pp. 11–13) and Hall (1988 pp. 140–2; 150–2).

rates. During this period, the rebirth of New England becomes apparent and its above-average rate of employment growth led Hall (1988) to suggest that it would be more realistic to see it as an extension of the Sunbelt rather than as part of the Manufacturing Belt, giving, a *New Perimeter*.

All these trends are apparent from the figures in Table 16.1, although the finer spatial scale used in Fig. 16.1 shows important intraregional variations. For example, not all states (e.g. West Virginia) participated in the growth of the periphery in the 1960s and 1970s, while the revival of New England in the first half of the 1980s was mainly concentrated in the states of New Hampshire, Vermont, and to a lesser extent Massachusetts. However, Weinstein and Gross (1988) assert that since 1980 the fortunes of the Sunbelt have undergone a reversal. Ten of the sixteen states that they classify as in the Sunbelt lost jobs during the 1980s, and by the latter part of the decade had unemployment rates well above the national average. This is a dramatic turn around from the situation in the 1970s.

The rapidity of the changing regional economic fortunes is well shown by the following three quotations taken from the writings of eminent academics who have analysed the pattern of regional economic development in the United States at different points in time over the last three decades. The first statement was based on data for the late 1940s during the period of maximum concentration of employment in the Manufacturing Belt; the second observation was made after over twenty-five years of significant decentralization of employment to the Sunbelt, and the final statement was made following the economic difficulties faced by the 'oil patch' states of the Sunbelt in the mid-1980s. The three quotations suggest that the perception of these academics was strongly affected by the trends which were prevalent at the time they were writing.

For the fringe areas to develop in the face of this formidable competition (from the Manufacturing Belt) poses an almost insuperable obstacle (Ullman, 1958 p. 180).

The 'natural' forces favouring the more rapid growth of the South are powerful indeed and it is debatable whether any feasible level of federal spending could counteract these forces in order to favour the North (Estall, 1980 p. 384).

A strong argument can be made that the Sunbelt is today the most distressed economic region in the U.S. (Weinstein and Gross, 1988 p. 10).

Attempts to explain these trends in theoretical terms have given rise to the regional convergence–uneven development debate (Perry and Watkins, 1977; Gober, 1984). Proponents of regional convergence point to the trends towards declining regional inequalities in income and occupational structures as evidence that the US economy is moving towards spatial equilibrium. On the other hand, advocates of the uneven development thesis emphasize Myrdal's (1957) theory of cumulative causation, which sees rapid industrial growth and capital accumulation as self-reinforcing processes (Weinstein *et al.*, 1985; Chapter 15.2). According to this view, the growth of the Sunbelt is not an adjustment process moving the economy towards spatial equilibrium, but a new stage of uneven development. However, both theses contain a strong element of determinism and are undermined by the recent role reversals of the Frostbelt and Sunbelt (Weinstein and Gross, 1988).

Clearly, a full explanation of the recent changes in the pattern of employment change in the United States needs to account both for variations in the comparative advantage of different regions and also for why the spatial patterns of comparative advantage have changed significantly within a relatively short period. The first part of the explanation may be attempted by examining the relevant *location factors* discussed in Part II of this book. A second and essentially complementary approach is to identify the wider set of national and international political and economic factors which have led firms to *restructure* the location of their activities. This restructuring perspective helps to account for both the reversal in fortunes of various regions and the timing of the changes.

Location factors

The effect of location factors on the pattern of recent regional economic change in the United States may be illustrated by examining the factors influencing the decline of the manufacturing belt and the growth of the periphery. A wide range of factors have been suggested as responsible, though some are more important than others (Perry and Watkins, 1977; House, 1983; Sawyers and Tabb, 1984; Weinstein *et al.*, 1985).

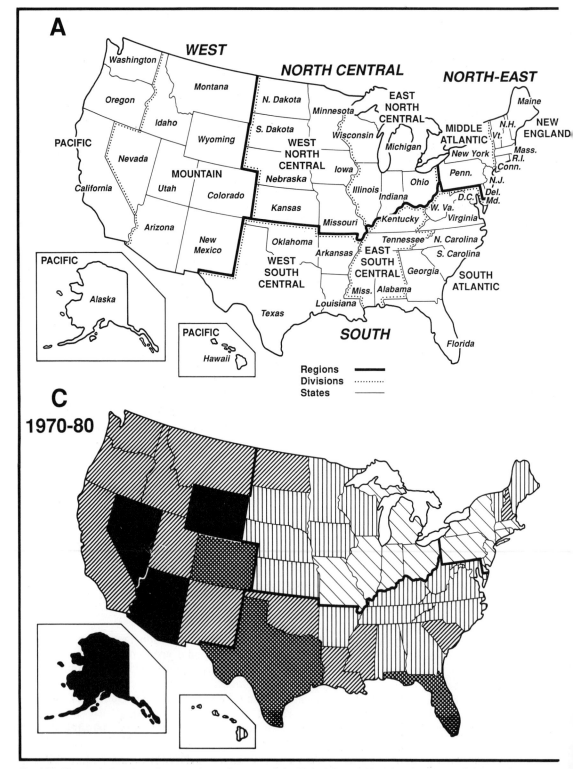

FIG 16.1 Non-agricultural employment change in states of the United States: (*a*) regional and state divisions; (*b*) 1960–70 percentage change per annum; (*c*) 1970–80 percentage change per annum; (*d*) 1980–5 percentage change per annum

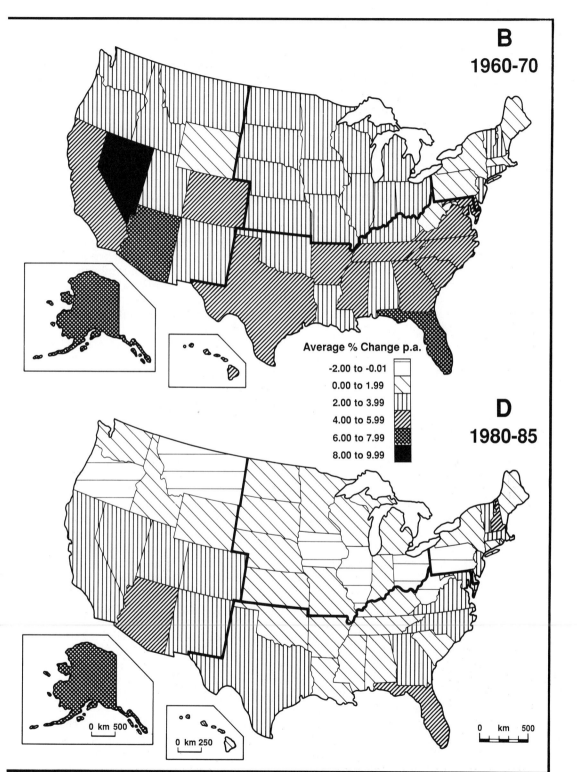

(*source*: based on data in US Department of Labor, Bureau of Labor Statistics, *Employment and Earnings*, various issues)

1. *Physical factors and natural resources*

Both warm climate and physical amenities have been suggested as factors encouraging entrepreneurs and population to migrate to the South and West (Estall, 1980; Bradshaw, 1988). Of course, physical factors such as a warm climate do not apply to all parts of the periphery. However, even where these elements do apply they have not changed significantly during the last 500 years of settlement of North America; so the key question becomes 'why have these features apparently become more important since the early 1960s?' One factor is the spread of air-conditioning of homes and workplaces, which has increased the attractiveness of the South during the hot humid summer months (Agnew, 1987). A further factor is the increased level of prosperity and personal mobility which has enabled people to take more advantage of the leisure opportunities provided by, for example, the mountains and coastline of the Sunbelt. Other factors include the general fall in the real cost of transport and the rapid growth of light industries, both of which have reduced the need for many manufacturing industries to locate in close proximity to their material sources and markets.

A similar argument applies to natural resources. For example, the oil and natural gas deposits in the South have been known and exploited for a long time—in the case of oil for over a century. However, the increase in the price of energy (and other commodities) in the 1970s increased the significance of differences in energy prices between states as a factor influencing industrial location. The Sunbelt thus gained in the 1970s both as a location with relatively cheap energy resources and as an exporter of energy, food, and other material resources (Weinstein and Gross, 1980).

2. *Factors of production*

It has often been suggested that the factors of production tend to favour the periphery. Land is generally cheaper and more available, the infrastructure of roads and housing is newer, the age of the capital stock is lower, and, perhaps most significantly, labour is perceived to be relatively cheaper and less militant. One common misconception is that only low-wage industries are attracted to the periphery. On the contrary, between 1940 and 1960, 90 per cent of the more than one and a half million new southern manu-

facturing jobs were in high-wage, fast-growing industries. However, these high-wage industries tend to pay lower wages in southern plants and this is an important attraction factor (Tabb, 1984). Probably more significant though is that many of the plants in the Sunbelt are newer and more capital-intensive than their counterparts in the Manufacturing Belt. Thus the wages *per unit of output* are much lower (Cruickshank, 1980). A related factor is the weakness of trade unions in the South and this is often taken by business as evidence of good labour relations, high labour productivity, and the likelihood of a co-operative work-force (Estall, 1980).

3. *Production technology and changes in demand*

The favourable situation of much of the periphery with respect to the factors of production has been particularly influential in encouraging the decentralization of the high-output, standardized forms of production from the Manufacturing Belt. This shift seems to support the locational interpretation of the product life cycle in which the mature stages of production are transferred to low labour cost locations (Chapters 6.3 and 15.2). If this was the sole source of growth in the Sunbelt, the economy would be very vulnerable to competition from low-cost locations overseas, particularly in the newly industrializing countries (Hansen, 1980). However, there is also evidence that the Sunbelt has attracted a significant proportion of high-growth and innovative industries. Indeed, Norton and Rees (1979 p. 142) ascribe the core region's industrial decline during the 1960s and 1970s to 'the cumulative effects of a more gradual *dispersal of innovative capacity* to the South and West' ... which has resulted 'in a reversal of the historical pattern, the periphery states now tend to specialize in the economy's "rapid growth" industries and the core states in slow growing ones.' The explanation for this shift of innovative industry to the Sunbelt is less clear, but it is suggested in Chapter 6.2 that high-technology industries tend to cluster in a few locations which lack a long history of industrialization, have a high-quality residential environment, and are often the sites of major scientific research institutions.

In more general terms, regional changes in employment may be interpreted as a product of shifts in the pattern of demand for different sectors of the US economy. For example, Clark

(1985 p. 107) argues that 'the manufacturing belt has gone into decline because its traditional re-source-based industries have been eclipsed by the science-based industries of the post-industrial era.'

4. Organizational structure

The organizational structure of industry in the periphery differs from that in the Manufacturing Belt. This is because corporation branch plants have been the major vehicle for industrial decentralization (Hansen, 1980), while head offices and research and development units have largely remained in the core (Knox et al., 1988). As Cohen (1977, p. 225) observes:

the rise of the Sunbelt, like the development of a third world nation, can be viewed as a new region's integration into the world as well as the national economy. And like a dependent nation, much of the Sunbelt's industry and a significant proportion of its finances remain under the control of outside economic actors.

Whether or not having a branch plant economy makes the Sunbelt more vulnerable in recession conditions is debatable (see Chapter 15.1). Cruickshank (1980 p. 100), for example, in writing about the situation in the 1970s, asserts that there is 'no indication that the area is regarded by management as a "peripheral region" ... "Marginal" plants must not be equated with spatially peripheral locations.' The experience of the latter half of the 1980s, however, suggests that management may have changed its view.

5. Government

The government has also had a significant influence on the development of high-technology industries in the periphery through the siting of research establishments and military bases and the placement of defence contracts. For instance, the location of military bases in the South-West during the 1940s is often cited as a catalyst for inducing the movement of military personnel and defence contracts into the region; while in the 1960s military–industrial contracts for the space race and the Vietnam war encouraged the avionics industry (Norton and Rees, 1979; Rees, 1979). Federal defence spending was also identified by Markusen et al. (1986) as a key factor in both the overall location of high-technology industry and its growth during the 1970s. The impact of defence contracts is, however, difficult

to assess, because although many of the 'prime contractors' are based in states in the periphery, they subcontract a considerable volume of the work to firms in the Manufacturing Belt (see Chapter 8.3). This suggests that the net flow of federal money from the North to the South (i.e. the difference between the money raised in federal taxes and federal expenditure) may not be quite as large as representatives of the North have often claimed (Estall, 1980; Rees and Weinstein, 1983).

Restructuring

The location factor approach has identified the main advantages that the periphery had over the Manufacturing Belt in the period after the Second World War until the early 1980s. It has highlighted the pattern of locational opportunities available to firms and individuals, but location factors cannot explain why the firms and individuals responded to these opportunities *when* they did. Neither can location factors, on their own, account for changes in spatial trends, such as occurred with the recent role-reversals of the Frostbelt and Sunbelt. To answer these questions an increasing number of authorities are arguing that it is necessary to examine wider changes affecting the economy as a whole which are leading firms to restructure the location of their activities.

Agnew (1987), for example, suggests that the primary cause in the rapid shift of manufacturing investment and employment from the core to the periphery lies in the strategies of firms adjusting to a crisis in the American economy as a whole. He infers that the fall in profitability experienced by manufacturing firms was forcing them to reduce costs and one way of doing this was to open new capacity in the lower-cost locations of the South and cut back in the higher cost locations in the core. Weinstein and Gross (1988) also argue that it is necessary to examine national and international factors to explain regional trends in the United States. They identify three key economic and political factors:

1. An evolving global economy

The post-war boom in the United States began to abate in the early 1970s in the face of growing competition from the reconstructed economies of Western Europe and Japan. This affected first the shoe, textile, steel, and automobile industries, then in the mid-1970s machine tools and ship-building felt the impact, while refining, chemicals, and semiconductors experienced increased competition in the early 1980s. The timing of the competition in different industrial sectors had a differential regional impact.

Initially, the regional impacts of this competition fell on the Frostbelt simply because the bulk of the U.S. shoe, textile, steel, automobile, and machine tool production was located in the Northeast, Mid-Atlantic, and Midwest, and not because those regions had somehow become inhospitable to competitive capitalism. Moreover the very same scenarios that were played out in traditional Frostbelt industries during the 1970s are today being repeated in other industries throughout the Sunbelt (Weinstein and Gross, 1988 p. 14).

2. *The international business cycle*
A major source of job growth in the Sunbelt during the 1970s was the inflationary cycle led by rapidly increasing commodity prices. This resulted in a substantial transfer of income and wealth occurring from the goods-producing economies of the Manufacturing Belt to the commodities-producing economies of the Sunbelt, most notably those based on energy resources and, to a lesser extent, agriculture. However, this situation was reversed after the early 1980s and the falling prices of commodities, associated with deflation of the international economy, crippled the agricultural and energy sectors which were the basis of the Sunbelt's industrial development.

3. *A changing federal environment*
The third factor affecting recent regional trends in the United States has been the redirection of federal policies since 1980 from an emphasis on redistributive equity to a concern for economic efficiency. Weinstein and Gross suggest that those states, such as Illinois and Florida, which have matched the federal reforms for the deregulation of interstate commerce are reaping the benefits of improved services at lower costs and a higher level of economic growth. Conversely, those Sunbelt states which had distressed economies in the late 1980s, such as Texas, Louisiana, and Oklahoma, and traditionally poor states, such as Mississippi, have been particularly hard hit by federal tax reforms and reductions in federal aid to local and state budgets.

Clearly, the changing pattern of regional economic development in the United States involves

more than simple convergence modified by elements of cumulative causation (Smith, 1987). To account for this 'see-saw' movement of capital (Smith, 1984 p. 148) requires an interpretation which views the impact of location factors in the context of the wider political and economic changes affecting society. A similar argument is used in the next section to understand the changing pattern of regional economic development in Britain. However, whereas most work on the geography of recent economic change in the United States has focused on analysing the rates of *employment growth* in different regions, most attention in Britain has concentrated on the rates of *decline in manufacturing employment* experienced by different places.

16.2 The geography of deindustrialization in Britain

Deindustrialization is a national phenomenon which has affected every British region. It has, however, been felt to varying degrees in different regions. The spatial pattern of deindustrialization depends to an extent, of course, on how the term is interpreted. There are a large number of definitions. They include a progressive deterioration in manufacturing trade (Singh, 1977), and the failure of a country or region to secure a rate of growth of output and net exports of all kinds sufficient to achieve full employment (Rhodes, 1986). But perhaps the simplest definition and the one which will be used here is: an 'absolute decline in industrial employment' (Thirwall, 1982 p. 24).

Manufacturing employment in Britain has been declining since 1966. Between 1966 and 1973 the main regional trend was towards spatial dispersion. The three regions with the main industrial concentrations, South-East, West Midlands, and North-West, all experienced above average rates of manufacturing employment decline, while the surrounding more peripheral regions declined at rates below the national average (Table 16.2). In the late 1970s and early 1980s, the decentralization trend reversed and a trend towards spatial concentration, which had previously been apparent in the 1950s and early 1960s, reappeared. However, the pattern of spatial concentration had changed in the intervening years. In the 1950s and early 1960s, manufacturing industry was concen-

TABLE 16.2 Regional manufacturing employment change in Great Britain, 1966–1988

Regions	1966 (000s)	% change in employment[a]			1988[b] (000s)
		1966–74	1974–84	1984–8	
South-East	2 363	− 14.4	− 20.6	− 11.1	1 321
East Anglia	173	+ 18.5	− 6.9	+ 14.7	218
South-West	429	+ 4.4	− 14.9	− 3.2	364
East Midlands	631	− 2.2	− 19.3	+ 1.0	493
West Midlands	1 197	− 9.7	− 28.6	− 1.7	697
Yorkshire and Humberside	860	− 11.2	− 31.7	− 8.7	443
North-West	1 251	− 12.9	− 32.0	− 10.6	600
North	461	+ 1.3	− 33.3	− 5.4	261
Wales	317	+ 5.7	− 31.8	+ 0.5	213
Scotland	726	− 5.1	− 28.7	− 11.3	385
GREAT BRITAIN	8 408	− 8.4	− 25.5	− 6.2	4 995

[a]Approximate because of changes in industrial classification.
[b]1988 figures are Department of Employment estimates.
Sources: Employment Gazette Aug. 1976, Oct. 1987, Nov. 1988.

trated in the already industrialized South-East and West Midlands (Keeble, 1976). However, during the late 1970s and 1980s the area experiencing an increase in the share of national manufacturing employment shifted to the South (South-East, South-West, East Anglia, and East Midlands) incorporating rural regions as well as industrialized areas, but excluding the West Midlands, resulting in a somewhat different 'north–south' divide (Massey, 1988b). The pattern began to change yet again in the late 1980s as the national economy began to recover. Most regions continued to experience deindustrialization, but at a lower rate than previously. Between 1984 and 1988, there was a more varied pattern of manufacturing employment change than previously. Regions both in the South and the North performed poorly (South-East and Scotland) and well (East Anglia and Wales), and the West Midlands experienced a rapid recovery.

Although regional differences in the rates of deindustrialization are significant, the variations within regions are greater. At this scale, the main trend since 1960 has been an urban–rural shift in the location of industry (Fothergill and Gudgin, 1982; Fothergill et al. 1986). As a general rule, the larger the settlement the greater the rate of decline in manufacturing employment. At one end of the hierarchy, London lost over half its manufactur-

ing workforce between 1960 and 1981, while at the other end rural areas increased their employment in manufacturing by almost a quarter (Table 16.3). Since 1974, however, rural areas have experienced a net loss of manufacturing jobs, though still at a lower rate than urban areas. So it is more appropriate to view the continuation of the urban–rural shift in Britain as a 'ruralization' of industry than as an industrialization of rural areas (Fothergill et al., 1985). The different rates of change in manufacturing employment between the main conurbations and the less industrialized counties are clearly shown in Fig. 16.2, both for the 1970s and the recession years of the early 1980s.

The main features of the geography of deindustrialization are not in dispute, but their explanation has 'provoked one of the widest-ranging and most interesting debates of recent years in economic geography' (Massey, 1988b p. 62). There are in very broad terms two main interpretations of the spatial shifts in manufacturing employment: one emphasizes the different characteristics of areas by focusing on location factors, while the other stresses the need to set the location factors within the wider context of the restructuring of industry. A similar classification of explanatory approaches was used in the last section and in the earlier discussion of the location of high-tech-

TABLE 16.3 The urban–rural contrast in manufacturing employment change in Great Britain, 1960–1981

	Change in number of manufacturing jobs	as % 1960
Rural areas	+128 000	+24.2
Small towns	−22 000	−1.4
Large towns	−165 000	−17.9
Free-standing cities	−381 000	−28.6
Conurbations	−987 000	−43.2
London	−688 000	−51.4
GREAT BRITAIN	−2 115 000	−26.3

Source: Fothergill et al. (1985 p. 149).

nology industries (Chapter 6.2). However, as in many debates it is not easy to assign protagonists to one camp or another and significant differences occur within both schools of thought.

Location factors

In this approach, differences in the rate of employment change in manufacturing between areas are accounted for by differences in the character of these areas. In other words, one spatial pattern is used to explain another. Some of the most detailed work using this approach has been carried out by Keeble (1976; 1980). He found, by using the statistical technique of multiple regression, that different location factors were important at different periods during the 1960s and first half of the 1970s. Whereas agglomeration diseconomies and industrial structure were important throughout the period, government regional policy was statistically significant only in the late 1960s and residential attractiveness disappeared as an important variable in the 1970s. Keeble suggests that the main reason why regional policy and residential attractiveness dropped out of the analysis during the 1970s was because these variables have most effect on mobile industry, which was decreasing in importance as a component of change as the national economy began to slip into recession.

Some of the same location factors also appear as significant in the analysis by Fothergill and Gudgin (1982), although they do not differentiate

sub-periods. They suggest that areas respond differently to national and international pressures, such as international competition and changes in technology, demand, and interest rates, because their inherited structures vary. They argue that there are four main factors which differentiate the response of an area—industrial structure, urban structure, plant size structure, and regional policy. To illustrate their relative influence, Table 16.4 shows the effect, according to Fothergill and Gudgin, that these four factors had on manufacturing employment trends in each of the economic planning regions of the United Kingdom between 1960 and 1975.

1. Industrial structure
This variable benefits those areas which have a higher proportion of industries which are growing, or declining more slowly, than the national average. In the United Kingdom, the regions with the most favourable industrial structure during the 1960s and 1970s were the South-East, East Anglia, South-West, and West Midlands. The inherited industrial structure thus helps to differentiate between the employment performance of different regions, but as the degree of regional specialization has been declining, the influence of industrial structure is decreasing. Further, it does not seem to be a significant factor influencing the urban–rural shift of manufacturing employment because there is no apparent relationship between industrial structure and the degree of urbanization.

FIG 16.2 Sub-regional employment change in manufacturing in Great Britain: (a) 1971–81 absolute change; (b) 1971–81 percentage change; (c) 1981–4 absolute change; (d) 1981–4 percentage change (source: based on unpublished Department of Employment statistics)

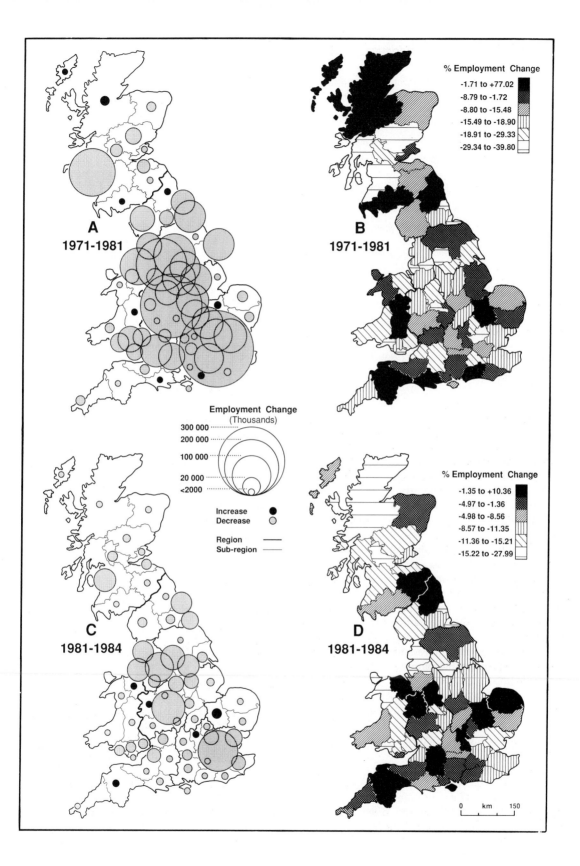

A
1971–1981

B
1971–1981

% Employment Change

-1.71 to +77.02
-8.79 to -1.72
-8.80 to -15.48
-15.49 to -18.90
-18.91 to -29.33
-29.34 to -39.80

Employment Change
(Thousands)

300 000
200 000
100 000
20 000
<2000

Increase ●
Decrease ○

Region
Sub-region

C
1981–1984

D
1981–1984

% Employment Change

-1.35 to +10.36
-4.97 to -1.36
-4.98 to -8.56
-8.57 to -11.35
-11.36 to -15.21
-15.22 to -27.99

0   km   150

TABLE 16.4 Employment accounts for manufacturing in regions of the United Kingdom, 1960–1975

	Net change	National change	Differences due to:				
			Industrial structure	Urban structure	Size structure	Regional policy	Residual
East Anglia	+28.6	−12.0	+3.8	+30.8	+1.2	−1.8	+6.6
Wales	+9.5	−12.0	+0.5	+13.6	−2.4	+15.1	−5.3
South-West	+7.4	−12.0	−3.4	+18.1	+0.1	+3.2	+1.4
North	+2.5	−12.0	−3.1	+8.6	−4.3	+14.1	−0.8
East Midlands	−0.4	−12.0	−1.8	+10.6	+2.4	−3.4	+4.6
West Midlands	−13.0	−12.0	+4.7	−2.2	−1.6	−3.6	+1.7
Scotland	−14.1	−12.0	−5.9	+8.1	−0.6	+6.5	−10.2
Yorkshire and Humberside	−14.4	−12.0	−10.4	+3.9	+1.5	−1.1	+3.7
Northern Ireland	−15.9	−12.0	−19.8	+14.7	+1.2	+11.9	−11.9
South-East	−18.5	−12.0	+10.1	−18.9	+1.2	−5.0	+6.1
North-West	−20.5	−12.0	−8.5	+3.8	−0.3	+0.5	−4.0

Note: figures represent percentage change from base-year level of manufacturing employment. Methods of estimation are described in Fothergill and Gudgin (1982), Appendix C.

Source: Fothergill and Gudgin (1983 p. 48).

2. *Urban structure*

The relationship between settlement size and the rate of decline in manufacturing employment has already been noted. Fothergill and Gudgin suggest that the degree of urbanization in a region is the major factor accounting for its rate of deindustrialization. Thus the South-East and the West Midlands have the least favourable urban structure (i.e. the most urbanized) and East Anglia and the South-West have the most favourable. Their explanation for this relationship between urban structure and manufacturing decline revolves around space constraints in towns and cities (see also Chapter 4.1). According to this argument, the space demands of industry are increasing in response to rising capital intensity. The effects of this national trend are felt unevenly, however, because constraints on land supply in the cities mean that a disproportionately large share of new factory floorspace and associated jobs are diverted to small towns and rural areas where space constraints are less (Fothergill *et al.*, 1986); this leads to a lower rate of job replacement in cities.

3. *Plant size structure*

From work in the East Midlands, Fothergill and Gudgin found that larger and older plants declined more rapidly, or grew more slowly, than smaller and younger plants. They also found that

areas dominated by large plants had a lower new firm formation rate than areas with a small plant structure. This difference, it was suggested in Chapter 7.2, reflects the greater relevance and variety of experience which entrepreneurs obtain in small firms. The regions which have the most favourable plant size structure are the East Midlands, Yorkshire and Humberside, South-East, East Anglia, Northern Ireland, and South-West, although the differences are not large. New firm formation rates are also generally higher in rural areas than in towns and cities and thus also make a contribution, if only a small one, to the urban-rural shift in manufacturing employment.

4. *Regional policy*

The diversion of jobs to the assisted areas has led to employment gains in Wales, the North, Northern Ireland, and Scotland and, to a lesser extent, in the South-West and North-West. By contrast, the negative effects of regional policy on the other regions are relatively small (Table 16.4). The most recent estimates of the effects of regional policy, as was noted in Chapter 8.3, suggest that some 450 000 surviving manufacturing jobs were diverted to the assisted areas between 1960 and 1981 (Moore *et al.*, 1986). Regional policy has therefore had an important impact on manufacturing trends in particular regions. On the other hand, regional policy is of little significance in explaining the urban–rural shift, because of the mix of urban and rural settlements in both assisted and non-assisted areas.

The final column of Table 16.4 shows the percentage manufacturing employment change not accounted for by these four factors (i.e. the residual percentage). Interestingly, the pattern of the residuals shows a distinct 'north–south' dimension. All the regions which declined more than expected are in the North, only Yorkshire and Humberside and the West Midlands, which at some periods has been classified as in the 'North', performed better than expected and this is partly accounted for because the study period began in 1960 when the West Midlands at least was still relatively prosperous.

Restructuring

According to this approach, location factors are inadequate on their own to account for spatial shifts in manufacturing employment. Rather they have to be set against the background of the changing national and international pressures on industry. One aspect of this argument was illustrated in Chapter 10.2 where the analysis by Lloyd and Shutt (1985) of industrial change in the North-West during the late 1970s was discussed. They suggested that the large companies (the prime movers) which dominate the regional economy restructured their activities during this period in response to three main forces—rationalization, internationalization, and technical change. Their main argument is that for a large part the causes of local events lie outside the local area. In the case of the decentralization of manufacturing employment in the 1960s, the restructuring approach argues that it needs to be interpreted in the context of increasing economic difficulties, in particular because of heightened international competition, faced by firms during this period (Massey, 1988b). The restructuring approach argues that decentralization in an effort to cut costs was one of the strategies followed by firms in response to these pressures. This is not to suggest that the proponents of the location factor approach ignore the significance of external factors (for example, Fothergill and Gudgin begin their analysis with a review of the national and international pressures which were changing the demand from industry for space); however, they put most emphasis in their explanations on the locational characteristics of different areas.

The differences between the two approaches are more than just matters of emphasis. Proponents of the restructuring approach reject the search for generalized relationships both on technical and theoretical grounds. In the first case, they point to the difficulty of disentangling variables in statistical analyses, such as the multiple regression analysis used by Keeble (1976; 1980). They suggest, for example, that labour is a critical factor influencing spatial shifts in manufacturing employment (e.g. Hudson, 1978; Massey, 1979b), but one reason why labour is not emphasized in Keeble's analyses is that its influence is hidden by that of other statistically significant variables which have similar spatial patterns (Massey, 1988b). For instance, the distribution of the unemployed (an indicator of labour availability) is closely related to the distribution of areas receiving government assistance, while the spatial pattern of female activity rates (an indicator of a pool of female labour) correlates with the spatial concentration of industry (a measure of agglomeration diseconomies).

Secondly, and more fundamentally, the restructuring approach rejects that it is possible to identify the relative importance of variables in statistical analyses on theoretical grounds (Sayer, 1982b). The approach suggests that there is no point in searching for general patterns because the way that restructuring works out differs from case to case. Thus the same factor can have different outcomes in different circumstances. For instance, in order to try to remain profitable in the face of increasing competition, one firm may cut costs by increasing its capital intensity at its existing site and laying off labour, while another firm may move to another location where labour costs are lower and the labour force is more compliant. Conversely, similar outcomes may result from the operation of different factors. Thus some firms moving to an assisted area may do so because of the receipt of government aid, while others may have moved there in any case in search of a pool of female labour. Firms respond in a wide range of different ways to the pressures placed upon them and the nature of these pressures varies between industries and between companies. Thus as Massey (1988 p. 68) notes:

The point, according to the restructuring school, is that the relative importance of these factors, and perhaps more importantly the way they are combined together, would depend on the characteristics of each case. Thus trying to find the best 'fit' between factors and outcomes was not very illuminating; what was necessary was to investigate combinations of causes at a more detailed and qualitative level.

Thus for the restructuring school explanation lies not in searching for empirical regularities, but in identifying the causal generative mechanisms, such as rationalization and technical change.

A further distinction between the location factor approach and the restructuring approach to explaining shifts in manufacturing employment in the United Kingdom is that they emphasize rather different questions. Whereas the location factor approach focuses directly on the issue of 'why did manufacturing employment change location in this way?' the restructuring approach argues that this question can only be tackled after asking 'why did the locational change take place in that period at all?' Thus if the way the questions are framed is different, it is not surprising

that the nature of the causes identified and the policies prescribed should also vary between the two approaches (Massey, 1988*b*).

This section has shown that deindustrialization has had an uneven impact on different areas of the country. Moreover, the pattern of new job creation by the restructuring of the economy has reinforced these differences. Thus not only has the industrial North suffered the largest rates of job loss in manufacturing, but it has also not received its share of new service sector jobs (Fig. 16.3).

16.3 Local economic change—the case of Coventry

The previous two sections have concentrated on analysing economic change between regions and sub-regions. In this section, attention focuses on

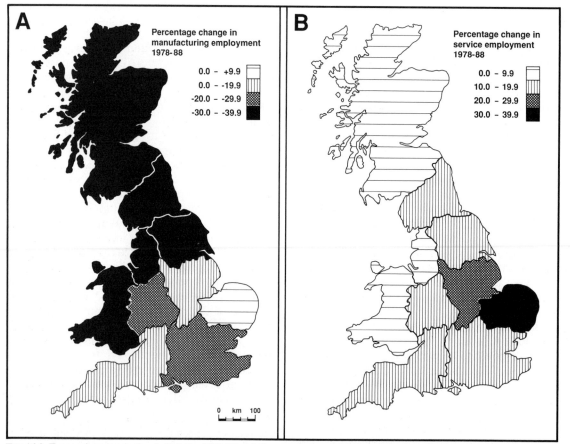

FIG 16.3 Economic restructuring in Britain, 1978–88: (*a*) the geography of deindustrialization; (*b*) the geography of tertiarization (*source:* based on data in *Employment Gazette*, Apr. 1985 and Nov. 1988)

intraregional economic change by examining one local economy, that of Coventry, England. The analysis of recent economic changes in Coventry is particularly interesting because Coventry has changed from a boom city into a depressed industrial area in less than twenty years.

Coventry has experienced a number of cycles of growth and decline during its history, associated with particular industries (Richardson, 1972; Friedman, 1977). For example, in the Medieval period prosperity was based on the woollen industry, while for about 100 years from the middle of the eighteenth century the fortunes of the city were tied to the silk ribbon weaving and watch industries. The most recent economic cycle began in about 1890. Based on the bicycle, car, and engineering industries, the growth phase lasted for about eighty years, but since about 1970 Coventry has experienced a massive cut-back in employment in its manufacturing industries. This case study is concerned with analysing the nature of Coventry's recent industrial decline and the reasons why it was hit harder during the 1970s and 1980s than most other local economies in the United Kingdom. The material used is drawn mainly from a research project in which one of the authors of this book was involved (Healey and Clark, 1984; 1985; 1986; Healey, 1985). The analysis concentrates particularly on the period 1974 to 1982.

Coventry is a free-standing city to the east of Birmingham. With a population of 310 000 in 1981, it is the eleventh largest city in Great Britain and the second largest in the West Midlands. In the 1950s and early 1960s it was described as a 'boom town' (Richardson, 1972 p. 98). Its prosperity in the first three-quarters of the twentieth century was based on the automobile, telecommunication, aerospace, and artificial fibre industries. The high level of demand for these industries enabled the population of Coventry, alone among industrial cities in Britain, to grow continuously between 1901 and 1971. Over this period the population increased from 70 000 to 337 000. The prosperity of the city is shown by the unemployment rate which before 1966 was commonly below 1 per cent. However, the general rise in unemployment since then gives an indication of the decline in employment opportunities. The 5 per cent barrier was passed in 1975 and the 10 per cent in 1981, while the average figure in 1982 was 14 per cent (Fig. 16.4). The position relative to the

country as a whole has also gradually worsened, though it is only since 1974 that the total unemployment rate has been consistently above the average for Great Britain.

The clearest evidence of industrial decline comes from the fall in manufacturing employment. Between 1974 and 1982, the city lost 53 000 jobs from the manufacturing sector. This represented a fall of 46 per cent, compared with a decline in the West Midlands region of 32 per cent and of 27 per cent in Great Britain over the same period. By far the greatest loss was in plants which survived but which shed labour. Almost 46 000 jobs were lost in this way; this was more than three times the number of jobs lost in complete closures (13 500). The city also gained some jobs in manufacturing, principally from expansions *in situ* (3700) and new enterprises (2200). However, for every one manufacturing job added Coventry lost nine others (Table 16.5). Despite this high rate of decline, manufacturing industries still accounted for almost half the jobs in the early 1980s, a dependence on manufacturing higher than for any similar sized city in the country.

The same classification of explanatory approaches which was applied in the previous two sections—location factors and restructuring—is used here to try to understand why the rate of decline of manufacturing industry in Coventry in the 1970s and early 1980s was so much more severe than that experienced by most other areas.

Location factors

Comment is made firstly on the application to Coventry of the four factors identified by Fothergill and Gudgin (1982) as largely accounting for the uneven urban and regional change in manufacturing employment in the United Kingdom (see earlier discussion of the reasons for the deindustrialization of Britain), before considering an additional factor, which several research workers have suggested has influenced the situation in Coventry.

1. *Industrial structure*
This had only a minor effect on the 46 per cent decline of manufacturing employment in Coventry during the study period. A shift-share analysis, which calculates the employment change which would occur in an area if each of its

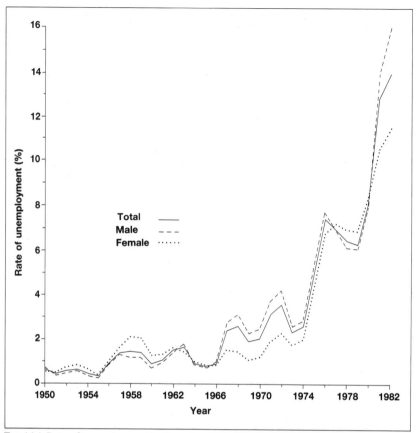

FIG 16.4 Rate of unemployment in Coventry, 1950–1982 (annual average figures)
(*source:* Healey and Clark, 1984 p. 306)

manufacturing industries changed at the same rate as in the country as a whole, shows that Coventry had only a slightly detrimental industrial structure. Nationally, as already noted, manufacturing employment declined by 27 per cent between 1974 and 1982; the structure of manufacturing industries in Coventry contributed a further 4 per cent to the rate of decline; leaving 15 per cent unaccounted for. In other words, manufacturing employment fell by almost a third more than would be expected on the basis of the national performance of the mix of manufacturing industries found in the city.

2. *Urban structure*

Large urban areas, according to Fothergill and Gudgin, perform less well in employment terms than nationally because they constitute a constrained location in which the expansion of manu-

facturing is restricted. How important this factor is during a period of severe contraction, when there are many empty and under-used factories is, however, debatable. It seems unlikely that manufacturing in Coventry performed poorly in the 1970s and early 1980s simply because it was located in a metropolitan area, though it probably had some effect.

3. *Size structure*

This also had only a minor influence. Local economies dominated by large factories, such as that in Coventry in which 79 per cent of manufacturing employment was in plants employing over 500 in 1974, are characterized by a low rate of new firm formation. However, as only 2200 jobs were created in new firms over the eight-year study period, a doubling or trebling of the rate of new firm formation would not have made a major dent in the net loss of 53 000 jobs.

TABLE 16.5 Components of change in manufacturing employment and establishments in Coventry, 1974–1982

Components	Employment	Establishments
JOB GAINS TO AREA		
Entries		
New enterprises	+2 163	+219
Branch openings	+781	+28
Transfers into city	+198	+7
	+3 142	+254
Expanding survivors[a]	+3 720	(115)
	+6 862	
JOB LOSSES TO AREA		
Exits		
Transfers out of city	−425	−13
Closures	−13 506	−248
	−13 931	−261
Contracting survivors	−45 778	(185)
	−59 709	
INTERNAL TRANSFERS		
Openings	+2 405	+94
Closures	−2 466	−105
	−61	−11
NET CHANGE	−52 908	−18
TOTAL 1974	115 317	666
TOTAL 1982	62 409	648

[a]Includes 38 plants which employed the same number of people in 1974 and 1982.

Source: based on Healey and Clark (1985 p. 1359).

4. *Regional policy*

Throughout the study period, Coventry was seen as a potential source of mobile industry for the areas receiving assistance under regional policy. The effect that this had on manufacturing employment trends in Coventry is, however, unclear. The major moves from Coventry occurred in the early 1960s, when Standard Triumph established a motor assembly plant at Speke in the North-West region and Rootes opened a similar unit in Scotland at Linwood. There is little evidence of local firms moving away from the city in the 1970s and early 1980s, although the lack of regional assistance may have deterred what mobile industry there was from locating in Coventry. On the other hand, it could be argued that without regional policy the local economy would have become more dependent on the motor industry and would have suffered even more with the onset of the recession.

5. *Labour market structure*

High wages and poor industrial relations may also have contributed to Coventry's industrial decline. Both these features characterized the local economy particularly in the 1950s and 1960s. Although in fact neither feature applied to the city by the late 1970s and early 1980s, an unfavourable industrial image may have deterred new investment, thereby constraining growth and diversification.

Restructuring

Together the various location factors provide an insight into the reasons why Coventry experienced a high rate of industrial decline, but on their own they do not give a full explanation. It is also necessary to take account of why local employers restructured the location of their activities in response to wider national and international forces. Among the wider influences which Spencer (1987 p. 13) suggests affected firms generally in the West Midlands were:

- declining competitiveness with rising imports and poor export performance, especially significant in the vehicle and metal goods industries;
- erosion of Commonwealth preference and entry into the EEC which necessitated a shift to a previously neglected market;
- domestic demand management and the use of the car industry as a regulatory tool which altered the working environment of many firms;
- national industrial policy and interventions which were made in the interests of the national economy and aimed at particular sectors or ailing companies, rather than with regard to local economic consequences.

The Coventry local economy is dominated by a few large employers. The 15 largest enterprises accounted for 82 per cent of manufacturing employment in 1974. Hence the investment and disinvestment strategies of a handful of companies was critical to the welfare of the city (Fig. 16.5). Whereas half the jobs in the top 15 were lost between 1974 and 1982, employment declined in the remaining companies by only 30 per cent. An important feature of these 'prime movers' is that most are not owned locally and they have only a small proportion of their national workforce in Coventry. Two aspects of the behaviour of these large companies are critical to understanding why the rate of decline of manufacturing employment in Coventry was almost a third higher than expected on the basis of its industrial structure. First, the particular companies located in the city may have performed less well than the average for the industries in which they operated, and, secondly, the companies may have cut back employment at their facilities in Coventry more than elsewhere. This may be illustrated with reference to the restructuring of BL and Talbot, which in 1974 were respectively the largest and third largest employers in manufacturing in the city. Together they accounted for two-thirds of the 31 300 jobs lost in Coventry in the motor vehicles industry between 1974 and 1982.

The British motor vehicle industry was facing severe pressures during the 1970s and 1980s. It was suffering from a declining level of international competitiveness, as illustrated by increasing import penetration, low levels of investment, and falling profitability. As Mallier and Rosser (1982 p. 20) note:

The worsening relative competitiveness of British cars was partly influenced by changes in tariff structures and currency exchange rates and partly by factors internal to the industry. It has been argued insufficient investment in production facilities and product development (and too much in merger activity), poor management and low productivity all increased unit production costs and/or reduced product quality.

In one sense Coventry was unfortunate to be a base for two of the companies which were not faring well. Both BL and Talbot shed a greater proportion of their United Kingdom work-force than did other companies in the motor industry. Whereas the industry nationally lost two in every five jobs between 1974 and 1982, BL shed half of its employees and Talbot lost almost three-quarters. Although employment in Talbot's Coventry factories did not fare as badly as elsewhere in the country, where, for example, the company's Linwood factory was closed down, the rate of job loss in Coventry was still above the rate for the industry. In contrast, BL cut-back much more severely in Coventry than elsewhere. Sir Michael Edwardes's survival plan led to the ending of volume car production in the city by BL. The ending of the assembly of Triumph cars at Canley left only Jaguar, with their luxury models, to continue the assembly of BL cars in Coventry, until 1984 when the Jaguar division was privatized. The main reasons for the decision by BL to run down Canley and the associated engine and body preparation plants and to concentrate assembly in Birmingham and Oxford were, first, that the models produced in Coventry, most of which were marketed under the Triumph marque, were unprofitable for the company; secondly, BL had no body-pressing facilities in Coventry; and, lastly, the plant at Canley was smaller than at Cowley or Longbridge and gave less potential for concentrating production and for achieving a minimum efficient scale of annual output.

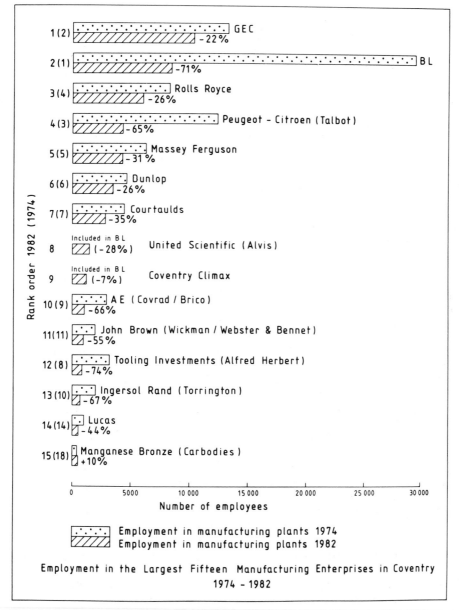

Rank order 1982 (1974)

1(2) GEC −22%

2(1) BL −71%

3(4) Rolls Royce −26%

4(3) Peugeot − Citroen (Talbot) −65%

5(5) Massey Ferguson −31%

6(6) Dunlop −26%

7(7) Courtaulds −35%

8 Included in BL (−28%) United Scientific (Alvis)

9 Included in BL (−7%) Coventry Climax

10(9) AE (Covrad / Brico) −66%

11(11) John Brown (Wickman / Webster & Bennet) −55%

12(8) Tooling Investments (Alfred Herbert) −74%

13(10) Ingersol Rand (Torrington) −67%

14(14) Lucas −44%

15(18) Manganese Bronze (Carbodies) +10%

0   5000   10 000   15 000   20 000   25 000   30 000

Number of employees

Employment in manufacturing plants 1974
Employment in manufacturing plants 1982

Employment in the Largest Fifteen Manufacturing Enterprises in Coventry
1974 – 1982

Fig 16.5 Employment in the largest fifteen manufacturing enterprises in Coventry, 1974–1982
(*source:* Healey and Clark, 1984 p. 311)

So both companies did relatively badly nationally, but only BL cut back to a greater extent in Coventry than elsewere. Talbot concentrated more of their activities in the city. Nevertheless, the result of the rationalization strategies adopted by Talbot and BL led to employment at the plants they operated in Coventry in 1974 being cut by a similar proportion, that is approximately two-thirds, but the different initial sizes of the two companies meant that whereas 2200 jobs were lost at Talbot, 18 200 went at BL.

It seems therefore that to understand the recent economic development of Coventry, it is necessary to consider both the distinctive features of the city, its people and its firms and its changing role in the wider national and international economy. A similar argument underlies the spatial division of labour approach to explaining regional economic change (Chapter 15.2). There are signs that the city is beginning to recover from the recession, with developments such as the opening of a Science Park at the University of Warwick (Chapter 6.2), the growth of an ethnic clothing industry (Chapter 12.2), and the increase in the attraction of mobile industry aided by the granting of Assisted Area status in 1984. However, the number of jobs involved in these developments has been small and it seems unlikely as yet that they will contribute to the city rising like a phoenix from the ashes, as happened when it recovered from the slump of the 1880s to enjoy nearly eighty years of almost uninterrupted economic growth and prosperity.

16.4 Regional economic policies

All countries with developed market economies have, to a greater or lesser extent, instituted regional economic policies in an attempt to relieve some of the spatial inequalities in economic health found within their boundaries. A common distinction is made between *interregional policies*, which are applied to whole regions, such as the Tennessee Valley or Scotland, and *intraregional* policies, which distinguish between different parts of regions, such as inner cities or rural areas. Often these two groups of policies are the responsibility of different government departments. For example, in Britain, interregional policies are largely the responsibility of the Department of Trade and Industry, while many intraregional policies originate from the Department of the Environment. Examples of a range of government policies which affect the location of economic activity are given in Chapter 8. Here the concerns are with the broader question of the validity and limitations of area-based economic policies.

Nature and justification

Regional economic policies are concerned for the most part with the problems of people and firms based in particular places. However, although these policies cover particular areas, the interdependencies between areas mean they also have wider national and even international consequences. Hence grants given to firms in one area

may be used to purchase supplies and to expand sales outside the area as well as within it. At the same time non-spatial policies, aimed at particular industrial sectors for example, have spatial consequences, because of the uneven distribution of the target groups and differences in the take-up rates of policies between areas (for an example see discussion of spatial impacts of small firm policies in Chapter 7.2).

Regional economic policies have an important role to play in a developed market economy (Regional Studies Association, 1983; Brook, 1985). The most common justification for such policies is on social grounds. They are seen as necessary to alleviate the worst effects of a free-enterprise system. By helping the 'victims' of the system, area-based economic policies provide a geographical welfare-net. The Conservative government, for instance, in its 1983 white paper (Cmnd 9111) reviewing regional industrial policy in Britain saw regional incentives in terms of satisfying largely 'social' needs. Attempting to meet such social needs also serves a political function. Area-based policies help to ameliorate the divisive effects of regional inequalities and their threat to national stability. Regional economic policies thus help to diffuse local problems and divert attention away from national issues. Indeed, area-based policies become almost inevitable given that local and central government politicians represent specific places. In the United States, for example, the term 'porkbarrel politics', mentioned in Chapter 8.3 in connection with the award of research, development, testing, and evaluation contracts, refers to the tendency for elected representatives to push the needs of their home region at every opportunity and to be swayed in their voting behaviour by promises of government assistance for their areas (Johnston, 1979). Regional interests are an important part of national policies in the United States, although regional policies have never been rigorously applied at the Federal level.

There are also economic justifications for regional economic policies, which suggest that a shift towards a regional balance may increase the prosperity of the whole area. Thus the social costs of overcrowding, congestion, and the high cost of land and providing the infrastructure in over-developed areas be reduced, while the under-utilization of labour resources and social capital (such as housing, roads, and schools) in depressed areas may be lessened by diverting investment to them. It is further often argued that, in times of labour shortage in growing regions, inflationary pressures on wages may be transmitted to other areas by national trade-union bargaining. The arguments vary in their validity (Keeble, 1976). For example, the suggestion that social capital in depressed areas may be under-utilized assumes that population is not growing and needs little modernization. Furthermore, the economic case is strongest in periods of national prosperity and is often ignored by governments in periods of recession.

Limitations

Regional economic policies also suffer from a number of weaknesses. Three main ones may be identified (Brook, 1985):

1. Area-based policies cover both individuals and businesses not requiring help and those needing aid. Such policies implicitly assume that all the people and firms in an area suffer from the same problems and have the same needs. Equally the policies omit many individuals and businesses suffering from similar problems, but who are resident or located outside the areas receiving assistance.

2. Regional economic policies stimulate competition between areas and divert attention away from other divisions in society, such as whether or not an individual is unemployed, or whether or not a firm is suffering from a shortage of skilled labour. Such groups often have more in common with others in the same situation than they do with other groups in the same locality. Area-based policies may lead to such problems being seen as narrow locational ones. For example, in the 1970s many inner-city areas in the non-assisted West Midlands and South-East regions had rates of unemployment as high or higher than many areas receiving assistance in the North of England and Scotland. This led many of the inhabitants of these areas to blame the operation of regional policy for the lack of manufacturing jobs (see Section 16.2).

3. Regional economic policies discriminate against those just outside the boundaries of the areas receiving assistance. This is most starkly illustrated when the designated area is small. For example, the boundaries around enterprise zones

in cities often distinguish between property on one side of a road from that on the other. This can lead to significant differences in the value of industrial property inside and outside the zone (Norcliffe and Hoare, 1982), and has lead one commentator (Anderson, 1983) to suggest that boundary effects may substantially increase the chances of blight in immediately adjoining areas (see also Chapter 8.4).

Despite these limitations, regional economic policies complement non-spatial economic policies. Whereas sector policies, for example, distinguish between differences in the performance of different industries, regional economic policies recognize that spatial differences in economic well-being are also important. Moreover, because economic problems are often concentrated in particular areas, such as inner cities, declining coalfield regions, and remote rural areas, there is often a significant overlap between spatial and non-spatial problems.

Theory and policy

The perceived strengths and weaknesses of regional economic policy depend in part on how regional problems and policies are conceptualized. For example, a neoclassical view of the regional problem sees regional inequalities as temporary, which in the long run will disappear as labour and capital respond to market forces to bring about equilibrium (Chapter 15.2). If this view is accepted, the main role of regional policy is social and political as a regional redistribution of resources is required to alleviate the pain caused by the adjustment, in the short to medium term, to market forces. This tends to be the kind of argument used by many Conservative politicians. At the other end of the political spectrum, a Marxist view of regional policies is that they are an attempt by the state to ameliorate the excesses of capitalism and to divert attention away from the structural problems which bring about regional inequalities. An intermediate viewpoint is that market forces will not produce the postulated equilibrium, since the factors of production are imperfectly immobile. Hence state intervention is required, partly in the form of regional policies, not only to alleviate the social costs of inequality but also to improve economic efficiency and encourage national growth.

However, the existence of a necessary relationship between theory and policy is a contentious one. Fothergill and Gudgin (1985, p. 115) argue that 'policy formulation is such an inherently political matter that policy recommendations should be clearly distinguished from research findings' (original quotation was in italics). For example, they suggest that the emphasis on small firm policies advocated by Birch (1979) in his study of the job generation process in the United States reflects his ideology and is only tentatively related to his research findings. He could equally have suggested policies to overcome the difficulties faced by large firms. Other research workers argue that different policy recommendations are related to the different theoretical frameworks and methodologies adopted (Massey and Meegan, 1985b). For example, it was suggested in Chapter 15.2 that the deterministic view of long wave theory adopted by Hall (1985) largely limited policies to those which foster and facilitate the trends, while the greater emphasis placed by other research workers on the social, economic, and political context in which long waves occur open up a greater range of policy options to steer and modify the outcomes. A further example comes from the attempt by Lloyd and Shutt (1985) to explain recent industrial changes in the North-West region of Britain by focusing on the role of key corporate enterprises (see Chapter 10.2). This led them to advocate policies which recognize that the causes of industrial change are primarily external to the region.

The recognition of the primacy of external factors raises an important issue, namely that although economic problems are often concentrated in particular areas, the causes of these problems are rarely the areas themselves. Area-based difficulties are problems found *in* particular areas and are rarely problems *of* those areas. Thus although it is often implied that area-based economic policies can solve regional economic difficulties, they, like other redistributional policies, tend to treat the symptoms of the problems rather than the underlying causes. They may thus alleviate economic problems, but not provide a solution. However, to treat the underlying causes may necessitate making fundamental changes to the economic system. Hence, a pattern of uneven development, albeit a changing one which may be modified by government policies, may have to be accepted as an inevitable consequence of maintaining the present economic system. Uneven

development seems to be a feature of all economic systems, but its underlying basis, which in capitalism is a search for profits (see Chapters 10 and 15.2), reflects the nature of the economic system in which the regional economic problems are found.

16.5 Summary

This chapter has been concerned mainly with analysing and explaining patterns of economic change between and within regions through three detailed case studies. The final section examined the justification and limitations of regional economic policies and discussed the relationship between theory and policy. Three major conclusions arise from the material discussed.

1. The nature of regional economic inequalities in countries with developed market economies can change dramatically over relatively short periods, sometimes leading to areas experiencing a complete reversal of fortunes.

- In the United States the main trend since 1960 has been decentralization of employment from the Manufacturing Belt to the periphery. This trend was popularized, though somewhat misleadingly, in the phrase 'Frostbelt versus Sunbelt'. However, since the early 1980s many parts of the Sunbelt have been in recession and New England has seen a revival in its fortunes.
- Britain also experienced interregional decentralization of manufacturing employment in the 1960s and early 1970s, but in the late 1970s and early 1980s this was replaced by a trend towards regioinal concentration. However, at the intraregional scale manufacturing employment was undergoing an urban–rural shift throughout the period.
- During the 1970s and 1980s Coventry changed from a boom city to a depressed industrial area, losing almost half its manufacturing employment in less than a decade.

2. To explain these changes it is necessary to examine both the different characteristics of areas, by focusing on location factors, and the wider set of national and international political and economic factors, which have led firms to restructure the location of their activities. Whereas the first approach attempts to explain why the

locational changes took place in the *way* they did, the second approach tries to account for why the changes occurred at all *when* they did. The different approaches ask different questions based on different assumptions and it is therefore not surprising that they often reach different conclusions as to the causal factors and policy implications.

3. Regional economic policies are concerned with the redistribution of resources between areas.

- They have a social welfare function in that spatial variations are seen as inequitable; a political role in that they promote national stability; and an economic function in that they can encourage a more efficient distribution of resources.

- However, they also have limitations in that they tend to treat individuals and firms alike in the designated areas regardless of whether or not they require aid; they encourage competition between areas and divert attention away from national issues; and they can create severe boundary effects, particularly where the area receiving assistance is small.

- The perceived strengths and weaknesses of regional economic policy depend in part on how regional problems and policies are conceptualized. However, the existence of a necessary relationship between theory and policy is a contentious one.

- Although it is often implied that area-based economic policies can solve regional economic difficulties, they tend to treat the symptoms of the problems rather than the underlying causes.

Whatever the relationship between theory and policy, it is increasingly being recognized that the process of economic change has unintended consequences on the environment, in the form of pollution and noise for example, as well as positive impacts such as job creation and the generation of wealth. The relationship between economic change and the environment is the topic of the final chapter in this book.

17

Economic Change and the Environment

This book provides insights into some of the many factors creating spatial differences in economic location and change. The emphasis, up until now, has been on how economic change leads both to the creation and loss of particular types of jobs and thus to variations in income and prosperity. Little attention, as yet, has been given to the effects of economic change on the environment in which people live. However, a two-way relationship exists between economic location and change and the environment. On the one hand, the environment can and does affect the spatial pattern of economic activity. In part this relates to the distribution of resources and to such concepts as physical margins and ecological optima (Chapter 3.2), although an attractive residential environment may also be a significant factor, for example in influencing new firm formation rates. On the other hand, economic location and change increasingly affects the environment, usually in an adverse manner. In this respect it is important to distinguish between such naturally occurring environmental problems as earthquakes and volcanoes and those created or exacerbated by the actions of humans, as in air and water pollution for example. The latter, which may result from economic change, form the focus of interest in this chapter.

It is usual for businesses, when seeking planning permission, to have to agree to comply with controls on the emission and dumping of dangerous substances and to meet minimum standards in terms of visual impacts and landscaping. However, there are indications that variations between countries and regions in the implementation of environmental controls may be a factor influencing the location decisions of some businesses, principally those which during the course of their actions produce potentially damaging environmental side-effects (Stafford, 1985; Leonard, 1988). There are still relatively few examples of entrepreneurs undertaking positive conservation measures.

At the time of writing (1989), there is mounting concern over 'green' issues and the global environmental threat from such problems as the greenhouse effect, acid rain, and depletion of the ozone layer—all resulting directly from economic change. Such forms of environmental degradation affect the natural ecosystem of the entire world and pay no respect to regional or international borders. Everyone is affected, even those not living in the most polluted areas. Environmental degradation is, therefore, a global problem and only international environmental policies can help to create a better balance between physical and human environments. This is a vast topic area and one that cannot be given adequate attention here (although acid rain is discussed briefly in section 17.2). However, economic change also creates environmental problems at smaller scales of analysis. These include the spatially extensive environmental impacts of, for example, agriculture and forestry, the more linear effects of major forms of transport (e.g. motorways and high-speed trains), and the environmental effects resulting from such site-specific activities as individual factories, quarries, and airports.

Consequently, this chapter provides a brief initial outline of environmental problems created by economic change. It has three main aims: first, to discuss the impacts of economic change on the environment in terms of positive and especially negative externalities; secondly, to look at the extent of environmental degradation in relation to air and water pollution and landscape deterioration; and thirdly, to stress the need for a change in attitude towards 'green' issues and examine recent government responses to environmental concerns.

17.1 Impacts of economic change

The impacts of economic change can be both beneficial and harmful to the local community and society at large. Positive impacts include the creation of jobs and the generation of income, with consequent multiplier effects upon other services (e.g. extra trade for local shops and businesses). Negative impacts, on the other hand, are of greater concern from a welfare point-of-view and include environmental problems, such as air and water pollution, and a wide range of social and economic difficulties associated with, for example, economic change in remote rural areas and increasing unemployment and dereliction in former industrial areas. The potential for environmental damage and other negative impacts has increased with the introduction of new technologies (Chapter 6.1) and the development of larger-scale operations (Chapter 7.1). However, these impacts are often ignored by entrepreneurs and given insufficient weight when the costs and benefits of economic change are evaluated. Positive and negative impacts can combine, as for example in the case of airports, where the benefits of increased employment and movement are mitigated by noise and pollution, and in the extraction of North Sea oil and gas, where new employment opportunities are often counterbalanced by dangers to human life (as was tragically demonstrated in the Piper Alpha accident in 1988).

Positive and negative impacts are usually discussed within the concept of *externalities* (Harvey, 1971; Smith, 1977; Bale, 1978; Chapman, 1981; Chapman and Walker, 1987). An externality can be defined as a side-effect which is not reflected in the costs and prices of a particular economic activity. For example, a power station without proper pollution controls is reducing its own costs at the expense of the health and welfare of others. This represents a deliberate transfer of the costs of production from the producer to society at large (Smith, 1977); the cost of the pollution is not borne by the polluter. Tragic examples of such side-effects have increased over the years, culminating in the horrendous accidents at Bhopal, India (1984) and Chernobyl (1986). Indeed, negative externalities are occurring under all modes of production and arise because emphasis is placed on economic growth rather than the satisfaction of fundamental human needs. However, not all negative impacts are deliberate and the wider external effects of economic change may be unknown to the 'culprits' and society (until confirmed by scientific research); an example would be the concern over leukaemia clusters near nuclear power plants.

Smith (1977 p. 90) emphasizes that 'the concept of externalities is intrinsically spatial.' The impacts of economic change extend beyond a confined boundary fence and can be of an international significance, as in the case of acid rain (Section 17.2), or of more local importance, as with an intensive livestock unit (factory farming). Most externalities (e.g. noise, smell, and traffic congestion) do in fact have a fairly localized impact and their effects are weakened by distance from the source (Chapman and Walker, 1987). Harvey (1971) visualizes this in terms of a spatial *externality field*, with a downward-sloping externality gradient in all directions from the source. This externality field can similarly be depicted in terms of a cone (where an even population distribution surrounds the source), or a set of contours (Fig. 17.1). Such uniform distance-decay functions can of course be modified, to take account of, for example, a dominant directional effect from the source (e.g. downwind of a power station) or a secondary node of concentration (e.g. a chemicals factory). Bale (1978) notes that with increasing distance from the source, the impact of negative externalities may be outweighed by positive externalities (Fig. 17.1); the example of an airport would again seem to be appropriate. Clearly, externality gradients and externality fields are going to vary, but as Dicken and Lloyd (1981 p. 317) comment 'whatever their precise spatial form ... the fact remains that the location of both public and private facilities has important consequences for individual and social well-being.'

It is clear that those responsible for initiating economic change (e.g. individuals, corporations, governments) have rarely taken account of the wider implications of their actions. Although businesses have 'social responsibilities', they seldom contribute to the solving of environmental problems and the improvement of welfare (Estall and Buchanan, 1980). Consequently, government measures are required to cover all aspects of economic change that have a bearing upon human welfare (see Chapter 8). This is a major task for policy-makers, made even more complex

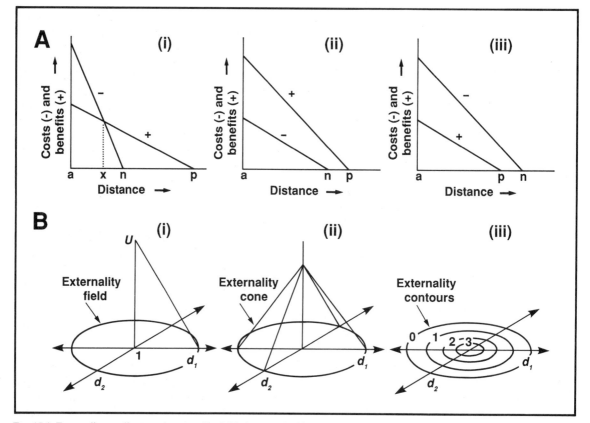

Fig 17.1 Externality gradients and externality fields (*source:* Smith, 1977 p. 92, and Bale, 1978 p. 335)

by two fundamental problems: first, the difficulty of predicting and objectively measuring the impacts of economic change (value judgements have to be made); and secondly, the deep-seated attitudes of individuals and governments which continue to put economic growth before human welfare (see section 17.3). As Chapman and Walker (1987 p. 262) aptly summarize: 'the maximisation of human welfare provides an elusive and intangible basis for policy-making.'

The environmental consequences of economic change represent just one component of human welfare. Nevertheless, they are of great contemporary concern and inextricably related to many of the aspects of economic change addressed in this book. Pressure-group activity has ensured that environmental problems or 'green' issues maintain a high media profile and remain on the political agenda. The rest of this chapter, therefore, examines the nature and extent of certain environmental issues and assesses attitudes and policy responses to them.

17.2 Nature and extent of environmental degradation

It has already been established that the environmental consequences of economic change can range in scale from global issues to site-specific problems. Despite this, many environmental problems are spatially concentrated in 'core' areas of economic activity. This is vividly portrayed in the older industrial regions of north-western Europe (e.g. the Ruhr, Sambre–Meuse trough, South Wales), where structural changes in industry have left a legacy of dereliction and decay (Hull *et al.*, 1988). Whilst recognizing that developments in the tertiary sector can have visual and other negative impacts on the landscape (Daniels, 1985*a*), the most spatially extensive environmental problems are associated with industry and agriculture. Consequently, the subsequent discussion concentrates on two broad areas that relate mainly to industry and agriculture: air and water pollution, and landscape deterioration.

Air and water pollution

The origins of air and water pollution can usually be traced to two main sources: agriculture and industry. Both produce a veritable 'cocktail' of pollutants, from waste and effluents, slurry and silage, and pesticides and fertilizers (Rose, 1985; Pearce, 1986) (Fig. 17.2a). Among the most serious by-products from agricultural and industrial activity are sulphur dioxide (SO_2) and nitrogen (N). Both are important ingredients of the truly international phenomenon of acid rain, which poisons lakes and rivers, damages forests and crops, and corrodes metal structures, stone monuments, and paintwork (Hull et al., 1988).

Initial research in Sweden and West Germany attributed forest damage and the acidification of lakes to air pollution and especially sulphur emitted from the burning of fossil fuels in the heavy industrial regions of Great Britain, West Germany, and the Benelux countries. Sulphur drifts in the prevailing winds, converts to sulphuric acid in the air and is 'washed' to the ground in an area that stretches from central England through Belgium and the Ruhr industrial zone of West Germany to the coalfields of Eastern Europe. It has been estimated that as much as 50 per cent of acid rain in Sweden comes from abroad and especially from the coal-rich nations of Western Europe (Hull et al., 1988). Acid rain is, therefore, a classic example of a negative externality which involves an international transfer of costs.

More recently, the importance of nitrogen as a source of acid rain has been recognized (Fig. 17.2b). Nearly two-thirds of nitrogen oxides (nitric acid) found in the air come from the exhausts of motor vehicles. This encouraged many countries (e.g. Switzerland, Austria, West Germany, Sweden, Norway, Canada, and the USA) to introduce lead-free petrol in the early 1980s; the United Kingdom has been slower on this issue. Nitrogen is similarly released in the form of ammonia (nitrogen and hydrogen atoms) from farm wastes (slurry in particular) and industrial solvents. This reacts with sulphur dioxide in the air to produce ammonium sulphate, which, in turn, settles on trees and invades the soil. In the latter, sulphate converts to sulphuric acid and the ammonia converts to nitric acid, producing a double dose of acid (Pearce, 1986). Ammonia released from slurry lagoons has increased as a source of pollution with the growth of intensive livestock units (Symes and Marsden, 1985). Such 'factory farming' is prevalent in Denmark, for example, where steps have been taken to ensure that farmers store slurry until it can be spread on the fields at a time when plant growth can absorb the nutrients immediately (Whittow, 1988). Total nitrogen fall-out, from factory farms and car exhausts, has doubled in most of Western Europe since the late 1950s (Pearce, 1986).

The deterioration in water quality, caused by a range of factors including the excessive use of fertilizers and pesticides in areas of intensive agriculture, effluent from slurry and silage pits and domestic sewerage systems, and chemical pollution (phosphorous) from industry, is yet another major issue of contemporary concern. Many rivers in Europe contain nitrates in excess of World Health Organization (WHO) and EC recommended levels. In the intensive arable and livestock farming area of East Anglia, for example, one-fifth of all rivers are so affected (Lowe et al., 1986). Similar levels have occurred in less prosperous agricultural areas too, like Devon and Cornwall where the length of rivers untouched by pollution fell from more than half to less than a quarter between 1950 and 1985 (Fig. 17.2c). Over 50 per cent of the prosecutions by water authorities in the United Kingdom for serious pollution of rivers are against farmers. Excessive nitrates in water cause eutrophication (the enrichment of water by nutrients), which, with the aid of bacteria from such polluting effluents as silage leaks (Fig. 17.2d), starves fish of oxygen. High nitrates have also been linked to methaemoglobinaemia in infants (blue babies).

The welfare of people and animals, therefore, is being adversely affected by the actions of others. In response to the deterioration in water quality, the EC drafted a new Directive in 1987. This recommended the imposition of limits on the use of nitrogenous fertilizers and the designation of water protection zones, within which the use of nitrates should be banned or strictly controlled (Whittow, 1988). In 1988, the United Kingdom made recommendations regarding Water Pollution Safeguard Areas (WPSAs), but at the time of writing (mid-1989) there has been little action and uncertainty remains over who, if anyone, should compensate farmers for their potential loss of

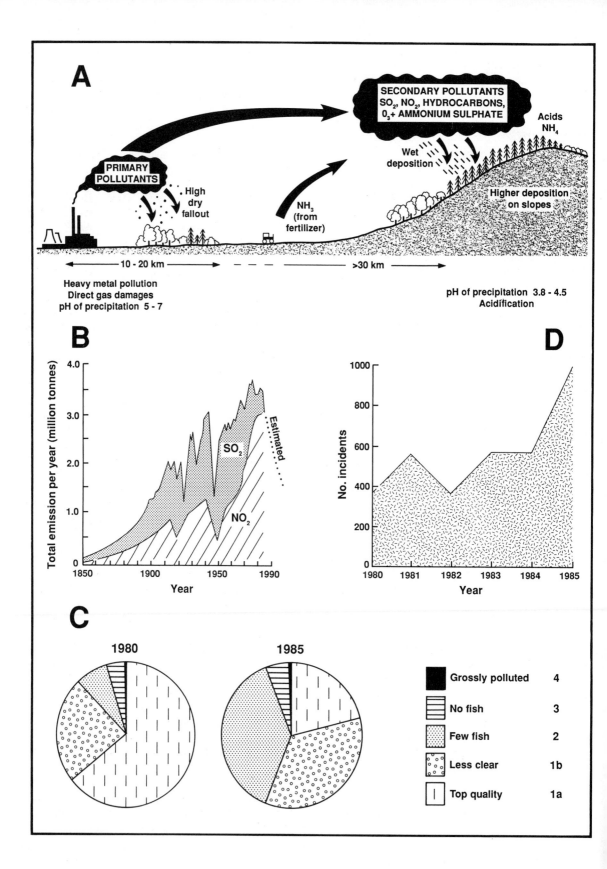

income (Harvey and Wilson, 1988; Radford, 1988). Even if implemented, there is no guarantee that WPSAs will be effective: much depends on farmers' attitudes (see section 17.3), which in Jersey for example (where WPSAs have existed since 1974) have been shown to be negative (Foster et al., 1989).

Air and water pollution do not only affect agricultural and rural regions. They create negative externalities in urban areas, where most people in Western economies reside. There has been a general lack of research on the distribution of pollution within cities. However, an investigation of 71 local-authority areas in Greater Manchester in the early 1970s, for example, revealed a general distance-decay pattern in sulphur dioxide pollution from the centre of the city outwards, much in line with Harvey's externality gradients (Wood et al., 1974; Fig. 17.3a). When a composite index of pollution was mapped (Fig. 17.3b), high concentrations occurred in two areas—Salford and Wigan—and coincided with the distribution of the most disadvantaged socio-economic groups in the Greater Manchester area. This provides further evidence that those suffering the most from negative externalities often benefit the least from economic change.

Landscape deterioration

The landscape has changed considerably in response to developments in the three main sectors of economic activity. Although change can bring positive environmental benefits, these are usually balanced or outweighed by a range of negative impacts. In relation to the service sector, for example, Bennison and Davies (1980) and Daniels (1985a) list the positive and negative environmental impacts of both retail renewal in city centres and the suburbanization of producer services (Table 17.1). Positive impacts include the modernization of outworn areas and the upgrading of some streets in city centres, and improved building design and landscaped development in suburban areas. These are counterbalanced by such negative impacts as the creation of new points of congestion and an artificial atmosphere

in city centres, and the visual intrusion of large unimaginative ground parking spaces in the suburbs (see Table 17.1 for details). Although the perception of what constitutes a positive or negative impact is open to interpretation, there can be no doubt that the landscape of city centres and suburban areas has been transformed.

Landscape deterioration is characteristic of many older industrial regions and inner cities. Both types of area have experienced a similar cycle of events—industrial growth, decline and dereliction, and regeneration. The lower Swansea Valley in South Wales is a classic example. Before 1750, it was an area of green fields and hedgerows; by 1800 it had become one of the world's leading centres of copper and zinc smelting. With the largest single concentration of industry in the United Kingdom—for the size of its area—the valley became a 'moonscape' of grey slag heaps and brick chimneys belching industrial smoke and fumes (Bromley and Humphrys, 1979). By 1950, the last tinplate works had been closed and the area was left with the largest legacy of industrial dereliction in Britain. In the process of planned redevelopment, including the designation of part of the area as an enterprise zone (Chapter 8.4), the breakdown and removal of toxic material from the waste tips was a major physical obstacle. With this overcome, the area has managed to restructure its economic base, attracting a wide range of manufacturing and service industries (Bromley and Thomas, 1988).

The most extensive changes to the landscape have occurred as a result of developments in the primary sector. The modernization of agriculture, whereby production has become intensified, specialized, and concentrated on fewer farms and in fewer areas (Bowler, 1985b and 1986), and the development of agribusinesses in many Western economies (Chapter 7.2) have had unfortunate secondary consequences for the landscape and environment. The rural landscape and wildlife have been systematically destroyed in such countries as the USA and the United Kingdom. Indeed, the famous dust bowl of the 1930s in the USA provided an early warning of the consequences of developing an intensive and specialized system of

---

FIG 17.2 Air and water pollution: (a) the natural history of acid rain; (b) emissions of sulphur and nitrogen in West Germany; (c) water pollution in the rivers of Devon and Cornwall, 1980–5; (d) pollution incidents caused by silage in England and Wales (source: (a) Rose, 1985 p. 55; (b) Pearce 1986 p. 43; (d) Pearce, 1986 p. 27)

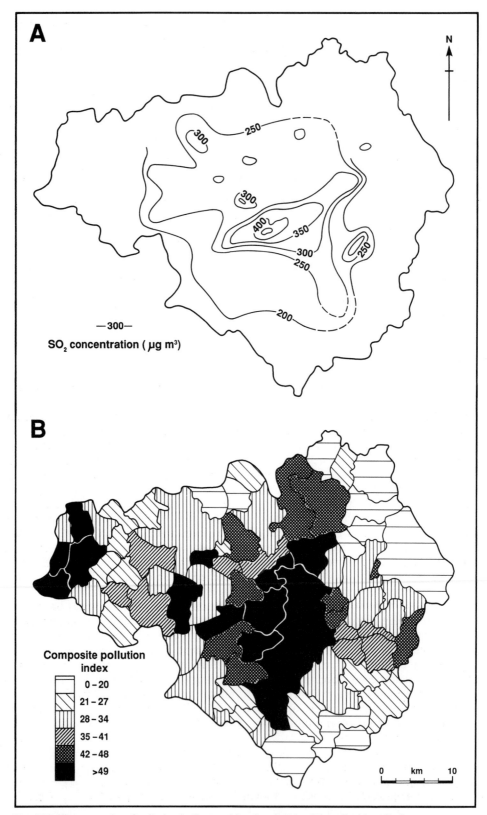

FIG 17.3 The geography of pollution in Greater Manchester: (*a*) sulphur dioxide pollution;
(*b*) composite index of pollution (*source:* Wood *et al.*, 1974 Figs. 11, 15)

TABLE 17.1 Environmental impacts of developments in the tertiary sector

(a) *Retail renewal in city centres*

Positive	Negative
Modernizes outworn areas	Changes traditional character
Reduces land-use conflicts	Creates new points of congestion
Scope for new design standards	Intrusive effects on older townscapes
Provides weather protection	Creates artificial atmosphere
Leads to upgrading of some streets	Causes blight on other streets
Integrates new transport	Causes pressure on existing infrastructures

(b) *Suburbanization of producer services*

Positive	Negative
Improved building design	Extensive unimaginative ground-level parking lots
Landscaped development	Sterilization of large areas of suburban land at low-use intensity
Upgrades existing suburban commercial centres	Increases congestion in established suburban centres
Reduced pedestrian/transport conflict	Visual intrusion of large areas of parked vehicles

Sources: Bennison and Davies (1980 p. 14) and Daniels (1985*a* p. 223).

farming, without due regard to the environment and soils in particular. Within Western Europe, large-scale farming is most advanced in the United Kingdom; not surprisingly most concern over the decline in landscape and environmental quality has been shown in this country.

In a penetrating account of conflicts in the countryside, Lowe *et al.* (1986) chronicle some of the losses which have occurred in the rural landscape of Great Britain between 1950 and the early 1980s. These include 95 per cent of lowland herb-rich grasslands; 80 per cent of chalk and limestone grasslands; 60 per cent of lowland heaths; 45 per cent of limestone pavements; 50 per cent of ancient woodlands; 50 per cent of lowland fens and marshes; 60 per cent of lowland raised bogs; and 33 per cent of upland grasslands and heaths. The habitats of plants, birds, and mammals have been lost with the large-scale removal of hedgerows—all in the name of increased efficiency and profit. Over 7000 ha of hedgerows were grubbed up each year between 1945 and 1970, especially in the main arable areas of eastern England (Norfolk alone lost half of its hedges between 1946 and 1970). Moorlands have been reclaimed for farming or converted into forests. Parry *et al.* (1981) estimate that 46 000 ha, or 10 per cent of the moorland in the National Parks of England and Wales, had been reclaimed since 1950. They dis-

tinguish between primary and secondary moorland loss and demonstrate how reclamation was formerly of the secondary type (i.e. moorland that had invaded abandoned farmland). However, up to 60 per cent of post-war reclamation in the Yorkshire Moors and Brecon Beacons has been primary in nature (i.e. land that has never been ploughed).

A common factor contributing to these losses has been government policy, in the form of price support and various drainage and reclamation schemes. In England and Wales, the Ministry of Agriculture, Fisheries, and Food (MAFF) increased the amount of grant-aided land for drainage from 25 000 ha in 1970 to over 100 000 ha in the mid-1980s; land drainage became the second largest component of grant aid after farm buildings. In theory, grants were only given when benefits exceeded costs. However, in an examination of cost-benefit appraisals for wetland drainage, Bowers (1983) reveals that the benefits have often been overestimated, especially as amenity and conservation losses are not assessed.

The bias of modern agriculture towards cereals and arable monoculture has brought with it other negative consequences for the landscape and environment. For example, straw-burning typifies the dilemma of modern farming. Cereals are so heavily treated with chemicals that waste straw is incapable of being broken down naturally. Instead, it is burnt, with the smoke (and sometimes the flames) affecting the welfare of others. Straw-burning is thus another example of a negative externality involving a transfer of costs, whereby farmers are trying 'to get away with it' at the public's expense. This was vividly portrayed by Lowe et al., (1986) in their account of a nine-car 'pile up' on the A19 in 1983, when two people died. The farmer involved had broken the voluntary National Farmers Union's code on straw-burning; however, with no statutory law he was fined a nominal figure of just £2000. The Royal Commission on Environmental Pollution (1984) did recommend a ban on straw-burning, to come into effect at the end of the 1980s. Yet again, enforcement of such a recommendation is made more difficult by the attitudes of farmers, who consider the burning of straw to be good for the soil.

Soil fertility has in fact been declining with continuous cereal production, and soil erosion has become a major international and political-economic issue (Blaikie, 1985; Boardman et al., 1990). The national soil map, published by the Soil Survey (1986), indicated that over 40 per cent of arable soils in England and Wales are at risk from erosion by water and wind (Aden-Clarke and Hodge, 1987). Erosion is especially likely on sandy and sandy loam soils, where more than 20 tonnes per ha can be removed in one year. Such losses are related to falling levels of organic matter in the soil, caused by the ploughing of permanent pasture and the use of inorganic fertilizers. However, more research is needed on the effects of different crop covers and tillage practices on rates of soil erosion, before practical soil conservation measures can be developed (Morgan, 1985; Boardman et al., 1990). The latter are, as yet, rather limited and if introduced could lead to fundamental social changes for those living in the affected areas (Blaikie, 1985). A growth in organic farming or a shift back to mixed farming would appear to provide the only long-term solution to the problem of soil erosion.

Governments in many developed economies are now aware of some of the environmental consequences of their own agricultural policies. A change in attitude is apparent and measures with a higher ecological and landscape value are slowly being introduced. Their objective is to maintain farming practices that both satisfy the requirements of 'protecting the countryside' and ensure an adequate income for farmers. However, these two are often not compatible and so an overall co-ordinated policy for agriculture and the environment has yet to emerge (see Section 17.3). Instead, various individual measures are being introduced, including the designation of Environmentally Sensitive Areas (Chapter 8.4), the set-aside of arable land, the encouragement of less intensive farming (extensification), and the diversification of agricultural land into woodland and such alternative land uses as golf courses, caravan parks, and recreational complexes (Ilbery, 1990a). Space does not permit an examination of these measures, all of which safeguard the welfare of farmers by offering financial incentives and/or compensation. Agricultural interests continue to be emphasized above environmental and conservation objectives (Potter, 1987), although pressure-group activity is beginning to affect policy measures. Much remains to be done, especially in changing the attitudes of policy and individual decision-makers.

17.3 Attitudes and environmental policy

Developed economies have long emphasized the positive externalities of economic growth, at the expense of environmental quality and human welfare. The conflict between economic and environmental interests in the countryside, for example, is well summarized by Lowe et al. (1986 p. 64):

Conservationists want essentially the products that low fertility brings. Modern agriculture, in contrast, aims to push up production through high inputs of chemical and mechanical energy and a heavily regulated and artificial environment, in which constant attention is given to the elimination of physical contraints, natural diversity and competing fauna and flora.

A major difficulty with economic growth policies is that they cannot maximize human welfare for everyone. Inevitably some benefit at the expense of others, with the outcome depending, in part, on location. Economic change, therefore, leads to spatial inequalities in such 'indicators' as income and unemployment levels, which later government measures may attempt to rectify. This paradox of government policy (policies introduced to remedy the problems partly created by previous policies) is apparent in the Common Agricultural Policy and regional policy measures for example (Chapters 8.3 and 16.4). Such policies are rather 'hit and miss', partly because of a lack of compatibility when applied at different geographical scales. This raises the whole issue of the desirability of area-based (spatial) policies over non-spatial policies. All government policies have spatial consequences (Chapter 8), but area-based policies have been criticized for cutting across other fundamental divisions of society and being a reaction to the symptoms rather than the causes of uneven development (see Chapter 16.4).

Whether national or regional, policies have continued to stress the benefits of economic growth over environmental issues. This is vividly portrayed in the development of oil and gas reserves in the North Sea, which has produced wealth at the expense of oil rig disasters and water pollution (e.g. oil slicks). It is necessary, therefore, to change the attitudes of those initiating change, whether government bodies, corporate organizations, or individual entrepreneurs. This remains a major challenge, however, as such people are reluctant to recognize that environmental values represent legitimate constraints upon their activities. In the USA, for example, the 1969 National Environmental Policy Act required that an environmental impact study (EIS) be produced by all Federal agencies proposing developments that would significantly affect the environment. However, great variability exists between states regarding the types of development which require an EIS; only a few demand an EIS for large private development proposals (Estall and Buchanan, 1980). Geographical variations exist, therefore, in the incidence of environmental control legislation, with some states developing an anti-business image or climate.

The attitudes of large US corporations to such legislation are examined by Stafford (1985). In a survey of 162 new branch plants, environmental factors ranked only eleventh in importance among the factors affecting their locational decisions. Traditional location factors—labour, markets, transport, materials—were the most critical, even for industries concerned with controlling the emission of pollutants. Indeed, environmental regulations still only ranked fifth for the 58 'less clean firms'. Stafford examined the location selection process (Chapter 10.1) at national, regional, sub-regional (state), and local (specific sites) levels and found environmental regulations to be significant only at the sub-regional scale (due to the effect of state environmental protection agencies). Overall, environmental regulations had not significantly altered the way firms conducted their location searches and thus are not likely to lead to major shifts in the location of industry within the USA.

Similar negative attitudes towards the environment have been revealed in the farming community. Westmacott and Worthington (1974) found that farmers in the United Kingdom were divided in their views as to whether they held any responsibility for the conservation of the landscape, although all thought they should be compensated for any financial losses from conservation! Positive conservation measures have been shown to be largely restricted to those with either large farms or a personal interest in conservation (MAFF, 1976; Newby et al., 1977; Gasson and Potter, 1988). However, not all of those with large farms are sympathetic to the needs of conservation, especially the large, owner-occupied agribusinesses. Indeed, large farms are both more hostile and sympathetic to conservation than farmers in general, suggesting that a more discriminating factor than farm size is needed. Consequently, Gasson and Potter (1988) produce a fourfold typology of farmers on the basis of two variables: first, their degree of financial constraint; and secondly, their commitment to conservation (Table 17.2a). Applying the typology to farmers involved in a survey of attitudes to voluntary land diversion schemes in the United Kingdom, they found that 42 per cent of the sample fell into group one (financially constrained with low conservation orientation), although they only covered 17 per cent of the sample area (with a mean farm size of 86 ha). In contrast, group four (less financially constrained with high conservation orientation) accounted for just 20 per cent of the sample, but 51 per cent of the total area (with an average farm size of 544 ha) (Table 17.2b). One of the implications of their findings is that land diversion schemes may not be very successful in instigating environmentally friendly land-use changes on farms which have no history of conservation management; a 'selectivity effect' is thus apparent, whereby land diversion schemes pay certain farmers to do what they would have done anyway (Ilbery, 1990a).

Despite the increasing significance of 'green'

TABLE 17.2 Attitudes of farmers towards conservation

(a) Typology of farmers

Financial constraint	Conservation orientation	
	low	high
more constrained	1	2
less constrained	3	4

(b) Relative importance of groups on the basis of financial status and conservation orientation

Group	No. farms	Mean farm size (ha)	Total area (ha)	% of sample area
1	61	85.6	5 222	16.8
2	34	124.4	4 228	13.6
3	21	276.1	5 799	18.7
4	29	543.6	15 763	50.9
TOTAL	145	213.9	31 012	100.0

Source: Gasson and Potter (1988 pp. 347, 348).

issues in the political arena, it would seem that most entrepreneurs are still to develop a positive attitude towards environmental issues. Yet they have social responsibilities and should contribute to the solving of welfare and environmental problems. Indeed, public pressure has been increasing and in 1987 an EC survey of the twelve member countries showed that 72 per cent of respondents considered the protection of the environment to be an immediate/urgent problem (Whittow, 1988); figures ranged from a high of 85 per cent in Italy to a low of 56 per cent in France and Ireland. A more recent Mori poll of 1902 adults in 146 constituencies of Britain suggested that over a half of the voters in the European Parliament elections in June 1989 would be swayed by environmental policies (Ardill, 1989); indeed, the 'green' vote increased substantially in those elections. Nuclear waste topped the list of environmental issues (63 per cent), followed by water pollution (46), toxic waste (44) and destruction of the ozone layer and/or the greenhouse effect (44); housing developments in rural areas (20), pesticides (19) and vehicle emissions (12) were of lesser importance.

Green politics are becoming more influential and the whole environmental movement has blossomed since the early 1970s. Consequently, governments are now more likely to act upon the blatant indicators of environmental damage and

human welfare. Many recommendations have been forwarded and individual policies introduced (e.g. Water Pollution Safeguard Areas, lead-free petrol, straw-burning regulations, and Environmentally Sensitive Areas). However, there has been little concerted action and no country has a coherent environmental policy. Regional, and even national, controls are of limited value anyway because major environmental problems pay no respect to national boundaries. Many problems are international and thus warrant international solutions, yet it is difficult to achieve agreements at this level.

This is exemplified in the case of the EC, which, in theory, has had an environmental policy since 1973. For the first eight years, it was somewhat peripheral to the Commission's activities. There was a lack of political will in the face of strong agricultural and industrial lobbies and the general view was that environmental protection and pollution control had a negative impact on economic interests. It was not until 1981 that Environmental Action Programmes were being outlined by the Commissioner for Environment, Consumer Protection and Nuclear Safety. However, these had no official power because the EC lacked the institutional and legal framework for implementing policy at the European level. Four years later, in 1985, the Directive on the Environmental Assessment of projects was published, advocating that all major development projects should be subject to an Environmental Impact Assessment (EIA) (see below). This too suffered from the same problem of lacking an institutional and legal framework that faced the environmental action programmes.

An important turning-point came in 1987 with the Single European Act (SEA), which paves the way for the single union in 1992. SEA made amendments to the original Treaty of Rome and provided the necessary legal and institutional framework for implementing policy at the international level. The environmental assessment Directive of 1985 now has a legal basis and so all major proposed projects, like coal-mines (Chapter 3.3), are subject to an EIA. Article 25 of the SEA ensures that environmental protection requirements shall be a component part of the Community's other policies (regional, social and agricultural), especially where this can be better attained at a Community, rather than an individual country, level. There are three main objectives to the protection of the environment under the SEA:

1. To preserve, protect and improve the quality of the environment.
2. To contribute towards protecting human health.
3. To ensure a prudent and rational utilization of natural resources.

The new legal powers under SEA have potentially far-reaching consequences for the environment and human welfare. A closer link between regional (spatial) policies and the environment has already been developed and the Directive on the Environmental Assessment of projects is building EIA into the process of approving proposals for funding by the European Regional Development Fund. Protection of the environment is, therefore, becoming an integral part of EC and national economic and social policies. This suggests that public pressure is causing attitudes to change. However, it is far from clear how these new ideas are going to work in practice. For example, agricultural policy-makers have been among the first to respond and incorporate environmental objectives into their set-aside policy (Regulation 1094/88). Yet this particular policy has been seen more in terms of alleviating surpluses (e.g. economic) than with environmental issues (Potter, 1987; Ilbery, 1990a). This may be a

case of environmental issues being used as an excuse to meet other objectives.

Another major problem relates to the technique of EIA itself (Chapman, 1981; Conacher, 1988). Although much further developed than original approaches (e.g. Leopold et al. 1971) and widely adopted in the USA, Canada, Australia, and New Zealand, EIA is essentially based on subjective evaluations of the likely impact of future developments. There is no objective method and quantification gives the false impression of objectivity, when qualitative data need to be incorporated. Indeed, there is a lack of baseline data on environmental and social conditions to assess the consequences of change. Further problems include who should actually undertake the EIA (e.g. consultants, local planning authorities, the developer) and who bears the cost (e.g. the government, developer, or both). EIA is usually based on checklists of possible impacts; but as Chapman (1981 p. 198) remarks, such pigeon-holing into specific categories 'tends to encourage a simple view of environmental systems in which the complex cause and effect relationships between the various elements are neglected'.

Environmental problems have come to the fore in recent years and there are clear signs that the attitudes of governments and individuals are beginning to change in response to pressures exerted by the general public and the environmental lobby. However, this is a very slow process and increasing international competition in a global economy has encouraged governments to pursue national policies for economic growth. The conflict between economic change and environmental quality remains therefore and there are no easy solutions to the issues involved. What is being recognized, however, is that something must be done quickly about environmental quality and that this can be achieved only through international agreements.

17.4 Summary

A two-way relationship exists between economic change and the environment. During the major post-war period of economic change in developed economies, the environment was perceived as presenting either opportunities or constraints for economic activity. However, in more recent years far greater attention has been given to the adverse environmental consequences of economic change. These range in scale from such global threats as the greenhouse effect to the localized impacts associated with the emission of smell and slurry leaks from intensive livestock units. Responses to any resulting environmental legislation may, in turn, affect location and land-use decisions, thus reinforcing the kind of feedback effect depicted in Figure 1.2. The main features to arise from this final chapter include:

- Positive and negative impacts of economic change are usually discussed within the concept of externalities, which is inherently spatial and suggests a distance-decay pattern away from the location of the relevant economic activity.
- Air and water pollution, in the form of acid rain and declining water quality, are good examples of the environmental consequences (negative externality) of economic change, especially associated with changes in agriculture and industry.

- The deterioration of the landscape, characterized by dereliction, soil erosion, and the removal of hedgerows and caused by developments in the primary and secondary sectors in particular, is another spatially extensive consequence of economic change.
- Environmental policies have been slow to be developed and implemented. This relates to the deep-seated attitudes of both entrepreneurs and governments, who have stressed the benefits of economic growth and change at the expense of the environment in which people live.
- A change in attitude towards environmental issues can, however, be detected. Pressure-group activity is beginning to affect government policies, although a co-ordinated approach to dealing with international problems of an environmental nature has not progressed very far. This is exemplified by the EC, which has theoretically had an environmental policy since 1973 but where little action occurred until 1987.

References

Aaronovitch, S., and Sawyer, M. C. (1975), *Big business: theoretical and empirical aspects of concentration and mergers in the United Kingdom* (Macmillan, London).

Abler, R. F. (1971), 'Distance, intercommunications and geography', *Proceedings of the Association of American Geographers*, 3: 1–4.

——Adams, J. S., and Gould, P. R. (1971), *Spatial organization: the geographer's view of the world* (Prentice-Hall, Englewood Cliffs, New Jersey).

ACARD (1979), *Technological change: threats and opportunities for the United Kingdom* (Advisory Council for Applied Research and Development, HMSO, London).

Aden-Clarke, C., and Hodge, D. (1987), 'Soil erosion: the answer lies in organic farming', *New Scientist*, 12 Feb., 42–3.

Aglietta, M. (1979), *A theory of capitalist regulation* (New Left Books, London).

——(1982), 'World capitalism in the eighties', *New Left Review*, 136: 25–36.

Agnew, J. (1987), *The United States in the world economy: a regional geography* (Cambridge University Press, Cambridge).

Agrawal, R. C., and Heady, E. O. (1968), 'Application of game theory models in agriculture', *Journal of Agricultural Economics*, 19: 207–18.

Albrecht, D. E., and Murdock, S. H. (1984) 'Toward a human ecological perspective on part-time farming', *Rural Sociology*, 49: 389–411.

Alexander, I. (1979). *Office location and public policy* (Longman, London).

Alic, J. A. (1986). 'Employment and job creation impacts of high technology', *Futures*, 18: 508–13.

Allen, J. (1988a), 'Service industries: uneven development and uneven knowledge', *Area*, 20: 15–22.

——(1988b), 'Towards a post-industrial economy', In J. Allen and D. Massey (eds.), *Restructuring Britain—the economy in question* (Sage, London), 91–135.

Allen, J. C., and Barnes, D. F. (1985), 'The causes of deforestation', *Annals of the Association of American Geographers*, 75: 163–84.

Allen, J. M., and Brown, R. H. (1984), '" Buy-British" policies and the regeneration of the British clothing industry', in B. M. Barr and N. M. Waters (eds.), *Regional diversification and structural change: proceedings of the Canada–United Kingdom Symposium*

on industrial geography held at the University of Calgary, Canada, in August 1983, B.C. Geographical Series, 39 (Tantalus Research, Vancouver), 73–86.

Allen, J., and Massey, D. (eds.) (1988), *Restructuring Britain: the economy in question* (Sage, London).

Altshuler, A., Anderson, M., Jones, D., Roos, D., and Womack, J. (1984), *The future of the automobile: the report of MIT's international automobile programme* (MIT Press, Cambridge, Massachusetts).

Ambrose, P., and Colenutt, P. (1975), *The property machine* (Penguin, London).

Amin, S. (1976), *Unequal development* (Harvester Press, Brighton).

Anderson, J. (1983), 'Geography as ideology and the politics of crisis: the Enterprize Zones experiment', in J. Anderson, S. Duncan and R. Hudson (eds.), *Redundant spaces in cities and regions* (Academic Press, London), 313–50.

Ardill, J. (1989), 'Nuclear waste tops green issue list for voters in European elections', *Guardian*, 6 Apr.

Armstrong, H., and Taylor, J. (1985), *Regional economics and policy* (Philip Allan, Deddington, Oxford).

Averitt, R. T. (1968), *The dual economy: the dynamics of American industry* (Norton, New York).

Aydalot, P. (1988), 'Technological trajectories and regional innovation in Europe', in P. Aydalot and D. Keeble (eds.), *High technology industry and innovative environments: the European experience* (Routledge & Kegan Paul, London), 22–47.

——and Keeble, D. (1988), 'High-technology industry and innovative environments in Europe: an overview', in P. Aydalot and D. Keeble (eds.), *High technology industry and innovative environments: the European experience* (Routledge & Kegan Paul, London) , 1–21.

Bagguley, P. (1986), *Service employment and economic restructuring in Lancaster: 1971–1981*, University of Lancaster, Lancaster Regionalism Group, Working Paper 20.

Bagnasco, A. (1981), 'Labour markets, class structure and regional formations in Italy', *International Journal of Urban and Regional Research*, 5: 40–4.

Balasubramanyam, V. N., and Rothschild, R. (1985), 'Free port zones in the United Kingdom', *Lloyds Bank Review*, 158: 20–31.

Bale, J. (1978), 'Externality gradients', *Area*, 10: 334–6.

Baran, B. (1985), *Technological innovation and de-*

regulation: the transformation of the labor process in the insurance industry, University of California, Berkeley, BRIE Working Paper.

Barney, G. O. (1980), *The Global 2000 Report to the President of the USA* (Pergamon, New York).

Barnum, H. G. (1966), *Market centres and hinterlands in Baden-Württemberg*, University of Chicago, Department of Geography, Research Paper 103.

Barras, R. (1979), *The returns from office development and investment*, Centre for Environmental Studies, Research Series, 35.

—— (1981), 'The causes of the London office boom', paper presented at the First CES London Conference, Feb.

—— (1985), 'Information technology and the service revolution', *Policy Studies*, 5(4): 14–24.

Bateman, M. (1985), *Office development: a geographical analysis* (Croom Helm, London).

—— (1988), *Shops and offices: locational change in Britain and the EEC,* (John Murray, London).

Bell, D. (1974), *The coming of post-industrial society: a venture in social forecasting* (Heinemann, London).

Bennison, D. J., and Davies, R. L. (1980), 'The impact of town centre shopping schemes in Britain: their impact on traditional retail environments', *Progress in Planning*, 14: 1–104.

Berry, B. J. L. (1967), *The geography of market centers and retail distribution* (Prentice-Hall, Englewood Cliffs, New Jersey).

Beyers, W. B., Tofflemire, J. M., Stranahan, H. A., and Johnsen, E. G. (1986), *The service economy: understanding growth of producer services in the central Puget Sound region* (Central Puget Sound Economic Development District, Seattle).

Birch, D. L. (1979), *The job generation process* (MIT Program of Neighbourhood and Regional Change, Cambridge, Massachusetts).

Blackbourn, A. (1972), 'The location of foreign owned manufacturing plants in the Republic of Ireland', *Tijdschrift voor Economische en Sociale Geografie*, 63: 438–43.

—— (1978), 'Multinational enterprises and regional development: a comment', *Regional Studies*, 12: 125–7.

—— (1982), 'The impact of multinational corporations on the spatial organisation of developed nations: a review', in M. J. Taylor and N. Thrift (eds.), *The geography of multinationals* (Croom Helm, London), 147–57.

Blackburn, P., Coombs, R., and Green, K. (1985), *Technology, economic growth and the labour process* (Macmillan, London).

Blaikie, P. M. (1978), 'The theory of the spatial diffusion of innovations: a spatial cul-de-sac', *Progress in Human Geography*, 2: 268–95.

—— (1985), *The political economy of soil erosion in developing countries* (Longman, London).

Bloomfield, G. T. (1978), *The world automotive industry* (David and Charles, Newton Abbot).

Bluestone, B., and Harrison, B. (1982), *The deindustrialization of America: plant closings, community abandonment, and the dismantling of basic industry* (Basic Books, New York).

—— and Baker, L. (1981), *Corporate flight* (Progressive Alliance, Washington DC).

Blunden, J. R. (1970), 'The renaissance of the Cornish tin industry', *Geography*, 55: 331–5.

—— (1977), 'Rural land use', in Open University D204 *Fundamentals of human geography, Section II, spatial analysis: area patterns*, Unit 15 (Open University, Milton Keynes), 5–55.

Boardman, J., Foster, I. D. L., and Dearing, J. (eds.) (1990), *Soil erosion on agricultural land* (Wiley, London).

Boas, C. W. (1961), 'Locational patterns of American automobile plants, 1895–1958', *Economic Geography*, 37: 218–30.

Boddy, M. J. (1987), 'Structural approaches to industrial location', in W. F. Lever (ed.), *Industrial change in the United Kingdom* (Longman, London), 56–66.

—— and Lovering, J. (1986), 'High technology industry in the Bristol sub-region: the aerospace/defence nexus', *Regional Studies*, 20: 217–31.

—— and Bassett, K. (1986), *Sunbelt city? A case study of economic restructuring in Britain's M4 growth corridor* (Oxford University Press, Oxford).

Bolton, J. (1971), *Small firms: Report of the Commission of Inquiry on Small Firms* (HMSO, London), Cmd 4811.

Borchert, J. R. (1978), 'Major control points in American economic geography', *Annals of the Association of American Geographers*, 68: 214–32.

Bowers, J. (1983), 'Cost-benefit analysis of wetland drainage', *Environment and Planning, A*, 15: 227–35.

—— (1985). 'The economics of agribusiness', in M. J. Healey and B. W. Ilbery (eds.), *Industrialization of the countryside* (Geo Books, Norwich), 29–43.

Bowler, I. R. (1979), *Government and agriculture: a spatial perspective* (Longman, London).

—— (1981), 'Regional specialisation in the agricultural industry', *Journal of Agricultural Economics*, 32: 43–54.

—— (1985a), *Agriculture under the Common Agricultural Policy: a geography* (Manchester University Press, Manchester).

—— (1985b), 'Some consequences of the industrialization of agriculture in the European Community', in M. J. Healey and B. W. Ilbery (eds.), *Industrialization of the countryside* (Geo Books, Norwich), 75–97.

—— (1986), 'Intensification, concentration and specialisation in agriculture: the case of the European community', *Geography*, 71: 14–24.

—— and Ilbery, B. W. (1987), 'Redefining agricultural geography', *Area*, 19: 327–32.

Bowler, J. (1971), *Small firms: report of the Commission of Inquiry on Small Firms* (HMSO, London), Cmnd 4811.

Boyce, R. B., and Williams, A. F. (1979), *The bases of economic geography* (Holt, Rinehart and Winston, London).

Bradbeer, J. B. (1986), 'The future of mineral extraction in the rural environment', in D. G. Lockhart and B. W. Ilbery (eds.), *The future of the British rural landscape* (Geo Books, Norwich), 97–114.

Bradbury, J. H. (1982), 'State corporations and resource based development in Quebec, Canada, 1960–80', *Economic Geography*, 58: 45–61.

Bradley, K., and Gelb, A. (1983). *Co-operation at work: the Mondragon experience* (Heinemann, London).

Bradshaw, M. (1988), *Regions and regionalisation in the United States* (Macmillan, Basingstoke, Hampshire).

Brady, T., and Liff, S. (1983), *Monitoring new technology and employment* (Manpower Services Commission, Sheffield).

Brandt, W. (1980), *North–south: a programme for survival* (Pan, London) (The Brandt Commission).

Breheny, M. J. (ed.) (1988), *Defence expenditure and regional development* (Mansell, London).

—— and McQuaid, R. (1985), *The M4 corridor: patterns and causes of growth in high technology industries*, University of Reading, Department of Geography, Geographical Papers, 87.

—— —— (1987), 'HTUK: the development of the United Kingdom's major centre of high technology industry', in M. J. Breheny and R. McQuaid (eds.), *The development of high technology industries: an international survey* (Croom Helm, London), 297–354.

Briggs, D. (1981), 'Environmental influences on the yield of spring barley in England and Wales', *Geoforum*, 12: 99–106.

Britton, J. N. H. (1974), 'Environmental adaptation of industrial plants: service linkages, locational environment and organisation' in F. E. I. Hamilton (ed.), *Spatial perspectives on industrial organisation and decision-making* (Wiley, London), 363–90.

—— (1985), 'Research and development in the Canadian economy: sectoral, ownership, locational and policy issues', in A. J. Thwaites and R. P. Oakey (eds.), *The regional economic impact of technological change* (Frances Pinter, London), 67–114.

—— (1987), 'High technology in Canada: locational and policy issues of the technology gap', in M. J. Breheny and R. McQuaid (eds.), *The development of high technology industries: an international survey* (Croom Helm, London), 143–91.

—— and Gilmour, J. M. (1978), *The weakest link: a technological perspective on Canadian industrial underdevelopment*, Science Council of Canada, Ottawa, Background Study 43.

Bromley, R. D. F., and Humphrys, G. (1979), *Dealing with dereliction: redevelopment of the Lower Swansea Valley* (University College of Swansea, Wales).

—— and Morgan, R. H. (1985), 'The effects of enterprise zone policy: evidence from Swansea', *Regional Studies*, 19: 403–15.

—— and Thomas, C. J. (1988), 'Retail parks: spatial and functional integration of retail units in the Swansea enterprise zone', *Transactions of the Institute of British Geographers*, 13: 4–18.

Brook, C. (1985), 'Area-based policy', in Open University *D205: Changing Britain, changing world: geographical perspectives*, iv. *Geography matters*, Block 7, Unit 27 (Open University, Milton Keynes).

—— and Hay, A. (1974). 'Export base theory and the growth and decline of regions' in Open University *D342: Regional analysis and development*, Unit 4 (Open University, Milton Keynes), 51–77.

Brookfield, H. C. (1975), *Interdependent development* (Methuen, London).

Browett, J. (1984), 'On the necessity and inevitability of uneven spatial development under capitalism', *International Journal of Urban and Regional Research*, 8: 155–76.

Brown, L. A. (1975), 'The market and infrastructure context of adoption: a spatial perspective on the diffusion of innovation', *Economic Geography*, 51: 185–216.

—— (1981), *Innovation diffusion: a new perspective* (Methuen, London).

Brown, S. (1987a), 'An integrated approach to retail change: the multi-polarisation model', *The Service Industries Journal*, 7: 153–64.

—— (1987b), 'Institutional change in retailing: a geographical interpretation', *Progress in Human Geography*, 11: 181–206.

Browning, C. E., and Gesler, W. (1979), 'The sun belt—snow belt: a case of sloppy regionalizing', *Professional Geographer*, 31: 66–74.

Brusco, S. (1982), 'The Emilian model: productive decentralisation and social integration', *Cambridge Journal of Economics*, 6: 167–84.

—— (1986), 'Small firms and industrial districts: the experience of Italy', in D. Keeble and E. Wever (eds.), *New firms and regional development in Europe* (Croom Helm, London), 184–202.

Buchanan, M. E. (1975), 'Immigrant tobacco growers in southern Queensland', *Australian Geographical Studies*, 13: 182–9.

Buck, N. (1988), 'Service industries and local labour markets: towards an anatomy of service job loss', *Urban Studies*, 25: 319–32.

Bunge, W. (1966), *Theoretical geography* (C. W. K. Gleerup, Lund).

Bunting, T., and Guelke, L. (1979), 'Behavioural and perception geography: a critical appraisal', *Annals of the Association of American Geographers*, 69: 448–63.

Burt, S. (1987), 'French shopping centre development:

trends and issues', paper presented to Institute of British Geographers' Urban Geography Study Group conference on 'Shopping centres—a geographical appraisal', Coventry Polytechnic, May.

—— Dawson, J. A., and Sparks, L. (1983), 'Structure plans and retailing policies', *Planner*, 69 (1): 11–13.

Burtenshaw, D., Bateman, M., and Ashworth, G. J. (1981), *The city in west Europe* (Wiley, Chichester).

Buswell, R. J., Easterbrook, R. P., and Morphet, C. S. (1985), 'Geography, regions and research and development activity: the case of the United Kingdom', in A. J. Thwaites and R. P. Oakey (eds.), *The regional economic impact of technological change* (Frances Pinter, London), 36–66.

—— and Lewis, E. W. (1970), 'The geographical distribution of industrial research activity in the United Kingdom', *Regional Studies*, 4: 297–306.

Bylinski, G. (1983), 'The race to the automatic factory', *Fortune*, 21 Feb., 52–64.

Cable, V. (1983), *Protectionism and industrial decline* (Hodder and Stoughton, London).

Cadden, P. C. (1975), 'Multi-plant firms and commodity flows: the case of the western Canadian flour milling industry', in B. M. Barr (ed.), *Western Canadian research in geography: the Lethbridge Papers*, B.C. Geographical Series, 21, Occasional Papers in Geography (Tantalus Research, Vancouver), 11–20.

Carr, M. (1983), 'A contribution to the review and critique of behavioural industrial location theory', *Progress in Human Geography*, 7: 386–402.

Castells, M. (1985), 'High technology, economic restructuring, and the urban-regional process in the United States', in M. Castells (ed.), *High technology, space and society*, Urban Affairs Annual Reviews, 28 (Sage, Beverly Hills, California), 11–40.

Chandler, A. D. (1963), *Strategy and structure: chapters in the history of the industrial enterprise* (MIT, Cambridge, Mass.).

Chapman, K. (1981), 'Issues in environmental impact assessment', *Progress in Human Geography*, 5: 190–210.

—— and Walker, D. (1987), *Industrial location* (Basil Blackwell, Oxford).

Checkland, S. (1975), *The Upas tree* (Glasgow University Press, Glasgow).

Chisholm, M. (1970), *Geography and economics* (Bell, London).

—— (1979), *Rural settlement and land use* (Hutchinson, London).

—— (1984), The Development Commission's factory programme, *Regional Studies*, 18: 513–17.

—— (1985), 'The Development Commission's employment programmes in rural England', in M. J. Healey and B. W. Ilbery (eds.), *Industrialization of the countryside* (Geo Books, Norwich), 279–305.

Chorley, R. J., and Haggett, P. (1967), *Models in geography* (Methuen, London).

Christaller, W. (1966), *Central Places in southern Germany*, trans. C. W. Baskin (Prentice Hall, Englewood Cliffs, New Jersey).

Christopherson, S., and Storper, M. (1986), 'The city as studio; the world as back lot: the impact of vertical disintegration on the location of the motion picture industry', *Environment and Planning D: Society and Space*, 4: 305–20.

Clairmonte, F., and Cavanagh, J. (1981), *The world in their web: dynamics of textile multinationals* (Zed Press, London).

Clark, C. (1940), *The conditions of economic progress* (Macmillan, London).

—— Wilson, F., and Bradley, J. (1969), 'Industrial location and economic potential in Western Europe', *Regional Studies*, 3: 197–212.

Clark, D. (1985), *Post-industrial America: a geographical perspective* (Methuen, London).

Clark, G. (1986), 'Diffusion of agricultural innovations' in M. Pacione (ed.), *Progress in agricultural geography* (Croom Helm, London), 70–92.

Clark, G. L. (1981), 'The employment relation and the spatial division of labour: a hypothesis', *Annals of the Association of American Geographers*, 71: 412–24.

—— (1986), 'The crisis of the Mid-West auto industry', in A. J. Scott and M. Storper (eds.), *Production, work, territory: the geographical anatomy of industrial capitalism* (Allen and Unwin, London), 125–48.

—— (1987), 'Regional development and planning: perspectives on foreign competition and the United States economy', *Progress in Human Geography*, 11: 549–57.

Clark, I. M. (1985), *The spatial organisation of multinational corporations* (Croom Helm, London).

Clout, H. D. (1971), *Agriculture: studies in contemporary Europe* (Macmillan, London).

—— (1984), *A rural policy for the EEC?* (Methuen, London).

—— (ed.) (1987), *Regional development in western Europe* (David Fulton, London).

—— Blacksell, M., King, R., and Pinder, D. (1985), *Western Europe: geographical perspectives* (Longman, London).

Coase, R. H. (1937), 'The nature of the firm', *Economica*, 4: 386–405.

Cohen, R. B. (1977), 'Multinational corporations, international finance, and the sunbelt', in D. C. Perry and A. J. Watkins (eds.), *The rise of the sunbelt cities* (Sage, Beverly Hills, California), 211–26.

Cohen, Y. S. (1972), *Diffusion of an innovation in an urban system*, University of Chicago, Department of Geography, Research Paper 140

Cohen, S., and Zysman, J. (1987), *Manufacturing matters: the myth of a post-industrial economy* (Basic Books, New York).

Conacher, A. (1988), 'Resource development and environmental stress: environmental impact assessment and beyond in Australia and Canada', *Geoforum*, 19: 339–52.

Conseil Économique et Social (1982), 'Le devenir des industries du textile et de l'habillement', *Journal Officiel*, Paris, 25 Feb.

Cooke, P. (1988), 'Flexible integration, scope economies, and strategic alliances: social and spatial mediations', *Environment and Planning D: Society and Space*, 6: 281–300.

—— (ed.) (1989), *Localities: the changing face of urban Britain* (Unwin Hyman, London).

—— Morgan, K., and Jackson, D. (1984), 'New technology and regional development in austerity Britain: the case of the semiconductor industry', *Regional Studies*, 18: 277–89.

—— and Rosa Pires, A. (1985), 'Production decentralisation in three European countries', *Environment and Planning A*, 17: 527–54.

Coombs, R., and Green, K. (1981), 'Microelectronics and the future of service employment', *Service Industries Journal*, 1(2): 4–20.

Cornwall County Council (1976), *County Structure Plan: topic report: employment, income and industry* (Cornwall County Council, Truro).

Country Landowners' Association (1973), *The future of land-ownership* (County Landowners' Association, London).

Cox, S. (1984), 'Ancient trade in modern form', *Geographical Magazine*, 56: 521–5.

Cromley, R. (1982), 'The von Thünen model and environmental uncertainty', *Annals of the Association of American Geographers*, 73: 404–10.

Cross, M. (1981), *New firm formation and regional development* (Gower, Farnborough, Hampshire).

Crow, B., and Thomas, A. (1982), *Third World atlas* (Open University Press, Milton Keynes).

Cruickshank, A. B. (1980) 'Development of the deep south: a reappraisal', *Scottish Geographical Magazine*, 96: 91–104.

Crum, R., and Gudgin, G. (1977), *Non-production activities in UK manufacturing industry* (European Economic Commission, Brussels).

—————— and Bailey, S. (1979), 'White collar employment in UK manufacturing industry' in P. W. Daniels (ed.), *Spatial patterns of office growth and location* (Wiley, Chichester), 127–57.

Cunningham, S. (1985), 'A new international division of labour, in Open University *D205: Changing Britain, changing world: geographical perspectives*, Unit 21, Block 6 (Open University, Milton Keynes).

Dalton, R. T. (1971), 'Peas for freezing: a recent development in Lincolnshire agriculture', *East Midlands Geographer*, 5: 133–41.

Daly, D. J. (1979), 'Weak links in the weakest link', *Canadian Public Policy*, 3: 307–17.

Damesick, P. J. (1987), 'The evolution of spatial economic policy', in P. J. Damesick and P. A. Wood (eds.), *Regional problems, problem regions, and public policy in the United Kingdom* (Oxford University Press, Oxford), 42–63.

Daniels, P. W. (1982), *Service industries: growth and location* (Cambridge University Press, Cambridge).

—— (1983), 'Service industries: supporting role or centre stage?' *Area*, 15: 301–9.

—— (1985a), *Service industries: a geographical appraisal* (Methuen, London).

—— (1985b), 'Service industries: some new directions', in M. Pacione (ed.), *Progress in industrial geography* (Croom Helm, London), 111–41.

—— (1986), 'Producer services and the post-industrial space economy', in R. Martin, and B. Rowthorn (eds.), *The geography of de-industrialisation* (Macmillan, Basingstoke, Hampshire), 291–321.

—— (1988), 'Some perspectives on the geography of services', *Progress in Human Geography*, 12: 431–40.

Daniels, T. L. (1986), 'Hobby farming in America: rural development or threat to commercial agriculture?' *Journal of Rural Studies*, 2: 31–40.

Darwent, D. F. (1969), 'Growth poles and growth centres in regional planning: a review', *Environment and Planning*, 1: 5–31.

Davies, R. L. (1976), *Marketing geography with special reference to retailing* (Retail and Planning Associates, Corbridge, Northumberland).

—— (1978), 'Issues in retailing', in P. Hall and R. L. Davies (eds.), *Issues in urban society* (Penguin, Harmondsworth), 132–60.

—— (1985), 'The Gateshead shopping and information service', *Environment and Planning B; Planning and Design*, 12: 209–20.

Davis, D. (1966), *A history of shopping* (Routledge and Kegan Paul, London).

Dawson, J. A. (1974), 'The suburbanization of retail activity', in J. H. Johnson (ed.), *Suburban growth: geographical processes at the edge of the western city* (Wiley, London), 155–73.

—— (1983a), *Shopping centre development* (Longman, London).

—— (1983b), 'Independent retailing in Great Britain: dinosaur or chameleon?' *Retail and Distribution Management*, 11: 29–32.

—— (1984), 'Structural-spatial relationships in the spread of hypermarket retailing', in E. Kaynak and R. Savitt (eds.), *Comparative marketing systems* (Praeger, New York), 156–82.

—— (1988), 'The changing high street', *Geographical Journal*, 154: 1–22.

—— and Kirby, D. A. (1980), 'Urban retail provision and consumer behaviour: some examples from Western society', in D. T. Herbert and R. J. Johnston (eds.), *Geography and the urban environment: progress in research and applications*, vol. iii (John Wiley, Chichester), 87–132.

—— and Lord, D. (eds.) (1985), *Shopping centre*

development: policies and prospects (Croom Helm, London).

De Lisle, D. (1982), 'Effects of distance on cropping patterns internal to the farm', *Annals of the Association of American Geographers*, 72: 88–98.

Demko, G. (ed) (1984), *Regional development problems and policies in Eastern and Western Europe* (Croom Helm, London).

Denman, D. R. (1965), 'Land ownership and the attraction of capital into agriculture: a British overview', *Land Economics*, 41: 209–16.

Dicken, P. (1976), 'The multi-plant business enterprise and geographical space: some issues in the study of external control and regional development', *Regional Studies*, 10: 401–12.

—— (1977), 'A note on location theory and the large business enterprise', *Area*, 9: 138–43.

—— (1986), *Global shift: industrial change in a turbulent world* (Harper and Row, London).

—— (1987), 'A tale of two NICs: Hong Kong and Singapore at the crossroads', *Geoforum*, 18: 151–64.

—— (1988), 'The changing geography of Japanese foreign direct investment in manufacturing industry: a global perspective', *Environment and Planning A*, 20: 633–53.

—— and Lloyd, P. E. (1981), *Modern western society: a geographical perspective on work, home and wellbeing* (Harper and Row, London).

Dickenson, J. P., and Salt, J. (1982), 'In vino veritas: an introduction to the geography of wine', *Progress in Human Geography*, 6: 159–89.

Dorfman, N. S. (1983), 'Route 128: the development of a regional high technology economy'. *Research Policy*, 12: 299–316.

Dosi, G. (1983), 'Technological paradigms and technical trajectories', *Research Policy*, 11: 147–64.

Drucker, P. F. (1986), 'The changed world economy', *Foreign Affairs*, 64: 768–91.

Duncan, J. S., and Ley, D. (1982), 'Structural Marxism and human geography: a critical assessment', *Annals of the Association of American Geographers*, 72: 30–59.

Dunford, M. F., and Perrons, D. C. (1983), *The arena of capital* (Macmillan, London).

—— and Perrons, D. (1986), 'The restructuring of the post-war British space economy', in R. Martin and B. Rowthorn (eds.), *The geography of de-industrialisation* (Macmillan, Basingstoke, Hampshire), 53–105.

Dunning, J. H. (1979), 'Explaining changing patterns of international production: in defence of the eclectic theory', *Oxford Bulletin of Economics and Statistics*, 41: 269–96.

—— (1980), 'Towards an eclectic theory of international production: some empirical tests', *Journal of International Business Studies*, 11: 9–31.

—— and Norman, G. (1983), 'The theory of multi-

national enterprise: an application to multinational office location', *Environment and Planning A*, 15: 675–92.

Durlacher, C. (1987), 'Satellite shopland: shopping centres of the future', in *Equinox: a guide to the 1987 series* (Channel 4 Television, London), 27–8.

Economist's Advisory Group (1979), *Factors influencing the location of offices of multinational enterprises* (EAG Ltd., London).

Edwards, L. E. (1983), 'Towards a process model of office-location decision making', *Environment and Planning A*, 15: 1327–42.

Edwards, S. (1975), 'Regional variations in freight costs', *Journal of Transport Economics and Policy*, 9: 115–26.

Enyedi, G. (1976), *Hungary: an economic geography* (Westview Press, Boulder, Colorado).

Erickson, R. A., and Leinbach, T. R. (1979), 'Characteristics of branch plants attracted to nonmetropolitan areas', in R. E. Lonsdale, and H. L. Seyler (eds.), *Nonmetropolitan industrialization* (V. H. Wilson, Washington, DC), 57–78.

Erlichman, J. (1988), 'Butter mountain melts but gloom spreads to cheese', *Guardian*, 9 Aug.

Estall, R. C. (1972), Some observations on the internal mobility of investment capital, *Area*, 4: 193–7.

—— (1980), 'The changing balance of the Northern and Southern regions of the United States', *Journal of American Studies*, 14: 365–86.

—— (1985), 'Stock control in manufacturing: the just-in-time system and its locational implications', *Area*, 17: 129–33.

—— and Buchanan, R. O. (1980), *Industrial activity and economic geography* (Hutchinson University Library, London).

European Commission (1986), *Europe's Common Agricultural Policy* (Commission of the European Communities, Brussels).

Everson, J. A., and Fitzgerald, B. P. (1969), *Settlement patterns* (Longman, London).

Ewald, U. (1976), 'The von Thünen principle and agricultural zonation in colonial Mexico', *Journal of Historical Geography*, 3: 123–34.

Farrands, C. (1982), 'The political economy of the Multi-Fibre Arrangement', in C. Stevens (ed.), *EEC and the Third World: a survey*, 2 (Hodder and Stoughton, London), 87–101.

Fertey, M. C., Lavelle, P. J., and White, R. (1986), *Report of the automotive industry human resources task force* (Department of Employment and Immigration, Canada, Ottawa).

Finn, D. (1984), *The employment effects of the new technologies: a review of the arguments* (Unemployment Unit, London).

Firth, M. (1976), *Management of working capital* (Macmillan, London).

Fisher, A. G. B. (1935), *The clash of progress and security* (Macmillan, London).

FitzSimmons, M. (1986), 'The new industrial agriculture: the regional integration of speciality crop production', *Economic Geography*, 62: 334–53.

Flockton, C. H. (1982), 'Strategic planning in the Paris region and French urban Policy', *Geoforum*, 13: 193–208.

Florence, P. S. (1948), *Investment, location and size of plant* (Cambridge University Press, Cambridge).

Florida, R. L., and Kenney, M. (1988), 'Venture capital, high technology and regional development', *Regional Studies*, 22: 33–48.

Forbes, D. K. (1984), *The geography of underdevelopment* (Croom Helm, London).

Foster, I. D. L., Ilbery, B. W., and Hinton, M. A. (1989), 'Agriculture and water quality: a preliminary examination of the Jersey nitrate problem', *Applied Geography*, 9: 95–113.

Foster-Carter, A. (1985), *The sociology of development* (Causeway, Ormskirk, Lancashire).

Fothergill, S., and Gudgin, G. (1982), *Unequal growth: urban and regional employment change in the United Kingdom* (Heinemann, London).

—— —— (1983), 'Trends in regional manufacturing employment: the main influences', in J. B. Goddard and A. G. Champion (eds.), *The urban and regional transformation of Britain* (Methuen, London), 27–50.

—— —— (1985), 'Ideology and methods in industrial location research', in D. Massey and R. Meegan (eds.), *Politics and method: contrasting studies in industrial geography* (Methuen, London), 92–115.

—— —— Kitson, M., and Monk, S. (1985), 'Rural industrialization: trends and causes', in M. J. Healey and B. W. Ilbery (eds.), *Industrialization of the countryside* (Geo Books, Norwich), 147–59.

—— —— —— (1986), 'The de-industrialisation of the city', in R. Martin and B. Rowthorn (eds.), *The geography of de-industrialisation* (Macmillan, Basingstoke, Hampshire), 214–37.

—— Monk, S., and Perry, M. (1987), *Property and industrial development* (Hutchinson, London).

Fotheringham, A. S., and Reeds, L. G. (1979), 'An application of discriminant analysis to agricultural land use prediction', *Economic Geography*, 55: 114–22.

Found, W. C. (1971), *A theoretical approach to rural land use patterns* (Edward Arnold, London).

Frank, A. G. (1967 and 1969), *Capitalism and underdevelopment in Latin America* (Monthly Review Press, New York), first and revised editions.

Franklin, S. H. (1971), *Rural societies: studies in contemporary Europe* (Macmillan, London).

Freeman, C. (1974), *The economics of industrial innovation* (Penguin, Harmondsworth).

—— (1986), 'The role of technical change in national economic development', in A. Amin and J. Goddard (eds.), *Technological change, industrial restructuring and regional development* (Allen and Unwin, London), 100–14.

—— Clark, J., and Soete, L. L. G. (1982), *Unemployment and technical innovation: a study of long waves and economic development* (Frances Pinter, London).

Freeman, D. B. (1985), 'The importance of being first: preemption by early adopters of farming innovations in Kenya', *Annals of the Association of American Geographers*, 75: 17–28.

French, R. A., and Hamilton, F. E. I. (eds.), (1979), *The socialist city: spatial structure and urban policy* (Wiley, New York).

Friedman, A. (1977), *Industry and labour: class struggle at work and monopoly capitalism* (Macmillan, London).

Frobel, F., Heinrichs, J., and Kreye, O. (1980), *The new international division of labour* (Cambridge University Press, Cambridge).

Gad, G. H. K. (1979), 'Face-to-face linkages and office decentralization potentials: a study of Toronto', in P. Daniels (ed.), *Spatial patterns of office growth and location* (John Wiley, Chichester), 298–319.

Galbraith, J. K. (1967), *The new industrial state* (Hamish Hamilton, London).

Ganguly, P. (1984), 'Business starts and stops: regional analysis by turnover size and sector 1980–83', *British Business*, 2 Nov. 350–3.

—— and Povey, D. (1983), 'Small firm survey: the international scene', *British Business*, 19 Nov. 486–91.

Gasson, R. M. (1969), 'Occupational immobility of small farmers', *Journal of Agricultural Economics*, 20: 279–88.

—— (1973), 'Goals and values of farmers', *Journal of Agricultural Economics*, 24: 521–42.

—— (1982), 'Part-time farming in Britain: research in progress', *Geo Journal*, 6: 355–8.

—— (1988), *The economics of part-time farming* (Longman, Harlow, Essex).

—— Crow, G., Errington, A., Hutson, J., Marsden, T., and Winter, D. M. (1988), 'The farm as a family business: a review', *Journal of Agricultural Economics*, 39: 1–41.

—— and Potter, C. (1988), 'Conservation through land diversion: a survey of farmers' attitudes', *Journal of Agricultural Economics*, 39: 340–51.

Gavin, A. (1988), 'Employment in retailing', paper presented to Centre for Local Economic Strategies Summer School, Barnsley, July.

Gershuny, J. (1978), *After industrial society? The emerging self-service economy* (Macmillan, London).

—— and Miles, I. (1983), *The new service economy: the transformation of employment in industrial societies* (Frances Pinter, London).

Gertler, S. (1988), 'The limits of flexibility: comments on the post-Fordist vision of production and its geography', *Transactions of the Institute of British Geographers*, 13: 419–32.

Gibbs, A. (1987), 'Retail warehouses: development

pressure and the planning response', *Estates Gazette*, 284, 31 Oct., 589–90, 596.

Gibbs, D. C. (1986*a*), *The changing international context of the clothing industry*, City of Manchester, Planning Department, Economic Briefing Note No. 70.

—— (1986*b*), *The changing national context of the clothing industry*, City of Manchester, Planning Department, Economic Briefing Note No. 71.

—— (1987), 'Technology and the clothing industry', *Area*, 19: 313–20.

—— (1988), 'Restructuring in the Manchester clothing industry: technical change and interrelationships between manufacturers and retailers', *Environment and Planning A*, 20: 1219–33.

Giggs, J. A. (1972), 'Retail change and decentralisation in the Nottingham metropolitan community', *Geographia Polonica*, 24: 173–88.

Gilbert, A. (1985), *An unequal world: the links between rich and poor nations* (Macmillan, London).

Gillespie, A. E., and Green, A. E. (1987), 'The changing geography of producer service employment in Britain', *Regional Studies*, 21: 397–411.

—— and Hepworth, M. E. (1988), *Telecommunications and regional development in the information society*, The University of Newcastle upon Tyne, Centre for Urban and Regional Development Studies, Newcastle Studies of the Information Economy, Working Paper 1.

Gillmor, D. A. (1986), 'Behavioural studies in agriculture: goals, values and enterprise choice', *Irish Journal of Agricultural Economics and Rural Sociology*, 11: 19–33.

Gillooly, J. F., and Dyer, T. (1979), 'On spatial and temporal variations of maize yields over South Africa', *South African Geographical Journal*, 61: 11–18.

Gilmour, J. M. (1974), 'External economies of scale, inter-industrial linkages and decision-making in manufacturing', in F. E. I. Hamilton (ed.), *Spatial perspectives on industrial organisation and decision-making* (Wiley, London), 335–62.

Glasmeier, A. K., and McCluskey, R. E. (1987), 'U.S. auto parts production: an analysis of the organization and location of a changing industry', *Economic Geography*, 63: 142–59.

—— (1988), 'The Japanese Technopolis programme: high-tech development strategy or industrial policy in disguise?', *International Journal of Urban and Regional Research*, 12: 268–84.

Glasson, J. (1978), *An introduction to regional planning* (Hutchinson, London).

Glyn, A., and Sutcliffe, R. (1972), *British capitalism, workers and the profits squeeze* (Penguin, Harmondsworth).

Gober, P. (1984), 'Regional convergence versus uneven development: implications for sunbelt SMSAs', *Urban Geography*, 5: 130–45.

Goddard, J. (1973), 'Office linkages and location: a study of communications and spatial patterns in Central London', *Progress in Planning*, 1: 109–232.

—— (1975), *Office location in urban and regional development* (Oxford University Press, Oxford).

—— (1980), 'Technology forecasting in a spatial context', *Futures*, 12: 90–105.

—— and Morris, D. (1976), 'The communications factor in office decentralisation', *Progress in Planning*, 6: 1–80.

—— and Pye, R. (1977), 'Telecommunications and office location', *Regional Studies*, 11: 19–30.

—— and Smith, I. J. (1978), 'Changes in corporate control in the British urban system 1972–77, *Environment and Planning A*, 10: 1073–84.

—— and Thwaites, A. T. (1980), *Technological change and the inner city*, Social Science Research Council, London, the Inner City in Context, Paper 4.

—— —— (1987), 'Technological change', in W. F. Lever (ed.), *Industrial change in the United Kingdom* (Longman, Harlow, Essex), 96–107.

Gooding, K. (1987), 'The motor industry: key held by US markets', *Financial Times*, 22 Oct.

Goodridge, J. C. (1966), 'The tin mining industry: a growth point for Cornwall', *Transactions of the Institute of British Geographers*, 38: 95–103.

Gordon, R., and Kimball, L. (1987), 'The impact of industrial structure on global high-technology location', in J. F. Brotchie, P. Hall and P. W. Newton, (eds.), *The spatial impact of technological change* (Croom Helm, London), 157–84.

Gore, C. (1984), *Regions in question: space, development theory and regional policy* (Methuen, London).

Gough, P. (1984), 'Location theory and the multi-plant firm: a framework for empirical studies', *Canadian Geographer*, 28: 127–41.

Gould, A., and Keeble, D. (1984), 'New firms and rural industrialisation in East Anglia', *Regional Studies*, 18: 189–201.

Gould, P. R. (1963), 'Man against his environment: a game-theoretic framework', *Annals of the Association of American Geographers*, 53: 291–7.

Green, A. (1988), 'The North–South divide in Great Britain: an examination of the evidence', *Transactions of the Institute of British Geographers*, 13: 179–98.

Green Europe (1985), *Perspectives for the Common Agricultural Policy* (European Commission, Brussels).

Greenfield, H. (1966), *Manpower and the growth of producer services* (Columbia University Press, New York).

Greenhut, M. L. (1956), *Plant location in theory and practice: the economics of an oligopolistic market economy* (Scott Foresman, Chicago).

—— (1981), 'Spatial pricing in the United States, West Germany and Japan', *Economica*, 48: 79–86.

Gregor, H. F. (1982), *Industrialization of US agriculture: an interpretative atlas* (Westview, Colorado).

Griffin, E. (1973), 'Testing von Thünen's theory in Uruguay', *Geographical Review*, 63: 500–16.

Griffin, M. (1982), 'European challenge for English hops' *Geographical Magazine*, 54: 564–71.

Griffiths, J. (1987), 'Close to true automation', *Financial Times*, 22 Oct.

Grigg, D. B. (1982), *The dynamics of agricultural change* (Hutchinson, London).

—— (1984), *An introduction to agricultural geography* (Hutchinson, London).

Griliches, Z. (1957), 'Hybrid corn: an exploration in the economics of technological change', *Econometrica*, 25: 501–22.

Gross, W. (1978), 'Revitalising downtown shopping requires more than cosmetification', *Journal of Marketing*, 42: 13–14.

Gudgin, G. (1978), *Industrial location processes and regional employment* (Saxon House, Farnborough, Hampshire).

—— (1984), *Employment creation by small and medium-sized firms in the UK*, Department of Applied Economics, University of Cambridge. Published in French as 'P.M.E, et créations d'emploi: le cas exemplaire du Royaume-Uni', in X. Greffe (ed.), *Les P.M.E: Créent-elles des emplois?* (Economica, Paris), 199–218.

—— Crum, R. E., and Bailey, S. (1979), 'White collar employment in UK manufacturing industry', in P. W. Daniels (ed.), *Spatial patterns of office growth and location* (Wiley, London), 127–57.

—— and Fothergill, S. (1984), 'Geographical variation in the rate of formation of new manufacturing firms', *Regional Studies*, 18: 203–6.

Guy, C. M. (1985a), 'Guest editorial', *Environment and Planning B: Planning and Design*, 12: 139–40.

—— (1985b), 'Some speculations on the retailing and planning implications of "push-button shopping" in Britain', *Environment and Planning B: Planning and Design*, 12: 193–208.

Hagerstrand, T. (1967), *Innovation diffusion as a spatial process* (University of Chicago Press, Chicago).

Haggett, P. (1971), 'Leads and lags in interregional systems: a study of the cyclic fluctuations in the South West economy', in M. Chisholm and G. Manners (eds.), *Spatial policy problems in the British economy* (Cambridge University Press, Cambridge), 69–95.

—— (1983), *Geography: a modern synthesis* (Harper and Row, London).

Haines, M. R. (1982), *An introduction to farming systems* (Longman, London).

Hall, P. (ed.) (1966), *Von Thünen's Isolated State* (Pergamon, London).

—— (1981a), 'The geography of the fifth Kondratieff cycle', *New Society*, 26 Mar. 535–7.

—— (ed.), (1981b), *The inner city in context: the final report of the Social Science Research Council Inner Cities Working Party* (Heinemann, London).

—— (1985), 'The geography of the fifth Kondratieff', in P. Hall and A. Markusen (eds.), *Silicon landscapes* (Allen and Unwin, London), 1–19.

—— (1987a), 'The anatomy of job creation: nations, regions and cities in the 1960s and 1970s', *Regional Studies*, 21: 95–106.

—— (1987b), 'The geography of high technology: an Anglo-American comparison', in J. Brotchie, P. Hall and P. W. Newton (eds.), *The spatial impact of technological change* (Croom Helm, London), 141–56.

—— (1987c), 'The geography of the post-industrial economy', in J. F. Brotchie, P. Hall and P. W. Newton (eds.), *The spatial impact of technological change* (Croom Helm, London), 3–17.

—— (1988), 'Regions in the transition to the information economy', in G. Sternlieb and J. W. Hughes (eds.), *America's new market geography: nation, region and metropolis* (Rutgers, The State University of New Jersey, New Jersey), 37–59.

—— and Breheny, M. (eds.) (1987), 'Theme biotechnology: the next industrial frontier', *Built Environment*, 13: 145–82.

—— —— McQuaid, R., and Hart, P. (1987), *Western sunrise: the genesis and growth of Britain's major high tech corridor* (Allen and Unwin, London).

—— and Markusen, A. (eds.) (1985), *Silicon landscapes* (George Allen and Unwin, Boston).

Hamilton, F. E. I. (1964), 'Location factors in the Yugoslav iron and steel industry', *Economic Geography*, 40: 46–64.

—— (1970), 'Aspects of spatial behaviour in planned economies', *Papers and Proceedings of the Regional Science Association*, 25: 83–105.

—— (1971a), 'Decision-making and industrial location in eastern Europe', *Transactions of the Institute of British Geographers*, 52: 77–94.

—— (1971b), 'The location of industry in east-central and southeastern Europe', in G. W. Hoffman (ed.), *Eastern Europe: essays on geographical problems* (Methuen, London), 173–224.

—— (1974), 'A view of spatial behaviour, industrial organisations and decision-making', in F. E. I. Hamilton (ed.), *Spatial perspectives on industrial organization and decision-making* (Wiley, Chichester), 3–46.

—— (1976), 'Multinational enterprise and the E.E.C.', *Tijdschrift voor Economische en Sociale Geografie*, 67: 258–78.

Hamnett, C. (1977), 'Non-explanation in urban geography: throwing the baby out with the bath water', *Area*, 9: 143–5.

Hansen, N. (1972), 'Criteria for a growth centre policy', in A. Kuklinski (ed.), *Growth poles and growth centres in regional planning* (Mouton, The Hague).

—— (1980), 'The new international division of labor

and manufacturing decentralization in the United States', *Review of Regional Studies*, 9: 1–11.

Harris, F., and McArthur, R. (1985), *High technology: an alternative viewpoint*, University of Manchester, North West Industry Research Unit, Working Paper 16.

Harris, L. (1988), 'The UK economy at a crossroads', in J. Allen and D. Massey (eds.), *Restructuring Britain—the economy in question* (Sage, London), 7–44.

Harris, N. (1986), *The end of the Third World: newly industrialising countries and the decline of an ideology* (I. B. Tauris, London).

Hart, P. W. E. (1978), 'Geographical aspects of contract farming, with special reference to the supply of crops to processing plants', *Tijdschrift voor Economische en Sociale Geografie*, 69: 205–15.

Hartshorne, R. (1939), *The nature of geography* (Association of American Geographers, Lancaster, Pennsylvania).

Harvey, D. R., Barr, C. J., Bell, M., Bunce, R. G. H., and others (1986), *Countryside implications for England and Wales of possible changes in the Common Agricultural Policy* (Centre for Agricultural Strategy, University of Reading, Reading).

Harvey, D. W. (1963), 'Locational change in the Kentish hop industry and the analysis of land-use patterns', *Transactions of the Institute of British Geographers*, 33: 123–44.

——(1969a), *Explanation in geography* (Edward Arnold, London).

——(1969b), 'Review of A. Pred, *Behaviour and location*, part 1', *Geographical Review*, 59: 312–14.

——(1971), 'Social processes, spatial form and the redistribution of real income in an urban system', in M. Chisholm *et al.* (eds.), *Regional forecasting* (Butterworth, London), 270–300.

——(1982), *The limits to capital* (Basil Blackwell, Oxford).

Harvey, J., and Wilson, R. (1988), 'Nitrates', *Farmers Weekly*, 30 Sept., 63–70.

Hasluck, C. (1987), *Urban unemployment* (Longman, London).

Haug, P. (1986), 'US high technology multinationals and Silicon Glen', *Regional Studies*, 20: 103–16.

Hay, A. (1976), 'A simple location theory for mining activity', *Geography*, 61: 65–76.

——(1985), 'The world as a spatial economic system', *Geography*, 70: 97–105.

Haynes, K. E., and Fotheringham, A. S. (1984), *Gravity and spatial interaction models* (Sage, London).

Hayter, R. (1978), 'Locational decision-making in a resource-based manufacturing sector: case studies from the pulp and paper industry of British Columbia', *Professional Geographer*, 30: 240–9.

——(1981), 'The role of foreign-controlled investments in the forest product sector of British Colum-

bia', *Tijdschrift voor Economische en Sociale Geografie*, 72: 99–113.

——(1982), 'Truncation, the international firm and regional policy,' *Area*, 14: 277–82.

——(1985), 'The evolution and structure of the Canadian forest product sector', *Fennia*, 163: 439–50.

——and Watts, H. D. (1983), 'The geography of enterprise: a re-appraisal', *Progress in Human Geography*, 7: 157–81.

Hazell, P. B. R., and Anderson, J. R. (1986), 'Public policy towards technical change in agriculture', in P. Hall (ed.), *Technology, innovation and economic policy* (St Martin's Press, New York), 201–30.

Healey, M. J. (1979), 'Changes in the location of production in multi-plant enterprises, with particular reference to the United Kingdom textile and clothing industries, 1967–72, University of Sheffield, unpublished Ph.D. thesis.

——(1981a), 'Locational adjustment and the characteristics of manufacturing plants', *Transactions of the Institute of British Geographers*, 6: 394–412.

——(1981b), 'Product changes in multi-plant enterprises', *Geoforum*, 12: 359–70.

——(1982), 'Plant closures in multi-plant enterprises—the case of a declining industrial sector', *Regional Studies*, 16: 37–51.

——(ed.) (1983), *Urban and regional industrial research: the changing UK data base* (Geo Books, Norwich).

——(1984), 'Spatial growth and spatial rationalisation in multi-plant enterprises', *GeoJournal*, 9: 133–44.

——(1985), 'Industrial decline, industrial structure and large companies', *Geography*, 70: 328–38.

——(ed.) (1991), *Economic activity and land use: the changing information base for local and regional studies* (Longman, Harlow, Essex).

——and Clark, D. (1984), 'Industrial decline and government response in the West Midlands: the case of Coventry', *Regional Studies*, 18: 303–18.

——— (1985), 'Industrial decline in a local economy: the case of Coventry, 1974–1982', *Environment and Planning A*, 17: 1351–67.

——— (1986), 'Employment growth in manufacturing and job creation policies during the recession: the experience of Coventry, 1974–1982', *The Journal of Industrial Affairs*, 13: 21–33.

——— and Shrivastava, V. (1987), *The clothing industry in Coventry*, Coventry Polytechnic, Department of Geography, Industrial Location Working Paper 10.

——and Ilbery, B. W. (eds.) (1985a), *Industrialization of the countryside* (Geo Books, Norwich).

——— (1985b), 'The industrialization of the countryside: an overview', in M. J. Healey and B. W. Ilbery (eds.), *Industrialization of the countryside* (Geo Books, Norwich), 1–26.

——and Watts, H. D. (1987), 'The multiplant enterprise', in W. F. Lever (ed.), *Industrial change in the United Kingdom* (Longman, Harlow, Essex), 149–66.

Henderson, J., and Scott, A. J. (1987), 'The growth and internationalisation of the American semiconductor industry', in M. J. Breheny and R. McQuaid (eds.), *The development of high technology industries: an international survey* (Croom Helm, London), 37–79.

Henry, P. (1981), *Study of the regional impact of the Common Agricultural Policy* (Commission of the European Communities, Brussels).

Henwood, F., and Wyatt, S. (1986), 'Women's work, technological change and shifts in the employment structure', in R. Martin and B. Rowthorn (eds.), *The geography of de-industrialisation* (Macmillan, Basingstoke, Hampshire), 106–37.

Hepworth, M. E. (1986), 'The geography of technological change in the information economy', *Regional Studies*, 20: 407–24.

—— (1987), 'The information city', *Cities*, Aug. 253–62.

Hetherington, P. (1988), 'Signposts on the Thatcher road to inner-city renewal', *Guardian*, 8 Mar.

Hewison, N., and Whitmarsh, D. (1981), 'Cornish tin mining: does it have a future?' *Geography*, 66: 58–60.

Hill, B. E. (1984), *The Common Agricultural Policy: past, present and future* (Methuen, London).

Hill, R. C. (1984), 'Economic crisis and political response in the motor city', in L. Sawyers and W. K. Tabb (eds.), *Sunbelt/snowbelt: urban development and regional restructuring* (Oxford University Press, New York), 313–38.

—— (1987), 'Global factory and company town: the changing division of labour in the international automobile industry', in J. Henderson and M. Castells (eds.), *Global restructuring and territorial development* (Sage, Newbury Park, California), 18–37.

Hine, R. C., and Houston, A. M. (1973), *Government and structural change in agriculture* (Universities of Nottingham and Exeter, for the Ministry of Agriculture, Fisheries, and Food).

Hirsch, S. (1967), *Location of industry and international competitiveness* (Clarendon Press, Oxford).

Hirschman, A. (1958), *The strategy of economic development* (Yale University Press, New Haven).

Hitchens, D. M. W. N., and O'Farrell, P. N. (1987), 'The comparative performance of small manufacturing firms in Northern Ireland and South East England', *Regional Studies*, 21: 543–53.

Hoare, A. G. (1985), 'Industrial linkage studies', in M. Pacione (ed.), *Progress in industrial geography* (Croom Helm, London), 40–81.

Holland, S. (1976a), *Capital versus the regions* (Macmillan, London).

—— (1976b), *the regional problem* (Macmillan, London).

Hollier, G. P. (1988), 'Regional development', in M.

Pacione (ed.), *The geography of the third world* (Routledge, London), 232–70.

Holly, B. P. (1987), 'Regulation, competition and technology: the restructuring of the U.S. commercial banking industry', *Environment and Planning A*, 19: 633–52.

Holmes, J. (1983), 'Industrial reorganisation, capital restructuring and locational change: an analysis of the Canadian automobile industry in the 1960s', *Economic Geography*, 59: 251–71.

—— (1986), 'The organization and locational structure of production subcontracting', in A. J. Scott, and M. Storper (eds.), *Production, work, territory: the geographical anatomy of industrial capitalism* (Allen and Unwin, London), 80–106.

—— (1987), 'Industrial change in the Canadian automotive products industry, 1973–84: the impact of technical change on the organisation and locational structure of automobile production', in K. Chapman and G. Humphrys (eds.), *Technical change and industrial policy* (Basil Blackwell, Oxford), 121–56.

Hood, N., and Young, S. (1982), *Multinationals in retreat: the Scottish experience* (Edinburgh University Press, Edinburgh).

Hoover, E. M. (1984), *The location of economic activity* (McGraw Hill, New York).

—— and Giarratani, F. (1984), *An introduction to regional economics* (Knopf, New York).

Horvath, R. J. (1969), 'Von Thünen's isolated state and the area around Addis Ababa, Ethiopia', *Annals of the Association of American Geographers*, 59: 308–23.

Hotelling, H. (1929), 'Stability in competition', *Economic Journal*, 3: 41–57.

House, J. W. (1983), 'Regional and area development', in J. W. House (ed.), *United States public policy: a geographical view* (Oxford University Press, Oxford), 34–79.

Howard, E. B. (1985), 'Teleshopping in North America', *Environment and Planning B: Planning and Design*, 12: 141–50

—— (1986), 'Measuring the impact of the big schemes', *Town and Country Planning*, 55: 282–4.

—— and Davies, R. L. (1988), *Change in the retail environment* (Oxford reports on retailing, Longman Harlow, Essex).

Howells, J. (1983), 'Filter-down theory: location and technology in the UK pharmaceutical industry', *Environment and Planning A*, 15: 147–64.

—— (1984), 'The location of research and development: some observations and evidence from Britain', *Regional Studies*, 18: 12–29.

—— (1987), 'Development in the location, technology and industrial organisation of computer services: some trends and research issues', *Regional Studies*, 21: 493–503.

—— and Green, A. E. (1986), 'Location, technology

and industrial organisation in UK services', *Progress in Planning*, 26: 83–184.

—— (1988), *Technological innovation, structural change and location in UK services* (Avebury, Aldershot).

Hudson, R. (1978), 'Spatial policy in Britain', *Area*, 10: 359–62.

—— (1988), 'Labour market changes and new forms of work on "old" industrial regions', in D. Massey and J. Allen (eds.), *Uneven re-development: cities and regions in transition* (Hodder and Stoughton, London), 147–66.

—— and Williams, A. (1986), *The United Kingdom* (Harper and Row, London).

Hull, A., Jones, T., and Kenny, S. (1988), *Geographical issues in western Europe* (Longman, London).

Humphrys, G. (1972), *South Wales* (David and Charles, Newton Abbot).

Hurst, M. E. (1974), *A geography of economic behaviour* (Prentice Hall, London).

Hymer, S. H. (1979), *The multinational corporation: a radical approach* (MIT Press, Cambridge, Massachusetts).

Ilbery, B. W. (1978), 'Agricultural decision-making: a behavioural perspective', *Progress in Human Geography*, 2: 448–66.

—— (1982), 'The decline of hop growing in Hereford and Worcestershire', *Area*, 14: 203–11.

—— (1983a), 'Harvey's principles reapplied: a case study of the declining West Midlands hop industry', *Geoforum*, 14: 111–23.

—— (1983b), 'Britain's uncertain future in the international hop market', *Outlook on Agriculture*, 12: 119–24.

—— (1983c), 'A behavioural analysis of hop farming in Hereford and Worcestershire', *Geoforum*, 14: 447–59.

—— (1983d), 'Goals and values of hop farmers', *Transactions of the Institute of British Geographers*, 8: 329–41.

—— (1984a), 'The marketing of hops in Great Britain: a study of changing structures and farmers' attitudes', *European Journal of Marketing*, 18: 45–55.

—— (1984b) 'Agricultural specialisation and farmer decision behaviour: a case study of hop farming in the West Midlands', *Tijdschrift voor Economische en Sociale Geografie*, 75: 329–34.

—— (1985a), *Agricultural geography* (Oxford University Press, Oxford).

—— (1985b), 'Factors affecting the structure of horticulture in the Vale of Evesham, UK: a behavioural interpretation', *Journal of Rural Studies*, 1: 121–33.

—— (1985c), 'Horticultural decline in the Vale of Evesham, 1950–80', *Journal of Rural Studies*, 1: 100–20.

—— (1986), *Western Europe: a systematic human geography* (Oxford University Press, Oxford).

—— (1987), 'Geographical research into farm diversification: lessons for the extensification proposals', in N. R. Jenkins and M. Bell (eds.), *Farm extensification: implications of EC Regulation 1760/87*, Institute of Terrestrial Ecology, Grange-over-Sands, Research and Development Report 112.

—— (1988), 'Farm diversification and the restructuring of agriculture', *Outlook on Agriculture*, 17: 35–9.

—— (1990a), 'The challenge of land redundancy', in D. Pinder (ed.), *Challenge and change in western Europe* (Belhaven Press, London), 211–25.

—— (1990b) 'Adoption of the arable set-aside scheme in England', *Geography*, 75: 69–73.

Illeris, S. (1986), 'New firm creation in Denmark, the importance of the cultural background', in D. Keeble and E. Wever (eds.), *New firms and regional development in Europe* (Croom Helm, London), 141–50.

Imrie, R. F. (1986), 'Work decentralisation from large to small firms: a preliminary analysis of subcontracting' *Environment and Planning A*, 18: 949–65.

Institute for Employment Research (1982), *Review of the economy and employment* (Institute for Employment Research, University of Warwick, Coventry).

Isard, W. (1956), *Location and space economy* (Wiley, New York).

—— (1960), *Methods of regional science: an introduction in regional science* (Wiley, New York).

Jaeger, C., and Durrenberger, G. (1987), 'Counter urbanisation and telework', paper presented at Colloquim on 'Espace et Périphérie', Lisbon, Sept.

Janelle, D. G. (1969), 'Spatial reorganisation: a model and concept', *Annals of the Association of American Geographers*, 59: 348–64.

Johnson, D. B. (1987), 'The West Edmonton Mall—from super-regional to mega-regional shopping centre', *International Journal of Retailing*, 2: 53–69.

Johnston, R. J. (1964), 'The measuring of a hierarchy of central places', *Australian Geographer*, 9: 315–17.

—— (1979), 'Congressional committees and the inter-state distribution of military spending', *Geoforum*, 10: 151–62.

—— (1980), 'On the nature of explanation in human geography', *Transactions of the Institute of British Geographers*, 5: 402–12.

—— (1984), 'The world is our oyster', *Transactions of the Institute of British Geographers*, 9: 443–59.

—— (1986), *Philosophy and human geography: an introduction to contemporary approaches* (Edward Arnold, London).

—— (1987), *Geography and geographers: Anglo-American human geography since 1945* (Edward Arnold, London).

—— and Taylor, P. J. (eds.) (1986), *A world in crisis? geographical perspectives* (Blackwell, Oxford).

Jones, D. T. (1983), 'Motor cars: a maturing industry?',

in G. Shepherd, F. Duchene and C. Saunders (eds.), *Europe's industries* (Frances Pinter, London), 110–38.

—— and Womack, J. P. (1985), 'Developing countries and the future of the automobile industry', *World Development*, 13: 393–407.

Jones, G. E. (1975), 'Innovation and farmer decision-making', in Open University *D203: Agriculture*, Block III, Part 2 (Open University, Milton Keynes), 23–56.

Jones, P. (1981), 'Retail innovation and diffusion—the spread of Asda stores', *Area*, 13: 197–201.

—— (1982), 'The locational policies and geographical expansion of multiple retail companies: a case study of M.F.I.', *Geoforum*, 13: 39–43.

—— (1984), 'Retail warehouse developments in Britain' *Area*, 16: 41–7.

Jussawalla, M. (1978), *T3: transportation/telecommunications/trade-offs* (East-West Communications Institute, Honolulu).

Keeble, D. E. (1967), 'Models of economic development', in R. J. Chorley and P. Haggett (eds.), *Models in geography* (Methuen, London), 243–87.

—— (1968), 'Industrial decentralisation and the metropolis', *Transactions of the Institute of British Geographers*, 44: 1–54.

—— (1971), 'Employment mobility in Britain', in M. Chisholm and G. Manners (eds.), *Spatial policy problems of the British economy* (Cambridge University Press, Cambridge), 24–68.

—— (1976), *Industrial location and planning* (Methuen, London).

—— (1977), 'Spatial policy in Britain: regional or urban?', *Area*, 9: 3–8.

—— (1987), 'Industrial change in the United Kingdom', in W. F. Lever (ed.), *Industrial change in the United Kingdom* (Longman, Harlow, Essex), 1–20.

—— (1988), 'High-technology industry and local environments in the United Kingdom', in P. Aydalot and D. Keeble (eds.), *High technology industry and innovative environments: the European experience* (Routledge, London), 65–98.

—— (1989a), 'Core–periphery disparities, recession and new regional dynamisms in the European Community', *Geography*, 74: 1–11.

—— (1989b), 'High-technology industry and local economic development: the case of the Cambridge phenomenon', *Environment and Planning C: Government and Policy*, 7: 153–72.

—— and Gould, A. (1985), 'Entrepreneurship and manufacturing firm formation in rural regions: the East Anglian case', in M. J. Healey and B. W. Ilbery (eds.), *Industrialization of the countryside* (Geo Books, Norwich), 197–219.

—— and Kelly, T. (1986), 'New firms and high technology industry in the United Kingdom: the case of

computer electronics', in D. Keeble and E. Wever (eds.), *New firms and regional development in Europe* (Croom Helm, London), 75–104.

—— Owens, P. L., and Thompson, C. (1982a), 'Regional accessibility and economy potential in the European community, *Regional Studies*, 16: 419–31.

—— —— —— (1982b), 'Economic potential and the Channel Tunnel', *Area*, 14: 97–103.

—— —— —— (1983), 'The urban-rural manufacturing shift in the European Community', *Urban Studies*, 20: 405–18.

—— and Wever, E. (eds.) (1986a), *New firms and regional development in Europe* (Croom Helm, London).

—— and Wever, E. (1986b), 'Introduction', in D. Keeble and E. Wever (eds.), *New firms and regional development in Europe* (Croom Helm, London), 1–34.

Kellerman, A. (1977), 'The pertinence of the macro-Thünen analysis', *Economic Geography*, 53: 255–64.

—— (1983), 'The suburbanisation of retail trade: the Israeli case', *Area*, 15: 219–22.

—— (1985a), 'The evolution of service economies: a geographical perspective', *Professional Geographer*, 37: 133–43.

—— (1985b), 'The suburbanisation of retail trade: a US nationwide view', *Geoforum*, 16: 15–23.

Kelly, T. (1987), *The British computer industry: crisis and development* (Croom Helm, London).

Kemp, T. (1983), *Industrialization in the non-western world* (Longman, London).

Kennelly, R. A. (1954–5), 'The localization of the Mexican steel industry', *Revista Geografica*, 15: 105–29; 16: 199–213; 17: 60–77.

King, R. L. (1975), 'The evolution of international labour migration movements concerning the EEC', *Tijdschrift voor Economische en Sociale Geografie*, 67: 66–8.

—— (1979), 'Return migration: a review of case studies from southern Europe', *Mediterranean Studies*, 1: 3–30.

Kirn, T. J. (1987),'Growth and change in the service sector of the US: a spatial perspective', *Annals of the Association of American Geographers*, 77: 353–72.

Kivell, P. T., and Shaw, G. (1980), 'The study of retail location', in J. A. Dawson (ed.), *The study of retail geography* (Croom Helm, London), 95–155.

Knowles, R., and Wareing, J. (1976), *Economic and social geography: made simple* (W. H. Allen, London).

Knox, P., Bartels, E. H., Bohland, J. R., Holcomb, B., and Johnston, R. J. (1988), *The United States: a contemporary human geography* (Longman, Harlow, Essex).

—— and Agnew. J. (1989), *The geography of the world economy* (Edward Arnold, London).

Kollmorgen, W. M. (1941 and 1943), 'A reconnaissance of some cultural-agricultural islands in the south', *Economic Geography*, 17: 409–30; and 19: 109–17.

Kondratieff, N. D. (1935), 'The long waves in economic life', *Review of Economic Statistics*, 17: 105–15.

Krume, G. (1969), 'Towards a geography of enteprise', *Economic Geography*, 45: 30–40.

—— (1981), 'Making it abroad: the evolution of Volkswagen's North American production plans', in F. E. I. Hamilton, and G. J. R. Linge, (eds.), *Spatial analysis, industry and the industrial environment*, vol, ii, *International industrial systems* (John Wiley, Winchester), 329–56.

Kuklinski, A. (1982), *Space economy and regional studies in Poland* (UNCRD, Nagoya).

Laaksonen, K. (1979), 'The effect of climatic factors on the hectare yields of barley, oats and spring wheat in Finland, 1972–7', *Fennia*, 157: 199–221.

Lambooy, J. G., and Renooy, P. H. (1985), 'The informal economy: a survey of national and regional dimensions', unpublished report for FAST II, Commission of the European Communities, Brussels.

Law, C. M. (1980), 'The foreign company's location investment decision and its role in British regional development', *Tijdschrift voor Economische en Sociale Geografie*, 71: 15–20.

—— (1983), 'The defence sector in British regional development', *Geoforum*, 14: 169–84.

—— Grime, E. K., Grundy, C. J., Senior, M. L., and Tuppen, J. N. (1988), *The uncertain future of the urban core* (Routledge, London).

Layton, R. L. (1979), 'Hobby farming', *Geography*, 65: 220–3.

Leadbeater, C. (1987), 'Managers gearing shopfloor to an era of change', *Financial Times*, 22 Oct.

Le Heron, R. (1988), 'Food and fibre production under capitalism: a conceptual agenda', *Progress in Human Geography*, 12: 409–30.

Leigh, R., and North, D. J. (1978), 'Regional aspects of acquisition activity in British manufacturing industry', *Regional Studies*, 12: 227–45.

—— and North, D. J. (1983), *The clothing industry in the West Midlands: structure, problems and policies* (Economic Development Unit, West Midlands County Council, Birmingham).

Lenon, B. (1987), 'The geography of the "Big Bang": London's office building boom', *Geography*, 72: 56–63.

Leonard, H. J. (1988), *Pollution and the struggle for the world product: multinational corporations, environment and international comparative advantage* (Cambridge University Press, Cambridge).

Leopold, L., Clarke, F. E., Hanshaw, B. B., and Balsley, J. R. (1971), *A procedure for evaluating environmental impact*, US Geological Survey, Washington, DC, Circular 645.

Lever, W. F. (1974), 'Manufacturing linkages and the search for suppliers and markets', in F. E. I. Hamilton (ed.), *Spatial perspectives on industrial organisation and decision-making* (Wiley, London), 309–33.

—— (1982), 'Urban scale as a determinant of employment growth or decline', in Collins, L. (ed.), *Industrial decline and regeneration: proceedings of the 1981 Anglo-Canadian symposium* (Department of Geography and the Centre of Canadian Studies, University of Edinburgh), 109–25.

—— (1987a), 'Labour and capital', in Lever, W. F. (ed.), *Industrial change in the United Kingdom* (Longman, Harlow, Essex), 69–85.

—— (1987b), 'Urban policy', in W. F. Lever (ed.), *Industrial change in the United Kingdom* (Longman, Harlow, Essex), 240–75.

Lewis, J. (1983), 'Women, work and regional development', *Northern Economic Review*, 7: 10–24.

—— (1984), 'The role of female employment in the industrial restructuring and regional development of postwar UK', *Antipode*, 6: 47–60.

Lewis, J. R. (1984) 'Regional policy and planning', in S. Bornstein, D. Held and J. Kreiger (eds.), *The state in capitalist Europe: a casebook* (Allen and Unwin, London), 138–48.

Lewis, R. (1977), 'Central place analysis', in Open University D204: *Fundamentals of human geography*, ii. *Spatial analysis, point patterns*, Unit 10 (Open University, Milton Keynes), 45–101.

Ley, D. (1981), 'Cultural/humanistic geography', *Progress in Human Geography*, 5: 249–57.

—— and Hutton, T. (1987), 'Vancouver's corporate complex and producer service sector: linkages and divergence within a provincial staple economy', *Regional Studies*, 21: 413–24.

Lindberg, O. (1953), 'An economic-geographical study of the localisation of the Swedish paper industry', *Geografiska Annaler*, 35: 28–40.

Lindley, P. D. (1985), 'The Merseyside Task Force', *Regional Studies*, 19: 69–73.

Lipietz, A. (1984), 'Imperialism or the beast of the apocalypse', *Capital and Class*, 22: 81–109.

—— (1986), 'New tendencies in the international division of labor: regimes of accumulation and modes of regulation', in A. J. Scott and M. Storper (eds.), *Production, work, territory: the geographical anatomy of industrial capitalism* (Allen and Unwin, London), 16–40.

Lipsey, R. G. (1983), *An introduction to positive economics* (Weidenfeld and Nicholson, London).

Litchenburg, R. M. (1960), *One-tenth of a nation* (Harvard University Press, Cambridge, Massachusetts).

Lloyd, P. E., and Dicken, P. (1972 and 1977), *Location in space: a theoretical approach to economic geography* (Harper and Row, London).

—— and Mason, C. M. (1984), 'Spatial variations in new firm formation in the United Kingdom: comparative evidence from Merseyside, Greater Manchester and South Hampshire', *Regional Studies*, 18: 207–20.

—— and Reeve, D. E. (1982), 'North West England, 1971–77: a study in industrial decline and economic restructuring', *Regional Studies*, 16: 345–59.

Lloyd, P., and Shutt, J. (1985), 'Recession and restructuring in the North West region 1975–82: the implications of recent events', in D. Massey and R. Meegan (eds.), *Politics and method: contrasting studies in industrial geography* (Methuen, London), 16–60.

Loasby, B. J. (1967), 'Making location policy work', *Lloyds Bank Review*, 83: 34–47.

Lord, J. D. (1987a), 'Shopping centre development trends in the USA', paper presented to Institute of British Geographers' Urban Geography Study Group Conference on 'Shopping centres—a geographical appraisal', Coventry Polytechnic, May.

—— (1987b), 'Interstate banking and the relocation of economic control points', *Urban Geography*, 8: 501–19.

—— and Lynds, C. D. (1984), 'Market area planning strategy: an example of interstate banking markets in the USA', *GeoJournal*, 9: 145–54.

Losch, A. (1954), *The economics of location* (Yale University Press, New Haven, Connecticut).

Lovejoy, P. (1988), 'Management buyouts and policy responses in the West Midlands', *Regional Studies*, 22: 344–7.

Lovering, J., and Boddy, M. (1988), 'The geography of military industry in Britain', *Area*, 20: 41–51.

Lowe, P., Cox, G., Macewen, M., O'Riordan, T., and Winter, M. (1986), *Countryside conflicts: the politics of farming, forestry and conservation* (Gower, Aldershot).

Luttrell, W. F. (1962), *Factory location and factory movement: a study of recent experience in Great Britain* (National Institute of Economic and Social Research, London).

McCarty, H. H., and Lindberg, J. B. (1966), *A preface to economic geography* (Prentice Hall, New Jersey).

McConnell, J. E. (1980), 'Foreign direct investment in the U.S.', *Annals of the Association of American Geographers*, 70: 259–70.

—— (1983), 'The international location of manufacturing investments: recent behaviour of foreign-owned corporations in the United States', in F. E. I. Hamilton and G. J. R. Linge (eds.), *Spatial analysis, industry and the industrial environment*, iii, *Regional economies and industrial systems* (Wiley, Chichester), 337–58.

McDermott, P. J. (1973), 'Spatial margins and industrial location in New Zealand', *New Zealand Geographer*, 29: 64–74.

McDowell, L., and Massey, D. B. (1984), 'A woman's place?', in D. Massey and J. Allen (eds.), *Geography

matters! A reader*, (Cambridge University Press, Cambridge), 128–47.

Macgregor, B. D., Langridge, J., Adley, J., and Chapman, B. (1986), 'The development of high technology industry in Newbury District', *Regional Studies*, 20: 433–48.

McMillan, C. H. (1987), *Multinationals from the Second World: growth of foreign investment by Soviet and East European enterprises* (Macmillan, London).

McNee, R. (1960), 'Towards a more humanistic economic geography', *Tijdschrift voor Economische en Sociale Geografie*, 51: 201–6.

McQuillan, D. A. (1978), 'Farm size and work ethic: measuring the success of immigrant farmers on the American grassland, 1875–1925', *Journal of Historical Geography*, 4: 57–76.

Mage, J. A. (1982), 'The geography of part-time farming—a new vista for agricultural geographers', *GeoJournal*, 6: 301–12.

Malecki, E. J. (1979), 'Locational trends in R & D by large U.S. corporations, 1965–1979', *Economic Geography*, 55: 309–23.

—— (1980), 'Corporate organisation of R and D and the location of technological activities', *Regional Studies*, 14: 219–34.

—— (1981), 'Public and private sector interrelationships, technological change, and regional development', *Papers of the Regional Science Association*, 47: 121–38.

—— (1982), 'Federal R and D spending in the United States of America: some impacts on metropolitan economies', *Regional Studies*, 16: 19–35.

—— (1983), 'Technology and regional development: a survey', *International Regional Science Review*, 8: 89–125.

—— (1984), 'Military spending and the US defence industry: regional patterns of military contracts and subcontracts', *Environment and Planning C*, 2: 31–44.

—— (1985), 'Public sector research and development and regional economic performance in the United States', in A. J. Thwaites and R. P. Oakey (eds.), *The regional economic impact of technological change* (Frances Pinter, London), 115–31.

Mallier, T., and Rosser, M. (1982), 'The decline and fall of the Coventry car industry', *Business Economist*, 13: 12–28.

Mandel, E. (1980), *Long waves of capitalist development* (Cambridge University Press, Cambridge).

Mandeville, T. (1983), 'The spatial effects of information technology', *Futures*, 15: 65–72.

Markusen, A. (1985), *Profit cycles, oligopoly and regional development* (MIT Press, Cambridge, Massachusetts).

—— and Bloch, R. (1985), 'Defensive cities: military spending, high technology, and human settlements', in M. Castells (ed.), *High technology, space, and society*, Urban Affairs Annual Review, 28 (Sage Publications, Beverly Hills, California), 106–20.

—— Hall, P., and Glasmeier, A. (1986), *High tech America: the what, how, where, and why of the sunrise industries* (Allen and Unwin, Boston).

Marquand, J. (1979), *The service and regional policy in the United Kingdom*, Centre for Environmental Studies, Research Series, 29.

—— (1983), 'The changing distribution of service employment', in J. B. Goddard and A. G. Champion (eds.), *The urban and regional transformation of Britain* (Methuen, London), 99–134.

Marsden, T. (1988), 'Exploring political economy approaches in agriculture', *Area*, 20: 315–22.

—— Whatmore, S., Munton, R., and Little, J. (1986*a*), 'The restructuring process and economic centrality in capitalist agriculture', *Journal of Rural Studies*, 2: 271–80.

—— Munton, R. J., Whatmore, S., and Little, J. (1986*b*), 'Towards a political economy of capitalist agriculture: a British perspective', *International Journal of Urban and Regional Research*, 10: 498–521.

Marshall, J. N. (1982), 'Linkages between manufacturing industry and business services', *Environment and Planning A*, 14: 523–40.

—— (1984), 'Information technology changes corporate office activity', *GeoJournal*, 9: 171–8.

—— (1985), 'Business services, the regions and regional policy', *Regional Studies*, 19: 353–63.

—— (1987), 'Industrial change, linkages and regional development', in W. F. Lever (ed.), *Industrial change in the United Kingdom* (Longman, Harlow, Essex), 108–22.

—— in collaboration with Wood, P., Daniels, P. W., McKinnon, A., Batchler, J., Damesick, N., Thrift, N., Gillespie, A., Green, A., and Leyshon, A. (1988), *Services and uneven development* (Oxford University Press, Oxford).

—— and Batchler, J. F. (1984), 'Spatial perspectives on technological change in the banking sector of the United Kingdom', *Environment and Planning A*, 16: 437–50.

—— Damesick, P., and Wood, P. (1985), 'Understanding the location and role of producer services', paper presented at the Regional Science Association Annual Conference, University of Manchester, Sept.

—— Damesick, P., and Wood, P. (eds.) (1987), 'Understanding the location and role of producer services in the United Kingdom', *Environment and Planning A*, 19: 569–710.

Marshall, M. (1987), *Long waves of regional development* (Macmillan, Basingstoke, Hampshire).

Martin, R. (1986), 'Thatcherism and Britain's industrial landscape', in R. Martin and B. Rowthorn (eds.), *The geography of de-industrialisation* (Macmillan, Basingstoke, Hampshire), 238–90.

—— (1988*a*), 'Industrial capitalism in transition: the contemporary reorganization of the British space-economy', in D. Massey and J. Allen (eds.), *Uneven re-development: cities and regions in transition* (Hodder and Stoughton, London), 202–31.

—— (1988*b*), 'The political economy of Britain's north–south divide', *Transactions of the Institute of British Geographers New Series*, 13: 389–418.

—— and Rowthorn, B. (eds.), *The geography of de-industrialisation* (Macmillan, Basingstoke, Hampshire).

Mason, C. M. (1983), 'Some definitional problems in new firm research', *Area*, 15: 53–60.

—— (1985), 'The geography of "successful" small firms in the United Kingdom', *Environment and Planning A*, 17: 1499–513.

—— (1987*a*), 'Venture capital in the United Kingdom: a geographical perspective', *National Westminster Bank Quarterly Review*, May, 47–59.

—— (1987*b*), 'The small firm sector', in W. F. Lever (ed.), *Industrial change in the United Kingdom* (Longman, Harlow, Essex), 125–48.

—— and Harrison, R. T. (1985), 'The geography of small firms in the UK: towards a research agenda', *Progress in Human Geography*, 9: 1–37.

Massey, D. (1979*a*), 'A critical evaluation of industrial location theory', in F. E. I. Hamilton and G. J. R. Linge (eds.), *Spatial analysis, industry and the industrial environment*, i. *Industrial systems* (Wiley, Chichester), 57–72.

—— (1979*b*), 'In what sense a regional problem?' *Regional Studies*, 13: 233–43.

—— (1981), 'The geography of industrial change', in D. Potter *et al.*, *Society and the social sciences* (Routledge & Kegan Paul in association with the Open University Press, London), 302–13.

—— (1982), 'Enterprise zones: a political issue', *International Journal of Urban and Regional Research*, 6: 429–34.

—— (1983), 'Industrial restructuring as class restructuring: production decentralization and local uniqueness', *Regional Studies*, 17: 73–89.

—— (1984*a*), 'Introduction: Geography matters', in D. Massey and J. Allen (eds.), *Geography Matters! A reader* (Cambridge University Press, Cambridge), 1–11.

—— (1984*b*), *Spatial divisions of labour* (Macmillan, London).

—— (1985), 'New directions in space', in D. Gregory and J. Urry (eds.), *Social relations and spatial structures* (Macmillan, London), 9–19.

—— (1986), 'The legacy lingers on: the impact of Britain's international role on its internal geography', in R. Martin and B. Rowthorn (eds.), *The geography of de-industrialisation* (Macmillan, Basingstoke, Hampshire), 31–52.

—— (1988a), 'Uneven development: social change and spatial divisions of labour', in D. Massey and J. Allen (eds.), *Uneven re-development: cities and regions in transition* (Hodder and Stoughton, London), 250–76.

—— (1988b), 'What's happening to UK manufacturing?' in J. Allen and D. Massey (eds.), *Restructuring Britain: the economy in question* (Sage, London), 45–90.

—— and Allen, J. (eds.) (1984), *Geography Matters! A reader* (Cambridge University Press, Cambridge).

—— and Catalano, A. (1978), *Capital and land* (Edward Arnold, London).

—— and Meegan, R. (1982) *The anatomy of job loss* (Methuen, London).

—————— (1983), *The anatomy of job loss: the how, why and where of employment decline* (Methuen, London).

—————— (1985a), *Politics and method: contrasting studies in industrial geography* (Methuen, London).

—————— (1985b), 'Introduction: the debate', in D. Massey and R. Meegan (eds.), *Politics and method: contrasting studies in industrial geography* (Methuen, London), 1–12.

—— and Miles, N. (1984), 'Mapping out the unions', *Marxism Today*, May, 19–22.

—— and Phillips, H. (1985), 'Land-use in Brazil', in Open University D205 *Changing Britain, changing world: geographical perspectives. Broadcast Handbook* (Open University, Milton Keynes), 28–32.

Mather, A. S. (1978), 'Patterns of afforestation in Britain since 1945', *Geography*, 63: 157–66.

—— (1986), *Land use* (Longman, London).

—— (1987), 'Global trends in forest resources', *Geography*, 72: 1–15.

Meegan, R. (1985), 'Are there two Britains? The north–south divide', in Open University D205 *Changing Britain, changing world: geographical perspectives*, Unit 19, Block 5 (Open University, Milton Keynes).

—— (1988), 'A crisis of mass production?' in J. Allen and D. Massey (eds.), *Restructuring Britain: the economy in question* (Sage, London), 136–83.

Mellor, R. E. H. (1975), *Eastern Europe: a geography of COMECON countries* (Macmillan, London).

Mendhan, S., and Barnock, G. (1982), 'Small business and international change', paper presented to International Congress on Small Business, Torremolinos, Spain, Oct.

Mensch, G. (1979), *Stalemate in technology: innovations overcome the depression* (Ballinger, Cambridge, Massachusetts).

Meyer, P. B. (1986a), 'Computer-controlled manufacture and the spatial distribution of production', *Area*, 18: 209–13.

—— (1986b), 'General Motors' Saturn plant: a quantum leap in technology and its implications for labour and community organising', *Capital and Class*, 30 (Winter): 73–96.

Michaels, P. (1982), 'Atmospheric pressure patterns, climatic change and winter wheat yields in North America' *Geoforum*, 13: 263–73.

Ministry of Agriculture, Fisheries and Food (1968), *Agricultural land classification map of England and Wales* (Agricultural Land Service, London).

—— (1976), *Wildlife conservation in semi-natural habitats on farms: a survey of farmers' attitudes and intentions in England and Wales* (HMSO, London).

Mitter, S. (1986), 'Industrial restructuring and manufacturing homework: immigrant women in the UK clothing industry', *Capital and Class*, 27 (Winter): 37–80.

Monck, C. S. P., Porter, R. B. Quintas, P. R., Storey, D. J., and Wynarzyk, P. (1988), *Science parks and the growth of high technology firms* (Croom Helm, Beckenham, Kent).

Moore, B., and Rhodes, J. (1973), 'Evaluating the effects of British regional economic policy', *Economic Journal*, 83: 87–110.

—————— and Tyler, P. (1977), 'The impact of regional policies in the 1970s', *Centre for Environmental Studies Review*, 1: 67–77.

—————— (1986), *The effects of government regional economic policy* (HMSO, London).

Morgan, A. D. (1978), 'Foreign manufacturing by UK firms', in F. Blackaby (ed.), *De-industrialisation* (Heinemann, London), 78–94.

Morgan, K. (1983), 'Restructuring steel: the crisis of labour and locality in Britain', *International Journal of Urban and Regional Research*, 7: 175–201.

—— (1986), 'Re-industrialisation in peripheral Britain: state policy, the space economy and industrial innovation', in R. Martin and B. Rowthorn (eds.), *The geography of de-industrialisation* (Macmillan, Basingstoke, Hampshire), 322–59.

—— and Sayer, A. (1983a), 'Regional inequality and the state in Britain', in J. Anderson, S. Duncan, and R. Hudson (eds.), *Redundant spaces in cities and regions? Studies in industrial decline and social change* (Academic Press, London), 17–49.

—————— (1983b), *The international electronics industry and regional development in Britain* University of Sussex, Urban and Regional Studies, Working Paper 34.

—————— (1985), 'A "modern" industry in a "mature" region: the remaking of management-labour relations', *International Journal of Urban and Regional Research*, 9: 383–403.

Morgan, R. P. C. (1985), 'Soil erosion measurement and soil conservation research in cultivated areas of the UK', *Geographical Journal*, 151: 11–20.

Morgan, W. B. (1978), *Agriculture in the Third World: a spatial analysis* (Bell and Hyman, London).

—— and Munton, R. J. C. (1971), *Agricultural geography* (Methuen, London).

Moriarty, B. M. (1983), 'Hierarchies of cities and the spatial filtering of industrial development', *Papers of the Regional Science Association*, 53: 59–82.

Morokvasic, M., Phizacklea, A., and Rudolph, H. (1986), 'Small firms and minority groups: contradictory trends in the French, German and British clothing industries', *International Sociology*, 1: 397–49.

Moseley, M. J., and Townroe, P. N. (1973), 'Linkage adjustment following industrial movement', *Tijdschrift voor Economische en Sociale Geografie*, 64: 137–44.

Moss, M. L. (1986), 'Telecommunications and the future of cities', *Land Development Studies*, 3: 33–44.

—— (1987), 'Telecommunications and international financial centres', in J. F. Brotchie, P. Hall and P. Newton (eds.), *The spatial impact of technological change* (Croom Helm, London), 75–88.

Moyes, A. (1980), 'Can spatially variable prices ever be fair? Some observations on the Price Commission's judgements on British cement prices', *Regional Studies*, 14: 37–53.

Munton, R. J. C. (1976), 'An analysis of price trends in the agricultural land market of England and Wales', *Tijdschrift voor Economische en Sociale Geografie*, 67: 202–12.

—— (1977), 'Financial institutions: their ownership of agricultural land in Great Britain', *Area*, 9: 29–37.

Murgatroyd, L., and Urry, J. (1983), 'The restructuring of a local economy: the case of Lancaster regional inequality and the state in Britain', in J. Anderson, S. Duncan and R. Hudson (eds.), *Redundant spaces in cities and regions?* Academic Press, London), 67–98.

Murray, F. (1983), 'The decentralisation of production—the decline of the mass-collective worker?' *Capital and Class*, 19: 74–99.

Myers, N. (1980), *Conversion of tropical moist forests* (Research Priorities on Tropical Biology of the National Research Council, National Academy of Sciences, Washington, DC).

Myrdal, G. (1957), *Rich lands and poor* (Harper and Row, New York).

Nelson, K. (1986), 'Labour demand, labour supply and the suburbanization of low-wage office work', in A. J. Scott and M. Storper (eds.), *Production, work and territory: the geographical anatomy of industrial capitalism* (Allen and Unwin, London), 149–71.

Neve, R. A. (1977), 'Hops—the years of change', *Brewers Guardian*, 106: 18.

Newby, H., Bell, C., Saunders, P., and Rose, D. (1977), 'Farmers' attitudes to conservation', *Countryside Recreation Review*, 2: 23–30.

—— and Utting, P. (1981), 'Agribusiness in the United Kingdom—social and political implications', paper presented to the British Sociological Association annual conference, University College, Aberystwyth.

Newson, J. (1986), 'New technology: the myths of new technology', *Local Government Policy Making*, 12: 23–33.

Newton, P. W., and O'Connor, K. (1987), 'The location of high technology: an Australian perspective', in J. F. Brotchie, P. Hall and P. W. Newton (eds.), *The spatial impact of technological change* (Croom Helm, London), 284–309.

Nicholson, N. K. (1984), 'Landholdings, agricultural modernization, and local institutions in India', *Economic Development and Cultural Change*, 34: 469–92.

Nilles, J. M., Carlson, R., Grey, P., and Heineman, G. (1976), *Telecommunications—transportation trade-offs: options for tommorow* (Wiley, New York).

Nishioka, H., and Takeuchi, A. (1987), 'The development of high technology industry in Japan', in J. F. Brotchie, P. Hall and P. W. Newton (eds.), *The spatial impact of technological change* (Croom Helm, London), 262–95.

Norcliffe, G. B. (1985), 'The industrial geography of the Third World', in M. Pacione (ed.), *Progress in industrial geography* (Croom Helm, London), 249–83.

—— and Hoare, A. G. (1982), 'Enterprise zone policy for the inner city: a review and preliminary assessment', *Area*, 14: 267–74.

North, D. C. (1955), 'Location theory and regional economic growth', *Journal of Political Economy*, 43: 243–58.

North, D. J. (1974), 'The process of locational change in different manufacturing organisations', in F. E. I. Hamilton (ed.), *Spatial perspectives on industrial organisation and decision-making* (Wiley, Chichester), 213–44.

North, J., and Spooner, D. J. (1976), 'Yorkshire coal crop from Selby farmland' *Geographical Magazine*, 48: 554–8.

Norton, R. D., and Rees, J. (1979), 'The product cycle and the spatial decentralization of American manufacturing', *Regional Studies*, 13: 141–51.

Noyelle, T. J., and Stanback, T. M. (1984), *The economic transformation of American cities* (Rowman and Allanheld, Totowa, New Jersey).

Oakey, R. P. (1984), 'Innovation and regional growth in small high technology firms: evidence from Britain and the USA', *Regional Studies*, 18: 237–51.

—— Thwaites, A. T., and Nash, P. A. (1980), 'The regional distribution of innovative manufacturing establishments in Britain', *Regional Studies*, 14: 235–53.

—— —— and —— (1982), 'Technological change and regional development: some evidence on regional variations in product and process innovation', *Environment and Planning A*, 14: 1073–86.

Oberhauser, A. (1987), 'Labour, production and the

state: decentralization of the French automobile industry, *Regional Studies*, 21: 445–58.

OECD (1979), *The impact of the NICs on production and trade in manufactures* (OECD, Paris).

—— (1988), *Industrial revival through technology* (OECD, Paris).

O'Farrell, P. N., and Crouchley, R. G. (1984), 'An industrial and spatial analysis of new firm formation in Ireland', *Regional Studies*, 18: 221–36.

Olsson, G. (1978), 'Of ambiguity or far cries from amemorializing mannafesta', in D. Ley and M. S. Samuels (eds.), *Humanistic geography: prospects and problems* (Maaroufa, Chicago).

Osleeb, J. P., and Cromley, R. G. (1978), 'The location of plants of the uniform delivered price manufacturer: a case study of Coca-Cola Ltd.', *Economic Geography*, 54: 40–52.

Owen, D. W., Gillespie, A. E., and Coombes, M. G. (1984), '"Job shortfalls" in British local labour market areas: a classification of labour supply and demand trends, 1971–1981', *Regional Studies*, 18: 469–88.

Palin, M. (1988), 'Changing transport', *Geography*, 73: 308–17.

Pallot, J., and Shaw, D. J. B. (1981), *Planning in the Soviet Union* (Croom Helm, London).

Parkinson, M. H., and Wilks, S. R. M. (1985), 'Testing partnership to destruction in Liverpool', *Regional Studies*, 19: 65–9.

Parry, M. L. (1975), 'Secular climatic and marginal agriculture', *Transactions of the Institute of British Geographers*, 64: 1–14.

—— (1976), 'Mapping of abandoned farmland in upland Britain', *Geographical Journal*, 142: 101–10.

—— Bruce, A., and Harkness, C. (1981), 'The plight of British moorland', *New Scientist*, May, 550–1.

Pearce, F. (1986), 'The strange death of Europe's trees', *New Scientist*, 4: Dec., 41–5.

Peck, F W., and Townsend, A. R. (1984), 'Contrasting experience of recession and spatial restructuring: British Shipbuilders, Plessey, and Metal Box', *Regional Studies*, 18: 319–38.

—— —— (1986), 'Corporate interaction in oligopolistic markets: the role of case studies of rationalisation', in M. Danson (ed.), *Recession and redundancy: re-structuring the regions* (Geo Books, Norwich), 49–63.

Peet, J. R. (1969), 'The spatial expansion of commercial agriculture in the nineteenth century: a von Thünen interpretation', *Economic Geography*, 45: 283–301.

—— (1983), 'Relations of production and the relocation of United States manufacturing industry since 1960', *Economic Geography*, 59: 112–43.

Penrose, E. (1959), *The theory of the growth of the firm* (Basil Blackwell, Oxford).

Perez, C. (1983), 'Structural change and the assimilation of new technologies in the economic and social system', *Futures*, 15: 357–75.

—— (1985), 'Microelectronics, long waves and world structural change', *World Development*, 13: 441–63.

Perloff, H., and Wingo, L. (1961), 'Natural resource endowment and regional economic growth', in J. J. Spengler (ed.), *Natural resources and economic growth* (Washington DC).

Perrons, D. C. (1981), 'The role of Ireland in the new international division of labour: a proposed framework for regional analysis', *Regional Studies*, 15: 81–100.

Perry, D. C., and Watkins, A. J. (eds.) (1977), *The rise of the sunbelt cities* (Sage, Beverly Hills, California).

Perry, R. (1979), *A summary of studies of the Cornish economy based upon surveys carried out 1974–8.* (Cornwall Industrial Development Association).

Phillips, K. (1968), 'The Balkanisation of America', *Harper's*, May, 37–48.

Phillips, P. (1982), *Regional disparities* (James Lorimer, Toronto).

Phizaclea, A. (1986), *Fashion clothing production in Britain, France and FRG—Final report* (Economic and Social Research Council, London).

Pigram, J. J. (1972), 'Resource appraisal and resistance to change: an Australian example', *Professional Geographer*, 24: 132–6.

Piore, M., and Sabel, C. (1984), *The second industrial divide* (Basic Books, New York).

Pizzano, W. (1985), 'Essential elements for scientific parks and programmes: three Appalachian models', *Seminar on Science Parks and technology complexes* (OECD, Paris).

Planning Exchange (1985), 'Mid Wales Development', Local Economic Development Information Service, Initiative A182.

Plant, R. (1981), *Industries in trouble* (International Labour Office, Geneva).

Pocock, D. C. D. (1957), 'England's diminished hop acreage', *Geography*, 42: 14–21.

Potter, C. (1987), 'Set-aside: friend or foe?' *Ecos*, 8: 36–9.

Potter, R. B. (1977), 'The nature of consumer usage fields in an urban environment: theoretical and empirical perspectives', *Tijdschrift voor Economische en Sociale Geografie*, 68: 168–76.

—— (1979), 'Perception of urban retailing facilities: an analysis of consumer information fields', *Geografiska Annaler*, 61B: 19–27.

Pottier, C. (1987), 'The location of high technology industries in France', in M. J. Breheny and R. McQuaid (eds.), *The development of high technology industries: an international survey* (Croom Helm, London), 192–222.

Prais, S. J. (1976), *The evolution of giant firms in Britain* (National Institute of Economic and Social Research, Cambridge).

Pratten, C. F. (1971), *Economies of scale in manufacturing industry*, University of Cambridge, Department of Applied Economics, Occasional Papers, 28.

—— (1986), 'The importance of giant companies', *Lloyds Bank Review*, 159: 33–48.

Pred, A. (1966), *The spatial dynamics of U.S. urban-industrial growth 1800–1914* (MIT Press, Cambridge, Massachusetts).

—— (1967), *Behaviour and location: foundations for a geographic and dynamic location theory: Part 1*, University of Lund, Lund Studies in Geography B, No. 27.

—— (1969), *Behaviour and location: foundations for a geographic and dynamic location theory: Part II*, University of Lund, Lund Studies in Geography B, No. 28.

—— (1974), 'Industry, information and city systems', in F. E. I. Hamilton (ed.), *Spatial perspectives on industrial organisation and decision-making* (Wiley, London), 105–339.

Preston, P. (1987), 'Technology waves and the future sources of employment and wealth creation in Britain', in M. J. Breheny and R. W. McQuaid (eds.), *The development of high technology industries: an international survey* (Croom Helm, London), 80–112.

Price, D. G., and Blair, A. M. (1989), *The changing geography of the service sector* (Belhaven Press, London).

Radford, T. (1988), 'Water nitrate cut will take decades', *Guardian*, 17 Nov.

Raitz, K. B. (1973), 'Ethnicity and the diffusion and distribution of cigar tobacco production in Wisconsin and Ohio', *Tijdschrift voor Economische en Sociale Geografie*, 64: 295–306.

—— and Mather, C. (1971), 'Norwegians and tobacco in western Wisconsin', *Annals of the Association of American Geographers*, 61: 684–96.

Rawlinson, M. (1989), 'The changing subcontracting relationships between motor vehicle firms and local suppliers: a case study in Coventry', paper presented to the Institute of British Geographers' Annual Conference, Coventry Polytechnic, Jan.

Rawstron, E. M. (1958), 'Three principles of industrial location', *Transactions of the Institute of British Geographers*, 25: 135–42.

Rees, J. (1974), 'Decision-making, the growth of the firm and the business environment', in F. E. I. Hamilton (ed.), *Spatial perspectives on industrial organisation and decision-making* (Wiley, Chichester), 189–212.

—— (1979), 'Technological change and regional shifts in American manufacturing', *Professional Geographer*, 31: 45–54.

—— and Stafford, H. (1986), 'Theories of regional growth and industrial location: their relevance for understanding high-technology complexes', in J. Rees and H. Stafford (eds.), *Technology, regions and policy* (Rowan and Littlefield, Totowa, New Jersey), 23–50.

—— and Weinstein, B. L. (1983), 'Government policy and industrial location', in J. W. House (ed.), *United States public policy: a geographical view* (Oxford University Press, Oxford), 213–62.

Reeves, R. (1980), 'Output of CVH engines builds up to Bridgend', *Financial Times*, 26 Sept.

Regional Studies Association (1983), *Report of an inquiry into regional problems in the United Kingdom* (Geo Books, Norwich).

Reilly, W. J. (1929), *Methods of the study of retail relationships*, University of Texas, Austin, University of Texas Bulletin No. 2944.

Reitsma, H. J. A. (1971), 'Crop and livestock production in the vicinity of the US-Canada border', *Professional Geographer*, 23: 216–23.

—— (1982), 'Development geography, dependency relations and the capitalist scapegoat', *Professional Geographer*, 34: 125–30.

—— (1986), 'Agricultural transboundary differences in the Okanagan region', *Journal of Rural Studies*, 2: 53–62.

Reynolds, J. (1983), 'Retail employment research: scarce evidence in an environment of change', *Service Industries Journal*, 3: 344–62.

Rhodes, J. (1986), 'Regional dimensions of industrial decline', in R. Martin and B. Rowthorn (eds.), *The geography of de-industrialisation* (Macmillan, Basingstoke, Hampshire), 138–68.

Richardson, H. W. (1978), *Regional and urban economies* (Penguin, Harmondsworth).

Richardson, K. (1972), *Twentieth-century Coventry* (City of Coventry, Coventry).

Roberts, P. W., and Shaw, T. (1982), *Mineral resources in regional and strategic planning* (Gower, Aldershot).

Robertson, I. (1987), 'Japanese plants abroad: global production on the way', *Financial Times*, 22 Oct.

Roberston, K. A. (1983), 'Downtown retail activity in large American cities 1954–77', *Geographical Review*, 73: 314–23.

Rogers, D. (1983), 'The changing pattern of American retailing', *Retail and Distribution Management*, 11: 8–13.

Rogers, E., and Larsen, J. (1984), *Silicon valley fever* (Basic Books, New York).

Rose, C. (1985), 'Acid rain falls on British woodlands', *New Scientist*, 14 Nov., 52–7.

Rostow, W. W. (1960), *The stages of economic growth: a non-communist manifesto* (Cambridge University Press, Cambridge).

Rothwell, R. (1982), 'The role of technology in industrial change: implications for regional policy', *Regional Studies*, 16: 361–69.

Rowe, D. (1988), 'Foreword: achievement from enterprise', in UK Science Park Association, *Science Parks as an opportunity for property and venture capital investment*, i. *Property* (CSP Economic Publications, Cardiff), pp. i–vii.

Rubenstein, J. M. (1986), 'Changing distribution of the American automobile industry', *Geographical Review*, 76: 288–300.

Rugg, D. S. (1985), *Eastern Europe* (Longman, New York).

Safarian, A. E. (1979), 'Foreign ownership and industrial behaviour: a comment on 'The weakest link', *Canadian Public Policy*, 3: 318–35.

Sawyers, L., and Tabb, W. K. (1984), *Sunbelt/snowbelt: urban development and regional resturing* (Oxford University Press, Oxford).

Saxenian, A. L. (1983), 'The urban contradictions of Silicon valley: regional development and the restructuring of the semiconductor industry', *International Journal of Urban and Regional Research* 7: 237–62.

——(1985), 'Silicon valley and Route 128: regional prototypes or historic exceptions', in M. Castells (ed.), *High technology, space and society*, Urban Affairs Annual Review, 28 (Sage Publications, Beverly Hills, California), 81–105.

Sayer, A. (1982*a*), 'Explaining manufacturing shift: a reply to Keeble', *Environment and Planning A*, 14: 119–25.

——(1982*b*), 'Explanation in economic geography', *Progress in Human Geography*, 6: 68–88.

——(1983), 'Theoretical problems in the analysis of technological change and regional development', in F. E. I. Hamilton and G. J. R. Linge (eds.), *Spatial analysis, industry and the industrial environment*, iii. *Regional economies and industrial systems* (Wiley, Chichester), 59–73.

——(1984), *Method in social science: a realist approach* (Hutchinson, London).

——(1985), The geography of industry: multinationals, in Open University *D205: Changing Britain, changing world: geographical perspectives*, Unit 5, Block 2 (Open University, Milton Keynes).

——(1986*a*), 'Industrial location and a world scale: the case of the semiconductor industry', in A. J. Scott and M. Storper (eds.), *Production, work, territory: the geographical anatomy of industrial capitalism* (Allen and Unwin, Boston), 107–23.

——(1986*b*), 'New developments in manufacturing: the just-in-time system', *Capital and Class*, 30 (winter): 43–72.

——(1989), 'Dualistic thinking and rhetoric in geography', *Area*, 21: 301–5.

——and Morgan, K. (1985), 'A modern industry in a declining region: links between method, theory and policy', in D. Massey and R. Meegan (eds.), *Politics*

and *method: contrasting studies in industrial geography* (Methuen, London), 144–68.

Schaefer, F. K. (1953), 'Exceptionalism in geography: a methodological examination', *Annals of the Association of American Geographers*, 43: 226–49.

Schiller, R. (1986), 'Retail decentralisation—the coming of the third wave' *Planner* (July), 13–15.

Schmenner, R. W. (1982), *Making business location decisions* (Prentice-Hall, Englewood Cliffs, New Jersey).

Schmitz, H. (1984), 'Industrialisation strategies in less developed countries: some lessons of historical experience', in R. Kaplinsky (ed.), *Third World industrialisation in the 1980s* (Frank Cass, London).

Schoenberger, E. (1987), 'Technological and organizational change in automobile production: spatial implications', *Regional Studies*, 21: 199–214.

Schumpeter, J. A. (1939), *Business cycles: a theoretical, historical and statistical analysis of the capitalist process* (McGraw Hill, London).

Scott, A. J. (1983*a*), 'Location and linkage systems: a survey and reassessment', *Annals of Regional Science*, 17: 1–39.

——(1983*b*), 'Industrial organization and the logic of intra-metropolitan location, I: Theoretical considerations', *Economic Geography*, 59: 231–49.

——(1983*c*), 'Industrial organization and the logic of intra-metropolitan location, II: A case study of the printed circuits industry in the Greater Los Angeles region', *Economic Geography*, 59: 343–67.

——(1984), 'Industrial organization and the logic of intra-metropolitan location, III: A case study of the women's dress industry in the Greater Los Angeles region', *Economic Geography*, 60: 3–27.

——(1986), 'High technology industry and territorial development: the rise of the Orange County Complex, 1955–1984', *Urban Geography*, 7: 1–43.

——(1987*a*), 'The semicondutor industry in South East Asia: organisation, location and the international division of labour', *Regional Studies*, 21: 143–60.

——(1987*b*), 'Industrial organisation and location: division of labour, the firm, and spatial process', *Economic Geography*, 63: 215–31.

——(1988), 'Flexible production systems and regional development: the rise of new industrial spaces in North America and western Europe', *International Journal of Urban and Regional Research*, 12: 171–86.

——and Angel, D. P. (1987), 'The U.S. semiconductor industry: a locational analysis', *Environment and Planning A*, 19: 875–912.

——and Storper, M. (1987), 'High technology industry and regional development: a theoretical critique and reconstruction' *International Social Science Journal*, 112: 215–32.

Scott, P. (1970), *Geography of retailing* (Hutchinson, London).

Scott, P. D. (1977), 'Hops in Britain and West Germany' *Outlook on Agriculture*, 9: 174–9.

Segal Quince and Partners (1985), *The Cambridge phenomenon: the growth of high-technology industry in a university town* (Segal Quince and Partners, Cambridge).

Selby, J. A. (1987), 'The operationalization of Pred's behavioural matrix', *Geografiska Annaler*, 69B: 81–90.

Sewell, J. W. (1979), 'Can the North prosper without growth and progress in the South?'; in M. M. McLaughlin (ed.), *The United States and world development: agenda 1979* (Praeger, New York), 45–76.

Shaw, A. B. (1987), 'Approaches to agricultural technology adoption and consequences of adoption in the Third World: a critical review' *Geoforum*, 18: 1–19.

Sheard, P. (1983), 'Auto-production systems in Japan: organization and locational features', *Australian Geographical Studies*, 21: 49–68.

Sheffield City Council (1987), *The retail revolution: who benefits?* (Sheffield City Council, Department of Employment and Economic Development, Sheffield).

Shepherd, G. (1981), 'Industrial strategies in textiles and clothing and motor cars' in C. Saunders (ed.), *The political economy of new and old industrial countries* (Butterworths, London), 132–56.

Short, J. (1981), 'Defence spending in the UK regions', *Regional Studies*, 15: 101–10.

Shutt, J. (1984), 'Tory enterprise zones and the labour movement', *Capital and Class*, 23: 19–44.

—— and Whittington. R. (1987), 'Fragmentation strategies and the rise of small units: cases from the North West', *Regional Studies*, 21: 13–23.

Silbertson, Z. A. (1984), *The Multi-fibre arrangement and the UK economy* (HMSO, London).

Simms, D., and Wood, M. (1984), *Car manufacturing at Linwood: the regional policy issues* (Department of Politics and Sociology, Paisley College, Paisley).

Simon, H. A. (1957), *Models of man: social and rational* (Wiley, New York).

—— (1960), *The new science of management decision* (Harper and Row, New York).

Simpson, E. S. (1987), *The developing world: an introduction* (Longman, London).

Singelmann, J. (1978), *From agriculture to services: the transformation of industrial employment* (Sage, Beverly Hills, California).

Singh, A. (1977), 'UK industry and the world economy: a case of deindustrialisation?', *Cambridge Journal of Economics*, 1: 113–36.

Sleigh, J., Boatwright, B., Irwin, P., and Stayon, R. (1979), *The manpower implications of microelectronics technology* (HMSO, London).

Smith, D. M. (1966), 'A theoretical framework for geographical studies of industrial location', *Economic Geography*, 42: 95–113.

—— (1977), *Human geography: a welfare approach* (Edward Arnold, London).

—— (1979), 'Modelling industrial location: towards a broader view of the space economy', in F. E. I. Hamilton and G. J. R. Linge (eds.), *Spatial analysis, industry and the industrial environment*, i. *Industrial Systems* (Wiley, Chichester), 37–56.

—— (1981), *Industrial location: an economic geographical analysis* (Wiley, London).

—— (1987), *Geography, inequality and society* (Cambridge University Press, Cambridge).

Smith, E. G. (1980), 'America's richest farms and ranches', *Annals of the Association of American Geographers*, 70: 528–41.

Smith, N. (1984), *Uneven development* (Blackwell, Oxford).

—— (1986), 'On the necessity of uneven development', *International Journal of Urban and Regional Research*, 10: 87–104.

Smyth, R. (1988), 'Danger—EEC at work in the sun', *Guardian*, 16 Jan.

Soja, E. W. (1985), 'Regions in context: spatiality, periodicity, and the historical geography of the regional question', *Environment and Planning D: Society and Space*, 3: 175–90.

Sparks, L. (1986), 'The changing structure of distribution in retail companies: an example from the grocery trade', *Transactions of the Institute of British Geographers New Series*, 11: 147–54.

—— (1988), 'Technological change and spatial change in UK retail distribution', paper presented to the Institute of British Geographers Annual Conference, Loughborough University of Technology, Jan.

Spencer, K. M. (1987), 'The decline of manufacturing industry in the West Midlands', *Local Government Studies*, 13, Mar./Apr.: 7–24.

Spooner, D. J. (1981), *Mining and regional development* (Oxford University Press, Oxford).

Stafford, H. A. (1972), 'The geography of manufacturers', *Progress in Geography*, 4: 181–215.

—— (1974), 'The anatomy of the location decision: content analysis of case studies', in F. E. I. Hamilton (ed.), *Spatial perspectives on industrial organisation and decision-making* (Wiley, Chichester), 169–88.

—— (1985), 'Environmental protection and industrial location', *Annals of the Association of American Geographers*, 75: 227–40.

Stanback, T. M. (1979), *Understanding the service economy* (John Hopkins University Press, Baltimore).

—— (1985), 'The changing fortunes of metropolitan economies', in M. Castells (ed.), *High technology: space and society*, Urban Affairs Annual Review, 28 (Sage, Beverly Hills, California), 122–42.

—— Bearse, P. J., Noyelle, T. J., and Karasek, R. A. (1981), *Services the new economy* (Allanfied Osman, Totowa, New Jersey).

Stanislawski, D. (1975), 'Dionysis westward: early religion and the economic geography of wine', *Geographical Review*, 65: 427–44.

Steed, G. P. F. (1981), 'International location and comparative advantage: the clothing industries and developing countries', in F. E. I. Hamilton and G. J. R. Linge (eds.), *Spatial analysis, industry and the industrial environment, ii. International industrial systems* (John Wiley, Winchester), 265–303.

—— and DeGenova, D. (1983), 'Ottawa's technology—oriented complex', *Canadian Geographer*, 27: 263–78.

Sternlieb, G., and Hughes, J. W. (1977), 'New metropolitan and regional realities', *Journal of American Institute of Planners*, 43: 227–41.

—— and Hughes, J. W. (eds.) (1981), *Shopping centers: USA* (Center for Urban Policy Research, Rutgers, State University of New Jersey, New Jersey).

Stohr, W. B. (1987), 'Regional economic development and the world economic crisis', *International Social Science Journal*, 112: 187–97.

Storey, D. J. (1980), *Job generation and small firms policy in Britain*, Centre for Environmental Studies, London, Policy Series, 11.

—— (1982), *Entrepreneurship and the new firm* (Croom Helm, Beckenham, Kent).

—— and Johnson, S. (1987a), *Job generation and labour market change* (Macmillan, London).

—— —— (1987b), *Are small firms the answer to unemployment?* (Employment Institute, London).

Storper, M., and Christopherson, S. (1987), 'Flexible specialisation and regional agglomerations: the case of the US motion picture industry', *Annals of the Association of American Geographers*, 77: 104–17.

—— and Walker, R. (1983), 'The theory of labour and the theory of location', *International Journal of Urban and Regional Research*, 7: 1–41.

—— —— (1984), 'The spatial division of labour: labour and the location of industries', in L. Sawyers and W. K. Tabb (eds.), *Sunbelt/snowbelt: urban development and regional restructuring* (Oxford University Press, New York), 19–47.

Symes, D., and Marsden, T. (1985), 'Industrialization of agriculture: intensive livestock farming in Humberside', in M. J. Healey and B. W. Ilbery (eds.), *Industrialization of the countryside* (Geo Books, Norwich), 99–120.

Symons, L. J. (1967), *Agricultural geography* (Bell, London).

Tabb, W. K. (1984), 'Urban development and regional restructuring, an overview' in L. Sawyers and W. K. Tabb (eds.), *Sunbelt/snowbelt: urban development and regional restructuring* (Oxford University Press, Oxford), 3–15.

Tarling, R. (1981), 'The relationship between employment and output: where does segmentation theory lead us?', in F. Wilkinson (ed.), *The dynamics of labour market segmentation* (Academic Press, London), 281–90.

Tarrant, J. R. (1974), *Agricultural geography* (David and Charles, Newton Abbot).

Taylor, M. J. (1970), 'The location decisions of small firms, *Area*, 2: 51–4.

—— (1975), 'Organisational growth, spatial interaction and location decision-making', *Regional Studies*, 7: 387–400.

—— (1978), 'Linkage change and organisational growth: the case of the West Midlands iron foundry industry', *Economic Geography*, 54: 314–36.

—— (1986), 'The product-cycle model: a critique', *Environment and Planning A*, 18: 751–61.

—— and Thrift, N. J. (1982a), 'Industrial linkage and the segmented economy, 1: Some theoretical proposals', *Environment and Planning A*, 14: 1601–13.

—— —— (1982b), 'Industrial linkage and the segmented economy, 2: An empirical reinterpretation', *Environment and Planning A*, 14: 1615–32.

—— —— (1983), 'Business organisation, segmentation and location', *Regional Studies*, 17: 445–65.

—— Wood, P. A. (1973), 'Industrial linkage and local agglomeration in the West Midlands metal industries', *Transactions of the Institute of British Geographers*, 59: 129–54.

Taylor, P. J. (1982), A materialist framework for political geography, *Transactions of the Institute of British Geographers*, 7: 15–34.

—— (1986), 'The World-Systems project', in R. J. Johnston and P. J. Taylor (eds), *A world in crisis? Geographical perspectives* (Blackwell, Oxford), 269–88.

—— (1988), 'World-systems analysis and regional geography', *Professional Geographer*, 40: 259–65.

TEST (1989), *Trouble in store? Retail locational policy in Britain and Germany* (Transport and Environmental Studies, London).

Thirwall, A. P. (1982), 'Deindustrialization in the United Kingdom', *Lloyds Bank Review*, 144: 22–37.

Thomas, C. J., and Bromley, R. (1987), 'The growth and functioning of an unplanned retail park: the Swansea Enterprise Zone', *Regional Studies*, 21: 287–300.

Thomas, H., and Logan, C. (1982), *Mondragon: an economic analysis* (Allen and Unwin, London).

Thomas, M. (1980), 'Explanatory frameworks for growth and change in multi-regional firms', *Economic Geography*, 56: 1–17.

Thompson, C. (1988), 'Some problems with R & D/SE & T-based definitions of high technology industry', *Area*, 20: 265–77.

Thorngren, B. (1970), 'How do contact systems affect regional development?', *Environment and Planning*, 2: 409–27.

Thrift, N. J. (1985), 'Research policy and review, 1: Taking the rest of the world seriously? The state of

British urban and regional research in a time of economic crisis', *Environment and Planning A*, 17: 7–24.

—— (1986), 'The geography of international economic disorder', in R. J. Johnston and P. J. Taylor (eds.), *A world in crisis? Geographical perspectives* (Blackwell, Oxford), 12–67.

Thwaites, A. T. (1982), 'Some evidence of regional variations in the introduction and diffusion of industrial products and processes within British manufacturing industry', *Regional Studies*, 16: 371–81.

Timmermans, H, (1979), 'A spatial preference model of regional shopping behaviour', *Tijdschrift voor Economische en Sociale Geografie*, 70: 45–8.

—— (1981), 'Spatial choice behaviour in different environmental settings: an application of the revealed preference approach', *Geografiska Annaler*, 63B: 57–67.

Toda, T. (1987), 'The location of high-technology industry and the Technopolis Plan in Japan', in J. F. Brotchie, P. Hall and P. W. Newton (eds.), *The spatial impact of technological change* (Croom Helm, London), 271–83.

Todd, D., and Brierley, J. S. (1977), 'Ethnicity and the rural economy: illustrations from southern Manitoba, 1961–71', *Canadian Geographer*, 21: 237–49.

Toffler, A. (1980), *The third wave* (Pan, London).

Tornqvist, G. (1973), 'Contact requirements and travel facilities: contact models of Sweden and regional development alternatives in the future', in A. Pred and G. Tornqvist (eds.), *Systems of cities and information flows*, University of Lund, Lund Studies in Geography B, 38.

Town and Country Planning Association (1987), *North–South divide: a new deal for Britain's regions* (Town and COuntry Planning Association, London).

Townroe, P. M. (1971), *Industrial location decisions: a study in management behaviour*, University of Birmingham, Centre for Urban and Regional Studies, Occasional Paper 15.

—— (1975), 'Branch plants and regional development', *Town Planning Review*, 46: 47–62.

—— (1979), Industrial movement: experience in the US and the UK (Saxon House, Aldershot).

Townsend, A. R. (1983), *The impact of recession* (Croom Helm, Beckenham, Kent).

—— (1986), 'Spatial aspects of the growth of part-time employment in Britain', *Regional Studies*, 20: 313–30.

—— (1987), 'Regional policy', in W. F. Lever (ed.), *Industrial change in the United Kingdom* (Longman, Harlow, Essex), 223–39.

—— and Peck, F. W. (1985*a*), 'An approach to the analysis of redundancies in the UK (post) 1976: some methodological problems and policy implications', in D. Massey and R. Meegan (eds.), *Politics and method: contrasting studies in industrial geography* (Methuen, London), 64–87.

—— —— (1985*b*) 'The geography of mass-redundancy', in M. Pacione (ed.), *Progress in industrial geography* (Croom Helm, Beckenham, Kent), 174–216.

Toyne, P. (1974), *Organisation, location, behaviour: decision making in economic geography* (Macmillan, London).

Tricker, M., and Bozeat, N. (1983), 'Encouraging the development of small businesses in rural areas: recent local authority initiatives in England', *Regional Studies*, 17: 201–4.

—— and Martin, S. (1984), 'The developing role of the Commission', *Regional Studies*, 18: 507–14.

Turnock. D. (1978), *Eastern Europe* (Dawson, Folkestone).

—— (1984), 'Postwar studies on the human geography of eastern Europe', *Progress in Human Geography*, 8: 315–46.

Tyler, P., and Kitson, M. (1987), 'Geographical variations in transport costs of manufacturing firms in Great Britain', *Urban Studies*, 24: 61–73.

Ullman, E. L. (1958), 'Regional development and the geography of concentration', *Papers and Proceedings of the Regional Science Association*, 4: 179–98.

Unwin, T. (1988), 'The propagation of agrarian change in North-West Portugal', *Journal of Rural Studies*, 4: 223–38.

URPI (1987), *Register of managed shopping schemes* (The Unit for Retail Planning Information Ltd., Reading).

Urry, J. (1987), 'Some social and spatial aspects of services', *Environment and Planning D: Society and Space*, 5: 5–26.

Vance, J. E. (1962), 'Emerging patterns of commercial structure in American cities', in *Proceedings of IGU Symposium in Lund* (Lund).

Varjo, U. (1979), 'Productivity and fluctuating limits of crop cultivation in Finland', *Geographia Polonica*, 40: 225–33.

Vernon, R. (1966), 'International investment and international trade in the product cycle', *Quarterly Journal of Economics*, 80: 190–207.

—— (1971), *Sovereignty at bay: the multinational spread of U.S. enterprises* (Basic Books, New York).

—— (1974), 'The location of economic activity', in J. H. Dunning (ed.), *Economic analysis and the multinational enterprise* (George Allen and Unwin, London), 89–114.

Vickerman, R. W. (1987), 'The Channel Tunnel: consequences for regional growth and development', *Regional Studies*, 21: 187–97.

Vogeler, I. (1981), *The myth of the family farm: agribusiness dominance of US agriculture* (Westview Press, Boulder, Colorado).

Walker, R. A. (1985), 'Technological determination

and determinism: industrial growth and location', in M. Castells (ed.), *High technology, space and society*, Urban Affairs Annual Review, 28 (Sage, Beverly Hills, California), 226–64.

—— and Storper, M. (1981), 'Capital and industrial location', *Progress in Human Geography*, 5: 473–509.

Wallace, I. (1985), 'Towards a geography of agribusiness', *Progress in Human Geography*, 9: 491–514.

—— and Smith, W. (1985), 'Agribusiness in North America', in M. J. Healey and B. W. Ilbery (eds.), *Industrialization of the countryside* (Geo Books, Norwich), 57–74.

Wallerstein, I. (1974), *The modern world system* (Academic Press, New York).

Walmsley, D. J., and Lewis, G. J. (1984), *Human geography: behavioural approaches* (Longman, London).

Ward, M. (1982), 'Political economy, industrial location and the European motor car industry in the postwar period', *Regional Studies*, 16: 443–53.

Ward, R., and Jenkins, R. (eds.) (1984), *Ethnic communities in business* (Cambridge University Press, Cambridge).

—— Randall, R., and Kromar, K. (1986), 'Small firms in the clothing industry: the growth of minority enterprise', *International Small Business Journal*, 4 (3): 46–56.

Warren, K. (1973), *Mineral resources* (David and Charles, Newton Abbot).

Watanabe, S. (1971), 'Subcontracting, industrialization and employment creation', *International Labour Review*, 104: 51–76.

Watts, H. D. (1971), 'The location of the beet sugar industry in England and Wales, 1912–36', *Transactions of the Institute of British Geographers*, 53: 95–116.

—— (1974), 'Spatial rationalisation in multi-plant enterprises', *Geoforum*, 17: 69–76.

—— (1977), 'Market areas and spatial rationalisation: the British brewing industry after 1945', *Tijdschrift voor Economische en Sociale Geografie*, 68: 224–40.

—— (1978), 'Inter-organisational relations and the location of industry', *Regional Studies*, 12: 215–25.

—— (1980a), *The large industrial enterprise: some spatial perspectives* (Croom Helm, London).

—— (1980b), 'Conflict and collusion in the British sugar industry, 1924 to 1928', *Journal of Historical Geography*, 6: 291–314.

—— (1980c), 'The location of European investment in the United Kingdom', *Tijdschrift voor Economische en Sociale Geografie*, 71: 3–14.

—— (1981), *The branch plant economy* (Longman, London).

—— (1987), *Industrial geography* (Longman, Harlow, Essex).

—— and Stafford, H. A. (1986), 'Plant closure and the multiplant firm: some conceptual issues', *Progress in Human Geography*, 10: 206–27.

Weber, A. (1929), *Alfred Weber's theory of the location of industries* (University of Chicago Press, Chicago).

Weinstein, B. L., and Firestine, R. E. (1978), *Regional growth and decline in the United States: the rise of the Sunbelt and the decline of the Northeast* (Praeger, New York).

—— and Gross, H. T. (1988), 'The rise and fall of sun, rust and frostbelts', *Economic Development Quarterly*, 2: 9–18.

—— Gross, H. T., and Rees, J. (1985), *Regional growth and decline in the United States* (Praeger, New York).

Wells, Jr., L. T. (1972), 'International trade: the product life cycle approach', in L. T. Wells, Jr. (ed.), *The product life cycle and international trade* (Division of Research, Harvard Business School, Boston), 3–33.

Westmacott, R., and Worthington, T. (1974), *New agricultural landscapes* (Countryside Commission, Cheltenham).

Wheaton, W. C. (ed.) (1979), *Interregional movements and regional growth* (Urban Institute, Washington DC).

White, H. P., and Senior, M. L. (1983), *Transport geography* (Longman, London).

White, R. L., and Watts, H. D. (1977), 'The birth of a new industry and its spatial pattern', *East Midlands Geographer*, 9: 349–60.

Whittington, R. C. (1984), 'Regional bias in new firm formation in the UK', *Regional Studies*, 18: 253–55.

Whittlesey, D. (1936), 'Major agricultural regions of the earth', *Annals of the Association of American Geographers*, 26: 199–240.

Whittow, J. (1988), 'Environmental concerns', *Progress in Human Geography*, 12: 451–8.

Williams, A. M. (1987), *The Western European economy: a geography of post-war development* (Hutchinson, London).

Williams, G. (1984), 'Promoting the rural economy: the role of Development Agencies in remoter rural areas', *Regional Studies*, 18: 73–88.

Wilson, M. G. A. (1968), 'Changing patterns of pit location on the New South Wales coalfields', *Annals of the Association of American Geographers*, 58: 78–90.

Wilson, R. K., and Woods, C. S. (1982), *Patterns of world economic development* (Longman Sorrett, Melbourne).

Winchester, H., and Ilbery, B. W. (1988), *Agricultural change: France and the EEC* (John Murray, London).

Winsberg, M. (1980), 'Concentration and specialisation in US agriculture, 1939–78', *Economic Geography*, 56: 183–9.

Withers, J., and Fawcett, A. (1984), 'Family that fashioned universal flair', *The Times*, 24 Aug.

Wolpert, J. (1964), 'The decision-making process in a spatial context', *Annals of the Association of American Geographers*, 54: 537–58.

Wood, C. M., Lee, N., Luker, J. A., and Saunders, P. J. (1974), *The geography of pollution: a study of Greater Manchester* (Manchester University Press, Manchester).

Wood, P. A. (1986), 'The anatomy of job loss and job creation: some speculations on the role of the "producer service" sector', *Regional Studies*, 20: 37–46.

Wooldridge, S. W., and East, W. G. (1958), *The spirit and purpose of geography* (Hutchinson, London).

World Bank (1988), *World development report 1988* (Oxford University Press, New York).

Wright, M., Coyne, J., and Lockley, H. (1984), 'Management buyouts and trade unions: dispelling the myths', *Industrial Relations Journal*, 15 (3): 45–52.

Wrigley, N. (1988), 'Retail restructuring and retail analysis', in N. Wrigley (ed.), *Store choice, store location and market analysis* (Routledge, London), 3–38.

Yapa, L. S., and Mayfield, R. G. (1978), 'Non-adoption of innovations: evidence from discriminant analysis', *Economic Geography*, 54: 145–56.

Zeitlin, J. (1985), 'Markets, technology and collective services: a strategy for local government intervention in the clothing industry', *Economic Policy Group Strategy Document 39* (Greater London Council, London).

Zimmerman, E. W. (1951), *World resources and industries* (Harper and Row, New York).

Index